Ethical Obligations and Decision Making in Accounting

Text and Cases   **Second Edition**

Ethical Obligations and Decision Making in Accounting

Text and Cases

Second Edition

Steven M. Mintz, DBA, CPA

Professor of Accounting
California Polytechnic State University,
San Luis Obispo

Roselyn E. Morris , PhD, CPA

Chair and Professor of Accounting
Texas State University–San Marcos

McGraw-Hill Irwin

ETHICAL OBLIGATIONS AND DECISION MAKING IN ACCOUNTING: TEXT AND CASES,
SECOND EDITION

Published by McGraw-Hill/Irwin, a business unit of The McGraw-Hill Companies, Inc., 1221 Avenue of the
Americas, New York, NY, 10020. Copyright © 2011 by The McGraw-Hill Companies, Inc. All rights reserved.
Previous edition © 2008. No part of this publication may be reproduced or distributed in any form or by any
means, or stored in a database or retrieval system, without the prior written consent of The McGraw-Hill
Companies, Inc., including, but not limited to, in any network or other electronic storage or transmission, or
broadcast for distance learning.

Some ancillaries, including electronic and print components, may not be available to customers outside the
United States.

1 2 3 4 5 6 7 8 9 0 QDB/QDB 1 0 9 8 7 6 5 4 3 2 1 0

ISBN 978-0-07-802528-0
MHID 0-07-802528-1

Vice President & Editor-in-Chief: *Brent Gordon*
Vice President EDP/Central Publishing Services: *Kimberly Meriwether David*
Editorial Director: *Stewart Mattson*
Publisher: *Tim Vertovec*
Executive Editor: *Richard T. Hercher, Jr.*
Associate Marketing Manager: *Dean Karampelas*
Development Editor: *Rebecca Mann*
Project Manager: *Erin Melloy*
Design Coordinator: *Margarite Reynolds*
Cover Image: *© Creatas/PunchStock*
Buyer: *Kara Kudronowicz*
Media Project Manager: *Balaji Sundararaman*
Compositor: *Laserwords Private Limited*
Typeface: *10/12 Times New Roman*
Printer: *Quad/Graphics*

All credits appearing on page or at the end of the book are considered to be an extension of the copyright page.

Library of Congress Cataloging-in-Publication Data

Mintz, Steven M.
    Ethical obligations and decision making in accounting : text and cases / Steven M. Mintz, Roselyn E. Morris.
— 2nd ed.
        p. cm.
    ISBN 978-0-07-802528-0 (alk. paper)
    1. Accountants—Professional ethics—United States—Case studies.   I. Morris, Roselyn E.   II. Title.
HF5616.U5M535   2011
174'.4—dc22

                                                                                            2010028835

www.mhhe.com

Dedication

"The choices we make dictate the life we lead."

A quotation by Danny De Vito's character to his students in the movie "The Renaissance Man."

We hope this book inspires students to make ethical choices in their lives and always strive for excellence in whatever they do.

About the Authors

STEVEN M. MINTZ, DBA, CPA, is a professor of accounting in the Orfalea College of Business at the California Polytechnic State University–San Luis Obsipo. Dr. Mintz received his DBA from George Washington University. His first book titled *Cases in Accounting Ethics and Professionalism* was also published by McGraw-Hill. Dr. Mintz develops courses in ethics for Bisk Education that meet state board of accountancy mandatory requirements for continuing education in ethics. He also serves on the California Board of Accountancy's Advisory Committee on Accounting and Ethics Curriculum. Dr. Mintz has received the Faculty Excellence Award of the California Society of CPAs.

ROSELYN E. MORRIS, PHD, CPA, is a professor of accounting and the chair of the Accounting Department at the McCoy College of Business, Texas State University–San Marcos. Dr. Morris received her PhD in business administration from the University of Houston. She is currently president of the Accounting Education Foundation and a member of the Qualifications Committee of the Texas Board of Public Accountancy. Dr. Morris has received the Outstanding Educator Award of the Texas Society of CPAs.

Preface

Why Did We Write This Book?

The first edition of *Ethical Obligations and Decision Making in Accounting: Text and Cases* was written in the wake of the dot.com bubble and accounting scandals at companies such as Enron and WorldCom. These scandals made it clear that ethics is of primary importance in the training of new accountants. The need for the second edition of the book comes on the heels of the housing bubble, the Bernie Madoff Ponzi scheme, the subprime housing scandal, government bailouts of AIG and Goldman Sachs, and the hubris of executives' compensation in these scandals.

Texas began requiring students sitting for the CPA exam to have passed a course in ethics after the Enron, Waste Management, and Andersen scandals; other states, such as New York, California, Ohio, Maryland, and Nebraska, have ethics requirements as part of the education criteria for CPA candidates. The National Association of State Boards of Accountancy (NASBA) has an ethics requirement in the suggested Uniform Accountancy Act. Accounting instructors should be at the forefront of the ethics education movement; in particular, those of us who have worked in the profession or who hold professional certifications understand the importance of following the profession's codes of ethics. All accounting instructors, regardless of background or teaching approach, know the importance of ethical behavior to the smooth functioning of the financial markets. In the classroom, we should serve as role models for students by channeling ethical behavior by respecting students, treating them fairly, and carrying out our obligations in a responsible manner.

Ethical Obligations and Decision Making in Accounting was written to guide accountants past a scandal-filled age. Our book is entirely devoted to helping students cultivate the ethical commitment needed to ensure that their work meets the highest standards of integrity, independence, and objectivity.

We wrote this book with these aims in mind:

- To help accounting students fully understand how a commitment to ethics can enable accounting professionals to meet their ethical obligations to investors and creditors, with a focus on professional judgment and professional skepticism.
- To define an integrated ethical framework built on ethical reasoning and detailed explanations of the principles of ethical behavior in the AICPA Code of Professional Conduct, IMA Statement of Ethical Professional Practice, IIA Code of Ethics, and Global Code of Ethics.
- This framework highlights the importance of adhering to generally accepted accounting principles (GAAP) and generally accepted auditing standards (GAAS), including auditors' responsibility for fraud.
- To provide the ethical grounding that accounting students need to reconcile conflicts between stakeholder interests that can occur in the performance of audit, tax, and consulting services with extensive coverage of corporate governance in the context of earnings management, auditor legal liabilities, and top management and board of director legal obligations.
- To examine the broad elements of the financial reporting system that dictate whether ethical decisions will be made in business and accounting, including the ethics of the

internal control environment, the effectiveness of accounting and auditing within an ethical framework, and board of director and audit committee responsibilities under the Sarbanes-Oxley Act.

- To aid students in understanding the failures of corporate governance that led to the financial scandals in the last decade.
- To expose students to differences in financial reporting and corporate governance around the world including the role of International Financial Reporting Standards (IFRS).

The philosophy of this text is that accounting ethics is best discussed in the context of professional obligations. CPAs serve as internal accountants and auditors, external auditors, tax preparers and advisors, and consultants to their clients. The ethical standards laid down in the AICPA Code pertain to the performance of professional services along with the IMA Statement of Ethical Professional Practice, IIA Code of Ethics, and Global Code of Ethics. Just knowing the ethics is only part of the story: The challenges for CPAs arise in the context of their roles as members of management and external auditors, and the pressures exerted by superiors and clients that test their commitment to ethical behavior.

About This Textbook

Ethical Obligations and Decision Making in Accounting is designed to provide the instructor with the best flexibility and pedagogical effectiveness of any book on the market. To that end, it includes numerous features designed to make both learning and teaching easier, such as:

- Coverage of IFRS and several international financial reporting cases
- 160 discussion questions
- Classic Harvard case, *The Parable of the Sadhu*
- 75 cases, half of which are from the SEC enforcement files
- Four additional major cases that can be used for comprehensive testing, a group project, or a research assignment
- Dozens of additional cases and instructional resources that are available to enrich student learning

In addition, the textbook offers these features:

- The book is comprehensive enough to serve as a stand-alone text yet flexible enough to act as a co-text or supplementary text across the accounting curricula or within an auditing or financial accounting course.
- There is sufficient case and problem material to allow the instructor to vary the course over at least two to three terms.
- The writing style is pitched specifically to students, making the material easy to follow and absorb.

The **Instructor Edition of the Online Learning Center,** www.mhhe.com/mintz2e, offers the finest teaching support of any accounting ethics text. A comprehensive **Instructor's Manual** provides teaching notes, grading suggestions and rubrics, sample syllabi, extra cases and projects, and guidelines for incorporating writing into the accounting ethics course; the **Test Bank** provides a variety of multiple-choice, short answer, and essay questions for building quizzes and tests; and **PowerPoint** presentations for every chapter make a convenient and powerful lecture tool.

Changes in This Edition

This edition of *Ethical Obligations and Decision Making in Accounting* has been greatly expanded to include more than 20 new cases taken from the files of the SEC and dozens of new discussion questions. We have broadened the coverage of fraud to include Ponzi schemes and the financial crisis of 2008, and both basic and complex earnings management cases. A new chapter on international financial reporting and ethics provides a foundation for instruction in international accounting, auditing, and corporate governance. Four new cases are provided for faculty to use as research projects or other major assignments. The Test Bank includes additional cases that can be assigned, including some that were not carried over from the first edition.

Acknowledgments

We greatly appreciate the insight and suggestions provided by the following reviewers of this text:

Nancy Batch
Mountain View College

Cathleen Burns
University of Colorado–Boulder

Dennis Elam
University of North Texas

Brian Elzweig
Texas A&M University–Corpus Christi

Michael Flores
Wichita State University

Aundrea Kay Guess
St. Edward's University

Cynthia Jeffrey
Iowa State University

Lawrence Kalbers
Loyola Marymount University

Carol Lawrence
University of Richmond

Lorraine Lee
University of North Carolina–Wilmington

Richard Mark
University of Texas at Arlington

L. Kevin McNelis
New Mexico State University

Michael Newman
University of Houston–Houston

Kevin M. Misiewicz
University of Notre Dame

Aileen Smith
Stephen F. Austin University

Charles Stanley
Baylor University

Wallace Wood
University of Cincinnati–Cincinnati

We also appreciate the assistance and guidance given us on this project by the staff of McGraw-Hill/Irwin, including Stewart Mattson, editorial director; Dick Hercher, executive editor; Dean Karampelas, marketing manager; Rebecca Mann, development editor; Erin Melloy, project manager; Kara Kudronowicz, buyer; Margarite Reynolds, design coordinator; and Balaji Sundararaman, media project manager. We greatly appreciate the role of Saradha Chandrahasan, project manager, and Sharon O'Donnell, copyeditor of the book.

Finally, we would like to acknowledge the contributions of our students, who have provided invaluable comments and suggestions on the content and use of these cases.

If you have any questions, comments, or suggestions concerning *Ethical Obligations and Decision Making in Accounting,* please send them to us through our publisher.

Steve Mintz

Rosie Morris

Case Descriptions

Chapter 1

Chapter 2

Chapter 3

Chapter 4

Case #	Case Name/Description

Chapter 5

Case #	Case Name/Description

Chapter 6

Chapter 7

Chapter 8

Case #	Case Name/Description
8-1	**SEC v. Siemens Aktiengesellschaft** *Massive bribery by German company totaling $1.4 billion with 4,283 separate payments using slush funds, off-book accounts, and business consultants and intermediaries to facilitate the illegal payments.*
8-2	**Parmalat: Europe's Enron** *Fictitious accounts at Bank of America and the use of nominee entities to transfer debt off books and remove impaired receivables led to one of Europe's largest fraud cases.*
8-3	**Satyam: India's Enron** *Known as India's Enron, Satyam's founder and CEO falsified financial information including revenues and bank balances while the auditors failed to follow appropriate standards to ferret out the fraud.*
8-4	**Royal Dutch Shell plc** *Overstatement of estimated recoverable proved oil and gas reserves in violation of SEC regulations.*
8-5	**Bat-A-Bing Construction Company** *Change in U.S. GAAP with respect to accounting for changes in accounting practices and policies in order to conform to IFRS standards.*

Major Cases

Chapter Coverage	Case Name/Description
Chapter 5	**Adelphia Communications Corporation** *SEC action against auditors for failing to exercise the proper degree of professional skepticism in examining complex related-party transactions and contingencies that were not accounted for in accordance with GAAP.*
Chapter 6	**Royal Ahold N.V. (Ahold)** *Court finds that the auditors did not have the necessary "scienter" to sustain legal proceedings against it for violating Section 10(b) of the Securities Exchange Commission Act of 1934.*
Chapter 7	**MicroStrategy, Inc.** *SEC action against MicroStrategy and its auditor for improper accounting for multiple deliverables and questionable auditor judgments.*
Chapters 1–7	**Cendant Corporation** *SEC action against Cendant for managing earnings by using techniques such as merger reserve manipulations and the failure of auditors to ferret out the fraud.*

Brief Contents

Contents

Chapter 4
AICPA Code of Professional Conduct   154

Chapter 7
Earnings Management and the Quality of Financial Reporting   323

Chapter 8
International Financial Reporting: Ethics and Corporate Governance Considerations   378

Ethical Reasoning: Implications for Accounting

Ethics Reflection

CAPITALISM AND ETHICS

Adam Smith, the father of modern economics, set out in his 1776 book *An Inquiry into the Nature and Causes of the Wealth of Nations* a philosophy that the pursuit of one's own interest led by the invisible hand of a free marketplace often leads to promoting the interests of society "more effectually than when [one] really intends to promote it."[1] Smith knew that a considerable structure was required in society before the invisible hand mechanism could work efficiently. For example, property rights must be strong, and there must be widespread adherence to *moral norms,* such as prohibitions against theft and misrepresentation. Therefore, laws and *moral values* such as honesty and integrity are a prerequisite for the invisible hand to work in the public interest.

THE 2008–2009 FINANCIAL CRISIS

The financial crisis that began in 2008 highlights the shortcomings of the invisible hand. Encouraged by the repeal in 1999 of the Glass-Steagall Act of 1933 that created a separation between commercial banking and the securities industry, large investment banks such as Lehman Brothers and Bear Stearns engaged in risky mortgage lending practices under the guise of subprime loans that facilitated the financial crisis. Loans were made to borrowers without proper documentation to support the amount of debt. Homeowners were either not informed of all the risks or lost in the "fine print." Once the economy started to falter as home values plunged and the jobless rate skyrocketed, some of these homeowners were unable to pay their monthly mortgage payments. The investment banks were not too concerned, perhaps because they had already sold off their loans as asset-based mortgages to Fannie Mae, a stockholder-based corporation chartered by Congress in 1968 to purchase these securitized mortgages so that funds would be available to institutions to lend again to new home buyers. The repeal of the Glass-Steagall Act fostered in a period of financial engineering and new forms of exotic securities such as credit default swaps that were sold by companies such as AIG to provide insurance for financial institutions in case borrowers could not repay debt.

WHO IS TO BLAME?

Existing regulations failed to cover the new forms of financial instruments. Some blame former Federal Reserve chair Alan Greenspan for failing to push for stronger regulation and for encouraging risky behavior as, in part, a way to encourage home ownership for those who might not otherwise qualify for mortgage loans. Others believe he was naive about the dangers of these new financial products. He always had believed that deregulation of financial markets and reliance upon self-regulation by self-interest was the way of both freedom and prosperity. However, in his testimony to Congress on October 23, 2008, during its investigation of the causes of the financial crisis, Greenspan sang a different tune. "Those of us who have looked to the self-interest of

(Continued)

lending institutions to protect shareholder's equity, myself included, are in a state of shocked disbelief. Such counter-party surveillance is a central pillar of our financial markets' state of balance. . . . The whole intellectual edifice [of risk management in derivative markets] . . . collapsed. . . . If it fails, as occurred this year, market stability is undermined."[2]

As you read this chapter think about the following: (1) Is laissez-faire capitalism a moral economic system? (2) What are the values essential to having an ethical free-market economy? (3) How can moral philosophies contribute toward making ethical decisions?

Have the courage to say no. Have the courage to face the truth. Do the right thing because it is right. These are the magic keys to living your life with integrity.

W. Clement Stone (1902–2002)

The quote by William Clement Stone, a businessman, philanthropist, and self-help book author, underscores the importance of integrity in decision making. Notice that the quote addresses integrity in one's personal life. That is because one has to act with integrity when making personal decisions to be best equipped to act with integrity on a professional level. Integrity, indeed all of ethics, is not a spigot that can be turned on or off depending on one's whims or whether the matter at hand is personal or professional. As the ancient Greeks knew, we learn how to be ethical by practice and exercising those virtues that enable us to lead a life of excellence.

In accounting, internal accountants and auditors may be pressured by superiors to manipulate financial results. The external auditors may have to deal with pressures imposed on them by clients to put the best face on the financial statements regardless of whether they conform to generally accepted accounting principles (GAAP). It is the ethical value of integrity that provides the moral courage to resist the temptation to stand by silently while a company misstates its financial statement amounts.

Integrity: The Basis of Accounting

According to Mintz, "Integrity is a fundamental trait of character that enables a CPA to withstand client and competitive pressures that might otherwise lead to the subordination of judgment."[3] A person of integrity will act out of moral principle and not expediency. That person will do what is right even if it means the loss of a job or client. In accounting, the public interest (i.e., investors and creditors) always must be placed ahead of the one's own self-interest or the interests of others, including a supervisor or client.

Integrity means a person acts on principle—a conviction that there is a right way to act when faced with an ethical dilemma. For example, assume that your tax client fails to inform you about an amount of earned income for the year and you confront the client on this issue. The client tells you not to record it and reminds you there is no W-2 or 1099 form to evidence the earnings. The client adds that you will not get to audit the company's financial statements anymore if you do not adhere to the client's wishes. Would you decide to "go along to get along"? If you are a person of integrity you should not allow the client to dictate how the tax rules will be applied in the client's situation. You are the professional and know the tax regulations best, and you have an ethical obligation to report taxes in accordance with the law. If you go along with the client and the Internal Revenue Service (IRS) investigates and sanctions you for failing to follow the IRS Tax Code, then you may suffer irreparable harm to your reputation. An important point is that a professional must never let loyalty to a client cloud good judgment and ethical decision making.

WorldCom: Cynthia Cooper, a Real Hero

Cynthia Cooper's experience at WorldCom illustrates how the internal audit function should work and how one person can put a stop to financial fraud. It all unraveled in April and May of 2002 after Gene Morse, an auditor at WorldCom, couldn't find any documentation to record $500 million in computer expenses. Morse approached his boss, Cynthia Cooper, the company's director of internal auditing, who instructed Morse to "keep going." A series of obscure tips led Morse and Cooper to suspect that WorldCom was cooking the books. Cooper formed an investigation team to determine whether their hunch was right. In its initial investigation, the team discovered $3.8 billion of misallocated expenses and phony accounting entries.[4] Cooper approached the chief financial officer (CFO), Scott Sullivan, but was dissatisfied with his explanations. The chief executive officer (CEO) of the company, Bernie Ebbers, had already resigned so Cooper went to the audit committee. The committee interviewed Sullivan about the accounting issues and did not get a satisfactory answer. Still, the committee was reluctant to take any action but Cooper persisted. Eventually, one member of the audit committee told her to approach the outside auditors to get their take on the matter. Cooper gathered additional evidence of fraud and ultimately KPMG, the firm that had replaced Arthur Andersen LLP—the auditors during the fraud—supported Cooper. Sullivan was asked to resign, refused to do so, and was fired.[5]

One tragic result of the fraud and cover-up at WorldCom is the case of Betty Vinson. It is not unusual for someone who is genuinely a good person to get caught up in fraud. Vinson, a former WorldCom mid-level accounting manager, went along with the fraud because her superiors told her to do so. She was convinced that it would be a one-time action. It rarely works that way because once an accounting fraud starts at a company it feels compelled to continue the charade into the future to keep up the appearance that each period's results are as good as or better than prior periods. The key to maintaining one's integrity and ethical perspective is not to take the first step down the proverbial *ethical slippery slope.*

Vinson pleaded guilty in October 2002 to participating in the financial fraud at the company. She was sentenced to five months in prison and five months of house arrest. Vinson represents the typical "pawn" in a financial fraud: an accountant who had no interest or desire to commit fraud but got caught up in it when Sullivan, her boss, instructed her to make improper accounting entries. The rationalization by Sullivan that the company had to "make the numbers appear better than they really were" did nothing to ease her guilty conscience. Judge Barbara Jones, who sentenced Vinson, commented that "Ms. Vinson was among the least culpable members of the conspiracy at WorldCom. . . . Still, had Vinson refused to do what she was asked, it's possible this conspiracy might have been nipped in the bud."[6]

Accounting students should reflect on what they would do if they faced a situation similar to the one that led Vinson to do something that was out of character. Once she agreed to go along with making improper entries, it was difficult to turn back. The company could have threatened to disclose her role in the original fraud and cover-up if Vinson all of a sudden developed a conscience.

Vinson became involved in the fraud because she had feared losing her job, her benefits, and the means to provide for her family. She must live with the consequences of her actions for the rest of her life. On the other hand, Cynthia Cooper on her own initiative ordered the internal investigation that led to the discovery of the $11 billion fraud at WorldCom. Cooper did all the right things to bring the fraud out in the open. Cooper received the Accounting Exemplar Award in 2004 given by the American Accounting Association and was inducted into the AICPA Hall of Fame in 2005.

Cooper truly is a positive role model. She discusses the foundation of her ethics that she developed as a youngster because of her mother's influence in her book *Extraordinary Circumstances: The Journey of a Corporate Whistleblower.* Cooper says: "Fight the good fight. Don't ever allow yourself to be intimidated. . . . Think about the consequences of your actions. I've seen too many people ruin their lives."[7]

Religious and Philosophical Foundations of Ethics

Virtually all of the world's great religions contain in their religious texts some version of the Golden Rule: "Do unto others as you would wish them do unto you." In other words, we should treat others the way we would want to be treated. This is the basic ethic that guides all religions. If we believe honesty is important, then we should be honest with others and expect the same in return. One result of this ethic is the concept that every person shares certain inherent human rights that will be discussed later in this chapter and the next. Exhibit 1.1 provides some examples of the universality of the Golden Rule in world religions provided by the character education organization "Teaching Values."[8]

Integrity is the key to carrying out the Golden Rule. A person of integrity acts with truthfulness, courage, sincerity, and honesty. Integrity means to have the courage to stand by your principles even in the face of pressure to bow to the demands of others. As previously mentioned, integrity has particular importance for certified public accountants (CPAs) who oftentimes are pressured by their employers and clients to give in to their demands. The ethical responsibility of a CPA in these instances is to adhere to the ethics of the accounting profession and not to subordinate professional judgment to others. Integrity encompasses the whole of the person and it is the foundational virtue of the ancient Greek philosophy of virtue.

The origins of Western philosophy trace back to the ancient Greeks including Socrates, Plato, and Aristotle. The ancient Greek philosophy of virtue deals with questions such as: What is the best sort of life for human beings to live? Greek thinkers saw the attainment of a good life as the *telos,* the end or goal of human existence. For most Greek philosophers, the end is *eudaimonia,* which is usually translated as "happiness." However, to the Greeks the end goal of happiness meant much more than to experience pleasure or satisfaction. The ultimate goal of happiness was to attain some objectively good status, the life of excellence. The Greek word for excellence is *arete,* the customary translation of which is "virtue." Thus for the Greeks, the "excellences" or "virtues" were the qualities that made a life admirable or excellent. They did not restrict their thinking to characteristics we regard as

EXHIBIT 1.1
The Universality of the Golden Rule in the World Religions

Religion	Expression of the Golden Rule	Citation
Christianity	All things whatsoever ye would that men should do to you, Do ye so to them; for this is the law and the prophets.	Matthew 7:1
Confucianism	Do not do to others what you would not like yourself. Then there will be no resentment against you, either in the family or in the state.	Analects 12:2
Buddhism	Hurt not others in ways that you yourself would find hurtful.	Udana-Varga 5,1
Hinduism	This is the sum of duty, do naught onto others what you would not have them do unto you.	Mahabharata 5, 1517
Islam	No one of you is a believer until he desires for his brother that which he desires for himself.	Sunnah
Judaism	What is hateful to you, do not do to your fellowman. This is the entire Law; all the rest is commentary.	Talmud, Shabbat 3id
Taoism	Regard your neighbor's gain as your gain, and your neighbor's loss as your own loss.	Tai Shang Kan Yin P'ien
Zoroastrianism	That nature alone is good which refrains from doing another whatsoever is not good for itself.	Dadisten-I-dinik, 94, 5

moral virtues, such as courage, justice, and temperance, but included others we think of as nonmoral such as wisdom.[9]

Modern philosophies have been posited as ways to living an ethical life. Unlike virtue theory, these philosophies rely more on methods of ethical reasoning and they, too, can be used to facilitate ethical decision making. We review these philosophies later in the chapter.

What Is Ethics?

The term *ethics* is derived from the Greek word *ethikos* which itself is derived from the Greek word *ethos*, meaning "custom" or "character." Morals are from the Latin word *moralis*, meaning "customs," with the Latin word *mores* being defined as "manners, morals, character." Therefore, ethics and morals are essentially the same.

In philosophy, ethical behavior is that which is "good." The Western tradition of ethics is sometimes called moral philosophy. The field of ethics or moral philosophy involves developing, defending, and recommending concepts of right and wrong behavior. These concepts do not change as one's desires and motivations change. They are not relative to the situation. They are immutable.

In a general sense, ethics (or moral philosophy) addresses fundamental questions such as: How should I live my life? That question leads to others such as: What sort of person should I strive to be? What values are important? What standards or principles should I live by?[10] There are various ways to define *ethics*. The simplest may be to say that ethics deals with "right" and "wrong." However, it is difficult to judge what may be right or wrong in a particular situation without some frame of reference.

Ethics must be based on accepted standards of behavior. For example, in virtually all societies and cultures it is wrong to kill someone or steal property from someone else. These standards have developed over time and come from a variety of sources including:

- The influence of religious writing and interpretations
- The influence of philosophical thought
- The influence of community (societal) values

In addition, the ethical standards for a profession, such as the accounting profession, are heavily influenced by the practices of those in the profession, state laws and board of accountancy rules, and the expectations of society. Gaa and Thorne define ethics as "the field of inquiry that concerns the actions of people in situations where these actions have effects on the welfare of both oneself and others."[11] We adopt that definition and emphasize that it relies on ethical reasoning to evaluate the effects of actions on others— *the stakeholders.*

Norms, Values, and the Law

Ethics deals with well-based standards of how people *ought* to act, does not describe the way people *do* act, and is prescriptive, not descriptive. Ethical people always strive to make the right decision in all circumstances. They do not rationalize their actions based on their own perceived self-interests. Ethical decision making entails following certain well-established norms of behavior. The best way to understand ethics may be to differentiate it from other concepts.

Values and Ethics

Values are basic and fundamental beliefs that guide or motivate attitudes or actions. In accounting, the values of the profession are embedded in its codes of ethics that guide the actions of accountants and auditors in meeting their professional responsibilities.

Values are concerned with how a person behaves in certain situations, whereas ethics is concerned with how a moral person should behave. A person who values prestige, power, and wealth is likely to act out of self-interest, whereas a person who values honesty, integrity, and trust will typically act in the best interests of others. It does not follow that acting in the best interests of others precludes acting in one's own self-interest. Indeed, the Golden Rule prescribes that we should treat others the way we want to be treated.

The Golden Rule requires that we try to understand how our actions affect others; thus we need to put ourselves in the place of the person on the receiving end of the action. The Golden Rule is best seen as a consistency principle in that we should not act one way toward others but have a desire to be treated differently in a similar situation. In other words, it would be wrong to think that separate standards of behavior exist to guide our personal lives but that a different standard (a lower one) exists in business.

Laws versus Ethics

Being ethical is not the same as following the law. Although ethical people always try to be law-abiding, there may be instances where their sense of ethics tells them it is best not to follow the law. These situations are rare and should be based on sound ethical reasons.

> Assume you are driving 45 miles-per-hour on a two-lane divided roadway (double yellow line) going east. All of a sudden you see a young boy jump out to retrieve a ball. The boy is close enough to your vehicle so that you know you cannot continue straight down the roadway and stop in time to avoid hitting him. You quickly look to your right and notice about 10 other children off the road. You cannot avoid hitting 1 or more of them if you swerve to the right to avoid hitting the boy in the middle of the road. You glance to the left on the opposite side of the road and notice no traffic going west or any children off the road. What should you do?
>
> **Ethical Perspective**
>
> If you cross the double yellow line that divides the roadway, you have violated the motor vehicle laws. We are told never to cross a double yellow line and travel into on-coming traffic. The ethical action would be to do just that given you have determined it appears to be safe. It is better to risk a ticket than hit the boy in the middle of your side of the road or those boys off to the side of the road.

Laws and Ethical Obligations

Benjamin Disraeli (1804–1881), the noted English novelist, debater, and former prime minister, said, "When men are pure, laws are useless; when men are corrupt, laws are broken." A person of goodwill honors and respects the rules and laws and is willing to go beyond them when circumstances warrant. As indicated by the previous quote, such people do not need rules and laws to guide their actions. They always try to do the right thing. On the other hand, the existence of specific laws prohibiting certain behaviors will not stop a person who is unethical (e.g., does not care about others) from violating those laws. Just think about a "Ponzi" scheme such as the one engaged in by Bernie Madoff whereby he duped others to invest with him promising huge returns that, unbeknownst to the investor, would come from additional investments of scammed investors and not true returns. Bernie's story will be discussed in Chapter 3.

Laws create a minimum set of standards. Ethical people often go beyond what the law requires because the law cannot cover every situation a person might encounter. When the facts are unclear and the legal issues uncertain, an ethical person should decide what to do on the basis of well-established standards of ethical behavior. This is where moral philosophies come in and, for accountants and auditors, the ethical standards of the profession.

Ethical people often do less than is permitted by the law and more than is required. A useful perspective is to ask:

What does the law require of me?

What do ethical standards of behavior demand of me?

How should I act to conform to both?

The Gray Area

When the rules are unclear, an ethical person looks beyond his own self-interest and evaluates the interests of the stakeholders potentially affected by the action or decision. Ethical decision making requires that a decision maker, at least sometimes, be willing to take an action that may not be in his best interest. This is known as the "moral point of view."

Sometimes people believe that the ends justify the means. Nothing could be further from the truth. The process you follow to decide on a course of action is more important than achieving the end goal. If this were not true from a moral point of view then we could rationalize all kinds of actions in the name of achieving a desired goal even if that goal does harm to others while, at the same time, satisfying our personal needs and desires.

Imagine that you work for a CPA firm and are asked to evaluate three software packages for a client. Your boss tells you that the managing partners are pushing for one of these packages that happens to be the firm's internal software. Your initial numerical analysis of the packages based on functionality, availability of upgrades, and customer service indicates that a competitor's package is better than the firm's software. Your boss in no uncertain terms tells you to redo the analysis. You know what she wants. Even though you feel uncomfortable with the situation, you decide to "tweak" the numbers to show a preference for the firm's package. The end result desired in this case is to choose the firm's package. The means to that end was to alter the analysis, an unethical act because it is dishonest and unfair to the other competitors to change the objectively determined results. In this instance, ethical decision making requires that we place the client's interests (to get the best software package for his needs) above those of the firm (to get the new business and not upset the boss).

Ethical Relativism

Ethical relativism is the theory that holds that morality is relative to the norms of one's culture. That is, whether an action is right or wrong depends on the moral norms of the society in which it is practiced. The same action may be morally right in one society but be morally wrong in another. For the ethical relativist, there are no universal moral standards—standards that can be universally applied to all peoples at all times. The only moral standards against which a society's practices can be judged are its own. If ethical relativism is correct, then there can be no common framework for resolving moral disputes or for reaching agreement on ethical matters among members of different societies.

Most ethicists reject the theory of ethical relativism. Some claim that while the moral practices of societies may differ, the fundamental moral principles underlying these practices do not. For example, in the 1990s there was a situation in Singapore where a young American spray-painted graffiti on several cars. The Singaporean government's penalty was to "cane" the youngster. In the United States, some said it was cruel and unusual punishment for such a minor offense. In Singapore, the issue is that to protect the interests of society, the government treats harshly those who commit relatively minor offenses. After all, it does send a message that in Singapore this and similar types of behavior will not be tolerated. While such a practice might be condemned in the United States, most people would agree with the underlying moral principle—the duty to protect the safety and security of the public (life and liberty concerns). Societies, then, may differ in their application of fundamental moral principles but agree on the principles.

The Six Pillars of Character

It has been said that ethics is all about how we act when no one is looking. In other words, ethical people do not do the right thing because someone observing their actions might conclude otherwise or they may be punished as a result of their actions. Instead, ethical people act as they do because their "inner voice" or conscience tells them it is the right thing to do.

What makes a person of goodwill? What enables a person to treat others with respect, caring, and fairness? It is someone who internalizes the ethical values described in the following sections and lives life consistently, both at home and at work, in accordance with those same values.

The Josephson Institute of Ethics identifies Six Pillars of Character that provide a foundation to guide ethical decision making. These ethical values include trustworthiness, respect, responsibility, fairness, caring, and citizenship. Josephson believes that the Six Pillars act as a multilevel filter through which to process decisions. So, being trustworthy is not enough—we must also be caring. Adhering to the letter of the law is not enough; we must accept responsibility for our actions or inactions.[12]

Trustworthiness

The dimensions of trustworthiness include being honest, acting with integrity, being reliable, and exercising loyalty in dealing with others.

Honesty

Honesty is the most basic ethical value and means that we should express the truth as we know it and without deception. In accounting, the full disclosure principle supports transparency and requires that the accounting professional should disclose all the information that owners, investors, creditors, and the government need to know to make informed decisions. To withhold relevant information is dishonest. Transparent information is that which helps one understand the process followed to reach a decision.

Let's assume you are a member of a discussion group in your Intermediate Accounting II class and in an initial meeting with all members the leader asks whether there is anyone who has not completed Intermediate I. You failed the course last term and are retaking it concurrently with Intermediate II. However, you feel embarrassed and say nothing. Now, perhaps the leader feels it is important because a case study assigned to your group uses knowledge gained from Intermediate I. You internally justify the silence by thinking: Well, I did complete the course, albeit with a grade of F. This is an unethical position. You are rationalizing silence by interpreting the question in your own self-interest rather than in the interests of the entire group. The other members need to know whether you have completed Intermediate I because the leader may choose not to assign a specific project to you that requires the Intermediate I prerequisite knowledge.

Integrity

The integrity of a person is an essential element in trusting that person. MacIntyre, in his account of Aristotelian virtue, states, "There is at least one virtue recognized by tradition which cannot be specified except with reference to the wholeness of a human life—the virtue of integrity or constancy."[13] A person of integrity takes time for self-reflection, so that the events, crises, and challenges of everyday living do not determine the course of that person's moral life. Such a person is trusted by others because that person is true to her word.

Going back to the previous example, if you encounter a conflict with another group member who pressures you to plagiarize a report available on the Internet that the two of you are working on, you will be acting with integrity if you refuse to go along. Integrity requires that you should have the courage of your convictions. You know it's wrong to plagiarize other material. Someone worked hard to get the report published. You would not want another person to take material you had published without permission and proper citation. Why do it to that person? If you do it simply because it might benefit you, then you act out of self-interest, or egoism, and that is wrong!

Reliability

The promises that we make to others are relied on by them and we have a moral duty to follow through with action. Our ethical obligation for promise-keeping includes avoiding bad-faith excuses and unwise commitments. Imagine that you are asked to attend a group meeting on Saturday and you agree to do so. That night your best friend calls and says he has two tickets to the basketball game between the Dallas Mavericks and San Antonio Spurs. The Spurs are in town, so you decide to go to the game instead of the meeting. You've broken your promise and you did it out of self-interest. You figured, who wouldn't want to see the Spurs play? What's worse is you call the group leader and say you can't attend the meeting because you are sick. Now you've also lied. You've started the slide down the ethical slippery slope and it will be difficult to climb back up to the top.

Loyalty

We all should value loyalty in friendship. After all, you wouldn't want the friend who called you to go to the basketball game to telephone the group leader later in the day and say you went to the game on the day of the group meeting.

Loyalty requires that friends not violate the confidence we place in them. In accounting, loyalty requires that we keep financial and other information confidential when it deals with our employer and client. For example, if you are the in-charge accountant on an audit of a client for your CPA firm-employer and you discover that the client is "cooking the books," you shouldn't telephone the local newspaper and tell the story to a reporter. Instead, you should go to the partner in charge of the engagement and tell her. Your ethical obligation is to report what you have observed to your supervisor and let her take the appropriate action.

A Word about Whistleblowing

There are limits to the confidentiality obligation. For example, let's assume that you are the accounting manager at a publicly owned company and your supervisor (the controller) pressures you to keep silent about the manipulation of financial information. You go to the CFO who tells you both the CEO and board of directors support the controller. Out of a misplaced duty of loyalty in this situation you might rationalize your silence. Ethical values sometimes conflict and loyalty is the one value that should never take precedence over other values such as honesty and integrity. Otherwise, we can imagine all kinds of cover-ups of information in the interest of loyalty or friendship.

Internal whistleblowing typically is appropriate to clarify the positions of your superiors and bring matters of concern to the highest levels within an organization including the audit committee of the board of directors. In fact, the ethics of the accounting profession (Interpretation 102-4 of the American Institute of Certified Public Accountants [AICPA] Code of Professional Conduct)[14] obligates the CPA to do just that. The prior example may

EXHIBIT 1.2
Ethical Responsibilities of Industry CPAs to Avoid Subordinating Judgment*

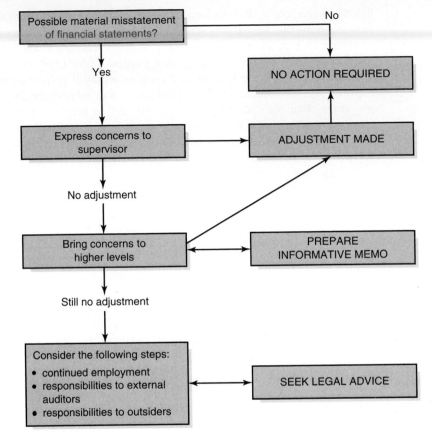

*A depiction of the requirements of Interpretation 102-4 developed by Steven Mintz.

represent a situation where you may be tempted to take the matter outside your employer or circumvent the firm-employer relationship to air your concerns. You should be careful if you choose to do this and get legal advice before acting. Informing parties outside an entity violates confidentiality. While acting out of conscience and a sense that the right thing to do is the highest ethical choice one can make, it is important to be aware of the consequences of one's actions before taking the ultimate step of external whistleblowing. Exhibit 1.2 describes the ethical standards for CPAs under Interpretation 102-4.

Notice that the process is clearly defined and requires bringing any concerns to higher-ups in the organization including the audit committee and preparing an informative memorandum that would summarize the various positions including that of members of top management. The memo should help provide a defense of due care and compliance with ethical standards in case it becomes a regulatory or legal matter.

While attending a Josephson Institute of Ethics training program for educators, one of your authors heard Michael Josephson make an analogy about loyal behavior that sticks with him to this day. Josephson said: "Dogs are loyal to their master while cats are loyal to the house." How true it is that dogs see their ultimate allegiance to their owner while cats get attached to the place they call home—their own personal space. Now, in a business context this means that a manager should try to encourage "cat" behavior in the organization (sorry dog lovers). In that way, if a cover-up of a financial wrongdoing exists, the cat loyalty mentality incorporated into the business environment dictates that the information be disclosed since it is not in the best interests of the organization to hide or ignore it. If we act with dog loyalty, we will cover up for our supervisor who has a say about what happens to us in the organization. It may be an understandable position, perhaps, but it is unethical all the same. Moreover, once we go along with the cover-up, we have started the slide down the ethical slippery slope and there may be no turning back. In fact, our supervisor may come to us next period and expect the same cover-up in a similar situation. If we refuse, the first instance may be brought up and used as a threat against us since we've already violated ethical standards once and don't want to get caught. It is important to emphasize that we should not act ethically out of fear of the consequences of hiding information. Instead, we should act ethically out of a positive sense that it is the right way to behave.

Oftentimes when we cover up information in the present, later on it becomes public knowledge. The results at that time are more harmful since trust is gone. Think about former President Richard Nixon, who went along with the cover-up in the Watergate break-in only to be forced to resign the presidency once the cover-up became public knowledge.

Respect

All people should be treated with dignity. We do not have an ethical duty to hold all people in high esteem, but we should treat everyone with respect, regardless of their circumstances in life. In today's slang language we might say that respect means "giving a person his 'props.'" The Golden Rule encompasses respect for others through notions such as civility, courtesy, decency, dignity, autonomy, tolerance, and acceptance.[15]

By age 16, George Washington had copied out by hand 110 *Rules of Civility & Decent Behavior In Company and Conversation.* They are based on a set of rules composed by French Jesuits in 1595. While many of the rules seem out of place in today's society, Washington's first rule is noteworthy: "Every Action done in Company, ought to be with Some Sign of Respect, to those that are Present."[16]

Washington's vernacular was consistent with the times as indicated by the last of his rules: "Labour to keep alive in your Breast that Little Spark of Celestial fire Called Conscience."[17] There are many definitions of conscience, but the one your authors find most relevant comes from the lexical database for the English language by the Cognitive Sciences Laboratory at Princeton University. The definition is: "Motivation deriving logically from ethical or moral principles that govern a person's thoughts and actions."[18]

As a member of the case discussion group in the previous example, it would be wrong to treat another member with discourtesy or prejudice because you have prejudged that person on the basis of national origin or some other factor rather than one's abilities and conduct. You would not want to be treated unfairly because of how you dress or walk or talk, so others should not be judged based on similar considerations. We should judge people based on their character.

The Nobel Prize peace activist Dr. Martin Luther King said it best in his "I Have a Dream" speech delivered on the steps at the Lincoln Memorial in Washington, DC, on August 28, 1963. Dr. King said the following in reference to the true meaning of the nation's creed: "'We hold these truths to be self-evident; that all men are created equal.' . . . I have a dream that my four little children will one day live in a nation where they will not be judged by the color of their skin but by the content of their character."[19]

Responsibility

Josephson points out that our capacity to reason and our freedom to choose make us morally autonomous for our actions and decisions. We are accountable for what we do and who we are.[20]

A responsible person carefully reflects on alternative courses of action using ethical principles. A responsible person acts diligently and perseveres in carrying out moral action. Imagine if you were given the task by your group to interview five CPAs in public practice about their most difficult ethical dilemma and you decided to ask one person, who was a friend of the family, about five dilemmas that person faced in the practice of public accounting. Now, even if you made an "honest" mistake in interpreting the requirement, it is clear that you did not exercise the level of care that should be expected in this instance in carrying out the instructions to interview five different CPAs. The due care test is whether a "reasonable person" would conclude that you had acted with the level of care, or diligence, expected in the circumstance. The courts have used this test for many years to evaluate the actions of professionals.

Fairness

A person of fairness treats others equally, impartially, and openly. In business we might say that the fair allocation of scarce resources requires that those who have earned the right to a greater share of corporate resources as judged objectively by performance measures should receive a larger share than those whose performance has not met the standard.

Let's assume your instructor told the case study groups at the beginning of the course that the group with the highest overall numerical average would receive an A grade, the group with second highest a B, and so on. At the end of the term the teacher gave the group with the second highest average—90.5—an A and the group with the highest average—91.2—a B grade. Perhaps the instructor took subjective factors into account in deciding on the final grading. You might view the instructor's action as unfair to the group with the highest average. As Josephson points out, "Fairness implies adherence to a balanced standard of justice without relevance to one's own feelings or inclinations."[21]

Caring

The late Edmund L. Pincoffs, a philosopher who formerly taught at the University of Texas at Austin, believed that virtues such as caring, kindness, sensitivity, altruism, and benevolence enable a person who possesses these qualities to consider the interests of others.[22] Josephson believes that caring is the "heart of ethics, and ethical decision-making."[23]

The essence of caring is empathy. Empathy is the ability to understand, be sensitive to, and care about the feelings of others. Caring and empathy support each other and enable a person to put herself in the position of another. This is essential to ethical decision making.

Let's assume that the morning of an important group meeting your child comes down with a temperature of 103 degrees. You call the group leader and say that you can't make it to the meeting. Instead, you suggest that the meeting be taped and you will listen to the discussions later that day and telephone the leader with any questions. The leader reacts angrily stating that you are not living up to your responsibilities. Assuming your behavior is not part of a pattern, you would have a right to be upset with the leader who seems uncaring. In the real world, emergencies do occur and placing your child's health and welfare above all else should make sense in this situation to a person of rational thought. You also acted diligently by offering to listen to the discussions and, if necessary, follow up with the leader.

Putting yourself in the place of another is sometimes difficult to do because the circumstances are unique to the situation. For example, what would you do if a member of your team walked into a meeting all bleary-eyed? You might ignore it or you might ask that person if everything is all right. If you do and are informed that the person was up all night with a crying baby, then you might say something like: If there's anything I can do to lighten the load for you today, just say the word.

A person who can empathize seems to know just what to say to make the other person feel better about circumstances. On the other hand, if you have never been married and have not had children, you might not be able to understand the feelings of a mother who has just spent the night trying to comfort a screaming child.

Citizenship

Josephson points out that "citizenship includes civic virtues and duties that prescribe how we ought to behave as part of a community."[24] An important part of good citizenship is to obey the laws, be informed of the issues, volunteer in your community, and vote in elections. President Barack Obama has called for citizens to engage in some kind of public service to benefit society as a whole.

Reputation

It might be said that judgments made about one's character contribute toward how another party views that person's reputation. In other words, what is the estimation in which a person is commonly held, whether favorable or not? The reputation of a CPA is critical to a client's trusting that CPA to perform services competently and maintain the confidentiality of client information, notwithstanding whistleblowing instances. One builds "reputation capital" through favorable actions informed by ethical behavior. You should never forget that it takes a long time to build a reputation of trust, but not very long at all to tear it down.

All too often in politics a well-respected leader becomes involved in some behavior that, once disclosed, tears down a reputation earned over many years of service. The case of former senator and presidential candidate John Edwards provides a clear example of how quickly one's reputation can be destroyed, in this case because of the disclosure of an extramarital affair that was covered up by Edwards.

John Edwards admitted to ABC News[25] in an interview with Bob Woodruff in August 2009 that he repeatedly lied about an extramarital affair with a 42-year-old campaign employee, Rielle Hunter. Edwards strenuously denied being involved in paying the woman hush money or fathering her newborn child. He admitted the affair was a mistake. "Two years ago I made a very serious mistake, a mistake that I am responsible for and no one else. In 2006, I told Elizabeth [his wife] about the mistake, asked her for her forgiveness, asked God for his forgiveness. And we have kept this within our family since that time." Edwards said he told his entire family about the affair after it ended in 2006, and that his wife Elizabeth was "furious" but that their marriage would survive.

In 2006, Edwards's political action committee (PAC) paid Hunter's video production firm $100,000 for work. Then the committee paid another $14,086 on April 1, 2007. The Edwards camp said the latter payment from the PAC was in exchange for 100 hours of unused videotape Hunter shot. The same day, the Edwards presidential campaign had injected $14,034.61 into the PAC for a "furniture purchase," according to federal election records.

Edwards, a U.S. senator representing North Carolina from 1998 until his vice presidential bid in 2004, acknowledged in May 2009 that federal investigators are looking into how he used campaign funds. Grand jury proceedings are secret, and the U.S. attorney's office in Raleigh has declined to confirm or deny an investigation.

A man who once claimed to have fathered the child of John Edwards's mistress, Andrew Young, says in a book that the former presidential candidate is the real father and that Edwards worked with Young, his former campaign finance chairman, to hide that secret. In the book, Young claims that he helped facilitate the affair between Edwards and Rielle Hunter. Young wrote that Edwards once told Hunter they would wed after Edwards's wife, who has cancer, died. Allegedly, Edwards told Hunter that the ceremony would be held on a rooftop in New York and the Dave Matthews Band would make an appearance.

During past interviews Edwards had always denied that he fathered Hunter's child. However, Young claimed that Edwards knew from the start that he was the father of the child and expended considerable effort trying to conceal that. Allegedly, Edwards even pleaded with Young to claim paternity. On January 21, 2010 (prior to Young's book being published), Edwards finally admitted to being the father stating: "It was wrong for me ever to deny she was my daughter and hopefully one day, when she understands, she will forgive me."

Edwards violated virtually every tenet of ethical behavior and destroyed his reputation. He lied about the affair and attempted to cover it up, including allegations that he fathered Hunter's baby. He violated the trust of the public and lied after telling his family about the affair in 2006. He even had the audacity to run for the Democratic nomination for president in 2008. One has to wonder what it says about Edwards's ethics that he was willing to run for president of the United States while hiding the knowledge of his affair without considering what might happen if he had won the Democratic nomination in 2008, and then campaigned for president during which time news of the affair became public knowledge. His behavior is the ultimate example of ethical blindness and the pursuit of one's own self-interests to the detriment of all others. Perhaps the noted Canadian American chemist and author Orlando Aloysius Battista (1917–1995), said it best: "An error doesn't become a mistake until you refuse to correct it." In other words, when you do something wrong, admit it, take responsibility for your actions, accept the consequences, and move on.

AICPA Code of Professional Conduct: The Foundation of Ethical Reasoning in Accounting

The accounting profession is a community with values and standards of behavior. These are embodied in the various codes of conduct in the profession. The AICPA is a voluntary association of CPAs. Its membership totals more than 350,000 professionals around the world. Since the vast majority of CPAs belong to the association, its code of conduct typically is used to discuss the ethical obligations of CPAs. We discuss the Principles section of the AICPA Code of Professional Conduct in this chapter since they mirror virtues-based principles, and we elaborate on the Rules of conduct that are the enforceable provisions of the Code's Rules section in Chapter 4.

The Principles of the AICPA Code are aspirational statements that form the foundation for the Code's enforceable rules. The Principles guide members in the performance of their professional responsibilities and call for an unyielding commitment to honor the public trust, even at the sacrifice of personal benefits. While CPAs cannot be legally held to the Principles, they do represent the expectations for CPAs on the part of the public in the performance of professional services. In this regard, the Principles are based on values of the profession and traits of character (virtues) that enable CPAs to meet their obligations to the public.

The Principles include (1) Responsibilities; (2) The Public Interest; (3) Integrity; (4) Objectivity and Independence; (5) Due Care; and (6) Scope and Nature of Services.[26]

The umbrella statement in the Code is that the overriding responsibility of CPAs is to exercise sensitive professional and moral judgments in all activities. By linking professional conduct to moral judgment, the AICPA Code recognizes the importance of moral reasoning in meeting professional obligations. That is one reason why we discuss the classic moral philosophies later in the chapter.

The second principle defines the public interest to include "clients, credit grantors, governments, employers, investors, the business and financial community, and others who rely on the objectivity and integrity of CPAs to maintain the orderly functioning of commerce." This principle calls for resolving conflicts between these stakeholder groups by recognizing the primacy of a CPA's responsibility to the public as the way to best serve the clients' and employers' interests.

Integrity has been discussed before. As a principle of CPA conduct, integrity recognizes that the public trust is served by (1) being honest and candid within the constraints of client confidentiality; (2) not subordinating the public trust to personal gain and advantage;

(3) observing both the form and spirit of technical and ethical standards; and (4) observing the principles of objectivity and independence and of due care.

Objectivity requires that all CPAs maintain a mental attitude of impartiality and intellectual honesty and be free of conflicts of interest in meeting professional responsibilities. Independence applies only to CPAs who provide attestation services (i.e., auditing) and it requires both independence in fact and in appearance. Since it is difficult to determine independence in fact, CPAs should avoid relationships with a client entity that may be seen as impairing objective judgment by a "reasonable" observer. The foundational standard of independence is discussed in the context of the audit function in Chapter 5.

The due care standard (diligence) calls for continued improvement in the level of competency and quality of services by (1) performing professional services to the best of one's abilities; (2) carrying out professional responsibilities with concern for the best interests of those for whom the services are performed; (3) carrying out those responsibilities in accordance with the public interest; (4) following relevant technical and educational standards; and (5) properly planning and supervising engagements. A CPA who undertakes to perform professional services without having the necessarily skills violates the due care standard. The requirement for continuing education to maintain one's CPA certificate helps meet the due care standard.

Imagine if a CPA were asked to perform an audit of a school district and the CPA never engaged in governmental auditing before and never completed a course of study in governmental auditing. While the CPA (CPA firm) may still obtain the necessary skills to perform the audit—for example, by hiring someone with the required skills—the CPA would have a hard time supervising such work without the proper background and knowledge.

The due care standard also relates to the scope and nature of services performed by a CPA. The latter requires that CPAs practice in firms that have in place internal quality control procedures to ensure that services are competently delivered and adequately supervised and that such services are consistent with one's role as a professional. Also, CPAs should determine, in their individual judgments, whether the scope and nature of other services provided to an audit client would create a conflict of interest in performing an audit for that client.

Virtue, Character, and CPA Obligations

Traits of character such as honesty, integrity, and trustworthiness enable a person to act with virtue and apply the moral point of view. Kurt Baier, a well-known moral philosopher, discusses the moral point of view as being one that emphasizes practical reason and rational choice.[27] To act ethically means to incorporate ethical values into decision making and to reflect on the rightness or wrongness of alternative courses of action.

Aristotle believed that deliberation (reason and thought) precedes the choice of action and we deliberate about things that are in our power (voluntary) and can be realized in action. The deliberation that leads to the action always concerns choices and not the ends. We take the end for granted—a life of excellence or virtue—and then consider in what manner and by what means it can be realized.[28]

Aristotle's conception of virtue can be equated with positive traits of character to identify ethical standards in the accounting profession. These virtues enable CPAs to have integrity—the inner strength of character to withstand pressures that might otherwise overwhelm and negatively influence their professional judgment. A summary of the virtues is listed in Exhibit 1.3.[29]

EXHIBIT 1.3
Virtues and Ethical
Obligations of CPAs

Aristotle's Virtues	Ethical Standards for CPAs
Trustworthiness, benevolence, altruism	**Integrity**
Honesty, **integrity**	Truthfulness, non-deception
Impartiality, open-mindedness	Objectivity, independence
Reliability, dependability, faithfulness	Loyalty (confidentiality)
Trustworthiness	Due care (competence and prudence)

Modern Moral Philosophies

The ancient Greeks believed that reason and thought precede the choice of action and that we deliberate about things we can influence with our decisions. In making decisions, most people want to follow the laws and rules. However, rules are not always clear and laws may not cover every situation. Therefore, it is the ethical foundation we develop and nurture that will determine how we react to unstructured situations that challenge our sense of right and wrong. In the end, we need to rely on moral principles to guide our decision making.

Moral philosophies provide specific principles and rules we can use to decide what is right or wrong in specific instances. They can help a business decision maker formulate strategies to deal with ethical dilemmas and resolve them in a morally appropriate way. There are many such philosophies, but we limit the discussion to those that are most applicable to the study of accounting ethics including teleology, deontology, justice, and virtue ethics. Our approach focuses on the most basic concepts needed to help you understand the ethical decision-making process in business and accounting. We do not favor any one of these philosophies since there is no one correct way to resolve ethical issues in business. Instead, we present them to aid in resolving ethical dilemmas in accounting. Exhibit 1.4 summarizes the basis for making ethical judgments for each of the major moral philosophies. The discussion that follows elaborates on these principles and applies them to a common situation in accounting.

Teleology

Recall that *telos* is the Greek word for "end" or "purpose." In *teleology,* an act is considered morally right or acceptable if it produces some desired result such as pleasure, the realization of self-interest, fame, utility, wealth, and so on. Teleologists assess the moral worth of behavior by looking at its consequences, and thus moral philosophers often refer to these theories as consequentialism. Two important teleological philosophies that typically guide decision making in individual business decisions are egoism and utilitarianism.

Egoism and Enlightened Egoism

Egoism defines right or acceptable behavior in terms of its consequences for the individual. *Egoists* believe that they should make decisions that maximize their own self-interest, which is defined differently by each individual. In other words, the individual should "Do the act that promotes the greatest good for oneself."[30] Many believe that egoistic people and companies are inherently unethical, are short-term oriented, and will take advantage of others to achieve their goals. Our laissez-faire economic system enables the selfish pursuit of individual profit so that a regulated marketplace is essential to protect the interests of those affected by individual (and corporate) decision making.

There is one form of egoism that emphasizes more of a direct action to bring about the best interests of society. *Enlightened egoists* take a long-range perspective and allow for the well-being of others because they help achieve some ultimate goal for the decision maker, although their own self-interest remains paramount. Enlightened egoists may, for

EXHIBIT 1.4 Ethical Reasoning Methods Basis for Making Ethical Judgments

	Teleology			Deontology	Justice	Virtue Ethics
	Egoism	Enlightened Egoism	Utilitarianism	Rights Theory		
Ethical Judgments	Defines "right" behavior by consequences for the decision maker	Considers well-being of others within the scope of deciding on a course of action based on self-interest	Evaluates consequences of actions (harms and benefits) on stakeholders *Act* — Evaluate whether intended *action* provides greatest net benefits *Rule* — Select action that conforms to the correct *moral rule* that produces greatest net benefits	Considers "rights" of stakeholders & related duties to them Treats people as an end and not merely as a means to an end *Universality Perspective:* Would I want others to act in a similar manner for similar reasons in this situation?	Emphasizes rights, fairness, and equality Those with equal claims to justice should be treated equally; those with unequal claims should be treated unequally	Only method where ethical reasoning methods–"virtues" (internal traits of character)–apply both to *decision maker* and the decision Judgments are made not by applying rules but by possessing those traits that enable the decision maker to act for the good of others. Similar to Principles of AICPA Code and IMA Standards
Problems with Implementation	Fails to consider interests of those affected by decision	Interests of others are subservient to self-interest	Can be difficult to assign values to harms and benefits	Relies on moral absolutes—no exceptions; need to resolve conflicting rights	Can be difficult to determine criteria to distinguish equal from unequal claims	Virtues may conflict requiring choices to be made

17

example, abide by professional codes of ethics, avoid cheating on taxes, and create safe working conditions. They do so not because their actions benefit others but because they help achieve some ultimate goal for the egoist, such as advancement within the firm.[31]

Let's examine the following example from the perspectives of egoism and enlightened egoism. The date is Friday, January 15, 2011, and the time is 5:00 p.m. It is the last day of fieldwork on an audit and you are the staff auditor in charge of receivables. You are wrapping up the test of subsequent collections of accounts receivable to determine whether certain receivables that were outstanding on December 31, 2010, and that were not confirmed by the customer as being outstanding have now been collected. If these receivables have been collected and in amounts equal to the year-end outstanding balances, then you will be confident that the December 31 balance is correct and this aspect of the receivables audit can be relied on. One account receivable for $1 million has not been collected even though it is 90 days past due. You go to your supervisor and discuss whether to establish an allowance for uncollectibles for part of or for the entire amount. Your supervisor contacts the manager in charge of the audit who goes to the CFO to discuss the matter. The CFO says in no uncertain terms that you should not record an allowance of any amount. The CFO does not want to reduce earnings below the current level because that will cause the company to not meet financial analysts' estimates of earnings for the year. Your supervisor informs you that the firm will go along with the client on this matter even though the $1 million amount is material. In fact, it is 10 percent of the overall accounts receivable balance on December 31, 2010.

The junior auditor faces a challenge to integrity in this instance. The client is attempting to circumvent GAAP. The ethical obligation of the staff auditor is to not subordinate judgment to others, including top management of the firm.

If you are an egoist you might conclude that it is in your best interests to go along with the firm's position to support the client's presumed interests. After all, you do not want to lose your job. An enlightened egoist would consider the interests of others including the investors and creditors, but still might reason that it is in her long-run interests to go along with the firm's position to support the client because she may not advance within the firm unless she is perceived to be a "team player."

Utilitarianism

Utilitarians follow a relatively straightforward method for deciding the morally correct course of action for any particular situation. First, we identify the various courses of action that we could perform. Second, we determine all of the foreseeable benefits and harms (consequences) that would result from each course of action for everyone affected by the action (stakeholders). And third, we choose the course of action that provides the greatest benefits after the costs have been taken into account.[32] Given its emphasis on evaluating the benefits and harms of alternatives on stakeholders, utilitarianism requires that we look beyond self-interest to consider impartially the interest of all persons affected by our actions.

The utilitarian theory was first formulated in the eighteenth century by the English writer Jeremy Bentham (1748–1832) and later refined by John Stuart Mill (1806–1873). Bentham sought an objective basis that would provide a publicly acceptable norm for determining what kinds of laws England should enact. He believed that the most promising way to reach an agreement was to choose the policy that would bring about the greatest net benefits to society once the harms had been taken into account. His motto became "the greatest good for the greatest number." Over the years, the principle of utilitarianism has been expanded and refined so that today there are many different variations of the principle. Modern utilitarians often describe benefits and harms in terms of satisfaction of personal preferences or in purely economic terms of monetary benefits over monetary costs.[33]

Utilitarians differ in their views about the kind of question we ought to ask ourselves when making an ethical decision. Some believe the proper question is: What effect will my doing this act in this situation have on the general balance of good over evil? If lying would produce the best consequences in a particular situation, we ought to lie.[34] These *act-utilitarians* examine the specific action itself, rather than the general rules governing the action, to assess whether it will result in the greatest utility. For example, a rule such as "don't subordinate judgment" would serve only as a general guide for an act-utilitarian. If the overall effect of giving in to the client's demands brings net utility to all of the stakeholders, then the rule is set aside.

Rule-utilitarians, on the other hand, claim that we must choose that act that conforms to the general rule that would have the best consequences. For the rule-utilitarian, actions are justified by appeal to rules such as "don't subordinate judgment." According to the rule-utilitarian, an action is selected because it is required by the correct moral rules that everyone should follow. The correct moral rule is that which maximizes intrinsic value and minimizes intrinsic disvalue. For example, a rule such as "don't deceive" might be interpreted as requiring the full disclosure of the possibility that the client will not collect on a material, $1 million receivable. A rule-utilitarian might reason that the long-term effects of deceiving the users of financial statements are a breakdown of the trust that exists between the users and preparers and auditors of financial information.

In other words, we must ask ourselves: What effect would everyone's doing this kind of action (subordination of judgment) have on the general balance of good over evil? So, for example, the rule "to always tell the truth" in general promotes the good of everyone and therefore should always be followed, even if in a certain situation lying would produce the best consequences. Notwithstanding differences between act and rule-utilitarians, most hold to the general principle that morality must depend on balancing the beneficial and harmful consequences of our conduct.[35]

While utilitarianism is a very popular ethical theory, there are some difficulties in relying on it as a sole method for moral decision making because the utilitarian calculation requires that we assign values to the benefits and harms resulting from our actions. But it is often difficult, if not impossible, to measure and compare the values of certain benefits and costs. Let's go back to our receivables example. It would be difficult to quantify the possible effects of going along with the client. How can a utilitarian measure the costs to the company of possibly having to write off a potential bad debt after the fact including possible higher interest rates to borrow money in the future because of a decline in liquidity? What is the cost to one's reputation for failing to disclose an event at a point in time that might have affected the analysis of financial results? On the other hand, how can we measure the benefits to the company of *not* recording the allowance? Does it mean the stock price will rise and, if so, by how much?

Deontology

Deontology is derived from the Greek word *deon* meaning "duty." Deontology refers to moral philosophies that focus on the rights of individuals and on the intentions associated with a particular behavior rather than on its consequences. *Deontologists* believe that moral norms establish the basis for action. Deontology differs from rule-utilitarianism in that the moral norms (or rules) are based on reason, not outcomes. Fundamental to deontological theory is the idea that equal respect must be given to all persons.[36] In other words, individuals have certain inherent rights and I, as the decision maker, have a duty (obligation, commitment, or responsibility) to respect those rights.

Philosophers claim that rights and duties are correlative. That is, my rights establish your duties and my duties correspond to the rights of others. The deontological tradition focuses on duties, which can be thought of as establishing the ethical limits of my behavior.

From my perspective, duties are what I owe to others. Other people have certain claims on my behavior; they have, in other words, certain rights against me.[37]

Unlike utilitarians, deontologists argue that there are some things we should never do, regardless of utilitarian benefits. For example, deontologists would consider it wrong for someone who has no money to steal bread. It violates the right of the storeowner to gain from his hard work baking and selling the bread. This is the dilemma in the classic story *Les Misérables* by Victor Hugo. The main character, Jean Valjean, serves a 19-year sentence at hard labor for stealing a loaf of bread to feed his starving family.

Rights Principles

A *right* is a justified claim on others. For example, if I have a right to freedom, then I have a justified claim to be left alone by others. Turned around, I can say that others have a duty or responsibility to leave me alone.[38] In accounting, since investors and creditors have a right to accurate and complete financial information, I have the duty to ensure that the financial statements "present fairly" financial position, results of operations, and changes in cash flows.

Formulations of *rights theories* first appeared in the seventeenth century in writings of Thomas Hobbes and John Locke. One of the most important and influential interpretations of moral rights is based on the work of Immanuel Kant (1724–1804), an eighteenth-century philosopher. Kant maintained that each of us has a worth or dignity that must be respected. This dignity makes it wrong for others to abuse us or to use us against our will. Kant expressed this idea in a moral principle: Humanity must always be treated as an end, not merely as a means. To treat a person as a mere means is to use a person to advance one's own interest. But to treat a person as an end is to respect that person's dignity by allowing each the freedom to choose for himself or herself.[39]

An important contribution of Kantian philosophy is the so-called categorical imperative: "Act only according to that maxim by which you can at the same time will that it should become universal law."[40] The "maxim" of our acts can be thought of as the intention behind our acts. The maxim answers the question: What am I doing and why?

Kant tells us that we should act only according to those maxims that could be universally accepted and acted on. For example, Kant believed that truth telling could, but lying could not, be made a universal law. If everyone lied whenever it suited them, rational communication would be impossible. Thus lying is unethical. Imagine if every company falsified its financial statements. It would be impossible to accurately evaluate the financial results of one company over time and in comparison to other companies. The financial markets might ultimately collapse because reported results were meaningless and even misleading. This condition of universality, not unlike the Golden Rule, prohibits us from giving our own personal point of view special status over the point of view of others. It is a strong requirement of impartiality and equality for ethics.[41]

One problem with deontological theory is that it relies on moral absolutes—absolute principles and absolute conclusions. Kant believed a moral rule must function without exception. The notions of rights and duties are completely separated from the consequences of one's actions. This could lead to making decisions that might adhere to one's moral rights and another's attendant duties to those rights but which also produce disastrous consequences for some. For example, imagine if you were the person hiding Anne Frank and her family in the attic of your home and the Nazis came banging at the door and demanded, Do you know where the Franks are? Now, a strict application of rights theory requires that you tell the truth to the Nazi soldiers. However, isn't this situation one in which an exception to the rule should come into play for humanitarian reasons?

Whenever we are confronted with a moral dilemma, we need to consider whether the action would respect the basic rights of each of the individuals involved. How would the action affect the well-being of those individuals? Would it involve manipulation or deception—either of which would undermine the right to truth that is a crucial personal right? Actions are wrong to the extent they violate the rights of individuals.[42]

Sometimes the rights of individuals will come into conflict and one has to decide which right has priority. There is no clear way to resolve conflicts between rights and the corresponding moral duties to respect those rights. One of the most widely discussed cases of this kind is taken from William Styron's *Sophie's Choice*. Sophie and her two children are at a Nazi concentration camp. A guard confronts Sophie and tells her that one of her children will be allowed to live and one will be killed. Sophie must decide which child will be killed. Sophie can prevent the death of either of her children, but only by condemning the other to be killed. The guard makes the situation even more painful for Sophie by telling her that if she chooses neither, then both will be killed. With this added factor, Sophie has a morally compelling reason to choose one of her children. But for each child, Sophie has an equally strong reason to save him or her. Thus the same moral precept gives rise to conflicting obligations.[43]

Now, thank goodness we do not face such morally excruciating decisions in accounting. The ultimate obligation of accountants and auditors is to honor the public trust. The public interest obligation that is embedded in the profession's codes of ethics requires that if a conflict exists between the obligations of a decision maker to others, the decision maker should always decide based on protecting the public's right (i.e., investors and creditors), such as in the receivables example, to receive accurate and reliable financial information about collectibility.

Justice

Justice is usually associated with issues of rights, fairness, and equality. A just act respects your rights and treats you fairly. Justice means giving each person what she or he deserves. *Justice* and *fairness* are closely related terms that are often used interchangeably, although differences do exist. While *justice* usually has been used with reference to a standard of rightness, *fairness* often has been used with regard to an ability to judge without reference to one's feelings or interests. When people differ over what they believe should be given, or when decisions have to be made how benefits and burdens should be distributed among a group of people, questions of justice or fairness inevitably arise. These are questions of *distributive justice.*[44]

The most fundamental principle of justice that was defined by Aristotle more than 2,000 years ago is that "equals should be treated equally and unequals unequally." In other words, individuals should be treated the same, unless they differ in ways that are relevant to the situation in which they are involved. The problem with this interpretation is in determining which criteria are morally relevant to distinguish between those who are equal and those who are not. It can be a difficult theory to apply in business if, for example, a CEO of a company decides to allocate a larger share of the resources than is warranted (justified) based on the results of operations, to one product line over another to promote that operation because it is judged to have more long-term expansion and income potential. If I am the manager in charge of the operation getting fewer resources but producing equal or better results, then I may believe that my operation has been (I have been) treated unfairly. On the other hand, it could be said that the other product line manager deserves to receive a larger share of the resources because of the long-term potential. That is, the product lines are not equal; the former deserves more resources because of its greater upside potential.

For purposes of our discussion, questions of fairness will be tied to making objective judgments. Auditors should render objective judgments about the fair presentation of financial results. In this regard, auditors should act as impartial arbiters of the truth just as should judges that make decisions in court cases. The ethical principle of objectivity requires that such judgments be made impartially, unaffected by pressures that may exist to do otherwise. An objective auditor with knowledge about the failure to allow for the uncollectible receivables would not stand idly by and allow the financial statements to be materially misleading.

Virtue Ethics

Virtue considerations apply both to the decision maker and to the act under consideration by that party. This is one of the differences between virtue theory and the other moral philosophies that focus on the act. To make an ethical decision, I must internalize the traits of character that make me an ethical (virtuous) person. This philosophy is called *virtue ethics,* and it posits that what is moral in a given situation is not only what conventional morality or moral rules require but also what a well-intentioned person with a "good" moral character would deem appropriate.

Virtue theorists place less emphasis on learning rules and instead stress the importance of developing *good habits of character,* such as benevolence. Plato emphasized four virtues in particular, which were later called cardinal virtues: wisdom, courage, temperance, and justice. Other important virtues are fortitude, generosity, self-respect, good temper, and sincerity. In addition to advocating good habits of character, virtue theorists hold that we should avoid acquiring bad character traits, or vices, such as cowardice, insensibility, injustice, and vanity. Virtue theory emphasizes moral education because virtuous character traits are developed in one's youth. Adults, therefore, are responsible for instilling virtues in the young. Virtue characteristics are particularly relevant to the cognitive moral development models discussed in Chapter 2.

The philosopher Alasdair MacIntyre states that the exercise of virtue requires "a capacity to judge and to do the right thing in the right place at the right time in the right way." Judgment is exercised not through a routinizable application of the rules, but as a function of possessing those dispositions (tendencies) that enables choices to be made about what is good for people and by holding in check desires for something other than what will help achieve this goal.[45]

MacIntyre relates virtues to the internal rewards of a practice. He differentiates between the external rewards of a practice (such as money, fame, and power) and the internal rewards, which relate to the intrinsic value of a particular practice. MacIntyre points out that every practice requires a certain kind of relationship between those who participate in it. The virtues are the standards of excellence that characterize relationships within the practice. To enter into a practice is to accept the authority of those standards, obedience to the rules, and the commitment to achieve the internal rewards. Some of the virtues that MacIntyre identifies are truthfulness and trust, justice, courage, and honesty.[46]

Mintz points out that the accounting profession is a practice with inherent virtues that enable accountants to meet their ethical obligations to clients, employers, the government, and the public at large. For instance, for auditors to render an objective opinion on a client's financial statements, auditors must be committed to perform such services without bias and to avoid conflicts of interest. Impartiality is an essential virtue for judges in our judicial system. CPAs render judgments on the fairness of financial statements. Therefore, they should act impartially in carrying out their professional responsibilities.

The virtues enable accounting professionals to resolve conflicting duties and loyalties in a morally appropriate way. They provide accountants with the inner strength of character to withstand pressures that might otherwise overwhelm and negatively influence their professional judgment in a relationship of trust.[47] For example, if your boss, the CFO, pressures you to overlook a material misstatement in the financial statements, it is the virtue of honesty that leads you to place your obligation to the public, including stockholders, above your employer's interest (loyalty to one's supervisor). It is the virtue of integrity that enables you to withstand the pressure to look the other way. Now, in the real world this is easier said than done. You may be tempted to be silent because you fear losing your job. However, the ethical standards of the accounting profession obligate accountants and auditors to bring these issues to the attention of those in the highest positions in an organization including the audit committee of the board of directors, as did Cynthia Cooper in the WorldCom fraud.

We realize for students it may be a difficult concept to internalize that, when forced into a corner by one's supervisor to go along with financial wrongdoing, you should stand up for what you know to be right even if it means losing your job. However, ask yourself the following questions: Do I want to work for an organization that does not value my professional opinion? If I go along with it this time, might the same demand be made at a later date? Will I begin to slide down that ethical slippery slope where there is no turning back? How much is my reputation for honesty and integrity worth? Would I be proud if others found out what I did (or didn't do)?

Application of Ethical Reasoning in Accounting

In this section we discuss the application of ethical reasoning in its entirety to a common dilemma faced by internal accountants and auditors. The case deals with the classic example of when pressure is imposed on accountants by top management to ignore material misstatements in the financial statements.

As we have seen, accountants have ethical obligations under the AICPA Code that obligate them to place the public interest ahead of all other interests including their own self-interest and that of an employer or client. Many internal accountants belong to the Institute of Management Accountants (IMA), a leading organization of management accountants and finance executives. About 60,000 professionals worldwide belong to the IMA. The IMA's Standards of Professional Practice[48] are presented in Exhibit 1.5. Notice how similar the standards are to the Principles of Professional Conduct in the AICPA Code. Most important, read through the "Resolution of Ethical Conflict" section that defines the steps to be taken by members when they are pressured to go along with financial statement improprieties. Specific steps to be taken include discussing matters of concern with the highest levels of the organization including the audit committee. Recall that Interpretation 102-4 of the AICPA Code contains a similar provision.

DigitPrint Case Study

DigitPrint was formed in March 2011 with the goal of developing an outsource business for high-speed digital printing. The company is small and does not yet have a board of directors. The comparative advantage of the company is that its founder and president, Henry Higgins, owned his own print shop for several years before starting DigitPrint. Higgins recently hired Liza Doolittle to run the start-up business. Wally Wonderful, who holds the Certified Management Accountant certification from the IMA, was hired to help set up a computerized system to track incoming purchase orders, sales invoices, cash receipts, and cash payments for the printing business.

DigitPrint received $2 million as venture capital to start the business. The venture capitalists were given an equity share in return. From the beginning, they were concerned about the inability of the management to bring in customer orders and earn profits. In fact, only $200,000 net income had been recorded during the first year. Unfortunately, Wonderful had just discovered that $1 million of accrued expenses had not been recorded at year-end. Had that amount been recorded, the $200,000 net income of DigitPrint would have changed to an $800,000 loss.

EXHIBIT 1.5 **Institute of Management Accountants Statement of Ethical Professional Practice**

Members of IMA shall behave ethically. A commitment to ethical professional practice includes overarching principles that express our values, and standards that guide our conduct.

Principles
IMA's overarching ethical principles include: Honesty, Fairness, Objectivity, and Responsibility. Members shall act in accordance with these principles and shall encourage others within their organizations to adhere to them.

Standards
A member's failure to comply with the following standards may result in disciplinary action.

I. Competence
Each member has a responsibility to:

1. Maintain an appropriate level of professional expertise by continually developing knowledge and skills.
2. Perform professional duties in accordance with relevant laws, regulations, and technical standards.
3. Provide decision support information and recommendations that are accurate, clear, concise, and timely.
4. Recognize and communicate professional limitations or other constraints that would preclude responsible judgment or successful performance of an activity.

II. Confidentiality
Each member has a responsibility to:

1. Keep information confidential except when disclosure is authorized or legally required.
2. Inform all relevant parties regarding appropriate use of confidential information. Monitor subordinates' activities to ensure compliance.
3. Refrain from using confidential information for unethical or illegal advantage.

III. Integrity
Each member has a responsibility to:

1. Mitigate actual conflicts of interest, regularly communicate with business associates to avoid apparent conflicts of interest. Advise all parties of any potential conflicts.
2. Refrain from engaging in any conduct that would prejudice carrying out duties ethically.
3. Abstain from engaging in or supporting any activity that might discredit the profession.

IV. Credibility
Each member has a responsibility to:

1. Communicate information fairly and objectively.
2. Disclose all relevant information that could reasonably be expected to influence an intended user's understanding of the reports, analyses, or recommendations.
3. Disclose delays or deficiencies in information, timeliness, processing, or internal controls in conformance with organization policy and/or applicable law.

Resolution of Ethical Conduct
In applying the Standards of Ethical Professional Practice, you may encounter problems identifying unethical behavior or resolving an ethical conflict. When faced with ethical issues, you should follow your organization's established policies on the resolution of such conflict. If these policies do not resolve the ethical conflict, you should consider the following courses of action:

1. Discuss the issue with your immediate supervisor except when it appears that the supervisor is involved. In that case, present the issue to the next level. If you cannot achieve a satisfactory resolution, submit the issue to the next management level. If your immediate superior is the chief executive officer or equivalent, the acceptable reviewing authority may be a group such as the audit committee, executive committee, board of directors, board of trustees, or owners. Contact with levels above the immediate superior should be initiated only with your superior's knowledge, assuming he or she is not involved. Communication of such problems to authorities or individuals not employed or engaged by the organization is not considered appropriate, unless you believe there is a clear violation of the law.
2. Clarify relevant ethical issues by initiating a confidential discussion with an IMA Ethics Counselor or other impartial advisor to obtain a better understanding of possible courses of action.
3. Consult your own attorney as to legal obligations and rights concerning the ethical conflict.

Wonderful approached his supervisor, Liza Doolittle, with what he had uncovered. She told him in no uncertain terms that the $1 million of expenses and liabilities could not be recorded. Doolittle warned Wonderful of the consequences of pursuing the matter any further. The reason was that the venture capitalists might pull out from financing DigitPrint because of the reduction of net income, working capital, and the higher level of liabilities. Wonderful is uncertain whether to inform Higgins. On one hand, he feels a loyalty obligation to go along with Doolittle. On the other hand, he believes he has an ethical obligation to the venture capitalists and other financiers that might help fund company operations.

We provide a brief analysis of ethical reasoning methods based on the following. First, consider the ethical standards of the IMA and evaluate potential actions for Wonderful. Then, use ethical reasoning with reference to the obligations of an accountant to analyze what you think Wonderful should do.

IMA Standards

Wonderful is obligated by the competence standard to follow relevant laws, regulations, and technical standards including GAAP in reporting financial information. He should ensure the credibility of the financial information with respect to the accrued expenses by insisting that the information be presented as objectively determined. Doolittle has refused to support his position and told him in no uncertain terms not to take the matter any further. However, Wonderful is obligated by the integrity standard not to simply stand by and do nothing; instead, he should inform Higgins of the conflict. If Higgins backs Doolittle's position of nondisclosure, then Wonderful should seek outside advice from a trusted adviser, including an attorney, to help evaluate legal obligations and rights concerning the ethical conflict.

Utilitarianism

Wonderful should attempt to identify the harms and benefits of (the act of) recording the transactions versus not recording them. The consequences of failing to inform the venture capitalists about the accrued expenses are severe not only for Wonderful but also for DigitPrint. These include a possible lawsuit, investigation by regulators for failing to record the information, and, most important, a loss of reputational capital in the marketplace. The primary benefit to Wonderful is acceptance by his superiors, and he is secure in the knowledge that he'll keep his job. Utilitarian values are difficult to assign to each potential act. Still, Wonderful should act in accordance with the moral rule that honesty requires not only truth telling but disclosing all the information that another party has a need (or right) to know.

Rights Theory

The venture capitalists have an ethical right to know about the higher level of payables, lower income, and the effect of the unrecorded transactions on working capital; the company has a duty to the venture capitalists to record the information. Wonderful should take the necessary steps to support such an outcome. The end goal of securing needed financing should not cloud Wonderful's judgment about the means chosen to accomplish the goal (i.e., nondisclosure). Wonderful should ask whether he believes others in a similar situation should cover up the existence of $1 million in accrued expenses. Assuming this is not the case, he shouldn't act in this way.

Justice

In this case the justice principle is linked to the fairness of the presentation of the financial statements. The omission of the $1 million of unrecorded expenses means that the statements would not "present fairly" financial position and results of operations. It violates the rights of the venture capitalists to receive accurate and reliable (fair presentation) financial information.

Virtue Considerations

The virtue of integrity requires Wonderful to have the courage to withstand the pressure imposed by Doolittle and not subordinate his judgment to that of hers. Integrity is the virtue that enables Wonderful to act in this way. While he has a loyalty obligation to his employer, it should not override his obligation to the venture capitalists who expect to receive truthful financial information. A lie by omission is dishonest and not consistent with the standards of behavior (virtues) in the accounting profession. The public relies on his ethics and integrity to ensure that the financial statements are free of material misstatement.

What Should Wonderful Do?

Wonderful should inform Doolittle that he will take his concerns to Higgins. That may force Doolittle's hand and cause her to back off from pressuring Wonderful. Higgins has a right to know as the president of the company. After all, he hired Doolittle because of her expertise and, presumably, based on certain ethical expectations. Higgins may decide to disclose the matter immediately and cut his losses since this is the right thing to do. On the other hand, if Higgins persists in covering up the matter, then, after seeking outside/legal advice, Wonderful must decide whether to go outside the company. His conscience may move him in this direction. However, the confidentiality standard requires that he not do so unless legally required.

A Message for Students

As you can tell from the DigitPrint case, ethical matters in accounting are not easy to resolve. On one hand, the accountant feels an ethical obligation to his employer or the client. On the other hand, the profession has strong codes of ethics that require accountants and auditors to place the public interest ahead of all other interests. Accounting professionals should analyze conflicting situations and evaluate the ethics by considering professional standards and the moral principles discussed in this chapter. A decision should be made after careful consideration of these factors and by applying logical reasoning to resolve the dilemma. Keep in mind that you may be in a position during your career where you feel pressured to remain silent about financial wrongdoing. You might rationalize that you didn't commit the unethical act so your hands are clean. That's not good enough as your ethical obligation to the public and the profession is to do whatever it takes to prevent a fraud from occurring and, if it does, take the necessary steps to correct the matter.

Scope and Organization of the Text

The overriding philosophy of this text is that the ethical obligations of accountants and auditors are best understood in the context of professional responsibilities including one's role in the corporate governance system, the requirements of financial reporting, the audit function, obligations to prevent and detect fraud, and legal liabilities. Given the rapid pace of globalization in the business world, we also believe that today's accounting students should gain an appreciation for ethical issues related to international financial reporting and global ethics standards.

CPAs serve as internal accountants and auditors, external auditors, tax preparers and advisers, and consultants to their clients. The ethics standards of the accounting profession provide the foundation for ethical decision making in the performance of professional responsibilities. These are discussed in the text as defined by the AICPA Code of Professional Conduct (Chapters 1 and 4), IMA's Statement of Ethical Professional Practice (Chapter 1), the Institute of Internal Auditors Code of Ethics (Chapter 4), and the Global Code of Ethics (Chapter 8).

Ethical decision making in accounting is predicated on moral reasoning. We have discussed moral philosophies in this chapter and discuss cognitive developmental theory and moral development in Chapter 2. We describe a variety of situations where such principles can help accounting professionals exercise ethical judgment.

Accounting professionals serve as members of management in positions such as controller, chief internal auditor, and CFO. In this regard, accounting professionals have an important role to play in the corporate governance system that is described in Chapter 3. The passage of the Sarbanes-Oxley (SOX) Act and New York Stock Exchange listing requirements strengthened the role and responsibilities of accountants and auditors in the governance process and require specific interactions with the audit committee.

The accounting profession has been investigated by Congress over a number of years following disclosures of financial fraud. A common question has been: Where were the auditors? Accounting scandals at companies such as Enron and WorldCom, and dozens of others that are discussed in the text, have led to the creation of the Public Company Accounting Oversight Board (PCAOB) that now sets audit, independence, and ethics standards for public companies that report to the Securities and Exchange Commission (SEC). These investigations and the standards of the PCAOB are discussed in Chapters 4 and 5.

CPAs are expected to approach an audit with a healthy dose of skepticism and exercise professional judgment informed by ethical principles. These issues are discussed throughout the text. The audit function is the foundation of the accounting profession. Virtually any person can perform tax and advisory services; only CPAs are allowed to conduct an (independent) audit of a client's financial statements. The ethical standards discussed in Chapter 4 are further explored in the context of auditing in Chapter 5 along with considerations related to internal controls and fraud detection and prevention. Certain "red flags" that may provide a warning signal about the existence of fraud and the auditors' responsibilities are explored in Chapters 5 and 7.

Accounting professionals are vulnerable to lawsuits when a company's financial statements fail to adhere to expected standards of reporting. Accountants and auditors are held to strict legal obligations under the Securities Act of 1933 and the Securities Exchange Act of 1934. Notwithstanding the passage of the Private Securities Litigation Reform Act that limited legal liability to a proportionate amount of the losses in a business failure, CPAs are often targets of lawsuits because they are perceived to have "deep pockets." Liability also exists under the Foreign Corrupt Practices Act that obligates accountants and auditors to look out for possible illegal payments that violate the act, and the act imposes internal control and reporting obligations. These issues are addressed in Chapters 6 and 8.

Perhaps no issue more than earnings management has been discussed as the cause of financial statement fraud. During the 1990s and early 2000s, companies financially engineered transactions to manage earnings and used devices such as "cookie jar reserves" and "channel stuffing" to alter the period in which earnings were recognized. These techniques have challenged the ethics of accounting professionals as they have been asked (expected) by their superiors and clients to go along with financial wrongdoing. We discuss a variety of cases throughout the book on earnings management, especially in Chapters 7 and 8.

The book concludes with Chapter 8 on ethics and corporate governance in the international environment. With the impending adoption of International Financial Reporting Standards (IFRS) in the United States and probable replacement of GAAP (at least for publicly owned companies), it is important for students to understand the ethical obligations of accountants and auditors with respect to international financial reporting. Examples are provided of international financial reports and corporate governance standards and practices as well as the Global Code of Ethics for Professional Accountants.

There are 160 discussion questions, 75 cases, and 4 major cases in the end-of-chapter materials. More than half of the cases have been taken from the files of the SEC to give a real-life dimension to the text. Many of the cases, at the end of the chapter or discussed in the text, deal with well-known examples of financial statement fraud both nationally and internationally.

This book covers a variety of areas in financial reporting and auditing. Most students will have taken the Intermediate Accounting sequence before using this book, so the financial reporting areas relevant to accounting ethics such as financial statement reporting and disclosure already will have been covered. As for auditing, the ethical responsibilities of CPAs that audit public companies cannot be separated from the audit function that is designed to provide reasonable assurance that the financial statements are free of material misstatements. We also address legal obligations because of the vulnerable position of accountants and auditors when fraud occurs. Coverage in the book is at a level that should be easily followed by students even if they have not completed courses in these areas.

Concluding Thoughts

Our culture seems to have morphed into exhibitionist tendencies where people do silly (stupid) things just to get their 15 minutes of fame with the promise of their own reality television show. Think about the "balloon boy" incident in October 2009, when the whole world watched a giant balloon fly through the air as a tearful family expressed fears that their six-year-old boy could be inside all the while knowing the whole thing was staged.

When was the last time you picked up a newspaper and read a story about someone doing the right thing because it was the right thing to do? It is rare these days. We seem to read and hear more about pursuing one's own selfish interests as the motivation for action. It might be called the "What's in it for me?" approach to life. Nothing could be more contrary to leading a life of virtue and, as the ancient Greeks knew, humility is an important virtue.

Ralph Waldo Emerson in his classic essay on friendship said: "The only reward of virtue is virtue; the only way to have a friend is to be one."[49] In other words, virtue is its own reward just as we gain friendship in life by being a friend to someone else. In accounting, integrity is its own reward because it builds trust in client relationships and helps honor the public trust.

Discussion Questions

1. Select one of the world's religions and give a concrete example of how the Golden Rule applies in that religion.

2. The following statements about virtue were made by noted philosophers/writers:

   a. MacIntyre, in his account of Aristotelian virtue, states that integrity is the one trait of character that encompasses all the others. How does integrity relate to, as MacIntrye said, "the wholeness of a human life"?

   b. David Starr Jordan (1851–1931), an educator and writer, said, "Wisdom is knowing what to do next; virtue is doing it." Explain the meaning of this phrase as you see it.

3. a. Do you think it is the same to act in your own-self interest as it is to act in a selfish way? Why or why not?

   b. Do you think "enlightened self-interest" is a contradiction in terms, or is it a valid basis for all action? Evaluate whether our laissez-faire, free-market economic system does (or should) operate under this philosophy.

4. a. What (who) has had the most influence on your personal ethics to this point in your life? Do you feel that your ethics are still evolving? What would cause you to change your ethics positively or negatively?

   b. Some believe that the absence of role models has negatively affected the overall ethics in society, especially with respect to young people. Do you agree or disagree?

5. One explanation about rights is that "there is a difference between what we have the right to do and what is the right thing to do." Explain what you think is meant by this statement.

6. In this chapter we discuss how John Edwards ruined his reputation by having an affair, covering it up, and then not admitting to fathering a child out of wedlock. Shortly after the Edwards disclosure, the public was stunned to find out that one of its most celebrated sports heroes—Tiger Woods—had also engaged in extramarital affairs. Do you think Tiger should be forgiven by the public for his transgressions? What about sponsors such as Nike? Should they drop Tiger and others who violate societal standards from their role as endorsers of products?

7. Steroid use in baseball is an important societal issue. Many members of society are concerned that their young sons and daughters may be negatively influenced by what apparently has been done at the major league level to gain an advantage and the possibility of severe health problems for young children from continued use of the body mass enhancer now and in the future. Barry Bonds and Roger Clemens, two potential future hall-of-famers for their accomplishments in home run productivity, should be listed in the record book with an asterisk after their names and an explanation that their records were established at a time when baseball productivity might have been positively affected by the use of steroids. Some even believe they should be denied entrance to the baseball Hall of Fame. Mark McGwire, who broke Roger Maris's 60-home-run record, initially denied using steroids. He has never come close to the 75 percent positive vote to be in the Hall of Fame. Some believe his admission in January 2010 that he did use steroids will help improve his maximum approval by sportscasters of 23.5 percent, but it still won't be enough to get him into the Hall. What do you think about these issues? Be sure to use ethical reasoning to support your position.

8. Your best friend is from another country outside the United States. One day after a particularly stimulating lecture on the meaning of ethics by your instructor, you and your friend disagree about whether culture plays a role in ethical behavior. You state that good ethics are good ethics and it doesn't matter where you live and work. Your friend tells you that in her country it is common to pay bribes to gain favor with important people. Comment on both positions. What do you believe?

9. Some people believe that ethics is relative to the situation. Others believe we should act the same way in similar situations. Comment on these opposing points of view.

10. a. What is the relationship between the ethical obligation of honesty and truth telling?

    b. Is it ever proper to not tell someone something he or she has a right to know? If so, describe under what circumstances this might be the case. How does this square with rights theory? If you believe it is never right to withhold such information, consider the virtue of caring or empathy to evaluate your action.

11. Assume you are coming home from the store one day and see a fast-moving fire approach your neighbor's house. You notice that the neighbor's car is in the garage. The garage door entrance to the house is locked as is the main entrance. You bang on the door and no one answers. You call the neighbor on your cell phone and no one answers. You don't think there is enough time to call the fire department 10 miles away before serious damage is done to the house. What would you do next and why?

12. In the discussion of loyalty in this chapter a statement is made that "your ethical obligation is to report what you have observed to your supervisor and let her take the appropriate action." We point out that you may want to take your concerns to others. Do you think there are any circumstances when you should go outside the company to report financial wrongdoing? If so, to what person/organization would you go? Why? If not, why would you not take the information outside the company?

13. In the new age of texting, blogging, tweeting, and updating one's Facebook, a variety of new activities have occurred that raise interesting ethical questions. For example, stay-at-home moms that blog often during the day are being wined and dined by giant food companies such as Nestlé in return for the unwritten understanding that they will blog positively about company products. In November 2009, Nestlé paid to put up 16 so-called mommy bloggers at the posh Langham Huntington Hotel in Pasadena, California. These bloggers were treated to a private show at the Magic Castle in Hollywood and sent packages of frozen Omaha steaks to their families to tide them over while the women were away learning all about the company's latest product lines. In return, the virtual sisterhood filed Twitter posts raving about Nestlé's canned pumpkin, Wonka candy, and Juicy Juice drinks. Is there anything wrong with these practices? Provide ethical support for your answer.

14. a. Assume you have been hired by the head of a tobacco industry group to do a cost–benefit analysis of whether the tobacco firms should disclose that nicotine is addictive. Assume this is before the federal government required such disclosure on all packages of cigarettes. Explain how you would go about determining what are the potential harms and potential benefits of disclosing this information voluntarily. Is there any information you feel cannot be included in the evaluation? What is it? Why can't you include it? If you could include it, would it impact your recommendation to the head of the industry group?

    b. Analyze the situation from a rights perspective, justice, and virtue theory. How might these considerations affect your recommendation to the head of the industry group?

15. Former associate justice of the U.S. Supreme Court Potter Stewart (1915–1985) said, "Fairness is what justice really is." How would you interpret this statement in the context of business decision making?

16. How does virtue theory apply to both the decision maker and the act under consideration by that party? Explain.

17. Distinguish between ethical rights and obligations from the perspective of accountants and auditors.

18. Assume in the DigitPrint case that the venture capitalists do not provide additional financing to the company even though the adjustments have not been made. The company hires an audit firm to conduct an audit of its financial statements to take to a local bank for a loan. The auditors become aware of the unrecorded $1 million in accrued expenses. Liza Doolittle pressures them to delay recording the expenses until after the loan is secured. The auditors do not know whether Henry Higgins is aware of all the facts. Identify the stakeholders in this case. What alternatives are available to the auditors? Use the AICPA Code of Professional Conduct and Josephson's Six Pillars of Character to evaluate the ethics of the alternative courses of action.

19. In their landmark book that was published in 1966, *Ethical Standards of the Accounting Profession*,[50] John Carey and William Doherty state: "The [AICPA] code [of ethics] in effect is an announcement that, in return for the faith which the public reposes in [CPAs], members of the profession accept the obligation to behave in a way that will be beneficial to the public." Comment on the meaning of this statement as you understand it.

20. Sir Walter Scott (1771–1832), the Scottish novelist and poet, wrote: "Oh what a tangled web we weave, when first we practice to deceive." Comment on what you think Scott meant by this phrase.

Endnotes

1. Adam Smith, *An Inquiry into the Nature and Causes of the Wealth of Nations* (London: Methuen, 5th ed., ed. Edwin Cannan, 1904).

2. Testimony of Dr. Alan Greenspan to the Committee of Government Oversight and Reform, October 23, 2008, www.oversight.house.gov/documents/20081023100438.pdf.

3. Steven M. Mintz, "Virtue Ethics and Accounting Education," *Issues in Accounting Education* 10, no. 2 (Fall 1995), p. 257.

4. Susan Pulliam and Deborah Solomon, "Ms. Cooper Says No to Her Boss," *The Wall Street Journal,* October 30, 2002, p. A1.

5. Lynne W. Jeter, *Disconnected: Deceit and Betrayal at WorldCom* (Hoboken, NJ: Wiley, 2003).

6. Securities Litigation Watch, *Betty Vinson Gets 5 Months in Prison,* http://slw.issproxy.com/securities_litigation_blo/2005/08/betty_vinson_ge.html.

7. Cynthia Cooper, *Extraordinary Circumstances* (Hoboken, NJ: Wiley, 2008).

8. Teaching Values, *The Golden Rule in World Religions,* www.teachingvalues.com/goldenrule.html.

9. William J. Prior, *Virtue and Knowledge: An Introduction to Ancient Greek Ethics* (London: Routledge, 1991).

10. William H. Shaw and Vincent Barry, *Moral Issues in Business* (Belmont, CA: Wadsworth Cengage Learning, 2010), p. 5.

11. James C. Gaa and Linda Thorne, "An Introduction to the Special Issue on Professionalism and Ethics in Accounting Education," *Issues in Accounting Education* 1, no. 1 (February 2004), p. 1.

12. Michael Josephson, *Making Ethical Decisions,* rev. ed. (Los Angeles: Josephson Institute of Ethics, 2002).

13. Alasdair MacIntyre, *After Virtue,* 2nd ed. (Notre Dame, IN: University of Notre Dame Press, 1984).

14. American Institute of Certified Public Accountants (AICPA), *AICPA Professional Standards. Volume 2 as of June 1, 2009,* Section 102-4 (New York: AICPA, 2009).

15. Josephson.

16. George Washington, *George Washington's Rules of Civility and Decent Behavior in Company and Conversation* (Bedford, ME: Applewood Books, 1994), p. 9.

17. Washington.

18. Cognitive Sciences Laboratory at Princeton University, *WordNet,* http.wordnet.princeton.edu.

19. Martin Luther King Jr., *The Peaceful Warrior* (New York: Pocket Books, 1968).

20. Josephson.

21. Josephson.

22. Edmund L. Pincoffs, *Quandaries and Virtues Against Reductivism in Ethics* (Lawrence: University Press of Kansas, 1986).

23. Josephson.

24. Josephson.

25. Rhonda Schwartz, Brian Ross, and Chris Francescani, "Edwards Admits Sexual Affair; Lied as Presidential Candidate" (Interview with *Nightline*), August 8, 2008.

26. American Institute of Certified Public Accountants, *Code of Professional Conduct* (New York: AICPA, 2002).

27. Kurt Baier, *The Rational and Moral Order: The Social Roots of Reason and Morality* (Oxford, England: Oxford University Press, 1994).

28. Aristotle, *Nicomachean Ethics,* trans. W. D. Ross (Oxford, England: Oxford University Press, 1925).

29. Steven M. Mintz, "Virtue Ethics and Accounting Education," *Issues in Accounting Education* 10, no. 2 (1995), p. 260.

30. O. C. Ferrell, John Fraedrich, and Linda Ferrell, *Business Ethics: Ethical Decision Making and Cases* (Mason, OH: South-Western, Cengage Learning, 2009 Update), pp. 150–151.

31. Ferrell et al., p. 151.

32. Manuel Velasquez, Claire Andre, Thomas Shanks, and Michael J. Meyer, "Calculating Consequences: The Utilitarian Approach to Ethics," *Issues in Ethics* 2, no. 1 (Winter 1989), www.scu.edu/ethics.

33. Velasquez et al., 1989.

34. Velasquez et al., 1989.

35. Velasquez et al., 1989.

36. Ferrell et al., p. 153.

37. Joseph Desjardins, *An Introduction to Business Ethics,* 3rd ed. (New York: McGraw-Hill, 2009), pp. 35–36.

38. Manuel Velasquez, Claire Andre, Thomas Shanks, and Michael J. Meyer, "Rights," *Issues in Ethics* 3, no. 1 (Winter 1990), www.scu.edu/ethics.

39. Velasquez et al., 1990.

40. Immanuel Kant, *Foundations of Metaphysics of Morals,* trans. Lewis White Beck (New York: Liberal Arts Press, 1959), p. 39.

41. Desjardins, pp. 35–36.

42. Velasquez et al., 1990.

43. William Styron, *Sophie's Choice* (London: Chelsea House, 2001).

44. Manuel Velasquez, Claire Andre, Thomas Shanks, and Michael J. Meyer, "Justice and Fairness," *Issues in Ethics* 3, no. 2 (Spring 1990).

45. Manuel G. Velasquez, *Business Ethics Concepts and Cases,* 4th ed. (Upper Saddle River, NJ: Prentice Hall, 1998), pp. 132–133.

46. MacIntyre, pp. 187–192.

47. Steven M. Mintz, *Cases in Accounting Ethics & Professionalism,* 3rd ed. (New York: McGraw-Hill, 1997), p. 26.

48. Institute of Management Accountants, *Statement of Ethical Professional Practice,* www.imanet.org.

49. Ralph Waldo Emerson, *Essays: First and Second Series* (New York: Vintage Paperback, 1990).

50. John L. Carey and William O. Doherty, *Ethical Standards of the Accounting Profession* (New York: AICPA, 1966).

Chapter 1 Cases

Case 1-1

A Student's Dilemma

Helen Kanell has a 4.0 grade point average and is in her last semester of college at Empire State University. Helen has already accepted a position to join the accounting firm of Big & Apple LLC. Still, she is determined to complete her career at Empire State and graduate with at least a 3.90 average to qualify for summa cum laude, the highest academic honor. However, she has a B average in all five courses going into the final exam. It seems as though Helen was distracted from her studies the last semester because she agreed to be the president of Beta Alpha Psi, the accounting student honor society, and it has required a great deal more work than anticipated. Helen is quite certain she will maintain her B average in four of the five courses but she knows she must get an A grade in at least one course to qualify for summa cum laude.

Prior to the final exam in Accounting 544, Accounting, Law & Governance, Helen is approached by her best friend who works in the accounting department office. Her friend is sensitive to Helen's situation and she had an opportunity to take a copy of the final exam from the professor's mailbox. She gives it to Helen and says, "You can thank me later."

Questions

1. Discuss Helen's responsibilities to each of the following groups in this situation:
   a. The accounting department and university
   b. Other students in the class and in the department
   c. Big & Apple LLC
   d. The professor of Accounting 544
   e. Her best friend (including possible consequences of Helen's action)
   f. Herself
2. What ethical values should guide Helen in her decision making?
3. If you were Helen, what would you do? Include in your answer to whom you might go for advice and the steps you would take to resolve the dilemma. Be specific. Would your answer change if Empire State University has an honor code? How about if it provides a $5,000 award to all students that graduate summa cum laude?

Case 1-2

Giles and Regas

Ed Giles and Susan Regas have never been happier than during the past four months since they have been dating each other. Giles is a 35-year-old CPA and a partner in the medium-sized accounting firm of Saduga & Mihca. Regas is a 25-year-old senior accountant in the same firm. Both Giles and Regas know the firm's policy on dating. Although it is acceptable for peers to date, the firm does not permit two members of different ranks within the firm to date. A partner should not date a senior in the firm any more than a senior should date a junior staff accountant. If such dating eventually leads to marriage, then one of the two must resign because of the conflict of interests. Giles and Regas have tried to be discreet about their relationship because they don't want to create any suspicions.

While most of the staff seem to know about Giles and Regas, it is not common knowledge among the partners that the two of them are dating. Perhaps that is why Regas was assigned to work on the audit of CAA Industries for a second year, even though Giles is the supervising partner on the engagement.

As the audit progresses, it becomes clear to the junior staff members that Giles and Regas are spending personal time together during the workday. On one occasion they were observed leaving for lunch together. Regas did not return to the client's office that day until three hours later. On another occasion Regas seemed distracted from her work, and later that day she received a dozen roses from Giles. A friend of Regas's, Ruth Revilo, inadvertently discovered this fact when she happened to see the card that accompanied the flowers. It was signed, "Love, Poochie." Regas had once told Revilo that it was the nickname Regas gave to Giles.

Revilo pulls Regas aside at the end of the day and says, "We have to talk."

"What is it?" Regas asks.

"I know the flowers are from Giles," Revilo says. "Are you crazy?"

"It's none of your business," Regas responds.

Revilo goes on to explain that others on the audit engagement team are aware of the relationship between the two. Revilo cautions Regas about jeopardizing her future with the firm by getting involved in a serious dating relationship with someone of a higher rank. Regas does not respond to this comment. Instead, she admits to being distracted lately because of an argument she had with Giles. She points out that the flowers are his way of saying he is sorry for some of the comments he had made about her. It all started when Regas had suggested to Giles that it might be best if they did not go out during the workweek because she was having a hard time getting to work on time. Giles was upset at the suggestion and called her ungrateful. He

said, "I've put everything on the line for you. There's no turning back for me."

Regas promises to talk to Giles and thanks Revilo for her concern. That same day, Regas telephones Giles and tells him she wants to temporarily put aside her personal relationship with him until the CAA audit is complete in two weeks. She suggests that, at the end of the two-week period, they get together and thoroughly examine the possible implications of their continued relationship. Giles reluctantly agrees, but he conditions his acceptance on having a "farewell" dinner at their favorite restaurant. Regas agrees to the dinner.

Giles and Regas have dinner that Saturday night. As luck would have it, the controller of CAA Industries, Mark Sax, is at the restaurant with his wife. Sax is startled when he sees Giles and Regas together. He wonders about the possible seriousness of their relationship, while reflecting on the recent progress billings of the accounting firm. Sax believes the number of hours billed is out of line with work of a similar nature and the fee estimate. He had planned to discuss the matter with Herb Morris, the managing partner of the firm. He decides to call Morris on Monday morning.

"Herb, you son of a gun, it's Mark Sax."

"Mark. How goes the audit?"

"That's why I'm calling," Sax responds. "Can we meet to discuss a few items?"

"Sure," Morris replies. "Just name the time and place."

"How about first thing tomorrow morning?" asks Sax.

"I'll be in your office at 8:00 a.m.," says Morris.

"Better make it at 7:00 a.m., Herb, before your auditors arrive."

Sax and Morris meet to discuss Sax's concerns about seeing Giles and Regas at the restaurant and the possibility that their relationship is negatively affecting audit efficiency. Morris asks whether any other incidents have occurred to make him suspicious about the billings. Sax says that he is only aware of this one instance, although he sensed some apprehension on the part of Regas last week when they discussed why it was taking so long to get the audit recommendations for adjusting entries. Morris listens attentively until Sax finishes and then asks him to be patient while he sets up a meeting to discuss the situation with Giles. Morris promises to get back to Sax by the end of the week.

Questions

1. Analyze the behavior of each party from the perspective of the Six Pillars of Character. Assess the personal responsibility of Ed Giles and Sue Regas for the relationship that developed between them. Who do you think is mostly to blame?

2. If Giles were a person of integrity but just happened to have a "weak moment" in starting a relationship with Regas, what do you think he would say when he meets with Herb Morris? Why?

3. Assume Ed Giles is the biggest "Rainmaker" in the firm. What would you do if you were in Herb Morris's position when you meet with Giles? In your response, consider how you would resolve the situation in regard to both the completion of the CAA Industries audit and the longer-term issue of the continued employment of Giles and Regas in the accounting firm.

Case 1-3

Jason Tybell

Jason Tybell has been employed as a junior accountant by the professional accountancy corporation of Rodgers & Philips for two years. Jason graduated with a bachelor's degree in accounting from State University. He became a CPA after passing all parts of the computerized CPA exam in one sitting. Jason is on the fast track with Rodgers & Philips, and he receives high evaluations from his seniors. He hopes to make partner in eight years. However, something just happened during an audit in his second year that makes him question whether that will ever happen—at least at Rodgers & Philips.

Jason is concerned about a meeting he will have later in the day with his mentor, William Jackson. The meeting concerns the fact that Jason was not asked to work on the current year's audit of two clients that he did work on during his first year. It is unusual for a second-year staff accountant not to continue unless something went wrong the first year. Jason is not aware of any such occurrence, but he is preparing for the worst. At a recent meeting of the partners of Rodgers & Philips, Jackson was informed that a third client has complained about Jason. As a result, Jason will be told by his mentor that he will not serve on the audit engagement of this client as well. Jackson discovered that Jason was given a good evaluation on the audit by the senior. However, the manager in charge of the audit requested that Jason not serve on the engagement team again because of complaints about Jason's inappropriate comments in meetings with client personnel. For example, Jason made a sarcastic comment to the office manager about the lack of organization of the computer files and records. Jason said, "Who set up this system, a five-year-old?" The comment was relayed to the indignant controller who informed the manager of the audit.

Jason enters William Jackson's office at 4:00 p.m. "Come in Jason." "Thanks, Bill. I gotta tell you I'm nervous about this meeting."

Jackson hesitated. He didn't expect Jason to be so blunt. Jackson decided to do the same.

"Jason, you have managed to upset some of our biggest clients."

"How so?" Jason responded.

"For starters, Cindi Laramie said that you made an inappropriate comment to her office manager last week and the controller was furious when he found out."

"Oh, you mean the comment about a five-year-old?" Jason asked.

"That's exactly what I mean," answered Jackson. "If you're aware that it was inappropriate, why did you make it?"

Jason said nothing.

"More important," Jackson said, "why didn't you apologize to the office manager and controller?"

Silence ensued for over a minute while Jason poured a glass of water and collected his thoughts. His mentor started to become impatient. Jackson walked over to Jason, put his hand on Jason's shoulder and asked, "Is everything okay at home?"

"Of course," Jason responded.

"Well, can you explain to me why you made the comment?" Jackson asked.

"I was just kidding. I thought the office manger had a good sense of humor."

At this point Jackson began to realize there was a big problem with Jason. Client contact is an important part of the responsibilities of all staff members in public accounting. Jackson now senses that Jason might not have what it takes. He decides to end the meeting by making an excuse that he had to go somewhere. Jackson did this to stall so that he could schedule an appointment with other key people in the firm to discuss the future of Jason Tybell.

Questions

1. Accountants are often judged on skills other than technical skills. What are those skills? Why are they important in public accounting?

2. Do you think it's ever appropriate for a staff accountant to joke around with a member of the client's organization? Why or why not? Identify ethical values to support your answer.

3. Is it right for a CPA firm or any other employer to give good evaluations to an employee and then turn around and fire that employee for something that was not noted in the evaluation? What's wrong with doing this from an ethical perspective? Use ethical reasoning to answer this question.

4. If you were making the decision in this case with respect to Jason's future in the firm, what would you do and why?

Case 1-4

Lone Star School District

Jose and Emily work as auditors for the state of Texas. They have been assigned to the audit of the Lone Star School District. There have been some problems with audit documentation for the travel and entertainment reimbursement claims of the manager of the school district. The manager knows about the concerns of Jose and Emily and he approaches them about the matter. The following conversation takes place:

Manager: Listen, I've requested the documentation you asked for but the hotel says it's no longer in their system.

Jose: Don't you have the credit card receipt or credit card statement?

Manager: I paid cash.

Jose: What about a copy of the hotel bill?

Manager: I threw it out.

Emily: That's a problem. We have to document all your travel and entertainment expenses for the city manager's office.

Manager: Well, I can't produce documents that the hotel can't find. What do you want me to do?

Questions

1. Assume Jose and Emily are CPAs and members of the AICPA. What ethical standards in the Code of Professional Conduct should guide them in dealing with the manager's inability to support travel and entertainment expenses?

2. Using Josephson's Six Pillars of Character as a guide, evaluate the statements and behavior of the manager.

3. a. Assume Jose and Emily report to Sharon, the manager of the school district audit. Should they inform Sharon of their concerns? Why or why not?

   b. Assume they don't inform Sharon but she finds out from another source. What would you do if you were in Sharon's position?

Case 1-5

Reneging on a Promise

Part A

Billy Tushoes recently received an offer to join the accounting firm of Tick and Check LLP. Billy would prefer to work for Foot and Balance LLP but has not received an offer from the firm the day before he must decide whether to accept the position at Tick and Check. Billy has a friend at Foot and Balance and is thinking about calling her to see if she can find out whether an offer is forthcoming.

Question

1. Should Billy call his friend? Provide reasons why you think he should or should not. Is there any other action you suggest Billy take prior to deciding on the offer of Tick and Check? Why do you recommend that action?

Part B

Assume Billy calls his friend at Foot and Balance and she explains the delay is due to the recent merger of Vouch and Trace LLP with Foot and Balance. She tells Billy that the offer should be forthcoming. However, Billy gets nervous about the situation and decides to accept the offer of Tick and Check. A week later he receives a phone call from the partner at Foot and Balance who had promised to contact him about the firm's offer. Billy is offered a position at Foot and Balance at the same salary as Tick and Check. He has one week to decide whether to accept that offer. Billy is not sure what to do. On one hand, he knows it's wrong to accept an offer and then renege on it. On the other hand, Billy hasn't signed a contract with Tick and Check and the offer with Foot and Balance is his clear preference because he has many friends at that firm.

Questions

1. Do you think it is ever right to back out of a promise you gave to someone else? If so, under what circumstances? If not, why not?

2. Identify the stakeholders and their interests in this case.

3. Evaluate the alternative courses of action for Billy using ethical reasoning. What should Billy do? Why?

Case 1-6

Serena Williams

At the 2009 U.S. Tennis Open, a line judge called a "foot fault" against Serena Williams, causing her to lose a point at a critical juncture of her championship match against the ultimate winner, Kim Clijsters. Williams menacingly turned toward the line judge and uttered an expletive. It was later reported that one of the things she said was, "You don't know where I'm from." (Williams grew up in Compton, a tough neighborhood outside Los Angeles.) The line judge ran up to the umpire to report the incident, which brought the tournament referee onto the court. Williams responded to statements by the line judge by proclaiming: "I never said I would kill you; are you serious?" Williams had picked up a first code violation for smashing her racket earlier in the match. After discussing the situation with the player, line judge, and chair umpire, Williams was handed a second code violation leading to her automatic disqualification and the match went to Clijsters.

Talking to the press 10 minutes after the match, Williams appeared calm but said she could not recall what she had said to the line judge.

> I said something that I guess they gave me a point penalty. Unfortunately, it was on match point. I didn't threaten. I didn't say, I don't remember any more. I was in the moment and everyone's fighting for every point. I've never foot faulted [all year] and then suddenly in this tournament they keep calling foot faults. I'm not going to sit here and make an excuse. If I foot fault, I did. It is what it is and that's basically all it was.

Williams, though, said she did not regret losing her temper: "I haven't thought about it to have any regrets. I try not to live my life saying, 'I wish' but I was out there and I fought and I tried and I did my best."

On the following day, Williams was set to play in the doubles final with her sister Venus. Some wondered whether Serena would be suspended for her actions and disqualified from playing in the women's doubles final. She was not and she and Venus won the double's title. Later, Serena was fined $10,500 by the tournament referee. In a statement released by her public relations firm, Serena apologized and said: "Everyone could truly see the passion I have for my job. Now that I have had time to gain my composure, I can see that while I don't agree with the unfair line call, in the heat of the battle I let my passion and emotion get the better of me and as a result handled the situation poorly."

Questions

1. People lose their temper all the time. Should we hold sports figures to a higher standard? Why or why not?

2. Evaluate Serena Williams's behavior and statements from an ethical perspective using Josephson's Six Pillars of Character.

3. The reactions to the Williams incident have been varied. Some believe her tantrum was bad for tennis and she should have been suspended. Others believe her tirade won't harm tennis one bit—the publicity and strong personality helps attract some in the public to tennis. Still others point out that men have acted badly in the past, including John McEnroe and Jimmy Connors, and no one seemed to blink an eye. Maybe there is a double standard. What do you believe?

Case 1-7

GMAT Cheating Scandal

The Graduate Management Admission Test (GMAT) is used by more than 4,000 graduate management programs worldwide and has been administered more than 200,000 times. It is a computer-adaptive exam that assembles a new test for every test taker from a pool of several thousand questions. The process virtually guarantees nobody gets the same test twice, or the same test as the person sitting at the next computer terminal. GMAC develops new test questions all the time—they cost GMAC about $2,400 each—and retires those that have been in circulation.

In the summer of 2008, 6,000 individuals who had taken the GMAT faced questions about possible unauthorized access to GMAT questions. This unprecedented action occurred after it was discovered that subscribers to a test-preparation service, Scoretop.com, may have received access to "live" GMAT questions—questions that were still currently in use by the Graduate Management Admission Council (GMAC) that develops the exam. GMAC sued Scoretop alleging copyright infringement and was awarded $2.3 million by the court plus legal costs, and the court allowed GMAC to seize Scoretop's domain name as well as a computer hard drive containing payment and other data. In the end, 84 individuals who generated 569 score reports to more than 100 business schools had their scores canceled by GMAC.

After investigating data on the subscribers to Scoretop from its hard drive, GMAC correlated the information with its own testing records—including the actual exam questions answered by the individual test takers—to identify individuals who used the site to break GMAC rules. Overall, it found 72 test takers who used the live questions, as well as 12 who posted questions after taking the test. Those who accessed the live questions were allowed to immediately retake the exam, but the 12 who posted questions from memory had to wait at least three years before retaking the GMAT. Students who posted live questions received harsher punishments because, according to the GMAC, they committed a worse offense. "Posters are taking our material and for the first time, putting it on a public site. They were involved in stealing our material," David Wilson, GMAC president, stated.

The Scoretop site offered a VIP service for $30 for 30 days that GMAC says gave visitors access to the "live" test questions. It is unclear whether everyone who used the site knew the questions were live. The site had described the questions as being "fully owned by Scoretop [and] written by our own . . . tutors." It is alleged that many of the posts

on the Scoretop site strongly suggested that visitors knew the questions were live. The messages referenced question "sets" and "JJs"—an acronym for "jungle juice"—which refer to groups of live questions that have been reconstructed by test takers and posted on the site. In one post cited by GMAC in its copyright infringement case, "h3adshOt" describes the value of the JJs as "inestimable," adding that he saw "10-12 JJs [when I took the GMAT,] word by word, and many of the other questions felt very familiar." In a "post-exam briefing" filed by "sammi," he described how he "got 3 successive [math] questions, of which all three were from Scoretop. . . . [T]he confidence you derive out of solving a seen problem is incomparable."

Those who take the GMAT must agree to GMAC's terms and conditions, which include a confidentiality agreement prohibiting the disclosure of test questions. To enter the test center, they must sign an agreement that gives GMAC the authority to cancel test scores if the test taker discloses a question "in any form or by any means." At the computer terminal itself, the test taker must agree to a second nondisclosure agreement. And in the 2008 *GMAT Bulletin,* GMAC reserves the right to cancel scores for any misconduct, including mere access to test content prior to the test, "even if a specific examinee's actual access to disclosed test content cannot be confirmed by GMAC."

Questions

1. Do you think the cancellation of GMAT scores by GMAC was warranted? Why or why not? Use ethical reasoning to support your answer.

2. Some who have blogged against GMAC's actions and the lawsuit claim that what the 84 students did was no big deal. Most test preparation consists of looking at old tests or sample questions and practicing on them. The fact that some live questions might also make it into the mix seems hardly likely to make much of a significant difference. Furthermore, it's not clear why Scoretop should be held responsible for the actions of its users. Comment on these statements.

3. From an ethical perspective, do you think it is wrong to subscribe to an online service that provides "live" GMAT test questions? What about posting those questions yourself after taking the test? Is this any different from buying a term paper from an Internet provider?

Case 1-8

A Faulty Budget

Jackson Daniels graduated from Lynchberg State College two years ago. Since graduating from the college, he has worked in the accounting department of Lynchberg Manufacturing. Daniels was recently asked to prepare a sales budget for the year 2011. He conducted a thorough analysis and came out with projected sales of 250,000 units of product. That represents a 25 percent increase over 2010.

Daniels went to lunch with his best friend, Jonathan Walker, to celebrate the completion of his first solo job. Walker noticed Daniels seemed very distant. He asked what the matter was. Daniels stroked his chin, ran his hand through his bushy, black hair, took another drink of scotch, and looked straight into the eyes of his friend of 20 years. "Jon, I think I made a mistake with the budget."

"What do you mean?" Walker answered.

"You know how we developed a new process to manufacture soaking tanks to keep the ingredients fresh?"

"Yes," Walker answered.

"Well, I projected twice the level of sales for that product than will likely occur."

"Are you sure?" Walker asked.

"I checked my numbers. I'm sure. It was just a mistake on my part," Daniels replied.

"So, what are you going to do about it?" asked Walker.

"I think I should report it to Pete. He's the one who acted on the numbers to hire additional workers to produce the soaking tanks," Daniels said.

"Wait a second," Walker said. "How do you know there won't be extra demand for the product? You and I both know

demand is a tricky number to project especially when a new product comes on the market. Why don't you sit back and wait to see what happens?"

"But what happens if I'm right and the sales numbers were wrong? What happens if the demand does not increase beyond what I now know to be the correct projected level?" Daniels asks.

"Well, you can tell Pete about it at that time. Why raise a red flag now when there may be no need?" Walker states.

As the lunch comes to a conclusion, Walker pulls Daniels aside and says, "Jack, this could mean your job. If I were in your position I'd protect my own interests first."

Questions

1. What should an employee do when he or she discovers that there is an error in a projection? Why do you suggest that action? Would your answer change if the error was not likely to affect other aspects of the operation such as employment? Why or why not?

2. Identify the stakeholders potentially affected by what Daniels decides to do. How might each stakeholder be affected by Daniels's action and decision? Use ethical reasoning to support your answer.

3. Assume Daniels is both a CPA and holds the Certified Management Accountant (CMA) certification granted by the IMA. Use the ethical standards of these two organizations to identify what Daniels should do in this situation.

Case 1-9

Cleveland Custom Cabinets

Cleveland Custom Cabinets is a specialty cabinet manufacturer for high-end homes in the Cleveland Heights and Shaker Heights areas. The company manufactures cabinets built to the specifications of homeowners and employs 125 custom cabinet makers and installers. There are 30 administrative and sales staff members working for the company.

James Leroy owns Cleveland Custom Cabinets. His accounting manager is Marcus Sims. Sims manages 15 accountants. The staff is responsible for keeping track of manufacturing costs by job and preparing internal and external financial reports. The internal reports are used by management for decision making. The external reports are used to support bank loan applications.

The company applies overhead to jobs based on direct labor hours. For 2011, it estimated total overhead to be $9,600,000 and 80,000 direct labor hours. The cost of direct materials used during the first quarter of the year is $600,000 and direct labor cost is $400,000 (based on 20,000 hours worked). The company's accounting system is old and does not provide actual overhead information until about four weeks after the close of a quarter. As a result, the applied overhead amount is used for quarterly reports.

On April 10, 2011, Leroy came into Sims's office to pick up the quarterly report. He looked at it aghast. Leroy had planned to take the statements to the bank the next day and meet with the vice president to discuss a $1 million expansion loan. He knew the bank would be reluctant to grant the loan based on the income numbers in Exhibit 1.

EXHIBIT 1
CLEVELAND CUSTOM CABINETS
Net Income for the Quarter Ended March 31, 2011

Sales	$6,400,000
Cost of goods manufactured	4,800,000
Gross margin	$1,600,000
Selling and administrative expenses	1,510,000
Net income	$ 90,000

Leroy asked Sims to explain how net income could have gone from 14.2 percent of sales for the year ended December 31, 2010, to 1.4 percent for March 31, 2011. Sims pointed out that the estimated overhead cost had doubled for 2011 when compared with the actual cost for 2010. He explained to Leroy that rent had doubled and the cost of utilities skyrocketed. In addition, the custom-making machinery was wearing out more rapidly so the company's repair and maintenance costs also doubled from 2010.

Leroy understood but wouldn't accept Sims's explanation. Instead, he told Sims that as the sole owner of the company, there was no reason not to "tweak" the numbers on a one-time basis. "I own the board of directors so no worries there. Listen, this is a one-time deal. I won't ask you to do it again," Leroy stated. Sims started to soften and asked Leroy just how he expected the tweaking to happen. Leroy flinched, held up his hands, and said, "I'll leave the creative accounting to you."

Questions

1. Do you agree with Leroy's statement that it doesn't matter what the numbers look like since he is the sole owner? Even if it is true that Sims "owns" the board of directors, what should be their role in this matter?

2. a. Assume Sims is a CPA and holds the CMA. What are the ethical considerations for him in deciding whether to tweak the numbers? What should Sims do and why?

   b. Assume Sims did a utilitarian analysis to help decide what to do. Evaluate the harms and benefits of alternative courses of action.

3. Assume Sims decided to reduce the estimated overhead for the year by 50 percent. How would that change the net income for the quarter? What would it be as a percentage of sales? Do you think Leroy would like the result? Do you think he will be content with the tweaking occurring just this one time?

Case 1-10

Telecommunications, Inc.

Telecommunications, Inc., is a U.S. company, a global leader in information technology, and it specializes in building data network systems. The company is a major player in the industry, although it is no match for companies like Cisco Systems. Recently, however, it has been more successful in securing contracts to build and support data network systems outside the United States. In one recent competitive bidding situation with companies from two other countries, the Latin American country of Bolumbia awarded Telecommunications a multi-million-dollar contract to develop a network for the corporate community. The job went so well that Telecommunications believes it will have a leg up on other companies in bidding for future contracts.

Telecommunications was the prime contractor on that job. It was responsible for the selection of subcontractors to perform the work that Telecommunications did not want to do, or when the company believed it was advantageous to use a local contractor. According to the company's contract with Bolumbia, only Latin American companies could be selected for subcontract work. In a recent competitive bidding selection process, Bolumbia National Communications (BNC), S.A.[1] was chosen to assist in infrastructure connectivity. BNC wasn't as well established as other companies such as Telefonica, the Spanish multinational company that operates throughout the Spanish- and Portuguese-speaking world, but it had submitted a bid that met all the specifications of the job including some that were unusual requests. Telefonica did not include these items in its subcontractor bid.

Ed Keller is employed as an engineer for Telecommunications, Inc. Keller recently graduated with a master's degree in engineering and joined the company six months ago. Keller had a 3.92 grade point average and could have worked for a variety of engineering firms. He chose Telecommunications because of the opportunity it afforded to travel around the world and as a result of its reputation for quality service and high moral standards.

During lunch at the office one day, Keller was talking to several of the more senior members of the engineering staff of Telecommunications, who told him about their recent trip to Bolumbia. They visited four cities and a resort in one week, and all their expenses were paid for by BNC. Keller knew that BNC had just completed its work on the contract for infrastructure connectivity. Out of curiosity Keller questioned the engineering staff about the propriety of accepting an all-expenses-paid trip from a major subcontractor. Keller was told that it was common practice for Latin American companies to make gestures of gratitude, such as free travel and entertainment. One of the senior engineers, Mike Stone,

[1]S.A., Sociedad Anonima, is the designation for a Spanish company.

stated: "There's nothing wrong with accepting such an offer. After all, the offer of free travel was made after the decision to accept the bid of BNC and the completion of the job. We were not responsible for making the selection decision. All we did was to establish the engineering specifications for the job."

Keller viewed this as an opportunity to learn more about the bidding process so he approached Sam Jennings, the head of the internal audit department of Telecommunications. Keller grew up with Jennings's son and Sam Jennings has been a close friend of the Keller family for many years.

Keller asked Jennings to have lunch with him one day. Jennings was curious about the request since they hadn't had lunch during the six months that Keller worked for Telecommunications. Keller said he had some questions about reporting expenses on trips that he might be assigned to in the future. Since it was a work-related request and their families go back a long time, Jennings cleared his calendar and agreed to have lunch with Keller.

During the lunch, Keller raised the issue of whether there was a conflict of interest when members of the senior engineering staff, such as those who worked on developing specifications for the BNC job, accept free travel and entertainment from a subcontractor. At first, Jennings was furious because Keller had misled him about the purpose of the lunch, but he gave Keller the benefit of the doubt and proceeded to answer the question.

Jennings informed Keller that the relationship between the engineers in question and BNC, and whether there was any inappropriate influence one way or the other, had been examined because of the company's concern about a possible violation of the Foreign Corrupt Practices Act (FCPA). Jennings went on to explain that the act prohibits U.S. multinationals or their agents from making payments that improperly influence government officials in another country, or their representatives, in the normal course of carrying out their responsibilities. Jennings told Keller that no evidence existed that the awarding of the contract was a prepayment for the promise of later free travel and entertainment, as Keller had expected. Moreover, explained Jennings, the decision to accept the BNC bid was made by Richard Kimble, the engineering division manager, and Bob Gerard, the vice president for engineering, and neither of them received any free travel or lodging. The fact was, according to Jennings, the rejected bids, while lower than BNC's, were inadequate and did not meet the specifications of the contract. Only BNC's proposal could do that.

Keller felt better about the situation after discussing it with Jennings. Still, he wondered about the values of a company that condones accepting free travel and entertainment from a subcontractor and those of the engineers who should be beyond reproach in carrying out their responsibilities.

Questions

1. Should U.S. multinationals that operate overseas conduct business using U.S. ethical standards or the standards of the host country?

2. Assume that the engineers of Telecommunications did influence the decision-making process by establishing engineering specifications that only BNC could meet. The engineers received free travel and lodging from BNC *but only after the job was completed.* Is there anything wrong with this picture?

3. Do you think that Ed Keller is right to be concerned about the values of Telecommunications and the senior engineers who accepted the offers of free travel and lodging? Why or why not? If you believe that Keller's concerns are warranted, which values should be of concern to him?

Chapter 2

Accountants' Ethical Decision Process and Professional Judgment

Ethics Reflection

One event more than any other that demonstrates the failure of professional judgment and ethical reasoning in the period of accounting frauds of the late 1990s and early 2000s is the relationship between Enron and its auditors Arthur Andersen LLP. Barbara Toffler points out in her book about the rise and fall of Andersen—*Final Accounting*[1]—that *The Powers Report,* named after an Enron director and the head investigator of Enron's failure, denounced Andersen for failing to fulfill its obligations in connection with its audit of Enron's financial statements and to bring to the attention of Enron's board of directors concerns about Enron's internal controls over the related-party transactions.[2]

The possibility of an accounting fraud at Enron was first discussed in an article by two *Fortune* magazine reporters—Bethany McLean and Peter Elkind. They wrote a book titled *The Smartest Guys in the Room*[3] in which they criticized Andersen for failing to use *professional skepticism.* Professional skepticism requires that an auditor should approach the audit with a questioning mind and a critical assessment of audit evidence. David Duncan, the lead auditor, had personal relationships with some of Enron's executives that clouded his judgment and he was influenced by the size of the fees earned from Enron. The firm didn't seem to care about the conflict of interest because Duncan was able to generate 20 to 25 percent in additional fees each year.

Andersen's independence was called into question shortly after Enron disclosed that a large portion of the 1997 earnings restatement consisted of adjustments the auditors had proposed at the end of the 1997 audit but had allowed to go uncorrected. Congressional investigators wanted to know why Andersen tolerated $51 million of known misstatements during a year when Enron reported only $105 million of earnings. Andersen CEO Joseph Berardino explained that Enron's 1997 earnings were artificially low due to several hundred million dollars of nonrecurring expenses and write-offs. The proposed adjustments were not material, Berardino testified, because they represented less than 8 percent of "normalized" earnings.[4]

Enron was known for its special-purpose entities (SPEs) that were set up as partnerships to borrow money from financial institutions, record the debt on its books and not Enron's (thereby creating off-balance sheet transactions), and then transfer the cash to Enron in return for its underperforming assets. The disclosure of SPE activities failed to describe the true extent of the transactions and its effect on the financial results of Enron. By any measure transparency was virtually nonexistent.

The Enron–Andersen relationship illustrates how a CPA firm can lose sight of its professional obligations. While examining Enron's financial statements, the auditors at Andersen knew that diligent application of strict auditing standards required one decision, but that the consequences for the firm were harmful to its business interests.

In this chapter we explore the relationship between ethical intention and action and the ability to make judgments that are consistent with the requirements of the profession's accounting and auditing standards. At Andersen, decision makers did not possess ethical intent and were therefore unwilling to look past self-interest and act in the public interest. Think about the following as you read this chapter: (1) What is the ethical aspect of auditors' professional judgment? (2) Why is professional skepticism critical to professional judgment? (3) What is the role of virtue in auditors' ethical decision making?

> Every act is to be judged by the intention of the agent.
>
> *Unknown author*

This quote from an unknown source emphasizes one's intent in making decisions. Moral intent is a critical component of ethical decision making. By internalizing the virtues discussed in the previous chapter and acting in accordance with the principles of the philosophical reasoning methods, an accountant is better equipped to make ethical, professional judgments.

Cognitive Development Approach

Cognitive development refers to the thought process followed in one's moral development. An individual's ability to make reasoned judgments about moral matters develops in stages. The psychologist Lawrence Kohlberg concluded, on the basis of 20 years of research, that moral development occurs in a specific sequence of six stages that may be divided into three levels of moral reasoning.[5] Kohlberg's views on ethical development are helpful in understanding how individuals may internalize moral standards and, as they become more sophisticated in their use, apply them more critically to resolve ethical conflicts.

Kohlberg developed his theory by using data from studies on how decisions are made by individuals. The example of Heinz and the Drug illustrates a moral dilemma used by Kohlberg to develop his stage-sequence model.

Heinz and the Drug

In Europe, a woman was near death from a rare type of cancer. There was one drug that the doctors thought might save her. It was a form of radium that a druggist in the same town had recently discovered. The drug was expensive to make, but the druggist was charging 10 times what the drug cost him to make. He paid $200 for the radium and charged $2,000 for a small dose of the drug. The sick woman's husband, Heinz, went to everyone he knew to borrow the money, but he could get together only about $1,000, which was half of what it would cost. He told the druggist that his wife was dying and asked him to sell it cheaper or let him pay later. But the druggist said, "No, I discovered the drug and I'm going to make money from it." Heinz got desperate and broke into the man's store to steal the drug for his wife.

Should the husband have done that? Was it right or wrong? Most people say that Heinz's theft was morally justified, but Kohlberg was less concerned about whether they approved or disapproved than with the reasons they gave for their answers. Kohlberg monitored the reasons for judgments given by a group of 75 boys ranging in age from 10 through 16 and

TABLE 2.1
Three Sample Responses to the Heinz Dilemma

A:	It really depends on how much Heinz likes his wife and how much risk there is in taking the drug. If he can get the drug in no other way and if he really likes his wife, he'll have to steal it.
B:	I think that a husband would care so much for his wife that he couldn't just sit around and let her die. He wouldn't be stealing for his own profit; he'd be doing it to help someone he loves.
C:	Regardless of his personal feelings, Heinz has to realize that the druggist is protected by the law. Since no one is above the law, Heinz shouldn't steal it. If we allowed Heinz to steal, then all society would be in danger of anarchy.

isolated the six stages of moral thought. The boys progressed in reasoning sequentially with most never reaching the highest stages. He concluded that the universal principle of justice is the highest claim of morality.[6] Kohlberg's justice orientation has been criticized by Carol Gilligan, a noted psychologist and educator,[7] claiming that it ignores the care-and-response orientation that characterizes female moral judgment. Gilligan believes that women need more information before answering the question: Should Heinz steal the drug? Females look for ways of resolving the dilemma where no one—Heinz, his wife, or the druggist—will experience pain. Gilligan sees the hesitation to judge as a laudable quest for nonviolence, an aversion to cruel situations where someone will get hurt. However, much of her theories have been challenged in the literature. For example, Kohlberg considered it a sign of ethical relativism, a waffling that results from trying to please everyone (Stage 3). Moreover, her beliefs seem to imply that men lack a caring response when compared to females.

The dilemma of Heinz illustrates the challenge of evaluating the ethics of a decision. Table 2.1 displays three types of responses.[8]

Kohlberg considered how the responses were different and what problem-solving strategies underlie the three responses. Response A presents a rather uncomplicated approach to moral problems. Choices are made based on the wants of the individual decision maker (egoism). Response B also considers the wife's needs. Here, Heinz is concerned that his actions be motivated by good intentions (ends justify the means). In Response C, a societywide perspective is used in decision making. Law is the key in making moral decisions[9] (rule utilitarianism; justice orientation).

The examples in Table 2.2 demonstrate the application of Kohlberg's model of cognitive development to possible decision making in business.

TABLE 2.2 **Kohlberg's Stages of Moral Development**

Level 1—Preconventional

At the preconventional level, the individual is very self-centered. Rules are seen as something external imposed on the self.

Stage 1. Obedience to Rules; Avoidance of Punishment

At this stage what is right is judged by one's obedience to rules and authority.

Example: A company forbids making payoffs to government or other officials to gain business. Susan, the company's contract negotiator, might justify refusing the advances of a government official to make a payment to gain a contract as being contrary to company rules, or Susan might make the payment if she believes there is little chance of being caught and punished.

Stage 2. Satisfying One's Own Needs

At Stage 2 the rules and authority are important only if acting in accordance with them satisfies one's own needs (egoism).

Example: Here, Susan might make the payment even though it is against company rules if she perceives that such payments are a necessary part of doing business. She views the payment as essential to gain the contract. Susan may believe that competitors are willing to make payments and that making such payments are part of the culture of the host country. She concludes that if she does not make the payment it might jeopardize her ability to move up the ladder within the organization and possibly forgo personal rewards of salary increases and/or bonuses.

Level 2—Conventional

At the conventional level, the individual becomes aware of the interests of others and one's duty to society. Personal responsibility becomes an important consideration in decision making.

Stage 3. Fairness to Others

At this stage an individual is not only motivated by rules but seeks to do what is in the perceived best interests of others, especially those in a family, peer group, or work organization. There is a commitment to loyalty in the relationship.

Example: Susan wants to be liked by others. She might be reluctant to make the payment but agrees to do so not because it benefits her interests but in response to the pressure imposed by her supervisor who claims the company will lose a major contract and employees will be fired if she refuses to go along.

Stage 4. Law and Order

Stage 4 behavior emphasizes the morality of law and duty to the social order. One's duty to society, respect for authority, and maintaining the social order become the focus of decision making.

Example: Susan might refuse to make the illegal payment even though it leads to a loss of jobs in her company because she views it as her duty to do so in the best interests of society. She does not want to violate the law.

Let's return to the receivables example in Chapter 1 for a moment. An auditor who reasons at Stage 3 might go along with the demands of a client out of loyalty or because she thinks the company will benefit by such inaction. At Stage 4, the auditor places the needs of society and law-abiding above all else so that Susan will insist on recording an allowance for uncollectibles.

Level 3—Postconventional

Principled morality underlies decision making at this level. The individual recognizes that there must be a society-wide basis for cooperation. There is an orientation to principles that shape whatever laws and role systems a society may have.

Stage 5. Social Contract

At this stage an individual is motivated by upholding the basic rights, values, and legal contracts of society. That person recognizes in some cases that legal and moral points of view may conflict. To reduce such conflict, individuals at this stage base their decisions on a rational calculation of benefits and harms to society.

Example: Susan might weigh the alternative courses of action by evaluating how each of the groups is affected by her decision to make the payment. For instance, the company might benefit by gaining the contract. Susan might even be rewarded for her action. The employees are more secure in their jobs. The customer in the other country gets what it wants. On the other hand, the company will be in violation of the Foreign Corrupt Practices Act that prohibits payments to foreign government officials assuming the government finds out about the violation. Susan then weighs the consequences of making an illegal payment including any resulting penalty against the ability to gain additional business. Susan might conclude that the harms of prosecution, fines, other sanctions, and the loss of one's reputational capital are greater than the benefits.

Stage 6. Universal Ethical Principles

Kohlberg was still working on Stage 6 at the time of his death. He believed this stage rarely occurred. Still, a person at this stage believes that right is determined by universal ethical principles that everyone should follow. Stage 6 individuals believe that there are inalienable rights, which are universal in nature and consequence. These rights, laws, or social agreements are valid, not because of a particular society's laws or customs, but because they rest on the premise of universality. Justice and equality are examples of principles that are deemed universal. If a law conflicts with an ethical principle, then an individual should act in accordance with the principle.

An example of such a principle is Immanuel Kant's categorical imperative, the first formulation of which can be stated as: "Act only according to that maxim [reason for acting] by which you can at the same time will that it would become a universal law."[10] Kant's categorical imperative creates an absolute, unconditional requirement that exerts its authority in all circumstances, and is both required and justified as an end in itself.

Example: Susan would go beyond the norms, laws, and authority of groups or individuals. She would act without regard to pressure from her supervisor or the perceived best interests of the company. Her action would be guided only by universal ethical principles that would apply to others in a similar situation.

Returning to the receivables example one last time, an auditor who reasons at Stage 5 would not want to violate the public interest principle embedded in the profession's ethical standards. Investors and creditors have a right to know about the uncertainty surrounding collectibility of the receivables. At Stage 6, the auditor would ask whether she would want other auditors to insist on providing an allowance for the uncollectibles if they were involved in a similar situation. Susan reasons that the orderly functioning of markets and a level playing field require that financial information should be accurate and reliable so that

another auditor should also decide that the allowance needs to be recorded. The application of virtues such as objectivity and integrity enables her to carry out the ethical action.

Kohlberg's model suggests that people continue to change their decision priorities over time and with additional education and experience. They may experience a change in values and ethical behavior.[11] In the context of business, an individual's moral development can be influenced by corporate culture, especially ethics training.[12] Ethics training and education have been shown to improve managers' moral development. More will be said about corporate culture in Chapter 3.

The DigitPrint Case

Returning to the DigitPrint case from Chapter 1, if Wonderful reasons at Stage 2 he will insist that GAAP be followed only if it satisfies his needs. Given that Doolittle has warned him against recording the $1 million of accrued expenses, Wonderful is not likely to go up the chain of command to the president, Henry Higgins, absent a strong ethical conviction that is the right thing to do. Wonderful may conclude that to do so may put his job at risk. Nothing will change if Wonderful reasons at Stage 3 since out of loyalty to his supervisor, Liza Doolittle, he will remain silent about the matter. Reasoning at Stage 4 should lead Wonderful to insist on complying with the law (GAAP) that requires recording of the accrued expenses regardless of the consequences for him or the company. At Stage 5, Wonderful recognizes the company's obligations to the venture capitalists that have a right to know about the accrued expenses because it directly and materially impacts recorded earnings. The $1 million liability might influence the venture capitalists' evaluation of DigitPrint's liquidity prior to deciding on whether to continue financing of the company. At Stage 6, Wonderful would take a universal perspective and ask whether he would want other accountants to ignore recording $1 million of accrued expenses in similar situations for similar reasons. If so, then financial statements would be unreliable and undermine the true value of companies. From an ethics point of view, the end result of securing needed capital does not justify the means of falsifying the statements.

The Ethical Domain in Accounting and Auditing

The ethical domain for accountants and auditors usually involves four key constituent groups including (1) the client organization that hires and pays for accounting services; (2) the accounting firm that employs the practitioner, typically represented by the collective interests of the firm's management; (3) the accounting profession including various regulatory bodies such as the Securities and Exchange Commission (SEC); and (4) the general public who rely on the attestations and representations of the practitioner and the firm.[13] Responsibilities to each of these groups may conflict. For example, fees are paid by the client organization rather than by the general public including investors and creditors who are the direct beneficiary of the independent auditing services.

The accounting profession has instituted mechanisms such as professional standards and codes of conduct (i.e., AICPA Code and IMA Ethical Standards) to encourage the individual practitioner's ethical behavior in a way that is consistent with the stated rules and guidelines of the profession. These positive factors work in conjunction with an individual's ethical reasoning capacity to influence professional judgment and ethical decision making.

Kohlberg's theory of ethical development provides a framework that can be used to consider the effects of conflict areas on ethical reasoning in accounting. For example, if an individual accountant is influenced by the firm's desire to "make the client happy," then the result may be reasoning at Stage 3. The results of published studies during the 1990s by accounting researchers indicate that CPAs reason primarily at Stages 3 and 4. One possible implication of these results is that a larger percentage of CPAs may be overly influenced by their relationship with peers, superiors, and clients (Stage 3) or by rules (Stage 4). A CPA who is unable to critically apply the technical accounting standards and rules of conduct when these requirements are unclear is likely to be influenced by others in the decision-making process.[14] If an auditor reasons at the postconventional level, then that person may refuse to give in to the pressure applied by the supervisor to overlook the client's failure to follow GAAP. This is the ethical position to take although it may go against the culture of the firm to "go along to get along."

Empirical studies have explored the underlying ethical reasoning processes of accountants and auditors in practice. Findings show that ethical reasoning may be an important determinant of professional judgment, such as the disclosure of sensitive information[15] and auditor independence.[16] Results also show that unethical and dysfunctional audit behavior, such as the underreporting of time on an audit budget, may be systematically related to the auditor's level of ethical reasoning.[17] In reviewing these and other works, Ponemon and Gabhart conclude the results imply that ethical reasoning may be an important cognitive characteristic that may affect individual judgment and behavior under a wide array of conditions and events in extant professional practice.[18]

Rest's Four-Component Model of Morality

Cognitive-developmental researchers also have attempted to understand the process of ethical decision making. In particular, James Rest asserts that ethical actions are not the outcome of a single, unitary decision process but result from a combination of various cognitive structures and psychological processes. Rest's model of ethical action is based on the presumption that an individual's behavior is related to her level of moral development. Rest distinguishes four components inherent to the ethical decision-making process.[19]

Moral Sensitivity

The first step in moral behavior requires that the individual interpret the situation as moral. Absent the ability to recognize that one's actions affect the welfare of others, it would be virtually impossible to make the most ethical decision when faced with a moral dilemma. For example, let's assume you go into a store to order a pizza. You go to the counter and place your order. As you move down to the cashier, you notice a $50 bill in the refrigerated open area that contains cold sodas just below the counter that spans the distance from the order line to the payment area. You notice that two people are ahead of you at the cashier and wonder whether either of them dropped the money. What would you do? Why?

This is an ethical situation because if you decide to keep the money, someone is $50 poorer. You, of course, are $50 richer. Should you act in your own self-interest? If so, how will you justify it? Will you say to yourself: Finders keepers, losers weepers? Or, will you say: If I had dropped the $50, then I would hope the money would be returned to me.

Our ability to identify an ethical situation enables us to focus on how alternative courses of action might affect ourselves and others. If we simply acted without reflecting on the ethics of the situation in the store, we probably would have looked around, made sure no one was watching, and then pocketed the money. The important point to remember is that ethics is all about how we act when no one is looking.

Moral Judgment

An individual's ethical cognition of what "ideally" ought to be done to resolve an ethical dilemma is called *prescriptive reasoning*.[20] The outcome of one's prescriptive reasoning is his ethical judgment of the ideal solution to an ethical dilemma. Generally, an individual's prescriptive reasoning reflects his cognitive understanding of an ethical situation as measured by his level of moral development.[21] Once a person is aware of possible lines of action and how people would be affected by the alternatives, a judgment must be made about which course of action is more morally justifiable (which alternative is just or right).

Moral Motivation

Moral motivation reflects an individual's willingness to place ethical values (e.g., honesty, integrity, trustworthiness, caring, and empathy) ahead of nonethical values (e.g., wealth, power, and fame) which relate to self-interest. An individual's ethical motivation influences his intention to comply or not comply with his ethical judgment in the resolution of an ethical dilemma. In the previous example, if you decide to keep the $50, then enhancing your wealth (self-interest) overtakes the ethical values of honesty and empathy.

Moral Character

Individuals do not always behave in accordance with their ethical intention. An individual's intention to act ethically and her ethical actions may not be aligned because of a lack of ethical character. As previously noted, individuals with strong ethical character will be more likely to carry out their ethical intentions with ethical action than individuals with a weak ethical character because they are better able to withstand any pressures (integrity) to do otherwise. Once a moral person has considered the ethics of the alternatives, she must construct an appropriate course of action, avoid distractions, and maintain the courage to continue.

Rest's model can be applied to the situation faced by Sherron Watkins in the Enron failure. Watkins had come up through the ranks of Andersen to become an audit manager. Later on she joined Enron, one of Andersen's largest clients, and rose to the position of vice president. Watkins was savvy about accounting issues and was the first person in Enron to point out to top management that the accounting maneuvers conducted over a number of years up until the time when the company went bankrupt in December 2001 had jeopardized its ability to remain in business. In a now-famous memo to the former chair of the board of directors of Enron, Ken Lay, Watkins commented on the sudden resignation of the company's CEO, Jeff Skilling, by stating: "Skilling's departure . . . [will] raise suspicions of accounting improprieties and valuation issues." Watkins went on to say that she is "incredibly nervous that [Enron] will implode in a wave of accounting scandals."[22]

Watkins clearly identified the ethical issues in the Enron debacle. She was motivated to do the right thing and managed to get the company to review its accounting treatments, although to no avail. Still, Watkins put her future in jeopardy both at Enron (somewhat of a moot point at the time) and possibly with other employers. She did not know how her actions would affect her ability to work and earn a living in the future.

It is difficult to hypothesize whether Watkins used proper moral judgment. She seemed to consider the interests of employees at Enron but may have been motivated by self-interest (enlightened egoism). One statement Watkins made in the memo to Lay appears to support this contention: "My 8 years of Enron work history will be worth nothing on my resume, the business world will consider the past successes as nothing but an elaborate accounting hoax." Notice how she thinks of herself and does not mention the interests of thousands of stockholders that lost millions of dollars from a decline in Enron stock and thousands of employees who lost their jobs and most of their retirement money if it had been invested in 401-k plans that included Enron stock. We don't mean to be too critical of Watkins; she took an important step that no one else at Enron was willing to take. She became somewhat of an outcast at the company that had blinders on with respect to Enron's unethical actions.

Watkins's actions illustrate the difference between blowing the whistle internally and external whistleblowing. Watkins did go to the board chair so that internal whistleblowing practices were followed. However, she did not go outside the company (i.e., to the SEC) and disclose what she knew. Had Watkins gone to the SEC with her story on or around August 15, 2001, the day Skilling resigned, instead of or in addition to writing the internal memo to Lay, her actions may have saved thousands of people millions of dollars because the stock price was at $36 on that day and ultimately, when all the dust settled on December 2, 2001, the stock sold for less than $1 a share. On the other hand, Watkins may have truly believed that Enron was still salvageable if Lay had acted on her concerns so that employees would still have their jobs and the stock price may have recovered. Moreover, the ethical obligation of confidentiality probably weighed heavily on Watkins's mind so that we can understand why she would have been reluctant to go to the SEC.

How does a person develop the courage to withstand pressures that challenge one's commitment to act in an ethical manner? An important element is to have a supportive environment in the organization. An ethical tone must be set by top management. When an organization attempts to foster an ethical culture, the employees feel they will be supported if they bring matters of concern out into the open. The notion of creating an ethical organization environment will be explored in the next chapter.

The culture at Enron was to make the deal regardless of which ethical standards had to be sacrificed "for the good of the organization." An amusing story that made the rounds on the Internet as described in a book written by Watkins and Mimi Swartz, titled *Power Failure: The Inside Story of the Collapse at Enron,* speaks volumes about what motivated behavior at Enron.[23] It deals with how Enron defined capitalism with respect to its activities.

Feudalism:	You have two cows. Your lord takes some of the milk.
Facism:	You have two cows. The government takes both, hires you to take care of them and sells you the milk.
Communism:	You have two cows. You must take care of them, but the government takes all the milk.
Capitalism:	You have two cows. You sell one and buy a bull. Your herd multiplies, and the economy grows. You sell them and retire on the income.
Enron Capitalism:	You have two cows. You sell three of them to your publicly listed company, using letters of credit opened by your brother-in-law at the bank, then execute a debt-equity swap with an option so that you get all four cows back, with a tax exemption for five cows. The milk rights of the six cows are transferred through an intermediary to a Cayman Island company secretly owned by the majority shareholder who sells the rights to all seven cows to your listed company. The Enron annual report says the company owns eight cows, with an option on one more.

Professional Judgment in Auditing

Professional judgment is judgment exercised with due care, objectivity, and integrity within the framework provided by applicable professional standards, by experienced and knowledgeable people.[24] The exercise of professional judgment requires more than just following rules. It involves the application of professional standards (i.e., Principles of the AICPA Code; Ethical Standards of the IMA) to situations where the rules are unclear or when explicit standards do not yet exist. It also requires that auditors possess the moral fortitude "to withstand client pressures to disclose selectively in the event a breach is discovered."[25]

Generally accepted auditing standards (GAAS) require that auditors should obtain "sufficient competent evidential matter . . . through inspection, observation, inquiries, and confirmations to afford a reasonable basis for an opinion regarding the financial statements under audit."[26] That evidence enables an auditor to make judgments that help determine whether the client's financial statements accurately record, in all material respects, the client's actual income, financial position, and cash flows. An example of when an auditor might fail to live up to this standard is if she relies extensively on information provided by the client, often in the form of oral representations of management, and fails to obtain sufficient documentary and other evidence from independent sources to verify management's representations.

GAAS also requires auditors to exercise due professional care in performing an audit and preparing the report. According to professional standards, in the course of performing an audit the auditor must employ "such skill as she possesses with reasonable care and diligence . . . undertaking for good faith and integrity, but not for infallibility." The matter of due professional care concerns what the auditor does and how well she does it.[27]

In her seminal paper on the role of virtue on auditors' ethical decision making, Thorne contends that Rest's model fails to provide a theoretical description of the role of personal characteristics, excepting level of moral development, in auditors' ethical decision processes. Thorne develops a model of individuals' ethical decision processes upon which a better understanding of auditors' actions and professional judgments may be developed. Her model relies on virtue-based characteristics which tend to increase the decision maker's propensity to exercise sound ethical judgment. Thorne believes virtue theory is similar to the approach advocated by the cognitive-developmental perspective in three ways. First, both perspectives suggest that ethical action is the end result of a rational decision-making process. Second, both perspectives are concerned with an individual's ethical decision process. Third, both perspectives acknowledge the critical role of cognition to individuals' ethical decision making. Figure 2.1 presents Thorne's integrated model of the ethical decision-making process.[28]

Figure 2.1 shows that in addition to level of moral development, an individual's virtue is important in resolving ethical dilemmas and acting ethically. Thorne believes that the model (1) identifies the influence of moral virtue in the determination of ethical

FIGURE 2.1
Thorne's Integrated Model of Ethical Decision Making[1]

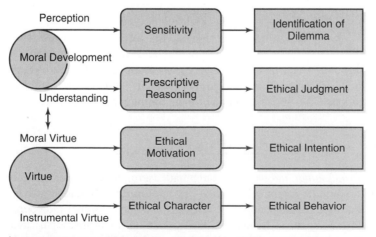

[1]Linda Thorne, "The Role of Virtue in Auditors' Ethical Decision Making: An Integration of Cognitive-Developmental and Virtue Ethics Perspectives," *Research on Accounting Ethics,* no. 4 (1998), pp. 291–308.

motivation, (2) identifies the influence of instrumental virtue[29] in the determination of one's ethical character, and (3) recognizes an association between an individual's moral virtue and prescriptive understanding.

Thorne explains the significance of each of the factors starting with moral virtue and ethical motivation, each of which are concerned with an individual's intention to act in accordance with her ethical judgment (informed by the philosophical reasoning methods). Moral virtue is the positive attribute of character that describes an individual's direct concern for the interests of others despite personal risks. Ethical motivation describes an individual's willingness to place the interests of others ahead of self-interest. According to virtue-ethics theory, the property of character critical to an individual's ability to implement her ethical intention is instrumental virtue. Therefore, the integrative perspective suggests that an individual's ethical character is a reflection of her instrumental virtue.[30]

The intention to exercise professional judgment requires an auditor to deliberate on whether or not to comply with the "ideal" professional judgment as established by codified rules or as determined by her prescriptive reasoning process. Thus, an auditor's intention to exercise professional judgment reflects her ethical motivation. The exercise of professional judgment describes the action of complying with one's intended professional judgment. Thorne's integrated framework suggests that auditors' intentions to exercise professional judgment are moderated by the strength of their instrumental virtue. Hence, the personal characteristics of moral virtue and instrumental virtue influence auditors' exercise of professional judgment, as well as moral development.[31]

Professional Skepticism

Auditor Expectations

"Professional skepticism is defined in the standards as an attitude that includes a questioning mind and a critical assessment of audit evidence. Standard setters suggest that partners of a CPA firm must set the proper tone at the top on all engagements for the benefits of professional skepticism to be realized and to increase the likelihood that auditors will uncover fraud."[32] *Statement on Auditing Standards (SAS) No. 99,* Considerations of Fraud in a Financial Statement Audit, emphasizes the need for auditors to exercise professional skepticism when considering and responding to the risk of material misstatement due to fraud.[33] The standard suggests that auditors should respond to increased fraud risk assessments with increased professional skepticism and additional audit procedures.[34]

The Public Company Accounting Oversight Board (PCAOB) was formed by the Sarbanes-Oxley (SOX) Act of 2002 to oversee public company audits. PCAOB reported in its 2008 inspections of firms that audit public companies that a lack of professional skepticism and selection of appropriate audit procedures are serious problems for auditors. PCAOB believes that the tone set by audit partners is critical for auditors' fraud investigations. The SEC enforcement division investigations suggest that a lack of professional skepticism was responsible for at least 60 percent of the commission's actions against auditors in 2008.

In a 2009 research paper, Nelson provided a model of professional skepticism in auditing that suggests there are links between evidential input that auditors receive and the incentives they are faced with and their skeptical judgments and actions.[35] Carpenter and Reimers found in a study of partner decision making that the degree of emphasis on professional skepticism and the presence or absence of fraud directly influences auditors' fraud risk assessments, consistent with Nelson's model.[36]

Hurtt, Eining, and Plumlee developed a scale to measure professional skepticism. Their findings indicate that while researchers have found that higher levels of skepticism are associated with individuals questioning data and collecting more evidence to support decisions, individuals who score low on the skepticism scale can be trained to exhibit behaviors consistent with those who score higher. The authors argue that the three characteristics of skepticism that deal with examining evidence are a questioning mind, suspension of judgment, and a search for knowledge. A questioning mind means skeptics are unlikely to accept information at face value; instead, they require proof or justification. Skeptics can see the other side of arguments and often enjoy the role of "devil's advocate." It has also been argued that skeptics suspend judgments to make additional inquiry and obtain evidence. Suspension of judgment means skeptics are slower to form judgments and not likely to jump to conclusions. Finally, a search for knowledge is equivalent to being generally curious. Skeptics are individuals who enjoy the learning process and seek knowledge for knowledge's sake.[37]

Responsibilities of Management Accountants

Preventing fraud is a responsibility for all levels of financial management from staff accountant to CFO. Even though management accountants are not under the same regulations as external auditors, they should adopt an elevated attitude of skepticism to detect fraud within their respective organizations. Because professional skepticism is the standard of behavior for fraud detection, it may be beneficial to understand how well management accountants utilize professional skepticism. Management accountants often have insights to details that may go unnoticed or unaudited by external or internal auditors. They typically have intimate knowledge of financial activities, the corporate environment, and employee actions. This insider perspective can put them in a position to detect many symptoms of fraud that may not be as obvious to an outsider, such as an employee who never takes vacations or invoices that come from unknown companies.

Charron and Lowe were the first to study the link between professional skepticism and management accountants. The authors point out that unlike auditors, who have a responsibility to explicitly consider fraud in every engagement, management accountants have no similar requirement. They note, however, that increasing fraud awareness can facilitate fraud detection.[38]

Charron and Lowe used Hurtt's scale and developed 30 skepticism questions to assess skepticism skills of management accountants. The results show that whereas others may conjecture that external and/or internal auditors have greater skepticism skills in detecting fraud or questioning red flags, this clearly is not the case and the skepticism of management accountants is similar to that of auditors—whether internal or external. One significant finding is the importance of understanding the motivations and integrity of evidence providers (Rest's approach). They note that a skeptic has the ability to recognize that different people will have different personal views of the same event. Skepticism aids individuals to see past the obvious to question the source of information even when a person appears completely trusting. A skeptic understands the other point of view and can investigate accordingly.[39] In public accounting, auditors are advised to be cautious regarding management assertions. The implication is that managers are just looking out for their or the firm's best interests (egoism) and will misrepresent the facts. The authors suggest that the truth may be that managers simply see things differently with respect to the interpretation of GAAP. The key is the motivation of the managers in making that determination.

Ethical Reflection and Decision Making

Reflection can be seen as consciously thinking about and analyzing what one has done (or is doing). A decision-making process can help organize the various elements of ethical reasoning and professional judgment. A good model should be based on the virtues discussed in Chapters 1 and 2 that mirror the obligations of accountants and auditors under the profession's ethics codes and standards. The model should allow for the use of ethical reasoning to evaluate stakeholder interests, analyze the relevant operational and accounting issues, and identify alternative courses of action. The recommended model that can be used to analyze the case studies in the book is presented as follows:

1. **Frame the ethical issue.** *What is the primary ethical issue in this case?* For example, in the DigitPrint case the ethical issue was whether the accountant should compromise his values and give in to the pressure of his supervisor not to report the $1 million of unrecorded expenses.

2. **Gather all the facts.** *Specify the relevant facts, including disagreements and other conflict situations.* Make a conscious effort to understand the situation and distinguish facts from mere opinion. An ethical judgment made after gathering the relevant facts is a more reasonable ethical judgment than one made without regard for the facts.

3. **Identify the stakeholders and obligations.** *Identify and consider all of the people affected by a decision—the stakeholders.* These include all of the groups and/or individuals affected by a decision, policy, operation, or the ethics standards of a firm or the accounting profession. Determine the obligations of the decision maker to each of the stakeholder groups.

4. **Identify the relevant accounting ethics standards involved in the situation.** *Identify the most important ethical values of the accounting profession that should be considered in evaluating the facts and alternative courses of action.* Emphasis must be placed on the profession's ethical standards (i.e., AICPA Principles and IMA Ethics Standards) because they provide the context within which ethical decision making takes place.

5. **Identify the operational issues.** Accounting decisions are not made in a vacuum so that factors such as reporting responsibilities, the culture of an organization and its own ethics standards, internal controls, and the corporate governance system must be considered to highlight operational problems that should be corrected.

6. **Identify the accounting and auditing issues.** Assuming the case deals with whether the financial reports are accurate and reliable, an important step is to clearly describe the accounting (GAAP) and auditing (GAAS) issues. These might include revenue and expense recognition, asset valuation, disclosures, audit independence, due care, and gathering of sufficient audit evidence to warrant the expression of an opinion.

7. **List all the possible alternatives that you can or cannot do.** Most ethical issues are not black or white—there are shades of gray and the alternatives should account for that uncertainty. Once you have examined the facts, identified the stakeholders, and described the operational and accounting issues, the next step is to consider the available alternatives. Creativity in identifying options, or "moral imagination," helps distinguish good people who make ethically responsible decisions from good people who do not.

8. **Compare and weigh the alternatives.**

Is it *legal* (in conformity with SEC laws and PCAOB rules)?

Is it *consistent with professional standards* (AICPA Principles and IMA Ethics Standards; GAAP and GAAS)?

Is it consistent with *in-house rules* (firm policies and its own code of ethics)?

Is it right?

What are the potential *harms and benefits* to the stakeholders?

Is it *fair* to the stakeholders?

Is it consistent with *virtue considerations?* This is where the decision maker should form a professional judgment after evaluating his moral intention and willingness to act in a principled manner including having the courage to stand by what he knows is the right thing to do.

9. Decide on a course of action. After evaluating the ethics of the alternatives, select the one that best meets the ethical requirements of the situation.

10. Reflect on your decision. Before taking action, think about what you are about to do and why. Double-check the correctness of your proposed action by asking: How would I feel if my decision was made public and I had to defend it? Would I be proud if I had to explain my decision to my spouse or child?

Figure 2.2 presents the ethical decision-making process. It is designed to facilitate an understanding of the issues in a case study. In using the model to analyze ethical issues, students should keep in mind that not every step needs to be addressed. The information given may limit the analysis. Also, there is some justification for simply explaining the rationale for using the ethical reasoning method that was chosen rather than analyzing the ethical issues from all perspectives, unless that is what is asked at the end of the case or required by your instructor. The key point is that the model presents criteria that should be considered before making a final decision in any case scenario in the text.

Some may view the model as onerous. However, the making of ethical decisions is not an easy task. Perhaps this is why so many decision makers fail to adequately consider the ethical issues before acting. Some just "fly by the seat of their pants."

FIGURE 2.2
An Ethical Decision-Making Model

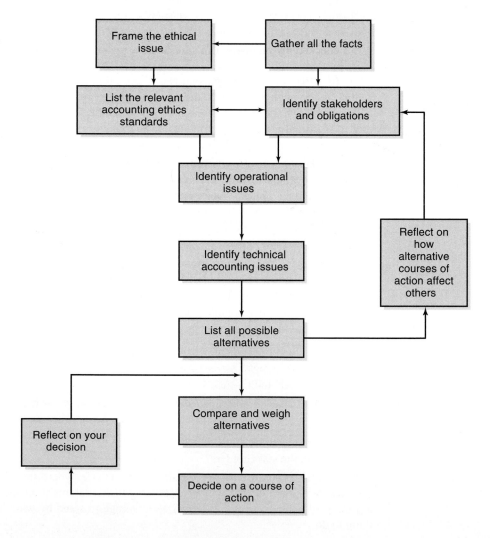

Applying the Ethical Decision Process and Professional Judgment

We use the *Faulty Budget* case in the back of Chapter 1 to illustrate the ethical decision-making process. The facts are repeated here.

A Faulty Budget

Jackson Daniels graduated from Lynchberg State College two years ago. Since graduating from the college, he has worked in the accounting department of Lynchberg Manufacturing. Daniels was recently asked to prepare a sales budget for the year 2011. He conducted a thorough analysis and came out with projected sales of 250,000 units of product. That represents a 25 percent increase over 2010.

Daniels went to lunch with his best friend, Jonathan Walker, to celebrate the completion of his first solo job. Walker noticed Daniels seemed very distant. He asked what the matter was. Daniels stroked his chin, ran his hand through his bushy, black hair, and looked straight into the eyes of his friend of 20 years. "Jon, I think I made a mistake with the budget."

"What do you mean?" Walker answered.

"You know how we developed a new process to manufacture soaking tanks to keep the ingredients fresh?"

"Yes," Walker answered.

"Well, I projected twice the level of sales for that product than will likely occur."

"Are you sure?" Walker asked.

"I checked my numbers. I'm sure. It was just a mistake on my part," Daniels replied.

"So, what are you going to do about it?" asked Walker.

"I think I should report it to Pete. He's the one who acted on the numbers to hire additional workers to produce the soaking tanks," Daniels said.

"Wait a second," Walker said. "How do you know there won't be extra demand for the product? You and I both know demand is a tricky number to project especially when a new product comes on the market. Why don't you sit back and wait to see what happens?"

"But what happens if I'm right and the sales numbers were wrong? What happens if the demand does not increase beyond what I now know to be the correct projected level?" Daniels asks.

"Well, you can tell Pete about it at that time. Why raise a red flag now when there may be no need?" Walker states.

As the lunch comes to a conclusion, Walker pulls Daniels aside and says, "Jack, this could mean your job. If I were in your position I'd protect my own interests first."

Analysis of the *Faulty Budget* Case Using the Decision-Making Model

1. **Frame the ethical issue:**
   - Should Daniels inform his superior (Pete) about the error in the sales budget forecast?

2. **Gather all the facts:**
   - Daniels put out a budget reflecting an unsupportable sales increase.
   - The company (Lynchberg Manufacturing) acted to hired more employees.
   - Daniels believes his forecast was wrong.
   - Daniels approaches his friend (Walker) for advice.
   - Walker suggests Daniels should wait to see if, in fact, the forecast turns out wrong and then decide whether to tell Pete about the error.

3. **Identify the stakeholders and obligations:**
   - Daniels—he should consider the consequences of his actions on others.

- Walker—to provide reliable advice to Daniels; consider Daniels's and company interests.
- Pete—as Daniels's superior, he has a right to be told about the inaccurate sales forecast since he acted on those numbers.
- Employees hired—have a right to expect the job will exist, at least in the short term.
- Company—has a right to expect employees to be honest and fully disclose all the information it needs to know.

4. **Identify the relevant accounting ethics standards involved in the situation:**
   - Honesty—fully disclosing both positive and negative information.
   - Integrity—acting in accordance with principled behavior; not being swayed to do what another party pressures you to do if you know it is wrong.
   - Due care in the performance of professional responsibilities—exercising care and caution in preparing budgeted information.

5. **Identify the operational issues:**
   - Are the lines of communication within the company open?
   - Is there someone to go to with concerns (i.e., hotline)?
   - Are there internal controls that should have caught the mistake; were they operating properly?
   - What role is played by corporate governance systems (i.e., board of directors)?

6. **Identify the accounting and auditing issues:**
   - Since the case does not deal with financial reporting per se, these issues are limited.
   - Extra employee costs (that may not be warranted) potentially have a negative impact on earnings.
   - Internal controls are an issue.
   - What is the role of the audit committee in oversight of financial reporting?

7. **List all the possible alternatives that you can or cannot do:**
   - Do nothing.
   - Wait to see what happens and then decide (Walker's recommendation).
   - Fully disclose the information about the mistake now.

8. **Compare and weigh the alternatives:**
   - Do nothing—keeps Daniels in the dark whether the company will catch the error (i.e., uncertainty about future events); integrity is challenged; fails to accept responsibility for his actions. The company has an ethical right to know about the error. If he covers it up and it becomes known to the company later on, the potential consequences for him at that time are much greater. The company's trust of Daniels as an employee and person will be breached.
   - Wait to see what happens—if the budget turns out to have been overstated and Daniels does not disclose this fact up front, the consequences for him could be worse; the company may question Daniels's technical skills because of the error; trust may be lost. Even if the sales equals the budgeted amount, Daniels will have to live with the fact that he was dishonest about not disclosing the error at the time he thought it was a error.
   - Full disclosure—while the company may wonder about Daniels's technical skills, he does take an ethical action and the company may respect him for his honesty. Daniels gets a big load off his mind and he may be respected by the company for telling the truth.

9. **Decide on a course of action:**
   - Full disclosure (transparency) is the way to go. Daniels should know that the company expects him to admit to his errors and move on. This is what others should do in similar situations for similar reasons (universality).

10. **Reflect on your decision:**
    - Remember, an error doesn't become a mistake until you refuse to correct it. Daniels should reason that the company will respect what he has done by fully disclosing the facts. He would be proud if his family knew about his actions. Indeed, he would be a good role model for his kids.

Daniels reasons at Stage 2 that if he covers up his error and acts in accordance with his perceived best interests, then, he should not admit to the error if there is no need to do so. At Stage 3, Daniels recognizes that out of fairness to the company and its employees, including the new ones hired as a result of the budget estimate, he should inform his superior, Pete, about the error.

Daniels seems to be motivated by good intentions. He needs to have the strength of character to carry out what he knows to be right with ethical action. The virtue of integrity gives him the courage to accept whatever consequences are forthcoming as a result of the faulty budget.

Concluding Thoughts

Professional skepticism, ethical intent, moral reasoning skills, and a decision-making process all contribute toward providing the framework that enables ethical decision making to take place. Ethical decision making starts with identifying that an ethical issue exists (i.e., my actions affect others) and then going on to analyze the ethics issues using specific reasoning methods to assess the possible affects of alternative courses of action on the stakeholders. Once the right decision has been determined, it is up to the decision maker to have the courage to carry through with ethical action.

Underlying ethical decision making in accounting is adherence to the profession's standards of conduct. Accountants and auditors should be guided by the principles and rules that define right conduct in meeting one's obligations to the stakeholders—investors and creditors who rely on the accuracy of financial statement information for their decision making. Remember that in some circumstances the rules in accounting may be unclear or nonexistent so that the public expects accounting professionals to exercise moral judgment in deciding on the proper course of action.

Discussion Questions

The following story applies to questions 1 and 2:

On October 15, 2009, in Fort Collins, Colorado, the parents of a six-year-old boy, Falcon Heene, claimed that he had floated away in a homemade balloon. The event attracted worldwide attention. At the time, it was reported that Falcon was apparently traveling at altitudes reaching 7,000 feet in a homemade helium balloon colored and shaped to resemble a silver flying saucer type of UFO. Falcon was nicknamed "Balloon Boy" by some in the media. After an hours-long flight that covered more than 50 miles across three counties, the balloon landed about 12 miles northeast of Denver International Airport. Authorities closed down the Denver airport and sent several National Guard helicopters and local police in pursuit. After the balloon landed and the boy was found not to be inside, authorities began a manhunt of the entire area, raising fears that he had fallen from the balloon. Later that afternoon the boy was reported to have been hiding at his house the entire time. Suspicions soon arose that the incident was a publicity stunt engineered by the boy's parents, Richard and Mayumi Heene, particularly following the Heenes' interview with Wolf Blitzer on *Larry King Live* that evening. In response to a question about why he was hiding, Falcon said to his father, "You guys said that, um, we did this for the show." On October 18, Larimer County sheriff Jim Alderden announced his conclusion that the incident was a hoax and that the father would be prosecuted. Richard Heene pleaded guilty on November 13, 2009, to the felony count of falsely influencing authorities to protect his wife, Mayumi, a Japanese citizen who he said may have faced deportation if convicted of a more serious crime. He began serving a 90-day sentence on January 11, 2010. Court documents later revealed the mother admitted to investigators that the incident was concocted as a reality show gimmick. The family previously had appeared on the ABC reality show *Wife Swap*.

1. Identify the stakeholders and how they were affected by Heene's actions?

2. What stage of moral reasoning is exhibited by Richard Heene's actions? Do you believe the punishment fit the crime? Why or why not?

3. Explain how the cognitive-developmental approach influences one's ability to make ethical judgments.

4. How do you assess at what stage of moral development in Kohlberg's model you reason at in making decisions? Are you satisfied with that stage? Do you believe there are factors or forces preventing you from reasoning at a higher level? If so, what are they?

5. Aristotle said, "Character is that which reveals moral purpose, exposing the class of things a man chooses or avoids." Explain what you think Aristotle meant by this statement.

6. Mahatma Gandhi, the famous Indian philosopher, said: "Cowards can never be moral." Explain what you think Gandhi meant by this statement.

7. In teaching about moral development, instructors often point out the threefold nature of morality: It depends on emotional development (in the form of ability to feel guilt or shame), social development (manifested by the recognition of the group and the importance of moral behavior for the group's existence), and cognitive development (especially the ability to take another's perspective). How does this perspective of morality relate to ethical reasoning by accountants and auditors?

8. Thorne believes that virtue-based reasoning tends to increase a decision maker's propensity to make sound ethical judgments. Discuss how this process occurs.

9. In this chapter we discussed the role of Sherron Watkins in the Enron fraud. Evaluate Watkins's thought process and actions from the perspective of Kohlberg's model. Do you think she went far enough in bringing her concerns out in the open? Why or why not?

10. Arthur Andersen LLP was the auditor for Enron, WorldCom, Waste Management, and other companies that committed fraud. The company was forced to shut its doors forever after a U.S. Department of Justice lawsuit against the firm concluded that it had obstructed justice and lied to the government in the Enron case. One thing Andersen had done was to shred documents related to its audit of Enron before the government could get its hands on them. Some in the profession thought the government had gone too far given the facts and mediating circumstances including top management's deception; others believed the punishment was unjustified because most accounting firms got caught up in similar situations during the late 1990s and early 2000s (pre-Sarbanes-Oxley). What do you believe? Use ethical reasoning to support your answer.

11. Explain how the elements of the ethical domain in accounting and auditing created conflicting responsibilities in the Enron case.

12. Comment on whether you believe that one's personal judgment is developed by an individual through practice in everyday decision making and/or whether it is cultivated by a professional firm.

13. In what ways does professional skepticism help an auditor evaluate the sufficiency and competency of evidence in the process of examining the financial statements of a client company?

14. Why is professional skepticism important for management accountants?

15. Some empirical research suggests that accountants and auditors may not achieve their higher levels of ethical reasoning. Why do you think this statement may be correct?

16. What is the role of the ethical principles and standards embedded in the accounting profession's codes of ethics in making professional judgments?

17. Libby and Thorne studied the association between auditors' virtue and professional judgment by asking members of the Canadian Institute of Chartered Accountants to rate the importance of a variety of virtues. The most important virtues identified were truthful, independent, objective, and has integrity. The authors note that the inclusion of these virtues in professional codes of conduct (such as the Principles of the AICPA Code of Professional Conduct) may account for their perceived importance.[40] Explain how these virtues relate to an auditor's intention to make ethical decisions.

18. Interpretation 102-4 of the AICPA Code of Professional Conduct that was discussed in Chapter 1 provides that a CPA should not knowingly misrepresent facts or subordinate her judgment when

performing professional services. Explain how Rest's model of moral development influences the steps a CPA should take to avoid subordinating professional judgment.

19. Explain what you think each of the following statements means in the context of moral development.

    a. How far are you willing to go to do the right thing?

    b. How much are you willing to give up to do what you believe is right?

    c. We may say we would do the right thing, but when it requires sacrifice, how much are we willing to give up?

20. In a June 1997 paper published in the *Journal of Business Ethics,* Sharon Green and James Weber reported the results of a study of moral reasoning of accounting students prior to and after taking an auditing course. The study also compared the results between accounting and nonaccounting students prior to the auditing course. The authors found that (1) accounting students, after taking an auditing course that emphasized the AICPA Code, reasoned at higher levels than students who had not taken the course; (2) there were no differences in moral reasoning levels when accounting and nonaccounting majors were compared prior to an auditing course; and (3) there was a significant relationship between the seniors' levels of ethical development and the choice of an ethical versus unethical action.[41] Comment on the results of this study.

Endnotes

1. Barbara Ley Toffler with Jennifer Reingold, *Final Accounting: Ambition, Greed, and the Fall of Arthur Andersen* (New York: Broadway Books, 2003), p. 217.

2. *Report of Investigation by the Special Investigative Committee of the Board of Directors of Enron Corp.* (Powers Report), February 1, 2002, http://news.findlaw.com/wp/docs/enron/specinv020102rpt1.pdf.

3. Bethany McLean and Peter Elkind, *The Smartest Guys in the Room: The Amazing Rise and Scandalous Fall of Enron* (New York: Penguin Group, 2003).

4. Paul M. Clikeman, *Called to Account: Fourteen Financial Frauds That Shaped the American Accounting Profession* (New York: Routledge, 2009).

5. Lawrence Kohlberg, "Stage and Sequence: The Cognitive Developmental Approach to Socialization," in *Handbook of Socialization Theory and Research,* ed. D. A. Goslin (Chicago: Rand McNally, 1969), pp. 347–480.

6. Immanuel Kant, "Fundamental Principles of the Metaphysics of Morals," in *Problems in Moral Philosophy: An Introduction,* 2nd ed., ed. Paul W. Taylor (Encino, CA: Dickenson, 1972), p. 229.

7. Carol Gilligan, *In a Different Voice: Psychological Theory and Women's Development* (Cambridge, MA: Harvard University Press, 1982).

8. James R. Rest and Darcia Narvaez, *Moral Development in the Professions: Psychology and Applied Ethics* (New York: Psychology Press, 1994), p. 4.

9. Rest and Narvaez, p. 4.

10. Muriel J. Bebeau and S. J. Thoma, "'Intermediate' Concepts and the Connection to Moral Education," *Educational Psychology Review* 11, no. 4 (1999), p. 345.

11. O. C. Ferrell, John Fraedrich, and Linda Ferrell, *Business Ethics: Ethical Decision Making and Cases* (Mason, OH: South-Western, Cengage Learning, 2009 Update), pp. 162–163.

12. Clare M. Pennino, "Is Decision Style Related to Moral Development Among Managers in the U.S.?" *Journal of Business Ethics* 41 (December 2002), pp. 337–347.

13. Lawrence A. Ponemon and David R. L. Gabhart, "Ethical Reasoning Research in the Accounting and Auditing Professions," in James R. Rest and Darcia Narvaez, *Moral Development in the Professions: Psychology and Applied Ethics* (New York: Psychology Press, 1994), p. 102.

14. See Michael K. Shaub, "An Analysis of the Association of Traditional Demographic Variables with the Moral Reasoning of Auditing Students and Auditors," *Journal of Accounting Education* (Winter 1994), pp. 1–26; and Lawrence A. Ponemon, "Ethical Reasoning and Selection Socialization in Accounting," *Accounting, Organizations and Society* 17 (1992), pp. 239–258.

15. D. Arnold and L. Ponemon, "Internal Auditors' Perceptions of Whistle-blowing and the Influence of Moral Reasoning: An Experiment," *Auditing: A Journal of Practice and Theory* (Fall 1991), pp. 1–15.

16. L. Ponemon and D. Gabhart, "Auditor Independence Judgments: A Cognitive Developmental Model and Experimental Evidence," *Contemporary Accounting Research* (1990), pp. 227–251.

17. L. Ponemon, "Auditor Underreporting of Time and Moral Reasoning: An Experimental-Lab Study," *Contemporary Accounting Research* (1993), pp. 1–29.

18. Ponemon and Gabhart, 1994, p. 108.

19. James R. Rest, "Morality," in *Handbook of Child Psychology: Cognitive Development,* Vol. 3, Series ed. P. H. Mussen and Vol. ed. J. Flavell (New York: Wiley, 1983), pp. 556–629.

20. Lawrence Kohlberg, *The Meaning and Measurement of Moral Development* (Worcester, MA: Clark University Press, 1979).

21. Rest and Narvaez, p. 24.

22. Mimi Swartz and S. Watkins, *Power Failure: The Inside Story of the Collapse of Enron* (New York: Doubleday, 2003).

23. Swartz and Watkins, pp. 350–351.

24. Linda Thorne, "The Role of Virtue in Auditors' Ethical Decision Making: An Integration of Cognitive-Developmental and Virtue Ethics Perspectives," *Research on Accounting Ethics,* no. 4 (1998), pp. 293–294.

25. Thorne, p. 294.

26. M. Gibbins and A. Mason, "Professional Judgment in Financial Reporting," *CICA Research Study* (Toronto, Ontario, Canada: Canadian Institute of Chartered Accountants, 1988).

27. James C. Gaa, "Discussion of Auditors' Ethical Decision Process," *Auditing: A Journal of Practice and Theory* (1992), pp. 60–67.

28. Thorne, p. 297.

29. Instrumental virtues are described by Pincoffs as properties of individuals' characters essential to the accomplishment of their ethical intentions (e.g., persistence, courage, carefulness, prudence, and determination).

30. Thorne, p. 298.

31. Thorne, pp. 302–303.

32. Thorne, pp. 303–304.

33. In its simplest form, fraud refers to a deliberate, knowing act designed to mislead another party. In accounting, fraud can exist in the financial statements with respect to material misstatements of amounts or the omission of disclosures. Fraud also occurs when an employee of an organization misappropriates assets for his personal benefit. More will be said about fraud in Chapters 3, 4, and 5.

34. American Institute of CPAs, *AICPA Professional Standards Volume 1, Statement on Auditing Standards (SAS) No. 99,* Considerations of Fraud in a Financial Statement Audit (New York: AICPA, June 2009).

35. M. Nelson, "A Model and Literature Review of Professional Skepticism in Auditing," *Auditing: A Journal of Practice & Theory* (2009).

36. Tina D. Carpenter and Jane L. Reimers, *Professional Skepticism: The Effects of a Partner's Influence and the Presence of Fraud on Auditors' Fraud Judgments and Actions,* 2009, Working Paper. Available at SSRN's Web site: http://ssrn.com/abstract=1068942.

37. Kathy Hurtt, Martha M. Eining, and David Plumlee, *An Experimental Examination of Professional Skepticism,* May 2008, Working Paper. Available at SSRN's Web site: http://ssrn.com/abstract=1140267.

38. Kimberly F. Charron and D. Jordan Lowe, "Skepticism and the Management Accountant: Insights for Fraud Detection," *Management Accounting Quarterly* (Winter 2008).

39. Charron and Lowe.

40. Theresa Libby and Linda Thorne, "The Development of a Measure of Auditors' Virtue," *Journal of Business Ethics* 71 (2007), pp. 89–99.

41. Sharon Green and James Weber, *Journal of Business Ethics* 16, no. 8 (June 1997), pp. 777–790.

Chapter 2 Cases

Case 2-1

Cynthia Cooper and WorldCom

Cynthia Cooper details her trials and tribulations about her experiences at WorldCom in the book *Extraordinary Circumstances: The Journey of a Corporate Whistleblower.* The following excerpts from the book describe the actions she took to uncover the fraud at WorldCom and reactions of key players in the accounting department, top management, the audit committee, and the external auditors.

Cooper was first alerted to the fact that there may have been a problem with capital expenditures when she read an article called "Accounting for Anguish" that appeared in the *Fort Worth* (Texas) *Weekly* on May 16, 2002. It described the ordeal of Kim Emigh, a former WorldCom financial analyst who was laid off from the company after complaining for many years about potential abuses related to capital spending. Glyn Smith, a senior manager in internal audit, suggested to Cooper that they do an internal audit of capital expenditures immediately. Cooper agreed. The first sign of a problem was when one of the finance directors provided capital spending schedules for the audit and two of them disagreed in amount. The director said the difference was due to something called "prepaid capacity." When asked to explain, the director couldn't and said that David Myers, the controller of WorldCom, provides the data to record.

Later on a member of the internal audit team with technology knowledge, Gene Morse, was asked to examine the system and see if there was anything designated as prepaid capacity. Morse found prepaid capacity amounts "jumping all over the place, from account to account." There were numerous examples of items moved from account to account apparently to mask the true nature of the expenditures. As news spread of the internal audit of capital expenditures, Myers suggested that the team was wasting its time on the audit and that their time would be better spent to find ways to save money in operating cost. The reaction of Myers only made Cooper more suspicious of what really was going on.

Cooper then approached Farrell Malone, the external audit partner at KPMG, the firm that replaced Andersen after its collapse following the Enron audit. Cooper explained about the movement of amounts to different accounts and unexplained prepaid capacity designations. Farrell recommended not going to the audit committee at that time. Still, Cooper decided to take a closer look. Morse downloaded thousands of entries searching accounts with more than 300,000 transactions each month spread across a hundred legal entities. Cooper learned that Scott Sullivan, the CFO, had found out about the audit. He questioned Morse about the work. This increased Cooper's suspicion since Sullivan rarely took such a direct interest in an internal audit matter. She asked her staff what they thought about Morse's discovery. Most believed

there was a good explanation. But Cooper knew as auditors they were obligated to stay with leads and keep reviewing the issues. In her book, Cooper states her philosophy of internal auditing as: "At times, it is a slow, plodding process of checking and re-checking facts, developing theories, trying to find connections, and thinking through the issues until you get it right."

On June 10, Morse found several entries labeled "prepaid capacity." They appeared to be moving large amounts from the income statement to the balance sheet—$743 million in the third quarter of 2001, $941 million in the fourth quarter of 2001, and $100 million in the first quarter of 2002. The auditors went about tracing the amounts from account to account through the system to see where they landed.

The next morning Cooper received a message that Sullivan wanted to speak to her right away. He talked about becoming more involved in internal audit matters, an unusual step for him. Cooper also overheard a conversation while in Sullivan's office that Max Bobbitt, the chair of the audit committee, would be leaving the committee. This was of concern to Cooper since she reported functionally to the audit committee and administratively to Sullivan. The audit committee provided internal audit with independence from management. She worried that the conversation may have been for her benefit to inform her that Bobbitt may not be there to support her.

At the meeting with Sullivan, Cooper bluntly asked about prepaid capacity. He explained that it represented costs associated with no or low-utilized Sonet Rings and (telecommunication) lines that were being capitalized. He stated: "While revenues have declined, the costs related to certain leases are fixed, creating a matching problem." Although not clear at the time, Cooper came to realize that the amounts represented costs related to the company's leased fiber (optic) lines that had little or no customer usage because of the implosion of telecommunications in the late 1990s and early 2000s. The company continued to pay for the leased capacity but they brought in little, if any, value. Instead of expensing the lease costs as they were incurred, the company reclassified the amounts as capital assets and expensed them over a longer period of time allowing it to stretch out the deduction to company earnings, buying time for revenue to catch up. Sullivan told her he was aware of the issues with the accounting treatment but they "will be cleared up in the second quarter of 2002." At that time he said a restructuring charge related to prepaid capacity would be recorded effectively writing off most of the amounts that had been capitalized. After that, the company would no longer capitalize line costs as prepaid capacity, "instead allocating these costs between a restructuring charge and an expense." Sullivan asked Cooper to postpone the audit until the third quarter of 2002.

Cooper thought about what had transpired in her meeting with Sullivan. She realized that some aspects of accounting depended on judgment. She thought, maybe the prepaid capacity was aggressive, but perfectly legal, accounting. She was uncomfortable with the matter in light of Farrell's admonition not to go to the audit committee. Cooper called Bobbitt to discuss the matter. She thought even though he was coming off the audit committee, that he would be interested in her findings. She told Bobbitt that her staff had identified accounting entries made in the third and fourth quarter of 2001 and the first quarter of 2002 that totaled $2.5 billion, and she was concerned about the accounting. Bobbitt told her to meet with Farrell, the KPMG partner, to discuss the issues.

The next day Bobbitt came to town for an audit committee meeting and asked Cooper to meet with her and Farrell. At first, a stressed-out Bobbitt chastised Cooper for discussing the matter with anyone else until after they could meet to discuss the entries. Cooper felt she needed to have Bobbitt focus on the real issue. However, Bobbitt had already decided not to discuss the matter with the whole committee and he was supported by Farrell.

At this point Cooper and Smith decided to interview Betty Vinson, the accounting director who entered some of the amounts into the accounting system. She asked for support for the prepaid capacity entries. Vinson admitted to making the entries but stated she did not know what they were for and had no support. Cooper asked where the amounts for the entries came from. Vinson said David Myers, the controller, or Buddy Yates, the director of general accounting. Cooper and Smith went to see Yates who told them to see Myers. Incredulously, she asked: "Can a person reporting to you book a billion-dollar journal entry without your knowledge?" Yates told her that Myers called people who report to him all the time to book entries. Besides, "most of the accounting is done in the field and not in my group." She thanked him for his answer but was in a state of disbelief. Cooper then went to see Myers who told her while he could construct support for the entries, he wouldn't do it. She asked him if there are any accounting standards to support the entries. He stated there aren't and that "we probably shouldn't have capitalized the line cost. But once it was done the first time, it was difficult to stop." He professed to be uncomfortable with the entries from the first time they were recorded. Smith wondered whether this was some sort of aggressive accounting technique. She asked Myers whether he was aware of other companies in the telecommunications industry who were using the same accounting treatment. He answered no, but offered that other companies must have been doing the same thing to keep their cost structure low.

Cooper decided to inform Bobbitt of what had transpired. Bobbitt suggested she should update Farrell and call him back after that. Farrell seemed surprised by the situation but said he would contact Bobbitt and Myers. Cooper called Myers to give him a heads-up. Later in the day, Bobbitt asked her to fly to Washington, DC, to meet with him and Farrell the next morning. At the meeting Cooper expressed her concern that only one member of the audit committee knew about the entries. Bobbitt cautioned that they had to be sure before going further and suggested it was now an external audit issue for KPMG, not an internal audit matter. Cooper offered that she didn't care "whose issue it [was] as long as it [was] addressed appropriately." They agreed that Farrell would meet with Scott Sullivan, the CFO, who was the mastermind behind the accounting and give him an opportunity to explain his rationale. Farrell told Cooper that Sullivan's explanation may have made sense from a business perspective, but not an accounting perspective.

By June 20, over $3 billion of improperly classified costs had been found. It had been eight days since Cooper first called Bobbitt about the audit findings and she was growing increasingly concerned that others on the audit committee were kept in the dark. She told Farrell that if Bobbitt didn't call a meeting of the audit committee immediately, she would. Later in the day Bobbitt called Cooper and told her there would be an audit committee meeting and she and Smith could attend if they wanted to. She asked why he seemed so agitated. Bobbitt remarked: "Do you have any idea what I'm about to have to do? I'm about to blow up this company!"

Farrell admitted at the meeting that he was not aware of any provision in GAAP that would support the line-cost entries. Sullivan defended the transfers by stating:

> Starting in 1999, WorldCom invested heavily in assets to expand the telecom network, anticipating enormous future demands in customer traffic. WorldCom not only purchased equipment and fiber, but also signed a significant number of long-term fiber leases with third parties to carry the expected telecom traffic. But when the telecom industry imploded, starting in 2000 and continuing through 2002, the customer usage anticipated never materialized. Now, large pieces of both owned and leased portions of the telecom network had no or very little customer traffic.

Sullivan had business reasons but no accounting rationale for the entries. He tried to use the matching principle to justify the accounting. However, it applied only if the original journal entries to account for the leases were correct. He also talked about taking an impairment charge in the second quarter of 2002, to write off the line cost amounts booked as capital assets. He insisted the entries weren't made to meet earnings; that the accounting for line costs required judgment and the transfers were made using estimates.

Following the audit committee meeting, Cooper's team found 49 prepaid capacity accounting entries, totaling $3.8 billion, recorded over all four quarters of 2001 and the first quarter of 2002. She concluded after reviewing the entries that they were sinister in intent. The pattern of movement between accounts changed from one quarter to the next but the entries had the same end result. She concluded: "It was a spider-web of amounts moving as many as three times and finally spread in smaller dollar increments across a multitude of assets, mostly telecom fiber and equipment. If the amounts are funneled through enough accounts and then spread out, someone seems to have thought, they'd come out on the other end less detectable by the external auditors."

On June 24, Cooper and Smith met with Troy Normand, the mid-level accounting director, who claimed to have relayed his concerns to Sullivan about another matter—the drawing down of "rainy-day" line-cost reserves, thereby reducing expenses. This occurred in 2000 when Normand observed that Sullivan was "forced" to manipulate these amounts to meet the earnings guidance he had provided to Wall Street. Sullivan drew on the business purpose of the transactions and assured Normand everything would be okay. Normand felt he didn't know enough to refute Sullivan's explanation so he went along with it. He shared with Cooper that he had considered resigning and never told internal or external audit about any of the entries because he was concerned for his job and had a family to support. He concluded, "In hindsight, I wish I had."

Questions

1. What are the rules in accounting for determining whether to expense certain costs against revenue versus capitalizing and amortizing the costs? How do the different treatments affect earnings? Explain the reasons given by Scott Sullivan for capitalizing line costs. Why did Cooper believe the treatment did not conform to GAAP?

2. Analyze Cooper's use of professional judgment in the WorldCom case. How do her actions relate to Rest's four stages of moral development?

3. What do you think motivated the behavior and actions of the following key people in this case:
   a. Max Bobbitt, chair of the audit committee
   b. Farrell Malone, the KPMG partner
   c. Scott Sullivan, the CFO
   d. David Myers, the controller
   e. Betty Vinson and Troy Normand, members of the accounting department staff

Case 2-2

Expectations for Professional Judgment by Auditors to Detect Fraud

Auditors today are subject to increased expectations from regulators and the investing public. At the same time, corporations are expanding, transactions have become more complex, and there are requirements for auditors to provide much greater levels of assurance related to financial fraud. A paper by the Institute of Chartered Accountants in Australia—titled *Professional Judgment: Are Auditors Being Held to a Higher Standard than Other Professionals?*[1]—contends that auditors are being held to higher standards for judgment than other professions such as law and medicine where the difficulty of making judgments is recognized. The paper suggests that even a well-conducted audit, following all appropriate audit standards, can fail to detect a material fraud in the financial statements, particularly where management has gone to great lengths to cover up the fraud. These considerations are important in an environment where audit standards have the force of law as is the case with public companies whose audits are overseen by the PCAOB, an entity that reports to the SEC.

The paper notes that judgment is the cornerstone of auditing. The auditor is expected to use professional judgment in

[1]www.charteredaccountants.com.au/files/.../Prof_Judgement_Report_0906.pdf.

light of the given circumstances. Even though auditors should exercise professional skepticism in an attempt to mitigate the risk of being deceived, there will always be some residual risk of material misstatement due to fraud.

With the increased complexity of accounting standards, these judgments for auditors are becoming even more difficult. This is due in part to the growing number and complexity of standards in areas such as fair value accounting and financial derivatives.

Questions

1. Do you think auditors should be held to higher standards than those in other professions? Why or why not? How do the expectations for professional judgment in the case of external auditors differ from those for internal accountants?

2. To what extent do you think the possession of certain virtues can help mitigate the risk that the audit might fail to detect a material fraud in the financial statements, particularly where management has gone to great lengths to cover up the fraud?

3. To what extent do you think the stage of moral development might influence an auditor's ability to take the necessary steps to identify and correct for fraud?

Case 2-3

The Tax Return

Brenda Sells sent the tax return she prepared for the president of Purple Industries, Inc., Harry Kohn, to Vincent Dim, the manager of the tax department at her accounting firm. Dim asked Sells to come to his office at 9:00 a.m. on Monday, April 12, 2010. Sells had no idea why Dim wanted to speak to her. The only reason she could come up with was the tax return for Kohn.

"Brenda, come in," Vincent said.

"Thank you, Vincent," Brenda responded.

"Do you know why I asked to see you?"

"I'm not sure. Does it have something to do with the tax return for Mr. Kohn?" asked Brenda.

"That's right," answered Vincent.

"Is there a problem?" Brenda asked.

"I just spoke with Kohn. I told him that you want to report his winnings from the lottery. He was incensed."

"Why?" Brenda asked. "You and I both know that the tax law is quite clear on this matter. When a taxpayer wins money by playing the lottery, then that amount must be reported as revenue. The taxpayer can offset lottery gains with lottery losses, if those are supportable. Of course, the losses cannot be higher than the amount of the gains. In the case of Mr. Kohn, the losses exceed the gains so there is no net tax effect. I don't see the problem."

"Let me tell you the problem," Vincent stated sharply. "It's taken me years to gain the trust of Kohn. Our firm now audits his company's books, prepares its annual tax return, prepares Kohn's personal tax return, and provides financial planning services for both. Kohn and Purple Industries together are the largest clients in our office. I can't afford to lose any of the business these clients provide for our firm. As you know, we are under increasing competition from larger regional firms that are looking for new clients. If we don't support Kohn, some other firm will step in and do it. Poof, there goes 20 percent of our revenues."

Brenda didn't know what to say. Vincent seemed to be telling her the lottery amounts shouldn't be reported. But that was against the law. She turned to Vincent and asked: "Are you telling me to forget about the lottery amounts on Mr. Kohn's tax return?"

"I want you to go back to your office and think carefully about the situation. Consider that this is a one-time request and we value our staff members who are willing to be flexible in such situations. Let's meet again in my office tomorrow at 9:00 a.m."

Questions

1. Assume Brenda has no reason to doubt Vincent's veracity with respect to the statement that it is "a one-time request." Should that make a difference in what Brenda decides to do? Why or why not?

2. Analyze the alternatives available to Brenda using Kohlberg's six stages of moral development. That is, what would Brenda's position be when she meets with Vincent assuming her judgment was influenced by relevant factors at each of the six different stages of moral development?

3. Assume Brenda decides to go along with Vincent and omits the lottery losses and gains. Next year the same situation arises, but now it's with gambling losses and gains. If you were Brenda, and Vincent asked you to do the same thing you did last year regarding omitting the lottery losses and gains, what would you do this second year? Why?

Case 2-4

Better Boston Beans

Better Boston Beans is a coffee shop located in the Faneuil Hall Marketplace near the waterfront and Government Center in Boston. The coffee shop specializes in exotic blends of coffee including Sumatra Dark Roast Black, India Mysore "Gold Nuggets," and Guatemala Antigua. It also serves blended coffees including Reggae Blend, Jamaican Blue Mountain Blend, and Marrakesh Blend. For those with more pedestrian tastes, the shop serves French Vanilla, Hazelnut, and Hawaiian Macadamia Nut. The coffee of the day varies, but the most popular is Colombia Supremo. The coffee shop also serves a variety of cold-blended coffees.

Cindie Rosen has worked for Better Boston Beans for six months. She took the job right out of college because she wasn't sure whether she wanted to go to graduate school before beginning a career in financial services. Cindie hoped that by taking a year off before starting her career or going on to graduate school, she would experience "the real world" and find out firsthand what it is like to work a 40-hour week. She did not have a full-time job during college because her parents helped pay for the tuition.

Since Cindie is the "new kid on the block," she is often asked to work the late shift from 4:00 p.m. to midnight. She works with one other person—Jeffrey Lyndell—who is the assistant shift supervisor. Lyndell has been with Boston Beans for three years but recently was demoted from shift supervisor.

For the past two weeks, Lyndell has been leaving before 11 p.m., after most of the stores in the Marketplace close down, and he has asked Cindie to close up by herself. Cindie felt this was wrong and it was starting to concern her, but she hasn't spoken to Lyndell and has not informed the store manager. However, something happened one night that caused Cindie to consider taking the next step.

At 11:00 p.m., 10 Japanese tourists came into the store for coffee. Cindie was alone and had to rush around and make five different cold-blended drinks and five different hot-blended coffees. While she was working, one of the Japanese tourists who spoke English very well approached her and said that he was shocked such a famous American coffee shop would only have one worker in the store at any time during the working day. Cindie didn't want to ignore the man's comments so she answered that her coworker had to go home early because he was sick. That seemed to satisfy the tourist.

It took Cindie almost 20 minutes to make all the drinks and field two phone calls that came in during that time. After she closed for the night, Cindie reflected on the experience. She realized it could get worse before it gets better because Jeffrey Lyndell was now making it a habit to leave work early. She had to either approach him about it or speak with the store manager. She felt much more comfortable talking to the store manager. In fact, in Cindie's own words, "Lyndell gives me the creeps."

Questions

1. Evaluate the actions of Lyndell from the perspective of the Six Pillars of Character. Consider Kohlberg's six stages of moral development. What would Cyndie do and why if she reasoned at each of the six stages?

2. Assume Cindie approached Lyndell about her concerns. Lyndell tells Cyndie that he has an alcohol problem. Lately, it's gotten to him real bad. That's why he's left early—to get a drink and calm his nerves. Lyndell also said that this is the real reason he was demoted. He was warned that if one more incident occurred, the store manager would fire him. He pleaded with Cindie to work with him through these hard times. How would you react to Lyndell's request if you were Cindie? Would you honor his request for confidentiality and support? Why or why not? What if Lyndell was a close personal friend—would that change your answer? Be sure to consider the implications of your decision on other parties potentially affected by your actions.

3. Assume Cindie keeps quiet. The following week another incident occurs where Cindie gets into a shouting match with a customer who became tired of waiting for his coffee after 10 minutes. Cindie felt terrible about it, apologized to the customer after serving his coffee, and left work that night wondering if it was time to apply to graduate school. The customer was so irate that he contacted the store manager and expressed his displeasure about service and Cindie's attitude. What do you think the store manager should do? Support your answer with ethical reasoning.

Case 2-5

Eating Time

Kevin Lowe is depressed. He has been with the CPA firm Stooges LLP for only three months. Yet the partners in charge of the firm—Bo Chambers and his brother Moe Chambers—have asked for a "sit-down." Here's how it goes:

"Kevin, we asked to see you because your time reports indicate that it takes you 50 percent longer to complete audit work than your predecessor," Moe said.

"Well, Bo and Moe, I am new and still learning on the job," replied Lowe.

"That's true," Bo responded, "but you have to appreciate that we have fixed budgets for these audits. Every hour over the budgeted time costs us money."

"Are you asking me to cut down on the work I do?" Lowe asked.

"We would never compromise the quality of our audit work," Moe said. "We're trying to figure out why it takes you so much longer than other staff members."

At this point Lowe started to perspire. He wiped his forehead, took a glass of water, and asked: "Would it be better if I took some of the work home at night and on weekends, completed it, but didn't charge the firm or the client for my time?"

Bo and Moe were surprised by Kevin's openness. On one hand, they valued that trait in their employees. On the other hand, they couldn't answer with a yes. Moe looked at Bo, and then turned to Kevin and said: "It's up to you to decide how to increase your productivity on audits. As you know, this is an important element of performance evaluation."

Kevin cringed. Was the handwriting on the wall in terms of his future with the firm? he wondered.

"I understand what you're saying," Kevin said. "I will do better in the future—I promise."

"Good," responded Bo and Moe. "Let's meet 30 days from now and we'll discuss your progress on the matters we've discussed today and your future with the firm."

Questions

1. Why do you think Bo and Moe did not want to respond directly to Kevin's comment about taking work home? Was that an ethical position to take?

2. Evaluate Bo and Moe's position of doing what it takes to avoid not exceeding budgeted time on audits from the perspective of Kohlberg's model of moral development. What are the implications of such a position for firm culture?

3. Assume on Kevin's very next audit he exceeds the budgeted time allowed for substantiating all capital expenditures. That is, he's already spent the allotted time to gather evidence, such as invoice descriptions, and he's only 50 percent through with the analysis. Given the facts of this case, what would you do if you were in Kevin's position? Consider the possible effect of your actions on the stakeholders.

Case 2-6

Supreme Designs, Inc.

Supreme Designs, Inc., is a small manufacturing company located in Detroit, Michigan. There are three stockholders of the company—Gary Hoffman, Ed Webber, and John Sullivan. Hoffman manages the business including the responsibility for the financial statements. Webber and Sullivan do most of the sales work, and they cultivate potential customers for Supreme Designs.

Hoffman recently hired his daughter, Janet, to manage the office. Janet has successfully managed a small clothing boutique in downtown Detroit for the past eight years. She sold the shop to a regional department store that wanted to expand its operations. Gary Hoffman hopes that his daughter will take over as an owner in a few years when he reaches retirement age. Webber and Sullivan are significantly younger than Gary Hoffman.

Janet is given complete control over the payroll, and she approves disbursements, signs checks, and reconciles the general ledger cash account to the bank statement balance. Previously, the bookkeeper was the only employee with such authority. However, the bookkeeper recently left the company, and Hoffman needed someone he could trust to be in charge of these sensitive operations. He did ask his daughter to hire someone as soon as possible to help with these and other accounting functions. Janet hired Kevin Greenberg shortly thereafter, based on a friend's recommendation.

Greenberg is a relatively inexperienced accountant but he was willing to work for less than what the company had paid the former bookkeeper. Greenberg holds a bachelor's degree in accounting from Detroit Pistons College. He had been working for Prince Brothers Enterprises for the past 16 months. However, Prince Brothers decided to go public and the company hired Hamilton LLP to do the accounting and auditing work.

On April 29, 2011, about one year after hiring Greenberg, Janet discovers that she needs surgery. Even though the procedure is fairly common and the risks are minimal, she plans on spending five weeks in recovery because of related medical problems that could flare up if she returns to work too soon. She tells Greenberg to approve vouchers for payment and present them to her father during this time, and her father will write the checks during her absence. Janet had previously discussed this plan with her father and they both agreed that Greenberg was ready to assume the additional responsibilities. They did not, however, discuss the matter with either Webber or Sullivan.

The bank statement for April arrives on May 3, 2011. Janet did not tell Greenberg to reconcile the bank statements. In fact, she specifically told him to just put those aside until she returns. However, Greenberg decides to reconcile the April bank statement as a favor to Janet and to lighten her workload after she returns.

Although everything appears to be in order, Greenberg is not sure what to make of his finding that Janet approved and signed five checks payable to herself for the same amount during April 2011. Each check appears in correct numerical sequence, 1 check of every 10 checks written during the month. Greenberg was surprised because if these were payroll checks, as he had suspected because they were for the same amount, it was highly unusual. This is because the payroll is processed once a month for all employees of Supreme Designs. In fact, he found only one canceled check for each of the other employees including himself.

Curiosity gets the better of Greenberg and he decides to trace the checks paid to Janet to the cash disbursements journal. He looked for supporting documentation but couldn't find any. He noticed that four of the five checks were coded to different accounts including supplies, travel and entertainment, books and magazines, and two to miscellaneous expenses.

After considering what his findings might mean and whether he should contact Janet, Greenberg decided to expand his search. He reviewed the bank statements for January through March of 2011. In all, there were 15 additional checks made payable to Janet, each for the same amount as the 5 in April. These 20 checks totaled $30,000. Greenberg still thought it was possible these amounts represented Janet's salary because he knows her annual salary is $50,000. Perhaps she took out a little more this year.

Greenberg doesn't know what to do. He could contact Janet, but he knows she would be unhappy that he opened the bank statements and went so far as to reconcile cash for April even though she specifically told him not to do it. Perhaps he should contact the three stockholders. Then again, it may be best if he keeps quiet about the entire matter.

Questions

1. Do you think Greenberg did the "right" thing by opening the April bank statement and reconciling it to the general ledger? Why or why not? What about the previous bank statements?

2. Explain what Greenberg should do if he reasons at each of the six stages of Kohlberg's model of moral development. Be sure to consider stakeholder effects in your answer.

3. Evaluate what steps should be taken in each of the following independent situations:

   a. If you were Janet and Greenberg dropped by the hospital to tell you about his discovery, how would you react?

   b. Assume Greenberg contacts Janet's father because he did not want to upset her after the surgery. Hoffman talks to his daughter, who informs him that she had a shortage in her personal funds and planned to repay the $30,000 after she returns. What would you do if you were Gary Hoffman? Why?

c. Assume Hoffman does nothing because of his daughter's explanation. Janet returns to work and fires Kevin Greenberg. What would you do if you were Greenberg. Why? How do you think his action (or inaction) might affect his opportunity for other jobs? Should that matter in terms of what he decides to do?

Case 2-7

Milton Manufacturing Company

Milton Manufacturing Company produces a variety of textiles for distribution to wholesale manufacturers of clothing products. The company's primary operations are located in Long Island City, New York, with branch factories and warehouses in several surrounding cities. Milton Manufacturing is a closely held company. Irv Milton is the president of the company. He started the business in 1999 and it grew in revenue from $500,000 to $5.0 million in 10 years. However, the revenues declined to $4.5 million in 2009. Net cash flows from all activities also were declining. The company was concerned because it planned to borrow $20 million from the credit markets in the fourth quarter of 2010.

Irv Milton met with Ann Plotkin, the chief accounting officer (CAO), on January 15, 2010, to discuss a proposal by Plotkin to control cash outflows. She was not overly concerned about the recent decline in net cash flows from operating activities because these amounts were expected to increase in 2010, as a result of projected higher levels of revenue and cash collections.

Plotkin knew that if overall capital expenditures continued to increase at the rate of 26 percent per year, Milton Manufacturing probably would not be able to borrow the $20 million. Therefore, she suggested establishing a new policy to be instituted on a temporary basis. Each plant's capital expenditures for 2010 would be limited to the level

of capital expenditures in 2008. Irv Milton pointedly asked Plotkin about the possible negative effects of such a policy, but in the end Milton was convinced it was necessary to initiate the policy immediately to stem the tide of increases in capital expenditures. A summary of cash flows appears in Exhibit 1.

Sammie Markowicz is the plant manager at the headquarters location in Long Island City. He was informed of the new capital expenditure policy by Ira Sugofsky, the vice president for operations. Markowicz told Sugofsky that the new policy could negatively affect plant operations because certain machinery and equipment, essential to the production process, had been breaking down more frequently during the past two years. The problem was primarily with the motors. New and better models with more efficient motors had been developed by an overseas supplier. These were expected to be available by April 2010. Markowicz planned to order 1,000 of these new motors for the Long Island City operation, and he expected that other plant managers would do the same. Sugofsky told Markowicz to delay the acquisition of new motors for one year after which time the restrictive capital expenditure policy would be lifted. Markowicz reluctantly agreed.

Milton Manufacturing operated profitably during the first six months of 2010. Net cash inflows from investing activities

---

EXHIBIT 1
MILTON MANUFACTURING COMPANY
Summary of Cash Flows
For the Years Ended December 31, 2009 and 2008 (000 omitted)

	December 31, 2009	December 31, 2008
Cash Flows from Operating Activities		
Net income	$ 372	$ 542
Adjustments to reconcile net income to net cash provided by operating activities	1,350	1,383
Net cash provided by operating activities	$ 1,722	$ 1,925
Cash Flows from Investing Activities		
Capital expenditures	$ (2,420)	$ (1,918)
Other investing inflows (outflows)	176	84
Net cash used in investing activities	$ (2,244)	$ (1,834)
Cash Flows from Financing Activities		
Net cash provided (used in) financing activities	$ 168	$ (376)
Increase (decrease) in cash and cash equivalents	$ (354)	$ (285)
Cash and cash equivalents—beginning of the year	$ 506	$ 791
Cash and cash equivalents—end of the year	$ 152	$ 506

exceeded outflows by $250,000 during this time period. It was the first time in three years there was a positive cash flow from investing activities. Production operations accelerated during the third quarter as a result of increased demand for Milton's textiles. An aggressive advertising campaign initiated in late 2009 seemed to bear fruit for the company. Unfortunately, the increased level of production put pressure on the machines and the degree of breakdown was increasing. A big problem was that the motors wore out prematurely.

Markowicz was concerned about the machine breakdown and increasing delays in meeting customer demands for the shipment of the textile products. He met with the other branch plant managers who complained bitterly to him about not being able to spend the money to acquire new motors. Markowicz was very sensitive to their needs. He informed them that the company's regular supplier had recently announced a 25 percent price increase for the motors. Other suppliers followed suit and Markowicz saw no choice but to buy the motors from the overseas supplier. That supplier's price was lower, and the quality of the motors would significantly enhance the machines' operating efficiency. However, the company's restrictions on capital expenditures stood in the way of making the purchase.

Markowicz approached Sugofsky and told him about the machine breakdowns and concerns of other plant managers. Sugofsky seemed indifferent. He reminded Markowicz of the capital expenditure restrictions in place and that the Long Island City plant was committed to make expenditures at the same level as it had in 2008. Markowicz argued that he was faced with an unusual situation and he had to act now. Sugofsky hurriedly left but not before he said to Markowicz: "A policy is a policy."

Markowicz reflected on the comment and his obligations to Milton Manufacturing. He was conflicted because he viewed his primary responsibility and that of the other plant managers to ensure that the production process operated smoothly. The last thing the workers needed right now was a stoppage of production because of machine failure.

At this time, Markowicz learned of a 30-day promotional price offered by the overseas supplier to gain new customers by lowering the price for all motors by 25 percent. Coupled with the 25 percent increase in price by the company's supplier, Markowicz knew he could save the company $1,500, or 50 percent of cost, on each motor purchased from the overseas supplier.

After carefully considering the implications of his intended action, Markowicz contacted the other plant managers and informed them that while they were not obligated to follow his lead because of the capital expenditure policy, he planned to purchase 1,000 motors from the overseas supplier for the headquarters plant in Long Island City.

Markowicz made the purchase in the fourth quarter of 2010 without informing Sugofsky. He convinced the plant accountant to record the $1.5 million expenditure as an operating (not capital) expenditure because he knew the higher level of operating cash inflows would mask the effect of his expenditure. In fact, Markowicz was proud that he had "saved" the company $1.5 million and he did what was necessary to ensure that the Long Island City plant continued to operate.

The acquisitions by Markowicz and the other plant managers enabled the company to keep up with the growing demand for textiles and the company finished the year with record high levels of net cash inflows from all activities. Markowicz was lauded by his team for his leadership. The company successfully executed a loan agreement with Second Bankers Hours & Trust Co. The $20 million borrowed was received on January 3, 2011.

During the course of an internal audit on January 21, 2011, Beverly Wald, the chief internal auditor, discovered that there was an unusually high level of motors in the inventory. A complete check of inventory determined that $1.0 million of motors remained on hand.

Wald reported her findings to Ann Plotkin and together they went to see Irv Milton. After being informed of the situation, Milton called in Ira Sugofsky. When Wald told him about her findings, Sugofsky's face turned beet red. He paced the floor, poured a glass of water, drank it quickly, and then began his explanation. Sugofsky told them about his encounter with Sammie Markowicz. Sugofsky stated in no uncertain terms that he had told Markowicz not to increase plant expenditures beyond the 2008 level. "I left the meeting believing that he understood the company's policy. I knew nothing about the purchase," he stated.

At this point Wald joined in and explained to Sugofsky that the $1 million is accounted for as inventory and not an operating cash outflow: "What we do in this case is transfer the motors out of inventory and into the machinery account once they are placed into operation because, according to the documentation, the motors added significant value to the asset." Sugofsky had a perplexed look on his face. Finally, Irv Milton took control of the accounting lesson by asking: "What's the difference? Isn't the main issue that Markowicz did not follow company policy?" The three officers in the room shook their head simultaneously, perhaps in gratitude for being saved the additional lecturing. Milton then said he wanted the three of them to brainstorm some alternatives on how best to deal with the Sammie Markowicz situation and present the alternatives to him in one week.

Question

Use the 10-step decision-making model explained in this chapter and develop the alternatives to be presented to Milton. Be sure to select the optimum alternative and explain why you chose it from an ethical perspective.

Case 2-8

Juggyfroot

"I'm sorry, Lucy. That's the way it is," Ricardo Rikey said.

"I just don't know if I can go along with it, Rikey," Lucy replied.

"We have no choice. Juggyfroot is our biggest client, Lucy. They've warned us that they will put the engagement up for bid if we refuse to go along with the reclassification of marketable securities," Rikey explained.

"Have you spoken to Fred and Ethel about this?" Lucy asked.

"Are you kidding? They're the ones who made the decision to go along with Juggyfroot," Rikey responded.

The previous scene took place in the office of Deziloo LLP, a large CPA firm in Beverly Hills, California. Lucy Spheroid is the partner on the engagement of Juggyfroot, a publicly owned global manufacturer of pots and pans and other household items. Ricardo Rikey is the managing partner of the office. Fred and Ethel are the two members of the firm that make final judgments on difficult accounting issues especially when there is a difference of opinion with the client. All four are CPAs.

Ricardo Rikey is preparing for a meeting with Norman Baitz, the CEO of Juggyfroot. Rikey knows that the company expects to borrow $5 million next quarter and it wants to put the best face possible on its financial statements to impress the banks. That would explain why the company had reclassified a $2 million market loss on a trading investment to the available-for-sale category so that the "loss" would now show up in stockholder's equity and not as a charge against current income. The result was to increase earnings in 2010 by 8 percent. Rikey also knows that without the change, the earnings would have declined by 2 percent and the company's stock price would have taken a hit.

In the meeting, Rikey points out to Baitz that the investment in question was marketable and in the past the company had sold similar investments in less than one year. Rikey adds there is no justification under generally accepted accounting principles to change the classification from trading to available-for-sale.

Questions

1. Explain the rules in accounting to determine whether an investment in a marketable security should be accounted for as trading, available-for-sale, or held-to-maturity. Include in your discussion how such classification affects the financial statements.

2. Who are the stakeholders in this case? What expectations should they have and what are the ethical obligations of Deziloo and its CPAs to the stakeholders? Use ethical reasoning to answer this question.

3. Using the AICPA Code of Professional Conduct as a reference, what ethical issues exist for Rikey, Lucy, Fred and Ethel, and Deziloo LLP in this matter? What role does auditor virtue play in determining what to do in this case?

Optional Question

Refer back to the ethics reflection introductory material on pages 1–2 in Chapter 1. Discuss why the accounting rules for valuing so-called securitized assets that were designed using a basket of outstanding mortgages came under attack in 2008–2009. Explain how the accounting rules for investments in securities changed following criticisms that the accounting rules were, at least in part, responsible for the financial crisis. Do you think accounting rules should be influenced by congressional pressure as was the case with the changes in accounting for investments? Why or why not?

Case 2-9

Phar-Mor

The Dilemma

The story of Phar-Mor shows how quickly a company that built its earnings on fraudulent transactions can dissolve like an Alka-Seltzer.

One day Stan Cherelstein, the controller of Phar-Mor, discovered cabinets stuffed with held checks totaling $10 million. Phar-Mor couldn't release the checks to vendors because it did not have enough cash in the bank to cover the amount. Cherelstein wondered what he should do.

Background

Phar-Mor was a chain of discount drugstores, based in Youngstown, Ohio, and founded in 1982 by Michael Monus and David Shapira. The company grew from 15 to 310 stores in less than 10 years and had 25,000 employees. According to Litigation Release No. 14716 issued by the SEC,[1] Phar-Mor had cumulatively overstated income by $290 million between 1987 and 1991. In 1992, prior to disclosure of the fraud, the company overstated income by an additional $238 million.

The Cast of Characters

Mickey Monus personifies the hard-driving entrepreneur who is bound and determined to make it big whatever the cost. He served as the president and chief operating officer of Phar-Mor from its inception until a corporate restructuring was announced on July 28, 1992.

David Shapira was the chief executive officer of Phar-Mor and the CEO of Giant Eagle, Phar-Mor's parent company and majority stockholder. Giant Eagle also owned Tamco, which was one of Phar-Mor's major suppliers. Shapira left day-to-day operations of Phar-Mor to Monus until the fraud became too large and persistent to ignore.

Patrick Finn was the CFO of Phar-Mor from 1988 to 1992. Finn, who holds the CMA, initially brought Monus the bad news that following a number of years of eroding profits, the company faced millions in losses in 1989.

John Anderson was the accounting manager at Phar-Mor. Hired after completing a college degree in accounting at Youngstown State University, Anderson became a part of the fraud.

[1] Securities and Exchange Commission, Litigation Release No. 14716, November 9, 1995, *SEC v. Michael Monus, Patrick Finn, John Anderson and Jeffrey Walley,* Case No. 4:95, CV 975 (N.D. OH, filed May 2, 1995), www.sec.gov/litigation/litreleases/lr14716.txt.

Coopers & Lybrand, prior to its merger with Price Waterhouse, were the auditors of Phar-Mor. The firm failed to detect the fraud as it was unfolding.

How It Started

The facts of this case are taken from the SEC filing and a Public Broadcasting System Frontline program, "How to Steal $500 Million." The interpretation of the facts is consistent with reports, but some literary license has been taken to add intrigue to the case.

Finn approached Monus with the bad news. Monus took out his pen, crossed off the losses, and then wrote in higher numbers to show a profit. Monus couldn't bear the thought of his hot growth company that had been sizzling for five years suddenly flaming out. In the beginning, it was to be a short-term fix to buy time while the company improved efficiency, put the heat on suppliers for lower prices, and turned a profit. Finn believed in Monus's ability to turn things around so he went along with the fraud. Finn prepared the reports and Monus changed the numbers for four months before turning the task over to Finn. These reports with the false numbers were faxed to Shapira and given to Phar-Mor's board. Basically, the company was lying to its owners.

The fraud occurred by dumping the losses into a "bucket account" and then reallocating the sums to one of the company's hundreds of stores in the form of increases in inventory amounts. Phar-Mor issued fake invoices for merchandise purchases and made phony journal entries to increase inventory and decrease cost of sales. The company overcounted and double-counted merchandise in inventory.

The fraud was helped by the fact that the auditors from Coopers observed inventory in only 4 out of 300 stores, and that allowed the finance department at Phar-Mor to conceal the shortages. Moreover, Coopers informed Phar-Mor in advance which stores they would visit. Phar-Mor executives fully stocked the 4 selected stores but allocated the phony inventory increases to the other 296 stores. Regardless of the accounting tricks, Phar-Mor was heading for collapse and its suppliers threatened to cut off the company for nonpayment of bills.

Stan Cherelstein's Role

Cherelstein, a CPA, was hired to be the controller of Phar-Mor in 1991 long after the fraud had begun. One day, John Anderson, Phar-Mor's accounting manager, called Cherelstein into his office and explained that the company had been keeping two sets of books—one that showed the true state of the company with the losses and the other, called the subledger, that showed the falsified numbers that were presented to the auditors.

Cherelstein and Anderson discussed what to do about the fraud. Cherelstein was not happy about it at all and demanded to meet with Monus. Cherelstein did get Monus to agree to repay the company for the losses from Monus's (personal) investment of company funds into the World Basketball League (WBL). But Monus never kept his word. In the beginning Cherelstein felt compelled to give Monus some time to turn things around through increased efficiencies and by using a device called exclusivity fees that were paid by vendors to get Phar-Mor to stock their products. Over time, Cherelstein became more and more uncomfortable as the suppliers called more and more frequently demanding payment on their invoices.

Accounting Fraud

Misappropriation of Assets

The unfortunate reality of the Phar-Mor saga was that it involved not only bogus inventory but also the diversion of company funds to feed Monus's personal habits. One example was the movement of $10 million in company funds to help start a new basketball league, the World Basketball League, that limited player participation to those six feet and under.

False Financial Statements

According to the ruling by the United States Court of Appeals that heard Monus's appeal of his conviction on all 109 counts of fraud, the company submitted false financial statements to Pittsburgh National Bank, which increased a revolving credit line for Phar-Mor from $435 million to $600 million in March 1992. It also defrauded Corporate Partners, an investment group that bought $200 million in Phar-Mor stock in June 1991. The list goes on including the defrauding of Chemical Bank, which served as the placing agent for $155 million in 10-year senior secured notes issued to Phar-Mor; Westinghouse Credit Corporation, which had executed a $50 million loan commitment to Phar-Mor in 1987; and Westminster National Bank, which served as the placing agent for $112 million in Phar-Mor stock sold to various financial institutions in 1991.

Tamco Relationship

The early financial troubles experienced by Phar-Mor in 1988 can be attributed to at least two transactions. The first was that the company provided deep discounts to retailers to stock its stores with product. There was concern early on that the margins were too thin. The second was that its supplier, Tamco, was shipping partial orders to Phar-Mor while billing for full orders. Phar-Mor had no way of knowing because it was not logging in shipments from Tamco.

After the deficiency was discovered, Giant Eagle agreed to pay Phar-Mor $7 million in 1988 on behalf of Tamco. Phar-Mor later bought Tamco from Giant Eagle in an additional effort to solve the inventory and billing problems. However, the losses just kept on coming.

Back to the Dilemma

Cherelstein looked out the window at the driving rain storm. He thought about the fact that he didn't start the fraud or the cover-up. Still, he knows about it now and feels compelled to do something. Cherelstein thought about the persistent complaints by vendors that they were not being paid and their threats to cut off shipments to Phar-Mor. Cherelstein knows that without any product in Phar-Mor stores, the company could not last much longer.

Questions

1. How do you assess blame for the fraud? That is, to what extent was it caused by Finn's willingness to go along with the actions of Monus? What about Shapira's lax oversight. Should the blame all go to Monus? What role did Coopers & Lybrand play with respect to its professional judgment?

2. Use the ethics standards of the AICPA and IMA to evaluate the actions of Finn and Cherelstein in the Phar-Mor fraud. Did they meet their ethical obligations?

3. What is the ethical message of Phar-Mor? That is, explain what you think is the "moral of the story."

Case 2-10

Imperial Valley Thrift & Loan—Part I*

Bill Stanley, of Jacobs, Stanley & Company, started to review the working paper files on his client, Imperial Valley Thrift & Loan, in preparation for the audit of the client's financial statements for the year ended December 31, 2010. The bank was owned by a parent company, Nuevo Financial Group, and it serviced a small western Arizona community by Yuma that reached south to the border of Mexico. The bank's preaudit statements are presented in Exhibit 1.

Bill Stanley knew there were going to be some problems to contend with during the course of the audit, so he decided to review several items in the file in order to refresh his memory about the client's operations.

*Part II of the case appears in Chapter 4.

Background

The first item Stanley reviewed was the planning memo he had prepared about two months ago. This memo is summarized in Exhibit 2.

The next item Stanley reviewed was an internal office communication on potential audit risks. This communication described three areas of particular concern.

1. The client charged off $420,000 in loans in 2009 and had already charged off $535,000 through July 31, 2010. Assume reserve requirements by law are a minimum of 1.25 percent of loans outstanding. However, given prior history, this statutory amount probably would not be large enough for the

---

EXHIBIT 1
IMPERIAL VALLEY THRIFT & LOAN
Balance Sheet (preaudit) December 31, 2010

Assets

Cash and cash equivalents	$1,960,000
Loans receivable	6,300,000
Less: Reserve for loan losses	(25,000)
Unearned discounts & fees	(395,000)
Accrued interest receivable	105,000
Prepayments	12,000
Real property held for sale	514,000
Property, plant, & equipment	390,000
Less: Accumulated depreciation	(110,000)
Contribution to Thrift Guaranty Corp.	15,000
Deferred start-up costs	44,000
Total assets	$8,810,000

Liabilities & Equity

Liabilities

Regular & money market savings	$2,212,000
T-bills & CDs	5,180,000
Accrued interest payable	190,000
Accounts payable & accruals	28,000
Total liabilities	$7,610,000

Equity

Capital stock	$ 700,000
Additional paid-in capital	1,120,000
Retained earnings (deficit)	(620,000)
Total equity	$1,200,000
Total liabilities and equity	$8,810,000

EXHIBIT 1 *(Continued)*
IMPERIAL VALLEY THRIFT & LOAN
Statement of Operations (preaudit)
For the Year Ended December 31, 2010

Revenues

Interest earned	$ 820,000
Discount earned	210,000
Investment income	82,000
Fees, charges, & commissions	78,000
Total revenues	$1,190,000

Expenses

Interest expense	$ 815,000
Provision for loan losses	180,000
Salary expense	205,000
Occupancy expense including depreciation	100,000
Other administrative expense	160,000
Legal expense	12,000
Thrift Guaranty Corp. payment	48,000
Total expenses	$1,520,000
Net loss for the year	$ 330,000

loan loss reserve. This, in combination with the prior auditors' concerns about proper loan underwriting procedures and documentation, indicates that we should carefully review loan quality.

2. The audit report issued on the 2009 financial statements contained an explanatory paragraph describing the uncertainty about the client's ability to continue as a going concern. The concern was caused by the "capital impairment" declaration by the Arizona Department of Corporations.

3. The client had weak internal controls according to the prior auditors. Some of the items to look out for, in addition to proper loan documentation, were whether the preaudit financial statement information provided by the client is supported by the general ledger, whether the accruals were appropriate, and whether all transactions were properly authorized and recorded on a timely basis.

Audit Findings

The audit was conducted during January and February 2011. Based on information gather during the audit, the following were the areas of greatest concern to Stanley:

1. **Adequacy of Loan Collateral.** A review of 30 loan files representing $2,100,000 of total loans outstanding (33.3 percent of the portfolio) indicated that much of the collateral for the loans was in the form of second or third mortgages on real property. This gave the client a potentially unenforceable position due to the existence of very large senior liens. For example, in the event foreclosure

became necessary to collect Imperial Valley's loan, the client would have to first pay off these large senior liens. Other collateral often consisted of personal items such as jewelry and furniture. In the case of jewelry, often there was no effort made by the client after granting the loan to ascertain whether the collateral was still in the possession of the borrower. The jewelry could have been sold without the client's knowledge.

2. **Collectibility of Loans.** Many loans were structured in such a way as to require interest payments only for a small number of years (two or three years), with a balloon payment for principal due at the end of this time. This structure made it difficult to properly evaluate the payment history of the borrower. Although the annual interest payments may have been made for the first year or two, this was not necessarily a good indication that the borrower would come up with the cash needed to make the large final payment, and the financial statements provided no additional disclosures about this matter.

3. **Weakness in Internal Controls.** Internal control weaknesses were a pervasive concern. The auditors recomputed certain accruals and unearned discounts, confirmed loan and deposit balances, and reconciled the preaudit financial information provided by the client to the general ledger. Some adjustments had to be made as a result of this work. A material weakness in the lending function was identified. Loans were too frequently granted merely because the borrowers were well known to Imperial Valley officials who

---

Exhibit 2
Planning Memo

1. The firm of Jacobs, Stanley & Co. succeeded the firm of Nelson, Thomas & Co. as auditors for Imperial Valley Thrift & Loan. The prior auditors conducted the 2008 and 2009 audits. Jacobs, Stanley & Co. communicated in writing with Nelson, Thomas & Co. prior to acceptance of the engagement. Additionally, authorization was given by the client for a review of the predecessor auditors' working papers. The findings of these inquiries are summarized in item 6 below and the previously discussed internal office communication.
2. Imperial Valley Thrift & Loan was incorporated in Arizona on June 12, 1994. It is a wholly owned subsidiary of Nuevo Financial Group, S.A., a Mexican corporation. As an industrial loan company, it is restricted to certain types of business, including making real estate and consumer loans and certain types of commercial loans.
3. Imperial Valley accepts deposits in the form of interest-bearing passbook accounts and investment certificates. Most of the depositors are of Spanish descent. The client primarily services the Spanish-speaking community in the Imperial Valley of southern Arizona, which is a rural community located on the Mexican border.
4. The principal officers of Imperial Valley are Jose Ortega and his brother Arturo. They serve as the chief executive officer and the chief financial officer, respectively. Two cousins serve as the chief operating officer and chief compliance officer.
5. Imperial Valley is subject to the regulations of the Arizona Industrial Loan Law and is examined by the Department of Corporations. It was last examined in December 2009 and was put on notice as "capital impaired." Additional capital was being sought from local investors.
6. Based on review of the prior auditors' working papers, the following items were noted:
    a. The client's lack of profitability was due to a high volume of loan losses resulting from poor underwriting procedures and faulty documentation.
    b. Imperial Valley has a narrow net interest margin due to the fact that all deposits are interest bearing and it pays the highest interest rates in the area.
    c. Due to the small size of the client and its focus on handling day-to-day operating problems, the internal controls are marginal at best. There were material weaknesses in their loan underwriting procedures and documentation, as well as in compliance with regulatory requirements.
    d. There are no reports issued by management on the internal controls.

---

believed they could be counted on to repay their outstanding loans. An ability to repay these loans was based too often on "faith" rather than on clear indications that the borrowers would have the necessary cash available to repay their loans when they came due. This was of great concern to the auditors, especially in light of the inadequacy of the loan reserve, as detailed in item 5 that follows.

4. **Status of Additional Capital Infusion.** We are working under the assumption that under Arizona regulatory requirements, a thrift and loan institution must maintain a 6:1 ratio of thrift certificates to net equity capital. Based on the financial information provided by Imperial Valley, the capital deficiency was only $32,000 below capital requirements (preaudit), as follows:

Thrift certificates ratio	$7,392,000
	6
Net equity capital required	$1,232,000
Net equity capital reported	$1,200,000
Deficiency	$ 32,000

However, audit adjustments explained in Exhibit 3 increased the capital deficiency to $622,000, as follows:

Net equity capital required	$1,232,000
Net equity capital (postaudit) (1,200,000–$590,000)	$ 610,000
Deficiency	$ 622,000

There was a possibility that the parent company, Nuevo Financial Group, would contribute the additional equity capital. Also, management had been in contact with a potential outside investor about the possibility of investing $600,000. This investor, Manny Gonzalez, has strong ties to the Imperial Valley community and to the family ownership of Imperial Valley.

5. **Adequacy of General Reserve Requirement.** The general reserve requirement of 1.25 percent had not been met. Based on the client's reported outstanding loan balance of $6,300,000, a reserve of $78,750 would be necessary. However, audit adjustments for the charge-off of uncollectible loan amounts significantly affected the amount actually required. Additionally, the auditors felt that a larger percentage

EXHIBIT 3
Audit Adjustments

AJE #1	Reserve for loan losses	$ 200,000	
	Loans receivable		$ 200,000
	To write down loans to net realizable value		
AJE #2	Reserve for loan losses	$ 300,000	
	Unearned discounts & fees	80,000	
	Loans receivable		$ 380,000
	To write off loans more than 180 days past due in compliance with statutes		
AJE #3	Provision for loan losses	$ 590,000	
	Reserve for loan losses		$ 590,000
	To increase the reserve balance to 2% of outstanding loans as follows:		
	Reserve balance (preaudit)		$ (25,000)

Less adjusting entry		
#1	$ 200,000	
#2	300,000	
		$ 500,000
Subtotal		$ 475,000
Add: Desired balance		
Loan balance (preaudit)	$ 6,300,000	
Less: AJE #1	(200,000)	
#2	(380,000)	
Loan balance (postaudit)	$ 5,720,000	
Reserve requirement	2%	
Desired balance (approx.)		115,000
Adjustment required		$ 590,000

would be necessary because of the client's history of problems with loan collections; initially, a 5 percent rate was proposed. Management felt this was much too high, arguing that the company had improved its lending procedures in the last few months and that it expected to have a smaller percentage of charge-offs in the future. A current delinquent report received in February 2011 showed only two loans from 2010 still on the past due list. The auditors agreed to a 2 percent reserve, and an adjusting entry (AJE #3) shown in Exhibit 3 was made.

Regulatory Environment

Imperial Valley Thrift & Loan was approaching certain regulatory filing deadlines during the course of the audit. Stanley had a meeting with the regulators at which representatives of management were present. Gonzalez also attended the meeting, since he had expressed some interest in possibly making a capital contribution. There was a lot of discussion about the ability of Imperial Valley to keep its doors open if the loan losses were recorded as proposed by the auditors. This was a concern because the proposed adjustments would place the

client in a position of having net equity capital significantly below minimum requirements.

The regulators were concerned about the adequacy of the 2 percent general reserve because of the prior collection problems experienced by Imperial Valley. The institution's solvency was a primary concern. At the time of the meeting, the regulators were quite busy trying to straighten out problems caused by the failure of two other savings and loan institutions in Arizona. Many depositors had lost money as a result of the failure of these S&Ls. The regulators were concerned that a domino effect might occur as had happened in the early 1990s, and Imperial Valley would get caught up in the mess. Also, the regulators were unable to make a thorough audit of the company on their own, so they relied quite heavily on the work of Jacobs, Stanley & Co. In this sense, the audit was used as leverage on the institution to get more money in as a cushion to protect depositors. The regulators viewed this as essential in light of the other S&L failures and the fact that the insurance protection mechanism for thrift and loan depositors was less substantial than depository insurance available through the Federal Deposit Insurance Corporation (FDIC) in commercial banks and in savings and loan institutions.

Summary of the Client's Position

The management of Imperial Valley Thrift & Loan placed a great deal of pressure on the auditors to reduce the amount of the loan write-offs. It maintained that the customers were "good for the money." Managers pointed out the payments to date on most of the loans had been made on a timely basis. The client felt that the auditors did not fully understand the nature of its business. Managers contend that a certain amount of risk had to be accepted in their business because they primarily made loans that commercial banks and savings and loan institutions did not want to make. "We are the bank of last resort for many of our customers," commented bank president Eddie Salazar. Salazar then commented that the auditors' inability to understand and appreciate this element of the thrift and loan business was the main reason the auditors were having trouble evaluating collectibility on the outstanding loans.

Questions

1. What is the role of professional skepticism in auditing financial statements? Do you think the auditors were skeptical enough in evaluating the operations of Imperial Valley?

2. a. Assume the auditors decide to support management's position and reduce the amount of loan write-offs. The decision was made in part because of concerns that regulators might force the bank to close its doors and many customers would have no where else to go to borrow money. Evaluate the auditors' stage of moral reasoning in making this decision.

   b. Assume instead that the auditors *insist* on a higher level of loan write-offs and allowance for uncollectibles and, if the client refuses, the auditors will issue a qualified opinion. What level of reasoning are they at in making this decision?

3. Are there parallels to be drawn between the facts of Imperial Valley Thrift & Loan and problems with subprime loans during the 2008–2009 period? Explain.

Chapter 3

Corporate Governance and Ethical Management

Ethics Reflection

Corporate governance has become one of the most commonly used phrases following the accounting frauds at Enron and WorldCom and the passage of the Sarbanes-Oxley (SOX) Act of 2002. In a general sense, corporate governance includes the control mechanisms (i.e., internal controls, internal audit, external audit, and the audit committee) that help ensure management operates in accordance with approved policies and regulations. One of the most glaring examples of an out-of-control corporate governance system occurred in the accounting fraud at Waste Management, a leading international provider of waste management services up until the late 1990s.

Despite being a leader in the industry, Waste Management was under increasing pressure from competitors and from changes in the environmental industry. Its 1996 financial statements showed that even though its consolidated revenue for the period from December 1994 to 1996 had increased 8.3 percent, its net income had declined during that period by 75.5 percent. The truth was that the income numbers had been manipulated to minimize the declines over time. The SEC's litigation against Waste Management indicated the following:[1]

Year	Originally Reported (thousands)	As Restated (thousands)	Percentage Overstated
1992	$850,036	$739,686	15%
1993	452,776	288,707	57
1994	784,381	627,508	25
1995	603,899	340,097	78
1996	192,085	(39,307)	100+
Q1–Q3 1997	417,600	236,700	76

The worst abuse of accounting occurred from 1988 through 1996 when management made unsupported changes to the estimated useful life or salvage value of one or more categories of vehicles, containers, or equipment, always resulting in a net reduction of depreciation expenses. The changes were recorded most often in the fourth quarter and then improperly applied cumulatively from the beginning of the year. Waste Management never disclosed the changes and their impact to investors, although disclosure was required by GAAP.

Arthur Andersen LLP, Waste Management's auditor, had proposed a plan called a "Summary of Action Steps" to correct past adjustments. The proposed plan outlined action steps to be taken that were characterized as "must do." The action steps were agreed to and signed off by Waste Management's CEO, CFO, and CAO. However, Waste Management officers did not follow the agreed-to plans and new items surfaced that brought into question the company's aggressive accounting and Andersen's willingness to go along. The board of directors failed in its fiduciary role by not making sure those steps were carried out.

On June 19, 2001, the SEC issued a civil injunction against Andersen in the Waste Management case whereby the firm consented to the entry of a permanent injunction enjoining it from violating Section 10(b) and Rule 10b-5 of the Securities Exchange Act of 1934. Andersen also agreed to pay a civil money penalty in the amount of $7 million and censure for engaging in improper professional conduct. The ink on the agreement barely had time to dry when, on December 2, 2001, Enron, Andersen's

(Continued)

most infamous client, filed for Chapter 11 protection in the United States. As you read this chapter think about how ethical management contributes toward developing an effective corporate governance system that supports issuing financial statements that present fairly financial position, results of operations, and changes in cash flows.

> Good corporate governance is about 'intellectual honesty' and not just sticking to rules and regulations, capital flowed towards companies that practised this type of good governance.
>
> *Mervyn King, chair of the King report*

This quotation by Mervyn King, chair of the King Commission on Corporate Governance in South Africa emphasizes the importance of being an ethical person and the exercise of ethical judgment in corporate governance systems. Transparency is an essential ingredient of good governance because it enables those outside the organization to understand just how the governance systems works and whether the financial statements contain all the information an informed user has a right to know.

Business Ethics

John Maxwell contends there is no such thing as "business" ethics. Maxwell believes that a single standard of ethics applies to both our business and to our personal lives. Maxwell identifies the standard as the Golden Rule. He says in making ethical decisions we should ask the question: How would I like to be treated in a particular situation? To Maxwell, the Golden Rule is an integrity guideline for all situations.[2] Maxwell's perspective implies that we should treat others the way we would like to be treated. His view is consistent with Kant's notion of universality; that is, we should act in ways that we would want others to act in similar situations for similar reasons. Predictability and consistency of behavior enhances the ethical judgment and enables an outsider to understand how we came to a conclusion.

While most people recognize that business must earn a profit to survive, it is the steps taken in business dealings and financial reporting to make the profit that concern ethicists. As Kant points out, the ends do not justify the means. If it did, then businesses could rationalize accelerating the recording of revenue into an earlier period to inflate profit. A company places its own self-interests, perhaps in the guise of maximizing shareholder wealth, ahead of the interests of society if it decides to artificially inflate revenue and earnings. In the financial crisis of 2008–2009, large financial institutions engineered and sold complex financial instruments to unsuspecting investors who had trusted these investments were based on solid financial analysis. Unfortunately, even these financial institutions did not fully understand the instruments and mislead investors into thinking a high level of returns would be forthcoming.

Stakeholder Perspective

The well-known ethicist Archie Carroll points out that questions of right, wrong, fairness, and justice permeate the organization's activities as it attempts to successfully interact with major stakeholder groups including employees (internal stakeholders), and customers, owners, government, and society at large (external stakeholders). He believes that the principal task of management is not only to deal with the various stakeholder groups in an ethical fashion but also to reconcile the conflicts of interest that occur between the organization and the stakeholder groups.[3] An important component of ethical management is to set a proper tone at the top so that a culture develops within the organization that it does not tolerate self-serving, egoistic-driven behavior in the pursuit of self-interest.

In this book we define business ethics in its simplest terms as the principles and standards adopted by a business organization to guide decision making. In the course of developing those principles and standards and making ethical decisions, a business must consider the interests of its stakeholders. By possessing certain dispositions (virtues), an ethical manager is guided by core values such as honesty, integrity, and trustworthiness in dealing with stakeholders.

Stakeholder management requires that an individual consider issues from a variety of perspectives other than one's own, and other than what local conventions suggest in promoting reasonable and responsible decision making. On the other hand, thinking and reasoning from a narrow and personal point of view virtually guarantee that we are likely to make a decision that does not give due consideration to other persons and perspectives.[4]

The Case of the Ford Pinto

The case of the Ford Pinto illustrates how a company can make a fatal mistake in its decision making by failing to adequately consider the interests of the stakeholders. The Pinto was Ford Motor Company's first domestic North American subcompact automobile marketed beginning on September 11, 1970. It competed with the AMC Gremlin and Chevrolet Vega, along with imports from makes such as Volkswagen, Datsun, and Toyota. The Pinto was popular in sales, with 100,000 units delivered by January 1971, and was also offered as a wagon and Runabout hatchback. Its reputation suffered over time, especially from a controversy surrounding the safety of its gas tank.

The public was shocked to find out that at speeds of only 30 miles per hour or less, the Pinto cars might become engulfed in flames and passengers could be burned or even die. Ford faced an ethical dilemma: what to do about the apparent unsafe gas tanks that seemed to be the cause of such incidents. At the time, the gas tanks were routinely placed behind the license plate so a rear-end collision was more likely to cause an explosion whereas today's gas tanks are placed on the side of the vehicle. However, the federal safety standards at the time did not address this issue so Ford was in compliance with the law. Ford's initial response was based on ethical legalism—the company complied with all the laws and safety problems so it was under no obligation to take any action.

Eventually, Ford did use ethical analysis to develop a response. It used a risk–benefit analysis to aid decision making. This was done because the National Highway Traffic Safety Administration excused a defendant from being penalized if the monetary costs of making a production change were greater than the "societal benefit" of that change. The analysis followed the same approach modeled after Judge Learned Hand's ruling in *United States v. Carroll Towing* in 1947 that boiled the theory of negligence down to the following: In that case it was ruled that if the expected harm exceeded the cost to prevent against it, the defendant was obligated to take the precaution, and if he did not, would be held liable. If the cost was larger than the expected harm, the defendant was not expected to take the precaution. If there was an accident, the defendant would not be found guilty.[5] A summary of the Ford analysis follows:

Ford's Risk–Benefit Analysis[6]

Benefits of Fixing the Pintos

Savings: 180 burn deaths, 180 serious burn injuries, 2,100 burned vehicles

Unit cost: $200,000 per death (figure provided by the government); $67,000 per burn injury and $700 to repair a burned vehicle (company estimates)

Total benefits: 180 × ($200,000) + 180 × ($67,000) + 2,100 × ($700) = **$49.5 million**

Costs of Fixing the Pintos

Sales: 11 million cars, 1.5 million light trucks

Unit cost: $11 per car, $11 per light truck

Total cost: 11,000,000 × ($11) + 1,500,000 × ($11) = **$137 million**

Based on this analysis and other considerations including not being required by law to change its product design, Ford decided to not change the placement of the fuel tank. Ford relied on ethical legalism reasoning to justify (rationalize) its actions.

In 2009, Toyota encountered a problem with some of its models when news broke that there may be a sudden unintended acceleration on certain models. Toyota was hesitant at first to do anything, but after being forced to explain its actions in the U.S. Congress, the company did take corrective action. You might say that Toyota was nudged by congressional and public opinion to see that the rights of the driving public outweighed inaction. Toyota's fix was to first cut the length of the accelerator pedals until replacement pedal assemblies become available and to install a brake-to-idle algorithm on affected models.

Returning to the Pinto problem, Ford's decision to do a risk–benefit analysis relying only on act-utilitarian reasoning focused only on costs and benefits, an approach that ignores the rights of various stakeholders. A rule-utilitarian approach might have led Ford to follow the rule "Never sacrifice public safety." A rights theory approach also would have led to the same conclusion based on the reasoning that the driving public has an ethical right to expect that their cars will not blow up if there is a crash at low speeds.

The other danger of utilitarian reasoning is that an important factor may be omitted from the analysis. Ford did not include as a potential cost the lawsuit judgments that might be awarded to the plaintiffs and against the company. For example, in May 1972, Lily Gray was traveling with 13-year-old Richard Grimshaw when their Pinto was struck by another car traveling approximately 30 miles per hour. The impact ignited a fire in the Pinto which killed Lily Gray and left Richard Grimshaw with devastating injuries. A judgment was rendered against Ford and the jury awarded the Gray family $560,000 and Matthew Grimshaw, the father of Richard Grimshaw, $2.5 million in compensatory damages. The surprise came when the jury also awarded $125 million in punitive damages. This was subsequently reduced to $3.5 million.[7]

Ethical Issues in Business

An ethical issue in business is a problem, situation, or opportunity that requires an individual decision maker, group of people, or the organization to choose among alternative actions that must be evaluated as (the better) right or (the lesser) wrong, ethical or unethical. Ferrell, Fraedrich, and Ferrell identify five major ethical issues in business including honesty and fairness, conflicts of interest, fraud, discrimination, and information technology.[8] While all issues can affect the practice of accounting, we focus on the first three since they are most directly related to the goal of producing accurate and reliable financial statements.

Honesty

Abraham Lincoln once said, "No man has a good enough memory to be a successful liar." A person who lies about a matter then has to remember what was said and be sure to provide a consistent response when questioned otherwise the story will come apart over time. It's easy to remember something said that is truthful. It's already etched in your mind.

Imagine that you and a friend were sent to a conference in New York City to learn about the growing field of "forensic accounting." Forensic accountants utilize accounting, auditing, and investigative skills when conducting an investigation of a matter such as fraud. You and your friend decide to skip out on the afternoon session. You go to the half-price theater ticket kiosk in Times Square and buy two tickets for the show *Chicago*. After you return to the office, your boss asks what you learned about litigation support. You look at each other somewhat perplexed but your friend "saves the day." She says: "It's a part of forensic accounting." "That's it?" your boss responds.[9]

Ask yourself what would happen if you or your friend, but not both of you, is asked by another supervisor in the firm about the forensics session. Did the two of you develop a script to respond consistently? What if one of you forgets his lines? Will it implicate only that person? Are you starting to see how much easier it is to simply tell the truth and avoid the ethical slippery slope?

Another problem with lying in this case is that the firm is paying for your registration and, perhaps, one or more nights at a fancy hotel in midtown Manhattan. Now you have squandered firm resources and will be reimbursed for hotel and lodging for part of the time that you were on "personal" business. It's just as if you had asked to be paid for time you didn't work. It is wrong to do this as it would be to make copies of personal documents on the company copier and on company time. You have an obligation to be honest and trustworthy. Remember, ethics involves consistent behavior based on underlying ethical principles. Also, what kind of example do you set for your son or daughter if you do improper things in business while touting ethical behavior at home in your personal life? The following example illustrates how dangerous this can be.

> You arrive home one night and see your daughter working on an art project. She has a variety of markers on the table to help with the project. Now, you know there are no such markers in the house so you ask your daughter where they came from. She admits taking them from the classroom to help with the project. You lecture her on how wrong it was to do that. She says to you: "But Daddy, you take supplies from your office and use them at home all the time."

Fairness

Fairness has already been addressed in the context of treating others equally. Fairness equates to just action in making ethical decisions. It is important to note that the idea of being "fair" is often shaped by vested interests. One or both parties to a business negotiation may view an action as unfair or unethical because the outcome was less beneficial than expected.

Fairness also implies objectivity in accounting and auditing. Objectivity depends on one's intellectual honesty. Accounting professionals should approach their roles as preparers of financial statements without bias or predisposition of how transactions should be reported and disclosed. There are two important points. First, the statements should be transparent—accurate, reliable, and reflect full disclosure. Second and related to the first requirement is for the statements to be prepared in accordance with GAAP and they should not be misleading.

Conflicts of Interest

A conflict of interest is a situation in which private interests or personal considerations may affect or be perceived to affect an employee's judgment to act in the best interests of the organization. Examples include using an employee's position, confidential information, or personal relationships for private gain or advancement or the expectation of private gain or advancement.

Objectivity and integrity are essential qualities for employees of any organization. It is the perception that one may be influenced by matters or relationships not relevant to a decision that creates many of the conflict of interest problems in business. For example, assume that a purchasing manager for a manufacturing company has to decide which of three suppliers should be given a contract to provide millions of dollars of raw material to the company. The brother-in-law of the purchasing manager is the sales manager of one of the three companies. If the purchasing manager selects that company for the contract, then the perception may be that her decision was tainted by the existence of a family relationship in awarding the contract.

Does that mean the purchasing manager should choose one of the other suppliers to avoid any questions about bias in the decision-making process? While that may protect the integrity of the decision, it's not fair to the brother-in-law or to his company assuming it provides the best product at the most reasonable price. So, what should the purchasing manager do? One possibility is to allow someone else to make the decision. She could step aside (recusal) from the matter and avoid the appearance of bias.

A good example of a conflict of interest policy is that of Johnson & Johnson. Selected sections appear in Appendix 1 at the end of this chapter. One of the most interesting aspects of the conflict of interest policy is its emphasis on disclosure. Disclosure is an element of honesty. Honest people not only avoid lying but also have as a goal the disclosure of all information that another party has a right to know. Disclosure enhances transparency and it is consistent with rights theory. Those who are honest typically look at disclosure as a positive obligation, not something one does after being caught violating a law or breaking a rule.

Fraud: Concept and Examples

Fraud can be defined as a deliberate misrepresentation to gain an advantage over another party. Fraud comes in many different forms including fraud in the financial statements, the misappropriation of assets (theft) and subsequent cover-up, and disclosure fraud. An example of the latter follows: On September 25, 1992, Lena Guerrero resigned as the head of the Texas Railroad Commission after it became public knowledge that Guerrero had claimed on her resume that she was a graduate of the University of Texas, when in fact she never graduated. She went to the university but never graduated—a disclosure fraud. Worse, she falsely claimed to be a member of Phi Beta Kappa, and failed classes on Texas government and Mexican Americans in the Southwest. Guerrero lied about her graduation during the process of running for election to head the commission having been initially appointed by then-governor Ann Richards.

Fraud in Organizations

Fraudulent Business Practices

Fraudulent business practices occur when an organization purposefully engages in an act that harms another person such as a customer. A good example is that of Sears.

The Sears case illustrates what can happen when the culture of an organization allows for deceptive business practices. One way to prevent this from happening is to establish an

In 1992, Sears paid $15 million to settle accusations in 41 states that auto-repair sales representatives were finding auto problems where none existed to get commissions on repair work. This was not an example of a few rogue employees acting alone to line their pockets with money they didn't rightfully earn. The company had instilled a culture of overcharging hundreds of customers at its auto-repair centers for performing four-wheel alignments even though only the front wheels can be aligned on many vehicles. Mechanics at Sears also told customers they would conduct a "free" vehicle inspection, but then went on to charge for unauthorized repairs supposedly discovered during the inspections. Sears's actions were repeated over and over again. In New Jersey alone there were at least 350 instances of the alleged overcharges for wheel alignments at 19 separate Sears stores. This wasn't the first time Sears was faced with lawsuits because of its fraudulent business practices. In 1992 Sears agreed to pay as much as $20 million to settle 19 class action lawsuits that stemmed from California state charges that it bilked auto-repair customers by recommending unneeded repairs. California state authorities sent in undercover investigators for simple brake jobs that Sears had advertised. The government subsequently charged that about half of the 72 auto centers had recommended unnecessary replacement of such parts. Under terms of the settlement, Sears offered a coupon worth $50 to some 933,000 customers nationwide who had the various (unnecessary) services performed at a Sears auto center from August 1, 1990, through January 31, 1992. There was a persistent and pervasive pattern of fraud and deception according to the lawsuits. The unassailable conclusion is that Sears was responsible for a moral erosion of business ethics in its auto-repair business. One has to wonder whether unethical behavior fed into other business lines of Sears.

ethical tone at the top that sends the message to employees that such practices will not be tolerated. Sears violated its obligations to its most important stakeholder—its customers. The company's reputation was tarnished as a result of these events. In the end, Sears had to shut down its auto-repair operation.

Occupational Fraud

In 2008 the Association of Certified Fraud Examiners (ACFE) released a follow-up study to its 2006 report titled *2008 Report to the Nation on Occupational Fraud and Abuse.* The ACFE defines occupational fraud as "the use of one's occupation for personal enrichment through the deliberate misuse or misapplication of the employing organization's resources or assets." The report is based on data compiled from 959 cases of occupational fraud that were investigated between January 2006 and February 2008. An important finding is that participants in the survey estimated that U.S. organizations lose 7 percent of their annual revenues to fraud. Applied to the 2008 U.S. gross domestic product, this 7 percent figure translates to approximately $994 billion in fraud losses. Also, the median dollar loss caused by fraud schemes was $175,000. More than one-quarter of the frauds involved losses of at least $1 million.[10]

ACFE identified three categories of fraud including corruption, asset misappropriation, and fraudulent financial statements. Examples of corruption include conflicts of interests, bribery, illegal gratuities, and economic extortion. Asset misappropriation includes, among others, fraudulent disbursements and the misuse or theft of assets. The most common occupational fraud schemes were corruption (27 percent) and fraudulent billing (24 percent). Financial statement fraud was the most costly with a median loss of $2 million. Fraudulent financial statements come in many forms including asset/revenue over- (under-) statements, delayed (accelerated) expense recognition, and the failure to accrue for liabilities. More will be said about financial statement fraud in Chapters 4 and 5. In 2010 the ACFE broadened its survey to include fraud cases around the world. The results of the 2010 Global Fraud Survey will be addressed in Chapter 8.

Detecting Fraud Schemes

The 2008 ACFE study reports how fraud was initially detected. These results appear in Exhibit 3.1.

EXHIBIT 3.1 **Initial Detection of Fraud 2008 (2006) ACFE Survey**

Year	Tip	Internal Audit	By Accident	Internal Controls	External Audit	Notified by Police
2008	51.7%	12.4%	17.4%	15.2%	16.3%	3.4%
2006	(46.2%)	(19.4%)	(20.0%)	(23.3%)	(9.1%)	(3.2%)

The rise in tip-based detection of fraud might be attributed to the increasing use of hotlines in businesses to report fraud. In fact, SOX mandated that all public companies implement a formal reporting mechanism, such as a hotline, so that employees and other parties can report fraudulent or inappropriate activity. Other possible contributing factors to the rise in tips include the presence of an ethics officer and whistleblower protections including a lessening of the stigma surrounding whistleblowing activities. Education and training in a company code of ethics also may contribute to the reporting of fraud.

The reduction in cases reported through internal audit and internal controls is somewhat surprising because of enhanced control procedures required under SOX and the standards established by the Public Company Accounting Oversight Board (PCAOB). An encouraging sign is the increase in fraud detection through the external audit. This may reflect SOX enhancements and the implementation of *Statement on Auditing Standards No. 99, Consideration of Fraud in a Financial Statement Audit.* This standard provides that "the auditor has a responsibility to plan and perform the audit to obtain reasonable assurance about whether the financial statements are free of material misstatement, whether caused by error or fraud." SAS 99 standards will be discussed in Chapter 5.[11]

In a disturbing finding, the Institute of Internal Auditors conducted a poll of nearly 300 chief audit executives in early 2010 that found fraudulent acts by employees and outsiders have risen since the beginning of the recession, and internal auditors predict the trend will continue through the rest of 2010. Among the 31 percent of survey participants from organizations where instances of fraud were detected since 2008, 43 percent report that fraud occurrences increased from 1 to 10 percent, 28 percent indicate fraud increased from 11 to 20 percent, and 14 percent say fraud increased by more than 20 percent. Theft of company property and resources—including proprietary information—is the fastest-growing fraud reported by respondents, followed by embezzlement, including expense account fraud and third-party or vendor fraud. Your authors are concerned that a lack of personal ethics may be contributing to the increase in fraudulent acts by employees.[12]

Sarbanes-Oxley (SOX) Act

The Sarbanes-Oxley (SOX) Act was adopted by Congress following massive accounting frauds at companies such as Enron and WorldCom. It is a landmark piece of legislation responsible for changing the way organizations approach their antifraud efforts. Organizations are required to implement several specific controls to help combat fraud to meet SOX requirements. Many of the provisions of the act have contributed to a strengthening on corporate governance. It is interesting to speculate whether the frauds at Enron and WorldCom would have occurred, or gone unreported for so long, if the provisions of the Act had been in place during that time.

The act defines internal control over financial reporting as

a process designed by, or under the supervision of, the issuer's [public company] principal executive and principal financial officers, or persons performing similar functions, and effected by the issuer's board of directors, management and other personnel, to provide reasonable assurance regarding the reliability of financial reporting and the preparation of financial statements for external purposes in accordance with generally accepted accounting principles and includes those policies and procedures that

(1) Pertain to the maintenance of records that in reasonable detail accurately and fairly reflect the transactions and dispositions of the assets of the issuer;

(2) Provide reasonable assurance that transactions are recorded as necessary to permit preparation of financial statements in accordance with generally accepted accounting principles, and that receipts and expenditures of the issuer are being made only in accordance with authorizations of management and directors of the issuer; and

(3) Provide reasonable assurance regarding prevention or timely detection of unauthorized acquisition, use or disposition of the issuer's assets that could have a material effect on the financial statements.[13]

Public companies were required to have the SOX-mandated controls in place during the period covered by the ACFE survey—with the exception of small public companies that were allowed extra time to develop and approve the controls. The report points out that the impact these controls had on the severity of the frauds that occurred in public companies is notable. Publicly traded companies with SOX controls in place incurred median losses 70 to 96 percent lower than corporations that had not yet implemented these controls. One surprising result of the study is that the one control associated with the largest reduction in the median loss—management certification of the financial statements—was the only control associated with a negative impact on the length of the scheme. Corporations that had management certify the company's financial statements suffered fraud schemes that continued for a median 18 months before being detected, compared with a median of 15 months for public companies lacking this control. One reason may have been the reluctance to admit to the fraud (and subsequent cover-up) by not certifying the financials.

Foundations of Corporate Governance Systems

The four pillars of corporate governance are responsibility, accountability, fairness, and transparency. To be effective, these principles must be part of the culture of an organization. They should emphasize conducting business and managing the company in a manner that promotes ethical and honest behavior, compliance with applicable laws and regulations, effective management of the company's resources and risks, and accountability of persons within the organization.

The role of the board of directors and executive officers, once they have agreed on the principles, is to establish an ethical culture and communicate these principles throughout the organization. As noted by Robert Noyce, the inventor of the silicon chip, "If ethics are poor at the top, that behavior is copied down through the organization."

Defining Corporate Governance

There is no single, accepted definition of corporate governance. A fairly narrow definition given by Shleifer and Vishny emphasizes the separation of ownership and control in corporations. They define corporate governance as dealing with "the ways in which the suppliers of finance to corporations assure themselves of getting a return on their investment."[14] Parkinson defines it as a process of supervision and control intended to ensure that the company's management acts in accordance with the interests of shareholders.[15]

Goergen, Manjonantolin, and Renneboog compare corporate governance mechanisms in Germany to those in other countries including the United States. German corporate governance includes a two-tier board structure—management and supervisory board—compared to the unitary system in the United States. The management board has responsibility for day-to-day operations while the supervisory board plays a role similar to the board of directors in the United States.[16] More will be said about the German board and those in other countries in our comparative analysis of global corporate governance systems in Chapter 8.

A corporate governance regime typically includes the mechanisms to ensure that the agent (management) runs the firm for the benefit of one or more principals (shareholders, creditors, suppliers, clients, employees, and other parties with whom the firm conducts its business). The mechanisms include internal ones such as the board of directors, its committees, executive compensation policies, internal controls, and external measures that include monitoring by large shareholders and creditors (in particular banks), external auditors, and the regulatory framework of a securities exchange commission, the corporate law regime, and stock exchange listing requirements and oversight.

The definition of corporate governance we like the best is by Tricker that governance is not concerned with running the business of the company per se, but with giving overall direction to the enterprise, with overseeing and controlling the executive actions of management, and with satisfying legitimate expectations of accountability and regulation by interests beyond the corporate boundaries.[17] In this regard, corporate governance can be seen as a set of rules that define the relationship between stakeholders, management, and board of directors of a company and influence how that company is operating. At its most basic level, corporate governance deals with issues that result from the separation of ownership and control. But corporate governance goes beyond simply establishing a clear relationship between shareholders and managers.

The Importance of Good Governance

The presence of strong governance standards provides better access to capital and aids economic growth. Various survey results in the decade of the 2000s indicate that the investment community is willing to pay more for a company with strong and effective corporate governance policies. A survey conducted by Economist Intelligence Unit indicates that more than 80 percent of European and U.S. institutional investors say they would pay more for companies with good governance.[18]

The importance of good governance to share prices can be seen in the results of a survey of 310 international executives in 2003 by the Economist Intelligence Unit. The results indicate that 70 percent believe the perception of good governance standards has a positive impact on stock prices and, in a related question, 79 percent state that a negative impact will occur if the perception is poor. These responses are consistent with the finding that 8, 32, and 37 percent, respectively, rate corporate governance as a top priority in their organization, one of the top 3 priorities, and among the top 10 priorities. Only 23 percent indicate it is not a priority.[19]

Good corporate governance ensures that the business environment is fair and transparent and that companies can be held accountable for their actions. Conversely, weak corporate governance leads to waste, mismanagement, and corruption. Good governance can deliver sustainable business performance. Properly designed rules of governance should focus on implementing the values of fairness, transparency, accountability, and responsibility to both shareholders and stakeholders.

Corporate governance is a multifaceted subject. An important theme of corporate governance deals with issues of accountability and fiduciary duty, essentially advocating the implementation of policies and mechanisms to ensure good behavior and protect shareholder interests. Another key focus is the economic efficiency view, through which the corporate governance system should aim to optimize economic results, with a strong emphasis on the welfare of shareholders. There are yet other aspects to the corporate governance subject, such as the stakeholder view, which calls for more attention and accountability to players other than the shareholders (i.e., the employees and the environment).

Agency Theory

In whose interests should corporations be governed? The traditional view in American corporate law has been that the corporate managers and directors (agents) owe their primary allegiance to the shareholders of the corporation (principal).

According to Core, Holthausen, and Larcker, the central problem in corporate governance then becomes to construct rules and incentives (that is, implicit or explicit "contracts") to effectively align the behavior of managers (agents) with the desires of the principals (owners). However, the desires and goals of management and shareholders may not be in accord and it is difficult for the shareholder to verify the activities of corporate management. This is often referred to as the agency problem.[20]

A basic assumption is that managers are likely to place personal goals ahead of corporate goals, resulting in a conflict of interests between stockholders and the management itself. (Recall our discussion of egoism.) An enlightened egoist would emphasize other interests including stockholders and creditors while trying to satisfy one's own self-interest. Critics of corporate behavior during the financial crisis of 2008–2009 blame corporate greed for many of the problems during that time.

Jensen and Meckling demonstrate how investors in publicly traded corporations incur (agency) costs in monitoring managerial performance. In general, agency costs also arise whenever there is an "information asymmetry" between the corporation and outsiders because insiders (the corporation) know more about a company and its future prospects than do outsiders (investors).[21]

Agency costs can occur if the board of directors fails to exercise due care in its oversight role of management. Allegedly, Enron's board of directors did not properly monitor the company's incentive compensation plans thereby allowing top executives to "hype" the company's stock so that employees would add it to their 401-k retirement plans. While the hyping occurred, oftentimes by positive statements about the company made by Ken Lay, the CEO, Lay himself sold about 2.3 million shares for $123.4 million.

The agency problem can never be perfectly solved and shareholders may experience a loss of wealth due to divergent behavior of managers. Investigations by the SEC and Department of Justice of 20 corporate frauds indicate that $236 billion in shareholder value was lost between the time the public first learned of the fraud and September 3, 2002, the measurement date.

Executive Compensation

One of the most common approaches to the agency problem is to link managerial compensation to the financial performance of the corporation in general and the performance of the company's shares. Typically, this occurs by creating long-term compensation packages and stock option plans that tie executive wealth to an increase in the corporation's stock price. These incentives aim to encourage managers to maximize the market value of shares.

Excessive Pay Packages

A problem arises when top management purposefully manipulates earnings amounts to drive up the price of stock and cash in with more lucrative stock options. During the financial crisis, Congress charged executives at some of the nation's largest companies with gaining pay packages in the millions while their companies suffered losses and they may have even accepted funds from the government to keep them liquid. The Obama administration named a "compensation czar," Kenneth Feinberg, to set salaries and bonuses at some of the biggest firms at the heart of the economic crisis, as part of a broader government campaign to reshape pay practices across corporate America. The initiative reflected public uproar over executive compensation at companies such as American International Group (AIG) that received a $180 billion bailout from the government and decided to pay $165 million in bonuses.

A study conducted by a professor at Purdue University in 2009 that used a new type of theoretical analysis found that chief executives in 35 of the top *Fortune* 500 companies were overpaid by 129 times their "ideal salaries" in 2008. The authors noted that the ratio of CEO pay to the lowest employee salary has gone up from about 40:1 in the 1970s to as high as 344:1 in recent years in the United States. At the same time, the ratio remained around 20:1 in Europe and 11:1 in Japan.[22]

Backdating Stock Options

An executive compensation scandal erupted in 2006 when it was discovered that some companies had changed the grant dates of their options to coincide with a dip in the stock price, making them worth more because less money would be needed to exercise the options and buy stock. Although backdating is legal, it must be properly expensed and disclosed in the financial statements. Legalities aside, it is difficult to justify such a practice from an ethical perspective since it purposefully manipulates the option criteria that determine their value.

In the wake of the scandal, hundreds of companies conducted internal probes and the SEC launched investigations into more than 140 firms. The agency filed charges against 24 companies and 66 individuals for backdating-related offenses, and at least 15 people have been convicted of criminal conduct. An interesting case is that of Nancy Heinen, Apple Computer's general counsel until leaving in 2006. She was investigated by the SEC for receiving backdated options and wound up agreeing to pay $2.2 million in disgorgement (return of ill-gotten gains), interest, and penalties. Steve Jobs, the CEO of Apple, apologized on behalf of the company stating that he did not understand the relevant accounting laws. Of course, ignorance of the law is no excuse for violating it—at least in spirit—especially by someone like Jobs who presumably has dozens of accountants on staff to advise on these matters. Notably, SOX includes stricter reporting requirements that are supposed to cut down on such practices.

Stakeholder Theory

Freeman suggests in his seminal book on stakeholder theory that successful managers must systematically attend to the interests of various stakeholder groups.[23] This "enlightened self-interest" position has been expanded upon by others who believe that the interests of stakeholders have intrinsic worth irrespective of whether these advance the interests of shareholders. Under this perspective, the success of a corporation is not merely an end in itself but should also be seen as providing a vehicle for advancing the interests of stakeholders other than shareholders.[24]

Boatright asserts that the shareholder–management relation is not unique because the fiduciary duties of officers and directors are owed not to shareholders but to the corporation as an entity with interests of its own, which can, on occasion, conflict with those of shareholders. Further, "corporations have some fiduciary duties to other constituencies, such as creditors [to remain solvent so as to repay debts] and to employees [in the management of a pension fund]."[25]

McDonnell supports employee governance as a way to ensure that corporations are governed in part in the interests of employees. He identifies three approaches: employee share ownership; electing employee representatives to the board of directors; and employee involvement in quality circles, work councils, or the like.[26] Employee representation on the management board in German companies is quite common, a practice known as co-determination.

Corporate Governance Mechanisms

In his book *Corporate Governance and Ethics,* Rezaee points out that corporate governance is shaped by internal and external mechanisms, as well as policy interventions through regulations. Internal mechanisms help manage, direct, and monitor corporate governance activities to create sustainable stakeholder value. Examples include the board of directors, particularly independent directors; the audit committee; management; internal controls; and the internal audit function. External mechanisms are intended to monitor the company's activities, affairs, and performance to ensure that the interests of insiders (management, directors, and officers) are aligned with the interests of outsiders (shareholders and other stakeholders). Examples of external mechanisms include the financial markets, state and federal statutes, court decisions, and shareholder proposals.[27] Two points of note include (1) independent directors enhance governance accountability and (2) separate meetings between the audit committee and external auditors strengthen control mechanisms.

Controlling Management through Board of Directors' Actions

The stockholders select the board of directors by electing its members to oversee managerial functions. Theoretically, boards of directors are charged with resolving the agency problems associated with the separation of a company's ownership controls from decision making. Unfortunately, all too often board members align their interests with those of management perhaps because of long-standing personal relationships that can impair independence or instill gratitude for holding a board position. Technically, managers that do not pursue stockholders' best interest can be replaced since the board of directors can hire and fire management. However, the accounting scandals taught us that boards can be controlled by management or be inattentive to their oversight responsibilities. For example, Andy Fastow, the now-indicted former CFO of Enron, directly or indirectly controlled many of the special-purpose entities that he had established. Yet, Enron's board waived the conflict of interest provision in the company's code of ethics to enable Fastow to wear both hats.

Board members have a fiduciary duty to safeguard corporate assets and make decisions that promote shareholder interests. They owe a duty of care in carrying out their responsibilities, which means to act in the best interests of the shareholders. This is typically defined as a level of care expected of a reasonable person under the same circumstances (notice the universality dimension). The board exercises diligence by the vigilant oversight of the company's business and financial affairs, ensuring that reliable financial information is reported, and monitoring compliance with applicable laws, rules, and regulations. Failure to adhere to these obligations may constitute a breach of the fiduciary duty of care expected of directors. For example, recall that the board of Waste Management agreed to take specific steps to resolve fraudulent accounting practices but failed to ensure that those steps were carried out by management.

The independence of the company's board of directors is essential to the proper and objective functioning of the board. The accounting scandals of the late 1990s and early 2000s shone the light on inadequate corporate governance systems and laws. SOX filled the void by requiring all members of the audit committee to be independent of management. National stock exchanges such as the New York Stock Exchange adopted listing requirements that a majority of directors must be independent of management.

Audit Committee

Following the passage of SOX, the audit committee was seen as the one body that was (should be) capable of preventing identified fraudulent financial reporting. The audit committee has an oversight responsibility for the financial statements. Indeed, the internal auditors should have direct and unrestricted access to the audit committee so that they can take any matters of concern directly to that group without having to go through top management. The external auditors rely on the support and actions of the audit committee to resolve differences with management over proper financial reporting. Section 401 of the act amended the Securities Exchange Act of 1934 to include the requirement that each financial statement filed with the SEC should reflect all material correcting adjustments that have been identified by the audit firm in accordance with GAAP and the rules and regulations of the commission.

"Tone at the Top," a publication of the Institute of Internal Auditors, a group that represents certified internal auditors and other accountants who perform internal audit functions, identifies 10 best practices of audit committees. These include to (1) establish effective internal auditing; (2) ensure organizational ethics; (3) communicate; (4) monitor use of inside information; (5) notice red flags (warning signs that should alert an audit committee to conduct more intensive and extensive audits); (6) control conflicts of interest; (7) ask questions (have a healthy dose of skepticism); (8) ensure external auditor independence; (9) seek tax services elsewhere;[28] (10) and consider impacts.[29] Notice how many of these practices are integral ingredients of establishing an ethical tone at the top of the organization.

An effective device to ensure audit committee independence is for the committee to meet separately with the senior executives, the internal auditors, and the external auditors. The perception of internal auditors as the "eyes and ears" of the audit committee suggests that the head of the internal audit department attend all audit committee meetings.[30] Recall the role of Cynthia Cooper at WorldCom. She informed the audit committee every step of the way as her department uncovered the fraud and ultimately gained the support of the external auditors.

Internal Controls as a Monitoring Device

The internal controls that are established by management should help prevent and detect fraud, including materially false and misleading financial reports, asset misappropriations, and inadequate disclosures in the financial statements. These controls are designed to ensure management policies are followed. However, even the best internal controls can be overridden by top management. For example, top executives at Tyco and Adelphia used corporate resources for their own benefit without getting proper authority from the board of directors, thereby violating their fiduciary duty and duty of care to the stockholders. The board at each company claimed to have been uninformed about the use of hundreds of millions of dollars from interest-free loans for personal purposes. We can assume that each company had a series of internal controls in place to prevent such an occurrence. Still, the CEOs circumvented their own controls to accomplish their self-interest-oriented goals. The tone at the top of these organizations apparently was that employees should do what the CEO says, not what he does. It creates a cynical attitude on the part of employees who may come to view the organization as not following its own ethical standards, while, at the same time, expecting its employees to adhere to those standards.

The risk that internal controls will not help prevent or detect a material misstatement in the financial statements is a critical evaluation to provide reasonable assurance. The system of internal controls and whether it operates as intended enables the auditor to either gain confidence about the internal processing of transactions or create doubt for the auditor that should be pursued. *Statement on Auditing Standards (SAS) No. 55* is a significant standard on internal control. The standard identifies five interrelated components of internal control as follows.[31]

1. The *control environment* sets the tone of an organization, influencing the control consciousness of its people. It is the foundation for all aspects of internal control, providing discipline and structure.

2. *Risk assessment* is the entity's identification and evaluation of how risk might affect the achievement of objectives.

3. *Control activities* are the strategic actions established by management to ensure that its directives are carried out.

4. *Information and communication* systems provide the information in a form and at a time that enables people to carry out their responsibilities.

5. *Monitoring* is a process that assesses the efficiency and effectiveness of internal controls over time.

SAS 78[32] amends *SAS 55* to reflect the changes necessary to recognize the definition and description of internal control contained in *Internal Control—Integrated Framework,* published by the Committee of Sponsoring Organizations (COSO) of the Treadway Commission in 1992. The framework defines internal control as a process, effected by an entity's board of directors, management, and other personnel, designed to provide reasonable assurance regarding the achievement of the following objectives: (a) effectiveness and efficiency of operations; (b) reliability of financial reporting; and (c) compliance with applicable laws and regulations.[33]

COSO utilizes the *SAS 55* framework and emphasizes the roles and responsibilities of management, the board of directors, internal auditors, and other personnel in creating an environment that supports the objectives of internal control. One important contribution of COSO is in the area of corporate governance. COSO notes that if members of the board and audit committee do not take their responsibilities seriously, then the system will likely break down as occurred in Enron and WorldCom. The COSO *Integrated Framework* is the foundation for control assessment of internal financial reporting required by SOX under Section 404. More will be said about the Framework in Chapter 5.

Internal Auditors

Internal auditors interact with top management and as such should assist them to fulfill their role in developing accurate and reliable financial statements and compliance with laws and regulations. Exhibit 3.2 presents the framework of financial reporting that supports a strong control environment identified in the Treadway Commission Report titled *Report of the National Commission on Fraudulent Financial Reporting.*[34] Notice how the internal auditors should have direct and unrestricted access to the audit committee. One problem for

EXHIBIT 3.2
Internal Control Environment— "Corporate Culture"

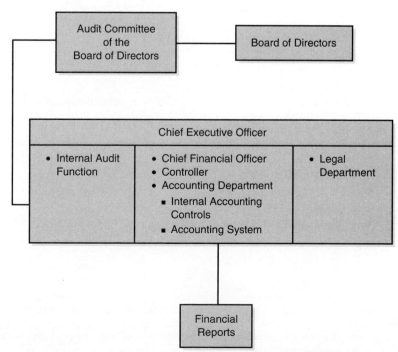

Cynthia Cooper as she struggled to get WorldCom to act on the fraudulent capitalization of line costs was periodic interference by Scott Sullivan, the CFO and mastermind of the fraud.

The ethics of the internal audit profession requires that internal auditors maintain their objectivity and independence from management. The Institute of Internal Auditors (IIA) that represents more than 120,000 members, many of whom hold the designation of certified internal auditor (CIA), has developed a code of ethics to guide actions and behaviors of its members. The code appears in Exhibit 3.3.[35]

EXHIBIT 3.3   **The IIA Code of Ethics**

Principles
Internal auditors are expected to apply and uphold the following principles:

1. Integrity
The integrity of internal auditors establishes trust and thus provides the basis for reliance on their judgment.

2. Objectivity
Internal auditors exhibit the highest level of professional objectivity in gathering, evaluating, and communicating information about the activity or process being examined. Internal auditors make a balanced assessment of all the relevant circumstances and are not unduly influenced by their own interests or by others in forming judgments.

3. Confidentiality
Internal auditors respect the value and ownership of information they receive and do not disclose information without appropriate authority unless there is a legal or professional obligation to do so.

4. Competency
Internal auditors apply the knowledge, skills, and experience needed in the performance of internal audit services.

Rules of Conduct

1. Integrity
Internal auditors:
- 1.1. Shall perform their work with honesty, diligence, and responsibility.
- 1.2. Shall observe the law and make disclosures expected by the law and the profession.
- 1.3. Shall not knowingly be a party to any illegal activity, or engage in acts that are discreditable to the profession of internal auditing or to the organization.
- 1.4. Shall respect and contribute to the legitimate and ethical objectives of the organization.

2. Objectivity
Internal auditors:
- 2.1. Shall not participate in any activity or relationship that may impair or be presumed to impair their unbiased assessment. This participation includes those activities or relationships that may be in conflict with the interests of the organization.
- 2.2. Shall not accept anything that may impair or be presumed to impair their professional judgment.
- 2.3. Shall disclose all material facts known to them that, if not disclosed, may distort the reporting of activities under review.

3. Confidentiality
Internal auditors:
- 3.1. Shall be prudent in the use and protection of information acquired in the course of their duties.
- 3.2. Shall not use information for any personal gain or in any manner that would be contrary to the law or detrimental to the legitimate and ethical objectives of the organization.

4. Competency
Internal auditors:
- 4.1. Shall engage only in those services for which they have the necessary knowledge, skills, and experience.
- 4.2. Shall perform internal audit services in accordance with the *International Standards for the Professional Practice of Internal Auditing*.
- 4.3. Shall continually improve their proficiency and the effectiveness and quality of their services.

Notice how similar the IIA standards are to the Ethical Standards of the IMA and the Principles of the AICPA that were discussed in Chapter 1.

Internal auditors also have a major role to play in ensuring that the internal controls are operating as intended. Section 302 of SOX requires management quarterly and annual certifications of both financial statements and financial reporting controls. Section 404 requires annual management assessment of the effectiveness of both the design and operation of the internal controls over financial reporting. Internal auditors can assist management in fulfilling the organization's compliance responsibilities.

Audited Financial Statements

The accounting statements prepared by management report the financial results in accordance with GAAP. The external auditor renders an independent opinion on those statements. The financial reports can be used to mitigate the conflict between owners and managers posited by agency theory. If owners perceive that accounting reports are reliable, then managers should be rewarded for their performance and for helping control agency monitoring costs. While management is responsible for the preparation of the financial reports, publicly owned companies must hire independent auditors to render opinions on the fairness of the presentations in the financial statements. Since the purpose of an audit is to provide "reasonable assurance" to investors and creditors that the financial statements are free of material misstatement, the audit plays an important role in corporate governance. The audit function will be discussed in greater detail in Chapter 5.

New York Stock Exchange Listing Requirements

Corporate governance provisions in the United States establish benchmark standards by which publicly owned companies should measure their practices. Control procedures required by the New York Stock Exchange (NYSE) provide a blueprint of good governance practices. While there is no required formal report on corporate governance as in many other countries outside the United States including Germany, listed companies in the United States must adopt and disclose corporate governance guidelines and CEOs must certify compliance. Non-U.S. companies listed on the NYSE must follow U.S. corporate governance provisions so that the listing requirements should be used as part of the comparative analysis. What follows are the final corporate governance rules of the NYSE (2003) approved by the SEC. Companies listed on the exchange must comply with standards regarding corporate governance as codified in Section 303A.

1. Listed companies must have a majority of independent directors.
2. To empower non-management directors to serve as a more effective check on management, they must meet at regularly scheduled executive sessions without management. "Non-management" directors are those who are not company officers and include directors who are not independent by virtue of a material relationship, former status or family membership, or for any other reason.
3. Listed companies must have an audit committee with a minimum of three members all of whom are independent of management and the entity.
4. The audit committee should meet separately, periodically, with management, internal auditors (or other personnel responsible for the internal audit function), and independent auditors.
5. The audit committee should review with the independent auditor any audit problems or difficulties and management's response.
6. The audit committee should report regularly to the board of directors.
7. Each listed company must have an internal audit function.

8. Each listed company CEO must certify to the NYSE each year that he or she is not aware of any violation by the company of NYSE corporate governance listing standards.

9. Listed companies must adopt and disclose corporate governance guidelines.

10. Listed foreign private issuers must disclose any significant ways in which their corporate governance practices differ from those followed by domestic companies under NYSE listing standards.

Building Ethics into Corporate Governance Systems

A critical issue for an organization that aspires to be ethical is how it should build ethics into its corporate governance systems. For example, how can an organization ensure that its management operates and makes decisions in a manner that promotes ethical behavior among all those in the organization?

As previously mentioned, an ethical tone at the top must be established throughout the organization. Oftentimes, new employees are influenced by what is and is not said to them when they first join the firm. Imagine that you just began working in the accounting department of a company and on your first day at work, after the usual meetings about human resource issues, the CEO meets with all new hires. The CEO walks into the conference room, welcomes everyone to the company, hands each one a copy of the code of ethics, and then says "make sure you read it." That's not very inspiring and it may not engender a great deal of enthusiasm for the code or the company's commitment to ethical behavior. Imagine instead that the CEO walks in, greets everyone, holds up the code, and then says:

> This is our code of ethics. We believe in it. It guides our actions. It's not just a piece of paper. In fact, next week you will go through a two-day ethics training program to learn just what the provisions mean to you in the performance of your services. Do not hesitate to question an action if you think it violates the code. We have an ethics hotline where you can discuss any matter anonymously with our ethics officer. If all else fails, come to me directly and we'll discuss it. This organization supports ethical behavior. No cutting of corners. No fudging numbers. No padding expense accounts. And be careful to avoid even the appearance of a conflict of interest.

The expected response from employees probably would be to identify with the company's ethical expectations. Wouldn't you feel proud to work for such a company?

Some companies use forms of communication to instill an ethical, socially responsible culture. One example is Microsoft. With hundreds of thousands of employees around the globe, the company finds it most valuable to commit to writing its standards of business conduct. These appear in Appendix 2 at the end of this chapter. One of the most impressive statements is the commitment of the company to foster, manage, and reward a culture of accountability and integrity within (employee) groups. The statement is supported by a set of values that are discussed in the following text.

Corporate Values

Recall that values are basic and fundamental beliefs that guide or motivate attitudes or actions. Ethics is revealed through a decision maker's behavior when solving business problems that emerge from carrying out corporate policies and operations. Thus, the underlying antecedents of behavior are values and, as such, values are the foundation of ethical decision making.[36]

Increasingly, companies around the world have adopted formal statements of corporate values, and senior executives now routinely identify ethical behavior, honesty, integrity, and social concerns as top issues on their companies' agendas. In 2004, the consulting firm

EXHIBIT 3.4
Corporate Values
Statements

Values	Percentage
Ethical behavior/integrity	90%
Commitment to customers	88
Commitment to employees	78
Teamwork and trust	76
Commitment to shareholders	69
Honesty/openness	69
Accountability	68
Social responsibility/corporate citizenship	65
Innovativeness/entrepreneurship	60
Drive to succeed	50
Environmental responsibility	46
Initiative	44
Commitment to diversity	41
Adaptability	31

of Booz Allen Hamilton teamed up with the Aspen Institute, an organization dedicated to promoting values-based leadership and public policy, to survey corporations in 30 countries and five regions. The purpose of the survey was to examine the way that companies define corporate values, to expand the research about the relationship of values to business performance, and to identify best practices for managing corporate values.[37]

The survey's most significant finding was that a large number of companies are making their values explicit. Exhibit 3.4 presents the results of a survey of the frequency of values included in corporate values statements.

This is a brief, yet forceful statement of values by Microsoft:

Microsoft Values

Our values guide our behaviors and must shine through in all our interactions with each other and our stakeholders. Microsoft employees are great people who share the following values:

- Integrity and honesty
- Passion for customers, partners, and technology
- Open and respectful with others and dedicated to making them better
- Willingness to take on big challenges and see them through
- Self-critical, questioning, and committed to personal excellence and self-improvement
- Accountable for commitments, results, and quality to customers, shareholders, partners, and employees

Code of Ethics for CEOs and CFOs

In virtually all of the frauds of the late 1990s and early 2000s, the CEOs and CFOs knew about the company's materially misstated financial statements. One important provision of SOX that helps protect the public against fraudulent financial statements is the requirement that the CEO and CFO must certify that to the best of their knowledge there are no material misstatements in the financial statements. Another requirement of SOX is that public companies must have a code of ethics for its CEO and principal financial officers. This code must be separate from the company's code of ethics. An excellent example of such a code is Microsoft's Finance Code of Professional Conduct that appears in Appendix 3. Notice how the code includes many provisions that are part of an ethical culture, reliance on virtues to instill the desired standards of behavior, and links to corporate governance. You know the company takes its ethical obligations seriously when it establishes a series of steps for employees to follow when reporting violations of the standards of business practice (whistleblowing) and concerns about questionable accounting or auditing practices.

Codes of Business Ethics

Recall that the Enron board approved a waiver of its code so that Andy Fastow, the CFO, could purchase an interest in one of the company's SPEs. Section 406 of SOX requires public companies to disclose whether they have codes of ethics and also to disclose any waivers of those codes for certain members of senior management. The SEC adopted specific rules implementing these requirements in January 2003. Item 406(a) of Regulation S-K requires companies to disclose[38]

- whether they have a written code of ethics that applies to their principal executive officer, principal financial officer, principal accounting officer or controller, or persons performing similar functions;
- any waivers of the code of ethics for these individuals; and
- any changes to the code of ethics.

Companies that do not have a code of ethics must explain why not. Companies were first required to comply with the code of ethics disclosure requirements in their annual reports for fiscal years ending on or after July 15, 2003. A company may file its code as an exhibit to the annual report, post the code on the company's Web site, or agree to provide a copy of the code upon request and without charge. Section 406 incorporates some, but not all, of the provisions regarding a code of ethics offered by the NYSE Corporate Accountability and Listing Standards Committee.[39]

In addition to a statement of values, standards of business practices, and a code of ethics, some companies use a credo to instill virtue. A credo is an aspirational statement that encourages employees to internalize the values of the company. A good example of a corporate credo is that of Johnson & Johnson. It appears in Exhibit 3.5.[40]

The Johnson & Johnson credo clearly sets a positive ethical tone. Notice how it emphasizes the company's primary obligations to those who use and rely on the safety of its products. The Johnson & Johnson credo implies that shareholders will earn a fair return if the company operates in accordance with its ethical values. Johnson & Johnson was credited with being an ethical organization in part because of the way it handled the Tylenol poisoning incidents in 1982.

Tylenol Poisoning

In the fall of 1982, seven people in the Chicago area collapsed suddenly and died after taking Tylenol capsules that had been laced with cyanide. These five women and two men became the first victims ever to die from what came to be known as product tampering.

McNeil Consumer Products, a subsidiary of Johnson & Johnson, was confronted with a crisis when it was determined that each of the seven people had ingested an Extra-Strength Tylenol capsule laced with cyanide. The news of this incident traveled quickly and was the cause of a massive, nationwide panic.

Tamara Kaplan, a professor at Penn State University, contends that Johnson & Johnson used the Tylenol poisonings to launch a public relations program immediately, in order to save the integrity of both their product and their corporation as a whole. We find this to be a vacuous position. By Kaplan's own admission, "Johnson & Johnson's top management put customer safety first, before they worried about their company's profit and other financial concerns."[41] This hardly sounds like a company that used a catastrophic event to boost its image in the eyes of the public.

Johnson & Johnson's stock price dropped precipitously after the initial incident was made public. In the end, the stock price recovered because the company's actions gained the support and confidence of the public. Johnson & Johnson acted swiftly to remove all the product from the shelves of supermarkets, provide free replacements of Tylenol

EXHIBIT 3.5
Johnson & Johnson Credo

We believe our first responsibility is to the doctors, nurses and patients,
to mothers and fathers and all others who use our products and services.
In meeting their needs everything we do must be of high quality.
We must constantly strive to reduce our costs
in order to maintain reasonable prices.
Customers' orders must be serviced promptly and accurately.
Our suppliers and distributors must have an opportunity
to make a fair profit.

We are responsible to our employees,
the men and women who work with us throughout the world.
Everyone must be considered as an individual.
We must respect their dignity and recognize their merit.
They must have a sense of security in their jobs.
Compensation must be fair and adequate,
and working conditions clean, orderly and safe.
We must be mindful of ways to help our employees fulfill
their family responsibilities.
Employees must feel free to make suggestions and complaints.
There must be equal opportunity for employment, development
and advancement for those qualified.
We must provide competent management,
and their actions must be just and ethical.

We are responsible to the communities in which we live and work
and to the world community as well.
We must be good citizens—support good works and charities
and bear our fair share of taxes.
We must encourage civic improvements and better health and education.
We must maintain in good order
the property we are privileged to use,
protecting the environment and natural resources.

Our final responsibility is to our stockholders.
Business must make a sound profit.
We must experiment with new ideas.
Research must be carried on, innovative programs developed
and mistakes paid for.
New equipment must be purchased, new facilities provided
and new products launched.
Reserves must be created to provide for adverse times.

When we operate according to these principles,
the stockholders should realize a fair return.

capsules with the tablet form of the product, and make public statements of assurance that the company would not sell an unsafe product. To claim the company was motivated by a public relations agenda, even though in the end its actions did provide a public relations boon for the company, is to ignore a basic point that Johnson & Johnson's management may have known all along. That is, good ethics is good business. But don't be fooled by this expression. It is good for the company if it benefits as a result of an ethical action. However, the main reason to make ethical decisions, as did Johnson & Johnson, is that it is the proper way to act.

Let's analyze Johnson & Johnson's actions from the perspective of the ethical decision-making model starting from the first public disclosure of the poisoning and how the company should have (and did) act in response.

1. **Frame the ethical issue.** *How should the company react to the Tylenol crisis to protect the interests of those who rely on the product?*

According to the company, its reaction was guided by the company's credo. If you read the credo, you'll notice how the company places the interests of the people who rely on the safety of the product ahead of its own self-interest. In fact, it links making a "fair profit" to its ethical action and social responsibility. The actions of Johnson & Johnson to the Tylenol crisis today are viewed as a model of business ethics.

2. **Gather all the facts.** Typically, these would be presented in summary or bullet form. Since the facts have already been described, they will not be repeated here.

3. **Identify the stakeholders and obligations.** This is arguably the most important step for Johnson & Johnson. The credo clarifies the stakeholders. In addition to the company's obligations to doctors, nurses, patients, and parents to provide a safe and reliable product, the company has an obligation to its employees to "walk the talk" of the credo. If it did not act in accordance with the company's written statement of core values, then employees might wonder about the company's commitment to its own credo. This would send a negative message concerning the tone at the top of the organization.

The company also has an important obligation to its investors. As noted earlier, even though the company's stock price declined at first, it ultimately recovered all of that loss. But the point is by acting ethically the company retained the trust of its stockholders, many of whom are parents and can relate to the parents of children who might accidentally ingest a tainted product.

Finally, Johnson & Johnson has an obligation to the government since the Food and Drug Administration regulates pharmaceutical products and is concerned about its role in protecting the public health. The issue of product tampering is one that has grown in importance since the Tylenol event as more and more companies have been questioned about the safety of products including automobile manufacturers, tire manufacturers, and makers of silicone gel breast implants.

4. **Identify the relevant accounting ethics standards involved in the situation.** These are limited by the facts of the case. However, the manner of disclosing the facts of the situation relates to being honest and transparent in financial reporting.

5. **Identify the operational issues.** The application of Johnson & Johnson's credo in handling the Tylenol incident is an operational issue. The company indicated that it turned to the credo immediately for guidance. This means it was guided operationally by one of its internal reporting controls—the credo—that enabled it to respond in an ethical manner.

Additional facts of the Tylenol poisoning indicate that the company established a 1-800 hotline for consumers to call for any inquiries about the safety of Tylenol. Operationally, this was another positive step to assure the public of the company's concern for its safety.

The company acted swiftly and responsibly to develop a safer packaging for Tylenol. It was a triple safety seal packaging—a glued box, a plastic seal over the neck of the bottle, and a foil seal over the mouth of the bottle. This is the industry standard today.

6. **Identify the technical accounting and auditing issues.** The main accounting issue was how to disclose information about the Tylenol poisonings and the ultimate legal liability of the company. Given that the Tylenol incident was the first of its kind, it would have been difficult for the accountants to determine the potential monetary liability in any lawsuit brought against the company. Still, the event itself should have been disclosed in the footnotes as a contingent liability since it was reasonably possible that there would have been a material liability for the company.

7. **List all the possible alternatives of what you can or cannot do.**
   a. Ignore the poisonings and let the government dictate what the company should do.

Chapter 3 Corporate Governance and Ethical Management 107

b. Do the minimum. Recall the tainted product.

c. Do all that the company can do to assure the public by acting in a responsible and ethical manner.

Undoubtedly, other alternatives can be identified. Of course, the company chose the last alternative as already explained. Imagine the public outcry if the company had ignored or downplayed the severity of the situation as so many companies have since the Tylenol incident. Recall the way Ford reacted to safety concerns of its Pinto brand by conducting a cost–benefit analysis of whether the company should fix the apparently unsafe placement of Pinto gas tanks behind the rear axle. Then there is the tobacco industry that hid information from the public that its studies showed nicotine was addictive. In that case Jeffrey Wigand, the former vice president of research and development at Brown & Williamson, blew the whistle on the company's actions to hide the information and even enhance the addictive component of cigarettes. Wigand went so far as to inform the television show *60 Minutes* that did an expose on the tobacco industry. His story was ultimately told in the movie *The Insider.*

8. **Compare and weigh the alternatives.**

Is it legal (in conformity with laws and rules)? Johnson & Johnson is not obligated to recall product unless so ordered by the FDA. Its actions did not violate any laws.

Is it consistent with professional standards? The main issue is full disclosure and honest, reliable financial reporting.

Is it consistent with in-house rules (i.e., codes of conduct)? Yes, the "rules" in this instance reflect the company's credo and they were diligently followed.

Is it right? This is the strength of the actions taken by Johnson & Johnson. The company respected the rights of the parties that used and relied on the safety of Tylenol in crafting a response to the crisis. Imagine if every company that faced a product tampering case did not act to assure the public of the safety of their product. All trust would be lost on the part of the public.

What are the potential harms and benefits to the stakeholders? It is difficult to see how a stakeholder would have benefited by a response other than the one developed by the company. The shareholders were harmed initially when the stock lost market value. However, in the long run they were better off monetarily. From the perspective of employees working for Johnson & Johnson, they should have been proud to work for the company based on its handling of the Tylenol incident.

Is it fair to the stakeholders? The company acted in accordance with its credo that emphasizes fair treatment for its stakeholders, especially the "doctors, nurses and patients, mothers and fathers, and all those who use [company] products and services."

Is it consistent with virtue considerations? Virtually all of Josephson's Six Pillars of Character are involved in the Tylenol situation. Honesty exists because the company has an obligation to fully disclose all of the information that the public has a right or need to know. Integrity requires that the company have the courage to stand up for the values in its credo regardless of the consequences. The company demonstrated accountability and responsibility by acting to remove the tainted form of Tylenol from the shelves of all supermarkets. At first, Johnson & Johnson acted only to remove the product from Chicago-area markets, but it eventually did a national recall of the capsule form of the product. By assuring the public that it would not allow a tainted product to be sold, the company garnered the trust of the public. Finally, since the company acted in a socially responsible manner, its commitment to citizenship was clearly established.

9. Decide on a course of action. We know what Johnson & Johnson did and why. Imagine if it had ignored the situation. The number of deaths may have risen before the government stepped in and forced a recall. The company's reputation might have suffered irreparable harm. The lawsuits would have been flowing.

10. Reflect on your decision. Johnson & Johnson's then-chair of the board of directors, James E. Burke, was quoted as saying in regard to questions about the survivability of the company after the poisonings were publicly reported: "It will take time, it will take money, and it will be very difficult; but we consider it a moral imperative, as well as good business, to restore Tylenol to its preeminent position."

How Employees View the Ethics of Their Organizations

The 2009 Ethics Resource Center (ERC) National Business Ethics Survey (NBES), *Ethics in the Recession,* provides valuable information about how employees view the ethics and ethical practices of organizations they work for. The survey indicates some positive results including misconduct at work is down; whistleblowing is up; ethical cultures are stronger; and pressure to cut corners is lower.[42] Most likely, the passage of SOX with its emphasis on strong internal controls, an ethical tone at the top, and independent audit committee accounts for the encouraging results.

Despite the positive overall picture, there is a toll that the recession has taken on ethics. When NBES asked about the effects of the recession, about 22 percent agreed that the recession has negatively impacted the ethical culture within respondents' companies. Also, 10 percent said that "to stay in business during the recession, my company has lowered its ethical standards." These are troubling results in part because they reflect ethical relativism in decision making, an approach that might have long-term negative consequences for business and our society. The problem is when the times get tough, the less ethical look to cut corners. As we have learned, good ethics requires practice and consistency of behavior in accordance with core values (e.g., Aristotle's virtues, Josephson's Six Pillars of Character). Unethical behavior tends to feed on itself, especially if those in and around it conclude it has became part of the culture.

The report provides many interesting perspectives on employee perceptions about fraud in their companies. For example, the percentage of employees observing misconduct increased from 46 percent following passage of SOX in 2002 to 56 percent in 2007. The top three types of observed misconduct reflect personal lapses, rather than organizational violations that further the company's agenda. Nevertheless, all pose significant risk to company reputation, value, and growth. They are conflicts of interest—putting one's own interests above the organization (observed by 23 percent of employees); abusive or intimidating behavior (observed by 21 percent of employees); and lying to employees (observed by 20 percent of employees).

NBES asked about transparency and accountability in financial reporting to identify whether signs existed that there may be material misstatements in the financial statements. The results indicate the following red flags:

- Falsifying or manipulating financial information
- Overriding routine procedures (altering cut-off revenue, holding books open, misdating revenue)
- Ignoring unusual activities happening at higher levels (e.g., side agreements, unusual business deals)
- Creating fictitious vendors or invoices
- Stealing or misappropriating assets

- Submitting false or misleading invoices to customers
- Entering into contracts that lack proper terms, conditions, or approvals
- Violating contract terms with customers or suppliers

More will be said about these techniques in Chapters 5 and 7.

An interesting part of the results is the reported retaliation against employees who observe and report misconduct (whistleblowing). Fifteen percent perceive they were retaliated against as a result of their actions. The forms of perceived retaliation include:

- Other employees gave them a cold shoulder.
- Their supervisor or management excluded them from decisions and work activity.
- They were verbally abused by their supervisor or someone else in management.
- They almost lost their job.
- They were verbally abused by other employees.
- They were relocated or reassigned.
- They were demoted.

These results seem to challenge the notion that whistleblower protection exists in organizations.

The Ethics and Compliance Officer Association (ECOA) has recognized its increased responsibilities resulting from SOX. The mission of the ECOA is to promote "ethical business practices and [serve] as a global forum for the exchange of information and strategies among organizations and individuals responsible for ethics, compliance and business conduct programs."[43] An important step in encouraging the reporting of wrongdoing is to appoint a trusted member of the management team to be the organization's ethics officer. This person should take the lead in ensuring that the organization is in compliance with the laws and regulations, including SEC securities laws and SOX, and serving as a sounding board for management to try out new ideas to see if it passes the ethics "smell" test. The ethics officer plays a critical role in helping create a positive ethical tone in organizations.

Whistleblowing

Section 806 of the Sarbanes-Oxley Act

Section 806 of the Sarbanes-Oxley (SOX) Act of 2002, Protection for Employees of Publicly Traded Companies Who Provide Evidence in Fraud Cases, confers legal protection upon employees of public companies that report suspected violations of a range of federal offenses—including those relating to fraud against shareholders.[44] This so-called whistleblower provision protects employees who provide information on a fraud by prohibiting the discharge, demotion, discrimination, suspension or threatening or harassing action against an employee who provides information in a federal or regulatory investigation or to Congress or to the employee's supervisor. A person who alleges discharge or discrimination under this section can file a complaint with the secretary of labor. An employee who brings a successful action will be entitled to "reinstatement with the same seniority status that the employee would have had, but for the discrimination; the amount of back pay with interest; and compensation for any special damages sustained as a result of the discrimination, including litigation costs, expert witness fees, and reasonable attorney fees."

The Department of Labor delegated to the Occupational Safety and Health Administration (OSHA) enforcement authority over the whistleblower provisions of SOX. OSHA's regulations require that an employee first establish a *prima facie* case of retaliation. This is generally interpreted as meaning that the employee must be engaged in a protected activity or conduct; that the employer knew "actually or constructively" that the conduct occurred; that the employee suffered an unfavorable personnel action; and that the circumstances "were sufficient to raise the inference that the protected activity was a contributing factor to the unfavorable action."

Department of Defense Whistleblower-Protection Rules Covering Contractor Employees

On November 19, 2009, the Department of Defense (DoD) published a final rule regarding whistleblower protections for federal contractors' employees who disclose to government officials information about wrongdoing. The new DoD rule defines the broadened whistleblower protections under the 2008 and 2009 amendments to the National Defense Authorization Act (NDAA), provides the procedural framework for agency action and a private cause of action by the employee, and requires contractors to inform employees in writing of federal whistleblower rights and protections.

The final regulation prohibits government contractors from discharging, demoting, or otherwise discriminating against employees as a reprisal for disclosing to government officials information that the employee reasonably believes is evidence of gross mismanagement of a DoD contract or grant, a gross waste of DoD funds, a substantial and specific danger to public health or safety, or a violation of law related to a DoD contract (including the competition for or negotiation of a contract). These protections are available to employees who disclose such information to a member of Congress, a representative of a committee of Congress, an inspector general, the Government Accountability Office, a DoD employee responsible for contract oversight or management, or an authorized official of an agency or the Department of Justice.

An employee who believes that he or she has been subject to reprisal in violation of the NDAA may file a complaint with the inspector general of the DoD. Unlike most whistleblower-protection laws, neither the NDAA nor the Defense Department rule contains a statute of limitations for filing a complaint. Upon receiving a complaint, the inspector general must determine whether a complaint is frivolous or merits further investigation. If the complaint calls for further investigation, the inspector general has 180 days to investigate the complaint and submit a report to the complaining employee, the respondent contractor, and the head of the agency with which the private party contracted. Additional time may be available if the complainant agrees.

Within 30 days after receiving a report from an inspector general, the agency head must determine whether sufficient basis exists to conclude that the employee was subjected to unlawful reprisal and grant or deny relief accordingly. If the agency denies relief or fails to file an order granting relief within 210 days after the complaint was filed, the employee will be deemed to have exhausted all administrative remedies with regard to the complaint.

Upon exhausting administrative remedies, the complaining employee may file a whistleblower-discrimination lawsuit against the contractor in federal district court, regardless of the amount of damages being sought. The employee or the contractor may request that the federal lawsuit be tried before a jury. Under DoD rules, the inspector general's determination and an agency head's order denying relief will be admissible in the employee's federal action. Successful plaintiffs may recover "make whole" relief, including reinstatement, compensation (including back pay), employment benefits, and restoration of pre-reprisal conditions of employment, as well as attorneys' fees and costs incurred in pursuing the litigation.

Employers that have contracts with a DoD agency are advised to adopt a formal policy prohibiting retaliation against employees for engaging in any of the whistleblower activities protected by the new DoD rule. That policy could also advise employees of their rights under the new rule, thereby satisfying the requirement that employees be informed in writing of their rights and protections under the NDAA. Defense contractors should consider obtaining signed acknowledgments from employees, so that the contractors will be able to demonstrate compliance with the written notice requirement.[45]

Lockheed Martin has been embroiled in a whistleblower lawsuit since October 2007. The facts of the case were originally sealed but opened up in February 2009. The facts of the case are summarized as follows:

Ex-Lockheed Engineer Claims F-22 Tech "Defective"

A former engineer for defense contractor Lockheed Martin Corporation claims in a federal whistleblower lawsuit brought on November 10, 2009, that the company knowingly used "defective" stealth coatings when building its F-22 Raptor stealth jets.

Darrol Olsen, a stealth engineer who was fired by Lockheed in 1999, claims Lockheed "falsely certified" the coatings between September 1995 and June 1999, saying they had passed stealth tests and concealing results that showed otherwise. Olsen said in the lawsuit he was told to "stay out of it" when he complained to his superiors.

Olsen contends Lockheed applied more than 600 pounds of extra layers of coatings so the jet could pass the stealth tests required by the Air Force. The layers were needed because the coating rubbed off when exposed to jet oil, fuel, and water, the complaint said. It left the supersonic fighters with "extremely thick coatings [that] have proved brittle" and the coatings designed to be paper-thin have now compromised the superfighter's velocity and maneuverability, the lawsuit said. It said the process has essentially painted a "bull's-eye target" on aircraft designed to avoid radar detection.

According to Bluestein, Olsen asked the judge in the lawsuit to order Lockheed to pay the federal government $50 million for each of the 183 F-22s built or under construction as part of the contract. He is also asking the judge to order Lockheed to pay his legal fees.[46]

Bernie Madoff's Ponzi Scheme

The case of Bernie Madoff illustrates what can happen when regulators ignore warnings by whistleblowers. Madoff engaged in a Ponzi scheme,[47] a fraudulent investment operation that pays returns to investors from their own money or money paid by subsequent investors rather than from any actual profit earned. To entice new investors the Ponzi scheme offered short-term returns that were either abnormally high or unusually consistent, but it required an ever-increasing flow of money from investors in order to keep the scheme going. Once the investment funds dried up or large numbers of investors asked for their invested capital back, the house of cards collapsed.

Madoff was a trusted investment adviser. After all, he had served as chair of the board of directors and served on the board of governors of the National Association of Securities Dealers (NASDAQ), a self-regulator securities industry organization. He had personal relationships with his investors and was a pillar of the community. Madoff used his "reputation" to gain favor with his investors and assure them about the promised level of returns.

As the stock market tanked in the period between 2007 and 2009, many Madoff investors asked to have their funds returned. Madoff could return some of the money, typically to favored investors, but he couldn't meet most of the claims. By the time the dust had settled, Madoff had perpetrated a $65 billion fraud. His sons notified the federal authorities on December 11, 2008, and Madoff was arrested. He was sentenced to serve a 150-year sentence on June 16, 2009, and $170 billion of his ill-gotten gains is supposed to be restored to the victims of his crime.

The SEC brought an action against Madoff's auditors, Friehling & Horowitz, CPA's, P.C., claiming that the firm enabled Madoff's conduct by falsely representing to investors that Bernard L. Madoff Investment Securities (BMIS) LLC was financially sound and that the firm employed independent auditors who conducted audits of BMIS each year.

In documents that the firm knew were distributed or submitted to investors and the SEC, Friehling knowingly or with reckless disregard falsely stated that[48]

- The firm audited BMIS' financial statements pursuant to Generally Accepted Auditing Standards (GAAS), including the requirements to maintain auditor independence, and to perform audit procedures regarding custody of securities;
- BMIS' financial statements were presented in conformity with Generally Accepted Accounting Principles (GAAP); and
- Friehling had reviewed the internal control environment at BMIS, including internal controls over the custody of securities, and found no material inadequacies.

According to the SEC, all of these statements were materially false because Friehling did not perform anything remotely resembling an audit of BMIS, and, critically, did not perform procedures to confirm the securities BMIS purportedly held on behalf of its customers even existed. Instead, Friehling merely pretended to conduct minimal audit procedures of certain accounts to make it seem like he was conducting an audit, and even then failed to document his purported findings and conclusions as required under GAAS. If properly stated, those financial statements, along with BMIS's related disclosures regarding reserve requirements, would have shown that BMIS owed tens of billions of dollars in additional liabilities to its customers and thus was insolvent. Similarly, Friehling did not conduct any procedures with respect to BMIS's internal controls, or he knew or recklessly disregarded that he had absolutely no basis to represent that BMIS had adequate internal controls. On November 3, 2009, Friehling agreed not to contest the SEC's findings and consented to a partial judgment without admitting or denying the allegations of the SEC's complaint.

Who is to blame for the fraud at Madoff? Clearly, Madoff himself violated every standard of ethical behavior and acted strictly in his own self-interests. He even ignored the interests of his family claiming that they knew nothing of the fraud (somewhat hard to believe) and left them to pick up the pieces of what he had done. Friehling shares the blame with Madoff for failing to live up to his ethical obligations as a CPA. Perhaps most important was the benign role played by the SEC in acting on tips it had received by an external whistleblower, Harry Markopolos, an investment adviser who was skeptical of Madoff's approach to earning the purported large returns for his investors.

Markopolos testified in February 2009, in hearings held by the U.S. House of Representatives, that the SEC ignored his repeated warnings about the dealings of Madoff. Markopolos asserted that he had submitted warnings about Madoff since 2000 and he assailed the agency for ignoring his warnings or brushing them aside. "Nothing was done," he declared. "There was an abject failure by the regulatory agencies we entrust as our watchdog," Markopolos said his experience with most SEC officials "proved to be a systemic disappointment, and lead me to conclude that the SEC securities lawyers, if only through their investigative ineptitude and financial illiteracy, colluded to maintain large frauds such as the one to which Madoff later confessed."

Markopolos said he began his investigation of Madoff after his superior at Rampart Investment Management asked him to try to match the returns of Madoff's firm. Markopolos said his analysis showed it was impossible for Madoff to consistently outperform the markets and other managers. He described Madoff as "one of the most powerful men on Wall Street" and said there was "great danger" in raising questions about him. During his years of investigation, "my team and I surmised that if Madoff gained knowledge of our activities, he may have felt threatened enough to seek to stifle us." He also said, "I became fearful for the safety of my family until the SEC finally acknowledged, after Madoff had been arrested, that it had received credible evidence of Madoff's Ponzi scheme several years earlier."

In the wake of the Madoff fraud, the SEC's office of the inspector general launched an internal investigation in December 2008 to determine why the agency did not detect the scheme. The SEC initiated a variety of actions to prevent such a regulatory failure from occurring in the future. Some of the more relevant steps affecting the accounting profession include:[49]

- Require all investment advisers who control or have custody of their clients' assets to hire an independent public accountant to conduct an annual "surprise exam" to verify those assets actually exist.
- Require all investment advisers who do not use independent firms to maintain their clients' assets to obtain a third-party written report assessing the safeguards that protect the clients' assets. The report—prepared by an accountant registered and inspected by the PCAOB—would, among other things, describe the controls that are in place to protect the assets, the tests performed on the controls, and the results of those tests.

In the aftermath of the Madoff fraud, the SEC is advocating for expanded authority from Congress to reward whistleblowers who bring forward substantial evidence to the agency about significant federal securities violations. It proposed legislation that a fund would be established to pay whistleblowers using money collected from wrongdoers that is not otherwise distributed to investors.

Concluding Thoughts

Fraud in business continues to persist in spite of efforts to improve the ethical climate of organizations and strengthen regulatory requirements and sanctions for wrongdoing. We believe one reason is the general decline in ethics in society at large. In today's environment, some people believe they can get away with anything they choose to do and, because they act out of self-interest, they delude themselves into thinking they'll never get caught. Many fail to acknowledge responsibility for their actions and show little, if any, remorse for their behaviors. Fraudsters see so many who have committed fraud go unpunished or given a "slap on the wrist" for their crime. People like Bernie Madoff are willing to use personal relationships and relationships of trust to dupe gullible investors into believing they can earn returns on their investments that can't be supported.

Why didn't the corporate governance systems work as intended in the frauds at companies like Enron, WorldCom, and Waste Management? It seems as though no one wanted to look too hard at what was going on. Red flags that were raised by professionals such as Sherron Watkins and Cynthia Cooper fell on deaf ears. One problem certainly was the lack of independence of members of the board of directors and an inattentive audit committee. The external auditors went along with the fraud because they didn't want to lose large amounts of revenue and the opportunity to earn even more fees from lucrative consulting contracts.

The failure of ethics in an organization typically occurs because top management fails to establish an ethical tone at the top. Employees may come to believe there is a culture of "make the deal at any costs" or that we must "meet projected earnings" regardless of what it takes. Former SEC chair Arthur Levitt, who testified in Congress following the accounting frauds, identified the cause of financial statements failures as a "culture of gamesmanship" in business rooted in the emphasis on achieving short-term results such as meeting or exceeding financial analysts' earnings expectations.[50]

Discussion Questions

1. Mahatma Gandhi is quoted as saying: "Capitalism as such is not evil; it is its wrong use that is evil." What do you think Gandhi meant by this statement? Give an example of when capitalism may have fallen short of its goal to promote the interests of society.

2. To whom do managers owe their allegiance? Is it to the shareholders? To other stakeholders? Be sure to support your answer with ethical thought and examples in the text from discussions about corporate governance.

3. Marvin Bower, the former managing partner of McKinsey & Company, said: "There is no such thing as business ethics. There is only one kind—you have to adhere to the highest standards." What does this statement mean to you?

4. Five major ethical issues in business were identified in the chapter. One of these issues is information technology. Discuss how information technology might create an ethical challenge for a business.

5. The four pillars of corporate governance are responsibility, accountability, fairness, and transparency. Discuss how each of these pillars helps create ethical corporate governance systems.

6. Why do you think there was a reduction of cases where fraud was detected by internal audit and internal controls in the 2006–2008 comparison survey by the ACFE? Does it mean that these elements of corporate governance are not working as intended?

7. In 2005, a group of concerned shareholders of Johnson & Johnson requested the board of directors establish a policy of, whenever possible, separating the roles of the chair and CEO, so that an independent director who has not served as an executive officer of the company serves as the chair of the board of directors. Do you think such a policy should improve corporate governance? Why or why not?

8. On August 9, 2005, Chancellor William B. Chandler III of the Delaware Chancery Court[51] ruled that the directors of the Walt Disney Company acted in good faith when Michael Ovitz was hired in 1995 to be the CEO of Disney and then allowed to walk away 15 months later after being fired by Michael Eisner, the chair of the Disney's board of directors, with a severance package valued at $130 million. Discuss the role and responsibilities of a board of directors in matters such as this? Is it "fair" that Ovitz was allowed to walk away with such a lucrative severance package only 15 months after being fired? Include in your discussion what is fairness in this instance from an ethical perspective.

9. COSO explains the importance of the control environment to internal controls by stating it sets the tone of an organization, influencing the control consciousness of its people. It is the foundation for all aspects of internal control, providing discipline and structure. Explain what is meant by this statement.

10. According to the IAA Code of Ethics, internal auditors should make a balanced assessment of all the relevant circumstances and should not be unduly influenced by their own interests or by others in forming judgments. Apply this statement to the actions of Cynthia Cooper in the WorldCom case.

11. In 2005, the Institute of Management Accountants reported the results of a survey of business, academic, and regulatory leaders conducted by the Center for Corporate Change that found the corporation's culture to be the most important factor influencing the attitudes and behavior of executives. The results also indicate that 88 percent of the representatives who took part in the survey believe that companies devote little management attention to considering the effect of the culture on their executives. What are the elements of the corporate culture? Do you think it is possible for a company to control the culture? Why or why not?

12. Evaluate the ethicality of the corporate governance systems at Microsoft based on the discussion in the text.

13. In the accounting fraud at the cable company Adelphia, top management had established a "cash management" system that enabled the founder of Adelphia and former CEO and chair of the board of directors, John Rigas, to dip into the fund for personal expenses whenever he wanted. The final approval for such expenditures rested with Timothy Rigas, the son of John Rigas and Adelphia's CEO during the final years that fraud had occurred. What's wrong with the founder of a company, its former CEO and board chair, utilizing corporate assets for personal reasons? Can you think of any circumstances where it would be permissible? That is, what would have to happen for this to be acceptable?

14. In the Bernie Madoff case, some investors who lost money are concerned about the potential for "clawback" suits that might be brought by the trustee in charge of liquidating Madoff's firm. Such suits would seek to reclaim funds that some investors were able to pull out from their Madoff investments and redistribute them to other investors not so lucky. The potential for clawbacks is prompting some investors to protect their remaining assets by transferring them to irrevocable trusts, homes, annuities, or life-insurance policies. The trustee intends to distribute clawed-back funds to investors who were wiped out. Under the bankruptcy code, those who will be most susceptible to a clawback are investors who withdrew any money in the 90 days before

Madoff's arrest on December 11, 2008. Do you think it is ethical for the trustee to go after the funds of investors in Madoff's enterprises simply because they were withdrawn in the 90 days before Madoff's arrest? Use ethical reasoning to answer this question.

15. The Institute of Internal Auditors states in its November 2005 issue of "The Tone at the Top" that businesses can rely on an industry standard, *Internal Control—Integrated Framework,* to comply with certain provision in SOX by assessing and enhancing companies' internal control systems. How do effective internal controls help an organization promote efficiency, minimize risks, help ensure the reliability of financial statements, and comply with regulations?

16. On the evening of January 27, 1986, the temperature outside the Kennedy Space Center in Florida dropped below freezing. The National Aeronautics and Space Administration (NASA) had a dilemma. In discussions with executives from the Morton Thiokol Corporation that produced the solid rocket boosters for the space shuttle program, it was decided there was insufficient evidence and specific testing about how the cold weather would affect the rocket booster seals even though engineers assigned to the launch thought otherwise. The engineers recommended not launching because of the cold temperature. The temperature had dropped to 27 degrees at launch time. It took only 75 seconds after the launch for tragedy to strike. Eleven miles above the earth, fire leaked from one of the booster seals and the *Challenger* erupted into flames killing all aboard including schoolteacher Christa McAuliffe, America's first private citizen in space. Did NASA do the right thing by allowing the launch to go on? Be sure to support your answer with ethical reasoning.

17. "Give me the 'McFacts,' ma'am, nothing but the McFacts!" So argued the defense attorney for McDonald's Corporation as she questioned Stella Liebeck, an 81-year-old retired sales clerk, two years after her initial lawsuit against McDonald's claiming it served dangerously hot coffee. Liebeck had bought a 49-cent cup of coffee at the drive-in window of an Albuquerque McDonald's, and while removing the lid to add cream and sugar, she spilled the coffee and suffered third-degree burns of the groin, inner thighs, and buttocks. Her suit claimed the coffee was "defective." During the trial it was determined that testing of coffee at other local restaurants found that none came closer than 20 degrees to the temperature at which McDonald's coffee is poured, about 180 degrees. The jury decided in favor of Liebeck and awarded her compensatory damages of $200,000, which they reduced to $160,000 after determining that 20 percent of the fault belonged with Liebeck for spilling the coffee. The jury then found that McDonald's had engaged in willful, reckless, malicious, or wanton conduct, the basis for punitive damages. It awarded $2.7 million in punitive damages. That amount was ultimately reduced by the presiding judge to $480,000. The parties then settled out of court for an amount reported to be less than the $480,000.

    For its part, McDonald's had suggested that Liebeck may have contributed to her injuries by holding the cup between her legs and not removing her clothing immediately. The company also argued that Liebeck's age may have made the injuries worse than they might have been in a younger individual, "since older skin is thinner and more vulnerable to injury."

    Who is to blame for the McSpill? Be sure to support your answer with a discussion of personal responsibility, corporate accountability, and ethical reasoning.

18. On February 26, 2009, the SEC accused Robert Allen Stanford of executing a "massive Ponzi scheme" over the last decade, in which he and his cohorts misappropriated funds and made more than $1.6 billion in "bogus" loans to Stanford and his bank—the Stanford International Bank. The agency also accused Stanford of falsifying financial statements to investors who bought $8 billion worth of certificates of deposit with promised large returns that turned out to be too good to be true. Numerous interviews with former Stanford employees and testimony provided in court documents indicate that over time, top managers surrounded themselves with a team of friends, family, and acquaintances who had little financial experience, but were as close-knit as the small Southern towns from which several of them came. The SEC said these ties created an environment that left "no independent oversight" over the assets of his bank. As many as 17 lawsuits that were brought by former investors for money lost in the alleged $8 billion Ponzi scheme were consolidated into a multidistrict litigation in Texas federal court. Stanford was indicted in June 2009 for his alleged role in defrauding thousands of investors through the sale of fraudulent certificates of deposit in his bank. He and some of his top corporate officers

are accused of lying to investors about the rates of return they could expect on their investments. As of February 2010, Stanford had pleaded not guilty and remained in custody in a Houston-area lockup, where various reports say he recently came out on the losing end of a prison brawl with a broken nose, black eyes, and other injuries.[52]

Evaluate the ethics of a person such as Bernie Madoff and Allen Stanford who develops a Ponzi scheme by using Kohlberg's stages of moral development ad with reference to the discussion about ethical behavior in Chapters 1 through 3.

19. Companies are sometimes faced with crisis management decisions. A good example is that of Ford with its Pinto brand that was discussed in the chapter. Compare Ford's reaction, from an ethical perspective, to the gas tank problem in Pinto vehicles to that of Toyota in January 2010, when the company admitted that faulty gas pedals in its cars and trucks may cause unexpected acceleration. What factors may be responsible for whether Toyota's image endures long-term versus short-term negative effects?

20. A report by *60 Minutes* in October 2009 claimed that the cost to the government from Medicare fraud is at least $60 billion each year. In the debates over health care reform in Congress during 2009 and 2010, one version of a bill called for the recovery of $500 billion from health care fraud as a way to finance reform. Review the cases described in Appendix 1 of Case 3-7. (Your instructor may ask you to look at only one or two cases.) Do you think it is reasonable to expect the U.S. government to recover half-a-trillion-dollars from Medicare fraud? Why or why not? If, in fact, there is $500 billion to recover, why wait for the health care reform act to identify that amount? Does it seem that the government acted with diligence in recovering this amount on a timely basis?

Endnotes

1. Securities and Exchange Commission, Litigation Release No. 17435, www.sec.gov/litigation/litreleases/complr17435.htm.

2. John C. Maxwell, *There's No Such Thing as "Business" Ethics* (New York: Warner Business Books, 2003).

3. Archie B. Carroll and Ann K. Buchholtz, *Business & Society: Ethics and Stakeholder Management* (Mason, OH: Cengage Learning, 2009).

4. Laura P. Hartman and Joe Desjardins, *Business Ethics: Decision-Making for Personal Integrity and Social Responsibility* (New York: McGraw-Hill Irwin, 2008).

5. *United States v. Carroll Towing,* 159 F.2d 169 (2d Cir. 1947).

6. Douglas Birsch and John H. Fiedler, *The Ford Pinto Case: A Study in Applied Ethics, Business, and Technology* (Albany: State University of New York, 1994).

7. *Grimshaw v. Ford Motor Co.,* 1 19 Cal.App.3d 757, 174 Cal. Rptr. 348 (1981).

8. O. C. Ferrell, John Fraedrich, and Linda Ferrell, *Business Ethics: Ethical Decision Making and Cases* (Boston: Houghton Mifflin, 2005).

9. Litigation support provides assistance to one or another party in a lawsuit. Forensic accountants provide litigation support on matters related to fraud where people have lost money as a result of a financial wrongdoing. Had you and your friend attended that session, you might have learned that the Association of Certified Fraud Examiners provides extensive education and training in this area and a person can study to become a certified fraud examiner.

10. Association of Certified Fraud Examiners, *2008 Report to the Nation on Occupational Fraud and Abuse* (Austin, TX: ACFE, 2008).

11. American Institute of CPAs, *AICPA Professional Standards. Volume 1 as of June 1, 2009, Statement on Auditing Standards (SAS) No. 99,* Consideration of Fraud in a Financial Statement Audit, AU Section 316.

12. *Auditors See Increase in Fraud,* www.webcpa.com/news/Auditors-See-Increase-in-Fraud-53221-1.html.

13. U.S. House of Representatives, H.R. 3763, Sarbanes-Oxley Act of 2002, www.findlaw.com.

14. Andrei Shleifer and Robert Vishny, "A Survey of Corporate Governance," *Journal of Finance* (1997).

15. J. E. Parkinson, *Corporate Power and Responsibility* (Oxford, England: Oxford University Press, 1994).

16. Marc Goergen, Miguel C. Manjonantolin, and Luc Renneboog, *Recent Developments in German Corporate Governance,* ECGI–Finance Working Paper Series No. 41/2002, Center Discussion Paper Series No. 2004-123.

17. R. I. Tricker, *Corporate Governance: Practices, Procedures and Powers in British Companies and Their Boards of Directors* (Aldershot, England: Gower Press, 1984).

18. Economist Intelligence Unit, "A Survey of Corporate Governance," *The Economist* (2001).

19. Economist Intelligence Unit, "Corporate Governance: Business under Scrutiny," *The Economist* (2003).

20. John E. Core, Robert W. Holthausen, and David F. Larcker, "Corporate Governance, Chief Executive Officer Compensation, and Firm Performance," *Journal of Financial Economics* (1999), pp. 371–406.

21. Michael Jensen and William H. Meckling, "Theory of the Firm: Managerial Behavior, Agency Costs, and Ownership Structure, *Journal of Financial Economics* (1976), pp. 305–360.

22. Venkat Venkatasuvramanian, *What Is Fair Pay for Executives? An Information Theoretic Analysis of Wage Distributions,* www.mdpi.com/1099-4300/11/4/766.

23. R. Edward Freeman, *Strategic Management: A Stakeholder Approach* (Boston: Pitman, 1984).

24. Oliver Hart, *Firms, Contracts, and Financial Structure* (Cambridge, England: Oxford University Press, 1995).

25. James R. Boatright, "Fiduciary Duties and the Shareholder-Management Relation: Or What's So Special about Shareholders?" *Business Ethics Quarterly* (1994), pp. 393–407.

26. Brett H. McDonnell, *Corporate Constituency Statutes and Corporate Governance,* Minnesota Public Law Research Paper No. 02–13, University of Minnesota Law School, October 2002.

27. Zabihollah Rezaee, *Corporate Governance and Ethics* (New York: Wiley, 2009).

28. SOX does not prohibit tax services for audit clients but requires approval of the audit committee before such services can be rendered.

29. Institute of Internal Auditors, "Tone at the Top," *The Audit Committee's "Top 10"* (December 2007), http://theiaa.org.

30. Rezaee, p. 130.

31. American Institute of CPAs, *AICPA Professional Standards. Volume 1 as of June 1, 2009, Statement on Auditing Standards (SAS) No. 55* (includes *SAS 78* and *SAS 94*), Consideration of Internal Control in a Financial Statement Audit, AU Section 319.06-.07.

32. AICPA, *SAS 78:* Consideration of Internal Control in a Financial Statement Audit. An amendment of *SAS 55.*

33. Committee of Sponsoring Organizations of the Treadway Commission, *Internal Control—Integrated Framework* (New York: AICPA, 1992).

34. National Commission on Fraudulent Financial Reporting (Treadway Commission Report), *Report of the National Commission on Fraudulent Financial Reporting,* October 1987.

35. Institute of Internal Auditors (IIA). *Code of Ethics,* http//theiia.org.

36. Milton Rokeach, *The Nature of Human Values* (New York: Free Press), 1973.

37. Reggie Van Lee, Lisa Fabish, and Nancy McGaw, "The Value of Corporate Values," *Strategy + Business* (Spring 2005), Booz Allen Hamilton Inc.

38. Release No. 33-8177 (January 23, 2003), www.sec.gov/rules/final/33-8177.htm. Separate provisions were adopted relating to investment companies.

39. The committee's report, dated June 6, 2002, is available through links at www.nyse.com.

40. Johnson & Johnson Credo, www.jnj.com/our_company/our_credo/.

41. Tamara Kaplan, "The Tylenol Crisis: How Effective Public Relations Saved Johnson & Johnson," Pennsylvania State University, www.personal.psu.edu/users/w/x/wxk/116/tylenol/crisis.html.

42. Ethics Resource Center (ERC), *National Business Ethics Survey: An Inside View of Private Sector Ethics,* 2007, www.ethics.org/files/u5/The_2007_National_Business_Ethics_Survey.pdf.

43. Ethics and Compliance Officer Association (ECOA), www.eoa.org.

44. U.S. House of Representatives, H.R. 3763, Sarbanes-Oxley Act of 2002, www.findlaw.com.

45. *Department of Defense Issues Final Whistleblower-Protection Rule Covering Contractor Employees,* November 24, 2009, www.kilpatrickstockton.com/publications/legal-alert.aspx?ID=400.

46. Greg Bluestein, *Ex-Lockheed Engineer Claims F-22 Tech "Defective,"* November 11, 2009, www.sfgate.com/cgibin/article.cgi?f=/n/a/2009/11/11/financial/f103556S38.DTL&type=printable.

47. The SEC Web site points out that a "Ponzi" scheme was named after Charles Ponzi, a crook who made his money by promising New England residents that he could provide 40 percent returns on their investment, compared to the 5 percent return they could receive from banks at the time. Ponzi believed he could take advantage of the difference between the U.S. and foreign currencies used in buying and selling international mail coupons. In reality he developed a pyramid scheme that used a "rob-Peter-to-pay-Paul" approach to make his money.

48. *Securities and Exchange Commission v. David G. Friehling, Friehling & Horowitz, CPA's, P.C.,* March 18, 2009, www.sec.gov/litigation/complaints/2009/comp20959.pdf.

49. SEC Web site, www.sec.gov/spotlight/secpostmadoffreforms.htm.

50. Arthur Levitt, "The 'Numbers Game,'" Remarks by Chairman Arthur Levitt, Securities and Exchange Commission, before the NYU Center for Law and Business," September 28, 1998, www.sec.gov.

51. The Delaware Court of Chancery is widely recognized as the preeminent forum in the United States for the determination of disputes involving the internal affairs of thousands of Delaware corporations and other business entities, especially matters of board of director responsibilities. The court has jurisdiction to hear all matters related to equity. Its decisions can be appealed to the Delaware Supreme Court.

52. *Stanford Ponzi Scheme Lawsuits Consolidated into Texas MDL,* www.attorneyatlaw.com/2009/10/stanford-ponzi-scheme-lawsuits-consolidated-into-texas-mdl/.

Appendix 1

Selected Sections from Johnson & Johnson's Conflict of Interest Policy

Every employee has a duty to avoid business, financial or other direct or indirect interests or relationships which conflict with the interests of the Company or which divides his or her loyalty to the Company. Any activity which even appears to present such a conflict must be avoided or terminated unless, after disclosure to the appropriate level or management, it is determined that the activity is not harmful to the Company or otherwise improper.

A conflict or the appearance of a conflict of interest may arise in many ways. For example, depending on the circumstances, the following may constitute an improper conflict of interest:

- Ownership of or an interest in a competitor or in a business with which the Company has or is contemplating a relationship (such as a supplier, customer, landlord, distributor, licensee/licensor, etc.) either directly or indirectly, such as through family members.
- Profiting, or assisting others to profit, from confidential information or business opportunities that are available because of employment by the Company.
- Soliciting or accepting gifts, payments, loans, services or any form of compensation from suppliers, customers, competitors or others seeking to do business with the Company.

- Influencing or attempting to influence any business transaction between the Company and another entity in which an employee has a direct or indirect financial interest or acts as a director, employee, partner, agent or consultant.
- Buying or selling securities of any other company using non-public information obtained in the performance of an employee's duties, or providing such information so obtained to others.

Disclosure is the key [when a conflict exists]. Any employee, who has a question about . . . a conflict of interest or the appearance of one, should disclose the pertinent details, preferably in writing, to his or her supervisor. Each supervisor is responsible for discussing the situation with the employee and arriving at a decision after consultation with or notice to the appropriate higher level of management. Each President, General Manager and Managing Director is responsible for advising his or her Company Group Chairman or International Vice President, as the case may be, in writing, of all disclosures and decisions made under this Policy. The Law Department should be consulted for advice as necessary.

To summarize, each employee is obligated to disclose her own conflict or any appearance of a conflict of interest. The end result of the process of disclosure, discussion and consultation may well be approval of certain relationships or transactions on the grounds that despite appearances those relationships are not harmful to the Company. But all conflicts and appearances of conflicts of interest are prohibited, even if they do not harm the Company, unless they have gone through this process.

Appendix 2

Letter from Steven A. Ballmer, Chief Executive Officer

Dear Fellow Employee:

Microsoft aspires to be a great company, and our success depends on you. It depends on people who innovate and are committed to growing our business responsibly. People who dedicate themselves to really satisfying customers, helping partners, and improving the communities in which we do business. People who are accountable for achieving big, bold goals with unwavering integrity. People who are leaders, who appreciate that to be truly great, we must continually strive to do better ourselves and help others improve.

We must expect the best from ourselves because who we are as a company and as individuals is as important as our ability to deliver the best products and services. How we manage our business internally—and how we think about

and work with customers, partners, governments, vendors and communities—impacts our productivity and success. It's not enough to just do the right things; we have to do them in the right way.

The Standards of Business Conduct are an extension of Microsoft's values and the foundation for our business tenets. They reflect our collective commitment to ethical business practices and regulatory compliance, and they provide information about Microsoft Business Conduct and Compliance Program. At a high level, they summarize, and are supported by, the principles and policies that govern our global businesses in several important areas: legal and regulatory compliance; trust and respect of consumers, partners, and shareholders; asset protection and stewardship; creation of a cooperative and productive work environment; and commitment to the global community.

These Standards of Business Conduct provide information, education, and resources to help you make good, informed business decisions and to act on them with integrity. In addition, managers should use this resource to foster, manage, and reward a culture of accountability and integrity within their groups. Working together, we can continuously enhance our culture in ways that benefit customers and partners, and that strengthen our interactions with one another. Then we can truly achieve our mission of enabling people and businesses throughout the world to realize their full potential.

All Microsoft employees are responsible for understanding and complying with the Standards of Business Conduct,

applicable government regulations, and Microsoft policies. As Microsoft employees, you also have a responsibility to raise compliance and ethics concerns through our established channels. This is the way to ensure that Microsoft is and continues to be a great company of great people.

Steven A. Ballmer
Chief Executive Officer

Appendix 3

Microsoft Finance Code of Professional Conduct

Microsoft Finance's mission includes promotion of professional conduct in the practice of financial management worldwide. Microsoft's Chief Executive Officer (CEO), Chief Financial Officer (CFO), Corporate Controller, and other employees of the finance organization hold an important and elevated role in corporate governance in that they are uniquely capable and empowered to ensure that all stakeholders' interests are appropriately balanced, protected, and preserved. This Finance Code of Professional Conduct embodies principles which we are expected to adhere to and advocate. These principles of ethical business conduct encompass rules regarding both individual and peer responsibilities, as well as responsibilities to Microsoft employees, the public, and other stakeholders. The CEO, CFO, and Finance organization employees are expected to abide by this Code as well as all applicable Microsoft business conduct standards and policies or guidelines in Microsoft's employee handbook relating to areas covered by the Code. Any violations of the Microsoft Finance Code of Professional Conduct may result in disciplinary action, up to and including termination of employment.

All employees covered by the Finance Code of Professional Conduct will

- Act with honesty and integrity, avoiding actual or apparent conflicts of interest in their personal and professional relationships.
- Provide stakeholders with information that is accurate, complete, objective, fair, relevant, timely, and understandable, including information in our filings with and other submissions to the U.S. Securities and Exchange Commission and other public bodies.
- Comply with rules and regulations of federal, state, provincial, and local governments, and of other appropriate private and public regulatory agencies.
- Act in good faith, responsibly, with due care, competence, and diligence, without misrepresenting material

facts or allowing one's independent judgment to be subordinated.
- Respect the confidentiality of information acquired in the course of one's work except when authorized or otherwise legally obligated to disclose.
- Not use confidential information acquired in the course of one's work for personal advantage.
- Share knowledge and maintain professional skills important and relevant to stakeholders' needs.
- Proactively promote and be an example of ethical behavior as a responsible partner among peers, in the work environment, and the community.
- Exercise responsible use, control, and stewardship over all Microsoft assets and resources that are employed by or entrusted to us.
- Not coerce, manipulate, mislead, or unduly influence any authorized audit or interfere with any auditor engaged in the performance of an internal or independent audit of Microsoft's system of internal controls, financial statements, or accounting books and records.

If you are aware of any suspected or known violations of this Code of Professional Conduct, the Standards of Business Conduct, or other Microsoft policies or guidelines, you have a duty to report such concerns promptly to one of the following:

- Your manager
- Another responsible member of management
- A Human Resources representative
- A Legal and Corporate Affairs (LCA) contact
- The Director of Compliance
- The 24-hour Business Conduct Line:

  Within the United States (toll-free number): (877) 320-MSFT (6738)

  International toll-free number: (1) (704) 540-0139

The procedures to be followed for such a report are outlined in the Standards of Business Conduct and the

Whistleblowing Reporting Procedure and Guidelines in the Employee Handbook.

If you have a concern about a questionable accounting or auditing matter, you can send a confidential e-mail message to the Microsoft Office of Legal Compliance. If you want to submit your concern anonymously, you may use one of the following methods:

- Submit a report through the Microsoft Integrity Web site
- Call the Business Conduct Line
- Send a letter to the Director of Compliance at the following address:
  Microsoft Corporation
  Legal and Corporate Affairs
  One Microsoft Way
  Redmond, WA 98052
  USA
- Send a confidential fax to the Director of Compliance at (1) (425) 705-2985.

Microsoft will handle all inquiries discreetly and make every effort to maintain, within the limits allowed by law, the confidentiality of anyone requesting guidance or reporting questionable behavior and/or a compliance concern. It is Microsoft's intention that this Code of Professional Conduct be its written code of ethics under Section 406 of the Sarbanes-Oxley Act of 2002 complying with the standards set forth in Securities and Exchange Commission Regulation S-K Item 406.

Chapter 3 Cases

Case 3-1

The Parable of the Sadhu

Bowen H. McCoy
(Reproduced with the permission of the Harvard Business Review)

Last year, as the first participant in the new six-month sabbatical program that Morgan Stanley has adopted, I enjoyed a rare opportunity to collect my thoughts as well as do some traveling. I spent the first three months in Nepal, walking 600 miles through 200 villages in the Himalayas and climbing some 120,000 vertical feet. My sole Western companion on the trip was an anthropologist who shed light on the cultural patterns of the villages that we passed through.

During the Nepal hike, something occurred that has had a powerful impact on my thinking about corporate ethics. Although some might argue that the experience has no relevance to business, it was a situation in which a basic ethical dilemma suddenly intruded into the lives of a group of individuals. How the group responded holds a lesson for all organizations, no matter how defined.

The Sadhu

The Nepal experience was more rugged than I had anticipated. Most commercial treks last two or three weeks and cover a quarter of the distance we traveled.

My friend Stephen, the anthropologist, and I were halfway through the 60-day Himalayan part of the trip when we reached the high point, an 18,000-foot pass over a crest that we'd have to traverse to reach the village of Muklinath, an ancient holy place for pilgrims.

Six years earlier, I had suffered pulmonary edema, an acute form of altitude sickness, at 16,500 feet in the vicinity of Everest base camp—so we were understandably concerned about what would happen at 18,000 feet. Moreover, the Himalayas were having their wettest spring in 20 years; hip-deep powder and ice had already driven us off one ridge. If we failed to cross the pass, I feared that the last half of our once-in-a-lifetime trip would be ruined.

The night before we would try the pass, we camped in a hut at 14,500 feet. In the photos taken at that camp, my face appears wan. The last village we'd passed through was a sturdy two-day walk below us, and I was tired.

During the late afternoon, four backpackers from New Zealand joined us, and we spent most of the night awake, anticipating the climb. Below, we could see the fires of two other parties, which turned out to be two Swiss couples and a Japanese hiking club.

To get over the steep part of the climb before the sun melted the steps cut in the ice, we departed at 3.30 a.m. The New Zealanders left first, followed by Stephen and myself, our porters and Sherpas, and then the Swiss. The Japanese lingered in their camp. The sky was clear, and we were confident that no spring storm would erupt that day to close the pass.

At 15,500 feet, it looked to me as if Stephen were shuffling and staggering a bit, which are symptoms of altitude sickness. (The initial stage of altitude sickness brings a headache and nausea. As the condition worsens, a climber may encounter difficult breathing, disorientation, aphasia, and paralysis.) I felt strong—my adrenaline was flowing—but I was very concerned about my ultimate ability to get across. A couple of our porters were also suffering from the height, and Pasang, our Sherpa sirdar (leader), was worried.

Just after daybreak, while we rested at 15,500 feet, one of the New Zealanders, who had gone ahead, came staggering down toward us with a body slung across his shoulders. He dumped the almost naked, barefoot body of an Indian holy man—a sadhu—at my feet. He had found the pilgrim lying on the ice, shivering and suffering from hypothermia. I cradled the sadhu's head and laid him out on the rocks. The New Zealander was angry. He wanted to get across the pass before the bright sun melted the snow. He said, "Look, I've done what I can. You have porters and Sherpa guides. You care for him. We're going on!" He turned and went back up the mountain to join his friends.

I took a carotid pulse and found that the sadhu was still alive. We figured he had probably visited the holy shrines at Muklinath and was on his way home. It was fruitless to question why he had chosen this desperately high route instead of the safe, heavily traveled caravan route through the Kali Gandaki gorge. Or why he was shoeless and almost naked, or how long he had been lying in the pass. The answers weren't going to solve our problem.

Stephen and the four Swiss began stripping off their outer clothing and opening their packs. The sadhu was soon clothed from head to foot. He was not able to walk, but he was very much alive. I looked down the mountain and spotted the Japanese climbers, marching up with a horse.

Without a great deal of thought, I told Stephen and Pasang that I was concerned about withstanding the heights to come and wanted to get over the pass. I took off after several of our porters who had gone ahead.

On the steep part of the ascent where, if the ice steps had given way, I would have slid down about 3,000 feet, I felt vertigo. I stopped for a breather, allowing the Swiss to catch up with me. I inquired about the sadhu and Stephen. They said that the sadhu was fine and that Stephen was just behind them. I set off again for the summit.

Stephen arrived at the summit an hour after I did. Still exhilarated by victory, I ran down the slope to congratulate him. He was suffering from altitude sickness—walking 15 steps, then stopping, walking 15 steps, then stopping. Pasang accompanied him all the way up. When I reached them, Stephen glared at me and said: "How do you feel about contributing to the death of a fellow man?"

I did not completely comprehend what he meant. "Is the sadhu dead?" I inquired.

"No," replied Stephen, "but he surely will be!"

After I had gone, followed not long after by the Swiss, Stephen had remained with the sadhu. When the Japanese had arrived, Stephen had asked to use their horse to transport the sadhu down to the hut. They had refused. He had then asked Pasang to have a group of our porters carry the sadhu. Pasang had resisted the idea, saying that the porters would have to exert all their energy to get themselves over the pass. He believed they could not carry a man down 1,000 feet to the hut, reclimb the slope, and get across safely before the snow melted. Pasang had pressed Stephen not to delay any longer.

The Sherpas had carried the sadhu down to a rock in the sun at about 15,000 feet and pointed out the hut another 500 feet below. The Japanese had given him food and drink. When they had last seen him, he was listlessly throwing rocks at the Japanese party's dog, which had frightened him.

We do not know if the sadhu lived or died.

For many of the following days and evenings, Stephen and I discussed and debated our behavior toward the sadhu. Stephen is a committed Quaker with deep moral vision. He said, "I feel that what happened with the sadhu is a good example of the breakdown between the individual ethic and the corporate ethic. No one person was willing to assume ultimate responsibility for the sadhu. Each was willing to do his bit just so long as it was not too inconvenient. When it got to be a bother, everyone just passed the buck to someone else and took off. Jesus was relevant to a more individualistic stage of society, but how do we interpret his teaching today in a world filled with large, impersonal organizations and groups?"

I defended the larger group, saying, "Look, we all cared. We all gave aid and comfort. Everyone did his bit. The New Zealander carried him down below the snow line. I took his pulse and suggested we treat him for hypothermia. You and the Swiss gave him clothing and got him warmed up. The Japanese gave him food and water. The Sherpas carried him down to the sun and pointed out the easy trail toward the hut. He was well enough to throw rocks at a dog. What more could we do?"

"You have just described the typical affluent Westerner's response to a problem. Throwing money–in this case, food and sweaters–at it, but not solving the fundamentals!" Stephen retorted.

"What would satisfy you?" I said. "Here we are, a group of New Zealanders, Swiss, Americans, and Japanese who have never met before and who are at the apex of one of the most powerful experiences of our lives. Some years the pass is so bad no one gets over it. What right does an almost naked pilgrim who chooses the wrong trail have to disrupt our lives? Even the Sherpas had no interest in risking the trip to help him beyond a certain point."

Stephen calmly rebutted, "I wonder what the Sherpas would have done if the sadhu had been a well-dressed Nepali, or what the Japanese would have done if the sadhu had been a well-dressed Asian, or what you would have done, Buzz, if the sadhu had been a well-dressed Western woman?"

"Where, in your opinion," I asked, "is the limit of our responsibility in a situation like this? We had our own well-being to worry about. Our Sherpa guides were unwilling to jeopardize us or the porters for the sadhu. No one else on the mountain was willing to commit himself beyond certain self-imposed limits."

Stephen said, "As individual Christians or people with a Western ethical tradition, we can fulfill our obligations in such a situation only if one, the sadhu dies in our care; two, the sadhu demonstrates to us that he can undertake the two-day walk down to the village; or three, we carry the sadhu for two days down to the village and persuade someone there to care for him."

"Leaving the sadhu in the sun with food and clothing–where he demonstrated hand-eye coordination by throwing a rock at a dog–comes close to fulfilling items one and two," I answered. "And it wouldn't have made sense to take him to the village where the people appeared to be far less caring than the Sherpas, so the third condition is impractical. Are you really saying that, no matter what the implications, we should, at the drop of a hat, have changed our entire plan?"

The Individual versus the Group Ethic

Despite my arguments, I felt and continue to feel guilt about the sadhu. I had literally walked through a classic moral dilemma without fully thinking through the consequences. My excuses for my actions include a high adrenaline flow, a superordinate goal, and a once-in-a-lifetime opportunity–common factors in corporate situations, especially stressful ones.

Real moral dilemmas are ambiguous, and many of us hike right through them, unaware that they exist. When, usually after the fact, someone makes an issue of one, we tend to resent his or her bringing it up. Often, when the full import of what we have done (or not done) hits us, we dig into a defensive position from which it is very difficult to emerge. In rare circumstances, we may contemplate what we have done from inside a prison.

Had we mountaineers been free of stress caused by the effort and the high altitude, we might have treated the sadhu differently. Yet isn't stress the real test of personal and corporate values? The instant decisions that executives make under pressure reveal the most about personal and corporate character.

Among the many questions that occur to me when I ponder my experience with the sadhu are: What are the practical limits of moral imagination and vision? Is there a collective or institutional ethic that differs from the ethics of the individual? At what level of effort or commitment can one discharge one's ethical responsibilities?

Not every ethical dilemma has a right solution. Reasonable people often disagree; otherwise there would be no dilemma.

In a business context, however, it is essential that managers agree on a process for dealing with dilemmas.

Our experience with the sadhu offers an interesting parallel to business situations. An immediate response was mandatory. Failure to act was a decision in itself. Up on the mountain we could not resign and submit our résumés to a head-hunter. In contrast to philosophy, business involves action and implementation–getting things done. Managers must come up with answers based on what they see and what they allow to influence their decision-making processes. On the mountain, none of us but Stephen realized the true dimensions of the situation we were facing.

One of our problems was that as a group we had no process for developing a consensus. We had no sense of purpose or plan. The difficulties of dealing with the sadhu were so complex that no one person could handle them. Because the group did not have a set of preconditions that could guide its action to an acceptable resolution, we reacted instinctively as individuals. The cross-cultural nature of the group added a further layer of complexity. We had no leader with whom we could all identify and in whose purpose we believed. Only Stephen was willing to take charge, but he could not gain adequate support from the group to care for the sadhu.

Some organizations do have values that transcend the personal values of their managers. Such values, which go beyond profitability, are usually revealed when the organization is under stress. People throughout the organization generally accept its values, which, because they are not presented as a rigid list of commandments, may be somewhat ambiguous. The stories people tell, rather than printed materials, transmit the organization's conceptions of what is proper behavior.

For 20 years, I have been exposed at senior levels to a variety of corporations and organizations. It is amazing how quickly an outsider can sense the tone and style of an organization and, with that, the degree of tolerated openness and freedom to challenge management.

Organizations that do not have a heritage of mutually accepted, shared values tend to become unhinged during stress, with each individual bailing out for himself or herself. In the great takeover battles we have witnessed during past years, companies that had strong cultures drew the wagons around them and fought it out, while other companies saw executives–supported by golden parachutes–bail out of the struggles.

Because corporations and their members are interdependent, for the corporation to be strong the members need to share a preconceived notion of correct behavior, a "business ethic," and think of it as a positive force, not a constraint.

As an investment banker, I am continually warned by well-meaning lawyers, clients, and associates to be wary of conflicts of interest. Yet if I were to run away from every difficult situation, I wouldn't be an effective investment banker. I have to feel my way through conflicts. An effective manager can't run from risk either; he or she has to confront risk. To feel "safe" in doing that, managers need the guidelines of an agreed-upon process and set of values within the organization.

After my three months in Nepal, I spent three months as an executive-in-residence at both the Stanford Business School and the University of California at Berkeley's Center for Ethics and Social Policy of the Graduate Theological Union. Those six months away from my job gave me time to assimilate 20 years of business experience. My thoughts turned often to the meaning of the leadership role in any large organization. Students at the seminary thought of themselves as antibusiness. But when I questioned them, they agreed that they distrusted all large organizations, including the church. They perceived all large organizations as impersonal and opposed to individual values and needs. Yet we all know of organizations in which people's values and beliefs are respected and their expressions encouraged. What makes the difference? Can we identify the difference and, as a result, manage more effectively?

The word *ethics* turns off many and confuses more. Yet the notions of shared values and an agreed-upon process for dealing with adversity and change–what many people mean when they talk about corporate culture–seem to be at the heart of the ethical issue. People who are in touch with their own core beliefs and the beliefs of others and who are sustained by them can be more comfortable living on the cutting edge. At times, taking a tough line or a decisive stand in a muddle of ambiguity is the only ethical thing to do. If a manager is indecisive about a problem and spends time trying to figure out the "good" thing to do, the enterprise may be lost.

Business ethics, then, has to do with the authenticity and integrity of the enterprise. To be ethical is to follow the business as well as the cultural goals of the corporation, its owners, its employees, and its customers. Those who cannot serve the corporate vision are not authentic businesspeople and, therefore, are not ethical in the business sense.

At this stage of my own business experience, I have a strong interest in organizational behavior. Sociologists are keenly studying what they call corporate stories, legends, and heroes as a way organizations have of transmitting value systems. Corporations such as Arco have even hired consultants to perform an audit of their corporate culture. In a company, a leader is a person who understands, interprets, and manages the corporate value system. Effective managers, therefore, are action-oriented people who resolve conflict, are tolerant of ambiguity, stress, and change, and have a strong sense of purpose for themselves and their organizations.

If all this is true, I wonder about the role of the professional manager who moves from company to company. How can he or she quickly absorb the values and culture of different organizations? Or is there, indeed, an art of management that is totally transportable? Assuming that such fungible managers do exist, is it proper for them to manipulate the values of others?

What would have happened had Stephen and I carried the sadhu for two days back to the village and become involved with the villagers in his care? In four trips to Nepal, my most interesting experience occurred in 1975 when I lived in a Sherpa home in the Khumbu for five days while recovering from altitude sickness. The high point of Stephen's trip was an invitation to participate in a family funeral ceremony in Manang. Neither experience had to do with climbing the high passes of the Himalayas. Why were we so reluctant to try the lower path, the ambiguous trail? Perhaps because we did not have a leader who could reveal the greater purpose of the trip to us.

Why didn't Stephen, with his moral vision, opt to take the sadhu under his personal care? The answer is partly because Stephen was hard-stressed physically himself and partly because, without some support system that encompassed our involuntary and episodic community on the mountain, it was beyond his individual capacity to do so.

I see the current interest in corporate culture and corporate value systems as a positive response to pessimism such as Stephen's about the decline of the role of the individual in large organizations. Individuals who operate from a thoughtful set of personal values provide the foundation for a corporate culture. A corporate tradition that encourages freedom of inquiry, supports personal values, and reinforces a focused sense of direction can fulfill the need to combine individuality with the prosperity and success of the group. Without such corporate support, the individual is lost.

That is the lesson of the sadhu. In a complex corporate situation, the individual requires and deserves the support of the group. When people cannot find such support in their organizations, they don't know how to act. If such support is forthcoming, a person has a stake in the success of the group and can add much to the process of establishing and maintaining a corporate culture. Management's challenge is to be sensitive to individual needs, to shape them, and to direct and focus them for the benefit of the group as a whole.

For each of us the sadhu lives. Should we stop what we are doing and comfort him; or should we keep trudging up toward the high pass? Should I pause to help the derelict I pass on the street each night as I walk by the Yale Club en route to Grand Central Station? Am I his brother? What is the nature of our responsibility if we consider ourselves to be ethical persons? Perhaps it is to change the values of the group so that it can, with all its resources, take the other road.

Questions

Consider corporate values and ethics as discussed in Chapter 3 and the ethical reasoning methods discussed in Chapters 1 and 2 in answering the following questions:

1. Bowen H. McCoy's friend Stephen is quoted as saying, "I feel that what happened with the sadhu is a good example of the breakdown between the individual and corporate ethic." Explain what you think Stephen meant by this statement. What is the nature of that breakdown between the individual and corporate ethic as you see it?

2. In reflecting on his discussion with Stephen about the sadhu McCoy says, "The instant decisions that executives make under pressure reveal the most about personal and corporate character." Do you think on-the-spot decisions better reflect the character of the decision maker and organization rather than those that might be more thoroughly thought through? Why or why not?

3. McCoy equates the parameters of the decision-making process about the sadhu with that in business. He believes there is an interesting parallel to business situations. Explain what you think McCoy meant by this statement. Do you agree with him?

4. McCoy concludes that the lesson of the sadhu is that "in a complex corporate situation, the individual requires and deserves the support of the group. When people cannot find such support in their organizations, they don't know how to act." What support in organizations do you think McCoy is referring to? If such support is not found, what should individuals do when they have an ethical dilemma such as that in the sadhu case?

5. What is the moral of the story of the sadhu from your perspective?

Case 3-2

Amgen Whistleblowing Case

Amgen, a Thousand Oaks, California–based company, had the unenviable task of dealing with lawsuits filed by 15 states in 2009 alleging a Medicaid kickback scheme.[1] To make matters worse, two additional whistleblowing lawsuits were filed against the company in Ventura County. The complaints, which don't appear related to the fraud alleged by the group of states, were brought by former employees who said they had uncovered wrongdoing at the biotech giant and were terminated after they raised red flags to superiors. One employee alleged the company violated federal law by under-reporting complaints and problems with the company's drugs after they hit the market. The facts of that lawsuit are described below.

Former Amgen employee Shawn O'Brien sued Amgen for wrongful termination on October 9, 2009, alleging he was laid off in October 2007 in retaliation for raising concerns about how the company reported complaints and problems with drugs already on the market. O'Brien worked as a senior project manager for Amgen's "Ongoing Change Program," according to the lawsuit filed in Ventura County Superior Court. His job was to improve Amgen's "compliance processes with high inherent risk to public safety, major criminal and civil liability, or both," according to the lawsuit.

The lawsuit alleged that in April 2007, Amgen's board of directors flagged the company's process for dealing with post-market complaints about drugs as a potential problem. Federal law requires drug companies to track and report to the Food and Drug Administration any problems with their drugs after they hit the market. In June 2007, O'Brien was put on the case. He soon uncovered facts that Amgen was not adequately and consistently identifying phone calls or mail related to post-marketing adverse events of product complaints. That year, O'Brien warned the company about the

[1]www.oag.state.ny.us.

seriousness of the issues but, he claims, the company would not take any action or offer any support. In August 2007, O'Brien took his complaint to a senior executive/corporate officer (unnamed) and warned that Amgen's process for dealing with post-market problems wasn't adequate.

In early September of 2007, O'Brien's managers instructed him to stop all work and not discuss the issues any further with anyone. Approximately four weeks later he was informed that he was being terminated as part of Amgen's October 12, 2007, reduction in the work force.

To help you answer the following questions, refer to the Amgen Web site on corporate compliance at: www.amgen.com/corporate compliance.html.

Questions

1. Amgen's Code of Ethics emphasizes "Doing the Right Thing." The code suggests that employees should resolve ethical dilemmas by considering the legality of proposed actions, compliance with company policies, Amgen's values, and an analysis of ethical issues including rights and respect. Identify the areas where the allegations by Shawn O'Brien and the alleged retaliation seem to contradict the principles and practices embodied in the code.

2. Explain what is meant by whistleblowing? Include in your discussion the difference between internal and external whistleblowing. Given the facts of the case, do you think O'Brien took the right steps to report his concerns about Amgen's process for dealing with post-market complaints about drugs as a potential problem? Are there any other steps he might have taken?

3. Evaluate O'Brien's actions from an ethical perspective. That is, what motivated him to act as he did? Consider in your response how O'Brien's actions fit in to Kohlberg's model of moral development.

Case 3-3

United Thermostatic Controls

United Thermostatic Controls is a publicly owned company that engages in the manufacturing and marketing of residential and commercial thermostats. The thermostats are used to regulate temperature in furnaces and refrigerators. United sells its product primarily to retailers in the domestic market, with the company headquartered in San Jose, California. Its operations are decentralized according to geographic region. As a publicly owned company, United's common stock is listed and traded on the New York Stock Exchange. The organization chart for United is presented in Figure 1.

Frank Campbell is the director of the Southern sales division. Worsening regional economic conditions and a reduced

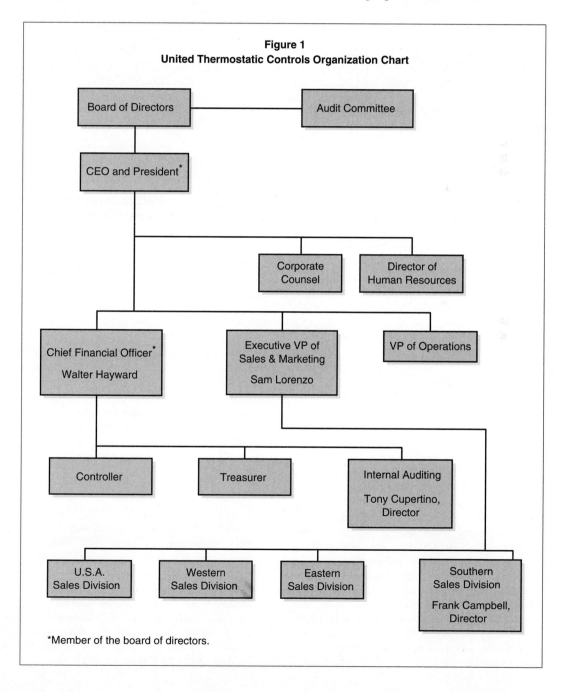

Figure 1
United Thermostatic Controls Organization Chart

*Member of the board of directors.

Exhibit 1
United Thermostatic Controls

Budgeted and Actual Sales Revenue
First Three Quarters in 2010

	U.S.A. Sales Division			Western Sales Division		
Quarter Ended	Budget	Actual	% Var.	Budget	Actual	% Var.
March 31	$ 632,000	$ 638,000	.009%	$ 886,000	$ 898,000	.014%
June 30	640,000	642,000	.003	908,000	918,000	.011
September 30	648,000	656,000	.012	930,000	936,000	.006
Through September 30	$1,920,000	$1,936,000	.008%	$2,724,000	$2,752,000	.010%

	Eastern Sales Division			Southern Sales Division		
Quarter Ended	Budget	Actual	% Var.	Budget	Actual	% Var.
March 31	$ 743,000	$ 750,000	.009%	$ 688,000	$ 680,000	(.012)%
June 30	752,000	760,000	.011	696,000	674,000	(.032)
September 30	761,000	769,000	.011	704,000	668,000	(.051)
Through September 30	$2,256,000	$2,279,000	.010%	$2,088,000	$2,022,000	(.032)%

rate of demand for United's products together have created pressures to nonetheless achieve sales revenue targets set by United management. Also, significant pressures exist within the organization for sales divisions to maximize their revenues and earnings for 2010 in anticipation of a public offering of stock early in 2011. Budgeted and actual sales revenue amounts, by division, for the first three quarters in 2010 are presented in Exhibit 1.

Campbell knows that actual sales lagged even further behind budgeted sales during the first two months of the fourth quarter. He also knows that each of the other three sales divisions exceeded their budgeted sales amounts during the first three quarters in 2010. He is very concerned that the Southern division has been unable to meet or exceed budgeted sales amounts. He is particularly worried about the effect this might have on his and the division managers' bonuses and share of corporate profits.

In an attempt to improve the sales revenue of the Southern division for the fourth quarter and for the year ended December 31, 2010, Campbell reviewed purchase orders received during the latter half of November and early December to determine whether shipments could be made to customers prior to December 31. Campbell knows that sometimes orders that are received before year-end can be filled by December 31, thereby enabling the division to record the sales revenue during the current fiscal year. It could simply be a matter of accelerating production and shipping to increase sales revenue for the year.

Reported sales revenue of the Southern division for the fourth quarter of 2010 was $792,000. This represented an 18.6 percent increase over the actual sales revenue for the third quarter of the year. As a result of this increase, reported sales revenue for the fourth quarter exceeded the budgeted amount by $80,000, or 11.2 percent. Actual sales revenue for the year exceeded the budgeted amount for the Southern division by $14,000, or .5 percent. Budgeted and actual sales revenue amounts, by division, for the year ended December 31, 2010, are presented in Exhibit 2.

During the course of their test of controls, the internal audit staff questioned the appropriateness of recording revenue of $150,000 on two shipments made by the Southern division in the fourth quarter of the year. These shipments are described as follows:

1. United shipped thermostats to Allen Corporation on December 31, 2010, and billed Allen $85,000, even though Allen had specified an earliest delivery date of February 1, 2011, to take control of the product. Allen intended to use the thermostats in the heating system of a new building that would not be ready for occupancy until March 1, 2011.

2. United shipped thermostats to Bilco Corporation on December 30, 2010, in partial (one-half) fulfillment of an order. United recorded $65,000 revenue on that date. Bilco had previously specified that partial shipments would not be accepted. Delivery of the full shipment had been scheduled for February 1, 2011.

Exhibit 2
United Thermostatic Controls

Budgeted and Actual Sales Revenue
for the Year Ended December 31, 2010

Quarter Ended	U.S.A. Sales Division			Western Sales Division		
	Budget	Actual	% Var.	Budget	Actual	% Var.
March 31	$ 632,000	$ 638,000	.009%	$ 886,000	$ 898,000	.014%
June 30	640,000	642,000	.003	908,000	918,000	.011
September 30	648,000	656,000	.012	930,000	936,000	.006
December 31	656,000	662,000	.009	952,000	958,000	.006
2010 Totals	$2,576,000	$2,598,000	.009%	$3,676,000	$3,710,000	.009 %

Quarter Ended	Eastern Sales Division			Southern Sales Division		
	Budget	Actual	% Var.	Budget	Actual	% Var.
March 31	$ 743,000	$ 750,000	.009%	$ 688,000	$ 680,000	(.012)%
June 30	752,000	760,000	.011	696,000	674,000	(.032)
September 30	761,000	769,000	.011	704,000	668,000	(.051)
December 31	770,000	778,000	.010	712,000	792,000	.112
2010 Totals	$3,026,000	$3,057,000	.010%	$2,800,000	$2,814,000	.005%

During their investigation, the internal auditors learned that Campbell had placed pressure on United's accounting department to record these two shipments early to enable the Southern division to achieve its goals with respect to the company's revenue targets. The auditors were concerned about the appropriateness of recording the $150,000 revenue in 2010 in the absence of an expressed or implied agreement with the customers to accept and pay for the prematurely shipped merchandise. The auditors noted that, had the revenue from these two shipments not been recorded, the Southern division's actual sales for the fourth quarter would have been below the budgeted amount by $70,000, or 9.8 percent. Actual sales revenue for the year ended December 31, 2010, would have been below the budgeted amount by $136,000, or 4.9 percent. The revenue effect of the two shipments in question created a 5.4 percent shift in the variance between actual and budgeted sales for the year. The auditors felt that this effect was significant with respect to the division's revenue and earnings for the fourth quarter and for the year ended December 31, 2010. The auditors decided to take their concerns to Tony Cupertino, director of the internal auditing department. Cupertino is a licensed CPA and holds the certified internal auditor (CIA) designation.

Cupertino discussed the situation with Campbell. Campbell informed Cupertino that he had received assurances from Sam Lorenzo, executive vice president of sales and marketing, that top management would support the recording of the $150,000 revenue because of its strong desire to meet or exceed budgeted revenue and earnings amounts. Moreover, top management is very sensitive to the need to meet financial analysts' consensus earnings estimates. The company, according to Campbell, is concerned that earnings must be high enough to meet analysts' expectations because any other effect might cause the stock price to go down. In fact, Lorenzo has already told Campbell that he did not see anything wrong with recording the revenue in 2010, since the merchandise had been shipped to the customers before year-end and the terms of shipment were FOB shipping point.

At this point, Cupertino is uncertain whether he should take his concerns to Walter Hayward, the chief financial officer, who is also a member of the board of directors, or take them directly to the audit committee. Cupertino knows that the majority of the members of the board, including those on the audit committee, have ties to the company and members of top management. Cupertino is not even certain that he should pursue the matter any further because of the financial performance pressures that exist within the organization. However, he is very concerned about his responsibilities and obligations to coordinate the work of the internal auditing department with that of the external auditors.

Questions

1. Describe the ethical responsibilities of Tony Cupertino as a CPA and CIA.

2. Explain how a strong corporate governance system should work to enhance the accuracy and reliability of the December 31, 2010, financial statements. Does the corporate governance system at United appear to comply with
   a. Provisions of the Sarbanes-Oxley Act? Explain.
   b. NYSE corporate governance guidelines? Explain.

3. Assume Tony Cupertino decides to delay contacting Walter Hayward and, instead, Cupertino contacts the CFO of Bilco Corporation and offers a 20 percent discount on the total $130,000 cost of merchandise if Bilco agrees to approve the partial shipment on December 30, 2010. Cupertino adds that the $26,000 would be deducted from the remaining $65,000 to be shipped during January 2011. Evaluate Cupertino's actions with respect to the following:
   a. Is the offer ethical or unethical? Why?
   b. Has Cupertino violated any of his reporting responsibilities in directly contacting the CFO of Bilco?

Case 3-4

SEC v. Jeanne M. Rowzee et al.: A Ponzi Scheme

On September 15, 2008, the SEC charged an Irvine, California, attorney and two other promoters with conducting a $52.7 million Ponzi scheme in which they sold investors bogus investments, promised unrealistic profits, and misappropriated more than $20 million of investors' funds that were used as their own personal piggy bank. The SEC's complaint alleges that attorney Jeanne M. Rowzee along with James R. Halstead of Santa Ana, California, and Robert T. Harvey of Prosper, Texas, told investors that Rowzee was an experienced securities attorney who personally screened and selected each investment after thorough due diligence. Halstead and Harvey instead used new investor funds to pay principal and returns to earlier investors, and to finance their own personal endeavors such as trips to Las Vegas, property purchases, and alimony payments. Basically, the three of them raised millions of dollars from unsuspecting investors and simply used the funds to enrich themselves.[1]

The defendants allegedly solicited business clients and acquaintances and generated word-of-mouth referrals. The SEC's complaint alleges that from at least March 2004 through December 2006, the defendants sold the purported investments to investors, promising returns of 19 to 54 percent within 12 to 16 weeks. The defendants were charged with securities fraud under Section 17(a) of the Securities Act of 1933 and Section 10(b) of the Securities Exchange Act of 1934 and Rule 10b-5 thereunder, and with

conducting an unregistered offering under Section 5 of the Securities Act. Rowzee and Harvey were also charged with investment adviser fraud under Sections 206(1) and 206(2) of the Advisers Act of 1940, and Halstead was charged with aiding and abetting violations of both sections. The commission's complaint seeks permanent injunctions, disgorgement of ill-gotten gains, and civil penalties against each defendant.

In March of 2009, Rowzee submitted an Offer of Settlement that was accepted by the SEC. Rowzee admitted to the SEC's findings. She was suspended from appearing or practicing before the commission as an attorney and was barred from any association with any investment adviser.[2]

Questions

1. The case states that the defendants told investors that Rowzee was an experienced securities attorney who personally screened and selected each investment after thorough due diligence. Describe the fiduciary obligations of an investment adviser to her client as you see it. Are there any similarities with the responsibilities of members of a board of directors?

2. What are the parallels in this case to that of Bernie Madoff?

3. From an ethical perspective, to what extent should we hold investors responsible for investing their money in schemes that they could have (should have) investigated before committing funds?

[1]Litigation Release No. 20719, *SEC v. Jeanne M. Rowzee, James R. Halstead, and Robert T. Harvey,* www.sec.gov/litigation/litreleases/2008/lr20719.htm.

[2]Administrative Proceeding File No. 3-13413.

Case 3-5

SEC v. Nanette Miller

In March of 2000 the SEC brought an action against Nanette Miller, a CPA in Maryland, charging her with violating professional standards. Miller submitted an Offer of Settlement to the SEC that was accepted. The facts of the case follow.[1]

Miller was a partner in Chadbourne & Miller, then a public accounting firm with offices located in Washington, DC. The firm was the outside auditor for Underwriters Financial Group, Inc. (UFG), formerly a public company engaged in the insurance brokerage business with principal offices in New York City. At the time of the transactions and events underlying the SEC's filing, UFG's common stock was registered with the commission pursuant to Section 12(b) of the Securities Act of 1933 and traded on the American Stock Exchange.[2]

In May 1995, UFG filed its annual report on Form 10-K for the year ended December 31, 1994. In financial statements that were contained in the 1994 10-K report, UFG reported pretax net income of $521,192, which was overstated by approximately $5,687,000. This overstatement was attributable to UFG's falsification of the books and records from which the financial statements were prepared and other fraudulent conduct described as follows.

During its year ended December 31, 1994, UFG misappropriated several million dollars from premium finance companies and other parties with whom UFG transacted insurance business. UFG used the misappropriated funds to pay UFG's operating expenses and for other purposes. UFG failed to record the liability arising from the misappropriation of funds and, instead, recorded a portion of the misappropriated funds as income to UFG. During the 1994 year, UFG also improperly purged certain accounts payable from its books and records and simultaneously recognized those purged amounts as income.

Chadbourne & Miller audited the financial statements that were contained in UFG's 1994 Form 10-K and issued an audit report that was included in the 10-K report. Miller participated in the fieldwork done in connection with the audit and signed the firm's name to the audit report. The report contained an opinion in which it represented that it conducted an audit in accordance with generally accepted auditing standards and that UFG's financial statements, presented fairly, in all material respects, UFG's financial position and results of operations in conformity with generally accepted accounting principles. Both of those representations were inaccurate.

Miller and another accountant requested that UFG management provide to the firm specific documentary evidence supporting a sampling of a material amount of commission

income recorded by UFG. Management represented to Miller that the requested documentation was unavailable and agreed to write off the unsupported commission income. Miller failed to question why the supporting documents were unavailable and why UFG agreed to a material write-off of purportedly bona fide income. She also did not conduct further procedures to determine whether there was other income that lacked sufficient competent evidential support.

Miller failed to maintain an independent mental attitude with respect to the UFG audit. Before fieldwork was complete, Miller and another accountant from Chadbourne & Miller advised counsel for UFG that they had concerns about possible illegal conduct at UFG and that the firm was considering the possibility of withdrawing from the audit. In response, counsel raised the possibility of litigation against the firm if it withdrew from the audit. As a result of this threat, Miller requested UFG to agree to hold Chadbourne & Miller harmless in the event of a withdrawal. The threat adversely affected Miller's independence and objectivity. Nevertheless, the firm completed the audit and, through Miller, issued an unqualified audit report. The financial statements that were contained in UFG's 1994 Form 10-K did not present fairly, in all material respects, UFG's financial position and results of operations for the year ended 1994 in conformity with GAAP.

According to the SEC's findings in this case, Miller failed to obtain sufficient competent evidential matter to determine whether UFG's financial statements accurately recorded, in all material respects, UFG's actual income and accounts payable. Miller relied extensively on information provided by UFG, often in the form of oral representations of management, and failed to obtain sufficient documentary and other evidence from independent sources to verify management's representations.

Questions

1. Did Miller conduct the audit with the degree of professional skepticism expected with respect to its audit procedures and judgments? Why or why not?

2. Due to the concerns of the auditors, Miller requested UFG to agree to hold Chadbourne & Miller harmless in the event of a withdrawal. Do a Google search of indemnification clauses in audit engagement letters. One such source is as follows: http://www.cpai.com/risk-management/professional-liability/letter-clauses.jsp. Explain what is meant by an indemnification clause ("hold harmless" clause) in an engagement letter. Evaluate the ethics of including such a clause using the ethical reasoning discussions in Chapters 1 and 2. In particular, how might the inclusion of such a clause influence the ability of the auditor to meet the standards of conduct in the AICPA Code of Professional Conduct?

3. The case is silent about corporate governance. What elements of good governance should have been in effect and how might they have helped prevent and detect the misappropriation of assets?

[1]Administrative Proceeding File No. 3-10167, *In the Matter of Nanette Miller,* www.sec.gov/litigation/admin/34-42586.htm.
[2]The American Stock Exchange no longer exists. On October 1, 2008, NYSE Euronext completed acquisition of the American Stock Exchange. Before the closing of the acquisition, NYSE Euronext announced that the exchange will be integrated with Alternext European small-cap exchange and renamed NYSE Alternext U.S. In March 2009, NYSE Alternext U.S. was again rebranded to NYSE Amex Equities.

Case 3-6

Bubba Tech, Inc.

Willie Carson and Waylon Boone are friends who grew up in Dallas, Texas. They both attended the University of Texas at Austin and graduated with degrees in accounting and computer science, respectively. They moved back to Dallas after graduation. Carson went to work for the accounting and assurances services firm of Randy Burnham LLP where he met his wife, Shania Hill. This firm is one of the largest non–Big 4 accounting firms in the world, and it is considered to be an expert in accounting for companies in the high-tech industry. Boone went to work for Alorotom, Inc., which is one of the largest manufacturers of high-tech products in the world.

Carson and Boone worked for these companies for seven years. During this time Carson became a certified public accountant, while Boone successfully completed a master's degree program in information systems at Southern Methodist University. In 2001 they decided to strike out on their own, and they formed a manufacturing company, Bubba Tech, Inc., in Austin. Boone became the chief executive officer and Carson the chief financial officer. Bubba Tech was privately owned by Carson, Boone, and a venture capital firm. The firm had complete confidence in the abilities of Boone and Carson so there was no board of directors. The venture capitalists built a provision into its agreement with Boone and Carson that they would receive a 10 percent return on their investment for five years and then, after the company went public, they would be repaid the amount of their investment.

Since Bubba Tech planned to go public within five years, it hired Randy Burnham & Co. to audit its December 31, 2005, financial statements. Hill was in charge of the audit. The firm completed its audit for 2005 and the following four years and rendered unqualified opinions on the audited financial statements. In 2010, Bubba Tech decided to go public. During a meeting with the auditors from Randy Burnham, Waylon Boone asked the partner in charge of the BTI audit, Clint Strait, to prepare a list of operational issues to consider as the company went from being privately held to a publicly held corporation.

Strait called a meeting of the audit engagement team to discuss how to proceed. Shania Hill suggested that as the manager in charge of the audit, she should head up the effort to prepare a list for discussion with BTI management. Strait agreed. Hill asked Faith Twain to join the team since Faith had been the senior in charge of the audit. Faith agreed to join the team. Faith suggested adding Garth Chesney from the tax department. Garth agreed and suggested that Kenny Brooks also should be on the team because Kenny is responsible for the information technology work related to the audit of BTI. Brooks agreed and the team was finalized.

Questions

1. Based on the limited facts of this case, prepare a list of the operational issues to present to top management at BTI. Include in your list any corporate governance issues of importance in relation to the management of BTI after it becomes a public company, and issues related to the relationship between BTI and Randy Burnham & Co.

2. Do you think there are any ethical issues that should have been addressed by Carson and Boone before they hired Randy Burnham & Co. as their auditors? Be specific and explain why they should have been issues of concern.

3. Assume the company went public in 2010. During that year the controller of Bubba Tech identified the following transaction as having been recorded as a capital asset. There was no amortization recorded in 2010.

> Bubba Tech engaged in extensive research activities into new voice-data transmission software that cost $2.5 million. As of December 31, 2010, the company had not yet completed the research process and no sales were pending.

Did Bubba Tech record the research expenditure in accordance with GAAP? Why or why not?

Case 3-7

Fraud Actions under the Federal False Claims Act

Background

The U.S. Department of Justice reported on November 7, 2007, that the government collected $2 billion in settlements and judgments in the fiscal year ending September 30, 2007, pursuing allegations of fraud against the federal government. This brings total recoveries since 1986, when Congress substantially strengthened the civil federal False Claims Act, to more than $20 billion. However, this is a drop in the bucket if we are to believe a CBS *60 Minutes* expose on Medicare fraud on October 25, 2009, that claims the amount of fraud is as high as $60 billion a year.

Of the $2 billion, $1.45 billion is associated with suits initiated by whistleblowers under the False Claims Act's qui tam provisions. These whistleblower provisions authorize individuals, known as "relators," to file suit on behalf of the United States against those who have falsely or fraudulently claimed federal funds. Such cases run the gamut of federally funded programs from Medicare and Medicaid to defense procurement contracts, disaster assistance loans, and agricultural subsidies. Persons who knowingly make false claims for federal funds are liable for three times the government's loss plus a civil penalty of $5,500 to $11,000 for each claim. Relators typically recover 15 to 25 percent of the proceeds of a successful suit if the United States intervenes in the qui tam action, and up to 30 percent if the government declines and the relator pursues the action alone. In fiscal year 2007, whistleblowers were awarded $177 million excluding relator shares.

As in the last several years, health care accounted for the lion's share of fraud settlements and judgments—$1.54 billion. This number includes both whistleblower claims and those initiated by the United States in independent fraud investigations. Cases involving fraud against the Department of Health and Human Services reaped the biggest recoveries, largely attributable to its Medicare program and the federal/state Medicaid program, which funds health care for the needy. The largest health care recoveries came from pharmaceutical companies and related entities. Settlements with Bristol-Myers Squibb Co., Aventis Pharmaceuticals, Inc., Medco Health Solutions, Inc., Purdue Pharma L.P. and Purdue Frederick Co., and InterMune, Inc., accounted for more than $800 million of the $1.5 billion. In addition to federal recoveries, pharmaceutical fraud cases returned $264 million to state Medicaid programs. Examples of health care lawsuit settlements appear in Appendix 1 of this case.

Outside the health care arena, fraud against the Department of Defense accounted for $48.4 million in settlements. Examples of these cases brought under the federal False Claims Act include:

- In a record General Services Administration settlement, Oracle Corporation paid the government $98.5 million to resolve allegations that PeopleSoft, Inc. (acquired by Oracle in 2005), engaged in defective pricing of its software and services under the company's multiple award schedule with GSA and violated the federal False Claims Act. The allegations arose from a qui tam suit filed by a former employee of PeopleSoft, who alleged that PeopleSoft provided GSA with pricing disclosures for its software and related maintenance services that were not complete, accurate, and current. As a result of the defective disclosures, federal agencies that purchased PeopleSoft software and services between March 17, 1997, and September 30, 2005, under the company's multiple award schedule with GSA, paid inflated prices. The relator received $17.7 million as his statutory award.[1]

- The government received $34.6 million from Mellon Bank, N.A., to resolve allegations that the bank violated the False Claims Act when in April 2001 several of its employees hid and then destroyed approximately 77,000 individual income tax returns, together with approximately $1.3 billion in tax payment checks, instead of processing the returns and checks as required by its Lockbox Depositary Agreement with the Internal Revenue Service (IRS). Through a massive effort lasting more than a year, the IRS was able to obtain copies of the tax returns and replacement checks from most of the taxpayers. Although Mellon Bank had paid the IRS for its costs and for interest on the destroyed tax revenue, the out-of-court settlement resolved the government's claim that the bank was liable for multiple damages and civil penalties under the False Claims Act.

Case Facts

A False Claims Act whistleblower lawsuit against the prime contractors for the Coast Guard's $26 billion Deepwater acquisition program will go to trial in November 2010, a U.S. District Court judge has ruled. Former Lockheed Martin Corp. engineer Michael J. DeKort filed the complaint against Integrated Coast Guard Systems, a joint venture of Lockheed Martin and Northrop Grumman Corp. DeKort accused the companies of being seriously deficient in carrying out the contract and caused major safety, security, and national security problems and wasted taxpayers' money. Lockheed Martin officials have previously said the allegations are without merit and that they would "vigorously defend" against the lawsuit. DeKort previously worked on Deepwater's command, control, and communication systems. He left Lockheed Martin in 2004 and is seeking damages of

---

[1] www.usdoj.gov/opa/pr/2006/October/06_odag_689.html.

up to $720 million along with civil penalties, legal costs, and other relief in the lawsuit, according to his attorney.[2]

Deepwater is the Coast Guard's largest acquisition program. It includes the production of new assets including national security cutters and patrol boats. The Coast Guard has acknowledged several significant problems with the program, and in 2007 the service rejected eight new patrol boats due to structural problems with the hulls. The Coast Guard is seeking a refund for $96 million for unsound patrol boats produced under Deepwater.

On October 2, 2009, U.S. District Judge Reed O'Connor of U.S. District Court for the Northern District of Texas rejected a request from the defendants to dismiss the case, saying their request for dismissal was "moot." On October 5, O'Connor issued a schedule for pleadings, naming of expert witnesses, identifying evidence, and a trial. He also instructed the parties to hire a mediator and attempt to come to an agreement to resolve the case. The trial will take place upon two days' notice at any time during the four weeks that start November 1, 2010.

[2]http://fcw.com/articles/2009/10/06/deepwater-false-claims-lawsuit-to-go-to-trial.aspx.

In False Claims Act lawsuits, plaintiffs can pursue a case either with or without the Justice Department. If the plaintiff wins, the government can collect damages of up to three times its losses and the plaintiff can collect 25 to 30 percent of the recovery amount. To date, the Justice Department had not joined the Deepwater case.

Questions

1. What motivates health care provider fraud and fraud against the government such as in the cases described in Appendix 1? Do you think additional legislation is the answer or are there better ways to reduce the reported $60 billion cost to the government of Medicare fraud each year? Be specific in answering the question.

2. Do you think it is ethical for a person to file a lawsuit under the federal False Claims Act with the sole motivation of the prospect of being awarded a significant amount of money as a result of a decision against the defendant?

3. Given the allegations that were in the 2009 lawsuit and expected 2010 court date to hear the case, what do you think should be disclosed in the financial statements about the Deepwater case in the calendar-year 2009 financial statements? Provide support for your answer.

Appendix 1

Examples of U.S. Government Settlement of Health Care Fraud Cases in 2007

Among the department's most significant settlements and judgments in fiscal year 2007 were:

1. $328 million from Bristol-Myers Squibb (BMS) Co. and its generic division, Apothecon, to resolve a broad array of allegations involving illegal drug pricing and marketing activities. BMS and Apothecon paid an additional $187 million to state Medicaid programs based on the same allegations. The civil settlement arises from seven qui tam actions and resolves allegations that (1) BMS and Apothecon set and maintained inflated prices knowing that federal health care programs used these prices for reimbursement, and then marketed the "spread"—the difference between the reported price and cost—to induce sales by increasing providers' profits; (2) BMS paid kickbacks to doctors in the form of bogus consulting fees to induce them to purchase BMS's drugs; (3) BMS paid kickbacks to wholesalers and retail pharmacies to induce purchases of generic products; (4) BMS promoted its atypical antipsychotic drug, Abilify, for juvenile use and to treat dementia-related psychosis—uses that were not approved by the Food and Drug Administration; and (5) BMS violated the Medicaid

Drug Rebate Act, 42 U.S.C. § 1396r-8, by reporting false "best prices" to the government for its drug Serzone, which resulted in BMS underpaying quarterly rebates owed to the Medicaid program. The six relators will share a $52 million award plus additional amounts from the states.[1]

2. $311 million from four manufacturers of hip and knee surgical implant products—Zimmer, Inc., Depuy Orthopaedics, Inc., Biomet Inc., and Smith & Nephew, Inc.—to settle claims that from at least 2002 through 2006 these companies used consulting agreements with orthopedic surgeons to induce the purchase of their devices. The government's investigation revealed that the firms paid surgeons hundreds of thousands of dollars a year for consulting contracts and lavished them with trips and other expensive perquisites in exchange for using the companies' products exclusively. In addition to the civil settlements, the four companies executed deferred prosecution agreements requiring new corporate compliance procedures and the appointment of federal monitors to review their compliance with these procedures.[2]

3. $180 million from Aventis Pharmaceuticals, Inc., to resolve allegations that the company engaged in a scheme (1) to set and maintain fraudulent and inflated prices for its

[1]www.usdoj.gov/opa/pr/2007/September/07_civ_782.html.
[2]www.usdoj.gov/usao/nj/press/files/pdffiles/hips0927.rel.pdf.

drug, Anzemet, knowing that federal health care programs established reimbursement rates based on those prices; and (2) to use the difference between the inflated prices reported and the actual prices charged to its customers to market, promote, and sell the drug. In addition, Aventis paid $10 million to several state governments based on the same allegations. The relators shared a $33 million award.[3]

4. $172 million judgment after trial against Amerigroup, Illinois Inc. finding that Amerigroup fraudulently skewed enrollment in its Medicaid HMO program by refusing to register pregnant women and by discouraging registration by individuals with preexisting conditions. Amerigroup had entered into contracts with the Illinois Department of Public Health requiring the company to provide health care services to Medicaid eligible individuals in Illinois. In violation of these contracts, Amerigroup engaged in a cherry-picking scheme to ensure that those who enrolled in its HMO program represented a disproportionately healthy population of Medicaid-eligible individuals. As a result, Amerigroup reduced its medical losses and increased its profits. Amerigroup has appealed the judgment.

5. $155 million from Medco Health Solutions, Inc., to settle allegations that Medco submitted false claims in connection with the mail-order prescription drug benefit offered under the Federal Employee Health Benefits Program. The government alleged that Medco cancelled prescriptions it could not fill timely to avoid late penalties, shorted pills, and billed for pharmacy services it didn't provide. The government also alleged that Medco solicited kickbacks from pharmaceutical manufacturers to favor their drugs on Medco's formulary, and paid kickbacks to health plans to obtain business. The settlement resolved two qui tam lawsuits and a separate federal investigation prompted by Medco's disclosure to the government concerning billing problems for diabetic supplies. The relators received $23.9 million as their award. Medco also entered into a corporate compliance agreement with the Department of Health and Human Services and the Office of Personnel Management.[4]

6. $100.6 million ($109 million including interest) from Purdue Pharma L.P. and Purdue Frederick Company, Inc., to settle allegations of fraud against Medicaid and other federal health care programs. The government alleged

that Purdue fraudulently misbranded OxyContin as being less addictive and less subject to abuse and diversion than other pain medications. The civil settlement resolved allegations that, based on these misleading marketing claims, Purdue knowingly caused the submission of false claims for OxyContin that were not eligible for federal reimbursement. In addition, Purdue paid $60 million to state Medicaid programs, forfeited $276 million to the United States, set aside $130 million to resolve private civil claims (with unclaimed amounts to revert to the United States), paid $5.3 million to the Virginia Attorney General's Medicaid Fraud Control Unit to fund future health care fraud investigations, and paid $20 million to fund the Virginia Prescription Monitoring Program. Finally, Purdue paid $500,000 in criminal fines—the maximum allowed under the statute.[5]

7. $42.65 million to settle allegations of fraud against Maximus, Inc., in connection with claims to the Medicaid program. The District of Columbia Child and Family Services Agency (CFSA) hired Maximus to assist it in submitting claims to Medicaid for targeted case management services provided by the District to children in its foster care program. The United States alleged that Maximus caused CFSA to submit claims for every child in the foster care program whether or not targeted case management services had been provided to the child. Maximus also entered into a deferred prosecution agreement with the U.S. Attorney's Office. The relator, a former division manager with Maximus, received $4.93 million as his share of the recovery.[6]

8. $30.2 million from InterMune, Inc., to resolve allegations that InterMune marketed its drug, Actimmune, for uses not approved by the Food and Drug Administration resulting in federal health program losses. The government alleged that InterMune marketed Actimmune for idiopathic pulmonary fibrosis (IPF), a fatal disease that causes scarring of lung tissue. Although the company had failed to demonstrate Actimmune's efficacy for IPF, it nevertheless misled physicians and the public to believe that the drug trial had been successful. The relator received $5.7 million as her share of the recovery. InterMune paid an additional $6.7 million to state Medicaid programs.[7]

[3]www.usdoj.gov/opa/pr/2007/September/07_civ_694.html.
[4]www.usdoj.gov/opa/pr/2006/October/06_civ_722.html.
[5]www.usdoj.gov/usao/vaw/press_releases/purdue_frederick_10may2007.html.
[6]www.usdoj.gov/opa/pr/2007/July/07_civ_535.html.
[7]www.usdoj.gov/opa/pr/2006/October/06_civ_728.html.

Case 3-8

Pension Benefit Guaranty Corporation

In 1974, Congress created the Pension Benefit Guaranty Corporation (PBGC) as part of the Employment Retirement Income Security Act to protect workers from pension failures. The PBGC protects the pensions of American workers and retirees in private single-employer and multiemployer defined benefit pension plans. The PBGC receives no funds from general tax revenues. Operations are financed by insurance premiums set by Congress and paid by sponsors of defined benefit plans, investment income assets from pension plans trusteed by PBGC, and recoveries from the companies formerly responsible for the plans. The PBGC collects premiums from U.S. pension plans and uses the money to pay partial retirement benefits if a plan cannot meet its pension obligations to workers. A 2009 study of the solvency of PBGC by the Brookings Institute points out that the deficit in the fund is $22 billion.[1]

This may be just the tip of the iceberg. In May of 1995 United Airlines was granted permission by the bankruptcy court to terminate its $9.8 billion in pension obligations. The PBGC will cover about $6.6 of the shortfall with retirees bearing the burden of reduced benefits of about $3.2 billion. The agency estimates that total underfunding of all traditional pensions is about $450 billion, including $96 billion for defaults it calls "reasonably possible."

There is a statutory limit on the amount that PBGC can guarantee. Under the single-employer program, the limit is adjusted annually based on changes in the Social Security contribution and benefit base and is permanently established for each pension plan based on the date the plan terminates except for cases in which termination occurs during a plan sponsor's bankruptcy or for certain airline industry plans.

For plans with a 2009 termination date, the maximum guarantee is $54,000 yearly ($4,500 monthly) for a single life annuity beginning at age 65. The maximum is adjusted downward for retirees younger than age 65. For example, the maximum guarantee for a participant who retires at age 62 is $42,660 yearly ($3,555 monthly) for a single-life annuity.

There are three main reasons for the PBGC's financial troubles. First, it has structural problems with its finances that date back to its inception in 1974. Its premium levels, which are set by legislation, have never been high enough to cover the risks it has faced over the long term, which are themselves largely determined by pension funding rules that are also legislated. This problem has been mitigated over the years by increases in premiums and tighter rules on corporate pension funding, but the deficit continues to get worse. Premium levels are not sufficient to hold the deficit steady;

[1]www.brookings.edu/papers/2009/0604_pbgc_elliott.aspx.

they would have to go up considerably further still to fill in the existing financial hole.

Second, the PBGC insures against corporate bankruptcies, so it is no surprise that a period of severe economic distress would cause claims on the PBGC to soar. The problem would have been worse still for the PBGC if the government had not rescued GM and Chrysler in 2009. (The state of the economy is not the only explanation, of course, since the PBGC had deficits of $11 billion and up during the bubble period of the mid-2000s.) In addition to the actual claims hitting the PBGC as a result of the recession of 2008 through 2010, there is also a much higher potential level of claims over the next few years.

Third, corporate pension funds have about three-fifths of their money invested in the stock market. There is an unfortunate tendency for bankruptcies to occur during periods when the stock market has also been hammered, since both are tied to the overall state of the economy. This gives the PBGC a large, indirect stake in the performance of the stock market, which is one reason why economists with pension expertise virtually unanimously have opposed increases in the PBGC's holdings of stock in its own portfolio. The stock market declined precipitously during the years 2007 through 2008, which directly reduced the value of the PBGC's stock holdings to a modest extent and raised the likely cost of bankruptcies that resulted in PBGC takeovers of pension funds.

Even more importantly is the estimated cost in today's dollars of paying all future pension claims that have gone up sharply. For example, the PBGC provides an estimate of the pension underfunding at financially weak companies. The 2008 report showed a figure of $47 billion for this exposure. Pension liabilities are measured by estimating the future pension payments, based on such things as life expectancies, and then calculating the cost in today's dollars of making those payments. The dramatic reduction in interest rates over the time period through 2010 makes the cost in today's dollars significantly higher, since there is less assumed investment income over the years due to the lower interest rates. Thus, the mismatch between the poor performance of the stock market and the large increase in estimates of the pension liability due to declines in interest rates was quite harmful to pension plans and to the PBGC.

In sum, the past few years have been bad ones for the PBGC. But, the results should not be dismissed as simply the sign of another victim of the financial crisis. There are serious structural problems with the PBGC's finances that will keep it on a long-term downward trend unless corrected. There will be periods when the cancer at its core seems to be in remission, especially during boom periods in the economy and markets, but the inevitable economic declines will show that the problem is still there, getting worse.

Questions

1. What are the ethical obligations of a company to meet pension obligations to its employees? Should companies be allowed to walk away from their commitments if it is the only reasonable step to forestall bankruptcy? Use ethical reasoning to answer this question.

2. What are the corporate governance implications of having a pension plan that fails to meet its employee obligations? In other words, which group(s) responsible for governance should shoulder the blame? What are their ethical obligations to those covered by the pension plan?

3. In late April of 2009, Lockheed Martin said its first-quarter earnings for 2009 fell 8.7 percent because rising pension costs outweighed an increase in sales. Is it "right" for a company to absorb pension costs so high that it exceeds sales revenue? Consider stakeholder interests in answering this question.

Case 3-9

Bhopal, India: A Tragedy of Massive Proportions

We are citizens of the world. The tragedy of our times is that we do not know this.

Woodrow T. Wilson (1856–1924),
28th president of the United States

At five past midnight on December 3, 1984, 40 tons of the chemical methyl isocynate (MIC), a toxic gas, started to leak out of a pesticide tank at the Union Carbide plant in Bhopal, India. The leak was first detected by workers about 11:30 p.m. on December 2, 1984, when their eyes began to tear and burn. According to AcuSafe,[1] "in 1991 the official Indian government panel charged with tabulating deaths and injuries counted more than 3,800 dead and approximately 11,000 with disabilities." However, estimates now range as high as 8,000 killed in the first three days and over 120,000 injured.[2] There were 4,000 deaths officially recorded by the government, although 13,000 death claims were filed with the government, according to a United Nations report, and hundreds of thousands more claim injury as a result of the disaster.[3] While the numbers may be debatable, there can be no doubt that the Bhopal incident raises a variety of interesting ethical questions including:

- Did the company knowingly sacrifice safety at the Bhopal plant?
- Did the Indian government properly oversee the functioning of the plant consistent with its regulatory authority?
- Did the company react quickly enough to avoid sustained health problems to those injured by the leak of toxic fumes?
- In the aftermath of the disaster, were the disclosures made by Union Carbide sufficiently transparent to enable a concerned public to understand the causes of the leak and the steps the company was taking to address all of the issues?
- Did the company and the Indian government reach a fair resolution of the thousands of claims filed by Indian citizens?

You make up your own mind as you read about the tragedy that is Bhopal.

[1]AcuSafe is an Internet resource for safety and risk management information that is a publication of AcuTech, a global leader in process safety and security risk management located in Houston, Texas, www.acusafe.com/Incidents/Bhopal1984/incidentbhopal1984.htm.
[2]According to CorpWatch, www.corpwatch.org/
[3]United Nations, *United Nations University Report (UNU Report) on Toxic Gas Leak,* www.unu.edu/unupress/unupbooks/uu21le/uu211eOc.htm.

In the Beginning

On May 4, 1980, the first factory exported from the West to make pesticides using methyl isocyanate (MIC) began production in Bhopal, India. The company planned to export the chemicals from the United States to make the pesticide, Sevin. The new CEO of Union Carbide had come over from the United States especially for the occasion.[4]

As you might expect, the company seemed very concerned about safety issues. "Carbide's manifesto set down certain truths, the first being that 'all accidents are avoidable provided the measures necessary to avoid them are defined and implemented.'" The company's slogan was: "Good safety and good accident prevention practices are good business."

Safety Measures

The Union Carbide plant in Bhopal was equipped with an alarm system with a siren that was supposed to be set off whenever the "duty supervisor in the control room" sensed even the slightest indication that a possible fire might be developing "or the smallest emission of toxic gas." The "alarm system was intended to warn the crews working on the factory site." Even though thousands of people lived in the nearby bustees (shantytowns), "none of the loudspeakers pointed outward" in their direction. Still, they could hear the sirens coming from the plant. The siren went off so frequently that it seemed as though the population became used to it and weren't completely aware that one death and several accidental poisonings had occurred before the night of December 2, and there was a "mysterious fire in the alpha-naphtol unit."

In May 1982, three engineers from Union Carbide came to Bhopal to evaluate the plant and confirm that everything was operating according to company standards. The investigators identified more than 60 violations of operational and safety regulations. An Indian reporter managed to obtain a copy of the report that noted "shoddy workmanship," warped equipment, corroded circuitry, "the absence of automatic sprinklers in the MIC and phosgene production zones," a lack of pressure gauges, and numerous other violations. The severest criticism was in the area of personnel. There was "an alarming turnover of inadequately trained staff, unsatisfactory instruction methods and a lack of rigor in maintenance reports."

The reporter wrote three articles proclaiming the unsafe plant. The third article was titled "If You Refuse to Understand, You Will Be Reduced to Dust." Nothing seemed to matter in the end because the population was assured by Union Carbide and government representatives that no one

[4]Dominique LaPierre and Javier Moro, *Five Past Midnight in Bhopal* (New York: Warner Books, 2002).

need be concerned because the phosgene produced at the plant was not a toxic gas.

The Accident

The accident occurred when a large volume of water entered the MIC storage tanks and triggered a violent chain reaction. Normally, water and MIC were separated but on the night of December 2, "metal barriers known as slip blinds were not inserted and the cleaning water passed directly into the MIC tanks." It is possible that additional water entered the tanks later on in trying to control the reaction. Shortly after the introduction of water, "temperatures and pressures in the tanks increased to the point of explosion."

The report of consultants that reviewed the facts surrounding the accident indicates that workers made a variety of attempts to save the plant including: [5]

- They tried to turn on the plant refrigeration system to cool down the environment and slow the reaction but the system had been drained of coolant weeks before and never refilled as a cost savings measure.
- They tried to route expanding gases to a neighboring tank but the tank's pressure gauge was broken and indicated the tank was full when it was really empty.
- They tried other measures that didn't work due to inadequate or broken equipment.
- They tried to spray water on the gasses and have them settle to the ground but it was too late as the chemical reaction was nearly completed.

The Workers and Their Reaction

It was reported that the maintenance workers did not flush out the pipes after the factory's production of MIC stopped on December 2. This was important because the pipes carried the liquid MIC produced by the plant's reactors to the tanks. The highly corrosive MIC leaves chemical deposits on the lining of the tanks that can eventually get into the storage tanks and contaminate the MIC. Was it laziness, as suggested by one worker?

Another worker pointed out that the production supervisor of the plant left strict instructions to flush the pipes but it was late at night and neither worker really wanted to do it. Still, they followed the instructions for the washing operation but the supervisor had omitted the crucial step to place solid metal discs at the end of each pipe to ensure hermetically sealed tanks.

The cleansing operation began when one worker connected a hosepipe to a drain cock on the pipe work and turned on the tap. After a short time it was clear to the worker that

the injected water was not coming out of two of four drain cocks. The worker called the supervisor who walked over to the plant and instructed the worker to clean the filters in the two clogged drain cocks and turn the water back on. They did that but the water did not flow out of one drain. After informing the supervisor who said to just keep the water flowing, the worker left for the night. It would now be up to the night shift to turn off the tap.

The attitude of the workers as they started the night shift was not good as Union Carbide had started to cut back on production and lay off workers. They wondered if they might be next. The culture of safety that Union Carbide tried to build up was largely gone as the workers typically handled toxic substances without protective gear. The temperature readings in the tanks were made less frequently and it was rare when anyone checked the welding on the pipe work in the middle of the night.

Even though the pressure gauge on one of the tanks increased beyond the "permitted maximum working pressure," the supervisor ignored warnings coming from the control room because he was under the impression that Union Carbide had built the tanks with special steel and walls thick enough to resist even greater pressures. Still, the duty head of the control room and another worker went to look directly at the pressure gauge attached to the three tanks. They confirmed the excessive pressure in one tank.

The duty head climbed to the top of that tank, examined the metal casing carefully, and sensed the stirring action. The pressure inside was increasing quickly leading to a popping sound "like champaign corks." Some of the gas then escaped and a brownish cloud appeared. The workers returned to where the pipes had been cleaned and turned off the water tap. They smelled the powerful gas emissions. They heard the fizzing sound as if someone was blowing into an empty bottle. One worker had a cool enough head to sound the general alarm, but it was too late for most of the workers and many of those living in the shantytowns below the plant.

The Political Response

Union Carbide sent a team to investigate the catastrophe but the Indian government had seized records and denied the investigators access to the plant and the eyewitnesses. The Madhya Pradesh state government tried to place the blame squarely on the shoulders of Union Carbide. It sued the company for damages on behalf of the victims. The ruling Congress Party was facing national parliamentary elections three weeks after the accident and it "stood to lose heavily if its partners in the state government were seen to be implicated, or did not deal firmly with Union Carbide."[6]

The government thwarted early efforts by Union Carbide to provide relief to the victims to block its attempt to gain the goodwill of the public. The strategy worked as the Congress

[5]Ron Graham, "FAQ on Failures: Union Carbide Bhopal," Barrett Engineering Consulting, www.tcnj.edu/rgraham/failures/UCBhopal.html.

[6]United Nations, *United Nations University Report (UNU Report) on Toxic Gas Leak.*

Party won both the state legislative assembly and the national parliament seats from Madhya Pradesh by large margins.

Economic Effects

The economic impact of a disaster like the one that happened in Bhopal is staggering. The $25 million Union Carbide plant in Bhopal was shut down immediately after the accident, and 650 permanent jobs were lost. The loss of human life means a loss of future earning power and a loss of economic production. The thousands of accident victims had to be treated and in many cases rehabilitated. The closure of the plant had peripheral effects on local businesses and the population of Bhopal. It is estimated that "two mass evacuations disrupted commercial activities for several weeks, with resulting business losses of $8 to $65 million."

In the year after the accident, the government paid compensation of about $800 per fatality to relatives of dead persons. About $100 was awarded to 20,000 victims. Beginning in March 1991, new relief payments were made to all victims who lived in affected areas and a total of $260 million was disbursed.

Union Carbide's Response

Shortly after the gas release, Union Carbide launched what it called "an aggressive effort to identify the cause." According to the company, the results of an independent investigation conducted by the engineering consulting firm Arthur D. Little were that "the gas leak could only have been caused by deliberate sabotage. Someone purposely put water in the gas storage tank, causing a massive chemical reaction. Process safety systems had been put in place that would have kept the water from entering the tank by accident."[7]

In a 1993 report prepared by Jackson B. Browning, the retired vice president of Health, Safety, and Environmental Programs at Union Carbide Corporation, Browning stated that he didn't find out about the accident until 2:30 a.m. on December 3. He claims to have been told that "no plant employees had been injured, but there were fatalities—possibly eight or twelve—in the nearby community."

A meeting was called at the company's headquarters in Danbury, Connecticut, for 6 a.m. The chair of the board of directors of Union Carbide, Warren M. Anderson, had received the news while returning from a business trip to Washington, DC. He had a "bad cold and a fever" so Anderson stayed at home and designated Browning as his "media stand-in" until Anderson could return to the office.[8]

At the first press conference called for 1:00 p.m. on December 3, the company acknowledged that the disaster had occurred at its plant in Bhopal. The company reported that it was sending "medical and technical experts to aid the people of Bhopal, to help dispose of the remaining [MIC] at the plant and to investigate the cause of the tragedy." Notably, Union Carbide halted production at its only other MIC plant in West Virginia and it stated its intention "to convert existing supplies into less volatile compounds."

Warren Anderson traveled to India and offered aid of $1 million and the Indian subsidiary of Union Carbide pledged the Indian equivalent of $840,000. Within a few months the company offered an additional $5 million in aid that was rejected by the Indian government. The money was then turned over to the Indian Red Cross and used for relief efforts.

The company continued to offer relief aid with "no strings attached." However, the Indian government rejected the overtures and it didn't help the company to go through third parties. Union Carbide believed that the volatile political situation in India—Prime Minister Indira Gandhi had been assassinated—hindered its relief efforts, especially after the election of Rajiv Gandhi on a government reform platform. It appeared to the company that Union Carbide was to be made an example of as an exploiter of Indian natural resources and the government may have wanted to "gain access to Union Carbide's financial resources."

Union Carbide had a contingency plan for emergencies but it didn't cover the "unthinkable." The company felt compelled to show its "commitment to employee and community safety and specifically, to reaffirm the safety measures in place at their operation." Anderson went to West Virginia to meet with the employees in early February 1985. At that meeting, as "a measure of the personal concern and compassion of Union Carbide employees," the workers established a "Carbide Employees Bhopal Relief Fund and collected more than $100,000 to aid the tragedy's victims."[9]

Analysis of Union Carbide's Bhopal Problems

Documents uncovered in litigation[10] and obtained by the Environmental Working Group of the Chemical Industry Archives, an organization that investigates chemical company claims of product safety, indicate that Union Carbide "cut corners and employed untested technologies when building the Bhopal Plant." The company went ahead with the unproven design even though it posed a "danger of polluting subsurface water supplies in the Bhopal area." The following is an excerpt from a document numbered UCC 04206 and included in the Environmental Working Group Report on

---

[7]Union Carbide started a Web site, www.bhopal.com, after the leak to provide its side of the story and details about the tragedy. In 1998 the Indian state government of Madhya Pradesh took full responsibility for the site.

[8]Jackson B. Browning, *The Browning Report*, Union Carbide Corporation, 1993, www.bhopal.com/pdfs/browning.pdf.

[9]*The Browning Report*, p. 8.

[10]*Bano et al. v. Union Carbide Corp & Warren Anderson*, *99cv11329 SDNY*, filed on 11/15/99.

Bhopal India.[11] It also reveals the indifferent attitude of the Indian government toward environmental safety.

> The systems described have received provisional endorsement by the Public Health Engineering Office of the State of Madhya Pradesh in Bhopal. At present there are no State or Central Government laws and/or regulations for environmental protection, though enactment is expected in the near future. It is not expected that this will require any design modifications.

Technology Risks

> The comparative risk of poor performance and of consequent need for further investment to correct it is considerably higher in the [Union Carbide-India] operation than it would be had proven technology been followed throughout . . . the MIC-to-Sevin process, as developed by Union Carbide, has had only a limited trial run. Furthermore, while similar waste streams have been handled elsewhere, this particular combination of materials to be disposed of is new and, accordingly, affords further chance for difficulty. In short, it can be expected that there will be interruptions in operations and delays in reaching capacity or product quality that might have been avoided by adoption of proven technology.
>
> [Union Carbide-India] finds the business risk in the proposed mode of operation acceptable, however, in view of the desired long term objectives of minimum capital and foreign exchange expenditures. As long as [Union Carbide-India] is diligent in pursuing solutions, it is their feeling any shortfalls can be mitigated by imports. Union Carbide concurs.

As previously mentioned there was one death and several accidental poisonings at the Bhopal plant before December 3, 1984. The International Environmental Law Research Center prepared a Bhopal Date Line that showed the death occurred on December 25, 1981, when a worker was exposed to phosgene gas. On January 9, 1982, 25 workers were hospitalized as a result of another leak. On October 5, 1982, another leak from the plant led to the hospitalization of hundreds of residents.[12]

It is worth noting that the workers had protested unsafe conditions after the January 9, 1982, leak but their warning went unheeded. In March 1982 a leak from one of the solar evaporation ponds took place and the Indian plant expressed its concern to Union Carbide headquarters. In May 1982 the company sent its U.S. experts to the Bhopal plant to conduct the audit previously mentioned.

The reaction to newspaper allegations that Union Carbide-India was running an unsafe operation was for the plants' works manager to write a denial of the charges as baseless. The company's next step was, to say the least, bewildering. It rewrote the safety manuals to permit switching off of the

refrigeration unit and a shutdown of the vent gas scrubber when the plant was not in operation. The staffing at the MIC unit was reduced from 12 workers to 6. On November 29, 1984, three days before the disaster, Union Carbide had completed a feasibility report and the company had decided to dismantle the plant and ship it to Indonesia or Brazil.

India's Position

The Indian government has itself acknowledged that 521,262 persons, well over half the population of Bhopal at the time of the toxic leak, were "exposed" to the lethal gas.[13] In the immediate aftermath of the accident, most attention was devoted to medical recovery. The victims of the MIC leak suffered damage to lung tissue and respiratory functions. The lack of medical documentation affected relief efforts. The absence of baseline data made it difficult to identify specific medical consequences of MIC exposure and to develop appropriate medical treatment. Another problem was that malnourishment of the poor Indians affected by the tragedy added to the difficulty because they already suffered from many of the postexposure symptoms such as coughing, breathlessness, nausea, vomiting, chest pains, and poor sight.[14]

In a paper on the Bhopal tragedy written by Pratima Ungarala, a student at Hindu University, he analyzed the *Browning Report* and characterized the company's response as one of public relations. He noted that the report identified the media and other interested parties such as customers, shareholders, suppliers, and other employees as most important to pacify. Ungarala criticized this response for its lack of concern for the people of India or the people of Bhopal. Instead, the corporation saw the urgency to assure the people of the United States that such an incident would not happen here.[15]

Browning's main strategy to restore Union Carbide's image was to distance the company from the site of the disaster. He points out early in the document that Union Carbide had owned only 50.9 percent of the affiliate, the Union Carbide India Ltd. He notes that all the employees in the company were Indians and that the last American employee had left two years before the leak.

The report contended that the company "did not have any hold over its Indian affiliate." This seems to be a contentious issue because while "many of the day to day details, such as staffing and maintenance, were left to Indian officials, the major decisions, such as the annual budget, had to

[11]Environmental Working Group, *Chemical Industry Archives,* www.chemicalindustryarchives.org/dirtysecrets/bhopal/index .asp.

[12]S. Muralidhar, "The Bhopal Date Line," International Environmental Law Research Centre, www.ielrc.org/content/ n0409.htm.

[13]Vinay Lal and Jamie Cassels, "Sovereign Immunity: Law in an Unequal World," *Social and Legal Studies* 5, no. 3 (1996), pp. 421–436.

[14]Paul Shrivastava, "Long-Term Recovery from the Bhopal Crisis," *The Long Road to Recovery: Community Responses to Industrial Disaster (*New York: United Nations University, 1996).

[15]Pratima Ungarala, *Bhopal Gas Tragedy: An Analysis,* Final Paper HU521/Dale Sullivan 5/19/98, www.hu.mtu.edu/ hu_dept/tc@mtu/papers/bhopal.htm.

be cleared with the American headquarters." In addition, by both Indian and U.S. laws, a parent company (United Carbide in this case) holds full responsibility for any plants it operates through subsidiaries and in which it has a majority stake. Ungarala concluded that Union Carbide was trying to avoid paying the $3 billion that India demanded as compensation and was looking to find a "scapegoat" to take the blame.[16]

After the government of Madhya Pradesh had taken over the information Web site from Union Carbide, it began to keep track of applications for compensation. Between 1985 and 1997, over 1 million claims were filed for personal injury. In more than half of those cases the claimant was awarded a monetary settlement. The total amount disbursed as of March 31, 2003, was about $345 million.[17] An additional $25 million was disbursed through July 2004 at which time the Indian Supreme Court ordered the government to pay to the victims, and families of the dead, the remaining $330 million in the compensation fund.

Lawsuits

The inevitable lawsuits began in December 1984 and March 1985, when the government of India filed against Union Carbide in India and the United States, respectively. Union Carbide asked for the case filed in the Federal District Court of New York to be moved to India because that was where the accident had occurred and most of the evidence existed. The case went to the Bhopal District Court—the lowest level court that could hear such a case. During the next four years the case made "its way through the maze of legal bureaucracy" from the state high court up to the Supreme Court of India.

The legal disputes were over the amount of compensation and the exoneration of Union Carbide from future liabilities. The disputes were complicated by a lack of reliable information about the causes of the event and its consequences. The government of India had adopted the "Bhopal Gas Leak Disaster Ordinance—a law that appointed the government as sole representative of the victims." It was challenged by victim activists who pointed out that the victims were not consulted about legal matters or settlement possibilities. The result was, in effect, to dissolve "the victims' identity as a constituency separate and differing from the government."[18]

In 1989, India had another parliamentary election and it seemed a politically opportune time to settle the case and win support from the voters. It had been five years since the accident and the victims were fed up with waiting. By that time, "hundreds of victims had died and thousands had moved out of the gas-affected neighborhoods." Even though the Indian government had taken Union Carbide to court asking for $3

billion, in January 1989 the company reached a settlement with the government for $470 million; the agreement gave Union Carbide immunity from future prosecution.

In October 1991, India's Supreme Court upheld the compensation settlement but cancelled Union Carbide's immunity from criminal prosecution. The money had been held in a court-administered account until 1992, while claims were sorted out. By early 1993 there were 630,000 claims filed of which 350,000 had been substantiated on the basis of medical records. The numbers are larger than previously mentioned because the extent of health problems grew continuously after the accident and hundreds of victims continued to die. Despite challenges by victims and activists to the settlement with Union Carbide, at the beginning of 1993 the government of India began to distribute the $470 million that had increased to $700 million as a result of interest earned on the funds.[19]

What Happened to Union Carbide?

The lawsuits and bad publicity affected Union Carbide's stock price. Before the disaster, the company's stock traded between $50 and $58 a share. In the months immediately following the accident it traded at $32 to $40. In the latter half of 1985, the GAF Corporation of New York made a hostile bid to take over Union Carbide. The ensuing battle and speculative stock trading ran up the stock price to $96 and it forced the company into financial restructuring.

The company's response was to fight back. It sold off its consumer products division and received over $3.3 billion for the assets. It took on additional debt and used the funds from the sale and borrowing to repurchase 38.8 million of its shares to protect the company from further threats of a takeover.

The debt burden had accounted for 80 percent of the company's capitalization by 1986. At the end of 1991, the debt levels were still high—50 percent of capitalization. The company sold its Linde Gas Division for $2.4 billion, "leaving the company at less than half its pre-Bhopal size."

The Bhopal disaster "slowly but steadily sapped the financial strength of Union Carbide and adversely affected" employee morale and productivity. The company's inability to prove its sabotage claim affected its reputation. In 1994 Union Carbide sold its Indian subsidiary, which had operated the Bhopal plant, to an Indian battery manufacturer. It used $90 million from the sale to fund a charitable trust that would build a hospital to treat victims in Bhopal.

Two significant events occurred in 2001. First, the Bhopal Memorial Hospital and Research Centre opened its doors. Second, the Dow Chemical Company purchased Union Carbide for $10.3 billion in stock and debt. Union Carbide became a subsidiary of Dow Chemical.

Subsequent to the initial settlement with Union Carbide, the Indian government took steps to right-the-wrong and its

[16]Ungarala.
[17]Madhya Pradesh Government, Bhopal Gas Tragedy Relief and Rehabilitation Department, www.mp.nic.in/bgtrrdmp/facts.htm.
[18]Michael R. Reich, *Toxic Politics: Responding to Chemical Disasters* (Ithaca, New York: Cornell University Press, 1991).

[19]*United Nations Report.*

aftereffects caused by the failure of management and the systems at Union Carbide in Bhopal. On August 8, 2007, the Indian government announced that it would meet many of the demands of the survivors by taking legal action on the civil and criminal liabilities of Union Carbide and its now owner, Dow Chemical Co. The government established an "Empowered Commission" on Bhopal to address the health and welfare needs of the survivors as well as environmental, social, economic, and medical rehabilitation.

Questions

1. How do you assess blame for the tragedy that is Bhopal? Use ethical reasoning to support your answer. What do the actions of Union Carbide say about its commitment to act as a socially responsible company?

2. The document uncovered by the Environmental Working Group Report refers to the acceptable "business risk" in the Bhopal operation due to questions about the technology. Is it ethical for a company to use business risk as a measure of whether to go ahead with an operation that may have safety problems?

3. Compare the decision-making process used by Union Carbide to deal with its disaster with that of Ford Motor Co. and Johnson & Johnson as described in this chapter. How do you assess the ethics and corporate governance decisions in each of these cases?

Case 3-10

The Hollinger Chronicles

Introduction

The case of Hollinger International resembles Enron, Adelphia, and Tyco all wrapped up in one. There is the improper removal of documents from the company by its chief executive officer during an investigation of its activities (Arthur Andersen destroyed thousands of documents related to its audit of Enron). Conflicts of interest existed because the CEO acted on behalf of two or more related-party entities (Andy Fastow held the position of CFO of Enron and he managed some of its SPEs). The CEO engaged in uncontrolled self-dealing by treating company funds as his own personal piggy bank (see discussion question 13 in this chapter about Adelphia). The Hollinger case has it all—a member of the British House of Lords, a former U.S. secretary of state, and a former governor of one of the nation's largest states. The Special Committee that was formed in June 2003 to investigate fraud made its report public on August 30, 2004, calling it the "Hollinger Chronicles." The committee characterized what went on at Hollinger as a "corporate kleptocracy." As the report points out, this is a story about how Hollinger was systematically manipulated and used by its controlling shareholders for their sole benefit, and in a manner that violated every concept of fiduciary duty."[1]

There was a complete breakdown in the corporate governance systems at Hollinger. Top management represented their own interests, not those of the shareholders, thereby violating the duty of care in making business judgments and the duty of loyalty in dealing fairly by managing the corporation with unselfish loyalty. The board of directors and audit committee did not act independently of management, especially the CEO, Lord Conrad Black. Black wore two hats, also serving as chair of the board of directors. The actions of the external auditors failed to measure up to the fraud standards in *Statement of Auditing Standards (SAS) No. 99: Consideration of Fraud in a Financial Statement Audit*. The internal controls either were nonexistent or were overridden by top management.

The timeline of the case occurs both before and after enactment of the SOX in August 2002. Prior to 2002, Black signed off on financial statements filed with the SEC. Black violated Section 302 when he did the same with the 2002 10-K report filed with the commission. That section prohibits the CEO and top accounting officials from certifying the accuracy of the financial statements filed with the SEC that contain materially false information or omit information that is necessary to make the statements not misleading.

The SEC issued its first complaint against Hollinger on January 19, 2004, in Accounting and Auditing Enforcement Release (AAER) No. 1946.[2] The filing occurred less than two weeks after the company had removed Black as its chair and he had resigned as CEO. This followed the announcement of a $200 million lawsuit against Black and David Radler, the deputy chair, president, and chief operating officer, charging that they had diverted corporate assets for personal purposes.

The commission followed up by filing a lawsuit in U.S. District Court for the Northern District of Illinois on November 15, 2004. The suit charged Black, Radler, and Hollinger, Inc., with multiple violations of the securities acts through the commission of fraud in relation to improper payments and related party transactions.[3]

Background

Organization Structure

Imagine that you and your brother set up a company primarily to own the controlling interest in another public company. Just for good measure, you set up a third private company to own a controlling interest in the first company. Now, the third company controls the first company that controls the second company, so the third company also controls the second company. Confused yet?

Of course, you and your brother really are all three companies because you are the chair of each board of directors and the chief executive officer of two of them, and your brother is the president or chief operating officer of all three and a deputy chair in two. It sounds like you can do pretty much whatever you want to do. That is what happened with Black and Radler through their ownership and management of all three companies. Figure 1 depicts the organization structure at Hollinger.

Hollinger, Inc., was a publicly held Canadian mutual fund company whose primary holding is its shares of stock in Hollinger, International. From about 1998 to the present, Hollinger, Inc. (referred to as "the Company"), had no operations. During that time it was the controlling shareholder of Hollinger, International (referred to as "Hollinger") through direct and indirect ownership of all shares of Class B common. This stock had a 10-to-1 voting preference over shares of Hollinger's Class A common. The Company owned approximately 18.2 percent of the combined equity but 68 percent of combined voting power in Hollinger.

---

[1]Special Committee of the Board of Directors to Investigate Hollinger International, www.cba.ca/news/background/black_conrad/hollinger_report.html.

[2]Securities and Exchange Commission, Accounting and Auditing Enforcement Release (AAER) No. 1946, www.sec.gov/litigation/litreleases/lr18550.htm.
[3]*United States Securities and Exchange Commission v. Conrad M. Black, F. David Radler, and Hollinger, Inc.*

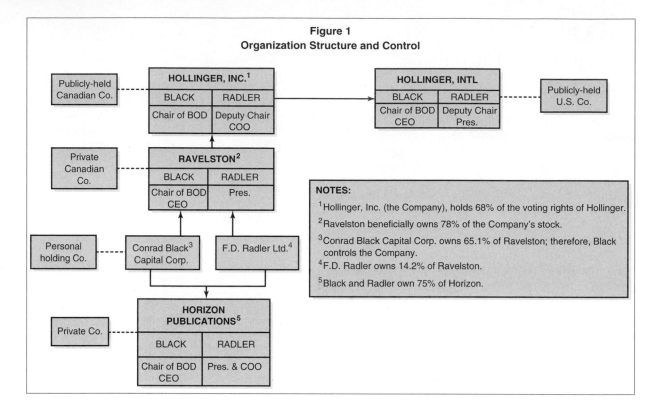

Figure 1
Organization Structure and Control

NOTES:

[1] Hollinger, Inc. (the Company), holds 68% of the voting rights of Hollinger.

[2] Ravelston beneficially owns 78% of the Company's stock.

[3] Conrad Black Capital Corp. owns 65.1% of Ravelston; therefore, Black controls the Company.

[4] F.D. Radler owns 14.2% of Ravelston.

[5] Black and Radler own 75% of Horizon.

Hollinger was a Delaware corporation with its principal place of business in Chicago. The company was listed on the New York Stock Exchange. Hollinger owned and operated newspaper publishing businesses in the United States and abroad. From 1998 through 2004 it owned, through its wholly owned subsidiaries, the *Chicago Sun-Times, The Daily Telegraph,* a London newspaper, and the *Jerusalem Post,* as well as almost 400 smaller newspapers and other entities.

Ravelston was a privately owned Canadian company that beneficially owned approximately 78 percent of the Company's stock. Ravelston, in turn, is owned by Conrad Black through Conrad Black Capital Corporation (65.1 percent), a personal holding company, and F. D. Radler Ltd. (14.2 percent). Ravelston, therefore, effectively owned Hollinger, and Black and Radler control Ravelston.

The top management at Hollinger, including Black and Radler, were employed through a contract with an affiliate of Ravelston that received payments from Hollinger for its management of that entity. These arrangements led to the top executives at Hollinger working for Black as the CEO and also they were subordinate to and drew benefits from Black in their roles at Ravelston. The overlapping ownership and management structure is analyzed in the *Special Committee Report* that appears in Table 1.

Cast of Characters

Conrad Black was born in Canada but renounced his Canadian citizenship in 2001 after unsuccessfully attempting to gain dual British-Canadian citizenship. The Canadian government would not approve and Black gave up his Canadian citizenship to become a British citizen and accept a peerage in the British House of Lords. Ironically, Black now seeks to restore his Canadian citizenship so he can request U.S. trials to be moved to Canada.

Between 1999 and 2003, Black signed Hollinger's annual 10-K reports as its chair and CEO. He certified Hollinger's annual and quarterly reports between August 2002 and August 2003 that were filed with the SEC pursuant to SOX.

David Radler signed Hollinger's 10-K reports between 1999 and 2003 as the deputy chair and president of Hollinger. Radler served as Black's right-hand man and supervised newspaper sales through which he and other managers siphoned off millions of dollars in fees that should have gone to Hollinger. On September 21, 2005, Radler pled guilty to a lesser charge, apparently as part of a deal for a lesser sentence in exchange for testimony against Black.

Peter Atkinson served as the executive vice president and was a director of Hollinger from 1996 until April 27, 2004. In January 2004, he resigned as executive vice president. John Boultbee served as a director from 1990 until 1995 and became executive vice president in 1998. He also served as the chief financial officer from 1995 through 2002. During the 1999 through 2002 period, Boultbee signed many of Hollinger's quarterly 10-Q reports. Both Atkinson and Boultbee owned, directly or indirectly, 0.98 percent of Ravelston. They shared to some extent in the diverted amounts.

Table 1
Hollinger International—Overlaps in Management, Board of Directors, and Ownership*

	Ravelston Shareholder	Hollinger, Inc. (Company)		Hollinger International (Hollinger)	
		Officer	**Director**	**Officer**	**Director**
Conrad M. Black	Yes 65.1%	Chair CEO	Yes	Chair[3] CEO[4]	Yes
F. David Radler	Yes 14.2%	Deputy chair President & COO	Yes	Deputy chair[5] President & COO[5]	Yes
	Yes	Executive VP	Yes	Executive VP[6]	Yes
Peter Atkinson		President	[1]		[5]
	0.98%	General counsel			
	Yes	Executive VP	Yes	Executive VP[7]	No
J.A. Boultbee		President			
	0.98%	Former CFO		Former CFO	
	Yes	Vice chair	Yes	Vice chair[8]	Yes
Daniel W. Colson			[2]		
	2.9%			Deputy chair & CEO of *Telegraph*	

[1]Resigned effective January 13, 2004.
[2]Resigned effective December 22, 2003.
[3]Removed on January 17, 2004.
[4]Resigned effective November 19, 2003.
[5]Resigned effective November 17, 2003.
[6]Resigned effective April 27, 2004.
[7]Terminated effective November 17, 2003.
[8]Resigned effective March 24, 2004.
*Taken from *The Special Committee Report.*

Hollinger's Board of Directors

Hollinger had 10 members of the board immediately before the events that led to the collapse of management and the board; 5 were inside directors and 5 were outsiders. The 5 inside directors included Black, his wife, Radler, Atkinson, and Daniel Colson, who was the deputy chair of Hollinger's board and CEO of the *London Telegraph*. He also owned stock in Ravelston.

Black and Radler were majority shareholders in Ravelston, and Ravelston received management fee payments for their services to Hollinger from Hollinger funds. Now, add to the equation the fact that the Company owned the majority voting power in Hollinger while Black was the chair and CEO of the Company and Radler served as its deputy chair, president, and chief operating officer, and it is easy to see how the organization's framework and overlapping ownership interests enabled the frauds to occur. Of course, Black and Radler were the ones who established a culture of deceit and selfishness.

With the exception of Shmuel Meitar, a communications and media business specialist, the outside board members reads like a list from "Who's Who" and included:

- Richard Burt, the former chief negotiator of the Strategic Arms Reduction Talks and an ambassador to Germany
- Henry Kissinger, the former secretary of state and national security advisor under Presidents Nixon and Ford
- Richard Perle, the former assistant secretary for the Department of Defense for International Security Policy during the Reagan administration
- James Thompson, the former four-term governor of Illinois

The Fraudulent Noncompetition Payments

The SEC civil fraud lawsuit (Litigation Release No. 18969) that was filed on November 15, 2004, in the U.S. District Court, Northern District of Illinois, against Black, Radler, and the Company alleged that from approximately 1999 through 2003, the defendants engaged in a fraudulent and deceptive scheme to divert cash and assets from Hollinger and concealed their self-dealing from Hollinger's public shareholders. The SEC complaint asks the court to:

- Enjoin the defendants from further violations of the securities laws
- Order the defendants to disgorge their ill-gotten gains and pay prejudgment interest
- Order the defendants to pay civil penalties
- Bar Black and Radler from serving as an officer or director of another public company
- Impose a voting trust upon the shares of Hollinger held directly or indirectly by Black and the Company

The SEC complaint (11–35) detailed several fraudulent noncompetition payments from approximately 1999 through 2001. The noncompetition payments were made in connection with a series of Hollinger sales of its U.S. and Canadian newspaper properties. As a result of these payments, portions of the sales proceeds that should have gone to Hollinger for the benefit of all its shareholders were diverted in the amount of $85 million to Black and Radler, the Company, Ravelston, and other corporate insiders. A summary of the payments appears in Table 2.

During the 1999–2001 period, the Company received $16.55 million, Black and Radler received $19 million each, Atkinson and Boultbee received $1.9 million each, and Ravelston, the company controlled by Black, received $26.3 million. These amounts represented 3.7 and 6.2 percent of Hollinger's gross and net income, respectively, for 1999 and increased to 11.6 and 54.2 percent in 2000. In 2001 Hollinger experienced a large loss, so the percentages are not computed.

The buyer of the properties did not request Hollinger's officers to execute the noncompetition agreements, and none of the Hollinger officers were asked to sign such agreements. All that was needed was for Hollinger, as a separate legal entity, to sign a noncompete agreement, which would have covered Black and Radler without the need for separate payments to these or other officers of Hollinger. On one occasion,

Black and Radler engineered purported noncompetition payments to themselves for their agreements not to compete with a wholly owned subsidiary of Hollinger in the absence of any purchase or sale of newspapers.

The amounts received by the Company from the noncompete payments in 1999 were used by it to repay debt due to Hollinger. This created a double benefit for the Company because not only was $15.2 million diverted from the sales proceeds that should have gone to Hollinger, but the Company then turned around and used that money to repay a loan due to Hollinger.

The CanWest Transaction

Perhaps no transaction more than CanWest illustrated the extent to which Black schemed to defraud Hollinger. On July 30, 2000, Hollinger and its subsidiaries executed a transaction agreement to sell several of its Canadian newspapers to CanWest for approximately $2.6 billion, of which $51.6 million was allocated as consideration for noncompetition agreements. The transaction was strictly between Hollinger and CanWest, yet the Company, Ravelston, Black, Radler, Atkinson, and Boultbee were identified in the transaction agreement as parties to the noncompetition agreement along with Hollinger.

Black negotiated the transaction on behalf of Hollinger. Black and Radler determined the allocation of the noncompete payment. Atkinson asked Black if he and Boultbee could be given "noncompetition" payments to serve as bonuses for their work on the CanWest transaction. Black agreed to add their names to the list of the chosen.

On July 25, 2000, the Hollinger board received a summary of the proposed CanWest transaction. The summary stated, "The purchase price was increased as a result of a reduction of Management Service Fees charged by Ravelston with respect to the ongoing management of the Newspaper Assets. Prior to closing, Ravelston and the Audit Committee will negotiate an appropriate sharing of such purchase price increase." Apparently, the purchase price was increased because the future operating results of CanWest would be

Table 2
Fraudulent Noncompetition Payments

Year	Amount	Recipient	Payment as a % of Hollinger	
			Gross Income	**Net Income**
1999	$15.2M	Company	3.7%	6.2%
2000	1.35M	Company	—	—
2000 – 2001	19.0M	Black		
	19.0M	Radler	11.6%	54.2% ('00)
	1.9M	Atkinson		
	1.9M	Boultbee		
	26.3M	Ravelston	$361.5M loss	$337.5M loss ('01)

higher since it would not have to pay the management service fee to Ravelston.

In preparation for an audit committee meeting on September 11, 2000, a memorandum was sent explaining that Black, Radler, Hollinger, Ravelston, Atkinson, and Boultbee had been requested to execute noncompetition agreements. At the same time, Ravelston proposed that it receive approximately 0.9 percent of the purchase price, "in consideration for Ravelston reducing its management fee and consenting to CanWest having an early termination of its management arrangements." The audit committee approved CanWest's desire for the noncompete agreements and Ravelston's termination fee request without knowing that CanWest had not requested the noncompete payments. Thompson, the audit committee chair, presented it to the board and it, too, approved based on the "fairness" of the allocations.

Hollinger did not disclose the CanWest noncompete transactions in its 2000 Form 10-K filed on April 2, 2001. It first disclosed the payments in its Form 10-Q for the quarter ended March 31, 2001, and then later in its 2001 Form 10-K and 2002 Form 10-K. These disclosures appear in Exhibit 1.

The disclosures identified CanWest as the originator of the request for noncompete payments, and the annual reports indicate the payments were approved by Hollinger's independent directors. The SEC charged Black and Radler with recklessness in not knowing that Hollinger's 2001 and 2002 Forms 10-K and Form 10-Q for the quarter ended March 31, 2001, were materially false and misleading because they contained misstatements and omissions of material facts. Black and Radler signed Hollinger's 2001 and 2002 Forms 10-K with the omissions and misstatements. Black also certified Hollinger's 2002 Form 10-K pursuant to Section 302 of SOX as the CEO of Hollinger. An example of Hollinger's disclosures on Form 10-K for 2001 and 2002 appears in Exhibit 2.

By policy and practice, Hollinger should have had all related party transactions reviewed and approved by the audit committee of the board of directors. According to the charges filed by the SEC, to perpetrate their scheme Black and Radler made misstatements and omissions of material fact regarding the purported noncompetition payments to the audit committee and board. On November 17, 2003, Hollinger filed a Form 8-K with the SEC along with a press release disclosing some of the payments. Perhaps the filing was motivated by the more stringent requirements for filing that formed in the aftermath of SOX.

Exhibit 1
Examples of Disclosures about the CanWest Transaction

Form 10-Q for the Quarter Ended March 31, 2001
Also, as required by CanWest as a condition to the transaction, Ravelston, [the Company], and Messrs. Black, Radler, Boultbee, and Atkinson, entered into noncompetition agreements with CanWest pursuant to which each agreed not to compete directly or indirectly in Canada with the Canadian businesses sold to CanWest for a five year period, subject to certain limited exceptions, for aggregate consideration received by Ravelston and the executives of $53 million paid by CanWest in addition to the purchase price referred to above, consisting of $38 million paid to Ravelston, $19 million paid to Mr. Black, $19 million paid to Mr. Radler, $2 million paid to Mr. Boultbee, and $2 million paid to Mr. Atkinson.

2001 Form 10-K
Also, as required by CanWest as a condition to the transaction, [Hollinger], Ravelston, the Company, Lord Black, and three senior executives entered into noncompetition agreements with CanWest pursuant to which each agreed not to compete directly or indirectly in Canada with the Canadian businesses sold to CanWest for a five year period, subject to certain limited exceptions, for aggregate consideration received by Ravelston and the executives of $53 million paid by CanWest in addition to the purchase price referred to above of which $25.2 million was paid to Ravelston and $27.8 million was paid to Lord Black and the three senior executives. [Hollinger's] independent directors have approved the terms of these payments.

2002 Form 10-K
Further, CanWest required as a condition to the transaction that, [Hollinger], Ravelston, the Company, Lord Black, and three senior executives entered into noncompetition agreements with CanWest pursuant to which each agreed not to compete directly or indirectly in Canada with the Canadian businesses sold to CanWest for a five-year period, subject to certain limited exceptions, for aggregate consideration received by Ravelston and the executives of $53 million paid by CanWest in addition to the purchase price referred to above of which $25.2 million was paid to Ravelston and $27.8 million was paid to Lord Black and the three senior executives. [Hollinger's] independent directors have approved the terms of these payments.

Exhibit 2
Examples of Disclosures about the Noncompete Agreements

2001

In connection with the sales of U.S. newspaper properties in 2000, to satisfy a closing condition, the Company, Lord Black, and three senior executives entered into noncompetition agreements with purchasers to which each agreed not to compete directly or indirectly in the United States with the U.S. businesses sold to purchasers for a fixed period, subject to certain limited exceptions, for aggregate consideration of $0.6 million paid in 2001. These amounts were in addition to the aggregate consideration paid in 2001 in respect to these noncompetition agreements of $15 million in 2000. Such amounts were paid to Lord Black and the three senior executives. The Company's independent directors have approved the terms of these payments.

2002

During 2000, we sold most of our remaining U.S. community newspaper properties for total proceeds of approximately $215 million. In connection with those sales, to satisfy a closing condition, the Company, Lord Black, and three senior executives entered into noncompetition agreements with purchasers to which each agreed not to compete directly or indirectly in the United States with the U.S. businesses sold to purchasers for a fixed period, subject to certain limited exceptions, for aggregate consideration paid of $0.6 million in 2001. These amounts were in addition to the aggregate consideration paid in 2001 in respect to these noncompetition agreements of $15 million in 2000. Such amounts were paid to Lord Black and the three senior executives. The Company's independent directors have approved the terms of these payments.

The Report of the Special Committee

Abusive Practices

The Report of the Special Committee of the board identified a variety of abusive practices, in addition to the noncompetition payments, that included the Company's taking approximately $80 million in Hollinger cash as "loans" without paying market levels of interest and, as previously mentioned, using Hollinger's own cash to repay debt. The report concluded that Black and Radler freely used Hollinger's cash and credit to benefit the Company without adequately compensating Hollinger, in part to maintain the Company's "stranglehold" control over Hollinger.

The report labeled the noncompetition payments as a form of unauthorized compensation and also identified another form of "compensation" in the use of Hollinger cash to pay personal expenses of Black and his wife, and of Radler and his family. While the total amount taken from the personal piggy bank set up by Black from Hollinger cash for these purposes was nowhere near that of John Rigas, the former founder and CEO of Adelphia, the two officers did manage to travel in style. Hollinger bought a Challenger aircraft for $11.6 million that was given to Radler and leased a Gulfstream IV at a cost of $3 to $4 million each year for the Blacks. Operating costs for both of these aircraft totaled over $23 million from 2000 to 2003.

Perhaps the most abusive practice was the substantial amounts that were taken out of Hollinger and paid to Ravelston on behalf of Black and Radler as their management fees. The report described a camouflaged system that was designed to make it more difficult for the audit committee and external auditors to know exactly how much was transferred from Hollinger to Ravelston for this purpose.

The Management Fees

The Special Committee's compensation experts concluded that "from 1997 to 2003, Black and Radler received 'management fees' of $218.4 million through [the Company] and Ravelston." The experts analyzed the fees and identified $196.9 million of the total amount that represented compensation to the five senior officers.

One issue that permeated the Hollinger case from a corporate governance perspective is the fairness of Black and Radler's practices to all of Hollinger's shareholders. The report noted that Hollinger did not benefit from the Ravelston structure. Moreover, shareholders could not learn what compensation Black and the others were receiving by reading Hollinger's proxy statement that was prepared before each annual meeting. The aggregate management fees to Ravelston were disclosed, but investors had no way of knowing that almost all of the fees represented compensation to the individuals. An analysis by compensation experts of total fees paid to Black, Radler, and their associates at Ravelston during the 1997 to 2003 period indicates that over $400 million was paid from all sources including the noncompete payments, personal expenses, and other transfers from Hollinger. This represented 95.2 percent of Hollinger's adjusted net income over the relevant period.

Black's public defense of the Ravelston management system was that the amount of the management fee each year was approved by the audit committee. Yet the Hollinger board was never given truthful and accurate information to enable it to understand how much Black or Radler made directly and indirectly in annual compensation from Hollinger. When the audit committee approved the Ravelston management fees, it did so without knowing the level of compensation for each officer and how this might compare to officers at other publishing companies. Also, the audit committee did not know how much more the Ravelston fee cost Hollinger compared with what it would have cost Hollinger to follow normal compensation and hiring practices for senior executives.

Where Were the Auditors?

Where were the KPMG auditors whose job it was to protect the interests of the shareholders? While Black failed to fully disclose to the auditors the information they needed to investigate the noncompete payments and management fees over a five-year period ending in 2003, the auditors had knowledge of the payments, at least in general, but it does not seem from the report that they were actively engaged in trying to find out what was going on at Hollinger. Ultimately, they gave up when on December 24, 2003, the firm announced that it was resigning from the engagement after the embattled holding company refused the firm's demands to make a number of management changes.

The Lawsuits Just Kept on Coming

In March 2005, Black learned that U.S. authorities had opened a criminal investigation into his activities. Also, the Ontario Securities Commission launched proceedings against Black, three former associates, and the Company for alleged violations of securities laws.

On March 30, 2005, the Company filed a $636 million lawsuit in Canada against Black and other former executives charging that they blocked corporate opportunities, breached their fiduciary responsibilities, and misappropriated management fees and noncompetition payments.

On May 3, 2005, a group of Hollinger directors settled a shareholder lawsuit and agreed to pay Hollinger $50 million that would come from directors' liability insurance policies. Earlier, on May 11, 2004, Hollinger had reached agreement with former director Atkinson. Atkinson paid $2.8 million, which represents 100 percent of the amount he received plus interest from noncompete payments and management fees. David Radler also pleaded guilty on September 21, 2005, and agreed to a 29-month jail term and a fine of $250,000. The lone hold-out other than Black was John Boultbee, the former CFO of Hollinger, who on December 7, 2005, pleaded not guilty to fraud charges. He was ordered released after posting bail of $1.5 million.

The scope of the legal proceedings against Black expanded on November 17, 2005, when Patrick Fitzgerald, U.S. attorney for the Northern District of Illinois, charged Black and other former top executives with 12 counts of fraud relating to the alleged diversion of millions from Hollinger. The charges included the fraud scheme that involved Hollinger's sale of Canadian newspapers to CanWest. Black pleaded not guilty and was released after posting a $20 million bond.

An expanded 15-count indictment was returned on December 15, 2005, that added four new charges against Black—one count each of racketeering, obstruction of justice, money laundering, and wire fraud. The obstruction charge referred to the removal of boxes from the Company headquarters. The racketeering count alleged that Black masterminded the activities of a group of individuals and entities that comprised the "Hollinger Enterprise." The indictment identified racketeering in the form of noncompete payments that improperly diverted funds away from Hollinger, the abuse of perquisites, and the making of false and fraudulent statements to Hollinger's shareholders and other outsiders including filings with the SEC that contained material falsehoods and omissions.

Black was convicted in Illinois U.S. District Court on July 13, 2007. He was sentenced to serve 78 months in federal prison and pay Hollinger $6.1 million and a fine of $125,000. Black was found guilty of diverting funds for personal benefit from money due Hollinger International when the company sold certain publishing assets and other irregularities. He also obstructed justice by taking possession of documents to which he was not entitled. The U.S. Supreme Court heard his case on December 8, 2009, and is expected to render a decision in June 2010.

Questions

1. Evaluate the actions of top management in the Hollinger case with respect to meeting its agency responsibilities to shareholders.

2. How do the actions of Conrad Black and other officers in the case match up with the ethics and values expected of corporations, top management, and the board of directors that were discussed in the chapter?

3. There was a massive failure of the corporate governance systems in the Hollinger case. Describe each of the failings.

Chapter 4

AICPA Code of Professional Conduct

Ethics Reflection

First, it was the Big Eight CPA firms. Then, Arthur Young and Ernst & Whinney combined to form Ernst & Young (EY). This was followed by the merger of Deloitte Haskins & Sells and Touche Ross & Co. (Deloitte & Touche), and then Price Waterhouse and Coopers & Lybrand (PricewaterhouseCoopers). The Big Five including KPMG existed until the early 2000s when Arthur Andersen (Andersen) was forced out of business as a result of the fallout from a criminal investigation of the firm by the U.S. Department of Justice. Now, it's the Big Four CPA firms—the four largest firms in the world that audit major international companies.

In her book *Final Accounting* that chronicles the rise and fall of Arthur Andersen, Barbara Ley Toffler describes Andersen's employees as "Androids." Toffler points to a culture at Andersen that led to a compromise of its ethical values by establishing a tone at the top for employees to live the mantra of "keep the client happy."[1]

The shortcomings with the Enron audit are generally credited with leading to the demise of Andersen. However, the firm had reportedly settled more than a dozen cases over a 25-year period pertaining to claims that auditors concealed or failed to reveal material misstatements within financial reports. Multimillion-dollar settlements preceded the Enron scandal, which at that time was the largest bankruptcy case in the history of the United States.[2] Accounting frauds at Andersen clients including Sunbeam, Waste Management, Enron, and WorldCom typified Andersen's failure to act in the public interest.

On December 2, 2001, Enron filed for Chapter 11 Bankruptcy, and two weeks later it fired Andersen as its auditor. On January 15, 2002, the main partner, David Duncan—who was responsible for the Enron audit—was fired by Andersen for his role in overseeing the mass destruction of Enron documents prior to the SEC's investigation of the firm. On January 28, 2002, the U.S. Department of Justice filed a criminal obstruction-of-justice charge against Andersen for its shredding of documents in the Enron case. Andersen pleaded not guilty to a charge of obstructing justice and explained that the destruction of Enron documentation and e-mails was just part of routine company procedures of destroying confidential client documentation. On April 9, 2002, in an agreement with the Department of Justice, Duncan pleaded guilty to illegally shredding Enron documents. Just a day before, Andersen announced a massive layoff of 7,000 of its workforce. On June 15, 2002, after 5 weeks of hearing evidence and 10 days of deliberation, the jury found Andersen guilty of obstructing the course of justice.

In a surprise reversal, the U.S. Supreme Court reviewed the original jury instructions given by Judge Melinda Harmon that defined the standards and hurdles the jury had to clear to reach a guilty verdict. The court ruled that the instructions "failed to convey the requisite consciousness of wrongdoing," Chief Justice William Rehnquist wrote in the unanimous opinion. "Indeed, it is striking how little culpability the instructions required."[3] Unfortunately for Andersen it was too late as the firm had already closed its doors for good.

As you read this chapter, think about the following: (1) How do the ethics rules in the AICPA Code of Professional Conduct define the CPA's obligations to the public? (2) Why is it important for a CPA to be independent of the client and how can CPAs manage the threats that exist to audit independence? (3) What roles do integrity and objectivity play in preventing a company from issuing materially false and misleading financial statements?

By certifying the public reports that collectively depict a corporation's financial status, the independent auditor assumes a public responsibility transcending any employment responsibility with the client. The independent public accountant performing this special function owes ultimate allegiance to the corporation's creditors and stockholders, as well as to the investing public. This "public watchdog" function demands that the accountant maintain total independence from the client at all times and requires complete fidelity to the public trust.[4]

Chief Justice Warren Burger, writing the unanimous opinion of the Supreme Court in United States v. Arthur Young & Co.

This important ruling of the U.S. Supreme Court reminds us that the independent audit provides the foundation for the existence of the accounting profession in the United States. Even though independent audits were common before the passage of the landmark legislation of the Securities Act of 1933 and the Securities Exchange Act of 1934, there is no doubt that CPAs derive their franchise as a profession from these two pieces of legislation that require independent audits of publicly owned companies.

The Burger Court opinion emphasizes the trust placed by the public in the independent auditor's opinion. The accounting profession is the only profession where one's public obligation supersedes that to a client. The medical profession recognizes the primacy of the physician's responsibility to a patient. The legal profession emphasizes the lawyer's responsibility to the client. The Public Interest Principle in the Code of Professional Conduct of the American Institute of CPAs (AICPA Code) states, "In discharging their professional responsibilities, members (of the AICPA) may encounter conflicting pressures from each of these groups [clients, employers . . .]. In resolving those conflicts, members should act with integrity, guided by the precept that when members fulfill their responsibility to the public, clients' and employers' interests are best served."[5]

Investigations of the Profession

The rules of conduct in the AICPA Code are best understood in light of the investigations of the accounting profession following high-profile frauds during the period of the 1970s and 1980s and following frauds at companies such as Enron and WorldCom. Congressional concern was that auditors were not living up to their ethical and professional responsibilities (as stated in the Burger Court opinion). The major themes of these investigations were (1) whether nonaudit services impair auditor independence, (2) the need for management to report on internal controls, and (3) the importance of developing techniques to prevent and detect fraud.

Metcalf Committee and Cohen Commission: 1977–1978

As CPA firms have become global entities, the profession's concern about ethics and regulation has grown. In 1977, a major study examined the relationship between auditors and clients and the provision of nonaudit services for those clients. The Metcalf (Moss) Report was the first real investigation of the accounting profession since the 1930s. An investigation was conducted between 1975 and 1977 by Senator Lee Metcalf and, on the

House side, Representative John Moss.[6] The Metcalf Report issued four recommendations, two of which are described here. The report did not lead to any new legislation at the time, although, in the aftermath of frauds at Enron and WorldCom, changes were made to enhance audits and financial reporting.

The first recommendation of the Metcalf Committee was to establish a self-regulatory organization of firms that audit publicly owned companies. It led to the AICPA's formation of a two-tier voluntary peer review program in 1977: one for firms with public-company clients and one for smaller firms with only private companies. In 2004, the Public Company Accounting Oversight Board (PCAOB) assumed the AICPA's responsibilities relating to firms that audit public clients ending the period of self-regulation by the profession, at least for public companies.* PCAOB instituted a mandatory quality inspection program for CPA firms that audit public companies. The AICPA continued its two-tier program to assist firms in meeting state licensing and AICPA membership requirements.[7]

The second recommendation of the Metcalf Committee was to limit types of management services to those relating directly to accounting. The accounting profession was upset at the implication that somehow the provision of management consulting services tainted the audit. It was left to the Cohen Commission to conduct an in-depth study of the issue. In the meantime, the SEC followed up the concern with a requirement that public companies disclose in their annual reports the aggregate fees they paid to their accountants for nonaudit services.

The profession's own Cohen Commission Report on auditors' responsibilities examined a variety of issues that are still debated today including the auditor's responsibility for detecting fraud and the expectation gap that exists between the profession's goals for the audit and what the public expects an audit to accomplish.[8] Beyond that, the commission recommended that management report on its internal controls to the users of the financial statements and the auditor should evaluate management's report. This recommendation was ultimately enacted into legislation as part of the Sarbanes-Oxley (SOX) Act of 2002.

The events that eventually led to change were two rounds of major scandals—one in the 1980s including the failures of savings and loan institutions and the second in the late 1990s and early 2000s led by Enron and WorldCom. After Enron and WorldCom, the profession agreed to go along with change in the form of the provisions passed by SOX and the creation of PCAOB, a new public oversight board.

The Cohen Commission headed by Manny Cohen, a former SEC commissioner, was important for two reasons. First, its final report included an instance that demonstrates the potential conflict when providing nonaudit services for an audit client. It was discovered that the audit of Westec Corporation had been compromised because of a consulting project. Second, it decried the lowballing of audit fees that raised the possibility of a decline in audit quality.[9] The latter concern along with opinion shopping have contributed over the years to a shift in the environment of professionalism that has existed in the accounting profession to one emphasizing the commercialization of accounting services.

The practice of lowballing consists of deliberately underbidding for an audit engagement to obtain the audit client and with the hope of securing more-lucrative management advisory or other consulting services from that client in the future. To a large extent the practice became less prevalent after the passage of SOX, which restricts providing certain nonaudit services for audit clients. Opinion shopping occurs when a client seeks out the views of various accountants until finding one that will go along with the client's desired—not necessarily

*On June 26, 2010, the U.S. Supreme Court ruled that the restriction on removal of PCAOB board members under SOX violates separation of powers principles, but found that the provision was severable from the remainder of the Act. The problem was that SOX's provisions making PCAOB board members removable by the SEC only for good cause were inconsistent with the Constitution's separation of powers. The Court stated that the Act remains fully operative as a law with the for-cause restrictions taken out, leaving the members of PCAOB subject to removal by the SEC without restriction.

most ethical—accounting treatment. This practice can lead to pressure being applied on the auditor to remain silent or risk losing the account, an intimidation threat to independence.

House Subcommittee on Oversight and Investigations

Representative Ron Wyden had introduced a bill in May 1986 to hold the accounting profession responsible for the detection of fraud in light of the failure at ESM Government Securities and bank failures in the early 1980s at Continental Illinois National Bank and Trust and Penn Square Bank.[10] Even though Continental Illinois had received a $4.5 billion federal bailout, the company ultimately was liquidated by the Federal Deposit Insurance Corporation just four months after receiving an unqualified opinion on its audit by Peat Marwick. The cry in Congress heard during the investigation was: "Where were the auditors?"

Wyden eventually changed his proposed legislation because of criticisms by the AICPA and SEC, the latter under then-chair John Shad, who believed the system was "working well" to protect the public from major financial fraud. The new legislation called once again for internal control reports and emphasized the need for auditors to detect material illegalities or irregularities.

Representative John Dingell was chair of both the House Committee on Energy and Commerce and its Subcommittee on Oversight and Investigations. In January and February 1988, the subcommittee held two hearings concerning the failure of ZZZZ Best Co., a corporation that had "created" 80 percent or more of its total revenue in the form of fictitious revenue from the restoration of carpets, drapes, and other items in office buildings after fires and floods. Chair Dingell characterized the fraud as follows:[11]

> The fact that auditors and attorneys repeatedly visited make-believe job sites and came away satisfied does not speak well for the present regulatory system. The fact that the audit firm discovering the fraud resigned the engagement without telling enforcement authorities is even more disturbing. . . . Cases such as ZZZZ Best demonstrate vividly that we cannot afford to tolerate a system that fails to meet the public's legitimate expectations in this regard.

Savings and Loan Industry Failures

By the late 1980s, the savings and loan (S&L) industry failures became the focus of the congressional hearings as a $300 million failure at Beverly Hills Savings & Loan and a $250 million failure at Sunrise Savings, a Florida S&L, engulfed Deloitte & Touche. Arthur Young, the firm that was to merge with Ernst & Whinney, had run into deep trouble in its S&L audits. In particular, it certified the financial statements of Western Savings Association in 1984 and 1985 that were overstated by $400 million. If Arthur Young had not merged with Ernst & Whinney, the firm may have been forced out of business. Eventually the firm paid the federal government $400 million to settle claims that the company's auditors failed to warn of disastrous financial problems that caused some of the nation's biggest thrift failures.

Perhaps the most publicized failure is that of Lincoln Savings & Loan. Thousands of California retirees lost their life savings after buying uninsured subordinated debentures issued by Lincoln's parent company, American Continental, and sold through Lincoln branches. Arthur Young, the auditors of American Continental, issued unqualified opinions on the entity's financial statements for fiscal years 1986 and 1987. The audit opinions were part of the annual reports of American Continental that were furnished to prospective buyers of the worthless debentures.

The cost to the public to clean up 1,043 failed thrift institutions with total assets of over $500 billion during the 1986–1995 period was reported to be $152.9 billion, including $123.8 billion of U.S. taxpayer losses. The balance was absorbed by the thrift industry itself. It was the greatest collapse of U.S. financial institutions since the Great Depression.[12] Little did we know that 20 years later banks and financial institutions would be embroiled in a scandal that involved risky investments including derivatives and worthless mortgage-backed securities, and some institutions would need federal bailout funds to stay in business while others were taken over by the government or other institutions.

The accounting issues in failed S&Ls centered on three issues: (1) the failure to provide adequate allowances for loan losses, (2) the failure to disclose dubious deals between the S&Ls and some of their major customers, and (3) the existence of inadequate internal controls to prevent these occurrences. The profession was already considering ways to address the large number of business failures in the 1980s when the S&L debacle occurred. The profession's response to deal with this new pressure was to form the Treadway Commission, and its work was given a new sense of urgency.

Treadway Commission Report

The National Commission on Fraudulent Financial Reporting, referred to as the Treadway Committee after its chair James C. Treadway, was formed in 1985 to study and report on the factors that can lead to fraudulent financial reporting. This independent private sector initiative was sponsored by five professional associations called the Committee of Sponsoring Organizations (COSO). The work of the Treadway Committee and COSO since 1985 has been extremely valuable to those who study how to enhance the ethics of an organization and strengthen its internal control environment. The Treadway Commission and COSO have emphasized the need to change the corporate culture and establish the systems necessary to prevent fraudulent financial reporting. It starts with the "tone at the top"; that is, top management should set an ethical tone that filters throughout the organization and influences everything and everyone.

While Metcalf-Moss, Dingell, and Wyden focused mainly on the role of the external auditor including independence matters, Treadway and COSO extended the review to include the role and responsibilities of internal accountants and auditors and the board of directors in preventing and detecting fraud. An important part of the framework and work of the Treadway Commission is to stress the importance of a strong control environment so that the internal auditors can have direct and unrestricted access to the audit committee of the board of directors (refer back to Exhibit 3.2 in Chapter 3).[13] If top management (i.e., the CEO and CFO) attempts to manipulate earnings or use company assets for inappropriate reasons, then the internal auditors supported by strong internal controls should detect and report the wrongdoing to the audit committee. The audit committee's responsibility is to do whatever is necessary to reverse top management's action.

Armadillo Foods, Inc: An Example of Integrity and Objectivity

Let's assume you are a CPA and the controller of Armadillo Foods, Inc., a large southwestern processor of armadillo-based food products. One day the CFO comes to you and says the earnings results for the quarter ending June 30, 2010, are 20 percent below the financial analysts' estimates. As a public company, you know the stock price is likely to decline, perhaps significantly, after public disclosure of the earnings reduction for the second straight quarter in 2010. The CFO tells you that the CEO insists the company must "make the numbers" this quarter. You are told to find a way to make it happen. What would you do? Why?

This is a hypothetical situation but one that occurred all too often during the accounting scandals of the 1990s and 2000s. The pressure applied by the CFO and CEO on the controller tests that person's commitment to act ethically. The controller is probably quite aware of her ethical obligations to act in accordance with the public interest. She also knows that integrity requires that she not subordinate her judgment and give in to the pressure to go along with materially misstated financial statements. Recall that Interpretation 102-4 that was discussed in Chapter 1 outlines the steps to be taken by internal accountants to avoid subordinating judgment. The controller has an ethical dilemma. Interpretation 102-4 requires that she bring her concerns to higher-ups in the organization including the audit committee and prepare an informative memorandum that summarizes the various positions including those of top management. The memo should help provide a defense of due care and the compliance with ethical standards in case it becomes a regulatory or legal matter.

If all parties refuse to support the controller, then the question is whether to inform the external auditors who, after all, rely on the objectivity and integrity of the controller in performing external audit services. The relationship of trust that exists between the controller and the external auditors may be compromised if the controller is silent.

Beyond informing the external auditors, the controller has no responsibility to bring accounting matters of concern to outsiders, and to do so violates confidentiality. As for considering one's continued employment with the company, that may be a moot issue since the controller may have been fired. In all seriousness, the situation portrayed is a difficult one for the controller. However, it is important to emphasize that studies such as those sighted in Chapter 3 by the ACFE clearly indicate that if fraud does not get by the internal accountants, then the external auditors' responsibility to find fraud is lessened. The external auditors' responsibilities to detect fraud will be discussed in Chapter 5.

AICPA Code of Professional Conduct

The AICPA Code is generally recognized as a model for the accounting profession. Each of the 50 states as well as Washington, DC, Puerto Rico, the Virgin Islands, and Guam have independent professional societies for CPAs. The state CPA societies also have codes of conduct for their membership that often mirror the AICPA Code. Even though only members of these voluntary organizations are bound by the codes, the provisions are generally similar to those of state boards of accountancy, so we use the AICPA Code as the model of ethical standards to be followed by CPAs.

CPAs are granted a license to practice in a given state by that state's board of accountancy. The board of accountancy carries out the intent of the state legislature in its statutes and the board promulgates its own rules of professional conduct. The state board of accountancy grants the right to practice accounting in a given state, establishes standards of professional conduct including ethics rules, investigates allegations that a CPA violated the rules, and issues sanctions against CPAs that can include a suspension or revocation of one's license to practice. Although we rely on the AICPA Code for our discussion of ethical standards, it is important to remember that when differences do exist between these standards and the rules of conduct of your state board of accountancy, it is the state board's rules that should be followed.

Rules of professional conduct, whether issued by the AICPA or a state board of accountancy, apply to CPAs in public accounting, private industry, government, and education. The rules apply to a variety of professional services including accounting; auditing and other assurance services; taxation; financial advisory services; and consulting services.

From time to time we will refer to the rules of conduct in California and Texas. The Public Accountancy Act directs the Texas State Board of Public Accountancy to promulgate rules of professional conduct for licensed CPAs "in order to establish and maintain high standards of competence and integrity in the practice of public accountancy and to insure that the conduct and competitive practices of licensees serve the purposes of the Act and the best interest of the public."[14]

One reason for using Texas as an example is the forward-looking ethics education requirement passed by that state's board of accountancy that took effect on July 1, 2005. To qualify to take the CPA Exam in Texas, individuals who hold a baccalaureate degree from a recognized educational institution must demonstrate, as part of the educational requirements, that they have passed a three-semester-hour course in ethics that includes "ethical reasoning, integrity, objectivity, independence and other core values."[15] Students should note that even if they are educated in another state, in order to be eligible to take the CPA Exam in Texas, that state's ethics requirement must be met.

The California Senate passed legislation in August 2009 that was signed into law by Governor Schwarzenegger and becomes effective as of January 1, 2014. It requires that candidates for certification in the state must complete a specified number of ethics hours that was still being defined as of June 2010. The ethics education must include "professional values and attitudes for exercising professional skepticism and other behavior that is in the best interest of the investing and consuming public and the profession." At a minimum, it should include a foundation for ethical reasoning and the core values of integrity, objectivity, and independence consistent with the International Education Standard-4 of the International Accounting Education Standards Board, the International Federation of Accountants Code of Ethics, and the [AICPA] Code of Professional Conduct.[16]

Of particular note is the reference to international education and professional standards that define ethical behavior on a global level. We devote all of Chapter 8 to international issues given the globalization of business and the accounting profession and the influence of International Financial Reporting Standards (IFRS) and uniform ethics and audit standards. We also explore fraud cases in non-U.S. companies, many of whom list their stock on U.S. exchanges and, therefore, come under the listing requirements of the New York Stock Exchange (NYSE) and SEC regulations.

The cornerstone ethical obligation of a CPA to society is to render an opinion on the financial statements of an entity. An opinion is rendered after auditing or examining the financial statements of that entity. All publicly owned companies that sell stock on an established exchange such as the NYSE and NASDAQ are required by the SEC to have their financial statements audited annually and their interim financial information reviewed. A review provides only limited assurance that there are no material modifications that should be made to the financial statements in order for them to be in conformity with GAAP, whereas an audit provides "reasonable assurance" that the financial statements are free of material misstatements. We explore audit standards in Chapter 5.

A CPA also might compile financial statements based on data provided by the client. Since a compilation entails putting together the statements from accounting data, both internal and external accountants can perform this service. Unlike the audit and review service that cannot be performed by an external CPA unless that person is independent of the client, a compilation can be performed when independence is lacking. The reason for not requiring independence with a compilation is that the CPA does not render an opinion along with the compiled statements.

SOX prohibits the performance of bookkeeping services for audit clients. Auditors should not record transactions or prepare the financial statements for an entity under audit. To do so would create a conflict of interests that impairs independence because the auditor would be placed in the position of examining and reporting on his own work. The client's management should prepare the financial statements. Typically, this means the accounting department prepares the statements with oversight by the controller. In most publicly owned companies the controller reports to the CFO. Recall that AICPA Interpretation 102-4 requires that when there is a difference of opinion between a controller and the CFO, specific steps should be taken to explore all avenues of change including taking the matter to the audit committee of the board of directors.

The *practice of public accounting* is defined under the AICPA Code as the performance for a client of specific services while "holding out" as a CPA. *Holding out* generally occurs by informing the public of being a CPA. The services include accounting, auditing, tax preparation and advice, personal financial planning, litigation support, and those services for which standards are established by authoritative organizations. The latter include, for example, Statements of Financial Accounting Standards, Statements on Auditing Standards, Statements on Standards for Tax Services, Statements on Standards for Accounting (Compilation) and Review Services, Statements on Standards for Consulting Services, Statements of Governmental Standards, and Statements on Standards for Attestation Engagements.[17]

You are likely to be most familiar with financial accounting standards established by the Financial Accounting Standards Board (FASB) and auditing standards established by the AICPA. The PCAOB now establishes ethics, independence, and auditing standards for public companies while the AICPA continues to establish such standards for privately held companies. Subsequent to its formation under SOX, the PCAOB adopted AICPA auditing standards as its interim standards. Since that time, the PCAOB has issued a variety of standards to elaborate on AICPA standards and develop new ones. We discuss PCAOB standards later in this chapter and in Chapter 5.

Link between Ethical Judgment and Professional Responsibilities

Ethical reasoning and judgment are critical components of ethical decision making. These skills can be learned through the application of philosophical reasoning methods, which were discussed in Chapter 1. CPAs should utilize these techniques when the accounting rules are unclear, where there is a difference of opinion with an employer or client on an accounting issue, and when there are conflicts between the interests of stakeholder groups. The Integrity Principle best illustrates the link between ethical reasoning and professional judgment.

> "Integrity" is measured in terms of what is right and just. In the absence of specific rules, standards, or guidance, or in the face of conflicting opinions, a [CPA] should test decisions and deeds by asking: "Am I doing what a person of integrity would do? Have I retained my integrity?" Integrity requires a [CPA] to observe both the form and the spirit of technical and ethical standards; circumvention of those standards constitutes subordination of judgment.[18]

Ethics principles are inextricably linked. Recall that the Integrity Principle links to moral behavior by emphasizing the rights of the stakeholders in decision making. A CPA cannot maintain integrity without judging situations with objectivity. Consider, for example, that a sole-practitioner CPA borrowed a significant amount of money from a friend who happened to be the CEO of a client entity under audit. The CPA is not independent because of the relationship with the CEO and objectivity is compromised.

An auditor must be independent in fact, that is, actually be objective, and also avoid actions that may appear to affect independence. Since it is difficult for the public to know whether a CPA has acted independently in providing professional services, the CPA must avoid creating the perception that independence may be impaired as would exist when a CPA borrows money from a client or members of top management.

AICPA Ethics Rules and Interpretations

The Principles of the AICPA Code were discussed in Chapter 1 to emphasize their similarity to virtue. The rules of conduct are the enforceable provisions of the Code. Interpretations of the rules provide guidance on the applicability of the rules in specific situations.

The rules and interpretations are divided into four sections for purposes of our discussion: (1) Independence, Integrity, and Objectivity; (2) Professional Standards and Quality of Work; (3) Responsibilities to Clients; and (4) Other Responsibilities and Practices. Although we discuss all four sections, we emphasize independence, integrity, and objectivity because these standards provide the foundation for all others and directly impact the quality of professional services.

Conceptual Framework for AICPA Independence Standards

Under Rule 101 of the AICPA Code, independence is required when performing audit and other attest-related (opinion) services. To meet the independence standard, the CPA should avoid certain relationships that might impair one's ability to be independent. Generally, these fall into three categories: (1) financial relationships, (2) business relationships, and (3) family relationships. Given the breadth and complexity of independence standards, we emphasize situations that might create an unacceptable risk to the CPA's independence. This risk-based approach is used by the AICPA in its conceptual framework for analyzing threats to independence.[19]

Independence in fact is defined as the state of mind that permits the performance of an attest service without being affected by influences that compromise professional judgment, thereby allowing an individual to act with integrity and professional skepticism. To *appear to be independent,* the CPA should avoid circumstances that might cause an informed third party to reasonably conclude that the integrity, objectivity, or professional skepticism of a firm or member of the audit (attest) engagement team has been compromised.

Threats to independence are situations where relationships develop with a client that could impair independence absent the necessary countervailing steps to prevent a loss of independence. For example, an intimidation threat exists when the client attempts to influence the CPA's judgment on a GAAP matter by threatening to change auditors if the CPA does not go along with the client's demands. Other threats are discussed in the following text.

Financial Relationships That Impair Independence

To avoid violating the independence standard, a CPA should not own a direct financial interest in the client. This would create a financial self-interest threat. The ownership of even one share of stock precludes independence. The CPA also should not own a material indirect financial interest in a client such as through ownership of a mutual fund that includes the client entity's stock. The problem with owning direct and material indirect financial interests is that these arrangements might create the impression in the mind of an outside observer that the CPA cannot make decisions without being influenced by the stock ownership. The logical conclusion is that the auditor's opinion would be tainted by the existence of these relationships.

Another example of a financial self-interest threat is when a CPA becomes involved in a loan transaction to or from a client including home mortgage loans from financial institution clients. This type of loan is prohibited under Interpretation 101-5. Permitted loans include automobile loans collateralized by the automobile, loans fully collateralized by cash deposits at the same financial institution (e.g., "passbook loans"), and aggregate credit card balances from credit cards and overdraft reserve accounts that are reduced to $10,000 or less on a current basis taking into consideration the payment due and any available grace period.[20]

Perhaps no other situation illustrates the danger of a CPA accepting loans from a client more than that of Jose Gomez, the lead partner of Alexander Grant (now Grant Thornton) during its audit of ESM Government Securities from 1977 to 1984. Over the eight-year period, ESM committed fraud and in the process used its leverage against Gomez from $200,000 in loans to him to gain his silence even though Gomez knew ESM's financial statements did not present fairly financial position and the results of operations. Top management of ESM also threatened to pull the audit from Gomez's firm if he spoke out about the fraud. Gomez compromised his integrity and the event ruined his reputation.

Ultimately, Gomez was sentenced to a 12-year prison term and served 4 ½ years, and the firm paid approximately \$175 million in civil payments.[21]

AICPA Interpretation 101-1 extends the Independence rule to certain family members of the CPA. The detailed provisions of this Interpretation are beyond the scope of this book, but we do want to emphasize two points to provide examples of familiarity threats to independence. First, when a CPA is part of the attest engagement team, which includes employees and contractors directly involved in an audit and those who perform concurring and second partner reviews, the rules extend to that CPA's immediate family members and close relatives. The former include the CPA's spouse, spousal equivalent, and dependents (whether or not related). These family members come under the Independence rules. The rules also extend to the CPA's close relatives including a parent, sibling, or nondependent child if they hold a key position with the client, that is, one that involves direct participation in the preparation of the financial statements or a position that gives the CPA the ability to exercise influence over the contents of the financial statements. Close relatives are subject to the Independence rule if they own a financial interest in the client that is material to that person's net worth and of which the CPA has knowledge, or if they own a financial interest in the client that enables the close relative to exercise significant influence over the client. The potential danger in these family relationships is that the family member's financial or employment relationship with the client might influence the perception that the CPA can be independent in fact or appearance. One problem with the rule is that the CPA might feign ignorance of the ownership interest even though he is aware of it—an unethical act.

There are other relationships that will bring a CPA under the Independence rules including when a partner or manager provides 10 hours or more of nonattest services to the attest client. The problem is it may appear to an outside observer that the partner or manager may be able to influence the attest work because of the significant number of hours devoted to the nonattest services.

Let's stop at this point and consider that the Independence rule is a challenging standard for the CPA and family members and it might present some interesting dilemmas. For example, imagine if a CPA knows that his or her father owns a financial interest in a client entity but does not know if that interest is material to the father's net worth. Should the CPA contact the father to find out? Or, might the CPA reason that it is better to not know because the Independence rule applies only if the CPA has knowledge of the extent of the father's financial interest in the client? From an ethical perspective, the CPA should make a good-faith effort to determine the extent of the father's financial interest in the client entity.

SEC Positions

Publicly owned companies are obligated to follow SEC rules. The SEC approach to independence emphasizes independence in fact and appearance in three ways: (1) proscribing certain financial interests and business relationships with the audit client, (2) restricting the provision of certain nonaudit services to audit clients, and (3) subjecting all auditor conduct to a general standard of independence. The general standard of independence is stated as follows: "The Commission will not recognize an accountant as independent, with respect to an audit client, if the accountant is not, or a reasonable investor with knowledge of all relevant facts and circumstances would conclude that the accountant is not, capable of exercising objective and impartial judgment on all issues encompassed within the accountant's engagement."

The general standard of independence is evaluated by applying four principles that are similar to the AICPA's conceptual framework and that indicate when auditor independence may be impaired by a relationship with the audit client. If a situation results in any of the following, the auditor's independence may be impaired: (1) creates a mutual or conflicting interest between an accountant and his audit client, (2) places an accountant in the position of auditing her own work, (3) results in an accountant acting as management or an employee of the audit client, and (4) places an accountant in a position of being an advocate for the audit client.[22]

The SEC believes that these principles are "general guidance and their application may depend on particular facts and circumstances . . . [but they do] provide an appropriate framework for analyzing auditor independence issues." To provide further guidance on implementing the principles, the SEC identified three basic overarching principles that underlie auditor independence: (1) an auditor cannot function in the role of management, (2) an auditor cannot audit her own work, and (3) an auditor cannot serve in an advocacy role for her client.

The PeopleSoft Case

On April 16, 2004, the SEC sanctioned Ernst & Young LLP (EY) because it was not independent in fact or appearance when it audited the financial statements of PeopleSoft for fiscal years 1994–1999. The SEC's sanctions included a six-month suspension from accepting new SEC audit clients, disgorgement of audit fees (more than $1.6 million), an injunction against future violations, and an independent consultant report on its independence and internal quality controls.[23]

The SEC found independence violations arising from EY's business relationships with PeopleSoft while auditing the company's financial statements. These relationships created a mutuality of interests between the firm and PeopleSoft, resulting in a financial self-interest threat.

The SEC action against EY states that the firm violated independence standards in its business dealings with PeopleSoft as a result of the relationship that developed between the two entities with respect to EY's Global Expatriate Management System (EY/GEMS). EY's Tax Group developed this in-house software program for assisting clients with the tax consequences of managing employees with international assignments. The EY/GEMS system was enhanced with the use of PeopleTools, a software product created by EY's audit client, PeopleSoft. A business relationship was created whereby a license to use People-Tools was granted to EY in return for a payment to the company of 15 percent of each licensee fee it received from outside customers purchasing the new software, 30 percent of each license renewal fee, and a minimum royalty of $300,000, payable in 12 quarterly payments of $25,000 each.

The licensing agreement provided that EY would make PeopleSoft a third-party beneficiary of each sublicense. PeopleSoft agreed to assist EY's efforts by providing technical assistance for a $15,000 quarterly fee. The agreement provided that EY could not distribute the derivative software to PeopleSoft's direct competitors. The agreement permitted EY to use PeopleSoft trademarks and trade names in marketing materials. PeopleSoft maintained a degree of control over the product by restricting EY's distribution rights and requiring the firm to work closely with PeopleSoft to ensure the quality of the product.

The SEC found that EY and PeopleSoft had a "symbiotic relationship" engaging in joint sales and marketing efforts, and sharing considerable proprietary and confidential business information, and that EY partnered with PeopleSoft to accomplish increased sales and boost consulting revenues for EY. The findings of the SEC indicate that EY and PeopleSoft entered into a direct business relationship and shared a mutual interest in the success of EY/GEMS for PeopleSoft and acted together to promote the product so that a reasonable investor with knowledge of all the facts would conclude that EY was closely identified in fact and appearance with its audit client.

Brenda P. Murray, the chief administrative law judge at the SEC, wrote in her opinion that "Ernst's day-to-day operations were profit-driven and ignored considerations of auditor independence." She pointed out some failings in EY's quality control monitoring system including (1) EY did not give its employees any formal training on a regular basis concerning the independence rules on business dealings with an audit client; (2) EY had no procedures in place that could reasonably be expected to deter violations and ensure compliance with the rules on auditor independence with respect to business dealings with audit clients; and (3) EY maintained a self-reporting system for firm partners and employees to report whether they abided by the firm's independence policies. There was no threat of random verification, a control that the SEC believes is essential to an effective independence compliance system.

Providing Nonattest Services to an Attest Client

As previously mentioned in our review of congressional investigations, the issue of when should a CPA be permitted to provide nonattest services to an attest client has been examined for many years. The concern is that by providing certain (lucrative) nonattest services for an attest client, the CPA risks creating a conflict of interests that gives the client leverage over the CPA firm and its audit opinion. An example of a prohibited activity under AICPA and SEC rules is that a CPA should not perform management functions or make management decisions for an attest client. The relationship creates a management participation threat that places the CPA in the compromising position of making decisions for the client and then auditing those decisions. On the other hand, the CPA may provide advice and recommendations to assist the client's management in performing its functions and making decisions.

Interpretation 101-3 establishes requirements that must be met during the period covered by the financial statements and the period of the attest engagement by the CPA in order to conduct nonattest services for the client without impairing audit independence. The client must agree to perform the following functions in connection with the nonattest engagement: (1) make all management decisions and perform all management functions; (2) designate an individual who possesses suitable skill, knowledge, and/or experience to oversee the services; (3) evaluate the adequacy and results of the services performed; (4) accept responsibility for the results of the services; and (5) establish and maintain internal controls, including monitoring ongoing activities.[24]

SOX Provisions

Similar to AICPA and SEC rules, SOX prohibits CPAs and CPA firms from providing certain nonattest services for public company attest clients. The potential for a conflict of interest exists because of a self-review threat to independence that occurs when a CPA reviews, as part of an attest engagement, evidence that results from the CPA's own (nonattest) or the attest firm's work.[25]

As previously discussed, the accounting profession had successfully fought off past challenges to restrict nonattest services for attest clients. However, the Enron scandal changed the dynamics. Andersen's revenue from Enron in its last year was $25 million in audit fees and $27 million in nonaudit fees. The firm had performed significant internal audit work for Enron, creating a self-review threat. Given that the firm seemed to have adopted a hands-off approach on certain accounting issues, the impression was that the firm had lost its audit independence. Perhaps the close relationship between Andersen professionals and Enron employees was attributable to the internal audit services. If so, the relationship may have affected Andersen's ability to approach audit issues with the professional skepticism required by audit standards and essential in making ethical judgments. It didn't help that dozens of former Andersen employees worked for Enron or that both entities had offices in the same building.

Restrictions on Nonattest Services

Section 201 of SOX provides that the following nonattest services may not be performed for attest clients in addition to bookkeeping or other services related to the accounting records or financial statements of the audit client:

1. Financial information systems design and implementation
2. Appraisal or valuation services, fairness opinions, or contribution-in-kind reports
3. Actuarial services
4. Internal audit outsourcing services
5. Management functions or human resources
6. Broker or dealer, investment adviser, or investment banking services
7. Legal services and expert services unrelated to the audit
8. Any other service that the board of directors determines, by regulation, is impermissible

SOX also requires that tax services provided for the audit client should be preapproved by the audit committee. Tax services are not restricted under the act but an audit committee may decide not to permit the audit firm to do taxes to help gain the public trust. As will be mentioned later in the chapter, the PCAOB does restrict certain kinds of tax services and fee payment arrangements.

Corporate Responsibility for Financial Reports

At the conclusion of an audit, it has been customary for the CEO and CFO to sign a letter of representation or other communication to the external auditor on behalf of the client about the GAAP conformity of the financial statements. This management representation is similar to the requirement in Section 302 of SOX for the CEO and CFO to certify the financial statements filed with the SEC. The certification states that "based on the officer's knowledge, the report does not contain any untrue statement of a material fact or omit to state a material fact necessary in order to make the statements, in light of the circumstances under which such statements were made, not misleading." Section 906 of SOX establishes penalties for the false certification of financial statements under Section 302. The maximum fine is $1 million and maximum imprisonment is 10 years, or both. If the false certification was made willfully, the penalties go up to $5 million and 20 years, or both.[26] An officer who signs such a compliance statement while knowing the financial statements contain a material misstatement compromises the relationship of trust that should exist between top management and the external auditor.

HealthSouth: The Case of Richard Scrushy

The first major test case of Section 302 occurred in 2003 when the SEC charged the CEO of HealthSouth Corporation, Richard Scrushy, and the CFO, William T. Owens, with certifying financial statements filed with the SEC on August 14, 2002, that they knew or were reckless in not knowing, contained materially false and misleading information. Other accounting personnel also were charged with participating in the falsification of HealthSouth's financial statements during the 1999–2002 reporting periods. The alleged fraud led to an earnings restatement of about $2.7 billion.[27]

The HealthSouth story is a sad one in that Scrushy was acquitted of all charges that he participated in the fraud and cover-up. Scrushy served as chair of the board at Health-South from 1984 through early 2003. He also served as CEO during that time, except for periods in late 2002 and early 2003. Still, the Birmingham, Alabama, jury chose to believe Scrushy's claims of ignorance even though five HealthSouth financial and accounting officers including William Owens had admitted to their role in the fraud and had accused Scrushy of knowing about it. As U.S. District County Judge Sharon Lovelace Blackburn stated on December 9, 2005, before sentencing Owens to five years in prison for his part in the financial scandal, "life is not always fair" and the sentence "should be sufficient to serve as a deterrent and provide just punishment."[28]

Even though Scrushy was acquitted in state court, the SEC brought a federal action against him that was successful and that led to the following sanctions/penalties:

- Permanently barred Scrushy from serving as an officer or director of a public company
- Permanently enjoined Scrushy from committing future violations of the antifraud and other provisions of the federal securities laws
- Required Scrushy to pay $81 million in disgorgement and civil penalties[29]

The HealthSouth case is discussed in greater detail in Case 4-8 at the end of this chapter.

Due Care in the Performance of Professional Responsibilities

Whereas independence, integrity, and objectivity relate to the quality of the individual CPA who performs professional services, the Principle of Due Care addresses the quality of services performed by the CPA. The codes of the IMA and IIA that were discussed in Chapters 1 and 3 contain competency standards that are similar to the AICPA's Due Care standard.

AICPA Rule 201 of the AICPA Code establishes standards for the quality of work performed by CPAs including professional competence, due professional care, planning and supervision, and obtaining of sufficient relevant data. Interpretation 201-1 of the rule also requires that a CPA gain the competence to perform services, if necessary, by consulting with experts in the area of those services.[30] An option exists to turn down the opportunity to provide services. In that case, as noted in Rule 501.74 of the Texas Administrative Code, the CPA should "suggest to the client the engagement of someone competent to perform the needed professional service, either independently or as an associate."

CPAs should be sensitive to situations when one's capabilities are limited and the conservative action is to recommend another practitioner to perform the services. After all, if you were doing a group project with other students to develop a business plan, you might feel comfortable working on the financial plan but, presumably, you would not want to be responsible for developing the marketing plan. You would expect the marketing students to assume that responsibility.

Other Professional Standards

Rule 203 of the AICPA Code

Rule 203 obligates CPAs to ensure that the financial statements and disclosures are in conformity with GAAP before rendering an opinion that the statements comply with those accounting standards. On July 1, 2009, the Financial Accounting Standards Board (FASB) issued FASB Standards Codification that became the official source of authoritative, non-governmental GAAP. A new research structure to access GAAP exists. There are now two sources of GAAP: (1) authoritative standards (i.e., FASB Standards and Interpretations and Technical Bulletins) represented by the Codification and (2) nonauthoritative represented by all other literature. Interpretation 203-4 emphasizes that GAAP requirement applies equally to internal and external accountants.[31]

Responsibilities to Clients

Two AICPA rules establish important standards that directly address a CPA's responsibilities to clients. The first, Rule 301 on confidential client information, emphasizes the CPA's obligation not to divulge client information. The second, Rule 302 on contingent fees, clarifies when contingent fees can and cannot be accepted as a form of payment for services.

Confidentiality

A CPA should not divulge confidential client information unless the client specifically agrees. The client may consent, for example, when there is a change of auditor and the successor auditor approaches the client for permission to discuss matters related to the audit with the predecessor. This step is required by generally accepted auditing standards (GAAS). Of course, the client can always deny permission and cut off any such contact in which case the successor probably should run in the opposite direction of the client as quickly as possible. In other words, the proverbial "red flag" will have been raised. The CPA should be skeptical and wonder why the client may have refused permission.

Rule 301 also permits the CPA to discuss confidential client information without violating the rule in the following situations: (1) in response to a validly issued subpoena or summons, or to adhere to applicable laws and government regulations; (2) to provide the information necessary for a review of the CPA's professional practice (peer review) under AICPA, state CPA society, or board of accountancy authorization; and (3) to provide the information necessary for one's defense in an investigation of the CPA.[32]

In Chapter 1 we pointed out that while internal whistleblowing is the expected standard of behavior under Interpretation 102-4, to go outside the company and externally blow the whistle on wrongdoing violates the confidentiality obligation to the client. If a CPA even contemplates such an action, legal advice should be sought out before making a final decision. This does not mean that a CPA should never go outside the company and bring certain matters to the attention of the SEC. For example, when the auditor believes a client has committed an illegal act that has a material effect on the financial statements, the matter must be reported to the audit committee. The board then has one business day to inform the SEC. If the board decides not to inform the SEC, the auditor must provide the same report to the board within one business day or resign from the engagement. More will be said about illegal acts in Chapter 5.

Conflicts of interest can arise in the course of deciding confidentiality issues. A classic case occurred in the early 1980s—*Fund of Funds Ltd. v. Arthur Andersen & Co.* In that case, Arthur Andersen had issued an unqualified opinion on the audit of Fund of Funds and then essentially the same audit team began the audit of King Resources, a natural resource company whose stock was part of Fund of Funds mutual funds holdings. Andersen had learned during its audit of King Resources that King's natural resource holdings were overvalued, affecting the investment's value as it related to Fund of Funds. Rather than withdrawing from the audit upon learning that there was a relationship between two of Andersen's clients, the firm decided not to tell Fund of Funds. Andersen was probably concerned about a lawsuit if it had told the mutual fund company and, instead, the firm gambled that the company would not find out that King's natural resource properties were overstated, thereby rendering the company's investment much less valuable.[33]

King Resources went bankrupt and the investors in Fund of Funds sued Andersen claiming the auditors should have disclosed that the properties were overvalued. The firm claimed a confidentiality obligation to King Resources in its defense, but the court did not buy it. The court found that the auditors were liable of, among other things, failing to use information they had obtained from another client (King) to determine which of the two clients' financial statements accurately portrayed the facts of the same transaction.[34] Thus, a legal precedent may exist for holding an auditor liable for failing to disclose and use information obtained from services rendered to one client that is relevant to the audit of another client.

Contingent Fees

In January 1985, the Federal Trade Commission (FTC) began an investigation of AICPA rules and interpretations that banned the acceptance of commissions and contingent fees. Around the same time, the profession formed the Anderson Committee that would issue *A Plan to Restructure the Profession.* In its report, the committee recommended modification of the rules prohibiting contingent fees and a possibility of future changes relating to commissions. The profession was sharply divided over these issues and eventually the AICPA Ruling Council voted 98 to 97 to defeat the two recommendations.[35] The AICPA acted to end the investigation in 1990 by signing a Final Order with the FTC narrowing the AICPA's ability to prohibit the acceptance of commissions and contingent fees. The AICPA amended Rule 302 to prohibit the acceptance of contingent fees (and commissions) only with respect to clients for whom the CPA performs attest services.

The AICPA rule also prohibits the acceptance of contingent fees when preparing original or amended tax returns or claims for tax refunds. Interpretation 302-1 provides that contingent fees in tax engagements can be accepted when the fee is considered determined based on the findings of governmental agencies. In other words, a governmental agency, such as the IRS, must either initiate a review of the client's tax return or review the return because of some automatic trigger such as exceeding the amount for a tax refund ($1 million at March 1991). A contingent fee can be accepted in a claim for a tax refund as long as it is based on a tax issue that is either the subject of a tax case (involving a different taxpayer) or where the taxing authority is developing a position on a matter.[36]

You may wonder why contingent fees are permitted in certain tax engagements and prohibited when performing tax services for an audit (attest) client. The reason is the extra level of protection for the public that is needed when an audit opinion is issued. The acceptance of a contingent fee when performing a nonattest service for an attest client may create the appearance of a lack of independence since these fee payments are predicated on the results of services performed thereby creating a self-review threat to independence. Assume that an auditor (or audit firm) agrees to do the audit of an entity's financial statements and also agrees to file its income tax return and be paid a 10 percent contingent fee based on the size of the tax refund. A reasonable observer may conclude that the auditor could be biased in conducting the audit. After all, an auditor who identifies a $500,000 overstatement of revenue by the client may decide to let it go since an adjustment of this size will lead to a $50,000 reduction in the fee for the tax services.

Other Responsibilities and Practices

Commissions

We have already talked about the FTC challenge to the contingent fee rule. A similar challenge occurred with AICPA Rule 503 that contained a complete ban on commissions. The rule was changed to permit the acceptance of commissions except for those clients who also received attest services. In the case of commissions, the rule change also requires the CPA to disclose the fact to the client that a commission is being paid to that CPA.[37] Many state boards also require the disclosure of the amount of the commission. Under the AICPA rules, commission amounts can be paid to a CPA for recommending a product to a nonattest client. CPAs can also accept referral fees for recommending or referring any service of a CPA or pay a referral fee to obtain a client as long as such acceptance or payment is disclosed to the client. In California, however, licensed CPAs are prohibited from accepting any fee or commission solely for referral of a client to a third party. Recall that when the rules of the AICPA differ from those of a state board of accountancy, then the state's rules must be followed.[38]

The interplay of other ethics rules with contingent fees and commissions is important because the former establish standards of behavior to protect the public interest when such amounts are received. For example, even though a CPA is not prohibited from accepting a commission for recommending a financial or investment product in a nonattest engagement, there still exists an obligation to be objective and exercise due care in identifying the best products for the client.

FTC Challenges to Ethics Rules: Advertising and Solicitation

Even before the FTC challenge on contingent fees and commissions, the AICPA had acted to head off FTC legal challenges to its ethics rules as being too prohibitive. In 1978, the U.S. Supreme Court ruled in *National Society of Professional Engineers v. U.S.* that the engineering profession's canon of ethics violated the Sherman Antitrust Act because its competitive bidding rule was an unreasonable restraint of trade. Following this decision, the AICPA decided to drop its ban on competitive bidding in the AICPA Code by reasoning that the 1978 decision affecting professional engineers was also meant to apply to other professions.[39]

The advertising and solicitation rules also came under attack when in 1977 the Supreme Court ruled in *Bates v. State Bar of Arizona* that the free flow of commercial information protects the public interest. The Court ruled that the ban on attorney advertisements in newspapers violated the First Amendment because it inhibited free (commercial) speech. This led to the end of the ban on CPA advertising.[40]

The Court followed with a ruling in *Edenfeld v. Fane* that Florida's ban on "direct, in-person, uninvited solicitation" to obtain new clients violated the First and Fourteenth (due process) Amendments. The CPA in the case, Scott Fane, had alleged that Florida's ban prevented him from soliciting new clients. The Court sided with Fane and, in his opinion for the Court, Justice Kennedy noted the considerable value of solicitation in facilitating communication between a buyer and seller of professional accounting services. Kennedy pointed out that Florida's ban on uninvited solicitation "threatens societal interests in broad access to complete and accurate commercial information that the First Amendment coverage of commercial speech is designed to safeguard."[41] The *Edenfeld* ruling led to the AICPA's ending its complete ban on uninvited solicitation. The accounting profession did not fully support the liberalization of the rules because it sensed this might lead the profession down the road of putting commercial interests ahead of the public's interest, a charge that has been made in recent frauds such as in Waste Management, Enron, and others. The profession did hold its ground on advertising by issuing Interpretation 502-2 that identifies examples of advertising practices that are not in the public interest because they create false and unjustified expectations of favorable results, or imply the ability to influence official bodies, and/or make deceptive and misleading statements about fees. Rule 502 also prohibits solicitation by the use of coercion, overreaching, or harassing conduct.[42]

Ethical Standards in Operating a CPA Practice

Ethics rules apply not only to individual CPAs who are licensed by state boards but also to accounting firms and certain members of alternative practice structures. State boards need to have regulatory authority over practice units as well as CPAs because the members of a CPA firm might pressure an individual CPA within that firm to do something unethical. The firm should be sanctioned for the inappropriate behavior, and so should the CPA if he or she gives in to the pressure.

Rule 505 of the Code provides that CPAs may practice public accounting only in a form of organization permitted by state law or regulation.[43] For example, in Texas the legal forms of ownership must contain the names of a corporation, professional corporation, limited liability partnership, or professional limited liability company. Sole proprietor CPA firms must contain the name of the sole proprietor. The AICPA and Texas and California rules all prohibit the use of a firm name that is misleading.

The right of an entity to call itself a CPA firm has changed over the years. There was a time when all partners had to be licensed CPAs. However, the profession has expanded its consulting services and the firms have hired specialists who have not always held the CPA designation. These experts wanted an ownership interest in the firm, so over time the rules have changed to permit an entity to call itself a CPA firm as long as "a majority of the ownership of the firm in terms of financial interests and voting rights . . . belong to CPAs."[44] One question about the relaxed ownership rules is whether the expansion of ownership rights in CPA firms to include those not educated in the strong ethical values of the profession may have been, at least in part, responsible for the demise of Andersen that resulted from a clash of cultures.

One of the recent changes in the way CPA services have been provided to the public is through the formation of alternative practice structures (APS). Typically, a CPA firm is purchased by an entity that is not majority owned by CPAs, a so-called APS. The latter assumes the nonattest services while the CPA firm continues, sometimes as a shell entity, to provide attest services. The CPA firm may be making payments to the APS such as for leasing space and payments for the use (in audit work) of former CPA firm members who now perform nonattest services for the APS.[45]

Imagine, for example, that a tax preparation entity purchased a small CPA firm. The tax entity (now called an APS) cannot do audit work because it is not majority CPA owned. It can, however, perform all nonattest services while the original CPA firm does the audit work. The CPA firm and the APS have a relationship as a result of the sale, and that may cause some problems. A potential danger is when the APS performs its services for the same client who uses the related CPA firm for audit services. Independence of CPA firm members may be impaired by virtue of the relationship because the APS has some control over the CPA firm and its members as a result of the acquisition.

To control for the possibility that a top management official of the APS may attempt to influence the decision making of a member of the CPA firm, the AICPA rules extend to direct superiors of the APS who can directly control the activities of those in the CPA firm and indirect superiors who might influence the decisions made by the CPA in its audit work for mutual clients. Interpretation 101-14 subjects direct superiors to Rule 101 and its interpretations while indirect superiors are included only if they have material financial relationships as defined under Rule 101 and its interpretations.[46]

Ethics and Tax Services

The rules of professional conduct in the AICPA Code apply to CPAs in the performance of all professional responsibilities including tax services. The relevant AICPA rules include:

- A tax practitioner must adhere to requirements in Rule 101 because audit independence may be impaired by performing certain tax services.
- Rule 102 requires maintaining integrity and objectivity in performing tax services.
- Rule 201 requires the exercise of due care.
- Rule 202 obligates CPAs to follow professional standards including *Statements on Standards for Tax Services (SSTSs)*.
- Other rules apply including confidentiality requirements (Rule 301) and the acceptance of contingent fees in performing tax services (Rule 302).

Tax Compliance Services

Interpretation 101-3 establishes rules when providing tax compliance services.[47] Tax compliance services include preparation of a tax return, transmittal of a tax return and transmittal of any related tax payment to the taxing authority, signing and filing of a tax return, and authorized representation of clients in administrative proceedings before a taxing authority. Preparing a tax return and transmitting the tax return and related tax payment to a taxing authority, in paper or electronic form, would not impair a CPA's independence provided she does not have custody or control over the client's funds and the individual designated by the client to oversee the tax services (1) reviews and approves the tax return and related tax payment; and (2) if required for filing, signs the tax return prior to the member transmitting the return to the taxing authority.

Authorized representation of a client in administrative proceedings before a taxing authority would not impair a member's independence provided the CPA obtains client agreement prior to committing the client to a specific resolution with the taxing authority. However, representing a client in a court or in a public hearing to resolve a tax dispute would impair audit independence because it establishes an advocacy relationship between the CPA and the client that may create the appearance of a loss of independence with respect to the audit of a client's financial statements.

Tax Advocacy Positions

Tax practitioners offer tax advice, prepare tax returns, and represent taxpayers before the IRS. Taxpayers are responsible for the information they provide. The decisions made by a CPA in providing advice, preparing returns, and representing clients are the product of following the *Statements on Standards for Tax Services (SSTSs)* and the ethics rules previously mentioned.

Interpretation 102-6 of the AICPA Code recognizes the potential advocacy position of a tax practitioner who may represent a client in an IRS investigation or other legal matter. The Interpretation reiterates the requirement to follow the ethics rules and notes that in certain cases the tax services may go beyond "sound and reasonable practice, or may compromise credibility, and therefore pose an unacceptable risk of impairing the reputation" of the CPA or CPA firm "with respect to independence, integrity, and objectivity." In such cases, the CPA/firm should "consider whether it is appropriate to perform the service."[48]

Statements on Standards for Tax Services

The AICPA has issued seven *Statements on Standards for Tax Services (SSTSs)* that explain CPAs' responsibilities to their clients and the tax systems in which they practice. The statements demonstrate a CPA's commitment to tax practice standards that balance advocacy and planning with compliance. At the federal level, Treasury Department Circular 230 applies to those practicing before the IRS. We focus only on the tax statements issued by the AICPA.

Tax services differ from audit services in two important respects. First, the independence requirement for an auditor does not pertain to the tax practitioner, although a CPA firm that performs both services would be required to be independent to conduct the audit. Under SOX requirements, the audit committee of a public client must approve the tax services. This is a check in the system to ensure the board of directors is comfortable with the audit firm also performing tax services.

The second difference is due to the way in which objectivity relates to tax services. Auditors must maintain an unbiased attitude in conducting the audit. An auditor should never do what the client asks just because the client asks it. The final decision must be made by the CPA based on ethical considerations and using one's professional judgment. CPAs sometimes serve as advocates for the client's tax position. If a reasonable level of support exists for that position, as discussed below, the CPA should support that position. The tax practitioner still has to be objective in determining the supportability of that position. However, once supportability has been affirmed, the CPA can advocate that position in tax and legal proceedings. The relationship between the CPA and tax client creates an advocacy threat to independence and is particularly worrisome when the CPA represents the client in U.S. Tax Court.

SSTS No. 1, Tax Return Position, and Interpretation 1-1 are the most important standards with respect to the goals of this book. These standards provide that tax return information is "primarily a taxpayer's representation of facts" and as client advocates, "CPAs have the duty to assist taxpayers in lawfully minimizing the tax burden, as long as any tax return position satisfies the 'realistic possibility' standard." Taxpayers have the final responsibility for any tax position taken on a return.[49] The ethical "control," so to speak, is the realistic possibility standard.

Tax positions are taken because the tax rules are not always clear. A tax practitioner is required by *SSTS 1* to "have a good faith belief that the tax return position is warranted in existing law or can be supported by a good-faith argument for an extension, modification, or reversal of existing law." Recall that when rules and laws are unclear, a CPA should use professional judgment and ethical reasoning to decide on the proper course of action.

This good-faith belief requirement in taking a tax position is further explained in Interpretation 1-1. It links a good-faith belief with the notion that "the tax return position being recommended has at least a realistic possibility of being sustained administratively or judicially on its merits, if challenged." Absent the realistic possibility requirement, the CPA still can recommend the position to the taxpayer if it is not frivolous and the practitioner recommends appropriate disclosure of the position. If the tax client does not disclose the position, then the CPA should not "prepare or sign the tax return containing the position." *SSTS 1* points out that "a frivolous position is one that is knowingly advanced in bad faith and patently improper."[50]

Other constraints exist in the standard such as the practitioner should not recommend a tax return position or prepare or sign a return reflecting a position that the CPA knows "exploits the audit selection process of the taxing authority." In other words, a CPA should not adopt a tax position with the hope the client's tax return will not be audited by the IRS.

A critical evaluation of the ethical standard to use moral reasoning with the realistic possibility standard illustrates a conflict in the level of required judgment. Ethically speaking, we should not make decisions based on whether "reasonable support" exists for that position. To be an ethical person is an absolute requirement and ethical decision making is not relative to the situation or a tax position. Having said that, it is important that the CPA not be influenced by the tax client in determining what should be the tax position. Moreover, once that position is adopted, the CPA should resist client pressures to deviate from the strict requirements of the *SSTSs*.

To illustrate the interplay of ethics and tax standards, assume that a tax practitioner decides to recommend a tax position to a client because it minimizes the client's tax liability even though the CPA is not sure it is the right thing to do. The tax statements do not say to recommend another position if it is (ethically) better. As long as there is reasonable support for the first position, it is acceptable to adopt it in a tax situation. So, the CPA can recommend the first position because there is sufficient support for it in a court of law, assuming the position were to be challenged, and it is the position desired by the client. The CPA's task is to gather enough evidence to support the position if challenged in court. The fact that the alternative position may seem to be fairer or the right one does not matter.

Tax Shelters

One of the most controversial aspects of the Enron collapse was the alleged involvement of Andersen in marketing aggressive tax planning ideas the IRS and the courts subsequently found to be abusive. The accounting profession received a second serious blow after the Enron scandal when in 2005 KPMG settled a criminal tax case with the Department of the Treasury and the IRS for $456 million to prevent the firm's prosecution over tax shelters sold between 1996 and 2002. This is the largest criminal tax case ever filed.

The creation of tax shelter investments to help wealthy clients avoid paying taxes has been part of tax practice for many years. The difference in the KPMG case, according to the original indictment, is that tax professionals in the firm prepared false documents to deceive regulators about the true nature of the tax shelters. There appeared to be a clear intent to deceive the regulators, and that makes it fraud.[51]

The indictment claimed that the tax shelter transactions broke the law because they involved no economic risk and were designed solely to minimize taxes. The firm had collected about $128 million in fees for generating at least $11 billion in fraudulent tax losses and it resulted in at least $2.5 billion in tax evaded by wealthy individuals. On an annual basis, KPMG's tax department was bringing in for the firm nearly $1.2 billion of its $3.2 billion total U.S. revenue. Ultimately, the $128 million in fees were forfeited as part of the $456 million settlement.[52]

Perhaps the most interesting aspect of the KPMG tax shelter situation is the apparent culture that existed in the firm's tax practice during the time the tax shelters were sold. In 1998 the firm had decided to accelerate its tax services business. The motivation probably was the hot stock market during the 1990s and increase in the number of wealthy taxpayers. The head of the KPMG's tax department, Jeffrey M. Stein, and its CFO, Richard Rosenthal, created an environment that treated those who didn't support the growth at all costs effort as not being team players. From the late 1990s, KPMG established a telemarketing center in Fort Wayne, Indiana, that cold-called potential clients from public lists of firms and companies. KPMG built an aggressive marketing team to sell tax shelters it created, with names like Blips, Flip, Opis, and SC2.[53]

In an unusual move, the Justice Department brought a lawsuit against two former KPMG managers on 12 counts of tax evasion using illegal tax shelters. On April 1, 2009, John Larson, a former senior tax manager, was sentenced to more than 10 years and ordered to pay a fine of $6 million. Robert Plaff, a former tax partner at KPMG, was sentenced to more than 8 years and fined $3 million. A third person convicted in the case, Raymond J. Ruble, a former partner at the law firm Sidley Austin, was sentenced to 6 years and 7 months. In handing down the ruling in the U.S. District Court in Manhattan, Judge Lewis A. Kaplan stated: "These defendants knew they were on the wrong side of the line," adding later they had cooked up "this mass-produced scheme to cheat the government out of taxes for the purposes of enriching themselves." The losses through the scheme were estimated at more than $100 million. It is expected that the decision will be appealed by the defendants. Some of KPMG's tax shelter clients are now suing KPMG for the liability exposure.[54]

PCAOB Rules

Following the KPMG case, the PCAOB adopted new rules for tax services that are designed to prevent auditors from providing (1) certain aggressive tax shelter services to their public company audit clients, (2) any other service for a contingent fee, and (3) tax services to members of the audit client's management who serve in financial reporting oversight roles, or to their immediate family members.[55] The PCAOB rule prohibits public company executives from calling on their audit firms for tax preparation and planning services. Second, the PCAOB does not make an exception in its contingent fee rule for certain tax services (where it is subject to tax review) as does the SEC and AICPA. All contingent fees paid to audit clients would be banned. Third, the new rule provides that an audit firm is not independent if it provides services to an audit client on specified classes on tax-motivated transactions. The suspect categories are transactions with a confidentiality requirement imposed by a tax adviser on a client and any transaction recommended by an auditor or tax adviser that has as its main purpose tax avoidance, unless the proposed tax treatment is at least more likely than not to be allowable under relevant tax laws.[56] In other words, a tax practitioner may be able to support a decision to assist a client in a tax avoidance transaction so long as she is more than 50 percent confident it is allowable under the rules. We believe that these tax standards (perhaps understandably) sanction the practice of ethical legalism that was discussed in Chapter 1. That is, if a transaction is legal under the law based on defined criteria, then it is considered to be an ethical transaction. As we have discussed before, ethical people use the law as a minimum standard and go beyond it when warranted such as when the rules are unclear and judgments have to be made.

Concluding Thoughts

Independence is the backbone of the accounting profession. The usefulness of the audit opinion depends on it. Yet, auditors are subjected to pressures that threaten to compromise independence. The key is to never lose sight of the fact that the public interest must come before all others, including that of an employer, client, or one's own self-interest. If accountants and auditors allow themselves to be influenced by employer and client demands, then they place the public trust at risk as occurred for Andersen in their audits of Enron and WorldCom.

Auditors must be independent in appearance as well as in fact because factual independence is difficult to assess. Threats to independence caused by relationships with a client must be carefully managed. The marketing of professional services creates other challenges that may lead to accepting forms of payment such as commissions and contingent fees that may, under certain circumstances, impair objectivity and threaten audit independence. The growth of tax services and expansion into providing tax-advantaged investments such as tax shelters tests the commitment of accounting professionals to make ethical decisions.

The profession has been investigated three times by Congress following a series of frauds. There seems to be about a 10-year gap between investigations. Does that mean the profession will be investigated again in the decade of 2010? We hope not because the next time may lead to even more government regulation of a profession that has prided itself for so many years as being self-regulated.

Discussion Questions

1. The opening quote in this chapter includes the statement: "By certifying the public reports that collectively depict a corporation's financial status, the independent auditor assumes a public responsibility transcending any employment responsibility with the client." Discuss what it means for the auditor to have a public responsibility that transcends any employment responsibility with the client.

2. In their landmark book that was published in 1966, *Ethical Standards of the Accounting Profession,* John Carey and William Doherty state: "The code [of ethics] in effect is an announcement that, in return for the faith which the public reposes in [CPAs], members of the profession accept the obligation to behave in a way that will be beneficial to the public."[57] Comment on the meaning of this statement as you understand it. Do you think this standard of behavior has changed in the past 40 years? Why or why not?

3. Do you think independence with respect to a client would be impaired if a partner leaves a CPA firm and is subsequently employed by a client of the firm that the partner audited? Why or why not?

4. Comment on the statement, "Independence is not easily achieved where an auditor is hired, paid, and fired by the same corporate managers whose activities are the subject of the audit." Can you think of a way around this dilemma?

5. States require accounting students, CPA candidates, and licensed CPAs to complete different forms of ethics education. Go to the Internet and look up the rules and regulations of the state board of accountancy in your state. Does your state have a requirement to complete a specified number of hours in ethics education prior to taking the CPA Exam? Is there a separate examination in ethics given after passing the Uniform CPA Exam prior to licensing? What are your state's requirements with respect to continuing education in ethics? That is, do licensees have to complete a specified number of hours of continuing education in ethics as a condition of relicensing? Prioritize the importance of these three sets of ethics requirements. Do you believe they should help minimize instances of ethical violations by licensed CPAs or are the ethics education rules designed simply to demonstrate that the state takes the matter of establishing ethics requirements for CPAs seriously?

6. The accounting profession has been investigated by Congress over a number of years. However, none of the investigations or recommendations for change seems to have made a difference in that fraud cases continued into the early 2000s. Why do you think instances of accountants going along with fraud continue to occur? Do you believe the trend will continue despite the passage of SOX? Why or why not?

7. Have you ever agreed to do something when you weren't sure that you had the skills to accomplish the job? Why did you agree to do it? Can you draw an analogy between your motivations and the ethical responsibilities of CPAs in the performance of professional services?

8. It has been said that ethical people try to observe both the form and spirit of ethical standards in making professional judgments. What does this mean? How does this relate to the "realistic possibility" and "good-faith belief" standards in tax practice?

9. Assume that the CPA firm of Giants & Jets LLP audits Knickerbocker Systems Inc. The controller of "the Knicks" happens to be a tax expert. During the current tax season, Giants & Jets gets far behind in processing tax returns for wealthy clients. It does not want to approach them and ask permission to file for an extension to the April 15 deadline. One alternative is for the firm to hire the controller as a consultant just for the tax season. Discuss the ethical issues that should be considered by Giants & Jets before deciding whether to hire the controller of a client including possible threats to independence.

10. The managing partner of the CPA firm of Giants & Jets is approached by the CEO of a major client in the firm's headquarters office in New York City. The CEO can't use two tickets to the Super Bowl between the Indianapolis Colts and the New York Giants. The CEO knows the partner is a huge New York Giants football fan and is looking forward to the Peyton Manning versus Eli Manning match-up. While both quarterbacks have won the Super Bowl in different years, the Manning brothers have never played against each other in the Super Bowl. In a gesture of gratitude for services rendered, the CEO offers the tickets to the partner. At first, the partner is excited about the prospects of going to the Super Bowl but also realizes there may be some ethical issues to be considered before deciding whether to accept the tickets. Assume the partner asks for your help. You are a CPA and a longtime friend of the partner. You hate football, so will be objective in your advice. What are the ethical issues that you would raise with the partner to help in deciding whether to accept the Super Bowl tickets? Be sure to cite specific ethics rules in the AICPA Code of Professional Conduct that would guide your actions.

11. Can a CPA be independent without being objective? Why or why not? Can a CPA be objective without being independent? Why or why not?

12. Integrity is said to be the backbone of ethical behavior. How does the integrity requirement of CPAs affect the performance of professional services by the following:

    a. A controller of a corporation
    b. The internal auditor of a company
    c. The external auditor

    Describe a situation where each professional's integrity may be challenged.

13. With respect to the Armadillo Foods case in this chapter, let's assume that the controller is being told by top management that to "make the numbers" the company must increase EPS by $.02 per share. This sounds innocent enough and it is only a 4 percent increase. Does the relative size of the increase make any difference in deciding whether to increase EPS by $.02? Would you go along with top management's demand? What ethical issues should you consider in deciding on a course of action?

14. What is the danger from an ethical perspective of having a CPA firm that conducts the audit of a public company also engaged in consulting with the company on the installation of a new financial information system? What about giving tax advice to an audit client? What are the possible ethical dangers of having the tax practitioners at a CPA firm that audits a client entity prepare the tax return for members of management of the client who have a financial reporting oversight role?

15. The following two questions directly relate to ethics standards in the AICPA Code of Professional Conduct:

    a. Is it ever improper for a CPA/CPA firm to accept a commission from a client for recommending an investment product to the client? What about accepting a contingent fee in a tax engagement?
    b. Read the following advertisement that appeared in the community newspaper where you live. Do you think the advertisement violates any of the ethics rules? Explain the reasons for your answer.

IRS TAX TERMINATOR, A Professional Services Corporation

We have 10 CPAs on staff and provide a full range of tax services. We guarantee a tax refund or you pay nothing for our services. Call us at 999-777-7711. Your call will be routed to one of our tax experts, who will take down all the relevant information and inform you of our fee structure that includes a fixed amount regardless of the service provided and a variable amount that is based on the type of service provided.

---

16. Assume you are a CPA and the controller of a *Fortune* 500 company. On January 2, 2011, your boss, the CFO, comes into your office to discuss the recording of revenue on a shipment of product received by the customer on that day. Your boss hands you the sales invoice that reflects FOB Destination terms and tells you to backdate the document for the $20 million shipment to December 30, 2010, the shipping date. What ethical issues should you consider in deciding whether to agree to the request? What provisions of the AICPA Code are relevant to your decision? What would you do and why?

17. Lew Walls is a CPA and a sole practitioner. Walls serves a small client base in the city of Tuscaloosa, Alabama. A potential client comes into Walls's office one day and asks to discuss the possibility of Walls preparing her 1040 tax return for the year 2010. Walls asks questions about the client's hair salon business and personal investments. Everything sounds all right to Walls, so he agrees to do the tax return. One week before the April 15 deadline the client comes into Walls's office with a shoebox filled with tax receipts. Walls asks, "What's this?" The client answers, "All the information you need to do my taxes." After drinking two glasses of water and doing some yoga exercises, Walls calmly tells the client he can't work with a shoebox full of tax information. The client assures Walls everything is in order, each taxable item or tax deduction category has been separated out, and there are explanations at the bottom of the shoebox for everything. Out of curiosity Walls removes the stacks and picks up the paper at the bottom, which is a receipt for a $200 pair of Nike shoes. Walls finds the explanation sheet for that purchase which says: "Required for comfort on the job." Later that day, after the client has left, Walls goes through the separate stacks and notices there is no earnings data from the salon. Walls calls the client, who explains that it is strictly a cash business and Walls should pick a number after looking at all the other tax information and then decide on the earnings amount from the business. She conditions the statement by saying she wants a $2,000 tax refund in 2010.

    a. What would you do if you were Lew Walls? Why?

    b. Assume the scenario just described occurs on April 14 and you know the client will not have enough time to find someone else to do her taxes if you decide to walk away from the engagement. Would that change your decision? Why or why not?

    c. Assume that the client was your sister. Would that change what you do? Why or why not?

18. A large, national accounting firm decides it is time to outsource the preparation of income tax returns to an organization in India that has performed outsource services for other U.S. CPA firms. The firm will transmit income tax information necessary to prepare the returns electronically and staff accountants in India will prepare the return. The return will then be transmitted back to the United States for final review and approval, and then given to clients. Assume the cost savings for the CPA firm are significant because of the lower salaries paid to chartered accountants in India, and the quality of work in India is as good as or better than that of U.S. tax accountants. Would you recommend that the firm outsource? Why or why not? Be sure to address ethical considerations with respect to the AICPA Code.

19. In August 2008, Ernst & Young LLP agreed to pay more than $2.9 million to the SEC to settle charges that it violated ethics rules by coproducing a series of audio CDs with a man who was also a director at three of EY's audit clients. According to the SEC, EY collaborated with Mark C. Thompson between 2002 and 2004 to produce a series of audio CDs called *The Ernst & Young Thought Leaders Series.* Thompson served on the boards at several of EY's clients during the period when the CDs were produced. What rules of conduct in the AICPA Code were

violated by EY and why? What are the potential harms of EY or any other accounting firm of engaging in this kind of relationship?

20. On January 16, 2008, the SEC charged two former employees of PricewaterhouseCoopers LLP with insider trading. According to the SEC's complaint, Gregory B. Raben, a former PwC auditor, and William Patrick Borchard, a former senior associate in PwC's Transaction Services Group, used their access to sensitive information about PwC's clients to allow Raben to buy stock ahead of a series of corporate takeovers. According to the complaint, Raben netted trading profits of more than $20,000 by buying stock ahead of public announcements disclosing the acquisitions and then selling his shares. Assume the actions of Raben and Borchard had no effect on the client or its operations. How would you evaluate the ethics of the stock acquisition by Raben and Borchard.

Endnotes

1. Barbara Ley Toffler with Jennifer Reingold, *Final Accounting: Ambition, Greed and the Fall of Arthur Andersen* (New York: Broadway Books, 2003).

2. The description of Andersen's demise is taken from an online document titled "The Demise of Arthur Andersen," http://utminers.utep.edu/.../Final%20Arthur%20Andersen%20Paper.doc.

3. U.S. Supreme Court, No. 04-368, *Arthur Andersen LLP v. U.S. on Writ of Certiorari to the U.S. Court of Appeals for the Fifth Circuit* [May 31, 2005], www.law.cornell.edu/supct/html/04-368. ZO.html.

4. *United States v. Arthur Young,* 465 U.S. 805, www.caselaw.lp.findlaw.com.

5. American Institute of CPAs, *AICPA Professional Standards. Volume 2 as of June 1, 2009,* AICPA Code of Professional Conduct (New York: AICPA, 2009).

6. Mike Brewster, *Unaccountable: How the Accounting Profession Forfeited a Public Trust* (Hoboken, NJ: Wiley, 2003).

7. William F. Messier Jr., Steven M. Glover, and Douglas F. Prawitt, *Auditing & Assurance Services: A Systematic Approach* (New York: McGraw-Hill Irwin, 2010).

8. American Institute of CPAs, *Journal of Accountancy: AICPA Centennial Issue 1987,* May 1987.

9. Brewster, pp. 153–154.

10. Jeff Baily, "Continental Illinois Dismisses Ernst & Whinney," *Wall Street Journal,* November 2, 1984, D1.

11. "Hearings Focus on ZZZZ Best," *Journal of Accountancy,* April 1988.

12. Timothy Curry and Lynn Shibut, "The Cost of the Savings and Loan Crisis: Truth and Consequences," www.fdic.gov/bank/analytical/banking/2000dec/brv13n2_2.pdf.

13. National Commission on Fraudulent Financial Reporting (Treadway Commission Report), *Report of the National Commission on Fraudulent Financial Reporting,* October 1987.

14. Texas State Board of Public Accountancy, *Texas Administrative Code Title 22, Part 22, Chapter 501, Subchapter A, Rule 501.5,* www.tsbpa.state.tx.htm.

15. *Texas Administrative Code Title 22, Part 22, Chapter 501, Subchapter A, Rule 501.5,* http://info. sos.state.tx.us.htm.

16. California Senate SB 819, As Amended September 10, 2009, http://.sen.ca.gov/.../bill/.../sb.../ sb_819_cfa_20090629_103137_asm_comm.html.

17. AICPA, *Professional Standards Volume 2,* AU Sections 92.11 and 92.25.

18. AICPA, *Professional Standards Volume 2,* AU Sections 101.06–.07.

19. AICPA, "A Conceptual Framework for AICPA Independence Standards—January 22, 2004," www.aicpa.org.

20. AICPA, *Professional Standards Volume 2,* AU Section 101.5.

21. Association of Certified Fraud Examiners, "Cooking the Books: What Every Accountant Should Know about Fraud," www.acfe.org.

22. Available at www.pcaobus.org/Rules/Docket_017/index.aspx.

23. SEC, Release No. 249, File No. 3-10933, *In the Matter of Ernst & Young LLP: Initial Decision,* April 16, 2004, www.sec.gov/litreleases.

24. AICPA, *Professional Standards Volume 2,* AU Section 101.3.

25. HR 3763, One Hundred Seventh Congress of the United States of America: The Sarbanes-Oxley Act, www.findlaw.com.

26. HR 3763.

27. SEC, Accounting and Auditing Enforcement Release (AAER) No. 1744, March 20, 2003, www.sec.gov/litigation/litreleases/lr18044.htm.

28. Michael Tomberlin, "Owens Sentenced to 5 Years in Prison," *The Birmingham News,* December 10, 2005.

29. SEC, Auditing and Enforcement Release No. 2599, April 23, 2007, www.sec.gov/litigation/litreleases/2007/lr20084.htm.

30. AICPA, *Professional Standards Volume 2,* AU Section 201.

31. AICPA, *Professional Standards Volume 2,* AU Section 203.

32. AICPA, *Professional Standards Volume 2,* AU Section 301.02.

33. 545 F. Supp. 1314 (S.D.N.Y. 1982).

34. Ibid.

35. Mary Beth Armstrong, *Ethics and Professionalism for CPAs* (Cincinnati, OH: South-Western Publishing, 1993).

36. AICPA, *Professional Standards Volume 2,* AU Section 302.02.

37. AICPA, *Professional Standards Volume 2,* AU Section 503.01.

38. California Board of Accountancy, Accountancy Act, Section 5061, www.ca.gov.

39. *National Society of Professional Engineers v. U.S.,* 435 U.S. 679 (1978).

40. *Bates v. State Bar of Arizona,* 433 U.S. 350 (1977).

41. *Edenfeld v. Fane,* 507 U.S. 761 (1993).

42. AICPA, *Professional Standards Volume 2,* AU Section 502.02.

43. AICPA, *Professional Standards Volume 2,* AU Section 505.3.

44. AICPA, "Council Resolution Regarding Rule 505—Form of Organization and Name," ET Appendix B.

45. AICPA, *Professional Standards Volume 2,* AU Section 505.3.

46. AICPA, *Professional Standards Volume 2,* AU Section 101.14.

47. AICPA, *Professional Standards Volume 2,* AU Section 101-3.

48. AICPA, *Professional Standards Volume 2,* AU Section 102-6.

49. AICPA Tax Executive Committee, *Statement on Standards for Tax Services (SSTS) No. 1,* Tax Return Positions, *AICPA Professional Standards. Volume 2 as of June 1, 2009* (New York: AICPA, 2009).

50. AICPA Tax Executive Committee, Interpretation 1-1, Realistic Possibility Standard of *SSTS No. 1,* Tax Return Positions, *AICPA Professional Standards. Volume 2 as of June 1, 2009* (New York: AICPA, 2009).

51. "KPMG Superseding Indictment: In Criminal Tax Case Related to KPMG Tax Shelters," www.justice.gov/usao/nys/pressreleases/.../kpmgsupersedingindictmentpr.pdf.

52. "KPMG to Pay $456 Million for Criminal Violations," Statement by IRS Commissioner Mark W. Everson, IR-2005-83, August 29, 2005.

53. "KPMG Superseding Indictment."

54. "2 Ex-KPMG Managers Sentenced Over Tax Shelters," www.nytimes.com/2009/04/02/business/02kpmg.html?page wanted=print.

55. Public Company Accounting Oversight Board (PCAOB), Ethics and Independence Rules, www.pcaobus.org.

56. Michael Hirsh, "New PCAOB Rules Affect Personal Tax Services for Key Management," *The CPA Journal,* December 2005.

57. John L. Carey and William O. Doherty, *Ethical Standards of the Accounting Profession* (New York: AICPA, 1966).

Chapter 4 Cases

Case 4-1

America Online (AOL)

Background[1]

In May 2000, America Online Inc. (AOL), the world's biggest Internet services provider at the time, settled charges that it improperly accounted for certain advertising costs in a case that was meant to be a stern warning to Internet start-ups. This was the first time the SEC had brought such an enforcement case against a public company for improper capitalization of advertising related to soliciting new customers and was meant as a warning to other start-up companies trying to draw in new customers.

The company reported profits for six of eight quarters during fiscal 1995 and 1996 instead of the losses it would have reported had advertising costs associated with acquiring new customers been accounted for as expenses instead of being deferred, according to the Securities and Exchange Commission. "This action reflects the Commission's close scrutiny of accounting practices in the technology industry to make certain that the financial disclosure of companies in this area reflects present reality, not hopes for the future," said Richard Walker, head of the agency's enforcement division.

AOL Subscribers

During fiscal year 1996, AOL had nearly $1.1 billion in revenues and at June 30, 1996, had approximately 6.2 million subscribers worldwide. AOL's common stock was registered with the SEC pursuant to Section 12(b) of the Exchange Act and was listed on the New York Stock Exchange.

During its fiscal years ended June 30, 1995, and June 30, 1996, AOL rapidly expanded its customer base as an Internet service provider through extensive advertising efforts. These efforts involved, among other things, distributing millions of computer disks containing AOL start-up software to potential AOL subscribers, as well as bundling AOL software with computer equipment. Largely as a result of its extensive advertising expenditures, this period was characterized by negative cash flows from operations.

For fiscal years 1995 and 1996, AOL capitalized most of the costs of acquiring new subscribers as "deferred membership acquisition costs" (DMAC)—including the costs associated with sending disks to potential customers and the fees paid to computer equipment manufacturers that bundled AOL software onto their equipment—and reported those costs as an asset on its balance sheet, instead of expensing the costs as incurred. Substantially all customers were derived from this direct marketing program. For fiscal years 1993, 1994, and

[1]Additional materials available on the AOL case can be found in Litigation Release No. 16552, www.sec.gov/litigation/litreleases/lr16552.htm.

1995, AOL (generally) amortized DMAC on a straight-line basis over a 12-month period. Beginning July 1, 1995, the company increased that amortization period to 24 months.

During fiscal year 1996, while the amount of DMAC reported on AOL's balance sheet grew from $77 million to $314 million, the uncertainties in the Internet marketplace became more pronounced. First, AOL's costs of subscriber acquisition increased substantially, as the response rate to its disk mailings decreased. Moreover, AOL's competition continued to increase, including competition from service providers offering unlimited Internet access for a flat monthly fee. To increasing numbers of Internet users, this unlimited access pricing was an attractive alternative to AOL's pricing plan, which charged customers on an hourly rate, and AOL's senior management was actively considering adoption of some variant of unlimited access pricing. In part as a result of this competition, AOL experienced declining rates of customer retention throughout fiscal year 1996. AOL introduced a modification to its pricing plan, offering a lower hourly rate for heavy users, on July 1, 1996, in hopes of improving customer retention. But AOL disclosed in its 1996 Form 10-K: "The Company cannot predict the overall future rate of retention."

Accounting for Advertising Costs

At July 1, 1994, the beginning of AOL's 1995 fiscal year, June 30, 1995, and June 30, 1996, the DMAC on AOL's balance sheets were $26, $77, and $314 million, respectively, or 17, 19, and 33 percent of total assets, and 26, 35, and 61 percent of shareholders' equity. Had these costs been properly expensed as incurred, AOL's 1995 reported pretax loss would have been increased from $21 to $98 million (including the write-off of DMAC that existed as of the end of fiscal year 1994), and AOL's 1996 reported pretax income of $62 million would have been decreased to a pretax loss of $175 million. On a quarterly basis, the effect of capitalizing DMAC was that AOL reported profits for six of eight quarters in fiscal years 1995 and 1996, rather than losses that it would have reported had the costs been expensed as incurred.

On October 29, 1996, AOL announced that as of September 30, 1996, it would write off all capitalized costs of membership acquisition carried as an asset at September 30, 1996, and would expense as incurred all such costs from October 1, 1996, forward. AOL reflected a one-time charge in the first quarter of fiscal year 1997 in the amount of $385 million to write off the DMAC asset. The company stated that the write-off was necessary to reflect changes in its evolving business model, including reduced reliance on subscribers' fees as the company developed other revenue sources. AOL had responded to competitive pressure by adopting an unlimited-use pricing plan and, by writing off DMAC, acknowledged that it could not rely on its revenue history under a different pricing model as support for the recoverability of DMAC. But the increasing competition and rapid changes in AOL's marketing merely confirmed that AOL, given its volatile business environment, could not comply with the requirements of AICPA *Statement of Position (SOP) 93-7*.[2]

The general rule as set forth in *SOP 93-7* is that "the costs of advertising should be expensed either as incurred or the first time the advertising takes place." To meet the requirements of the narrow exception to this general rule (allowing capitalization), an entity must operate in a sufficiently stable business environment that the historical evidence upon which it bases its recoverability analysis is relevant and reliable.[3] AOL did not meet the essential requirements of *SOP 93-7* because the unstable business environment precluded reliable forecasts of future net revenues. AOL was not operating in a stable environment, and its business was characterized, during the relevant period, by the following factors:

- AOL was operating in a nascent business sector characterized by rapid technological change.
- AOL's business model was evolving.
- Extraordinarily rapid growth in AOL's customer base caused significant changes to its customer demographics.
- AOL's customer retention rates were unpredictable.
- AOL's product pricing was subject to potential change.
- AOL could not reliably predict future costs of obtaining revenues.
- AOL's competition was increasing.
- AOL was experiencing negative cash flow.

SEC Ruling

Due to the previously mentioned factors, AOL did not have sufficient reliable evidence that its DMAC asset was recoverable, and AOL did not, therefore, satisfy the capitalization and amortization requirements of *SOP 93-7*. As a consequence, AOL's financial statements as filed with the commission in quarterly reports on Form 10-Q and annual reports on Form 10-K, from the quarter that began July 1, 1994, through the quarter beginning July 1, 1996, were rendered inaccurate by AOL's accounting treatment for DMAC. Therefore, AOL violated Section 13(a) of the Exchange Act that requires issuers of registered securities to file with the commission factually accurate annual and quarterly reports. Financial statements incorporated in commission filings must comply with Regulation S-X, which in turn requires conformity

with generally accepted accounting principles. The filing of a periodic report containing inaccurate information constitutes a violation of these regulations.

Registered companies are also required to make and keep books, records, and accounts that accurately reflect the transactions and disposition of their assets. AOL violated Section 13(b) of the Exchange Act during its fiscal years 1995 and 1996, and the quarter beginning July 1, 1996, by recording as an asset advertising costs that could not be capitalized in accordance with the requirements of *SOP 93-7*.

In settlement of the matter in a cease-and-desist order with the SEC, AOL agreed to pay $3.5 million to settle financial reporting violations. AOL ultimately combined with Time Warner in January 2001.

Questions

1. *SOP 93-7* requires the capitalization and amortization of direct response advertising costs only when "persuasive historical evidence exists that allows the entity to reliably predict future net revenues that will be obtained as a result of the advertising." Review *SOP 93-7* and explain what is meant by "persuasive historical evidence" and how a company such as AOL can support capitalization.

2. Subsequent to its merger with Time Warner, AOL became embroiled in another legal matter with the SEC when four members of its top management were sued by the commission for fraudulently funding its own online advertising revenue by giving counterparties the means to pay for advertising they would not have otherwise purchased. To do so, AOL mischaracterized the substance of the business transactions, utilizing "round-trip" transactions, including, among others, agreeing to pay inflated prices for, or forgo discounts on, goods and services it purchased in exchange for the vendors' purchases of online advertising in the amount of the markup or forgone discount. Review the complaint filed against the four officers of AOL on May 19, 2008,[4] and answer the following questions:
   a. Explain what is meant by a "round-trip" transaction.
   b. The complaint cites three round-trip transactions between AOL and other parties. Choose one and explain why AOL's accounting did not conform to GAAP.

3. The SEC filings do not address corporate governance failings at AOL in any meaningful way. With respect to the round-trip transactions, the complaint states that "senior finance managers at AOL signed representation letters to Ernst & Young claiming that the advertising revenues were being properly recognized." What conclusions can you draw about failings of the corporate governance system at AOL? How do you assess the ethics of AOL in capitalizing costs that should have been expensed?

[2]AICPA Statements of Position are part of the authoritative literature in the GAAP Codification.
[3]American Institute of CPAs, Accounting Standards Executive Committee, *Statement of Position (SOP) 93-7*, Reporting on Advertising Costs, www.aicpa.org.

[4]U.S. District Court of Southern District of New York, *Securities and Exchange Commission v. David M. Colburn, Eric L. Keller, James F. MacGuidwin, and Jay B. Rappaport*, 08 CV 4611, www.sec.gov/litigation/complaints/2008/comp20586_colburn.pdf.

Case 4-2

Beauda Medical Center

Lance Popperson woke up in a sweat. He felt an anxiety attack coming on. Popperson popped two anti-anxiety pills, laid down to try and sleep for the third time that night, and thought once again about his dilemma. Popperson is an associate with the accounting firm of Scoop and Shovel LLP. He recently discovered, through a casual conversation with Brad Snow, a friend of his on the audit staff, that one of the firm's clients managed by Snow recently received complaints that its heart monitoring equipment was malfunctioning. Cardio-Systems Monitoring, Inc. (CSM), called for a meeting of the lawyers, auditors, and top management to discuss what to do about the complaints from health care facilities that had significantly increased between the first two months of 2010 and the last two months of that year. Doctors at these facilities claimed the systems shut off for brief periods and, in one case, the hospital was unable to save a patient that went into cardiac arrest.

Popperson tossed and turned and wondered what he should do about the fact that Beauda Medical Center, his current audit client, plans to buy 20 units of Cardio-Systems' heart monitoring equipment for its brand-new medical facility in the outskirts of Beauda.

Questions

1. Assume both Popperson and Snow are CPAs. Do you think Snow violated his confidentiality obligation under the AICPA Code by informing Popperson about the faulty equipment at CSM? Why or why not.

2. Popperson has not told anyone connected to the Beauda Medical Center audit about the situation at CSM. What do you think he should do with the information? Be sure to consider Popperson's ethical obligations in answering this question.

3. Assume Popperson informs the senior in charge of the Beauda Medical audit and the senior informs the manager, Kelly Korn. A meeting is held the next day with all parties in the office of Iceman Cometh, the managing partner of the firm. Here's how it goes:

Iceman: If we tell Beauda about the problems at CSM, we will have violated our confidentiality obligation as a firm to CSM. Moreover, we may lose both clients.

Kelly: Lance, you are the closest to the situation. How do you think Beauda's top hospital administrators would react if we told them?

Lance: They wouldn't buy the equipment.

Iceman: Once we tell them, we're subject to investigation by our state board of accountancy for violating confidentiality. We don't want to alert the board and have it investigate our actions. What's worse, we may be flagged for the confidentiality violation in our next peer review.

Kelly: Who would do that? I mean, CSM won't know about it and the Beauda people are going to be happy we prevented them from buying what may be faulty equipment.

Senior: I agree with Kelly. They are not likely to say anything.

Iceman: I don't like it. I think we should be silent and find another way to warn Beauda Medical without violating confidentiality.

Lance: What about contacting the state board for advice?

  a. Discuss all ethical and professional matters of concern for the firm of Scoop and Shovel LLP, in deciding whether to do as Iceman Cometh suggests and not tell the administrators at Beauda Medical Center.

  b. What do you think about Lance's suggestion to contact the state board for advice on the matter? Is that the function of a state board of accountancy?

Case 4-3

Family Games, Inc.

"Yeah, I know all of the details weren't completed until January 2, 2011, but we agreed on the transaction on December 30, 2010. By my way of reasoning it's a continuation transaction and the $12 million revenue belongs in the results for 2010." This comment was made by Carl Land, the CFO of Family Games, Inc. The company has annual sales of about $50 million from a variety of manufactured board and electronic games that are designed for use by the entire family. However, during the past two years the company reported a net loss due to cost-cutting measures that were necessary to compete with overseas manufacturers and distributors.

Land made the previous comment to Helen Strom, the controller of Family Games, after Strom had expressed her concern that since the lawyers did not sign off on the transaction until January 2, the revenue should not be recorded in 2010. Strom emphasized that the product was not shipped until January 2 and there was no way of justifying its inclusion in the previous year's operating results.

Land felt Strom was being hypertechnical since the merchandise had been placed on the carrier (truck) on December 31, 2010. The items weren't shipped until January 2 because of the holiday. "Listen, Helen, this comes from the top," Land said. "The big boss said we need to have the $12 million recorded in the results for 2010."

"I don't get it," Helen said to Land. "Why the pressure?"

"The boss wants to increase his performance bonus by increasing earnings in 2010. Apparently, he lost some money in Vegas over the Christmas weekend and left a sizable 'I Owe U' at the casino," Land responded.

Helen shook her head in disbelief. She didn't like the idea of operating results being manipulated based on the personal needs of the CEO. She knows that the CEO has a gambling problem. It had happened before. The difference this time is it has the prospect of affecting the reported results and she is being asked to do something that she knows is wrong.

"I can't change the facts," Helen said.

"All you have to do is backdate the sales invoice to December 30 when final agreement was reached," Land responded. "As I said before, just think of it as a revenue-continuation transaction that started in 2010 and, but for one minor technicality, should have been recorded in 2011."

"You're asking me to 'cook the books,'" Helen said. "I won't do it."

"I hate to play hardball with you, Helen, but the boss authorized me to tell you he will stop reimbursing you in the future for child care costs so that your kid can have a live-in nanny 24-7, unless you are a team player on this issue. Remember, Helen, this is the only time we will request that you go along."

Helen was surprised by the threat and dubious of the one-time-event explanation. She sat down in her chair and reflected on the fact that the reimbursement payments are $35,000, 35 percent of her annual salary. She is a single working mother. Helen knows there is no other way that she can afford to pay for the full-time care needed by her autistic son.

Questions

1. Briefly discuss the rules for revenue recognition in accounting. Does the proposed handling of the $12 million violate those rules? Be specific.

2. Assume Carl Land and Helen Strom are both CPAs. What ethical issues exist for them in this situation? Identify the stakeholders in this case and Strom's ethical obligations to them.

3. To what extent should Helen consider the gambling problems of her boss in deciding on a course of action? To what extent should Helen consider her child care situation and the threatened cutoff of reimbursements? If you were Helen Strom, what would you do? Why?

Case 4-4

First Community Church

First Community Church is the largest church in the city of Perpetual Happiness. Yes, it's in California!

A meeting was held on Friday, November 16, to address the fact that money had been stolen from the weekly collection box during the course of the year and church leaders were getting quite concerned. At first, no one paid much attention as the amounts were small and could have been attributed to inadvertent errors due to discrepancies between the actual count and what really was collected. However, after 45 weeks of the continuous discrepancies, the total amount of differences had become alarming. Eddie Wong, the controller for the church, estimated the total was now $23,399. That represents well over 5 percent of their annual collections from church members totaling about $400,000.

The meeting began at 9 a.m., a time that was early for the church leaders who often had late evening calls to make. The church staff brought donuts, bagels, and coffee to help get the meeting off to a good start. But that's not the way it happened.

"I want an explanation," said Allen Yuen, the executive director of the church. The board of trustees are on my back on this matter. Some of them talk about this Sarbanes-Oxley Act and our lack of internal controls. It's all foreign to me but I know indignation when I see it!"

"I can't explain it, Allen," responded Eddie Wong.

"Jennie. How about you?" Yuen asked. He was addressing Jennie Lin, the member of the executive committee of the board of trustees who was directly responsible for the count each week.

Jennie seemed uncomfortable. She hesitated before saying: "I think my count is correct. I take the money given to me by Joey, put it in the safe, and then Eddie opens the safe on Monday morning. He records the cash receipts and makes a bank deposit."

Eddie said, "That's right. My deposit always matches the amount of money reported by Jennie."

"That doesn't make sense," Yuen said. "Someone is getting his or her hands on the money between the collection process and recording of the amount. I trust you, Jennie, to watch over these things and the internal control matter."

"Perhaps the recorded tally amount independently submitted by the church volunteers has been overstated," Jennie said.

"Why would that happen?" Yuen asked. "I mean, while it could happen and it would be an honest mistake, it seems unlikely."

Jennie was starting to sweat. She decided a diversion was in order. "Maybe someone gets their hands on the collection box after the tally and before Joey gives it to me." Joey Ching is the accounting manager who delivers the collection box and tally sheet to Jennie after each service. Joey goes to church on a regular basis and volunteered to do the job in order to establish a control in the process.

At this point Jennie lowered her head while she waited for a response. It came from Alex Yuen. "Jennie, are you accusing Joey of stealing money from the church collection box?"

Jennie shook her head as if to say no. She was visibly upset. A phone call came in for Yuen and the meeting had to break up. The group agreed to continue the discussion in two days. In the meantime, Alan Yuen said he'd call Joey Ching and ask him to attend the next meeting.

Jennie went back to her office, closed the door, and started to reflect on what she had just done. The truth is that Jennie had been taking the money each week and giving it to a homeless shelter two blocks from the church. Some of the homeless attend church services and Jennie has befriended many of them. She knew it was wrong to take money from the collection box, but she thought it was for a very good cause and that the church clergy would approve. She never thought about getting caught since she told the bookkeeper to record the lower amount. Now, she feels guilty about bringing Joey into the picture.

Questions

1. Assume Jennie Lin is a CPA. Evaluate her actions from an ethical perspective. Jennie believed her actions were proper because taking the money from the church and giving it to the homeless served a greater good. Do you agree with her position from an ethical perspective?

2. As a member of the board of trustees of the church, what are Jennie's ethical obligations to the church? Do you think it is more difficult to establish strong internal controls in a nonprofit such as First Community Church as compared to a public or privately owned company? Explain your answer.

3. a. Assume Jennie calls Joey and explains the situation. She tells Joey about the impending call from Alex Yuen and, as a friend, asks him not come to the meeting so she could explain what she has done without his involvement. If you were Joey, would you stay away from the meeting? Why or why not.

   b. Assume Joey stays away, Jennie explains why she did what she did, and, after due deliberation, Yuen fires Jennie and tells her she must replace the money she "stole" from the collection box. How would you evaluate Yuen's actions from an ethical perspective?

Case 4-5

The New CEO

Liza Perky was recently selected to be the CEO of a small company in Oklahoma City on October 11, 2010. The company is owned by venture capitalists and it plans to go public in 2011, after five years of growth in sales from $200,000 to $1,500,000. Texarkoma Products manufactures fax and copy machines and other office machines and sells them primarily to customers in the Oklahoma, Texas, and Arkansas tristate area. Increased competition from Kanecola, a start-up company in the Kansas, Colorado, and Nebraska tristate area, forced Texarkoma to cut prices and the losses started to mount. In 2008 the company lost $500,000 and in 2009 it lost $700,000. For the first nine months of 2010, the company lost an additional $600,000. That's when it fired the former CEO and hired Perky, a turn-around artist who had seemingly saved dozens of companies by eliminating unprofitable product lines.

Perky believes that the company will soon turn things around because Kanecola was recently taken over by Clips, Inc., a national company that is located in 40 states. Texarkoma now has a competitive advantage in the local tristate area since small businesses in the Southwest tend to be loyal to local and regional distributors because of the personal service and long-standing ties to the community.

During the last three months of 2010, the company reported a preliminary loss of $250,000, a total projected loss of $850,000 for the year. On January 8, 2011, Perky took a look at the results and seemed disappointed. She summoned her chief accounting officer, Joe Boreing, who is a CPA in Oklahoma. The following dialogue took place:

Perky: Joe, I've been looking over the results for the last three months and the supporting numbers and I can't understand how you only put through a $200,000 write-down (40 percent) of the "Gobble" line of commercial copiers.

Boreing: I think we can salvage something from a discount sales drive of the machines.

Perky: How so, Joe? We haven't sold very many of these machines during the past three months.

Boreing: We have sold 50 machines.

Perky: And what was our loss?

Boreing: It was 50 percent of the cost of each machine.

Perky: And your numbers indicate there are still 500 machines in stock.

Boreing: That's right.

Perky: Well, you're the math wiz but I figure that means a potential loss of at least $250,000.

Boreing: That's right but I cut it to $200,000 because I have a potential buyer. It's the Texas School District. The superintendent wants to buy the copiers for all K–12 schools and she doesn't care that it's not the latest model with all the bells and whistles.

Perky: Do you have a signed contract?

Boreing: No. I expect that to happen by the end of January.

Perky: Well, aren't you always preaching conservatism to me in terms of the numbers?

Boreing: Not always but in general; the accounting rules require that we provide for all potential losses immediately.

Perky: Right. So I want you to do that with the Gobble copiers.

Boreing: Okay. I'll add $50,000 to the write-down.

Perky: That's not enough. I want you to double the amount.

Boreing: You want me to increase the write-down to $300,000?

Perky: No. I want you to record a total write-off of the Gobble inventory.

Boreing: You want me to write off all $500,000?

Perky: That's what I said.

Boreing started to resist, but after 10 more minutes of discussion he knew it was no use. Perky cut him off and told him it was a direct order and she expected him to comply, or else.

Questions

1. What do you think is the motivation for Perky's position? What is she trying to accomplish by having Joe record a complete $500,000 write-down? Is there anything wrong with what she wants to do?

2. Use the relevant elements of the ethical decision-making model discussed in Chapter 2 to reason what Boreing should do.

Case 4-6

ZZZZ Best[1]

The story of ZZZZ Best is one of greed and audaciousness. It is the story of a 15-year-old boy from Reseda, California, who was driven to be successful regardless of the costs. His name is Barry Minkow.

Minkow had high hopes to make it big—to be a millionaire very early in life. He started a carpet cleaning business in the garage of his home. Minkow realized early on that he was not going to become a millionaire cleaning other people's carpets. He had bigger plans than that. Minkow was going to make it big in the insurance restoration business. In other words, ZZZZ Best would contract to do carpet and drapery cleaning jobs after a fire or flood. Since the damage from the fire or flood probably would be covered by insurance, the customer would be eager to have the work done. The only problem with Minkow's insurance restoration idea was that it was all a fiction. There were no insurance restoration jobs, at least for ZZZZ Best. Allegedly, over 80 percent of his revenue was from this work. In the process of creating the fraud, Minkow was able to dupe the auditors, Ernst & Whinney, into thinking the insurance restoration business was real. The auditors never caught on until it was too late.

How Barry Became a Fraudster

Minkow wrote a book, *Clean Sweep: A Story of Compromise, Corruption, Collapse, and Comeback,*[2] that provides some insights into the mind of a 15-year-old kid who was called a "wonder boy" on Wall Street until the bubble burst. He was trying to find a way to drum up customers for his fledgling carpet cleaning business. One day, while he was alone in the garage-office, Minkow called Channel 4 in Los Angeles. He disguised his voice to sound not like a teenager and told a producer that he had just had his carpets cleaned by the 16-year-old owner of ZZZZ Best. He sold the producer on the idea that it would be good for society to hear the success story about a high school junior running his own business. The producer bought it lock, stock, and carpet cleaner. Minkow gave the producer the phone number of ZZZZ Best and waited. It took less than five minutes for the call to come in. Minkow answered the phone and when the producer asked to speak with Mr. Barry Minkow, Minkow said: "Who may I say is calling?" Within days a film crew was in his garage shooting ZZZZ Best at work. The story aired that night and it was followed by more calls from radio stations and other television shows wanting to do interviews. The calls flooded

in with customers demanding that Barry Minkow personally clean their carpets.

As his income increased in the spring of 1983, Minkow found it increasingly difficult to run the company without a checking account. He managed to find a banker that was so moved by his story that the banker would agree to allow someone underaged to open a checking account. Minkow used the money to buy cleaning supplies and other necessities. Even though his business was growing, Minkow ran into trouble paying back loans and interest when due.

Minkow developed a plan of action. He was tired of worrying about not having enough money. He went to his garage—where all his great ideas first began—and looked at his bank account statement, which showed that he had more money than he thought he had based on his own records. Minkow soon realized it was because some checks he had written had not been cashed by customers so they didn't yet show up on the bank statement. Voila! Minkow started to kite checks between two or more banks. He would write a check on one ZZZZ Best account and deposit it into another. Since it might take a few days for the check written on bank number one to clear that bank's records, at least back then when checks weren't always processed in real time, Minkow could pay some bills out of the second account and the first bank would not know—at least for a few days—that Minkow had written a check on his account when, in reality, he had a negative balance. The bank didn't know it because some of the checks that Minkow had written before the visit to bank number two had not cleared his account in bank number one.

It wasn't long thereafter that Minkow realized he could kite checks big time. Not only that, he could make the transfer of funds at the end of a month or a year and show a higher balance than really existed in bank number one and carry it on to the balance sheet. Since Minkow did not count the check written on his account in bank one as an outstanding check, he was able to double-count.

Time to Expand the Fraud

Over time, Minkow moved on to bigger and bigger frauds like having his trusted cohorts confirm to banks and other interested parties that ZZZZ Best was doing insurance restoration jobs. Minkow used the phony jobs and phony revenue to convince bankers to make loans to ZZZZ Best. He had cash remittance forms made up from nonexistent customers with whatever sales amount he wanted to appear on the document. He even had a co-conspirator write on the bogus remittance form, "job well done." Minkow could then show a lot more revenue than he was really making.

[1]The facts are derived from a video by the ACFE, *Cooking the Books: What Every Accountant Should Know about Fraud.*
[2]Barry Minkow, *Clean Sweep: A Story of Compromise, Corruption, Collapse, and Comeback* (Nashville, TN: Thomas Nelson, 1995).

Minkow's phony financial statements enabled him to borrow more and more money and expand the number of carpet cleaning outlets. However, Minkow's personal tastes had become increasingly more expensive including purchasing a Ferrari with the borrowed funds and putting a down payment on a 5,000-square-foot home. So, the question was: How do you solve a perpetual cash flow problem? You go public! That's right, Minkow made a public offering of stock in ZZZZ Best. Of course he owned a majority of the stock to maintain control of the company.

Minkow had made it to the big leagues. He was on Wall Street. He had investment bankers, CPAs, and attorneys all working for him—the 15-year-old kid from Reseda who had turned a mom and pop operation into a publicly owned corporation.

Barry Goes Public

Minkow's first audit was for the 12 months ended April 30, 1986. A sole practitioner performed the audit. (There are eerie similarities in the Madoff fraud with its small practitioner firm—Friehling & Horowitz—conducting the audit of a multibillion-dollar operation and that of the sole practitioner audit of ZZZZ Best.)

Minkow had established two phony front companies that allegedly placed insurance restoration jobs for ZZZZ Best. He had one of his cohorts create invoices for services and respond to questions about the company. There was enough paperwork to fool the auditor into thinking the jobs were real and the revenue was supportable. However, the auditor never visited any of the insurance restoration sites. If he had done so, there would have been no question in his mind that ZZZZ Best was a big fraud.

Pressured to get a big-time CPA firm to do his audit as he moved into the big leagues, Minkow hired Ernst &Whinney to perform the April 30, 1987, fiscal year-end audit. Minkow continued to be one step ahead of the auditors; that is, until the Ernst & Whinney auditors insisted on going to see an insurance restoration site. They wanted to confirm that all the business—all the revenues—that Minkow had said was coming in to ZZZZ Best was real.

The engagement partner drove to an area in Sacramento, California, where Minkow did a lot of work—supposedly. He looked for a building that seemed to be a restoration job. Why he did that isn't clear, but he identified a building that seemed to be the kind that would be a restoration job in process.

Earlier in the week, Minkow had sent one of his cohorts to find a large building in Sacramento that appeared to be a restoration site. As luck would have it, Minkow's associate picked out the same site as had the partner later on. Minkow's cohorts found the leasing agent for the building. They convinced the agent to give them the keys so that they could show the building to some potential tenants over the weekend. Minkow's helpers went up to the site before the arrival

of the partner and placed placards on the walls that indicated ZZZZ Best was the contractor for the building restoration. In fact, the building was not fully constructed at the time but it looked as if some restoration work would have been going on at the site.

Minkow was able to pull it off in part due to luck and in part because the Ernst and Whinney auditors did not want to lose the ZZZZ Best account. It had become a large revenue producer for the firm and Minkow seemed destined for greater and greater achievements. Minkow was smart and used the leverage of the auditors not wanting to lose the ZZZZ Best account as a way to complain whenever they became too curious about the insurance restoration jobs. He would even threaten to take away his business from Ernst and Whinney and give it to other auditors.

Minkow also took a precaution with the site visit. He had the auditors sign a confidentiality agreement that they would not make any follow-up calls to any contractors, insurance companies, the building owner, or other individuals involved in the restoration work. This prevented the auditors from corroborating the insurance restoration contracts with independent third parties.

The Fraud Starts to Unravel

It was a Los Angeles housewife who started the problems for ZZZZ Best that would eventually lead to the company's demise. Since Minkow was a well-known figure and flamboyant character, the *Los Angeles Times* did an expose about the carpet cleaning business. The Los Angeles housewife read the story about Minkow and recalled that ZZZZ Best had overcharged her for services in the early years by increasing the amount of the credit card charge for carpet cleaning services.

Minkow had gambled that most people don't check their monthly statements so he could get away with the petty fraud. However, the housewife did notice the overcharge, complained to Minkow, and eventually he returned the overpayment. She couldn't understand why Minkow would have had to resort to such low levels back then if he was as successful as the *Times* article made him out to be. So, she called the reporter to find out more and that ultimately led to the investigation of ZZZZ Best and future stories that weren't so flattering.

Since Minkow continued to spend lavishly on himself and his possessions, he always seemed to need more and more money. It got so bad over time that he was close to defaulting on loans and had to make up stories to keep the creditors at bay, and he couldn't pay his suppliers. The complaints kept coming in and eventually the house of cards that was ZZZZ Best came crashing down.

During the time that the fraud was unraveling, Ernst and Whinney decided to resign from the ZZZZ Best audit. The firm never did issue an audit report. It had started to doubt the veracity of Minkow and the reality of business at ZZZZ Best.

The procedure to follow when a change of auditor occurs is for the company being audited to file an 8-K form with the SEC and the audit firm to prepare an exhibit commenting on the accuracy of the disclosures in the 8-K. The exhibit is attached to the form that is sent to the SEC within 30 days of the change. Ernst & Whinney waited the full 30-day period, and the SEC released the information to the public 45 days after the change had occurred. Meanwhile, ZZZZ Best had filed for bankruptcy. During the period of time that had elapsed, Minkow had borrowed more than $1 million and the lenders never were repaid. Bankruptcy laws protected Minkow and ZZZZ Best from having to make those payments.

Legal Liability Issues

The ZZZZ Best fraud was one of the largest of its time. ZZZZ Best reportedly settled a shareholder class action lawsuit for $35 million. Ernst & Whinney was sued by a bank that had made a multimillion-dollar loan based on the financial statements for the three-month period ending July 31, 1986. The bank claimed that it had relied on the review report issued by Ernst & Whinney in granting the loan to ZZZZ Best. However, the firm had indicated in its review report that it was not issuing an opinion on the ZZZZ Best financial statements. The judge ruled that the bank was not justified in relying on the review report since Ernst & Whinney had expressly disclaimed issuing any opinion on the statements.

Barry Minkow was charged with engaging in a $100 million fraud scheme. He was sentenced to a term of 25 years. Minkow was paroled after serving 8 years in jail. During his time in prison, Minkow became involved in Christian ministry, which continued after his probationary release from prison in April 1995. Today he is senior pastor of the Community Bible Church in San Diego, California, having renounced his felonious acts. Minkow is recognized as an expert on fraud, and speaks on the subject to university students and the business community in an effort to prevent fraud.

Questions

1. Do you believe that auditors should be held liable for failing to discover fraud in situations such as ZZZZ Best where top management goes to great lengths to fool the auditors? Why or why not.

2. The AICPA Code obligates CPAs to follow specific standards of conduct in carrying out audits. Answer the following questions with respect to those standards and the related ethical expectations.
   a. Why is it important to exercise sensitive moral judgments when conducting an audit? Did Ernst & Whinney meet its obligations in this regard? If not, describe why it failed to meet its obligations.
   b. What are the criteria for audit independence? Comment on the independence of Ernst & Whinney in conducting its audit of ZZZZ Best.
   c. Auditors are expected to exercise due care in the performance of professional services. Explain the purpose of the due care standard. Based on the facts of the case, do you think Ernst & Whinney met its due care obligations? Why or why not.

3. These are selected numbers from the financial statements of ZZZZ Best for fiscal years 1985 and 1986:

	1985	1986
Sales	$1,240,524	$4,845,347
Cost of goods sold	576,694	2,050,779
Accounts receivable	0	693,773
Cash	30,321	87,014
Current liabilities	2,930	1,768,435
Notes payable—current	0	780,507

What calculations or analyses would you make with these numbers that might help you assess whether the financial relationships are "reasonable"? Given the facts of the case, what inquiries might you make of management based on your analysis?

Case 4-7

Bubba and Rufus

Background

Tax avoidance is the legal utilization of the tax regulations to one's advantage to reduce the amount of tax that is payable by means that are within tax law. Examples of tax avoidance include purchasing a home to deduct the interest portion of mortgage payment amounts, property taxes, and other possible expenses such as the costs related to an office in one's home (subject to strict tax requirements). Many people rent apartments without the benefit of any of these write-offs.

Tax evasion occurs when an individual, firm, trust, and other entities use illegal means to evade taxes. Tax evasion usually entails deliberately misrepresenting or concealing the true state of the individual's tax situation and activities to the tax authorities to reduce taxable income, thereby lowering the tax liability. Simple examples include underreporting income or overstating deductions. More elaborate ones might include setting up offshore accounts to illegally hide income from the government and establishing an abusive tax shelter.

Tax fraud cases have been on the rise for several years. Criminal tax fraud is very difficult to prove. The government first reviews the evidence to decide whether it has a *prima facie* case and a reasonable probability of conviction. If the government has a *prima facie* case—that is, minimal evidence supporting a jury's finding on each element of the crime—then the government survives the taxpayer's motion to dismiss and the case is presented in front of a jury.

Legal Trusts versus Abusive Tax Trust Evasion Schemes

According to the IRS, trust/estate matters are the third highest area of growth among top CPA firms.[1] The trend in trust and estate tax practice is likely to grow increasingly with the aging population in the United States.

A *trust* is a legal entity formed under state law. To create a trust, legal title to property is conveyed to a trustee, who is then charged with the responsibility of using that property for the benefit of another person, called the *beneficiary,* who really has all the benefits of ownership, except for bare legal title.

Legal trusts are used in estate planning to shelter income, to facilitate the genuine charitable transfer of assets, and to hold assets for minors and those unable to handle their financial affairs. For example, you may want to establish a trust to set aside money for your teenage son or daughter. That money can then be released to your child at an appropriate age in the future.

A *trustee* is designated to hold legal title to the trust property, to exercise independent control over it, and to be responsible for its management. Trustees have strict fiduciary obligations under the law.

Trusts established to hide the true ownership of assets and income or to disguise the substance of financial transactions are considered fraudulent trusts. Some examples include wiring income overseas and failing to report it and attempting to protect transactions through bank secrecy laws in tax haven countries.

Trusts file Form 1120. Trust tax rates are high compared to comparable income tax rates for individual tax payers that file Form 1040. For 2009, the maximum tax rate on trusts is 35 percent, and it is reached by trusts with $11,150 of taxable income. Individuals filing separately are taxed at 10 percent up to $8,025 of income and 15 percent over $8,025 up until $32,550. A taxpayer with $11,150 would pay a tax of $3,902.50 as a trust entity and $1,270.50 as an individual. Individuals do not reach the 35 percent tax rate until their income reaches $357,700, and then the rate of taxation, which is the maximum rate on individuals, would be at 35 percent. (It is expected that the rates will go up to 39.6 percent in 2010 after the expiration of tax cuts passed during the Bush administration.)

The tax rate differential raises the question of why an individual would set up a trust unless it was for estate purposes or the benefit of a minor child. In the former case, the rate of tax on a trust might be less than the estate tax on property owned at the date of death. Typically, these trusts benefit wealthy people because, as of 2009, the first $3,500,000 of estate assets is not taxed. If the estate owned $4.0 million in 2009, then only $500,000 would be subject to tax. The tax rate on the $500,000 million would be 45 percent. This compares with 35 percent, the maximum rates for trusts. The difference in tax on $500,000 for an estate and for a trust is $50,000. However, that amount increases with higher estate incomes beyond the $3.5 million exemption.

Enough of the tax lecture. The point is why an individual would set up a trust to shelter his income when the trust rate is higher than individual tax rates. One possibility might be to withhold funds from a minor child after the death of a parent by having a trustee administer the trust on behalf of the child, and not distribute the estate inheritance automatically to the child. Of course, another reason could be if a taxpayer is duped by an unscrupulous tax accountant who is mainly interested in earning higher fees for setting up the trust. While we would like to think this is a rarity, it has happened before and the following case describes one instance of a fraud using trusts.

[1] Abusive Tax Evasion Schemes, www.irs.gov/businesses/small/article/0,,id=106549,00.html.

The Case

Bubba Toothless decided, after failing out of engineering school, to become an accountant. He graduated from Alabama State Polytechnic Institute with a master's degree in taxation. He passed the four parts of the CPA Exam in consecutive attempts during 2009. Bubba worked for a small firm in Birmingham during 2009, until he decided to strike out on his own. He hung out his shingle in downtown Birmingham on January 17, 2010. Bubba struggled with his tax practice during that first busy season. Most people in town were used to going to other tax providers. Bubba quickly realized he had to do something that would "add value" to his tax services for clients.

Bubba started marketing "common-law trust" packages to clients throughout the southeast via group seminars, individual client meetings, and an attractive Web site that promised 100 free lottery tickets to the first 100 people who purchased a trust package for $3,995. Bubba netted $3,795 on the 100 $2 lottery tickets given to clients for purchasing the common-law trust package. By April 16, 2010, Bubba had made over $450,000 from the sale of the packages.

Bubba marketed common-law trusts that alleged legitimate tax deductions for individuals who set up the trust (with Bubba, of course) and then "transferred" ordinary living expenses paid by the taxpayer such as the cost of utilities, food, clothing, vehicles, and education through a common-law trust.

One day Rufus Stoneman came to Bubba's office. They talked about the good old days when a boy could drink six packs of beer while driving his pickup down the highway and, if stopped by the highway patrol, the officer was more likely to ask for a beer rather that write up a ticket for the violation of the motor vehicle code. Bubba and Rufus hit it off so well that Bubba decided to tell Rufus about his common-law trusts. Rufus thought it was the best thing since sliced cheese, so he agreed to let Bubba set up a common-law trust. Rufus gave Bubba $2,000 as a down payment on the final product. By April 15, 2010, Rufus had filed his first trust return, given Bubba the remaining $2,000, and left the office happy as a clam that he had saved over $10,000 in taxes through the trust.

Fifteen months later, Rufus received the dreaded letter in the mail that he was the target of an IRS investigation into fraudulent common-law trusts that had been sold throughout the United States during the period 2007 through 2010. Rufus immediately called Bubba, but reached a recording that the number was no longer in service. No forwarding phone number was available.

Questions

1. What are the ethical responsibilities of a CPA who prepares tax returns? Assuming the common-law trust set up by Bubba was fraudulent, discuss the ethical and professional obligations violated by Bubba with respect to his professional services for Rufus.

2. Tax avoidance is legal under income tax regulations. Even though it is legal, do you think it is ethical to engage in tax avoidance when advising a tax client? Are there any "tipping points" when you would not engage in a tax advisory service for a client even though it can be rationalized under the law? Be specific.

3. Do you think it is right for the IRS to charge a taxpayer with fraud when that person does not realize that the devices set up by her tax accountant, who was implicitly trusted by the taxpayer, are fraudulent? Why or why not?

Case 4-8

HealthSouth Corporation

The HealthSouth case is unique because the CEO, Richard Scrushy, was initially acquitted on all accounts while five former HealthSouth employees were sentenced by a federal judge for their admitted roles in a scheme to inflate revenues and reported earnings of the company from 1999 through mid-2002. These amounts are presented in Exhibit 1.

HealthSouth was the nation's largest provider of outpatient surgery, diagnostic imaging, and rehabilitative services. In 2003, the SEC filed a complaint against the company and Scrushy for violating provisions of the Securities Act of 1933 and the Securities Exchange Act of 1934.[1] The complaint alleges that HealthSouth, under Scrushy's direction and with the help of key employees, falsified its revenue to inflate earnings and "meet their numbers." Specifically, false accounting entries were made to an account called "contractual adjustment." The contractual adjustment account is a revenue allowance account that estimates the difference between the gross amount billed to the patient and the amount that various health care insurers will pay for a specific treatment. HealthSouth deducted this account from gross revenues to derive net revenues, which were disclosed on the company's periodic reports filed with the SEC. The allowances were deliberately understated to help meet financial analyst earnings estimates.

The SEC contended that in mid-2002, certain senior officers of HealthSouth discussed with Scrushy the impact of the scheme to inflate earnings because they were concerned about the consequences of the August 14, 2002, financial statement certification required under Section 302 of SOX. Allegedly, "Scrushy agreed that, going forward, he would not insist that earnings be inflated to meet Wall Street analysts' expectations."

The filing also alleged that Scrushy received at least $6.5 million from HealthSouth during 2001 in "Bonus/Annual Incentive Awards." Also, from 1999 through 2002, HealthSouth paid Scrushy $9.2 million in salary. Approximately $5.3 million of this salary was based on the company's achievement of certain budget targets. On December 10, 2003, U.S. District Judge Inge P. Johnson sentenced former vice president of finance Emery Harris, who pleaded guilty in March 2003 to a charge of conspiracy and willfully falsifying books and records, to a term of five months in prison on each count to run concurrently, three years of supervised release with five months of unsupervised house detention, and payment of a $3,000 fine and a $200 special assessment. Harris was also ordered to pay $106,500 in forfeiture.[2]

On June 28, 2005, Richard Scrushy, the former CEO of HealthSouth, was acquitted on all charges despite the testimony of more than a half-dozen former lieutenants who said Scrushy had presided over a $2.7 billion accounting fraud while running the HealthSouth national hospital chain. The jury had even heard secretly recorded conversations between Scrushy and a CFO, William T. Owens, in March 2003 discussing balance sheet problems, with Scrushy asking "You're not wired, are you?"

In an ironic twist in the HealthSouth saga, the key prosecution witness in the government's case against Scrushy, William Owens, was sentenced on December 9, 2005, to five years in prison for his role in the accounting fraud at HealthSouth. Owens had manipulated the company's books and instructed subordinates to make phony accounting entries. He also falsely certified the 2002 financial statements filed with the 10-K report to the SEC.

U.S. District Judge Sharon Lovelace Blackburn knocked three years from the prosecutor's sentencing request stating to Owens, "I believe you told the truth." Blackburn called Scrushy's acquittal a "travesty." Nonetheless, Blackburn said white-collar criminals merit stiff sentences, if only to send a message of deterrence to other business executives.

[1] Securities and Exchange Commission, Civil Action No. CV-03-J-0615-S, U.S. District Court Northern District of Alabama, *Securities and Exchange Commission v. HealthSouth Corporation and Richard M. Scrushy, Defendants.*

[2] Department of Justice, "Five Defendants Sentenced in HealthSouth Fraud Case," www.usdoj.gov.

EXHIBIT 1
Misstatement of Net Income by HealthSouth Corporation

Net Income (in millions)	1999 Form 10-K	2000 Form 10-K	2001 Form 10-K	For Six Months Ended June 30, 2002
Actual	$(191)	$194	$ 9	$157
Reported	230	559	434	340
Misstated amount	421	365	425	183
Misstated percentage	220%	188%	4,722%	119%

"Corporate offenders are nothing more than common thieves wearing suits and wielding pens," Blackburn said.[3]

The Fraud Investigation— Implications of Whistleblowing

HealthSouth said a forensic audit by PricewaterhouseCoopers found fraudulent entries to raise the total to a range of $3.8 to $4.6 billion, up from $3.5 billion, the government's original estimate. The fraud included $2.5 billion in fraudulent accounting entries from 1996 to 2002, $500 million in incorrect accounting for goodwill and other items involved in acquisitions from 1994 to 1999, and $800 million to $1.6 billion in "aggressive accounting" from 1992 to March 2003.

Allegedly, HealthSouth's auditors—and maybe even government regulators—were tipped off to a possible massive accounting fraud at the company five years before it became public knowledge, or at least that's the takeaway from a shareholder's memo that was released by a congressional committee during its investigation. The memo, dated November 1998, was apparently written by an anonymous HealthSouth shareholder and sent to auditor Ernst & Young (EY). In it, the shareholder alerts the audit firm to alleged bookkeeping violations at the rehabilitation-services company. Reportedly HealthSouth's top lawyer assured its independent auditor that it would conduct an internal investigation of the allegations. The committee notes no record of such an inquiry, however. "You bring the smoke, I'll bring the mirrors," the unnamed shareholder wrote in the memo.

The shareholder's list of alleged violations at HealthSouth included an assertion that the company booked charges to outpatient clinic patients before checking that insurers would reimburse the claims. The shareholder also alleged that HealthSouth continued to record these charges as revenue even after payments were denied. "How can the company carry tens of millions of dollars in accounts receivable that are well over 360 days?" the shareholder asked in the letter.

More questions followed: "How can some hospitals have NO bad debt reserves? How did the EY auditors in Alabama miss this stuff? Are these clever tricks to pump up the numbers, or something that a novice accountant could catch?" In a statement issued by EY, the firm stated it had conducted a review at the time the allegations were made and determined the issues raised did not affect the presentation of HealthSouth's financial statements. "You people and I have been hoodwinked," the shareholder concluded in the memo. "This note is all that I can do about it. You all can do much more, if all you do is look into it to see if what I say is true." At 10:06 a.m. on February 13, 2003, someone made a sensational claim on the Yahoo bulletin board devoted to discussion of HealthSouth to this effect: "What I know about the accounting at HealthSouth will be the blow that will bring the company to its knees."

Michael Vines, a former bookkeeper in HealthSouth's accounting department, tried to spread the word about alleged questionable practices while at HealthSouth but was turned away at every corner. According to Vines's testimony at the April 2002 federal court hearing, he came to believe that people in the department were falsifying assets on the balance sheet. The accountants, he testified, would move expenses from the company's income statement—where the expenses would have to be deducted from profits immediately—to its balance sheet, where they wouldn't have to be deducted all at one time. Thus, the company's expenses looked lower than they should have been, which helped artificially boost net income.

The individual expenses were relatively small—between $500 and $4,999 apiece, according to Vines's testimony—because EY examined expenses over $5,000. Overall, according to the SEC complaint, about $1 billion in fixed assets were falsely entered. In his testimony, Vines identified about $1 million in entries he believed were fraudulent. He told his immediate superior, Cathy C. Edwards, a vice president in the accounting department, that he wouldn't make such entries unless she first initialed them. "I wanted her signature on it," Vines testified. Edwards, according to Vines's testimony, signed off on the entries, and he logged them. Vines also testified that he saw Edwards falsifying an invoice, which according to his testimony was a way to cover up the larger fraud involving the accounts. On April 3, Edwards pleaded guilty to conspiracy to commit wire and securities fraud. As part of the plea, she admitted to falsifying records, although the plea didn't mention specific incidents.

Over time, Vines had grown more concerned about the accounting practices particularly in light of the scandal that had recently erupted at Enron Corp. He quit his job and moved to the accounting office of a Birmingham country club. Not long afterward, he sent an e-mail to EY alleging fraudulent transactions and identified three account numbers that Ernst should investigate. The accounts covered expenses for "minor equipment," "repairs and maintenance" and "public information," which included costs for temporary workers and advertising job openings, he said in an interview and in court testimony.

Vines's e-mail was passed on to James Lamphron, a partner in Ernst's Birmingham office. Lamphron testified that he had contacted William T. Owens, who was then president and chief operating officer at HealthSouth, and George Strong, who served as chair of the audit committee of HealthSouth's board. A HealthSouth spokesperson said Strong felt the matter was being resolved. According to Lamphron's testimony, Owens defended the company's accounting practices. He acknowledged that the company had moved expenses from one category to another, but argued that the company had done it for several years and that it was an acceptable practice. Lamphron testified that Owens called Vines a "disgruntled employee." On March 26, 2004, Owens pleaded guilty

---

[3]Carrie Johnson, "5 Years for HealthSouth Fraud: Former Chief Financial Officer Was Key Witness," *Washington Post,* December 10, 2005, D1.

to wire and securities fraud and certifying a false financial report to the SEC.

Lamphron testified that EY had conducted "audit-related procedures" with the accounts Vines pointed out. The result: Ernst "reached a point where we were satisfied with the explanation that the company had provided to us. . . . We then closed the process." According to Lamphron's testimony, Vines never specified that invoices were being falsified—only that there was a problem with the three accounts he mentioned. So EY never investigated the falsified invoices and didn't find any evidence of fraud. Ernst defended itself by stressing the difficulty of detecting accounting fraud in the midst of a conspiracy involving senior executives and allegedly false documentation. Ernst wasn't named or charged as a defendant in the government cases and the firm cooperated with investigators.

Questions

1. Do you think lower-level employees should be excused from any liability for their actions that contribute toward financial statement fraud when the person in charge of the fraud is found not guilty in a court of law? Use ethical reasoning to support your answer.

2. What is the nature of the contractual allowance account? Can you equate it to other allowance accounts? Explain the rules under GAAP to account for such allowances.

3. EY wasn't named or charged as a defendant in the government case against HealthSouth. Based on the limited facts of the case, do you think EY should have been charged for its failure to exercise due care in the audit of HealthSouth? Be specific.

Case 4-9

Ethics of Using Indemnification Clauses

About Indemnification Clauses

"An indemnification or hold harmless clause in an engagement letter typically provides that the client will indemnify or hold the CPA harmless in the event the CPA sustains a loss resulting from claims arising from the CPA's work on the client engagement. Indemnification clauses are not intended to preclude the CPA from incurring liability for professional malpractice. Instead, such a clause is intended to preclude liability where the client knowingly makes misrepresentations to the CPA, causes or participates in a fraud, conceals information from the CPA, or otherwise leads the CPA astray."[1]

Indemnification and hold harmless clauses can provide valuable protection to CPAs where they are permitted and enforceable. They not only serve as a deterrent against a client considering a potential claim against a CPA, but also can be used to require the client to indemnify the CPA for attorney fees and costs, as well as the costs of any judgments or awards arising from claims made against the CPA by third parties. In addition to indemnification or hold harmless clauses, some CPAs use limitation of liability clauses, which typically limit the CPA's liability to a portion of their fee or a defined dollar value.

"While CPAs may view the use of an indemnification clause as attractive, clients may have a differing opinion leading to resistance from a client if such a clause is proposed to be included in an engagement letter. The use of such a clause then becomes a matter of negotiation with the client. The enforceability of indemnification clauses may be dependent upon the requirements of public policy and subject to the dictates of the controlling legal jurisdiction. Hence, the use of an indemnification clause may only provide false security to the CPA."[2]

For some time the position of the SEC with regard to the use of an indemnification provision by a CPA auditing a public company has been that an agreement that provides complete indemnification to an auditor impairs independence in attest engagements.

Can CPAs Use Indemnification Clauses in Engagement Letters?

CPAs can use indemnification clauses in engagement letters except when prohibited by applicable law, regulation, or ethics rules. The SEC, federal banking regulators and many state insurance departments prohibit indemnification or limitation of liability arrangements between the regulated entities and CPA firms performing audit or other attest services. According to AICPA Ethics Interpretation 501-8, use of indemnification and liability limitation clauses disregarding the rules and requirements of regulators would be considered an ethics violation.[3] As a result, when considering the use of indemnification and liability limitation clauses in an audit or other attest engagement letter, if the client is in a regulated industry, the CPA should check for regulatory rules prohibiting the use of these clauses. AICPA ethics rules also apply. With respect to indemnification and limitation of liability clauses, an AICPA Ethics Ruling indicates that clauses which limit liability resulting from knowing misrepresentations by client management do not impair independence. Accordingly, if indemnification clauses are limited in this manner and are not prohibited by regulation, they are permissible in engagement letters for attest services.

For non-attest services, there are typically no restrictions on the use of indemnification and liability limitation clauses in engagement letters. The terms in those clauses are subject to negotiation between the CPA and client. While CPAs usually prefer the use of such clauses, they often face resistance from their clients. So, it's necessary to explain the rationale for using those clauses to clients. For example, in engagements to prepare a compilation report for management use only, you can explain that because your work product is intended solely for their use, your firm should not be responsible for claims arising from use by others.

Are They Legally Enforceable?

In addition to ensuring that a CPA can use indemnification and liability limitation clauses in an engagement letter without violating applicable law, regulations, or ethics rules, the CPA should find out whether such clauses are enforceable in the applicable jurisdiction. The enforceability of such clauses is often a question of equity and public policy, subject to the dictates of the controlling legal jurisdiction. In many jurisdictions, an important enforceability factor is the ability to show that such clauses were negotiated between two parties with relatively equal bargaining power, and that the clauses were clearly set forth in the engagement letter, and understood and consented to by both parties to the agreement.

---

[1]McFadden, J. and Wolfe, J. 2009. "Engagement Letter Indemnification Clauses: Should You Use Them?" found at http://www.cpai.com/risk-management/professional-liability/letter-clauses.jsp.
[2]Ibid.

[3]AICPA Ethics Interpretation 501-8, Failure to Follow Requirements of Governmental Bodies, Commissions, or Other Regulatory Agencies on Indemnification and Limitation of Liability Provisions in Connection with Audit and Attest Services (effective July 1, 2008). Available at: http://www.aicpa.org/download/ethics/EDITED_Adopted_501_8_final.pdf.

Where permissible, CPAs can consider using indemnification, hold harmless and limitation of liability clauses in engagement letters to limit their liability to clients and third parties. No single clause or wording is appropriate in all situations. Instead, clauses should be tailored to fit individual client situations and the assessed risks. CPAs contemplating the use of such clauses in engagement letters should consult with their attorney regarding both the wording to be used and enforceability under applicable law.

Questions

1. Discuss the specific independence concerns when CPAs use indemnification clauses in engagement letters with clients. Include in your discussion whether there are any specific threats to independence as discussed in the chapter.

2. The case states that: "Indemnification and hold harmless clauses can provide valuable protection to CPAs where they are permitted and enforceable. They not only serve as a deterrent against a client considering a potential claim against a CPA, but also can be used to require the client to indemnify the CPA for attorney fees and costs, as well as the costs of any judgments or awards arising from claims made against the CPA by third parties. In addition to indemnification or hold harmless clauses, some CPAs use limitation of liability clauses, which typically limit the CPA's liability to a portion of their fee or a defined dollar value. Evaluate the ethics of this statement and whether you believe the use of indemnification clauses are ethical.

Case 4-10

Independence Violations at PricewaterhouseCoopers

On January 6, 2000, the SEC made public the report by independent consultant Jess Fardella, who was appointed by the commission in March 1999 to conduct a review of possible independence rule violations by the public accounting firm PricewaterhouseCoopers (PwC) arising from ownership of client-issued securities. The report found significant violations of the firm's, the profession's, and the SEC's auditor independence rules.

Background

On January 14, 1999, the commission issued an Opinion and Order Pursuant to Rule 102(e) of the Commission's Rules of Practice, *In the Matter of PricewaterhouseCoopers LLP* (Securities Exchange Act of 1934, Release No. 40945) ("Order"),[1] which censured PwC for violating auditor independence rules and improper professional conduct. Pursuant to the settlement reached with the commission, PwC agreed to, among other things, complete an internal review by Fardella to identify instances in which the firm's partners or professionals owned securities of public audit clients of PwC in contravention of applicable rules and regulations concerning independence.

The independent consultant's report discloses that a substantial number of PwC professionals, particularly partners, had violations of the independence rules, and that many had multiple violations. The review found excusable mistakes, but also attributed the violations to laxity and insensitivity to the importance of independence compliance. According to Fardella's report, PwC acknowledged that the review disclosed widespread independence noncompliance that reflected serious structural and cultural problems in the firm.

Results of the Independent Consultant's Report

The report summarizes results of the internal review at PwC, which included two key parts: PwC professionals were requested in March 1999 to self-report independence violations; and the independent consultant randomly tested a sample of the responses for completeness and accuracy. The results are as follows:

1. Almost half of the PwC partners—1,301 out of a total of 2,698—self-reported at least one independence violation. The 1,301 partners who reported a violation reported an average of 5 violations; 153 partners had more than 10 violations each. Of 8,064 reported violations, 81.3 percent were reported by partners and 17.4 percent by

[1]Available at www.sec.gov/pdf/pwclaw.pdf.

managers; 45.2 percent of the violations were reported by partners who perform services related to audits of financial statements.

2. Almost half of the reported violations involved direct investments by the PwC professional in securities, mutual funds, bank accounts, or insurance products associated with a client. Almost 32 percent of reported violations, or 2,565 instances, involved holdings of a client's stock or stock options.

3. Six out of 11 partners at the senior management level who oversaw PwC's independence program self-reported violations. Each of the 12 regional partners who help administer PwC's independence program reported at least 1 violation; one reported 38 violations and another reported 34 violations.

4. Thirty-one of the 43 partners who comprise PwC's Board of Partners and its U.S. Leadership Committee self-reported at least 1 violation. Four of these had more than 20 violations; one of these partners had 41 violations and another had 40 violations.

These random tests of the self-reporting process indicated that a far greater percentage of individuals had independence violations than were reported. Despite clear warnings that the SEC was overseeing the self-reporting process, the random tests of those reports indicated that 77.5 percent of PwC partners failed to self-report at least one independence violation. The combined results of the self-reporting and random tests of those reports indicated that approximately 86.5 percent of PwC partners and 10.5 percent of all other PwC professionals had independence violations.

The independent consultant's report identifies key weaknesses in the systems PwC had used to prevent or detect independence violations.

1. Reporting systems relied on the individuals themselves to sort through their own investments and interests for violations.

2. Efforts to educate professionals about the independence rules and their responsibilities to the client to comply with the rules were insufficient.

3. Resolution of reported violations was not adequately documented.

4. Reporting systems did not focus on the reporting of violations that were deemed to be resolved before annual confirmations were submitted.

The consultant's report concludes that the numbers of violations alone, as PwC acknowledged, reflect serious structural and cultural problems that were rooted in both its legacy firms (Price Waterhouse and Coopers & Lybrand). Although a large percentage of the reported and unreported violations is attributable solely to the merger, an even larger portion is not; thus, the situation revealed by the internal investigation is not a one-time breakdown explained solely by the merger. Nor can the magnitude of the reported and unreported violations be attributed simply to less familiar independence rules such as those pertaining to brokerage, bank, and sweep accounts. At least half of the reported and unreported violations consisted of interests held by a reporting PwC professional himself or herself, and most of the violations arose from either mutual fund or stock holdings. Independence compliance at PwC and its legacy firms was dependent largely on individual initiative. This system failed, as PwC has acknowledged.

Changes Needed

As accounting firms have grown larger, acquired more clients, and provided more services, and as investment opportunities and financial arrangements have increased in number and complexity, well-designed and extensive controls are needed both to facilitate independence compliance and to discourage and detect noncompliance. The violations discussed in the consultant's report had come to light as a result of a commission-ordered review after professional self-regulatory procedures failed to detect such violations. As a result, the SEC requested the then-current Public Oversight Board (largely replaced by PCAOB) to sponsor similar independent reviews at other firms and oversee development of enhancements to quality control and other professional standards. The firm also agreed in a settlement to conduct the review and create a $2.5 million education fund after the SEC alleged that some of its accountants compromised their independence by owning stock in corporations they audited.

PricewaterhouseCoopers promised at the time to take steps to ensure that it didn't happen again. As a result of the inquiry, five partners of the firm and a slightly larger number of other employees had been dismissed, and other employees were disciplined but not fired.

Two changes that resulted from the problems at PwC were (1) to clearly define family members and other close relatives of members of the attest engagement team that might create an independence impairment for the auditors because of the formers' ownership interests in a client and/or their position within the client including having a financial reporting oversight role (Interpretation 101-1); and (2) to restrict the ability of audit personnel from having loans to or from banks and other financial institution clients (Interpretation 101-5).

Questions

1. In commenting on the findings in the consultant's report, the then-chief accountant of the SEC, Lynn E. Turner, said, "This report is a sobering reminder that accounting professionals need to renew their commitment to the fundamental principle of auditor independence." Why is it so important for auditors to be independent of their clients? Explain the nature of the independence impairments at PwC with respect to the threats to independence discussed in the chapter.

2. Review question 19 at the end of the chapter and the PeopleSoft case in the chapter. What are the commonalities between the facts of these two cases with respect to independence violations and the facts of PwC's independence violations? How might the independence violations in these cases negatively affect the ability of an auditor to be objective in performing professional services and maintain her integrity?

3. We have discussed the need for an ethical tone at the top and strong internal controls at public companies to help prevent and detect fraud. In Chapter 2 we pointed out that studies have shown most CPAs reason at Stages 3 or 4 in Kohlberg's model. Given the independence violations at PwC, do you think it is indicative of a Stage 3 or 4 reasoning capacity? Or, is it Stage 1 or 2? Explain.

Chapter 5

Audit Responsibilities and Accounting Fraud

Ethics Reflection

CALIFORNIA MICRO DEVICES AND THE FAILURE TO CONDUCT AN AUDIT IN ACCORDANCE WITH GENERALLY ACCEPTED AUDITING STANDARDS

Michael Marrie and Brian Berry, as employees of the accounting firm Coopers & Lybrand LLP, acted as engagement partner and manager, respectively, for Coopers's 1994 audit of California Micro Devices, Inc., which designed, manufactured, and distributed electric circuits and semiconductors. On August 25, 1994, Marrie and Berry presented the firm's independent accountants' report addressed to Cal Micro's shareholders and directors, stating that Cal Micro's financial statements complied with GAAP and that the audit had been conducted in accordance with GAAS. Following an independent investigation, Cal Micro filed a revised financial report with the commission on February 6, 1995, showing a net loss of $15.2 million instead of earnings of $5 million, total revenue of $30.1 million rather than the previously reported $45.3 million, accounts receivable of $6.3 million instead of $16.9 million, $5.1 million in inventories instead of $13.9 million, and net property and equipment of $7.4 million instead of the previously reported $10.4 million. On August 10, 1999, the SEC initiated proceedings against Marrie and Berry in conjunction with accounting fraud at Cal Micro. The commission charged that the auditors had engaged in improper professional conduct in that they "violated GAAS by *failing to exercise appropriate professional skepticism, obtain sufficient competent evidential matter, or*

adequately supervise field work" in connection with three aspects of the 1994 audit:[1]

1. The write-off of $12 million of accounts receivable
2. The confirmation of the accounts receivable
3. The accounting of the sales returns and allowances

The commission also claimed that Marrie's and Berry's failures to examine the write-off, to investigate discrepancies in the confirmation responses, and to analyze Cal Micro's sales returns and the adequacy of its allowance for returns were "an extreme departure from professional standards." Further, Marrie and Berry were reckless in ignoring "unmistakable red flags" that indicated potential accounting irregularities in the areas of revenue recognition, accounts receivable confirmations, sales returns, sales cutoff, and cash collections. As a result, the commission alleged that Cal Micro's financial statements for the fiscal year 1994 were materially false and misleading and were not prepared in conformity with GAAP.

The SEC charges against Marrie and Berry were eventually overturned by an administrative law judge who ruled that the auditors had not intended to aid in the fraud being perpetrated by Cal Micro; therefore, their conduct was not reckless.[2] Nevertheless, the Cal Micro Devices case illustrates that auditors have an ethical obligation to follow the profession's standards and perform services with the level of care expected under the circumstances.

As you read this chapter, think about how the existence of red flags can help an auditor identify problem areas in an audit and the role of professional judgment and ethical reasoning in conducting an audit in accordance with GAAS.

I would want [the auditor], on the basis of his credentials, his professional responsibility and integrity, to assert that, from the alternatives in GAAP he has determined the options and the particular alternatives that he deemed to be most appropriate and fairest under the circumstances. Note the superlatives "most appropriate" and "fairest." . . . At present, the words used by the auditor when he "certifies" the financial statements make it appear that this is precisely what he is presently doing; but those of us who are sophisticated know that the words in the auditor's certificate about the statements presenting the financial condition and operations fairly [present fairly] are specious. I am presently urging that this appearance become reality. While our profession usually prefers to gloss over this condition, namely, the auditor's abdication of primary responsibility for the statements, when it suits the profession's purposes the condition is permitted to surface. This usually occurs in the process of litigation, when an accountant is found with his procedures down.

Abraham Briloff, a frequent critic of the account profession and a well-regarded academician, commenting on whether responsibility for financial statements should be shifted from management to the independent auditor

The Nature of Auditing and the Audit Report

Abe Briloff made these prescient comments in 1978. They ring true today as they did more than 30 years ago. The series of congressional investigations of the accounting profession that were discussed in Chapter 4 seem to indicate that auditors may not have learned their lesson over the years as accounting frauds rear their ugly head about once every 10 years.

An *audit* is an examination of the financial statements prepared by management and rendering of an independent opinion that the statements have been prepared in accordance with GAAP. SEC rules require that publicly owned companies have an audit. Students should become familiar with the requirements of an audit conducted in accordance with GAAS and different reporting situations. The unqualified report is desirable from the company's point of view. However, the auditor may choose to deviate from such an opinion if GAAP concerns exist or the auditor is unable to gather the qualitative evidence required to issue an unqualified report. The exact wording of the unqualified audit report for public companies appears in Exhibit 5.1.

Contents of the Audit Report

Introductory Paragraph

The three important features of the introductory paragraph follow:

1. Identifies the financial statements being examined
2. Clarifies management's responsibilities for the statements
3. States the auditor's responsibility to express an (independent) opinion on those statements

EXHIBIT 5.1
**Unqualified Opinion
of Mintz & Morris
LLP, Independent
Registered Public
Accounting Firm**

To the Board of Directors and Stockholders, XYZ Company

We have audited the accompanying consolidated balance sheets of XYZ Company as of December 31, 2010, and 2009, and the related consolidated statements of income, stockholders' equity, and cash flows for each of the three years in the period ended December 31, 2010. These financial statements are the responsibility of the company's management. Our responsibility is to express an opinion on these financial statements based on our audits.

We conducted our audit in accordance with the standards of the Public Company Accounting Oversight Board (United States). Those standards require that we plan and perform the audit to obtain reasonable assurance about whether the financial statements are free of material misstatement. An audit includes examining, on a test basis, evidence supporting the amounts and disclosures in the financial statements. An audit also includes assessing the accounting principles used and significant estimates made by management, as well as evaluating the overall financial statement presentation. We believe that our audit provides a reasonable basis for our opinion.

In our opinion, the financial statements referred to above present fairly in all material respects, the consolidated financial position of XYZ Company at December 31, 2010, and 2009, and the consolidated results of its operations and its cash flows for each of the three years in the period ended December 31, 2010, in conformity with U.S. generally accepted accounting principles.

We have also audited, in accordance with the standards of the Public Company Accounting Oversight Board (United States), the effectiveness of XYZ Corporation's internal control over financial reporting as of December 31, 2010, based on criteria established in *Internal Control—Integrated Framework* issued by the Committee of Sponsoring Organizations of the Treadway Commission, and our report dated January 31, 2011, expressed an unqualified opinion thereon.

[Signature]
[City and State]
[Date]

Financial statements typically are prepared under the direction of the controller who reports to the CFO. The CFO reports to the CEO. In virtually all of the frauds in the late 1990s and early 2000s, either the CFO gave in to the pressure of the CEO to prepare materially false and misleading financial statements and/or the CFO personally directed the fraud.

The controller's position is a difficult one because of the dual obligations of loyalty to one's employer and adherence to ethical standards. The IMA standards that were discussed in Chapter 1 obligate the controller to communicate information fairly and objectively and disclose all relevant information that could reasonably be expected to influence an intended user's understanding of the reports, analyses, or recommendations. A controller who is a CPA should be cognizant of the requirements under Interpretation 102-4 that was discussed in Chapter 1. It requires that the controller take whatever steps are necessary by going up the chain of command in the company to ensure that the financial statements are accurate and reliable. To review the 102-4 requirements, first, the controller should inform the CFO of any material misstatement in the financial statements. If the CFO does not support correcting the statements, then the controller should go to the CEO. If the CEO takes no action to correct the matter, then the controller should go to the audit committee of the board of directors. Although one's ethical obligations are satisfied after these steps have been taken, it is also recommended that the controller should prepare an informative memorandum outlining the discussions with respect to correcting the material misstatement of the financial statements just in case the matter winds up in the courts.

As a student, you may think it is unlikely you will be faced with a similar situation in your career. While this may be true with respect to the GAAP conformity of the financial statements, other situations may arise where your ethics are tested. For example, what would you do if you see a coworker steal a significant amount of money from petty cash and you confront that person who says it is a "one-time fix" to solve personal cash flow problems. Would you remain silent? No one likes to inform on a coworker. Recall from Chapter 1, however, that loyalty is the one ethical value that should never take precedence over other values such as honesty and integrity. Otherwise, we can imagine all kinds of cover-ups of information in the interest of loyalty or friendship.

We recommend that a controller (and a student) look at the big picture when expected by the company to go along with fraud and ask whether this is the kind of organization she wants to be associated with on a long-term basis. After all, it is the controller who has the technical expertise to decide GAAP matters, yet that person's skills and knowledge are not respected by the CFO and CEO. They make decisions from an egoistic perspective when pressuring the controller to go along with materially misstated financial statements. The danger of going along with fraud is that the controller may be blamed later on when (and if) the bubble bursts. The controller becomes a part of the cover-up and that is the first step down the ethical slippery slope.

Scope Paragraph

The scope paragraph contains four important statements that define the auditor's responsibility in conducting an audit:

1. The auditor followed GAAS.
2. The audit provided "reasonable assurance" that the statements are free of "material" misstatement.
3. The auditor assessed the accounting principles used and the significant estimates made by management, and evaluated the overall financial statement presentation.
4. The audit provided a "reasonable" basis for the opinion.

The word *reasonable* is critical to the public's understanding of the value of the audit opinion. It is an ethical judgment by the auditor in the sense that what is reasonable to one auditor may not be to another. In addition to stating a reliance on following GAAS as the basis for the reasonableness statements in the auditor's report (the "legal" perspective explained in the following text), the professional judgment of the auditor should have an ethical basis to make such a judgment. The Rights Theory might posit the question: Would I want other auditors to decide on reasonableness the same way I am about to do (universality perspective)?

GAAS is to the audit what GAAP is to the financial statements. GAAP represents the rules for the recording, reporting, and disclosure of financial statement information. GAAS establishes the audit standards and procedures that should be followed in conducting an audit. By following these standards the auditor increases the likelihood of being able to defend herself should the matter become the basis for a legal proceeding. SOX requires a report on management's assessment of internal controls. The examination of the financial statements and the internal controls are part of the same audit and, taken together, are referred to as an integrated audit.

Audit Opinions

Auditors can express an unqualified (clean opinion), unqualified opinion with an explanatory paragraph, qualified opinion, adverse opinion, or a disclaimer. An auditor also can withdraw from the engagement under restricted circumstances.

Opinion Paragraph—Unqualified

An auditor should give an unqualified opinion when the financial statements "present fairly" financial position, results of operations, and cash flows. Certain situations may call for adding a fourth, explanatory paragraph. Adding the explanatory language is not considered to be a qualification; rather, the language merely draws attention to a significant situation such as an uncertainty about the company's ability to continue as a going concern, an inconsistency in the application of accounting principles, and to emphasize a matter (i.e., significant related party transactions).

Statement on Auditing Standards (SAS) No. 59 states that although auditors are not required to perform procedures specifically designed to test the going-concern assumption, they must evaluate the assumption in relation to the results of the normal audit procedures.[3] Conditions that may cause the auditors to question the going-concern assumption include negative cash flows from operations, defaults on loan agreements, and adverse financial ratios. When such conditions or events are identified, the auditors should gather additional information and consider whether management's plans for dealing with the conditions are likely to mitigate the problem. If the auditors conclude that the substantial doubt is resolved, they may issue the standard unmodified report. On the other hand, if the auditors conclude that substantial doubt still exists about the company's ability to continue as a going concern for a period of one year from the balance sheet date, then the auditors should modify their report by adding a final paragraph. Exhibit 5.2 shows the language of a fourth paragraph.[4]

A going-concern issue may exist where the entity's ability to survive is attributable to continuing operating losses and/or the projected excess of cash outflows over cash inflows over an extended period of time and/or the inability of the company to raise needed funds to continue operations. Start-up companies sometimes have these kinds of problems as would a company facing bankruptcy. During the 2008–2009 financial crisis, well-established companies like General Motors faced going-concern problems.

If a company makes a change in accounting principle, the nature of, justification for, and effect of the change are reported in a note to the financial statements for the period in which the change is made. To determine general acceptance of the new principle, the auditor should evaluate whether (1) the newly adopted principle is generally accepted, (2) the method of accounting for the effect of the change is in conformity with GAAP, and (3) management's justification for the change is reasonable. When the auditors believe that the new principle is generally accepted, the accounting is proper, and the change is justified, the audit report is modified to highlight the lack of consistent application of

EXHIBIT 5.2
Unqualified Opinion with an Explanatory Paragraph—Going-Concern Issue

The accompanying consolidated financial statements have been prepared assuming that the Company will continue as a going concern. As discussed in note 1 to the consolidated financial statements, the Company has suffered negative cash flows from operations and has an accumulated deficit that raise substantial doubt about its ability to continue as a going concern. Management's plans in regard to these matters are also described in note 1. The consolidated financial statements do not include any adjustments that might result from the outcome of this uncertainty.

EXHIBIT 5.3
Unqualified Opinion with an Explanatory Paragraph—Change in Accounting Principle

> As discussed in note 2 to the consolidated financial statements, the Company adopted *Statement of Financial Accounting Standards (SFAS) No. 166*, Accounting for Transfers of Financial Assets—an amendment of *FASB Statement No. 140*, as of December 31, 2009.

acceptable accounting principles, but the opinion remains unqualified. An example of the fourth paragraph in the audit report under these circumstances appears in Exhibit 5.3.[5]

Opinion Paragraph—Qualified

A qualified opinion expresses the auditors' reservations or uncertainty about fair presentation in some areas of the financial statements. The opinion states that except for the effects of some deficiency in the statements, or some limitation in the scope of the auditor's examination, the financial statements are presented fairly. All qualified reports include a separate explanatory paragraph before the opinion paragraph disclosing the reasons for the qualification. The materiality of the exception governs the use of the qualified opinion. The exception must be sufficiently significant to warrant mention in the auditors' report, but not so significant as to necessitate a disclaimer of opinion or an adverse opinion. Thus, the determination of the appropriateness of issuing a qualified opinion in the event of a significant exception is a matter for careful professional judgment by the auditors. Exhibit 5.4 shows an example of the added paragraph and change in the language of the auditor's report.[6]

The auditor qualifies whenever there is a difference of opinion with management on the application of GAAP that is "material" in amount or material because of the nature of the difference. One example of a qualification because of the nature of the difference is an illegal payment under the Foreign Corrupt Practices Act. Even if the monetary amount of the payment is not material, an unlikely event, it still would lead to a qualification because it is qualitatively material.

Recall that the concept of ethical legalism equates compliance with the law as an ethical position. GAAP rules represent "the law" so that an insignificant amount of misstatement may be omitted from the financial statements under the guise of not being material. For example, an expenditure of $1,000 might be expensed rather than capitalized, even though it benefits future periods, because total assets are $100,000; therefore, the item in question is only 1 percent of the comparison total and immaterial.

EXHIBIT 5.4
Qualified Opinion for a Difference of Opinion on a GAAP Matter and the Explanatory Paragraph

> The Company has excluded from property and debt in the accompanying balance sheets certain lease obligations that, in our opinion, should be capitalized in order to conform to accounting principles generally accepted in the United States. If these lease obligations were capitalized, property would be increased by $15,000,000, long-term debt by $14,500,000, and retained earnings by $500,000 as of December 31, 2010. Additionally, net income would be increased by $500,000 and earnings per share would be increased by $1.22 for the year then ended.
>
> In our opinion, except for the effects of not capitalizing certain lease obligations as discussed in the preceding paragraph, the financial statements referred to above present fairly, in all material respects, the financial position of XYZ Company as of December 31, 2010, and the results of its operations and its cash flows for the year then ended in conformity with accounting principles generally accepted in the United States.

The rationale for treating "immaterial" expenditures as an expense rather than an asset to be written off over a period of time may be that it is the most expeditious treatment. The fact is that auditors make compromises all the time when differences of opinion with management exist. The monetary amount of the difference is typically used as the basis for that compromise. Notwithstanding that explanation of practicality, it is indefensible from an ethical perspective to ignore something that is wrong.

Here's a final example of materiality. Assume that the auditor estimates the market value of inventory to be $500,000 below its cost. GAAP requires that inventory be recorded at the lower of cost or market. The auditor approaches management and explains that a loss of $500,000 should be recorded. Management responds by saying the write-down is unacceptable because it will lower net income below financial analysts' estimates for the year. Management may also be concerned that net income below the targeted amount may lead to a reduction in the share price of stock and the value of their stock options. Hence, earnings must be "managed" to meet desired goals.

The auditor has three choices: (1) insist on recording the $500,000 loss, (2) ignore the loss, or (3) negotiate with management for an acceptable amount of loss to record. While in the "real world" the result may be a negotiation process between the auditor and management, the auditor's ethical responsibility is to insist on recording the loss that is justified by GAAP. The auditor should inform the audit committee and seek its help with the difference of opinion with management. Unfortunately, during the "dark days" of Enron and WorldCom practically all boards and audit committees either ignored their fiduciary obligations to shareholders or passively supported management.

In a worst-case scenario for the auditor, management might threaten to change auditors because of the disagreement. If a change occurs, then an 8-K report is filed with the SEC explaining the reason for the change in auditor. The filing of an 8-K may trigger an SEC investigation.

"Opinion shopping" occurs when management threatens an auditor with putting up the engagement for competitive bidding when the auditor refuses to support management's position. The goal of opinion shopping is to seek out a different (more favorable) opinion from the auditors. There is nothing (ethically) wrong with a client exercising its due diligence and putting out an audit for competitive bids, especially if a concern exists about the quality of work or size of the audit fees. However, when the client seeks other views until finding an auditor who will go along with the client's desired—not necessarily most ethical—accounting treatment, we have the classic example of opinion shopping.

Opinion Paragraph—Adverse Opinion

In limited situations, the auditor could conclude that the financial statements taken as a whole do not present fairly financial position or the results of operations or cash flows in conformity with GAAP. When the auditor expresses an adverse opinion, he must have accumulated sufficient evidence to support this unfavorable opinion. Typically, adverse opinions result from material departures from GAAP that, when taken as a whole, make the financial statements misleading. Adverse opinions should be preceded by a separate paragraph in the audit report that provides all the substantive reasons for the auditor's conclusion and the principal effects of the subject matter of the adverse opinion on financial position, results of operations, and cash flows, if practicable. An example of an adverse opinion appears in Exhibit 5.5.[7]

In reality, an auditor who contemplates giving an adverse opinion should follow the same procedures as one considering a qualified opinion and first attempt to influence management, with the help of the audit committee, to make the change necessary to avoid that opinion. Management may conclude it is better to make the change than to risk having either a qualified, or certainly an adverse opinion. There is no doubt in the latter case the stock market reaction would be negative.

EXHIBIT 5.5
Adverse Opinion Due to a Very Material Departure from GAAP

In our opinion, because of the effects of the matters discussed in the preceding paragraph, the financial statements referred to above do not present fairly, in conformity with generally accepted accounting principles in the United States, the financial position of XYZ Company as of December 31, 2010, or the results of operations or its cash flows for the year then ended.

Opinion Paragraph—Disclaimer

A disclaimer of opinion is no opinion. Auditors issue a disclaimer whenever they are unable to form an opinion or have not formed an opinion as to the fairness of presentation of the financial statements. In an audit engagement, a disclaimer is issued when substantial or client-imposed scope restrictions preclude the auditors' compliance with GAAS.

If a scope restriction is so severe that a qualified opinion is inappropriate, the auditors should issue a disclaimer. An example would be if the auditors were engaged after year-end and the client did not take a physical inventory. The observation of the physical inventory by the auditor is a required audit procedure. In this case, a disclaimer of opinion should be issued because, at least for most companies that produce and sell products, the inventory balance is material and it affects both the balance sheet and income statement.

When a disclaimer is appropriate, the auditor should omit the scope paragraph from the standard auditor's report and replace it with an explanatory paragraph describing the scope limitation. The wording of the opinion paragraph will change considerably because the auditors are not expressing an opinion—rather, they are saying they have no opinion.[8] Exhibit 5.6 illustrates the language of a disclaimer of opinion.

Disclaimers of opinion because of scope restrictions are rare. In the planning stages of the engagement, the auditor should ask questions about the physical inventory and other important aspects of the audit to assess possible scope limitations. The client does not want to incur the cost of an audit when a disclaimer may be issued, so these matters typically are resolved early on.

A summary of the wording that would appear to report modifications of the standard audit report language is presented in Exhibit 5.7.

EXHIBIT 5.6
Disclaimer Due to Substantial Scope Limitation

We were engaged to audit the accompanying balance sheet of XYZ Company as of December 31, 2010, and the related statements of income, retained earnings, and cash flows for the year then ended. These financial statements are the responsibility of the Company's management.

The Company did not make a count of the physical inventory, stated in the accompanying financial statements at $6,000,000 at December 31, 2010. Further, evidence supporting the cost of property and equipment acquired prior to December 31, 2009, is no longer available.

The Company's records do not permit the application of other auditing procedures to inventories or property and equipment. Since the Company did not take physical inventories and we were not able to apply other auditing procedures to satisfy ourselves as to inventory quantities and the cost of property and equipment, the scope of our work was not sufficient to enable us to express, and we do not express, an opinion on these financial statements.

EXHIBIT 5.7 Example of Modification Language in Auditors' Report*

Type of Report/Opinion	Introductory/Scope Paragraph	Explanatory Paragraph	Opinion Paragraph
Unqualified: Going-concern issue	None	Describe going-concern uncertainty	None
Unqualified: Inconsistent GAAP application	None	Describe change in accounting principle	None
Qualified: Difference of opinion on a GAAP matter	None	Describe departure from GAAP and effects on financial statements	"Except for [the GAAP problem] the financial statements present fairly . . . "
Qualified: Scope restriction	"Except as explained in the following paragraph . . ." (scope paragraph)	Describe scope restriction	" . . . except for the effects of the adjustments determined to be necessary . . . the financial statements present fairly . . ."
Adverse: Very material exception to GAAP	None	Describe substantial reasons for adverse opinion	" . . . the financial statements do not present fairly . . ."
Disclaimer: Client imposed or other material scope restriction	"We were engaged . . ."; Omit "Our responsibility . . ." (in introductory paragraph) Omit scope paragraph	Describe scope restriction and any reservations	" . . . we do not express an opinion on the financial statements."

*Adapted from Whittington and Pany, *Principles of Auditing and Other Assurance Services*, 17th ed. (New York: McGraw-Hill Irwin, 2010), p. 672.

Withdrawal from the Engagement

From time to time an auditor might consider withdrawing from an engagement. Withdrawal generally is not appropriate since an auditor is hired by the client to do an audit and render an opinion, not walk away from one's obligations when the going gets tough. However, if a significant conflict exists with management or the auditor decides management cannot be trusted, then a withdrawal may be justified. This would trigger the filing of the 8-K form by management. Trust issues are a matter of ethics. Once pressure builds up in the auditor–client relationship and it boils to the top, the auditor must consider whether the breakdown in the relationship has advanced to the point that any and all information provided by the client is suspect. An auditor should not allow himself to be in the position of questioning the client's motives with every statement made and piece of evidence gathered.

Generally Accepted Auditing Standards—Overview

GAAP is established by the Financial Accounting Standards Board, a private body with seven members who represent a variety of stakeholder interests. GAAS is established by two organizations. For many years the AICPA had sole responsibility for GAAS through its Auditing Standards Board. Following the passage of SOX, the SEC established the PCAOB to set auditing standards for public companies that file 10-K reports with the commission. PCAOB reports to the SEC in carrying out its responsibilities. The AICPA's Auditing Standards Board continues to set auditing standards for privately owned businesses.

This two-tier system can be confusing because the GAAS that existed before PCAOB was established have been incorporated by PCAOB as its standards effective on April 16, 2003. Therefore, GAAS still has widespread applicability to the audits of public companies (incorporated into PCAOB standards), and nonpublic companies and not-for-profit entities. PCAOB now establishes its own auditing standards for public companies. PCAOB audit standards are considered to be required, not "generally accepted." PCAOB's position is that its standards should be used regardless of what might be "generally accepted" in practice.

PCAOB also establishes independence rules and quality control standards for registered CPA firms. The board conducts a peer review program whereby its representatives review the quality controls in effect at registered firms and issue an opinion to firm management. The opinion can be unmodified if the quality control system provides the firm with reasonable assurance of complying with professional standards. A modified report means the quality control system fails to provide reasonable assurance. An adverse report identifies significant deficiencies in the control system.

GAAS Requirements

An independent auditor plans, conducts, and reports the results of an audit in accordance with GAAS. *Auditing standards* provide a measure of audit quality and the objectives to be achieved in an audit. Auditing standards differ from auditing procedures because the procedures are steps taken by the auditor during the course of the audit to comply with GAAS.

General Standards

There are three general standards that relate to the quality of the professionals who perform the audit. These include (1) adequate technical training and proficiency, (2) independence in mental attitude, and (3) due care in the performance of the audit and preparation of the report. Independence is a basic standard in the AICPA Code of Professional Conduct. As discussed in Chapter 4, to be independent means to avoid all appearances that one's judgment may be clouded by events and relationships. Due care in performing an audit is also included in the Code; it requires diligence and competence.

Standards of Fieldwork

Standards of fieldwork establish the criteria for judging whether the audit has met quality requirements. These standards should guide the auditor in meeting the expectations for a quality examination. The standards include (1) to adequately plan the audit work and supervise assistants so that the audit is more likely to detect a material misstatement; (2) to obtain a sufficient understanding of the entity and its internal control, to assess the risk of material misstatement of the financial statements, whether due to error or fraud, and to effectively plan the nature, timing, and extent of further audit procedures; and (3) to gather sufficient competent evidential matter through audit procedures including inspection, observation, inquiries, and confirmations to provide a reasonable basis (support) for an opinion regarding the financial statements under audit.

The standards of fieldwork provide the basis for determining whether the audit has been carried out with the level of care expected by the public. It is an integral part of providing the degree of support needed to make a statement that the audit provides a "reasonable basis" for the opinion and that the opinion provides "reasonable assurance" that the financial statements are free of material misstatement.

Standards of Reporting

Just as the financial statements are the end product of the accountants' work, the audit report is the end product of an auditor's work. The audit report carries particular significance for investors and creditors who rely on financial statements to help make decisions such as buying or selling stock and granting loans. Moreover, the report can be used to identify red flags that create questions about the entity's ability to continue as a going concern and point out any material nonconformity with GAAP.

There are three reporting standards that guide auditors in rendering an audit report and in determining the degree of responsibility the auditor is taking with respect to the expression of an opinion of the financial statements. They include (1) determination of whether the statements have been prepared in conformity with GAAP; (2) identification of situations where the accounting principles have not been consistently observed in the current period in relation to the preceding period; and (3) discussion in the report of any situation identified in the footnotes to the financial statements where informative disclosures are not adequate.

Audit Procedures

Audit procedures are specific acts performed by the auditor to gather evidence about whether specific assertions are being met. For example, the client may state that the inventory value is $1,000,000. That is a specific assertion. The auditor then uses the procedure of observing the physical count of inventory to assess inventory quantity and traces certain year-end purchases and sales of inventory to invoices and other documentation as part of the cutoff process to determine whether year-end transactions should be part of the inventory. Typically, the auditor also tests the pricing of the inventory to assess the application of methods such as first-in, first-out (FIFO); last-in, first-out (LIFO); and the weighted average methods. The current market value of the inventory also has to be assessed.

Audit procedures help obtain an understanding of the entity and its environment, including its internal control, to assess the risks of material misstatements. Such audit procedures are referred to as risk assessment procedures. Audit procedures also test the operating effectiveness of controls in preventing or detecting material misstatements.[9] More will be said about risk and internal control assessment later in the chapter.

Limitations of the Audit Report

Three phrases in the audit report are critical to understanding the limits of the report: (1) *reasonable assurance,* (2) *material,* and (3) *present fairly.* These expressions are used to signal the reader about specific limitations of the audit report.

Reasonable Assurance

The term *reasonable* is often used in law to define a standard of behavior to decide legal issues. For example, an auditor should exercise a *reasonable* level of care (due care) to avoid charges of negligence and possible liability to the client. The *reasonable* (prudent) person standard is typically used to judge whether an uninvolved individual looking at the behavior of an auditor internally, perhaps in relation to independence and client relationships, can conclude that the auditor has maintained the appearance of independence.

Reasonable assurance is not an absolute guarantee that the financial statements are free of material misstatement. Auditors do not examine all of a company's transactions. The transactions selected for examination are determined based on materiality considerations and risk assessment. Even then, only a small percentage of transactions are selected often by statistical sampling techniques.

The auditor makes the reasonable assurance statement in the context of GAAS. It means that the auditor has followed GAAS in carrying out audit responsibilities including gathering sufficient competent evidential matter. The auditor uses professional judgment to decide whether available evidence is sufficient to justify an opinion. If the auditor fails to follow GAAS in making that decision, then an allegation of negligence is supportable. If the auditor was to purposefully ignore justified audit procedures or evidence that, for example, has negative implications for the client, then a charge of constructive fraud or fraud may be sustained in a court of law. These charges can be brought by clients as well as third parties, as will be discussed in Chapter 6.

The auditor obtains and evaluates audit evidence to obtain reasonable assurance about whether the financial statements are presented fairly, in all material respects, in accordance with GAAP. The concept of reasonable assurance acknowledges that there is a risk the audit opinion is inappropriate. The risk that the auditor expresses an inappropriate audit opinion when the financial statements are materially misstated is known as *audit risk.*

Materiality

The concept of *materiality* recognizes that some matters are important to the fair presentation of financial statements, while others are not. The materiality concept is fundamental to the audit because the audit report states that an audit is performed to obtain reasonable assurance about whether the financial statements are free of material misstatement.

Materiality judgments require the use of professional judgment and are based on management and auditor perceptions of the needs of a reasonable person who will rely on the financial statements. *Materiality* is defined in the glossary of *Statement of Financial Accounting Concepts (SFAC) No. 2,* Qualitative Characteristics of Accounting Information, as[10]

> The magnitude of an omission or misstatement of accounting information that, in the light of surrounding circumstances, makes it probable that the judgment of a reasonable person relying on the information would have been changed or influenced by the omission or misstatement.

Statement on Auditing Standards (SAS) No. 99, Consideration of Fraud in a Financial Statement Audit, notes that "the auditor has a responsibility to plan and perform the audit to obtain reasonable assurance about whether the financial statements are free of material misstatement, whether caused by error or fraud."[11] The concept of materiality is perhaps one of the most challenging concepts in accounting. The application of professional judgment to the surrounding circumstances in which materiality is at issue provides the setting to assess whether an item or event is either quantitatively or qualitatively significant enough to warrant financial reporting or disclosure.

Judging Materiality

Materiality in the context of an audit reflects the auditor's judgment of the needs of users in relation to the information in the financial statements and the possible effect of misstatements on user decisions as a group. Materiality is judged by assessing whether the omissions or misstatements of items in the statements could, individually or collectively, influence the economic decisions of users taken on the basis of financial statements. Materiality depends on the size and nature of the omission or misstatement judged in the surrounding circumstances.

Each *Statement of Financial Accounting Standards (SFAS)* adopted by FASB states, "The provisions of this Statement need not be applied to immaterial items." The SEC has ruled in *Staff Accounting Bulletin (SAB) No. 99* that this does not mean that a public company filing financial statements with the commission, or its auditor, may rely solely on a quantitative threshold as a "rule of thumb" to determine materiality.[12] As previously mentioned, an auditor might use a percentage for the numerical threshold such as 5 percent. Materiality is then judged by comparing an item in question to some amount such as total assets or net income. If the questionable item is equal to or greater than 5 percent of the comparison amount, then it is material and must be reported in the financial statements.

Assume a company has one item in inventory that cost $400,000. The auditor believes the current market value is $381,000, or $19,000 (4.75 percent) below cost. Under the 5 percent rule, the item may be judged immaterial and the write-down ignored. However, what if the net income for the year is only $300,000? Then the $19,000 write-down becomes material since it equals 6.33 percent of net income.

One unintended consequence of the accounting profession's approach to materiality is that a controller—knowing the 5 percent rule is in effect—may attempt to decrease expenses or increase revenues by an amount less than 5 percent to increase earnings by an amount that will not be challenged by the auditor. It is somewhat ironic that the auditor can let the difference go unchallenged even though it may be due to the misapplication of GAAP simply because it is not "material" in amount.

SAB 99 provides that a percentage test may be used to form a preliminary assumption that—without considering all relevant circumstances—a "deviation of less than the specified percentage with respect to a particular item on the registrant's financial statements is unlikely to be material." However, the auditor must go beyond using such a "bright line" test based on the magnitude of misstatement as the sole source of judgment about materiality. According to *SAB 99,* "It cannot be used as a substitute for a full analysis of all relevant considerations."

The U.S. Supreme Court noted in *TSC Industries v. Northway, Inc.* that judgments of materiality require "delicate assessments of the inferences a 'reasonable shareholder' would draw from a given set of facts and the significance of those inferences to him."[13] In other words, the Court and the accounting profession have similar interpretations that a fact is material if there is a substantial likelihood that it would have been viewed by the reasonable investor as having significantly altered the "total mix" of information made available.

SAS 99 greatly advances the accounting profession's assessment of materiality by linking it to the obtaining of information needed to identify the risks of material misstatement due to fraud. This standard provides guidance to auditors in fulfilling their responsibilities to plan and perform the audit to obtain reasonable assurance about whether the financial statements are free of material misstatement, whether caused by error or fraud.[14]

Present Fairly

Without an understanding of the term *present fairly,* the users of the financial statements would be unable to assess the reliability of the financial statements. The expression to present fairly is linked to GAAP. *SAS No. 69,* The Meaning of Present Fairly in Conformity with GAAP, points out that the phrase "generally accepted accounting principles" is a technical accounting term that encompasses the conventions, rules, and procedures necessary to define accepted accounting practice at a particular time. GAAP provides a framework to measure financial presentations. The independent auditor's judgment concerning the "fairness" of the overall presentation of financial statements should be applied within the framework of GAAP.[15]

The auditor's assessment of fair presentation depends on whether (1) the accounting principles selected and applied have general acceptance; (2) the accounting principles are appropriate in the circumstances; (3) the financial statements, including the related notes, are informative of matters that may affect their use, understanding, and interpretation; (4) the information presented in the statements is classified and summarized in a reasonable manner—that is, neither too detailed nor too condensed; and (5) the financial statements reflect transactions and events within a range of reasonable limits.

Let's examine lease accounting rules and apply these criteria. A *lease* is a form of property rental where the party using the asset (lessee) makes periodic payments to the legal owner of the asset (lessor). GAAP for leases comes from a variety of FASB statements, but the *Statement of Financial Accounting Standards (SFAS) No. 17,* Accounting for Leases, establishes the lease standards in accounting. *SFAS 17* provides that the lessee (user of the property) determine the present value of future lease payments (PV) and record an asset and liability if any one of four criteria exists.

The capital lease criteria include (1) transfer of ownership to the lessee at the end of the lease term, (2) bargain purchase option for the lessee, (3) lease life of 75 percent or more of the economic life of the leased asset, and (4) the PV equals 90 percent or more of the fair value of the leased asset (plus any guaranteed residual value) at the date of the lease.[16] Only one of the four criteria needs to be met to treat the lease as a capital item thereby recording an asset and liability at present value. Absent all four criteria, the lease is treated as an operating lease and each lease payment is debited to an expense account, offset by a credit to cash, and the asset remains on the books of the lessor, the legal owner of the leased asset. Operating leases lead to "off-balance sheet financing" since the amount due to the lessor over the lease contract is not recorded on the lessee's balance sheet. This creates a potentially troublesome practice from the perspective of the user of the financial statements who might be interested in knowing the company's future cash obligations. GAAP deals with this issue by requiring the lessee to disclose the scheduled lease payments for the next five years.

In a capital lease, the lessor essentially finances the acquisition for the lessee by allowing a period of time for the lessee to make lease payments. Each payment includes an amount representing interest, and the difference between the total amount and the interest portion decreases the lease liability. Capital lease information in the balance sheet should reflect the carrying value of the leased asset and a breakdown of the current lease liability and long-term balance. Users would be misled if a company were to combine those numbers and just present the total as a long-term lease. The combined number also affects liquidity analysis such as the current ratio. The result of combining the liability amounts into one number is that the financial statements would not "present fairly" financial position.

The capital lease treatment of the discounted future lease payments as an asset on the balance sheet of the lessee (and removal of the asset and liability from the lessor's books) exemplifies putting the economic substance of a transaction over its legal form. Legally, the lessor owns the asset. There has been no sale. However, if any one of the four criteria is met, the accounting treatment reflects the conclusion that, for all intents and purposes, the lessee effectively owns the asset and is merely being given a fixed period of time to pay for it.

Expectations Gap

The independent auditor's responsibility is to audit and report on the financial statements prepared by management. Perceptions of the shortcomings in the effectiveness of independent audits erode public confidence in the integrity of the financial reporting system. To address these concerns, the AICPA's Auditing Standards Board issued, in 1988, nine new auditing standards to help close the "expectations gap"—that is, the difference between what the public and the users of financial statements perceive as the responsibilities of accountants and auditors and what accountants and auditors themselves see as their responsibilities.

A survey of investor views of audit assurance in 1994 by Epstein and Geiger indicates that the investing public holds auditors to a much higher level of accountability for detecting material misstatements due to error and fraud than the profession has assumed. The authors conclude that the profession's perception that an audit should provide only reasonable assurance of financial statement accuracy is held by a minority of investors. The majority of investors expect an audit to provide absolute assurance that the financial statements are free of all types of material misstatements, thereby confirming the existence of the gap.[17]

Many members of the public expect auditors to detect fraud, whereas auditors fall back on the claim that an audit provides only *reasonable assurance* that financial statements are free of material misstatement. The profession recognizes its obligation to look for fraud by being alert to certain red flags, assessing the control environment of the organization, and passing judgment on internal controls. However, this is a far cry from guaranteeing that fraud will be detected especially when top management goes to great lengths to hide it from the auditors.

One of the nine expectations gap standards issued in 1988 is *SAS No. 55,* Internal Control in a Financial Statement Audit. *SAS 55* attempts to narrow the gap by incorporating the auditor's assessment of the ethics of the organization and top management as an integral part of the internal control system. One of the five components of internal control is the control environment. The control environment sets "the tone of the organization, influencing the control consciousness of its people. It is the foundation for all other components of internal control, providing discipline and structure."[18]

SAS 55 differs from prior definitions of internal control in two important ways: (1) it broadens the definition of internal control and the parties that affect it by linking sound controls to the actions of the board of directors, management, and other personnel; and (2) it identifies five interrelated components of internal control including the control environment, risk assessment, control activities, information and communication systems, and the monitoring of controls.

The AICPA tried once again to close the gap when it released *SAS 99,* the so-called fraud standard. *SAS 99* was one of the last standards issued by the AICPA before being replaced by the PCAOB (for public company audits). *SAS 99* is discussed in full later in the chapter.

Errors, Fraud, and Illegal Acts

Material errors, fraud, and illegal acts represent situations where the financial statements should be restated. The following briefly describes the nature and effects of such acts.

Errors

An *error* can occur due to unintentional misstatements or omissions of amounts or disclosures in the financial statements. Errors may involve mistakes in gathering or processing data, unreasonable accounting estimates arising from oversight or misinterpretation of facts, or mistakes in the application of GAAP. Auditors are responsible for detecting errors that have a material effect on the financial statements and reporting their findings to the audit committee. Errors are typically recorded by adjusting the opening balance of retained earnings for the prior period adjustment to net income.

Fraud

Fraud, as the term is used in *SAS 99,* relates to intentional acts that cause a misstatement of the financial statements. Misstatements due to fraud may occur due to either (1) fraudulent financial reporting or (2) misappropriation of assets. It is important to remember that fraud does not occur by accident. Fraud exists when there is a deliberate decision made to deceive another party, such as the investors and creditors. As will be discussed in Chapter 6, the auditor has a legal liability for fraud to both the client and third parties who may have relied on the misstatement to their detriment.

Let's assume Risky Software, Inc., records revenue from the sale of software of $1 million on December 28, 2010. The sale requires Risky to provide support services including a 24-hour help desk for three years. Risky records all of the $1 million of revenue in 2010. However, GAAP requires that the company should separate out from the sale price the relevant amount that represents support services and record it as deferred revenue. This is known as *accounting for the multiple elements of a transaction.* The deferred amount would then be matched with the support services provided over the next three years.

The intent of management determines whether the misapplication of GAAP is an error in judgment or a deliberate decision to inflate revenues. In a court of law it typically comes down to the credibility of the CFO and CEO who are charged with fraud. Absent a "smoking gun," the court might look for parallel actions by these top officers such as selling their own shares of corporate stock after the fraudulent act but before it becomes public knowledge, as occurred at Enron and WorldCom.

Illegal Acts

Statement on Auditing Standards (SAS) No. 54, Illegal Acts, defines illegal acts as violations of laws or governmental regulations. For example, a violation of the Foreign Corrupt Practices Act constitutes an illegal act. *SAS 54* characterizes illegal acts as those attributable to the entity whose financial statements are under audit or as acts by management or employees acting on behalf of the entity. Such acts expose the company to both legal liability and public disgrace. The auditor's responsibility is to determine the proper accounting and financial reporting treatment of a violation once it has been determined that a violation has in fact occurred.[19]

The auditor's responsibility is to detect and report misstatements resulting from illegal acts that have a direct and material effect on the determination of financial statement amounts (i.e., they require an accounting entry). The auditors' responsibility for detecting such violations is greater than their responsibility to detect illegal acts arising from laws that only indirectly affect the client's financial statements.[20] An example of the former would be violations of tax laws that affect accruals and the amount recognized as income tax liability for the period. Tax law would be violated, triggering an adjustment in the current period financial statements if, for example, a company, for tax purposes, were to expense an item all in one year that should have been capitalized and written off over three years. Examples of items with an indirect effect on the statements include the potential violation of laws such as occupational safety and health, environmental protection, and equal employment. The events are due to operational, not financial, matters and their financial statement effect is indirect—for example, a possible contingent liability that should be disclosed in the notes to the financial statements.

The auditor's obligation when she concludes that an illegal act has or is likely to have occurred is first to assess the impact of the actions on the financial statements. This should be done regardless of any direct or indirect effect on the statements. The auditor should consult with legal counsel and any other specialists in this regard. Illegal acts should be reported to those charged with governance such as the audit committee. The auditor should consider whether the client has taken appropriate remedial action concerning the act. Such remedial action may include taking disciplinary actions, establishing controls to safeguard against recurrence, and, if necessary, reporting the effects of the illegal acts in the financial statements. Ordinarily, if the client does not take the remedial action deemed necessary by the auditor, then the auditor should withdraw from the engagement.[21] This action on the part of the auditor makes clear that she will not be associated in any way with illegal activities.

The Private Securities Litigation Reform Act (PSLRA) of 1995 places additional requirements upon public companies registered with the SEC and their auditors when (1) the illegal act has a material effect on the financial statements, (2) senior management and the board of directors have not taken appropriate remedial action, and (3) the failure to take remedial action is reasonably expected to warrant departure from a standard audit report (or to warrant resignation).

When the auditor believes the illegal act has a material effect on the financial statements and the matter has been reported to the client, the board of directors have one business day to inform the SEC. If the board decides not to inform the SEC, the auditor must provide the same report to the board within one business day or resign from the engagement and give the SEC the report.[22] In either case the ethical obligation of confidentiality is waived so that the SEC may live up to its responsibility to protect investor interests.

Auditors' Responsibilities for Fraud Prevention, Detection, and Reporting

Auditors are responsible for detecting material fraud and reporting it to the board of directors. The requirements are similar to those for illegal acts with a direct effect on the financial statements. Louwers, Ramsay, Sinason, and Strawser provide a useful summary of the auditor's responsibility to detect errors, illegal acts, and fraud.[23] The summary appears in Exhibit 5.8.

The first line of defense against fraud is to have an effective system of internal controls and an independent internal audit function. As described in Chapter 2, the internal auditors should have direct and unrestricted access to the audit committee. The head of internal auditing should not have to discuss matters pertaining to the existence of material misstatements in the financial statements with the CFO and CEO, both of whom may be responsible for the fraud. Recall that at WorldCom, Cynthia Cooper eventually bypassed

EXHIBIT 5.8   Auditors' Responsibility to Detect Errors, Illegal Acts, and Fraud

	Responsible for Detection		Required to Communicate Findings	
	Material	**Immaterial**	**Material**	**Immaterial**
Errors	Yes	No	Yes (audit committee)	No
Illegal acts	Yes (direct effect)	No	Yes (audit committee)	Yes (one level above)
Fraud	Yes	No	Yes (audit committee)	Yes (by low-level employee, to one level above) (by management-level employee, to audit committee)

Scott Sullivan, the CFO, after she concluded that he was not about to do anything about the fraud—a fraud that he had initiated. Instead, she approached the chair of the audit committee with her concerns and, after dealing with some resistance and soliciting help from the external auditors, she was successful in getting the company to come clean about its improper accounting.

Fraud comes in a variety of shapes and sizes but has one common element—the underlying action that results in a material misstatement of the financial statements is intentional. *SAS 99* identifies two types of misstatements that are relevant to the auditor's consideration of fraud: (1) misstatements arising from fraudulent financial reporting (management fraud) and (2) misappropriation of assets (defalcations).[24]

The auditor's fraud risk assessment involves identifying risks of material misstatement of the financial statements due to fraud and determining the appropriate audit response. To identify fraud risks the auditor performs a number of procedures including making inquiries of management and considering fraud risk factors.[25]

Albrecht and colleagues identify nine elements that caused the financial frauds during the years 2000–2002.[26]

1. A booming economy
2. Decay of moral values
3. Misplaced incentives
4. High analysts' expectations
5. High debt levels
6. Focus on accounting rules rather than principles
7. Lack of auditor independence
8. Greed
9. Educator failures

Some of these causes have already been discussed, including high analysts' expectations and the lack of auditor independence. The decline in moral values follows our general observation that today's young people are not as clearly focused on ethical behavior as were previous generations perhaps due to a downward shift in cultural norms, societal influences, and egoism.

The Fraud Triangle

SAS 99 defines *fraudulent financial reporting* as "intentional misstatements or omissions of amounts or disclosures in financial statements designed to deceive financial statement users where the effect causes the financial statements not to be presented, in all material respects, in conformity with GAAP." The reasons for the deception are many and are identified by *SAS 99* as part of "the fraud triangle" depicted in Exhibit 5.9.[27]

Incentives/Pressures to Commit Fraud

The incentive to commit fraud typically is a self-serving one. It may be caused by internal budget pressures or financial analysts' earnings expectations that are not being met. Personal pressures also might lead to fraud if, for example, a member of top management is deep in personal debt or has a gambling or drug problem.

Techniques Used to Falsify Financial Information

The techniques used to falsify financial information range from the basic to the exotic. The Waste Management fraud involved the arbitrary lengthening of the useful lives of trash hauling equipment to reduce annual depreciation charges and increase earnings.

EXHIBIT 5.9
The Fraud Triangle

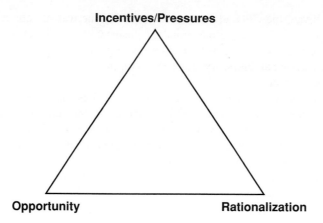

The Enron fraud involved financially structured transactions that created special-purpose entities (SPEs) that borrowed funds and then shifted the amounts to Enron in return for some underperforming asset. The liability was kept off Enron's books, a form of off-balance-sheet financing. The Enron saga will be discussed in full in Chapter 7.

Financial results can be manipulated through the use of bogus invoices to record revenue, as was the case at ZZZZ Best. In some instances a company might manipulate its own accounting records to achieve its goal. MicroStrategy is a company that back-dated sales agreements to push revenue back into the preceding period, for example, by dating a transaction on December 31, 2010, that was legally approved on January 3, 2011.

Misappropriation of Assets

The misappropriation of assets involves the theft of company assets where the action leads to financial statements that do not conform to GAAP. For example, an employee might write company checks payable to himself for personal expenses. The diversion of company funds for personal purposes understates cash and overstates expenses. Often, the guilty employee tries to "bury" the personal expense in an innocuous account such as miscellaneous or sundry expenses. The audit procedure that should catch such activities is to prepare a bank reconciliation or proof of cash and examine each check for proper authorization and recording.

Some fraudsters seem to have no shame. In the ZZZZ Best fraud, Barry Minkow set up front companies as clients that issued checks from its bank account to pay for services never performed. The checks were then deposited into the ZZZZ Best account and revenue was recorded. Minkow would then use some of the money to pay for personal expenses and would bury the expense in those accounts. The original funds paid by the fictitious company to ZZZZ Best came from funds diverted by Minkow and his cohorts to create the illusion of the front company.

Opportunity to Commit Fraud

The second side of the fraud triangle connects the pressure or incentive to commit fraud with the opportunity to carry out the act. Employees who have access to assets such as cash and inventory should be monitored closely through an effective system of internal controls that helps safeguard assets. For example, the company should segregate cash processing responsibilities including the opening of mail that contains remittance advices along with checks for the payment of services; the recording of the receipts as cash and a reduction of receivables; the depositing of the money in the bank; and the reconciling of the balance in cash on the books with the bank statement balance.

The opportunity to commit fraud also can be seen when top management backdates stock options to increase the potential gain for those executives receiving the options. For example, if a company's stock price is rapidly increasing and top management wants to attract new employees to the company, management may agree to set a strike (exercise) price that is dated weeks or months prior to the grant date. The executive gains because of the increased spread between the exercise price and future market price, assuming the stock price continues to rise. The backdating options problem first became public in the summer of 2006 and was investigated throughout the decade of the 2000s. The SEC Web site describes dozens of such cases including that of Monster Worldwide Inc.[28] Details of the fraud follow.

Backdating Stock Options—Monster Worldwide, Inc.

On May 18, 2009, the SEC charged that employment search company Monster Worldwide, Inc., schemed to secretly backdate stock options granted to thousands of Monster officers, directors, and employees. Monster agreed to pay a $2.5 million penalty to settle the SEC's charges that the company defrauded investors by granting backdated, undisclosed "in-the-money" stock options (current market value exceeds option price) while failing to record required noncash charges for option-related compensation expenses.[29]

According to the SEC, "Monster misled investors by failing to report hundreds of millions of dollars of expenses. Backdating stock options made the company look like it had more money than it really did." The SEC's complaint alleged that in connection with this scheme, Monster filed false and materially misleading statements concerning the true grant date and exercise price of stock options in its annual, quarterly, and current reports, proxy statements, and registration statements. Many of these documents also falsely represented that stock options were being granted at fair market value. Further, Monster failed to record and disclose the compensation expense associated with the in-the-money portion of stock option grants. As a result, Monster materially overstated its quarterly and annual earnings in its financial statements and was required to restate its historical financial results for 1997–2005 in a cumulative pretax amount of approximately $339.5 million and to record additional noncash charges for option related compensation expenses.[30]

Rationalization for the Fraud

Fraud perpetrators typically have some way to explain away their actions as acceptable. For corporate executives, rationalizations to commit fraud might include thoughts such as "we need to protect our shareholders and keep the stock price high," "all companies use aggressive accounting practices," "it is for the good of the company," or "the problem is temporary and will be offset by future positive results."[31] The latter rationalization was the one used to convince Betty Vinson, a mid-level accounting manager at WorldCom, to go along with the fraud. The details of her dilemma were discussed in Chapter 1. Disgruntled employees might rationalize fraud with thoughts such as "my boss doesn't pay me enough" or "I'll pay the money back before anyone notices it's gone." The underlying motivation for the fraud in these instances is dissatisfaction with the company. *SAS 99* provides an extensive list of examples of the elements of fraud that can lead to fraudulent financial reporting. These are presented in Exhibit 5.10.

Tyco: A Case of Corporate Greed

You probably have heard about the Tyco fraud. The actions of former CEO Dennis Kozlowski epitomize the selfishness and greed that overwhelmed some companies in the late 1990s and early 2000s. He and his second-in-command Mark Swartz (the CFO) were charged with stealing $170 million and pocketing an additional $430 million through the sale of company stock, while lying about Tyco's financial condition. The jury convicted Kozlowski of 22 counts of grand larceny, conspiracy, and securities fraud. He was ordered

EXHIBIT 5.10

Risk Factors Relating to Misstatements Arising from Fraudulent Financial Reporting

Incentives/Pressures

a. *Incentives* exist because financial stability or profitability is threatened by economic, industry, or entity operating conditions, such as (or as indicated by):

- High degree of competition or market saturation, accompanied by declining margins
- High vulnerability to rapid changes, such as changes in technology, product obsolescence, or interest rates
- Significant declines in customer demand and increasing business failures in either the industry or overall economy
- Operating losses making the threat of bankruptcy, foreclosure, or hostile takeover imminent
- Recurring negative cash flows from operations and an inability to generate cash flows from operations while reporting earnings and earnings growth
- Rapid growth or unusual profitability, especially compared to that of other companies in the same industry
- New accounting, statutory, or regulatory requirements

b. Excessive *pressure* exists for management to meet the requirements or expectations of third parties due to the following:

- Profitability or trend level expectations of investment analysts, institutional investors, significant creditors, or other external parties (particularly expectations that are unduly aggressive or unrealistic), including expectations created by management in, for example, overly optimistic press releases or annual report messages
- Need to obtain additional debt or equity financing to stay competitive—including financing of major research and development or capital expenditures
- Marginal ability to meet exchange listing requirements or debt repayment or other debt covenant requirements
- Perceived or real adverse effects of reporting poor financial results on significant pending transactions, such as business combinations or contract awards

c. Information available indicates that management's or those charged with governance's personal financial situation is threatened by the entity's financial performance arising from the following:

- Significant financial interests in the entity
- Significant portions of their compensation (for example, bonuses, stock options, and earn-out arrangements) being contingent upon achieving aggressive targets for stock price, operating results, financial position, or cash flow
- Personal guarantees of debts of the entity

d. There is excessive pressure on management or operating personnel to meet financial targets set up by those charged with governance or management, including sales or profitability incentive goals.

Opportunities

a. The nature of the industry or the entity's operations provides opportunities to engage in fraudulent financial reporting that can arise from the following:

- Significant related-party transactions not in the ordinary course of business or with related entities not audited or audited by another firm
- A strong financial presence or ability to dominate a certain industry sector that allows the entity to dictate terms or conditions to suppliers or customers that may result in inappropriate or non-arm's-length transactions
- Assets, liabilities, revenues, or expenses based on significant estimates that involve subjective judgments or uncertainties that are difficult to corroborate
- Significant, unusual, or highly complex transactions, especially those close to period end that pose difficult "substance over form" questions
- Significant operations located or conducted across international borders in jurisdictions where differing business environments and cultures exist
- Significant bank accounts or subsidiary or branch operations in tax-haven jurisdictions for which there appears to be no clear business justification

b. There is ineffective monitoring of management as a result of the following:

- Domination of management by a single person or small group (in a nonowner-managed business) without compensating controls
- Ineffective oversight over the financial reporting process and internal control by those charged with governance

c. There is a complex or unstable organizational structure, as evidenced by the following:
- Difficulty in determining the organization or individuals that have controlling interest in the entity
- Overly complex organizational structure involving unusual legal entities or managerial lines of authority
- High turnover of senior management, counsel, or board members

d. Internal control components are deficient as a result of the following:
- Inadequate monitoring of controls, including automated controls and controls over interim financial reporting (where external reporting is required)
- High turnover rates or employment of ineffective accounting, internal audit, or information technology staff
- Ineffective accounting and information systems, including situations involving significant deficiencies or material weaknesses in internal control

Attitudes/Rationalizations

Risk factors reflective of attitudes/rationalizations by those charged with governance, management, or employees, that allow them to engage in and/or justify fraudulent financial reporting, may not be susceptible to observation by the auditor. Nevertheless, the auditor who becomes aware of the existence of such information should consider it in identifying the risks of material misstatement arising from fraudulent financial reporting. For example, auditors may become aware of the following information that may indicate a risk factor:

- Ineffective communication, implementation, support, or enforcement of the entity's values or ethical standards by management or the communication of inappropriate values or ethical standards
- Nonfinancial management's excessive participation in or preoccupation with the selection of accounting principles or the determination of significant estimates
- Known history of violations of securities laws or other laws and regulations, or claims against the entity, its senior management, or board members alleging fraud or violations of laws and regulations
- Excessive interest by management in maintaining or increasing the entity's stock price or earnings trend
- A practice by management of committing to analysts, creditors, and other third parties to achieve aggressive or unrealistic forecasts
- Management failing to correct known significant deficiencies or material weaknesses in internal control on a timely basis
- An interest by management in employing inappropriate means to minimize reported earnings for tax-motivated reasons

to pay $97 million in restitution and $70 million in fines. Kozlowski was sentenced to a jail term of from 8 1/3 to 25 years in 2005 and will be eligible for parole in 2012.

Kozlowski was brazen. Manhattan District Attorney Robert Morgenthau successfully prosecuted him for using Tyco funds to purchase millions of dollars of artwork for his $18 million apartment in New York City, an apartment that was also paid for from Tyco funds. Kozlowski was charged with fraudulently transporting $13 million worth of art to Tyco's headquarters in New Hampshire to avoid more than $1 million in New York state and city sales taxes—New York does not tax purchases of merchandise for use outside the state. Kozlowski had the artwork, or, in some cases, empty boxes, sent to New Hampshire where there is no sales tax. He then had the boxes sent back to his Manhattan apartment.

Kozlowski used company "loans" for the purchases, allowing him to avoid paying income tax on the money used. (The loan amounts should have been declared as compensation on his tax return.) Of all the excesses, perhaps none more than his use of corporate funds for his own creature comforts illustrates Kozlowski's apparent lack of conscience. For example, he bought a $15,000 doggy umbrella stand and the ultimate symbol of his downfall: Kozlowski spent $6,000 of Tyco funds on a gold-plated shower curtain!

Kozlowski had deluded himself into thinking he would never get caught but, in reality, many fraudsters do get caught by their own growing greed that demands more and more of the excesses to keep up the charade of a certain lifestyle and/or to impress others, as was the case with Bernie Madoff.

Kozlowski was interviewed by *60 Minutes* reporter Morley Safer in his prison cell in a segment originally broadcast on March 25, 2007, and updated on July 23, 2007, as shown in Exhibit 5.11.[32]

EXHIBIT 5.11
60 Minutes **Interview: A Case of Greed**

According to Kozlowski, Wall Street couldn't get enough of his aggressive actions as a CEO. He also began making staggering amounts of money, among the top-earning CEOs in the country. "We had a pay-for-performance culture at Tyco," explains Kozlowski. "So, most of the money I earned was in the appreciation of Tyco stock."

The prosecution accused Kozlowski of granting himself unauthorized bonuses and running hundreds of millions of dollars' worth of personal expenses through interest-free Tyco loan programs. No expense was too great or too small to run through Tyco. None of this, claimed the prosecution, was authorized by the Tyco board. Asked what it was like to earn that kind of money, Kozlowski said, "It's a way of keeping score, I guess." Keeping score meant keeping up with the masters of the universe—$30 million to build a mansion in Florida, plus acquiring homes in Nantucket and Colorado. And for $16 million, he bought a vintage yacht *Endeavour*.

He elaborated on his guilt: "I am absolutely not guilty of the charges brought upon me," Kozlowski said. "There was no criminal intent here. Nothing was hidden. There were no shredded documents. Nobody was told not to say anything. All the information the prosecutors got was directly off the books and records of the company." He had claimed, in the trial, that everything he did was authorized. But he did not have a single document to prove it.

Kozlowski said the media coverage was "horrible." "Yet [I] did sign off on the décor. I signed off on a decorator to decorate the Tyco apartment. And, beyond that, that was my involvement. The first time I heard about that shower curtain was after I was out of the company and I read about it in a newspaper. And I was calling around asking: 'Where is this shower curtain?' But to this day, I wouldn't know it if it fell on me," he told Safer.

And then there was the 40th birthday party for Kozlowski's wife Karen on the Italian island of Sardinia. It was a four-day festival of the flesh outfitted by a Roman theme and togas galore. Jimmy Buffett was flown in for the music and guests were treated to a special cake: an anatomically correct woman with exploding breasts. The cost of the party was over $2 million; since Kozlowski claimed it was in part a work retreat (e.g., there was a board meeting at the end of the four days), Tyco footed half the bill. During the trial, jurors were shown a tape of the party. Kozlowski said it was "absolutely horrible. . . . It was over the top [and] I was taken aback by it, but I smiled and worked my [way] through it, wanted the night to end as fast as I could," he recalled.

Kozlowski told Safer that he had already repaid many of the loans and claimed he was simply an overworked executive who left the details for underlings to handle. "I was pushing the company, and growing the company and pushing all aspects of it to continue to grow and I just don't think we put enough infra-structure in place to support some of that growth." Safer asked, "Yeah, but some of the lines got blurred, correct? Some of the lines between what was your money, what was Tyco's money became very fuzzy." Kozlowski replied, "I think I did everything according to the way the programs were outlined, and the way it was done by my predecessors." (Notice the rationalization for his unethical actions.)

Whatever Kozlowski did, it was clear that the Tyco board was not exactly meticulous in carrying out its oversight. But the jury believed that Kozlowski was guilty of grand larceny. Even so, Kozlowski believes he was a "dead duck" from the start. "I was a guy sitting in a courtroom who made $100 million a year. And I think a juror sitting there just would have to say, 'All that money, he musta done somethin' wrong.' I think it's as you know, it's as simple as that," he said.

Kozlowski told Safer he was done in by bad timing: the Enron and WorldCom catastrophes. He felt that most people believe that's what happened to Tyco—that employees were left high and dry. But, he pointed out, Tyco remained a thriving $60 billion company. "The company went on after I left there. The company is alive today. It's doing well," Kozlowski said. Asked if it makes him angry to be lumped together with Ken Lay (Enron) and Bernie Ebbers (WorldCom), he replied: "That just frustrated me to no end. These are companies that had financial and accounting schemes, that had major scams, and that wasn't Tyco."

Failure of the Corporate Governance System

The corporate governance system at Tyco completely broke down. Most members of Tyco's board of directors benefited personally as a result of Tyco's practices. For example, one board member worked for a law firm that "just happened" to receive as much as $2 million in business from Tyco. This person's pay at the law firm was linked to the amount of work he helped bring in from Tyco. Another director received a $10 million payment for help in engineering an acquisition for Tyco. The problem here was (1) Tyco board members did business with the company, (2) directors and officers borrowed money from the company, and (3) related-party disclosures were not made in the financial statements. Clearly, board members lacked independence from management and the company and their own greed contributed to lax oversight at Tyco.

Exhibit 5.12 applies the fraud triangle concept to Tyco. Notice how the opportunities to commit fraud because of lax oversight and the complicity of those in corporate governance enabled the fraud. Also, Kozlowski seemed to come up with every excuse imaginable to rationalize the fraud.

The news was not any better for PricewaterhouseCoopers LLP, the auditors for Tyco. On August 13, 2003, the SEC issued a cease and desist order against Richard P. Scalzo, the PwC engagement partner for the firm's audits of Tyco's financial statements for fiscal years 1997 through 2001. The commission's order found that Scalzo recklessly violated the antifraud provisions of the federal securities laws and engaged in improper professional conduct.[33]

Of particular note with respect to the culture at Tyco that enabled the fraud to occur is the finding by the SEC that both PwC and its lead engagement partner failed to follow GAAS and failed in their professional obligations. Accounting and Auditing Enforcement Release No. 1839 notes:

> Multiple and repeated facts provided notice to Scalzo regarding the integrity of Tyco's senior management and that Scalzo was reckless in not taking appropriate audit steps in the face of this information. By the end of the Tyco annual audit for its fiscal year ended September 30, 1998, if not before, those facts were sufficient to obligate Scalzo, pursuant to GAAS, to reevaluate the risk assessment of the Tyco audits and to perform additional audit procedures, including further audit testing of certain items (most notably, certain executive benefits, executive compensation, and related party transactions).[34]

The Tyco fraud serves as a shocking example of what can happen when all systems involved in the governance of a corporation fail at the same time. Kozlowski sold $258 million of Tyco stock back to the company, on top of salary and other compensation valued near $30 million. By the time Kozlowski quit under indictment for sales tax fraud in 2002, $80 billion of Tyco's shareholder wealth had evaporated.

Kozlowski bought off the board of directors by providing personal favors. The audit committee was irrelevant. The company and its top officers violated its duty of care and loyalty to shareholder interests that is the foundation of good governance. The external auditors for their part didn't look too hard to find the fraud, or looked the other way when it should have been detected.

Fraud Considerations in the Audit

SAS 99 details 10 areas of fraud considerations that should improve the auditor's ability to detect and report fraud: (1) describing the characteristics of fraud; (2) exercising professional skepticism; (3) discussing with engagement personnel the risks of material misstatement due to fraud; (4) obtaining the information needed to identify risks of material misstatement due to fraud; (5) identifying risks that may result in a material misstatement

EXHIBIT 5.12   Application of the Fraud Triangle to Tyco

Incentive	Pressure	Opportunity	Rationalization
Pursuit of self-interest: Keeping up with the "masters of the universe"	Keep up with Wall Street expectations that were enamored with Kozlowski's aggressive management style	There was lack of internal controls to support growth	Claimed to need to push the company, to continue to grow without putting into place the infrastructure to support some of that growth
Pursuit of self-interest: Use of corporate funds for personal purposes		Kozlowski was in a position to sign off on home purchases and elaborate use of corporate funds for personal purposes	Victim of Enronitis and the jury's alleged distaste for the $100 million man; actions did not negatively affect employees as was the case with Enron's share price decline in 401-k employee retirement funds
Pursuit of self-interest: What's in it for me?	Mark Swartz (CFO) wanted in on the action	Swartz benefited from the misuse of corporate assets for personal purposes so one element of oversight was compromised	Did everything the way the "programs" were authorized; did the same things as his predecessors
Pursuit of self-interest: What's in it for me?	Concessions to get the board to buy into the fraud	Members of the board also benefited; some misused corporate resources for personal purposes, thereby compromising this element of governance	Did everything the way the "programs" were authorized
Pursuit of self-interest: Go along to get along	Auditors didn't want to lose Tyco as a client	Auditors failed to properly assess the culture at Tyco (control environment)	Activities were approved at the top management and board level

due to fraud; (6) assessing the identified risks after taking into account an evaluation of the entity's programs and controls; (7) responding to the results of the assessment; (8) evaluating audit evidence; (9) communicating about fraud to management, the audit committee, and others; and (10) documenting the auditor's consideration of fraud.[35]

Fraud Risk Assessment

Most of the requirements of *SAS 99* call for the auditor to engage in risk assessment during the audit. Actually, the assessment of risk starts with an evaluation of evidence about the potential client before agreeing to do the audit. One important step is to communicate with the predecessor auditor to find out the reasons for the firing or the reasons for no longer servicing the client. Of particular importance is to assess the integrity of the top management and key accounting personnel. The successor auditor also should clarify with the predecessor whether there were any differences of opinion with management over the application of accounting principles and how these were handled, including the role of the audit committee.

To support risk assessment, the auditor should approach each engagement with a healthy dose of skepticism. This means to be skeptical of the truth in gathering information, asking questions, and evaluating the corporate culture. In making the assessment, the auditor should not, of course, approach the audit with an attitude toward management of "You are crooks. Prove me wrong." Instead, a healthy attitude is one that informs management in word and deed that the auditor's responsibility is to ask the tough questions, thoroughly examine relevant documentation, and probe to determine whether the organization culture promotes ethical decision making and there is support for financial statement amounts and disclosures.

The auditor should obtain information needed to identify the risk of material misstatement due to fraud. According to *SAS 99,* the goal should be to (1) make inquiries of management and others within the organization to obtain their views about the risks of fraud and how they are addressed; (2) consider any unusual or unexpected relationships that have been identified in performing analytical procedures (i.e., financial statement comparisons over time and ratio analysis) in planning the audit; (3) consider whether one or more fraud risk factors exist; and (4) consider other information (i.e., interim financial results and factors associated with the acceptance of the client) that may be helpful in identifying risks of material misstatement due to fraud.[36]

Audit Committee Responsibilities

SAS 99 addresses the responsibilities of the audit committee with respect to fraud risk assessment. Specifically, "the audit committee or those charged with governance where no audit committee exists should evaluate management's identification of fraud risks, implementation of antifraud measures, and creation of the appropriate tone at the top." Active oversight by the audit committee can help reinforce management's commitment to create a culture with "zero tolerance" for fraud. An entity's audit committee also should ensure that senior management (in particular, the CEO) implements appropriate fraud deterrence and prevention measures to better protect investors, employees, and other stakeholders.[37]

The audit committee's evaluation and oversight not only helps ensure that senior management fulfills its responsibility, but also can serve as a deterrent to senior management engaging in fraudulent activity (that is, by ensuring an environment is created whereby any attempt by senior management to involve employees in committing or concealing fraud would lead promptly to reports from such employees to appropriate persons, including the audit committee).

The audit committee also plays an important role in helping those charged with governance fulfill their oversight responsibilities with respect to the entity's financial reporting process and the system of internal control. In exercising this oversight responsibility, the audit committee should consider the potential for management override of controls or other inappropriate influence over the financial reporting process. Some examples follow:

- The audit committee should solicit the views of the internal auditors and independent auditors with respect to management's involvement in the financial reporting process and, in particular, the ability of management to override information processed by the entity's financial reporting system (for example, the ability of management or others to initiate or record nonstandard journal entries).
- The audit committee should consider reviewing the entity's reported information for reasonableness compared with prior or forecasted results, as well as with peers or industry averages.
- Information received in communications from the independent auditors can assist the audit committee in assessing the strength of the entity's internal control and the potential for fraudulent financial reporting.

As part of its oversight responsibilities, the audit committee should encourage management to provide a mechanism for employees to report concerns about unethical behavior, actual or suspected fraud, or violations of the entity's code of conduct or ethics policy. The committee should then receive periodic reports describing the nature, status, and eventual disposition of any fraud or unethical conduct. A summary of the activity, follow-up, and disposition also should be provided to all of those charged with governance.

Fraud Risk Factors

Fraud risk factors are explained in *SAS 99* by linking them to one of the three sides of the fraud triangle. Essentially, they represent red flags that should serve as a warning to the auditor that financial stability, operating, and/or corporate culture factors exist that may be a precursor to fraud or indicative that fraud has occurred. The auditor's role is to follow up on these warning signs by asking the tough questions, gathering the necessary information to support or refute the signs, and not to give in to client pressures to look the other way. For example, the auditors of Waste Management (Andersen) were satisfied with explanations of highly questionable transactions and the related accounting and they accepted management's promise to "clean up their act" in the future. In restrospect it made no sense since the firm was choosing to accept the word of those who had already committed fraud.

Revisiting the Expectation Gap

In March 2006, the AICPA's Auditing Standards Board issued eight *Statements on Auditing Standards (SAS 104–111)* relating to the assessment of risk in an audit of financial statements. These statements establish standards and provide guidance concerning the auditor's assessment of the risks of material misstatement (whether caused by error or fraud) in a financial statement audit, and the design and performance of audit procedures whose nature, timing, and extent are responsive to the assessed risks. The statements also establish standards and provide guidance on planning and supervision, the nature of audit evidence, and the evaluation of whether the audit evidence obtained affords a reasonable basis for an opinion regarding the financial statements under audit.[38] There is no doubt that these standards were motivated by the continuing expectation gap between the public's perception of auditors' responsibilities to ferret out fraud and the accounting profession's traditional role of providing only reasonable assurance that the financial statements are free of material misstatement due to fraud.

The goal of the eight risk assessment standards is to enhance auditors' evaluation of audit risk by specifying, among other things:

1. More in-depth understanding of the entity and its environment, including its internal control, to identify the risks of material misstatement in the financial statements and what the entity is doing to mitigate them.
2. More rigorous assessment of the risk of material misstatement of the financial statements based on that understanding.
3. Improved linkage between the assessed risks and the nature, timing, and extent of audit procedures performed in response to those risks.

Of particular note is the distinction between two types of misstatements: known and likely, defined as follows:[39]

> *Known misstatements.* These are specific misstatements identified during the audit arising from the incorrect selection or misapplication of accounting principles or misstatements of facts identified, including, for example, those arising from mistakes in gathering or processing data and the overlooking or misinterpretation of facts.
>
> *Likely misstatements.* (1) These arise from differences between management's and the auditor's judgments concerning accounting estimates that the auditor considers unreasonable or inappropriate (for example, because an estimate included in the financial statements by management is outside the range of reasonable outcomes the auditor has determined). (2) The auditor considers the differences likely to exist based on an extrapolation from audit evidence obtained (for example, the amount obtained by projecting known misstatements identified in an audit sample to the entire population from which the sample was drawn).

The misapplication of accounting principles, misstatement of facts, and differences in judgment with respect to accounting estimates taken together create conditions whereby the risk of material misstatement in the financial statements increases. The auditor should be sensitive to these events as they bear directly on the type of audit opinion to be given.

The risk assessment standards were issued by the AICPA after its responsibilities for setting auditing standards for public companies ended. Still, the AICPA does set auditing standards for nonpublic companies. While PCAOB has not formally adopted these standards for public companies, on August 25, 2009, it did issue *Auditing Standard (AS) No. 5,* An Audit of Internal Control over Financial Reporting That Is Integrated with an Audit of Financial Statements, which incorporates much of the risk assessment concepts in the AICPA standards. It also requires a management report on internal control that should be assessed by the external auditors as part of an integrated audit of the financial statements and internal controls.[40]

Internal Control Assessment

The risk that internal controls will not help prevent or detect a material misstatement in the financial statements is a critical evaluation to provide reasonable assurance. The system of internal controls and whether it operates as intended enables the auditor to gain either confidence about the internal processing of transactions or doubt, which the auditor should pursue.

Internal Control—Integrated Framework

SAS 78 amends *SAS 55* to reflect the changes necessary to recognize the definition and description of internal control contained in *Internal Control—Integrated Framework,* published by the Committee of Sponsoring Organizations (COSO) of the Treadway Commission in 1992. The framework defines internal control as a process effected by an entity's board of directors, management, and other personnel, designed to provide reasonable assurance regarding the achievement of the following objectives: (1) effectiveness and efficiency of operations, (2) reliability of financial reporting, and (3) compliance with applicable laws and regulations.[41] COSO utilizes the *SAS 55* framework that was introduced in Chapter 3 and explained earlier in this chapter and emphasizes the roles and responsibilities of management, the board of directors, internal auditors, and other personnel in creating an environment that supports the objectives of internal control. COSO notes that if members of the board and audit committee do not take their responsibilities seriously, then the system will likely break down as occurred in the accounting frauds of the 1990s and 2000s.

The 1992 COSO *Internal Control—Integrated Framework* is a widely used tool to assess internal controls, and is recognized by the PCAOB as an appropriate internal control framework in *AS No. 5,* An Audit of Internal Control over Financial Reporting Performed in Conjunction with an Audit of Financial Statements.[42] According to *AS 5,* the COSO framework "provides a suitable and available framework" for assessing a company's internal controls and financial reporting.

Additional professional guidance may be found in *SAS No. 109,* Understanding the Entity and Its Environment and Assessing the Risks of Material Misstatement.[43] *SAS 109* deals with an auditor's understanding of internal control. The standard specifically includes the five interrelated components of internal control identified in the 1992 COSO framework. A survey of members of the Institute of Management Accountants and the Institute of Internal Auditors reports that approximately 90 percent of respondents rely to some extent on the COSO framework to evaluate controls.[44]

COSO Findings on Financial Statement Fraud

COSO analyzed the financial reporting by public companies from 1987 to 1997, a period during which business failures were high due to accounting fraud at companies such as ZZZZ Best. It is noteworthy that most of its findings were precursors to what happened during the business frauds and accounting failures of the 1998–2003 period.

COSO examined 200 cases of financial statement fraud and found the following:

1. Some companies committing the fraud were experiencing net losses or were in close to breakeven positions in periods before the fraud. These pressures may have led some companies to commit fraud to reverse downward spirals while others may have been motivated to preserve upward trends.

2. Top senior executives were frequently involved. In the SEC investigation and subsequent actions as reflected in the AAERs, 72 percent named the CEO and 43 percent the CFO. When considered together, in 83 percent of the cases the AAERs named one or the other officer, or both of them.

3. Most audit committees met infrequently or not at all. Twenty-five percent of the companies did not have an audit committee. Sixty-five percent of the committees did not have a member with expertise in accounting or finance.

4. Boards were dominated by insiders and "gray" directors (outsiders with special ties to the company or management) with significant equity ownership and little experience. Collectively, the directors and officers owned nearly one-third of the companies' stock, with the CEO/president personally owning about 17 percent.

5. Family relationships among directors and officers were fairly common, as were individuals who seemed to have significant power. The founder and current CEO were the same person or the original CEO/president in nearly half of the companies.

6. A majority of the audit reports were issued during the fraud period; 55 percent of reports in the last year of the fraud contained unqualified opinions.

7. The remaining 45 percent of the reports issued in the last year contained departures from the unqualified opinion. The reasons were substantial doubt about the entity's ability to continue as a going concern, litigation and other uncertainties, changes in accounting principles, and changes in auditors between fiscal years comparatively reported. Three percent of the audit reports were qualified due to a GAAP departure during the fraud period.

8. Financial statement fraud occasionally implicated the external auditor. Auditors were explicitly named in 29 percent of the fraud cases. Auditors were also named for alleged involvement in the fraud (30 of 56 cases) or for negligent auditing (26 of 56 cases).

9. Some of the companies changed auditors during the fraud period. Just over 25 percent changed auditors during the time frame between the beginning of the last clean financial statement period and ending with the last fraudulent financial statement period. A majority of the auditor changes occurred during the fraud period.

One obvious conclusion from the findings is the link between SOX provisions and the deficiencies noted by COSO, in particular strengthening the role of the audit committee and board of directors through independence requirements.

Enterprise Risk Management—Integrated Framework

In 2001, COSO initiated a project to develop a framework that would be readily usable by managements to evaluate and improve their organizations' enterprise risk management (ERM). The framework incorporates internal control principles that enhance corporate governance and risk management. *ERM* is defined as a process, effected by an entity's board of directors, management, and other personnel, applied in strategy setting and across the enterprise, designed to identify potential events that may affect the entity and to manage risk within its risk appetite.[45]

According to COSO, ERM encompasses six elements:

1. *Aligning risk appetite and strategy.* Risk appetite is considered by management in evaluating strategic alternatives, setting related objectives, and developing mechanisms to manage related risks.

2. *Enhancing risk response decisions.* ERM provides the discipline to identify and select among alternative risk responses—risk avoidance, reduction, sharing, and acceptance.

3. *Reducing operational surprises and losses.* ERM provides the capability to identify potential events and establish responses, reducing surprises and associated costs or losses.

4. *Identifying and managing multiple and cross-enterprise risks.* ERM facilitates effective responses to interrelated aspects of risk that affect different parts of the organization, and integrated responses to multiple risks.

5. *Seizing opportunities.* ERM allows management to consider a full range of potential events, positioning it to identify and proactively realize opportunities.

6. *Improving deployment of capital.* The risk information provided by ERM enables management to effectively assess overall capital needs and enhance capital allocation.

COSO's ERM is designed to help an entity get to where it wants to go and avoid pitfalls and surprises along the way. The components of ERM are similar to those of *SAS 55* and the COSO Integrated Framework. ERM adds strategic issues including objective setting by management, identification of risks and opportunities affecting achievement of an entity's objectives, and risk responses selected by management to align risk tolerance and risk appetite.[46]

The ERM framework represents the accounting profession's response to the increased need to manage risk in the aftermath of the accounting scandals and business failures that caused substantial harm to investors, company personnel, and other stakeholders.

The framework adopts the position that management should determine its risk appetite and align it with strategic objectives. Unfortunately, ERM seems to place emphasis in the wrong areas by focusing on risk appetite. The usefulness of the ERM framework in establishing an ethical culture can be questioned since it does not place emphasis on the ethical dimensions of making strategic decisions. Instead, the focus is on the company's "hunger" for risk and its strategic objectives.

In 2009, COSO issued *Guidance on Monitoring Internal Control Systems,* an integral part of its framework. Monitoring should be done to assess the quality of internal control performance over time. To provide reasonable assurance that an entity's objectives will be achieved, management should monitor controls to determine whether they are operating effectively and whether they need to be redesigned when risks change.[47]

According to COSO's *Guidance,* effective monitoring involves (1) establishing a baseline for control effectiveness; (2) designing and executing monitoring procedures that are based on the significance of business risks relative to the entity's objectives; and (3) assessing and reporting results, including follow-up on corrective actions.[48]

Monitoring can be done through ongoing activities or separate evaluations that are built into the normal, recurring activities of the entity and include regular management and supervisory activities. Management can use internal auditors or personnel performing similar functions to monitor the operating effectiveness of internal control. For example, management might review whether bank reconciliations are being prepared on a timely basis and reviewed by the internal auditors.[49]

PCAOB Standards

PCAOB issues standards for the audit of public companies by registered CPA firms. In it standards, PCAOB recognizes the importance of internal control over financial reporting as the foundation for the financial statement audit. The usefulness of financial statement amounts can be questioned if the underlying system that produced the numbers is not reliable. PCAOB requires auditors to examine the design and effectiveness of internal control sufficient to render an opinion on its effectiveness.

Auditing Standard No. 4: Reporting on Previously Reported Material Weakness

AS 4 describes the steps to be used by auditors when a company voluntarily engages them to report on whether a material weakness, previously identified in the SOX Section 404 report on internal controls, no longer exists. The auditor's objective in performing work under *AS 4* is to obtain reasonable assurance as to whether the previously reported material weakness still exists. The auditor focuses on whether the controls specified by management as addressing the material weakness were designed and operating effectively, as of the date chosen by management. The auditor's opinion is not an opinion on the effectiveness of internal controls over financial reporting overall, nor is it an update to a previous internal control over financial reporting opinion.

AS 4 establishes the following steps to be taken by auditors engaged to report on whether a previously reported material weakness still exists:[50]

(A) Evaluate whether conditions for engagement performance have been met including:
   (1) Management accepts responsibility for the effectiveness of internal control
   (2) Management has evaluated controls it believes have addressed the material weakness
   (3) Management asserts that the controls are effective in correcting the material weakness

      (4) Management has obtained sufficient evidence, including documentation, supporting its assessment

      (5) Management presents a report to accompany the auditor's report

(B) Plan the engagement.

(C) Evaluate whether to use the work of others.

(D) Obtain evidence about the effectiveness of controls.

(E) Obtain written representations from management and evaluate management's report.

(F) Form a conclusion and report.

(G) Communicate with the audit committee.

Auditing Standard No. 5: An Audit of Internal Control over Financial Reporting That Is Integrated with an Audit of Financial Statements

AS 5 establishes requirements and provides direction that applies when an auditor is engaged to perform an audit of management's assessment of the effectiveness of internal control over financial reporting.[51] It provides that "effective internal control over financial reporting [ICFR] provides reasonable assurance regarding the reliability of financial reporting and the preparation of financial statements for external purposes. If one or more material weaknesses exist, the company's ICFR cannot be considered effective." The standard emphasizes that the general standards are applicable to an audit of ICFR. Those standards require technical training and proficiency as an auditor, independence, and the exercise of due professional care, including professional skepticism. The standard also establishes fieldwork and reporting standards applicable to an audit of ICFR.

    The audit of ICFR should be integrated with the audit of financial statements. While the objectives of the audits are not identical, the auditor must plan and perform the work to achieve the objectives of both audits. In an integrated audit, the auditor should design testing procedures for internal controls to accomplish the objectives of both audits simultaneously (1) to obtain sufficient evidence to support the auditor's opinion on ICFR at year-end, and (2) to obtain sufficient evidence to support the auditor's control risk assessments for purposes of the audit of financial statements.

    AS 5 standards include obtaining reasonable assurance about whether the financial statements are free of material misstatement, whether caused by error or fraud, and whether management's assessment of the effectiveness of the company's ICFR is fairly stated in all material respects. Accordingly, there is some risk that a material misstatement of the financial statements or a material weakness in internal control over financial reporting would remain undetected. Although not absolute assurance, reasonable assurance is, nevertheless, a high level of assurance. Also, an integrated audit is not designed to detect error or fraud that is immaterial to the financial statements or deficiencies in internal control over financial reporting that, individually or in combination, are less severe than a material weakness. If, for any reason, the auditor is unable to complete the audit or is unable to form or has not formed an opinion, he may decline to express an opinion or decline to issue a report as a result of the engagement.

Auditing Standard No. 6: Evaluating Consistency of Financial Statements

AS 6 establishes requirements and provides direction for the auditor's evaluation of the consistency of the financial statements, including changes to previously issued financial statements, and the effect of that evaluation on the auditor's report on the financial statements. The comprehensive and far-reaching nature of the standard precludes complete coverage. Therefore, what follows is a description of its major provisions with respect to restatements of the financial statements due to errors and misstatements.[52]

AS 6 states that a change in accounting principle is a change from one GAAP to another GAAP when (1) there are two or more generally accepted accounting principles that apply, or when (2) the accounting principle formerly used is no longer generally accepted.

Second, according to *AS 6*, a change in the method of applying an accounting principle also is considered a change in accounting principle. A change from an accounting principle that is not generally accepted to one that is generally accepted is a *correction of a misstatement*. The term *error*, as used in *SFAS 154*, is equivalent to *misstatement*, as used in the auditing standards. Recall that such errors are recorded as an adjustment to the beginning balance of retained earnings and prior years' income amounts would be restated.

Third, *AS 6* states that the correction of a material misstatement in previously issued financial statements should be recognized in the auditor's report on the audited financial statements through the addition of an explanatory paragraph. The accounting pronouncements generally require certain disclosures relating to restatements to correct misstatements in previously issued financial statements. If the financial statement disclosures are not adequate, the auditor should address the inadequacy of disclosure and decide on the proper course of action with respect to the audit opinion.

Finally, *AS 6* says that changes in classification in previously issued financial statements do not require recognition in the auditor's report, unless the change represents the correction of a material misstatement or a change in accounting principle. Accordingly, the auditor should evaluate a material change in financial statement classification and the related disclosure to determine whether such a change also is a change in accounting principle or a correction of a material misstatement. For example, certain reclassifications in previously issued financial statements, such as reclassifications of debt from long-term to short-term or reclassifications of cash flows from the operating activities category to the financing activities category, might occur because those items were incorrectly classified in the previously issued financial statements. In such situations, the reclassification also is the correction of a misstatement. If the auditor determines that the reclassification is a change in accounting principle or if the auditor determines that the reclassification is a correction of a material misstatement in previously issued financial statements, he should address the matter as required by reporting standards.

Restatements of Financial Statements

Public companies are subject to SOX Section 404 requirements that include having their internal controls reviewed by management and evaluated independently by auditors. The need for an integrated audit of internal control and the financial statements elevates the importance of internal controls to providing accurate and reliable financial statements. Early results seemed to have supported that perspective because 15 percent of public companies that file financial statements with the SEC in the first full year of implementation of PCAOB *AS 2* (superseded by *AS 5*) restated their financial statements. This is double the number of 2004. In fact, an estimated range from 11 to 15 percent of public companies have identified in their filings with the SEC at least one material weakness in the internal controls over financial reporting.[53]

In 2007 the number of restatements declined by 31.4 percent (from 1,800 to 1,235). This decline continued in 2008, during which a total of 869 restatements were filed by 778 unique companies. These figures represent a 31.4 percent drop in the amount of restatements (1,235 down to 869) and a 30 percent drop in the number of unique filers (1,111 down to 778). The downward trend appears to be attributable to the improved reliability of ICFR implemented in response to SOX, but some observers suggest that the drop in restatements, at least to some extent, is due to a more relaxed approach adopted by the SEC regarding materiality and the need to file restatements. In addition to a drop in quantity, calendar year 2008 experienced an equivalence or drop in the severity of restatements as compared to prior years. Restatements are also taking a smaller cut out of profits. The typical reduction to net income for a company restating financials in 2008 was only $6.1 million, compared to $7.4 million in 2007 and $20 million in both 2006 and 2005. Restatements also took less time to file and cited fewer accounting problems.[54]

The study results show that "Companies . . . have been able to focus their attention on a smaller number of more impactful controls, so they're able to catch errors earlier, before the financial statement phase." The causes behind restatements are also shifting, the study notes. Problems with cash flow classifications, for example, have steadily risen as a cause for restatements, while revenue recognition problems have declined. Topping the list in 2008—even ahead of revenue recognition, which has been accounting's primary cause of financial statement fraud for years—are problems with debt, payroll, cash flow, compensation, and mergers and acquisitions. The rise in cash flow problems may be indicative of the economic climate in 2007 through 2009, where a cash flow perspective gained in importance due to liquidity problems at many large financial institutions and other companies.

Another important undercurrent in restatements is how often companies are filing "stealth" restatements—that is, restatements filed without a prior Form 8-K disclosure that the original numbers are wrong and unreliable. The raw number of stealth restatements was down in 2008 from the peak year of 2006, but they still made up 51 percent of all restatements filed in 2008.

Companies are allowed to skip the Form 8-K disclosure if the adjustment to financial statements is deemed immaterial. That led one analyst to wonder if a larger percentage of restatements are immaterial corrections, or if companies are improperly portraying them as such. He reiterated his concerns that SEC enforcement may be light in this area. If so, it may be a recipe for disaster if the abusive practices of the past and lax audit oversight continue in the future.

Concluding Thoughts

An audit opinion provides reasonable assurance that the financial statements are free of material misstatements including fraud. The basis for making that assertion is compliance with GAAS. The foundation of one's ethical and professional obligations in the audit of a client's financial statements is to meet (1) the general standards that address professional qualifications and competency, (2) fieldwork standards that identify required audit procedures, and (3) the reporting standards that guide the auditor in determining the proper opinion. Audit standards have come a long way since the AICPA issued the expectation gap standards in 1988. In particular, the standards today provide a framework to evaluate internal controls and assess audit risk, and they do a better job of identifying the red flags that indicate fraud may be present. COSO guidelines provide that internal controls are an integral part of the reasonable assurance given in an audit report and that an entity's objectives will be achieved.

The common element in fraud is a knowing attempt by management to make the financial results appear the way management wants (earnings management) rather than in accordance with GAAP. The best way to prevent the fraud from happening is to establish a culture that informs employees that such actions will not be tolerated. Internal controls over financial reporting should help establish an ethical control environment. Independent directors and members of the audit committee should be responsive to the concerns of internal auditors and support the external auditors in their efforts to resolve differences with management over the proper application of GAAP.

From time to time, accountants seem to lose sight of the critical role the independent audit plays in our free market economic system. Shareholders must be reassured that the financial statement numbers present fairly financial position and the results of operations. Creditors need to know that the financial results on which they make decisions about loans to companies are accurate and reliable. All parties expect that the financial statements are in conformity with GAAP and the audit has been conducted in accordance with GAAS.

Accounting professionals are subject to legal liability if they fail to follow the GAAP and GAAS and are unable to meet their ethical and professional obligations. In Chapter 6 we will look at a variety of classic cases that have established precedents for the legal liabilities of accountants and auditors to clients and third parties. We conclude this chapter by reiterating the need for a strong set of ethical values, including professional skepticism, ethical judgment, and integrity, to ferret out fraud and report it in accordance with professional standards.

Discussion Questions

1. Which of the three paragraphs of the audit report do you think is the most important? Why?

2. Give one example each of when an auditor might render an unqualified opinion with an explanatory paragraph, a qualified opinion, and an adverse opinion. When might a disclaimer be an acceptable substitute for a qualified or adverse opinion?

3. Assume a local health club, Texas Two-Step (TTS), records 100 percent of amounts received from annual membership fees in the month the cash is received, which is the first month of the new year. The reason given is that TTS does not specifically provide any services for members after the time the fees are paid. Do you agree with TTS's accounting? Why or why not? Assuming the accounting does not comply with GAAP, explain how the books should be corrected if the error is discovered in the subsequent year.

4. Assume the successor auditor requests permission from a potential client to discuss with the predecessor the reasons and circumstances for the firm's withdrawal from the engagement. What ethical considerations exist for both the predecessor and successor auditors in pursuing the contact? What is the purpose of speaking with the predecessor with respect to planning for the audit?

5. Professor Slim Pickens makes the following statement in his Intermediate II Accounting class: "The standards of fieldwork provide the foundation to ensure that the financial statements present fairly financial position and results of operations." Discuss what you think Pickens means by the statement. Why do you think he would make such a statement in an intermediate class?

6. Some criticize the accounting profession for using expressions in the audit report that seem to build in deniability should the client commit a fraudulent act. What expressions enable the CPA to build a defense should the audit wind up in the courtroom? How does your analysis relate to the opening statement in the chapter by Abe Briloff?

7. The audit report on General Motors for 2008 issued by Deloitte & Touche included the following statement: "The corporation's recurring losses from operations, stockholders' deficit, and inability to generate sufficient cash flow to meet its obligations and sustain its operations raise substantial doubt about its ability to continue as a going concern." Are you surprised to learn of this going-concern alert at a company such as General Motors? What signs might the auditors look for prior to issuing their report on the 2009 financial statements that help them reevaluate the going-concern assessment?

8. Do you think the concept of materiality is incompatible with ethical behavior? Why or why not?

9. Distinguish between an auditor's responsibilities to detect errors, illegal acts, and fraud. What role does materiality have in determining the proper reporting and disclosure of such events?

10. How do materiality judgments impact the consistency and comparability of financial statements over a period of time?

The following information should be used to answer questions 11 and 12.

In its 2008 Report to the Nation on Occupational Fraud and Abuse, *the Association of Certified Fraud Examiners reported the following results with respect to ranking of controls' importance in detecting or limiting the losses from the specific fraud scheme they investigated and their relative effectiveness in reducing the amount of losses.*[55]

Control	Rank	Average Score	% Reduction in Medium Losses
Internal audit	1	3.81	52.8%
Surprise audit	2	3.51	66.2
Management review of internal controls	3	3.17	45.0
Fraud hotline	4	3.03	60.0
Mandatory job rotation/vacations	5	3.02	61.0
Reward for whistleblowers	6	2.86	28.7
Audit of ICFR	7	2.65	47.8
Audit of financial statements	8	2.53	40.0

11. Why do you think mandatory job rotation and vacations are effective controls to reduce instances of fraud?

12. Does it surprise you that the audit of ICFR and external audit were ranked at the bottom as effective tools to prevent/detect fraud? Why or why not?

13. *SAS 99* points to three conditions that enable fraud to occur. Briefly describe each condition. How does one's propensity to act ethically as described by Rest's model of morality influence each of the three elements of the fraud triangle?

14. In 2005, the Institute of Management Accountants reported the results of a survey of business, academic, and regulatory leaders conducted by the Center for Corporate Change that found the corporation's culture to be the most important factor influencing the attitudes and behavior of executives. The results indicate that 88 percent of the representatives who took part in the survey believe that companies devote little management attention to considering the effect of the culture on their executives. What are the elements of the corporate culture? How do the standards in *SAS 55, SAS 78,* and COSO's *Integrated Framework* help define a strong control environment?

15. What is the purpose of audit "risk assessment"? What are its objectives, and why is it important in assessing the likelihood that fraud may occur?

16. Kinetics, Inc., included the following footnote in its December 31, 2009, financial statements:

    We corrected the misstatement of capitalized advertising costs recorded in 2008 by adjusting operating expenses for 2009, and crediting the asset account. The result of this correction is to reduce income by $500,000 for 2009 [a material amount] and reduce recorded assets by a like amount.

    Do you think the company should mention the change in its audit report? Why or why not? How would you determine whether its inclusion should affect the type of audit opinion?

17. According to *SAS 112,* the auditor must evaluate the control deficiencies that he has become aware of to determine whether those deficiencies, individually or in combination, are significant deficiencies or material weaknesses. What is the purpose of the auditor's evaluation of internal controls with respect to conducting an audit in accordance with GAAS?

18. In Europe, the audit reports use the expression "true and fair view" to characterize the results of the audit. Do you think there is a meaningful difference between that language and the "present fairly" statement made in U.S. audit reports? As a user of the financial statements in each instance, does one expression more than the other give you a greater comfort level with respect to the conformity of the financial statements with generally accepted accounting principles? Why or why not?

19. In a 2005 poll sponsored by *Wall Street Journal* Online and Harris Interactive, 2,061 U.S. investors were asked whether the regulations and costs of SOX were too strict. Overall, 55 percent called the rules too lenient and that punishment for poor corporate governance should be directed at certain individuals rather than the company as a whole. Are you surprised by these results? Why or why not?

20. Mr. Arty works for Smile Accounting Firm as a senior accountant. Currently he is doing a review of rental property compliance testing completed by the staff accountants. He is testing rental receipts and expenses of the property owned by the client. Arty realizes that the staff accountants tested only two tenants per property instead of the required three by the audit program based on materiality considerations. However, to request more information from the client would cause massive delays and the manager on the engagement is pressing hard for the information before Christmas vacation. Assume the manager approaches the client, who states that she does not

want any additional testing: "I needed the report yesterday." The manager points out to Arty that no problems were found from the testing of the two properties. Moreover, the firm has never had any accounting issues with respect to the client. Assume the firm decides it is not necessary to do the additional testing. What would you do if you were Arty? Consider in your answer the ethics of the situation and reporting obligations of the firm.

Endnotes

1. Securities and Exchange Commission, *In the Matter of the Application of Michael J. Marrie, CPA and Brian L. Berry, CPA,* Accounting and Auditing Enforcement Rel. No. 1823, July 29, 2003, www.sec.gov/litigation/opinions/34-48246.htm.

2. U.S. Court of Appeals for the District of Columbia Circuit, No. 03-1265, *Michael J. Marrie and Brian L. Berry, Petitioners v. SEC, Respondent,* www.sec.gov/litigation/opinions/34-48246_appeal.pdf.

3. American Institute of CPAs, *AICPA Professional Standards. Volume 1 as of June 1, 2009, Statement on Auditing Standards (SAS) No. 59,* The Auditor's Consideration of an Entity's Ability to Continue as a Going Concern (New York: AICPA, 2009), AU Section 341.

4. O. Ray Whittington and Kurt Pany, *Principles of Auditing and Other Assurance Services,* 17th ed. (New York: McGraw-Hill Irwin, 2010).

5. Whittington and Pany, pp. 663–664.

6. Ibid., pp. 667–668.

7. Ibid., pp. 670–671.

8. William F. Messier Jr., Steven M. Glover, and Douglas F. Prawitt, *Auditing and Assurance Services: A Systematic Approach,* 7th ed. (New York: McGraw-Hill Irwin, 2010).

9. Whittington and Pany, p. 197.

10. Financial Accounting Standards Board, *Statement of Financial Accounting Concepts (SFAC) No. 2,* Qualitative Characteristics of Accounting Information (Stamford, CT: FASB, May 1980).

11. AICPA, *Professional Standards Volume 1,* AU Section 316.

12. Securities and Exchange Commission, *SEC Staff Accounting Bulletin: No. 99—Materiality,* www.sec.gov/interps/account/sab99.htm.

13. *TSC Industries v. Northway, Inc.,* 426 438, 449 (1976), http://caselaw.lp.findlaw.com/scripts/getcase.pl?court=us.

14. AICPA, *SAS 99.*

15. American Institute of CPAs, *AICPA Professional Standards. Volume 1 as of June 1, 2009, Statement on Auditing Standards (SAS) No. 69* (includes *SAS 91* and *SAS 93*), The Meaning of Present Fairly in Conformity with Generally Accepted Accounting Principles (New York: AICPA, 2009), AU Section 411.

16. Financial Accounting Standards Board, *Statement of Financial Accounting Standards (SFAS) No. 17,* Accounting for Leases (Stamford, CT: FASB, November 1977).

17. Marc J. Epstein and Marshall Geiger, "Investor Views of Audit Assurance: Recent Evidence of the Expectations Gap," *Journal of Accountancy,* January 1994.

18. American Institute of CPAs, *AICPA Professional Standards. Volume 1 as of June 1, 2009, Statement on Auditing Standards (SAS) No. 55,* Internal Control in a Financial Statement Audit (New York: AICPA, 2009), AU Section 319.

19. American Institute of CPAs, *AICPA Professional Standards. Volume 1 as of June 1, 2009, Statement on Auditing Standards (SAS) No. 54,* Illegal Acts (New York: AICPA, 2009), AU Section 317.

20. Whittington and Pany, pp. 40–41.

21. Timothy J. Louwers, Robert J. Ramsay, David H. Sinason, and Jerry R. Strawser, *Auditing and Assurance Services* (New York: McGraw-Hill Irwin, 2008).

22. Ibid., pp. 77–78.

23. Ibid., p. 78.

24. AICPA, *SAS 99,* AU Sections 316.05–.06.

25. Whittington and Pany, p. 203.

26. W. Steve Albrecht, Conan C. Albrecht, Chad O. Albrecht, and Mark F. Zimbelman, *Fraud Examination,* 3rd ed. (Mason, OH: South-Western Cengage Learning, 2009).

27. AICPA, *SAS 99.*

28. Available at www.sec.gov/spotlight/optionsbackdating.htm.

29. Available www.sec.gov/news/press/2009/2009-113.htm.

30. SEC, Litigation Release No. 21042, May 18, 2009, Accounting and Auditing Release No. 2970, May 18, 2009, *SEC v. Monster Worldwide, Inc.,* U.S. District Court for the Southern District of New York, Civil Action No. 09 CV 4641 (S.D.N.Y. May 18, 2009), www.sec.gov/litigation/litreleases/2009/lr21042.htm.

31. Albrecht et al., p. 360.

32. Available at www.cbsnews.com/stories/2007/03/22/ . . . /main2596123.shtml.

33. Securities and Exchange Commission, *SEC v. Tyco International Ltd.,* Litigation Release No. 19657, April 17, 2006, www.sec.gov/litigation/litreleases/2006/lr19657.htm.

34. *SEC v. Tyco International Ltd.*

35. AICPA, *SAS 99,* AU Sections 316.06–.07.

36. Ibid.

37. Ibid.

38. AICPA, *Statement on Auditing Standards (SAS) No. 104–No.111,* Risk Assessment Standards, March 2006, www.aicpa.org/audit and attest standards/risk assessmentstandards.html.

39. AICPA, *Statement on Auditing Standards (SAS) No. 10,* Audit Risk and Materiality in Conducting an Audit, March 2006, www.aicpa.org/audit and attest standards/risk assessmentstandards.html.

40. Public Company Accounting Oversight Board, *Auditing Standard No. 5,* An Audit of Internal Control over Financial Reporting That Is Integrated with an Audit of Financial Statements, November 15, 2007, www.pcaobus.org/Standards.html.

41. Committee of Sponsoring Organizations of the Treadway Commission, *Internal Control—Integrated Framework* (New York: AICPA, 1992).

42. PCAOB, *AS 5.*

43. *Statement on Auditing Standards (SAS) No. 109,* Understanding the Entity and Its Environment and Assessing the Risks of Material Misstatement (New York: AICPA, 2006).

44. Parveen P. Gupta and Jeffrey C. Thomson, "Use of COSO 1992 in Management Reporting on Internal Control, *Strategic Finance,* March 2007.

45. COSO, *Enterprise Risk Management (ERM)—Integrated Framework: Executive Summary* (New York: AICPA, September 2004).

46. Ibid.

47. COSO, *Guidance on Monitoring Internal Control Systems,* Vol. 1, p. 4, 2009.

48. Ibid.

49. Messier, pp. 195–196.

50. Public Company Accounting Oversight Board, *Auditing Standard No. 4,* Reporting on Whether a Previously Reported Material Weakness Continues to Exist, April 27, 2006, www. pcaobus.org/Standards.html.

51. PCAOB, *AS 5.*

52. Public Company Accounting Oversight Board, *Auditing Standard No. 6,* Evaluating Consistency of Financial Statement, August 25, 2009, www.pcaobus.org/Standards.html.

53. These results were reported in *Report on the Effective Application of Section 404 of the Sarbanes-Oxley Act of 2002,* prepared by the international CPA firm of Grant Thornton. The results come from two studies: (1) Audit Analytics, Section 404 Internal Control Material Weaknesses Results for the First Three Quarters of Section 404; Disclosures based on filings as of November 15, 2005, and (2) Report generated on December 17, 2005, using SEC filings from the Russell 3000.

54. Tammy Whitehouse, "Restatements Tumble as Internal Controls Hit Stride," *Compliance Week,* March 10, 2009, www.complianceweek.com/article/5300/restatements-tumble-as-internal controls-hit-stride.

55. Association of Certified Fraud Examiners, *2008 Report to the Nation on Occupational Fraud and Abuse* (Austin, TX: ACFE, 2008).

Chapter 5 Cases

Case 5-1

General Electric Accounting Fraud

On August 4, 2009, the SEC filed a civil injunctive action alleging civil fraud and other charges against General Electric Company (GE). The suit, filed in U.S. District Court for the District of Connecticut, alleges that GE misled investors by reporting materially false and misleading results in its financial statements. The SEC alleges that GE used improper accounting methods to increase its reported earnings or revenues and avoid reporting negative financial results. GE has agreed to pay a $50 million penalty to settle the SEC's charges.

According to the commission's complaint,[1] GE met or exceeded final consensus analyst earnings per share (EPS) expectations every quarter from 1995 through filing of its 2004 annual report. However, on four separate occasions in 2002 and 2003, high-level GE accounting executives or other finance personnel approved accounting that was not in compliance with GAAP. In one instance, the improper accounting allowed GE to avoid missing analysts' final consensus EPS expectations. The four accounting violations were (1) beginning in January 2003, an improper application of the accounting standards to GE's commercial paper funding program to avoid unfavorable disclosures and an estimated approximately $200 million pretax charge to earnings; (2) a 2003 failure to correct a misapplication of financial accounting standards to certain GE interest-rate swaps; (3) in 2002 and 2003, reported end-of-year sales of locomotives that had not yet occurred in order to accelerate more than $370 million in revenue; and (4) in 2002, an improper change to GE's accounting for sales of commercial aircraft engines' spare parts that increased GE's 2002 net earnings by $585 million.

Without admitting or denying the SEC's allegations, GE agreed to the financial penalty and consented to the entry of an order permanently enjoining it from violating Section 17(a) of the Securities Act of 1933 and Sections 10(b), 13(a), 13(b)(2)(a), and 13(b)(2)(b) of the Securities Exchange Act of 1934. The charges announced concluded the SEC's investigation with respect to the company.

Specifics of the Claims against GE

Offer or Sale of GE Securities during the Relevant Period

Throughout the relevant period, shares of GE common stock were continuously offered for sale, sold, and purchased on the New York Stock Exchange. In addition, GE itself offered

[1]Securities and Exchange Commission, Litigation Release No. 21166, August 4, 2009, *Securities and Exchange Commission v. General Electric Company,* 3:09 CV 1235 (RNC) (D. Conn.),www.sec.gov/litigation/litreleases/2009/lr21166.htm.

securities for sale at the same time its financial statements contained materially false statements. For instance, in March 2004, GE offered approximately 119 million shares of newly issued GE common stock for sale to the public at $31.83. In April 2004, GE used approximately 342 million shares of newly issued shares of GE common stock to acquire Amersham plc. In addition, in March 2003, June 2003, January 2004, and December 2004, GE made additional acquisitions that were paid for in whole or in part with GE common stock.

GE, in its sale of stock, directly or indirectly—by use of the means or instruments of transportation or communication in interstate commerce or by the use of the mails—knowingly or recklessly (1) employed devices, schemes, or artifices to defraud; (2) obtained money or property by means of untrue statements of material fact or omissions to state material facts necessary in order to make the statements made, in the light of the circumstances under which they were made, not misleading; or (3) engaged in transactions, practices, or courses of business that operated or would operate as a fraud or deceit upon certain purchasers, including purchasers of GE securities. The conduct of GE involved fraud, deceit, manipulative or deliberate or reckless disregard of regulatory requirements, and directly or indirectly resulted in substantial losses to other persons.

Failure to Keep Accurate Books and Records in Violation of Exchange Act Section 13(b)(2)(A)

GE failed to maintain and keep books, records, and accounts that, in reasonable detail, accurately and fairly reflected the transactions and dispositions of GE's assets in violation of Section 13(b)(2)(A) of the Exchange Act.

Failure to Maintain Internal Controls in Violation of Exchange Act Section 13(b)(2)(B)

GE failed to devise and maintain a system of internal accounting controls sufficient to provide reasonable assurances that the company's transactions were recorded as necessary to permit preparation of financial statements in conformity with GAAP or other criteria applicable to such statements and to maintain accountability for assets in violation of Section 13(b)(2)(B) of the Exchange Act.

Questions

1. From an ethical perspective, what's wrong with a company selling shares during a period of fraud?

2. Identify the stakeholders affected by GE's actions. Do you think GE management and the board of directors met their fiduciary obligations? Use ethical reasoning to help answer this question.

3. Refer to the data in discussion questions 11 and 12. Based on the limited facts in the GE case, which of the specified controls do you believe either did not exist or were inefficient in detecting/reporting the fraud? Are there any additional controls that may have helped to prevent or detect the fraud?

Case 5-2

Kazweski and Dooktaviski

Kazweski and Dooktaviski (KD) were general partners in a limited partnership located in Cincinnati, Ohio, that was created in the year 2003 to generate profits for its limited partners from trading in real estate. The partnership had its financial statements audited by Rench & Bose LLP, a Cincinnati-based accounting firm with offices throughout Ohio. The firm gave unqualified opinions on its audits of KD for the years 2007–2009, and stated that the audits were conducted in accordance with generally accepted auditing standards.

Moe Jorgan was the audit manager for Rench & Bose in charge of these audits and Pony Terez was the partner in charge of the engagement. On August 20, 2010, Jorgan and Terez called a meeting of the KD audit engagement team. The purpose of the meeting was to review the findings of a peer review of Rench & Bose that was conducted by another CPA firm under AICPA rules; the review included the KD audits. The peer reviewers issued a modified opinion on the firm's quality controls and its adherence to professional standards. The firm does not audit any SEC clients, so it is subject to only the peer review requirements of the AICPA that are sanctioned by the Ohio State Board of Accountancy. A discussion of peer reviews in general and the specific AICPA standards are described in Exhibit 1.

In addition to Jorgan and Terez, the other members of the KD audit engagement team included four staff members who had been hired after graduating from State University of Ohio at Cincinnati. The staff members began working for Rench & Bose on July 1, 2010. The audit senior was Tod Kazweski, the son of one of the general partners of KD.

Exhibit 1
Peer Review of CPA Firms: An Overview of AICPA Requirements

Purpose of This Tool

This tool is prepared to educate audit committee members about the practice-monitoring programs over the accounting and auditing practices of the substantial majority of U.S. CPA firms. This tool is intended to help audit committee members understand the obligations and oversight of CPA firms. CPA firms that audit public companies are also subject to periodic inspections by the Public Company Accounting Oversight Board. See the section "Public Company Accounting Oversight Board Inspection."

Over the course of the 1990s, peer review requirements for CPA firms, and the schedule for administering them, changed considerably. Currently, most CPA firms undergo a review of their accounting and auditing practice at least once every three years. This tool will help audit committee members understand the requirements for a peer review, how to interact with auditors concerning their peer review, and why the auditor's peer review should be important to an audit committee member.

Peer Review of a CPA Firm

A peer review of a CPA firm can be used by an audit committee as a tool to assess whether the CPA firm it hires or is considering hiring:

1. Has a system of quality control for its accounting and auditing practice that has been designed to meet the requirements of the AICPA's Statements on Quality Control Standards (SQCSs).

2. Is complying with that system of quality control during the peer review year(s) to provide the firm with reasonable assurance of complying with professional standards.

The AICPA's standards regarding quality control provide requirements in the quality control areas of auditor independence, integrity, and objectivity; audit personnel management; acceptance and continuance of audit clients and engagements; audit engagement performance; and firm quality control monitoring. Professional standards include generally accepted auditing standards (GAAS), generally accepted accounting principles (GAAP), generally accepted government auditing standards (GAGAS), and the standards on auditor independence.

To have its peer review, a CPA firm will engage another CPA firm to perform the review. However, in selecting its peer reviewer, the reviewing CPA firm must be independent of the CPA firm, and must be qualified to perform the review. The Peer Review Committee (the body responsible for evaluating and accepting peer reviews) monitors firm independence and approves the peer review team prior to the peer review taking place.

Peer Review Reports

There are three types of peer review reports, namely, unmodified, modified, and adverse.

1. An unmodified report means the reviewed firm's system of quality control has been designed to meet the requirements of the quality control standards for an accounting and auditing practice and the system was being complied with during the peer review year(s) to provide the firm with reasonable assurance of complying with professional standards.

2. A modified report means the design of the firm's system of quality control created a condition in which the firm did not have reasonable assurance of complying with professional standards or that the firm's degree of compliance with its quality control policies and procedures did not provide it with reasonable assurance of complying with professional standards.

3. An adverse report means there are significant deficiencies in the design of the firm's system of quality control, pervasive instances of noncompliance with the system as a whole, or both, resulting in several material failures to adhere to professional standards on engagements.

Typically, unmodified and modified reports are accompanied by a letter of comments. A letter of comments describes matters that the peer reviewer believes resulted in conditions in which there was more than a remote possibility that the firm would not comply with professional standards and sets forth recommendations regarding those matters. A letter of comments is not prepared when an adverse report is issued as all deficiencies, comments, and recommendations are contained in the report itself.

The reviewed firm is required to respond in writing to the peer reviewer's comments on matters in the peer review report and/or in the letter of comments (called the letter of response). The response describes the actions taken or planned with respect to each matter in the report and/or the letter.

We recommend that audit committees request a copy of the auditor's latest peer review report and discuss both the report and the letter of comments with the auditor. If a report is modified or adverse, the audit committee should discuss the reasons as part of its assessment as to whether or not it should engage or continue to engage the auditor.

Common Misconceptions of Peer Review

1. Fiction: A peer review evaluates every engagement audited by a CPA firm. Fact: A peer review is performed using a risk-based approach. A peer reviewer must review enough engagements to obtain reasonable assurance that the reviewed firm is complying with its quality control policies and procedures. Therefore, it is possible that the review would not disclose all weaknesses in the system of quality control or all instances of lack of compliance with it.

2. Fiction: An unmodified report provides assurance with respect to every engagement conducted by the firm. Fact: Every engagement conducted by a firm is not included in the scope of a peer review nor is every aspect of each engagement reviewed. The peer review includes reviewing all key areas of engagements selected.

3. Fiction: If a firm receives a letter of comments, its system of quality control is inadequate. Fact: The criterion for including an item in the letter of comments is whether the item resulted in a condition being created in which there was more than a remote possibility that the firm would not comply with professional standards on accounting and auditing engagements. Because this is a very low threshold, most peer reviews result in the issuance of a letter of comments.

Questions for the Auditor Regarding Peer Review

The following questions are ones that the audit committee should consider asking its auditors in order to gain a better understanding of the firm's peer review experience.

Questions for the Auditor Regarding Peer Review			
Question	**Yes**	**No**	**Comments**
1. Is the firm subject to peer review? If not, please explain.			
2. What do the findings and recommendations in the letter of comments mean?			
3. Does the firm's letter of response demonstrate that the firm is committed to making the changes necessary to improve its practice? If not, please explain.			
4. If the peer review report was modified, explain why.			
5. Did the firm correct the deficiencies noted in either the peer review report and/or the letter of comments? If not, please explain.			

Question	Yes	No	Comments
6. Did the Peer Review Committee request any follow-up actions? If so, have these actions been carried out?			
7. Was our company selected for review during the peer review? If so, were any negative responses noted?			
8. Was the engagement partner (and other key engagement team members) selected for review during the peer review? If so, were any negative responses noted on audits performed by them?			

Public Company Accounting Oversight Board Inspection

The Sarbanes-Oxley Act of 2002 ("Act") established the Public Company Accounting Oversight Board (PCAOB) to oversee the audits of issuers as defined in the Act. The PCAOB established an inspection program that will assess the degree of compliance of each registered public accounting firm and firm personnel with the Act, the rules of the PCAOB, the rules of the SEC, and professional standards, in connection with its performance of audits, issuance of audit reports, and related matters involving issuers as defined in the Act. Registered public accounting firms auditing more than 100 issuers are subject to inspection by the PCAOB on a yearly basis. All other registered firms will be subject to an inspection every three years.

Source: Adapted from the AICPA Audit Committee Toolkit, Copyright © 2004 by the AICPA, Inc., New York.

The peer review pointed out several deficiencies that had to be addressed in a report to be filed with the Ohio State Board of Accountancy. The following summarizes the findings of the peer review:

1. KD assets that were supposedly being held by a brokerage firm called "Pennant Co." were not confirmed in writing. Instead, Tod Kazweski obtained verbal confirmation from Pennant for the $25 million balance. Kazweski failed to inform either Jorgan or Terez about the verbal confirmation from Pennant of the $25 million balance. The auditors failed to consider obtaining audit evidence from other sources to verify the brokerage account balance.

2. The auditors did not discover that KD had been audited prior to Rench & Bose's engagement, even though the firm's permanent file contained a document that referred to KD's prior CPA.

3. The auditors had not discussed audit matters with the prior auditors and did not discover that the prior auditors were fired from the audit of KD due to a difference of opinion over the application of an accounting principle.

4. There were no memos in Rench & Bose's KD audit working papers or anywhere else that discussed the fact that Tod Kazweski is the son of one of the general partners of KD.

Questions

1. Criticisms of the profession-run peer review program under the auspices of the AICPA and state CPA societies contributed to the takeover of the process by the PCAOB for public accounting firms that audit public companies that report to the SEC. In virtually all of the accounting frauds in the late 1990s and early 2000s, it was discovered that the peer reviewers noted no significant problems with the firms' quality controls.

Why was it important for the profession (through the regulations established by SOX that created the PCAOB) to "clean up its act" with respect to the usefulness of peer review reports? In other words, who are the stakeholders of the process and what are the needs that drive the peer review process?

2. What's wrong with accepting oral confirmation of balance sheet account balances with respect to conducting an audit in accordance with GAAS? Explain how the firm's failure to confirm the brokerage accounts might affect other areas of the audit where similar procedures are required.

Optional Question

PCAOB *Auditing Standard No. 7*, Engagement Quality Review,* establishes standards for peer reviewers of public companies with respect to audits and interim reviews. Review this standard and answer the following questions: (1) How do the standards established in *AS 7* relate to our discussion of ethics in Chapter 4 and the virtues discussed in Chapter 1? (2) What role does professional judgment play in conducting an audit and review with respect to the evaluation made by the peer reviewer?

*PCAOB, *Auditing Standard No. 7*, Engagement Quality Review, December 15, 2009, http://pcaobus.org/Standards/Auditing/Pages/Auditing_Standard_7.aspx.

Case 5-3

Imperial Valley Thrift & Loan—Part II[*]

Part I of the case in Chapter 2 describes the audit and internal control issues that arose in the audit of Imperial Valley Thrift & Loan. That part emphasizes the client's position on the collectibility of loan amounts and current value of the collateral for the loan. Part II explores the auditor's positions on verification matters and going-concern issues. If you were not assigned to do Part I, then you should go back to Chapter 2 and review the facts of Case 2-10.

Outstanding Loans

The management of Imperial Valley Thrift & Loan placed a great deal of pressure on the auditors (Jacobs, Stanley & Co.) to reduce the amount of the loan write-offs. It maintained that the customers were "good for the money." Managers pointed out those payments to date on most of the loans had been made on a timely basis. However, it was the auditors' contention that the payments to date, which were mostly annual interest amounts, were not necessarily a good indication that timely balloon principal payments would be made. They felt it was very difficult to adequately evaluate collectibility of the balloon payments, primarily because the borrowers' source of cash for loan repayment had not been identified. They could not objectively audit or support borrowers' good intentions to pay or undocumented resources as represented by client management.

To ensure that they were not being naïve about the thrift and loan industry, the auditors checked with colleagues in another office of the firm who knew more about this type of business. One professional in this office explained that the real secret to this business is to follow up ruthlessly with any nonpayer. The auditors certainly did not feel this was being done by Imperial Valley management.

The auditors knew that Manny Gonzalez was a potential source of investment capital for Imperial Valley. They believed it was very important to give Gonzalez an accurate picture because if a rosier picture were painted than actually existed, and Gonzalez made an investment, then the audit firm would be a potential target for a lawsuit.

Board of Trustees

The auditors approached the nine-member board of trustees that oversaw the operations of Imperial Valley, three of whom also served on the audit committee. Of the nine board members, four were officers with the banks and five were outsiders. All members of the audit committee were outsiders. The auditors had hoped to solicit the support of the audit committee in dealing with management over the audit opinion issue, as detailed in the next section. However, the auditors were concerned about the fact that all five outsiders had loans outstanding from

Imperial Valley that carried 2 percent interest payments until the due date in two years. Perhaps not coincidentally, all five had supported management with respect to the validity of collateral and loan collectibility issues with customers.

Auditor Responsibilities

The management of Imperial Valley Thrift & Loan was pressuring the auditors to give an unqualified opinion. If the auditors decided to give a qualified or an adverse opinion or to disclaim an opinion, then, in the client's view, this would present a picture to their customers and the regulators that their financial statements were not accurate. The client maintained this would be a blow to its integrity and would shake depositors' confidence in the institution.

On one hand, the auditors were very cognizant of their responsibility to the regulatory authority, and they were also concerned about providing an accurate picture of Imperial Valley's financial health to Manny Gonzalez or other potential investors. On the other hand, they wondered whether they were holding the client to standards that were too strict. After all, the audit report issued in the preceding year by the previous auditors contained only an explanatory paragraph on the capital impairment issue. They also wondered whether the doors of the institution would be closed by the regulators if they gave an adverse opinion or disclaimed an opinion. What impact could this action have on the depositors and the economic health of the community? Bill Stanley wondered whose interests they were really representing—depositors, shareholders, management, the local community, or regulators, or all of these.

Stanley knew that he would soon have to make a recommendation about the type of audit opinion to be issued on the 2010 financial statements of Imperial Valley Thrift & Loan. Before approaching the advisory partner on the engagement, Stanley drafted the memo on the next page to file:

Questions

1. Assume Imperial Valley Thrift & Loan was a publicly owned financial institution subject to the requirements of SOX with its stock listed on the New York Stock Exchange. Using the facts of the case and any other assumptions you may want to make, evaluate the bank's compliance with internal controls and other corporate governance requirements of the act and the NYSE. (These requirements are discussed in Chapter 3.)

2. Assume you were asked to review the information in Parts I and II as the advisory partner on the audit of Imperial Valley Thrift & Loan. Using the relevant steps in the decision-making model presented in Chapter 2, analyze the case and come up with a decision on what type of opinion to recommend to management.

*The first part of this case appears in Chapter 2 (Case 2-10).

Memo: Going-Concern Question

The question of the going-concern status of Imperial Valley Thrift & Loan is being raised because of the client's continuing operating losses and high level of loan losses. The client lost $920,000 after audit adjustments in 2010. This is in addition to a loss of $780,000 in 2009. Imperial Valley has also reported a loss of $45,000 for the first two months of 2011.

Imperial Valley is also out of compliance with regulatory capital requirements. After audit adjustments, the client has net equity capital of $610,000 as of December 31, 2010. The Arizona Department of Corporations requires a 6:1 ratio of thrift certificates to capital. As of December 31, 2010, these regulations would require net equity capital of $1,232,000. Imperial Valley was therefore undercapitalized by $622,000 at that date, and no additional capital contributions have been made subsequent to December 31. It is possible, however, that either the parent company, Nuevo Financial Group, or a private investor, Manny Gonzalez, will contribute additional equity capital.

We have concluded that there is a substantial doubt about the bank's ability to continue in business. The reasons for this conclusion include the following:

- The magnitude of losses, particularly loan losses, implies that Imperial Valley is not well managed.
- The losses are continuing in 2011. Annualized losses to date, without any provision for loan losses, are $270,000.
- Additional equity capital has not been contributed to date, although Gonzalez has $600,000 available.
- Our review of client loan files and lending policies raises an additional concern that loan losses may continue. If this happens, it would only exacerbate the conditions mentioned herein.

We also believe that it is not possible to test the liquidation value of the assets at this time should Imperial Valley cease to operate. The majority of client assets are loans receivable. These would presumably have to be discounted in order to be sold. In addition, there is some risk that the borrowers will simply stop making payments.

In conclusion, it is our opinion that a going-concern question exists for Imperial Valley Thrift & Loan at December 31, 2010. Pending the resolution of the question of capital adequacy, at a minimum, our audit report will include an explanatory paragraph describing the substantial doubt we have about Imperial Valley's ability to continue as a going concern. We should also consider the possibility of issuing a qualified opinion.

Case 5-4

Audit Client Considerations

Lanny Beaudean joined the CPA firm of Cardinal & Coyote LLP in 2008 after working for two years for the IRS in Phoenix, Arizona. The firm is a second-tier CPA firm just below the Big Four in size. Beaudean had passed all four parts of the CPA Exam in Arizona and decided to work for a locally based CPA firm with international clients to gain a broad base of experience that might help him become a CFO at a public company in the future. Beaudean has been advancing rapidly and just became a senior at Cardinal & Coyote.

Yancy Corliss is a new audit partner at Cardinal & Coyote. One day Corliss was summoned to the office of Sharon Rules, the managing partner of the firm. Rules told Corliss that she had been approached by a new client, Jost Furniture International. Jost is a large southwestern chain of home furniture rental catering to young upscale individuals who might live in a city for two years or so and then move on. It recently opened an office in Canada and plans to expand to Europe in the not-too-distant future. Top management at Jost seemed to imply that the firm would get the audit as long as it submitted a reasonable bid.

Rules asked Corliss to do background checks on Jost and make whatever inquiries were necessary to assess the potential business risk of Jost as a future client. Corliss was given three days to do the work and report back to Rules with a recommendation. If the decision is to go ahead, then Cardinal & Coyote would submit a bid and compete with one other CPA firm for the account. The firm believes it will be a lucrative account, especially since the company has been in an expansion mode and will require advice on acquisitions and other advisory services in the future.

Corliss assembled his team to review the background and other information about Jost Furniture. Corliss asked Beaudean to head up the assessment and report back to Corliss in two days. During that time, Beaudean would have two other staff members to help with the assignment. Beaudean was excited about his first opportunity to work on new client assessment.

Beaudean met with Vinnie Gabelli, a transplanted Brooklyn native who had graduated from Arizona State University (ASU) at Phoenix. Gabelli was like a fish out of water in Arizona even though he had spent 16 months in the master's of accounting program at ASU. Gabelli thought a prickly pear was someone who could not make it in Staten Island and moved to Brooklyn for a better life.

Gabelli told Beaudean that he welcomed the opportunity to work with a native of Phoenix and learn about its colorful history. Beaudean also asked Jackie Oloff, a native of Minneapolis, to join the team. Jackie had moved to Phoenix two years ago with her husband, who is a professor of accounting at ASU. The team discussed mutual responsibilities, data sources for the information, key areas of risk, and then they broke up to start their work. At the end of the day, the team reassembled to share information. Here is a brief list of the findings:

1. The predecessor firm had helped Jost Furniture with its initial public offering and audited the financial statements of the company for five years. The firm resigned the account in 2007, following the issuance of a modified opinion on the 2006 financial statements. The firm had issued an unqualified opinion with an explanatory paragraph that raised questions about the ability of Jost to continue as a going concern because of persistent operating losses that threatened the company's ability to secure needed financing.

2. A second firm audited the financial statements for 2007. That firm also raised going-concern questions and was dismissed by Jost's top management.

3. Jost's financial statements for 2008 and 2009 were audited by a third firm that was dismissed after two years.

4. The financial statements for 2010 had not been audited and on March 19, 2011, the CEO of Jost Furniture, Jerry Jost, approached Sharon Rules at a community event and asked her to submit a bid for the Jost audit. Jost asked that the bid be submitted by March 23.

5. A memorandum to the file prepared by Rules indicated that Jost had admitted to Rules that the company had past problems with various auditors, but Jost assured Rules the going-concern issues had been resolved. He also told Rules that the company's controller had recently quit, the third time in four years there had been a turnover at that position. Jost told Rules the company had two candidates and he wanted her to help with the final decision since the CPA firm would work closely with the controller.

6. Beaudean, with the help of Gabelli and Oloff, reviewed the financial statements of Jost Furniture for the past four years during which time going-concern explanatory paragraphs had been issued. They went through a checklist of risk assessment issues for new clients and stopped when they came to the following: Verify the circumstances of any prior auditor dismissal or withdrawal by first asking the client for permission to approach the predecessor auditor(s). All three auditors felt this should be done by Yancy Corliss.

At the meeting at the end of the first day, the auditors discussed the unusual number of auditor changes in a short period of time apparently due to going-concern issues that were raised in the audit reports for the years 2006 through 2009. Beaudean asked Gabelli to contact the two banks where the company does business and check into its payment record. Oloff had a past business relationship with Miles

Frazer, the attorney for Jost Furniture. Oloff agreed to contact Frazer to determine whether there are any outstanding litigation issues or other legal matters that the firm should know about. They all agreed to get these matters done by the end of the second day and a meeting was set for 5:00 p.m.

Gabelli found out that a $1 million loan payable to Phoenix Second National Bank had been overdue before payment had been made March 15, 2011. The president of the bank told Gabelli that Jost had been in violation of a debt covenant agreement that obligated Jost to maintain a current ratio of 1.5:1 at all times and that the bank was concerned about Jost's ability to continue as a going concern, pointing out that Jost had gone below the ratio twice. The first time Jost had violated the covenant, the bank accepted the explanation of a temporary cash flow problem. The bank granted the company a three-month extension to meet the requirements of the debt covenant. The bank subsequently found out the cash flow problem had been due to the fact Jerry Jost withdrew $500,000 from the Jost cash account at Second National Bank to help put a down payment on a mortgage loan to buy an upscale house in Scottsdale. The second time it occurred, the bank began foreclosure on the loan on January 31, 2011, but by the time the process had been completed, Jost had paid off the entire $1 million balance.

Oloff had no luck with the Frazer, the attorney for Jost. When she called his offices, the secretary always told Oloff that Frazer was on another line and she'd take a message. When Oloff asked to leave a voice-mail message, she was told Frazer did not have voice mail. How about leaving an e-mail message? she asked. No e-mail either. Can I text him, tweet him, or just do it the old-fashioned way and set up an appointment? No, no, no were the answers. Oloff had left five messages for Frazer in the time before the meeting. She had nothing to report except to make an editorial comment about lawyer responsiveness, or lack thereof.

At first, Jost had side-stepped Corliss's request for permission to speak with the predecessor auditor. Jost claimed that there had been a "personality conflict" and Jost was afraid the auditor would speak negatively about the company. Jost did agree after Corliss reminded him it was a required part of the procedures auditors follow in making the client acceptance decision.

At 5:00 p.m. on March 22, the auditors met in the firm's conference room to discuss their findings. After hearing about Gabelli's concerns and Oloff's lack of success with Frazer, Beaudean expressed serious concerns about taking on Jost as a client.

Questions

1. Why is it important to do the kind of due diligence testing and risk assessment review conducted by Cardinal & Coyote prior to determining whether to make a bid for the audit of a potential client? What are the potential red flags with respect to the Jost audit? If you were Yancy Corliss, would you go ahead and recommend to Sharon Rules that the firm should submit a bid for the Jost audit? Why or why not?

2. Regardless of your answer to question 1, assume Corliss decides to recommend to Rules that the firm should make a bid for the Jost Furniture audit. Beaudean seems surprised and asks what other factors Corliss might have considered in making the decision. Corliss is quite blunt and says: "I am a new partner in the firm. I have to bring in new business. This client is a slam dunk. If we make a reasonably competitive bid, we will get the account."

   a. Why do you think there is so much pressure in public accounting to bring in new clients? Is this a good thing or are there potential risks that might go unnoticed or ignored? How might the decision by Corliss present an impediment to making sound audit decisions later on?

   b. Some CPA firms have started to add indemnification clauses to their engagement letters that state the firm is not responsible for fraud when the client knowingly misrepresented financial information during the course of gathering evidence and testing account balances. Do you think these clauses are ethical? Why or why not?

3. Typically, when there is a going-concern issue with a client, the CPA firm issues an unqualified opinion with an explanatory paragraph. Given the limited facts of the case, do you believe this type of opinion is justified? Do you think the firm should consider issuing a qualified opinion or disclaim an opinion? Why or why not? How about withdrawal from the engagement?

Case 5-5

Krispy Kreme Doughnuts, Inc.

On March 4, 2009, the SEC reached an agreement with Krispy Kreme Doughnuts, Inc., and issued a cease-and-desist order to settle charges that the company fraudulently inflated or otherwise misrepresented its earnings for the fourth quarter of its 2003 fiscal year, and each quarter in 2004. By its improper accounting, Krispy Kreme avoided lowering its earnings guidance and improperly reported for that time period earnings per share; these amounts exceeded its previously announced EPS guidance by one cent.[1]

The primary transactions described in this case are "round-trip" transactions. In each case, Krispy Kreme paid money to a franchise with the understanding that the franchise would pay the money back to Krispy Kreme in a pre-arranged manner that would allow the company to record additional pretax income in an amount roughly equal to the funds originally paid to the franchisee.

There were three round-trip transactions cited in the SEC consent agreement. The first occurred in June 2003, the second quarter of fiscal 2004. In connection with the reacquisition of a franchise in Texas, Krispy Kreme increased the price it paid for the franchise by $800,000 (i.e., from $65,000,000 to $65,800,000) in return for the franchise purchasing from Krispy Kreme certain doughnut-making equipment. On the day of the closing, Krispy Kreme debited the franchise's bank account for $744,000, which was the aggregate list price of the equipment. The additional revenue boosted Krispy Kreme's quarterly net income by approximately $365,000 after taxes.

The second transaction occurred at the end of October 2003, four days from the closing of Krispy Kreme's third quarter of fiscal 2004, in connection with the reacquisition of a franchise in Michigan. Krispy Kreme agreed to increase the price it paid for the franchise by $535,463, and recorded the transaction on its books and records as if it had been reimbursed for two amounts that had been in dispute with the Michigan franchise. This overstated Krispy Kreme's net income in the third quarter by approximately $310,000 after taxes.

The third transaction occurred in January 2004, in the fourth quarter of fiscal 2004. It involved the reacquisition of the remaining interests in a franchise in California. Krispy Kreme owned a majority interest in the California franchise and, beginning on or about October 2003, initiated negotiations with the remaining interest holders for acquisition of their interests. During the negotiations, Krispy Kreme demanded payment of a "management fee" in consideration

of Krispy Kreme's handling of the management duties since October 2003. Krispy Kreme proposed that the former franchise manager receive a distribution from his capital account, which he could then pay back to Krispy Kreme as a management fee. No adjustment was made to the purchase price for his interest in the California franchise to reflect this distribution. As a result, the former franchise manager received the full value for his franchise interest, including his capital account, plus an additional amount provided that he paid back that amount as the management fee. Krispy Kreme, acting through the California franchise, made a distribution to the former franchise manager in the amount of $597,415, which was immediately transferred back to Krispy Kreme as payment of the management fee. The company booked this fee, thereby overstating net income in the fourth quarter by approximately $361,000.

In May 2004, Krispy Kreme disclosed disappointing earnings for the first quarter of fiscal 2005 and lowered its future earnings guidance. Subsequently, as a result of the transactions already described, as well as the discovery of other accounting errors, on January 4, 2005, Krispy Kreme announced that it would restate its financial statements for 2003 and 2004. The restatement reduced net income for those years by $2,420,000 and $8,524,000, respectively.

In August 2005, a special committee of the company's board issued a report to the SEC following an internal investigation of the fraud at Krispy Kreme. The report states that every Krispy Kreme employee or franchisee who was interviewed "repeatedly and firmly" denied deliberately scheming to distort the company's earnings or being given orders to do so; yet, in carefully nuanced language, the Krispy Kreme investigators hinted at the possibility of a willful cooking of the books. "The number, nature and timing of the accounting errors strongly suggest that they resulted from an intent to manage earnings," the report said. "Further, CEO Scott Livengood and COO John Tate failed to establish proper financial controls and the company's earnings may have been manipulated to please Wall Street." The committee also criticized the company's board of directors, which it said was "overly deferential in its relationship with Livengood and failed to adequately oversee management decisions."

Krispy Kreme materially misstated its earnings in its financial statements filed with the SEC between the fourth quarter of fiscal 2003 and the fourth quarter of fiscal 2004. In each of these quarters, Krispy Kreme falsely reported that it had achieved earnings equal to its EPS guidance plus one cent in the fourth quarter of fiscal 2003 through the third quarter of fiscal 2004 or, in the case of the fourth quarter of fiscal 2004, earnings that met its EPS guidance.

The SEC cited Krispy Kreme for violations of Section 13(a) of the Exchange Act and Rules 12b-20, 13a-1, and 13a-13

---

[1] Securities and Exchange Commission, Accounting and Auditing Enforcement Release No. 2941, *In the Matter of Krispy Kreme Doughnuts, Inc.,* March 4, 2009, www.sec.gov/litigation/admin/2009/34-59499.pdf.

thereunder, which require every issuer of a security registered pursuant to Section 12 of the Exchange Act to file with the commission all the necessary information to make the financial statements not misleading. The company was also sanctioned for its failure to keep books, records, and accounts that, in reasonable detail, accurately and fairly reflect their transactions and dispositions of their assets. Finally, Krispy Kreme was cited for failing to devise and maintain a system of internal accounting controls sufficient to provide reasonable assurances that transactions are recorded as necessary to permit preparation of financial statements in accordance with generally accepted accounting principles.

On March 4, 2009, the SEC reached agreement with three former top Krispy Kreme officials, including one-time chair, CEO, and president Scott Livengood. Livengood, former COO John Tate, and Randy Casstevens, the CFO, all agreed to pay more than $783,000 for violating accounting laws and fraud in connection with their management of the company.

Livengood was found in violation of fraud, reporting provisions, and false certifications. Tate was found in violation of fraud, reporting provisions, record keeping, and internal controls. Casstevens was found in violation of fraud, reporting provisions, record keeping, internal controls, and false certifications. Livengood's settlement required him to pay about $542,000, which included $467,000 of what the SEC considered as the "disgorgement of ill-gotten gains and prejudgment interest" and $75,000 in civil penalties. Tate's settlement required him to return $96,549 and pay $50,000 in civil penalties, while Casstevens had to return $68,964 and pay $25,000 in civil penalties. Krispy Kreme was not required to pay a civil penalty because of its cooperation with the SEC in the case.

Questions

1. Why did the round-trip transactions engaged in by Krispy Kreme and its franchisees violate revenue recognition rules?

2. The internal report prepared by the special committee of the board states: "The number, nature and timing of the accounting errors strongly suggest that they resulted from an intent to manage earnings." Explain why you think the board came to this conclusion?

3. Evaluate the ethics of Krispy Kreme's accounting for franchise amounts.

Optional Question

Prime accounting issues with respect to accounting for franchise activities include how to recognize revenue on the individual sale of franchise territories and on the transactions that arise in connection with the continuing relationship between the franchisor and franchisee. The *Krispy Kreme* case describes three transactions between the company and its franchisees that created false earnings. Review *Statement of Financial Accounting Standards (SFAS) No. 45,* Accounting for Franchise Fee Revenue, and explain specifically how Krispy Kreme's transactions violated *SFAS 45.* (See www. fasb.org/pdf/fas45.pdf.)

Case 5-6

Marcus Yamabuto

Marcus Yamabuto graduated from Washington State University in June 2010. He began his career working for Dunco, a public company that manufactures plasma television monitors. Dunco is the original equipment manufacturer (OEM) of 42- through 64-inch plasma screens. The company sells its monitors to major manufacturers in the United States and overseas. Marcus was hired directly by the internal audit department and reports to Francey Gordon, the director of internal auditing.

Marcus was assigned to review sale documents and freight bills to determine the amount of freight, the terms of the sale, and the proper cutoff treatment. During the course of his examination, Marcus discovered $2.4 million that was prematurely recognized as revenue by the accountants for the year ended December 31, 2010. He identified the problem by matching the invoices with corresponding freight bills and found that the shipping date of the transaction was January 2, 2011. However, there was a note signed by the freight forwarder: "picked up for shipment at Dunco warehouse on December 31, 2010."

Questions

1. Marcus Yamabuto is a staff internal auditor with virtually no real-world experience. He questions the appropriateness of recording the $2.4 million as earned revenue in 2010. He's not sure what to do, but does know one thing: he doesn't want to rock the boat. Given that Marcus is not a CPA, CMA, and he doesn't hold the CIA, why should he be concerned about ethical standards in this case?

2. How should Marcus determine whether the $2.4 million transaction was material? What factors would you consider in making that determination?

3. Assume you are Marcus and have been told that the company will adjust for the $2.4 million revenue transaction by putting through a prior period adjustment in 2011. Would you be willing to go along with this treatment? Why or why not?

Case 5-7

The Audit Report

Zoe Foster is the manager in charge of the audit of Sky Hook, Inc., a publicly owned professional sports consulting organization located in Oklahoma City. Sky Hook's stock is listed on the New York Stock Exchange. Foster reviewed the draft audit report on Sky Hook in Exhibit 1 that was prepared by the senior in charge of the audit, Frank D'Amato. Foster calls D'Amato to his office and has the following conversation:

Foster: Listen, Frank, you need to go back and redo the audit report for Sky Hook.

D'Amato: Why? What's wrong?

Foster: I think you need to figure that out for yourself. I realize this is the first time you have been asked to do an audit report, and there were a few complications in this audit, but some of the mistakes are Audit 101 issues.

D'Amato: Can you give some guidance here?

Foster: Let's just say we can't issue an unqualified opinion because of the difference of opinion with the client on the value to be used for the inventory held at various locations in Oklahoma. We had differences with the client

on current value for the limited number of locations we looked at and we believe the amount is material. We need to somehow come up with a number for the inventory write-down for all locations based on those limited observations. That amount undoubtedly will necessitate a qualification.

D'Amato: When do you want the revised draft?

Foster: Yesterday!

D'Amato went back to his office and reviewed the hardcopy file to look for workpapers that might provide support for the audit opinion. The problem was that no other information about the opinion existed. That meant D'Amato would have to look at the computer files to see if backup inventory information existed. Instead, D'Amato decided to telephone Thunder Hawkins, the sole staff member on the Sky Hook audit. Hawkins had served on the audit engagement team for three years. She had been assigned to another audit, so she told D'Amato she could talk for only a few minutes. D'Amato asked whether she recalled any issues with the Sky Hook inventory held in various Oklahoma locations.

Exhibit 1
Independent Auditor's Report

To the Management of Sky Hook, Inc.

We have audited the accompanying balance sheet of Sky Hook, Inc., as of December 31, 2010, and the related statements of income and retained earnings for the year then ended. These statements are the responsibility of the Company's management. Our responsibility is to express an opinion on these financial statements based on our audit.

We conducted our audit in accordance with generally accepted auditing standards prepared by the American Institute of CPAs. Those standards require that we plan and perform the audit to determine whether the financial statements are free of material misstatement. An audit includes examining evidence supporting the amounts and disclosures in the financial statements. An audit also includes assessing the accounting principles used and significant estimates that we made as well as evaluating the overall financial statement presentation. We believe that our audit provides a reasonable basis for an opinion.

In our opinion, the financial statements referred to above present fairly the financial position of Sky Hook as of December 31, 2010, and the results of its operations for the year then ended in conformity with generally accepted accounting principles established by the Financial Accounting Standards Board.

Sooners & Cowboys, LLC
Oklahoma City, Oklahoma

December 31, 2010

Hawkins told D'Amato that the physical inventory in Oklahoma City was never observed and, as far as she knew, the inventory was verified in only 3 of 20 locations. There was a difference of opinion with management on valuation at those 3 locations of about $100,000. She stated, "We didn't know what to do about the other locations so we just accepted management's numbers." D'Amato asked whether anyone on the audit questioned this position. "No," replied Hawkins. "We never had any problems with management so we accepted their numbers unquestioningly."

Questions

1. Describe the deficiencies in generally accepted auditing standards with respect to the audit of Sky Hook.

2. Assume Sky Hook, with D'Amato's help, traced inventory transactions and determined that the inventory was overstated by about $500,000 at December 31, 2009, and by $750,000 at December 31, 2010. Redraft the audit report using appropriate language.

Case 5-8

Edvid, Inc.

Charles Hutton is the partner in charge of the Edvid, Inc., audit for the year ended December 31, 2010. Hutton's firm was hired on September 30, 2010, to replace the previous auditor, who had audited the company's financial statements since it was formed in 2007.

Edvid is a privately owned company that produces training programs on DVD for sale to businesses and government agencies. The company has built up a library of DVDs that it offers to business customers on two-year contracts. After that, the training programs typically become outdated so the customers turn them in for replacement products. The old DVDs are sold at a discount to the Federal Emergency Management Administration (FEMA).

Edvid's business model is unique in that business customers must pay a $1,000 fee to join the program and then they are eligible to rent up to 10 DVDs over a two-year period. The tapes are developed by Edvid based on the needs of the members of its program. Edvid mails out questionnaires frequently to determine customer interest in training topics. It has its own professional instructors who develop the material and then it is produced on DVDs for distribution.

A typical contract with a customer who *rents 10 tapes for two years* appears in Exhibit 1:

EXHIBIT 1
EDVID, INC.
Terms of Rental Contract

Total contract price/10 DVDs	$1,000	
Contract life (2 years)		
Payment terms:		
Initial payment	$ 300	
Quarterly payments (7 quarters @ $100)	700	1,000
Costs associated with each 10 DVD rental contract:		
Royalties paid to instructors	75	
Advertising and promotion	25	
Commissions	60	
Telephone, postage, and printing	40	200

Edvid recognizes revenue on each contract, as shown in Exhibit 2:

EXHIBIT 2
EDVID, INC.
Revenue Recognition on Rental Contract

Payment Designation	Portion Recognized	Year
Initial payment ($300)	100%	1
Balance due ($700)	0	1
Balance due ($700)	100	2

Given its accounting approach, Edvid recognizes $300 net income from DVD rental in year 1 and $700 in year 2. During the audit of Edvid, Charles Hutton questions the delay in recognizing 70 percent of revenue. He points out to George Mutton, the CFO of Edvid, that since all of the costs are incurred up front with no service costs beyond that time, the company shows an arbitrarily low net income in the first year and relatively high net income in the second year. Mutton points out that by recognizing 70 percent of the revenue on all DVD contracts in the second year of the two-year period, the company is likely to show an increasing trend in profits over time as long as the number of contracts increases each year. Mutton emphasizes that such results have enabled Edvid to secure needed funding from venture capitalists each year since 2006.

Hutton is surprised that Mutton chose to delay recognition of 70 percent of the revenue. Typically, most of his clients would want to recognize as much revenue as possible in the first year of a two-year contract. He decides to review income data for the past three years. Assume all these amounts are material (see Exhibit 3).

EXHIBIT 3
EDVID, INC.
Contract Revenue Compared with Net Income
For the Years Ended December 31, 2007–2009

Year	Total Revenue (all contracts: in millions)	Net Income (in millions)
2007	$108	$ 8.6
2008	132	11.2
2009	164	14.8

Hutton speaks with Shirley Sutton, the firm's technical advisory partner. Sutton points out that there is no justification for delaying the recording of 70 percent of the revenue. Hutton agrees and asks her to work with him to develop an alternative that would conform to GAAP so that he can approach the client with the proposed new method of accounting for DVD rental revenue.

Questions

1. Compute the following:
   a. The percentage of net income to revenue for each of the three years.
   b. The percentage increase in revenue for the time period 2007 through 2009.
   c. The percentage increase in net income for the time period 2007 through 2009.

Do these numbers seem to support Hutton's concerns about Edvid's current accounting for DVD contracts?

2. Briefly describe the general rules for recognizing revenue in accounting? Explain why Edvid's current accounting method does not comply with GAAP. Assume you are Shirley Sutton. Identify a method of accounting for the revenue that would better reflect the true earnings of Edvid on DVD rentals.

3. Assume Hutton informs Mutton of the firm's opinion that, going forward, the company must change its accounting for the DVD contracts to comply with the method you described in the previous answer. What impact should the decision have on the reported results prior to 2010? What, if any, disclosures should be made in the audit report on the December 31, 2010, financial statements?

Case 5-9

Fannie Mae: The Government's Enron

Background

The Federal National Mortgage Association (Fannie Mae) and the Federal Home Loan Mortgage Corporation (Freddie Mac) are government-sponsored entities (GSEs) that operate under congressional charters to "help lower- and middle-income Americans buy homes." Both entities receive special treatment aimed at increasing home ownership by decreasing the cost for homeowners to borrow money. They do this by purchasing home mortgages from banks, guaranteeing them, and then reselling them to investors. This helps the banks eliminate the credit and interest rate risk as well as lengthening the mortgage period. Fannie Mae and Freddie Mac receive advantages over commercial banks including (1) the U.S. Treasury can buy $2.25 billion of each company's debt; (2) Fannie Mae and Freddie Mac receive exemption from state and local taxes; and (3) the implied government backing gives them the ability to take on large amounts of home loans without increasing their low cost of capital.

Fannie Mae makes money either by buying, guaranteeing, and then reselling home mortgages for a fee or by buying mortgages, holding them, and then taking on the risk. By selling the mortgages, Fannie Mae eliminates the interest rate risk. There is less profit from this conservative approach than by holding the mortgages they buy. By holding the mortgages, Fannie Mae can make money on the spread because it has such a low cost of capital. In 1998, Fannie Mae's holdings hit a peak of $375 billion of mortgages and mortgage-backed securities on its own books, not to mention the more than $1 trillion of mortgages it guaranteed. This process of holding mortgages on its books helped Fannie Mae expand rapidly. It also stimulated unprecedented profit growth because there was more profit to be made by keeping the mortgages than by guaranteeing and then reselling to other investors.

The reasons for growth in the telecommunications sector in the 1990s were, in part, the building of overcapacity in telecommunications equipment inventory based on the belief the economic growth bubble of the early 1990s would never end. Fannie Mae was similarly affected by the bubble in making and holding home mortgage loans. Just as telecommunication companies such as Global Crossing and Qwest were motivated to keep revenue and net income increasing quarter after quarter, the pressure also was on the top management of Fannie Mae to keep up the pace of growth. Fannie Mae's CEO, Franklin Raines, was so optimistic that at an investor conference in May 1999 he claimed, "The future is so bright that I am willing to set as a goal that our earnings per share will double over the next five years."[1]

As growth pressures continued, Fannie Mae began to use more derivatives to hedge interest rate risk. Critics looked at Fannie Mae's portfolio and expressed concern that with the risk involved in using derivatives, it may be at risk of defaulting. They pointed out that unlike federally guaranteed commercial bank deposits and the partial government guarantee of pension obligations through the Pension Benefit Guaranty Corporation (PBGC), there was no federal guarantee of Fannie Mae. Behind the scenes Fannie Mae encouraged the concept that if it did default, the government would back it. This "too big to fail" philosophy turned out to be true later on, after the initial crisis in the 1990s, when the government bailed out Fannie Mae during the 2008–2009 financial crisis.[2]

In the 1990s, Fannie Mae was growing and the market loved it. Top executives were receiving large bonuses for the growing profits. The growth was due to increased risk but people believed that, at the end of the day, the government would come to the rescue of Fannie Mae if that became necessary.

The Accounting Scandal

The discovery of Fannie Mae's accounting scandal began in 2001 when Freddie Mac fired its auditor, (Arthur) Andersen, right after Enron's scandal exploded and the firm's existence seemed untenable. Freddie Mac then hired PricewaterhouseCoopers.

PwC looked very closely at Freddie Mac's books and found it had understated its profits in an attempt to smooth earnings. Freddie Mac agreed to a $5 billion restatement and fired many of its top executives. Meanwhile, Fannie Mae continued on its course and accused Freddie Mac of causing "collateral damage." The Fannie Mae Web site even included the statement, "Fannie Mae's reported financial results follow [GAAP] to the letter. There should be no question about our accounting." To a cynic, that statement may have had the unintended consequence of raising suspicion about Fannie Mae's accounting. After all, the markets had already been through it with Enron.

The government agency that regulated Fannie Mae and Freddie Mac at the time, the Office of Federal Housing Enterprise Oversight (OFHEO), had stated days before Freddie Mac's restatement that its internal controls were "accurate and reliable." Once the restatement was made public, OFHEO had no choice but to look deeper into Fannie Mae's

[1]Bethany McLean, "Fannie Mae: The Fall of Fannie Mae," *Fortune,* January 10, 2005.

[2]With a growing sense of crisis in U.S. financial markets, Fannie Mae and Freddie Mac were placed into conservatorship and the U.S. government committed to backstop the two government-sponsored enterprises (GSEs) with up to $200 billion in additional capital.

accounting to make sure such a serious misjudgment did not happen again.

OFHEO was much weaker than most regulatory agencies such as the SEC and Justice Department that went after Enron in the obstruction of justice case. Fannie Mae essentially established OFHEO in 1992 as the regulatory agency that oversaw its operations and accounting. Fannie Mae was able to control its own regulator because it had enough influence in Congress to have OFHEO's budget cut. Fannie Mae had political influence because of its connections with realtors, homebuilders, and trade groups. Fannie Mae also made large contributions to various organizations and gained political clout.

After the Enron debacle, the White House wanted to make sure to avoid another scandal. The government provided the funding needed to bring in an independent investigator—Deloitte & Touche—that uncovered massive accounting irregularities. In September 2004, OFHEO released results of its investigation and "accused Fannie of both willfully breaking accounting rules and fostering an environment of 'weak or nonexistent' internal controls."

The investigation focused on the use of derivatives and Fannie Mae's deferring derivative losses on the balance sheet, thus inflating profits. OFHEO and Deloitte believed that the derivative losses should be recorded on the income statement. The dispute involved the application of *Statement of Financial Accounting Standards (SFAS) No. 133,* Accounting for Derivative Instruments and Hedging Activities. The SEC's chief accountant determined that Fannie Mae failed to comply with the requirements for hedge accounting—including *SFAS 133*'s rigorous documentation requirements. Fannie Mae was required by law to document its derivative use and file with the SEC. But, "Fannie Mae's application of *SFAS 133* (and its predecessor standards, *SFAS 91*) did not comply in material respects with the accounting requirements" of GAAP.[3] In particular, Fannie Mae's practice of putting losses on the balance sheet rather than on the income statement resulted in overstated earnings and excess executive compensation.

OFHEO issued a report charging that in 1998 Fannie Mae recognized only $200 million in expenses when it was supposed to recognize $400 million. The underreporting of expenses led to earnings of $3.23 per share and a total of $27 million in executive bonuses. These charges prompted investigations by the SEC and the Justice Department.[4]

Two weeks after the OFHEO report and charges against Fannie Mae, the House of Representatives Subcommittee on Capital Markets called a hearing. Raines initially deflected criticisms by saying, "These accounting standards are highly complex and require determinations on which experts often disagree." Raines was quite convincing in defense of OFHEO charges that Fannie Mae executives had manipulated earnings in an attempt to increase bonuses. In the end, Raines won because the tone of the OFHEO reports made it seem as though the regulator was out to get Fannie Mae.

Perhaps feeling his oats after the victory in the House, Raines demanded that the SEC review OFHEO's findings. On December 15, 2004, the SEC announced that "Fannie did not comply 'in material respects' with accounting rules, and that as a result, Fannie would have to restate its results by more than $9 billion." Other than the $11 to $13 billion WorldCom fraud, the Fannie Mae fraud has the "dubious" honor of being the next largest fraud during the dark days of the late 1990s and early 2000s.

The OHFEO had been vindicated. The Fannie Mae board was told that both Raines and CFO Tim Howard had to be fired. Soon after, both resigned and Fannie Mae fired KPMG and appointed Deloitte & Touche as the new auditor. Deloitte was asked to audit the 2004 statements of Fannie Mae and reaudit previous statements from 2001.

OFHEO Report May 23, 2006

On May 23, 2006, OFHEO issued a more extensive report of a comprehensive three-year investigation that officially charged senior executives at Fannie Mae with manipulating accounting to collect millions of dollars in undeserved bonuses and to deceive investors. The fraud led to a $400 million civil penalty against Fannie Mae, more than three times the $125 million penalty imposed on Freddie Mac for understating its earnings by about $5 billion from 2000 to 2002 to minimize large profit swings. The $400 million is one of the largest penalties ever in an accounting fraud case. Of this amount, $350 million will be returned to investors damaged by the alleged violations as required by the Fair Funds for Investors provision of SOX.[5]

The OFHEO review involves nearly 8 million pages of documents and details what the agency calls an arrogant and unethical corporate culture. The report, which concluded an 18-month investigation led by former Senator Warren Rudman, was commissioned by Fannie Mae's board of directors. The final 2,600 page report charges Fannie Mae executives with perpetrating an $11 billion accounting fraud in order to meet earnings targets that would trigger $25 million in bonuses for top executives. The report charged former CFO J. Timothy Howard and former controller Leanne G. Spencer as the chief culprits. Along with former chair and CEO Franklin Raines, who earned $20 million (including $3 million in stock options) in 2003 and $17.7 million in 2002, these executives created a "culture that improperly stressed stable earnings growth." Rudman told reporters that the management

[3] Securities and Exchange Commission, SEC Form 8-K for Federal National Mortgage Association (Fannie Mae), December 28, 2004.

[4] Office of the Federal Housing Oversight, *Report of the Findings to Date: Special Examination of Fannie Mae,* September 17, 2004, www.ofheo.gov/media/pdf/FNMfindingstodate17septo4.pdf.

[5] OFHEO, *Report of the Findings to Date: Special Examination of Fannie Mae,* September 17, 2004, www.fanniemae.com/media/pdf/newsreleases/FNMSPECIALEXAM.pdf.

team Raines hired was "inadequate and in some respects not competent."[6]

Criticisms of Internal Environment

From 1998 to mid-2004, the smooth growths in profits and precisely hit earnings targets each quarter reported by Fannie Mae were illusions deliberately created by senior management using faulty accounting. The report shows that Fannie Mae's faults were not limited to violating accounting standards but included inadequate corporate governance systems that failed to identify excessive risk-taking and poor risk management. Randal Quarles, U.S. Treasury undersecretary for domestic finance at the time, said in a statement, "OFHEO's findings are a clear warning about the very real risk the improperly managed investment portfolios of [Fannie Mae and Freddie Mac] posed to the greater financial system."[7]

Fannie Mae agreed to make these changes in its operations:

- Limit the growth of its multibillion-dollar mortgage holdings, capping them at $727 billion.

- Make top-to-bottom changes in its corporate culture, accounting procedures, and ways of managing risk.

- Replace the chair of the board's audit committee. The board named accounting professor Dennis Beresford to replace audit committee chair Thomas Gerrity.

The report also faulted Fannie Mae's board of directors for failing to discover "a wide variety of unsafe and unsound practices" at the largest buyer and guarantor of home mortgages in the country. It signaled out senior management for failing to make investments in accounting systems, computer systems, other infrastructure, and staffing needed to support a sound internal control system, proper accounting, and GAAP-consistent financial reporting.

KPMG's Audits

As for the role of KPMG as Fannie Mae's auditors, the report alleges that external audits performed by the firm failed to include an adequate review of Fannie Mae's significant accounting policies for GAAP compliance. KPMG also improperly provided unqualified opinions on financial statements even though they contained significant departures from GAAP. The failure of KPMG to detect and disclose the serious weaknesses in policies, procedures, systems, and controls in Fannie Mae's financial accounting and reporting, coupled with the failure of the board of directors to oversee

KPMG properly, contributed to the unsafe and unsound conditions at Fannie Mae.

SEC Civil Action

The SEC filed a civil action against Fannie Mae on May 23, 2006, charging that it engaged in a financial fraud involving multiple violations of GAAP in connection with the preparation of its annual and quarterly financial statements. These violations enabled Fannie Mae to show a stable earnings growth and reduced income statement volatility, and—for the year ended 1998—Fannie Mae was able to maximize bonuses and meet forecasted earnings.[8] The SEC action thoroughly details a variety of deficiencies in accounting and financial reporting. Four of the more serious situations are described below.

Improper Accounting for Loan Fees, Premiums, and Discounts

Statement of Financial Accounting Standards (SFAS) No. 91 requires companies to recognize loan fees, premiums, and discounts as an adjustment over the life of the applicable loans, to generate a "constant effective yield" on the loans.[9] Because of the possibility of loan prepayments, the estimated life of the loans may change with changing market conditions. *SFAS 91* requires that any changes to the amortization of fees, premiums, and discounts caused by changes in estimated prepayments be recognized as a gain or loss in its entirety in the current period's income statement. Fannie Mae referred to this amount as the "catch-up adjustment." In the fourth quarter of 1998, Fannie Mae's accounting models calculated an approximate $439 million catch-up adjustment, in the form of a decrease to net interest income. Rather than book this amount consistent with *SFAS 91,* senior management of Fannie Mae directed employees to record only $240 million of the catch-up amount in that year's income statement. By not recording the full catch-up adjustment, Fannie Mae understated its expenses and overstated its income by a pretax amount of $199 million. The unrecorded catch-up amount represented 4.3 percent of the 1998 earnings before taxes and 4.9 percent of 1998 net interest income for the fiscal year 1998.

Improper Hedge Accounting

Fannie Mae used debt to finance the acquisition of mortgages and mortgage securities and it turned to derivative

[6]Stephen Labaton and Eric Dash, "Report on Fannie Mae Cites Manipulation to Secure Bonus," *New York Times,* February 23, 2006, www.nytimes.com/2006/02/23/business/23cnd-fannie.htm.

[7]*Under Secretary Randal K. Quarles Statement on Treasury Reaction to OFHEO Report,* May 23, 2006, www.ustreas.gov/press/releases/js4278.htm.

[8]Securities and Exchange Commission, Case Number 1:06CV00959, *Securities and Exchange Commission v. Federal National Mortgage Association,* May 23, 2006.

[9]Financial Accounting Standards Board, *Statement of Financial Accounting Standards (SFAS) No. 91,* Accounting for Nonrefundable Fees and Costs Associated with Origination or Acquiring Loans and Initial Direct Costs of Leases (Norwalk, CT: FASB, 1982).

instruments to hedge against the effect of fluctuations in interest rates on its debt costs. Application of *SFAS 133* required that Fannie Mae adjust the value of its derivatives to changing market values.[10] Critics contended that this standard opened the door to earnings volatility, and it would appear that Fannie's desires to create earnings stability was used as the motivation for the application of the standards in *SFAS 133.*

Accounting for Loan Loss Reserve

During the period 1997 through 2003, management failed to provide any quantitative estimate of losses in their loan portfolio, instead relying on a qualitative judgment. The failure to establish and implement an appropriate model for determining the size of the loan loss reserve was a violation of the GAAP rules in *SFAS 5.*[11]

Fannie Mae maintained an unjustifiably high level of loan loss reserve in case it was needed to compensate for possible future changes in the economic environment. This violates the GAAP requirement that the estimate of loss reserves should be based on losses currently inherent in the loan portfolio. At year-end 2002, Fannie Mae's reserve was overstated by at least $100 million. This overstatement resulted in a $100 million understatement of earnings before tax, which represented 1.6 percent of the earnings before tax and $.08 of additional earnings per share on the year-end 2002 figure of $4.52.

Classifications of Securities Held in Portfolio

SFAS 115 requires the classification of securities acquired as either trading, available-for-sale, or held-to-maturity at the time of acquisition.[12] Rather than follow the *SFAS 115* rules, Fannie Mae initially classified the securities it acquired as held-to-maturity and then, at the end of the month of acquisition, decided on the ultimate classification.

GAAP requires that the accounting classification be made at the time of acquisition. Once a security is classified, it can be reclassified only in narrow circumstances. Both trading and available-for-sale securities are valued at current market value, with any declines over time (or recaptures) in trading securities reported as a loss (or gain) in the income statement and as other comprehensive income in the equity section of the balance sheet for available-for-sale securities.

[10]Financial Accounting Standards Board, *Statement of Financial Accounting Standards (SFAS) No. 133,* Accounting for Derivatives Instruments and Hedging Activities (Norwalk, CT: FASB, 1998).

[11]Financial Accounting Standards Board, *Statement of Financial Accounting Standards (SFAS) No. 5,* Accounting for Contingencies (Norwalk, CT: FASB, 1975).

[12]Financial Accounting Standards Board, *Statement of Financial Accounting Standards (SFAS) No.115,* Accounting for Certain Investments in Debt and Equity Securities (Norwalk, CT: FASB, 1993).

Postscript

On October 27, 2008, Congress formed the Federal Housing Finance Agency (FHFA) by a legislative merger of OFHEO, the Federal Housing Finance Board (FHFB), and the U.S. Department of Housing and Urban Development (HUD) government-sponsored enterprise mission team. FHFA now regulates Fannie Mae, Freddie Mac, and the 12 Federal Home Loan Banks.

The meltdown in the mortgage-backed securities market that occurred during the financial crisis of 2007–2009 took place after the facts of this case. One can only wonder how bad things would have been for Fannie Mae had the entity been exposed to huge market losses in the mortgages it held in addition to the financial fraud discussed in the case.

During the financial crisis, the market prices of many securities, particularly those backed by subprime home mortgages, had plunged to fractions of their original prices. That forced banks to report hundreds of billions of dollars in losses during 2008. The business community turned its attention to the accounting standards established by FASB for some relief. Bankers bitterly complained that the current market prices were the result of distressed sales and that they should be allowed to ignore those prices and value the securities instead at their value in a normal market.

At first, FASB resisted making changes, but that changed within a few days of a congressional hearing at which legislators from both parties demanded that the board act. FASB approved three changes to the rules, one of which would allow banks to keep some declines in asset values off their income statements. Reluctant FASB board members rationalized going along with this change by stating that improved disclosures would help investors. The American Bankers Association, which pushed legislators to demand the board make changes, praised the board stating that the "decision should improve information for investors by providing more accurate estimates of market values." The change that met with the most dissent was to allow banks to write down these investments to market value only if they conclude that the decline is "other than temporary." This change will now enable banks to keep many losses off the income statements, although the declines will still show up in the institutions' balance sheets.

Questions

1. Lawrence W. Smith, a member of the FASB, commented after passing the "other-than-temporary" market standard: "We are an independent standard setter, and it is important that we maintain our independence." He added, "At the same time, how can we ignore what is going on around us?"

   a. Compare the importance of having an independent accounting-standard-setting body with the need for independence in an audit. Are there commonalities in why independence is required in both instances? Explain.

b. Do you think economic and political considerations should be considered by FASB in making decisions on proper accounting standards? Why or why not?

2. Fannie Mae's corporate governance system failed to identify excessive risk-taking. Describe those risks and the mechanisms that should have been used by Fannie Mae and KPMG to enhance risk assessment.

3. According to the case, KPMG failed to review Fannie Mae's significant accounting policies for GAAP compliance.

One item in particular was the failure of Fannie Mae to make a quantitative estimate of losses on its loan portfolio. In the end, KPMG gave an unqualified opinion even though the financial statements contained significant departures from GAAP. What ethical and professional standards did KPMG violate in taking that position? Use the elements of the fraud triangle discussed in the chapter to identify internal control risks that should have influenced KPMG's position.

Case 5-10

Royal Ahold N.V. (Ahold)

Summary of the Charges against Ahold

On October 13, 2004, the SEC charged Royal Ahold N.V. (Ahold) with multiple violations of Section 17(a) of the Securities Act, Section 10(b) of the Exchange Act, and Exchange Act Rule 10b-5. Charges were also filed against three former top executives: Cees van der Hoeven, the former CEO and chair of the executive board; A. Michael Meurs, the former CFO and executive board member; and Jan Andreae, the former executive vice president and executive board member. The commission also filed a related administrative action charging Roland Fahlin, a former member of Ahold's supervisory board and audit committee, with causing violations of the reporting, books and records, and internal controls provisions of the securities laws.[1]

As a result of two frauds and other accounting errors and irregularities that are described in the following text, Ahold made materially false and misleading statements in SEC filings and in other public statements for at least fiscal years 1999 through 2001 and for the first three quarters of 2002. The company failed to adhere to the requirements of the Exchange Act and related rules that require each issuer of registered securities to make and keep books, records, and accounts that, in reasonable detail, accurately and fairly reflect the business of the issuer. The company also failed to devise and maintain a system of internal controls sufficient to provide reasonable assurances that, among other things, transactions are recorded as necessary to permit preparation of financial statements and to maintain the accountability of accounts.

About the Company

Ahold is a publicly held company organized in the Netherlands with securities registered with the SEC pursuant to Section 12(b) of the Exchange Act. Ahold's securities trade on the New York Stock Exchange and are evidenced by American Depositary Receipts.[2]

As a foreign issuer, Ahold prepared its financial statements pursuant to Dutch generally accepted accounting principles (GAAP) but included, in its filings with the commission, a reconciliation to U.S. GAAP and condensed financial statements prepared pursuant to U.S. GAAP.[3]

U.S. Foodservice (USF), a food service and distribution company with headquarters in Columbia, Maryland, is a wholly owned subsidiary of Ahold. USF was a publicly held company with securities registered with the SEC pursuant to Section 12(b) of the Exchange Act prior to being acquired by Ahold in April 2000.

Summary of Complaint

The SEC's complaints, filed in the U.S. District Court for the District of Columbia, alleged that, as a result of the fraudulent inflation of promotional allowances at USF, the improper consolidation of joint ventures through fraudulent side letters, and other accounting errors and irregularities, Ahold's original SEC filings for at least fiscal years 2000 through 2002 were materially false and misleading. For fiscal years 2000 through 2002, Ahold overstated net sales by approximately €33 billion ($30 billion).[4] For fiscal years 2000 and 2001 and the first three quarters of 2002, Ahold overstated operating income by approximately €3.6 billion ($3.3 billion) and net income by approximately €900 million ($829 million).

Ahold agreed to settle the commission's action, without admitting or denying the allegations in the complaint, by consenting to the entry of a judgment permanently enjoining the company from violating the antifraud and other provisions of the securities laws. Various officers of the company also settled charges, without admitting or denying the allegations in the complaint, by consenting to permanent injunctions and officer and director bars.

The SEC did not seek penalties in the enforcement actions because the Dutch Public Prosecutor's Office, which conducted a parallel criminal investigation in the Netherlands,

[1]U.S. Securities and Exchange Commission, Litigation Release No. 18929, October 13, 2004, www.sec.gov/litigation/litreleases/lr18929.htm.
[2]An American Depositary Receipt (or ADR) represents ownership in the shares of a non-U.S. company and trades in U.S. financial markets. The stock of many non-U.S. companies trade on U.S. stock exchanges through the use of ADRs. ADRs enable U.S. investors to buy shares in foreign companies without the hazards or inconveniences of cross-border and cross-currency transactions. ADRs carry prices in U.S. dollars, pay dividends in U.S. dollars, and can be traded like the shares of U.S.-based companies.

[3]Starting in 2005, members of the European Union (EU), including the Netherlands, adopted International Financial Reporting Standards (IFRS) as the only acceptable standards for EU companies when filing statements with securities commissions in the EU. Subsequent to the adoption, the SEC in the United States announced it would accept IFRS-based financial statement filings for foreign companies listing their stock on the NYSE and NASDAQ without reconciliation to U.S. GAAP. The United States has not adopted IFRS, although the SEC is studying the issue and has set forth a "roadmap" for adoption of IFRS in the United States that would begin to be phased in around 2015. These issued are discussed in Chapter 8.
[4]€ = euro, which is the currency in the European Union including in the Netherlands.

requested that the commission not seek penalties against the individuals because of potential double jeopardy issues under Dutch law. Because of the importance of this case in the Netherlands and the need for continued cooperation between the SEC and regulatory authorities in other countries, the commission agreed to the Dutch prosecutor's request.

The commission did not seek a penalty from Ahold because of, among other reasons, the company's extensive cooperation with the commission's investigation. Ahold self-reported the misconduct and conducted an extensive internal investigation. On its own initiative, Ahold expanded its internal investigation beyond the fraud at USF and the improper joint venture accounting to analyze accounting practices and internal controls at 17 operating companies. Ahold promptly provided the staff with the internal investigative reports and the supporting information and waived the attorney–client privilege and work product protection with respect to its internal investigations. Ahold also made its current personnel available for interviews or testimony and significantly assisted the staff in arranging interviews with, or testimony from, former Ahold personnel located in the United States and, of even greater importance, abroad. Ahold promptly took remedial actions including, but not limited to, revising its internal controls and terminating employees responsible for the wrongdoing.

In a separate action, on June 17, 2009, Ahold reached a final settlement with plaintiffs in a class action securities lawsuit that requires the company to pay the lead plaintiffs $1.1 billion to resolve all claims against Ahold. The settlement applies to all qualifying common shareholders around the world and covers Ahold, its subsidiaries and affiliates, the individual defendants, and the underwriters.[5]

Statement of Facts

The following summarizes the main facts of the case with respect to transactions between Ahold and USF.

Budgeted Earnings Goals

From the time it acquired USF in April 2000, Ahold and USF budgeted annual earnings goals for USF. Compensation for USF executives was based on, among other things, USF's meeting or exceeding budgeted earnings targets. USF executives each received a substantial bonus in early 2002 because USF purportedly satisfied earnings goals for fiscal year 2001. USF executives were each eligible for a substantial bonus if USF met earnings targets for fiscal year 2002. Certain USF executives engaged in or substantially participated in a scheme whereby USF reported earnings equal to or greater than the targets, regardless of the company's true performance.

[5] Securities and Exchange Commission, U.S. District of Columbia, December 5, 2009, www.sec.gov/litigation/complaints/comp 19034-6.pdf.

Promotional Allowances

A significant portion of USF's operating income was based on payments by its vendors, referred to in various ways such as promotional allowances, rebates, discounts, and program money (referred to below as "promotional allowances"). During at least fiscal years 2001 and 2002, USF made no significant profit on most of its end sales to its customers. Instead, the majority of USF's operating income was derived from promotional allowances.

In a typical promotional allowance agreement, USF committed to purchase a minimum volume from a vendor. The vendor in turn paid USF a per-unit rebate of a portion of the original price it charged USF, according to an agreed-upon payment schedule.

Sometimes the volume-based promotional allowances were paid as they were earned, but it was a common practice for the vendor to "prepay" on multiyear contracts at least some portion of the amounts that would be due if USF met all of the projected purchase volume targets in the contract. Promotional allowances were critical to USF's financial results—without them, USF's operating income for fiscal years 2001 and 2002 would have been materially reduced.

False Confirmations and Statements to Auditors

USF executives engaged in or substantially participated in a scheme whereby USF reported earnings equal to or greater than its earnings targets, regardless of the company's true performance. The primary method used to carry out this fraudulent scheme to "book to budget" was to improperly inflate USF's promotional allowance income. USF executives booked to budget by, among other things, causing USF to record completely fictitious promotional allowances sufficient to cover any shortfall to budgeted earnings.

USF executives covered up the false earnings by making it appear that the inflated promotional allowance income had been earned by (1) inducing vendors to confirm false promotional allowance income, payments, and receivable balances; (2) manipulating the promotional allowance accounts receivable from vendors and manipulating and misapplying cash receipts; and (3) making false and misleading statements, and material omissions, to the company's independent auditors, other company personnel, and/or Ahold personnel.

USF executives falsely represented to the company's independent auditors that there were no written promotional allowance contracts for the vast majority of promotional allowance agreements when, in fact, they knew, or were reckless in not knowing, that such written contracts existed. These executives falsely represented that USF had only handshake deals with its vendors that a USF executive would renegotiate at the end of each year to arrive at a mutually agreed-upon final amount due from each vendor for the year. They knew, or were reckless in not knowing, that these representations were false when they were made.

Nonexistent Internal Controls

USF had no comprehensive, automated system for tracking the amounts owed by the vendors pursuant to the promotional allowance agreements. Instead, USF, for purposes of interim reporting, purported to estimate an overall "promotional allowance rate" as a percentage of sales and recorded periodic accruals based on that rate. Information provided by USF executives caused the estimated rate to be inflated. The intended and actual result of inflating USF's promotional allowance income was that USF, and Ahold, materially overstated their operating incomes.

Corrupting the Audit Process

USF executives participated in a systematic effort to corrupt the audit process to keep the fraud from being discovered. Ahold's auditors attempted at the end of each fiscal year to confirm with the vendors that they actually paid, or still owed, the promotional allowances recorded by USF. To satisfy the auditors, USF executives successfully convinced vendors to sign audit confirmation letters even though they knew that the letters were false.

For each vendor subject to the confirmation process, USF executives prepared a schedule purportedly reflecting the promotional allowances earned by USF for the year, the amount paid by the vendor, and the balance due. USF executives grossly inflated the figures contained in these schedules. The schedules were used both by USF to support the related amounts recorded in its financial statements and by its auditors to perform the year-end audit.

USF executives provided information used to prepare confirmation request letters that they signed and that were sent to major vendors reflecting the inflated aggregate promotional allowances purportedly paid or owed to USF during the year. The promotional monies earned, paid, and receivable that were stated in the confirmations were grossly inflated and in many cases were simply fictitious, having no relationship to the actual promotional allowances earned, paid, or receivable.

Fraudulent Acts by Management

As a further part of the fraud, USF executives contacted or directed subordinates to contact vendors to alert them that they would receive confirmation letters and to ask them to sign and return the letters without objection. If a vendor balked at signing the fraudulent confirmation, USF executives pressed the vendor by, for example, falsely representing that the confirmation was just "an internal number" and that USF did not consider the receivable reflected in the confirmation to be an actual debt that it would seek to collect. USF executives sent, or directed subordinates to send, side letters to vendors who continued to object to the fraudulent confirmations. The side letters assured the vendors that they did not, in fact, owe USF amounts reflected as outstanding in the confirmation letters.

USF executives attempted to prevent the discovery of the fraudulent scheme by making accounting entries that unilaterally deducted material amounts from the balances that USF owed to certain vendors for the products USF had purchased, and simultaneously credited the promotional allowance receivable balance for the amount of such deductions. These "deductions" were made at year-end and had the net effect of making it appear that USF had made material progress in collecting promotional allowance payments allegedly due.

The large year-end deductions facilitated the fraudulent recording of promotional allowance income because these deductions made it appear that the amounts recorded had been earned and paid. The USF executives concealed the fact that the deductions were not authorized, were not legitimate, and that a substantial percentage of the deductions were reversed in the early part of the following fiscal year.

USF executives also knew, or were reckless in not knowing, that the amounts paid by some vendors included prepayments on multiyear contracts. But they falsely represented to USF personnel, Ahold personnel, and/or the company's independent auditors that none of the promotional allowance agreements included such prepayments. As a result, USF treated the prepayments by vendors as if they were payments for currently owed promotional allowances. This made it falsely appear that USF was making material progress in collecting the inflated promotional allowance income it had recorded.

Role of the Auditors

Deloitte & Touche had been Ahold's group auditor (the consolidated entity) since the company went public. A few years after Ahold had acquired USF and the accounting fraud surfaced, investors sued the firm for being engaged in deceptive conduct and recklessly disregarding misstatements in Ahold's financial statements. The charges were dismissed because it was concluded that Deloitte was being deceived by Ahold executives, many of whom went to great lengths to conceal the fraud.

When Deloitte took over the auditing of USF after being taken over by Ahold, the firm uncovered multiple accounting errors that not only had a material effect on USF's profits, but also materially distorted the net income of Ahold as well.

Financial Statement Misstatements and Restatements

As a result of the schemes already described, USF materially overstated its operating income during at least fiscal years 2001 and 2002. On February 24, 2003, Ahold announced that it would issue restated financial statements for previous periods and would delay filing its consolidated 2002 financial statements as a result of an initial internal investigation based, in part, on the overstatement of income at USF. Ahold announced in May 2003 that USF's income had been overstated by more than $800 million since April 2000. Ahold's stock price plummeted from approximately $10.69 per share to $4.16 per share.

On or about October 17, 2003, Ahold filed its Form 20-F (filing with the SEC for foreign entities) for the fiscal year ended December 29, 2002, which contained restatements for the fiscal years 2000 and 2001, corrected accounting adjustments for fiscal year 2002, and restated amounts for fiscal years 1998 and 1999 included in the five-year summary data. The restatements indicated that, in its original SEC filings and other public statements, Ahold had overstated (1) net income by approximately 17.6, 32.6, and 88.1 percent for the fiscal years 2000, 2001, and first three quarters of 2002, respectively; (2) operating income by approximately 28.1, 29.4, and 51.3 percent for the fiscal years 2000, 2001, and first three quarters of 2002, respectively; and (3) net sales by approximately 20.8, 18.6, and 13.8 percent for the fiscal years 2000, 2001, and 2002, respectively. Ahold and three of the individual defendants agreed to settlements with the commission.

Ahold Today

Ahold operates a number of grocery chains throughout the United States and Europe. Its common shares are listed and traded on the NYSE Euronext.[6]

[6]NYSE Euronext is the result of a merger on April 4, 2007, between the NYSE and stock exchanges in Paris, Amsterdam, Brussels, and Lisbon, as well as the NYSE Liffe derivatives markets in London, Paris, Amsterdam, Brussels, and Lisbon. NYSE Euronext is a U.S. holding company that operates through its subsidiaries. NYSE Euronext is a listed company. NYSE Euronext common stock is dually listed on the NYSE and Euronext Paris under the symbol "NYX." Each of the Euronext exchanges holds an exchange license granted by the relevant national exchange regulatory authority and operates under its supervision. Each market operator is also subject to national laws and regulations in its jurisdiction in addition to the requirements imposed by the national exchange authority and, in some cases, the central bank and/or the finance ministry in the relevant European country. Regulation of Euronext and its constituent markets is conducted in a coordinated fashion by the respective national regulatory authorities pursuant to memoranda of understanding relating to the cash and derivatives markets.

Questions

1. Explain how Ahold used promotional allowances to manipulate earnings. Refer to the fraud triangle described in this chapter and analyze the incentives, pressures, and opportunities to commit fraud at Ahold.

2. Utilize the COSO *Integrated Framework* and discussion of risk assessment in the chapter and evaluate the deficiencies in the internal control system at Ahold. Include in your discussion whether it seems as though Ahold adequately monitored its internal controls as suggested in COSO's *Guidance on Monitoring Internal Control Systems* discussed in the chapter.

3. The court ruled that Deloitte was not responsible for the fraud at Ahold because its management deceived the auditors and hid information from the firm. Given that the firm was not found liable for fraud, do you think that means the firm conducted its audit in accordance with GAAS? Why or why not? Are there other steps it could have taken to enhance its audit of Ahold? Be specific.

Optional Question

In addition to the deficiencies in accounting for promotional allowances, Ahold engaged in joint venture transactions that materially misstated the financial statements. Review the litigation referred to in the case and describe the nature and scope of the joint venture transactions and what problems existed with the company's accounting and financial reporting.

a. Evaluate the operation of internal controls with respect to accounting for the joint venture transactions. How might the company have strengthened its controls?

b. From a corporate governance perspective, what were the deficiencies that seem to have contributed to the fraud in accounting for and reporting the joint venture transactions? Can you identify corporate governance mechanisms that might have helped prevent or detect the fraud at Ahold but that were nonexistent?

Legal and Regulatory Obligations in an Ethical Framework

Ethics Reflection

The *Cenco, Inc. v. Seidman & Seidman* case deals with common-law legal standards governing the liability of independent auditors for failing to detect fraud.[1] Between 1970 and 1975, managerial employees of Cenco engaged in a massive fraud that involved inflating inventories in the Medical/Health Division far above their actual value. While the fraud was occurring, the market price of its stock had increased dramatically but after the dust had settled, Cenco's stock price had declined by 75 percent.

Cenco benefited from the fraud while the stock price was rising. It was able to borrow money at lower rates and buy other companies to expand in the marketplace. If inventory was lost or destroyed, Cenco could get insurance companies to pay larger amounts because of inflated inventory values. Thus, those involved in the fraud were not stealing from the company, as in the usual corporate fraud case, but were instead aggrandizing the company (and themselves) at the expense of outsiders.

The unmasking of the fraud led to the filing of a class action lawsuit against Cenco, its corrupt managers, and Seidman. The suit charged defendants with having violated various federal securities laws and SEC rules, notably Rule 10b-5. Cenco filed a cross-claim against codefendant Seidman, alleging that Seidman was liable to Cenco for failing to prevent the fraud by Cenco managers. Seidman filed its own cross-claim against Cenco, alleging that Seidman had been one of the victims of Cenco's fraud.

Cenco alleged breach of contract, professional malpractice (negligence), and fraud. The company's evidence tended to show that in the early stages of the fraud Seidman had been careless in checking Cenco's inventory figures and its carelessness had prevented the fraud from being nipped in the bud. The evidence supported the following conclusions: (1) As the fraud expanded, Seidman's auditors became suspicious, but, perhaps to protect the very high fees that Seidman was getting from Cenco (about $1 million a year, which was 70 percent of Seidman's total billings), concealed their suspicions and kept giving Cenco a clean bill of health in their audit reports. (2) Seidman's evidence tended to show that the firm had diligently attempted to follow up all signs of fraud, but had been thwarted by the efforts of the large group of managers at all levels at Cenco. The jury found that Seidman was not liable for breach of contract, negligence, or fraud. In upholding the decision, the U.S. Court of Appeals ruled it was appropriate to impugn the actions of corrupt management to the corporation. Thus, the corporation was a party to the fraud and not entitled to recover losses from the auditors.

The court ruling stated that the representatives of the owners—a board of directors on which dishonesty and carelessness were well represented—failed in their oversight and shared responsibility for the fraud with Seidman. In addition, the scale of the fraud both complicated the task of discovery for Seidman and made the failure of oversight

(Continued)

by Cenco's shareholders and board of directors harder to condone. As you read this chapter think about the following: (1) How do courts determine the legal liability of auditors to their clients and to third parties such as stockholders? (2) How do the actions of top management and the board of directors influence court decisions against auditors for failure to detect and report fraud? (3) Why is it important for auditors to show that they have adhered to the standards of the profession, both ethical and professional, to provide a defense in lawsuits alleging the failure to detect fraud?

It's not that we are trying to avoid our legitimate responsibilities. We are trying to put reasonable limitations on our exposure. Excessive liability creates an incentive for accountants to restrict the free flow of commercial information which is so important to our free enterprise system. When someone wishes to rely on an accountant's report for a significant business decision, it is only fair that the accountant have knowledge of the intended reliance.

Robert Mednick

In this statement made by Robert Mednick, the former chair of (Arthur) Andersen's Worldwide Committee on Professional Standards and worldwide Managing Partner—Professional and Regulatory Matters, he was responding to a question posed by an interviewer for *The CPA Journal* with respect to the effort led by the AICPA in the mid-1980s to reform accountants' legal liability.[2] Mednick served at that time as chair of the AICPA Task Force on Accountants Liability.

Mednick pointed out in the interview that was held prior to passage of the Private Securities Litigation Reform Act (PSLRA) that the number of lawsuits against accountants in the years 1975 to 1985 increased from 117,000 to 273,600. In many of the cases, the courts and juries found someone to compensate the injured parties for their losses. Under the joint and several liability principle (pre-PSLRA), each negligent party could be held liable for the total of damages suffered, even though it was deemed responsible for only a small portion of the loss. In other words, a $10 million class action lawsuit bought by the shareholders of a public company that named the investment bankers, accountants, and lawyers, could be recovered 100 percent from the accountants. During the 1970s and 1980s, accountants and auditors were deemed to have "deep pockets," and sometimes the firms preferred to settle out of court rather than become involved in protracted litigation.

In the mid-1990s, the accounting profession lobbied Congress for securities litigation reform and in 1995 the PSLRA was passed.[3] The act establishes a proportionate liability standard where each defendant is liable solely for the portion of the damages that correspond to the percentage of responsibility of that defendant. John Coffee, a noted professor of securities law at Columbia University, believes that the act decreased the threat of private enforcement against accountants while, at the same time, the SEC had turned its attention to CPA firms that were cross-selling services to clients and otherwise loosening audit independence standards.[4] One implication of proportionate liability is that accountants and auditors may have unconsciously veered away from the due care standard that is an essential part of carrying out professional responsibilities in an ethical manner.

Duty of Care—Managers and Directors

Directors and officers are deemed fiduciaries of the corporation because their relationship with the corporation and its shareholders is one of trust and confidence. As fiduciaries, directors and officers owe ethical—and legal—duties to the corporation and to the shareholders. These fiduciary duties include the duty of care and the duty of loyalty.

Directors and officers must exercise due care in performing their duties. The standard of *due care* provides that a director or officer act in good faith, exercise the care that an ordinarily prudent person would exercise in similar circumstances, and act in the way that he or she considers to be the best interests of the corporation. Directors and officers who have not exercised the required duty of care can be held liable for the harms suffered by the corporation as a result of their negligence.

Duty of Loyalty

Loyalty can be defined as faithfulness to one's obligations and duties. In the corporate context, the duty of loyalty requires directors and officers to subordinate their personal interests to the welfare of the organization. For example, directors may not use corporate funds or confidential corporate information for personal advantage. They must also refrain from self-dealing such as when a director opposes a stock tender offer that is in the corporation's best interest simply because its acceptance may cost the director her position.

Liability of Directors and Officers

Directors and officers are liable for crimes and torts committed by themselves or by corporate employees under their supervision. Additionally, shareholders may perceive that the corporate directors are not acting in the best interests of the corporation and may sue the directors, in what is called a shareholder's derivative suit, on behalf of the corporation.

Business Judgment Rule

A corporate director or officer may be able to avoid liability to the corporation or to its shareholders for poor business judgments under the *business judgment rule.* Directors and officers are expected to exercise due care and to use their best judgment in guiding corporate management, but they are not insurers of business success. Honest mistakes of judgment and poor business decisions on their part do not make them liable to the corporation for resulting damages.

The business judgment rule generally immunizes directors and officers from liability for the consequences of a decision that is within managerial authority, as long as the decision complies with management's fiduciary duties and as long as acting on the decision is within the powers of the corporation. Therefore, if there is a reasonable basis for a business decision, it is unlikely that a court will interfere with that decision, even if the corporation suffers as a result.

Chancery Court

The Chancery Court located in Delaware is the preeminent forum for the resolution of commercial business litigation matters including the duties of officers and directors. Many matters that involve the management of a corporation's inner workings are within the jurisdiction of Chancery Court. The Chancery Court is a court of equity, as opposed to a court of law. Most states do not separate the types of legal remedies available to litigants into equity and law the way that Delaware does. An equity court is the type that can issue temporary injunctions and declaratory judgments.

Caremark Opinion

In 1991, state and federal authorities began to investigate Caremark International for alleged violations of Medicare's antireferral law. The investigations led to indictments, substantial fines, and a shareholder's derivative suit alleging that the company directors had breached their fiduciary duty of care.

When the proposed settlement of the derivative action reached the Delaware Court of Chancery, it ruled in *Caremark International Derivative Legislation* that directors have an affirmative fiduciary obligation to ensure that adequate information and reporting systems exist in a corporation to provide timely and accurate information to the board and management about compliance with legal requirements.[5] The *Caremark* view of this duty of care goes beyond the more passive standard that allows a board to rely on the integrity of employees to comply with legal and regulatory requirements.

Shareholder Derivative Suit—Citigroup Subprime Lending

On February 25, 2009, Chancellor William B. Chandler III dismissed all but one of the claims in a shareholder suit in the Delaware Chancery Court against the board of Citigroup. The shareholders principally alleged that the board had breached their fiduciary duties by allowing the company to invest in, and sustain significant losses in, the subprime lending market.

The decision is important for two reasons. First, it shows that attempts to hold boards liable for some extremely bad decisions (bad in hindsight, at least) made prior to the financial crisis are going to be met with heavy skepticism by the Delaware courts. Here is one of the quotes from the opinion on this point: "Oversight duties under Delaware law are not designed to subject directors, even expert directors, to personal liability for failure to predict the future and to properly evaluate business risk."

Second, Chancellor Chandler dismissed the plaintiffs' breach of fiduciary duty claim. The plaintiffs had phrased this claim as a failure of the board "to properly monitor and manage the risks [Citigroup] faced from problems in the subprime lending market and for failing to properly disclose Citigroup's exposure to subprime assets."

The court ruled that the Citigroup case is a Caremark claim. Since the original ruling, the Delaware courts have struggled with the scope and content of this duty. In *Stone v. Ritter,*[6] the Delaware Supreme Court held that these Caremark-type duties were properly thought of as a subset of the duty of loyalty. This was important because under Delaware law, if a Caremark claim were classified as a duty-of-care claim, then a company could exculpate the directors from monetary liability, something Citigroup had done in its charter. Chandler's opinion notes the high standard under Caremark:

> To establish oversight liability a plaintiff must show that the directors knew they were not discharging their fiduciary obligations or that the directors demonstrated a conscious disregard for their responsibilities such as by failing to act in the face of a known duty to act. The test is rooted in concepts of bad faith; indeed, a showing of bad faith is a necessary condition to director oversight liability.[7]

Applying this standard to the facts of the *Stone v. Ritter* case, the judge held that the red flags before the board at the time, signaling that the subprime market was deteriorating, were insufficient to meet this standard. The court stated that the "warning signs alleged by plaintiffs are not evidence that the directors consciously disregarded their duties or otherwise acted in bad faith."[8]

Chancellor Chandler went on to distinguish regular Caremark duties to prevent fraud and wrongdoing from business decisions such as those in the Citigroup case stating:

> Such oversight programs allow directors to intervene and prevent frauds or other wrongdoing that could expose the company to risk of loss as a result of such conduct. While it may be tempting to say that directors have the same duties to monitor and oversee business risk, imposing Caremark-type duties on directors to monitor business risk is fundamentally different. Citigroup was in the business of taking on and managing investment and other business risks. To impose oversight liability on directors for failure to monitor "excessive" risk would involve courts in conducting hindsight evaluations of decisions at the heart of the business judgment of directors. Oversight duties under Delaware law are not designed to subject directors, even expert directors, to personal liability for failure to predict the future and to properly evaluate business risk.[9]

Legal Liability of Auditors: An Overview

University of Southern California Professor Zoe-Vonna Palmrose identifies the four general stages in an audit-related dispute: (1) the occurrence of events that result in losses for users of the financial statements, (2) the investigation by plaintiff attorneys before filing to link the user losses with allegations of material omissions or misstatements of financial statements, (3) the legal process that commences with the filing of the lawsuit, and (4) the final resolution of the dispute.[10] The first stage comes about as a result of some loss-generating event including client bankruptcy, fraudulent financial reporting, and the misappropriation of assets. The latter two events will be discussed later in the chapter.

Auditors can be sued by clients, investors, creditors, and the government for failure to perform services adequately and in accordance with the profession's ethics standards. Auditors can be held liable under two classes of law: (1) common law and (2) statutory law. Common-law liability evolves from legal opinions issued by judges in deciding a case. These opinions become legal principles that set a precedent and guide judges in deciding similar cases in the future. Statutory law reflects legislation passed at the state or federal level that establishes certain courses of conduct that must be adhered to by covered parties.[11]

Exhibit 6.1 summarizes the types of liability and auditors' actions that result in liability.

Common-Law Liability

Common-law liability requires the auditor to perform professional services with due care. Recall that due care is a basic principle and rule of conduct in the AICPA Code. Evidence of having exercised due care exists if the auditor can demonstrate having performed

EXHIBIT 6.1
Summary of Types of Liability and Auditors' Actions Resulting in Liability

Source: William F. Messier Jr., Steven M. Glover, and Douglas F. Prawitt, *Auditing and Assurance Services: A Systematic Approach* (New York: McGraw-Hill Irwin, 2010), p. 686.

Types of Liability	Auditors' Actions Resulting in Liability
Common law—clients	Breach of contract (privity relationship)
	Negligence
	Gross negligence/constructive fraud
	Fraud
Common law—third parties	Negligence
	Gross negligence/constructive fraud
	Fraud
Federal statutory law—civil liability	Negligence
	Gross negligence/constructive fraud
	Fraud
Federal statutory law—criminal liability	Willful violation of federal statutes

services with the same degree of skill and judgment possessed by others in the profession. Typically, an auditor would cite adherence to generally accepted auditing standards as evidence of having exercised due care in conducting the audit.

Liability to Clients—Privity Relationship

An accountant has a contractual obligation to the client that creates a *privity relationship*. A client can bring a lawsuit against an accountant for failing to live up to the terms of the contract.

Ultramares v. Touche

In the 1933 landmark case, *Ultramares v. Touche,* the New York State Court of Appeals held that a cause of action based on negligence could not be maintained by a third party who was not in contractual privity. The court did leave open the possibility that a third party could successfully sue for gross negligence that constitutes fraud (constructive fraud) and fraud.[12]

Ultramares had loaned $100,000 to Fred Stern & Company. Before making the loan, the company had asked Stern to provide an audited balance sheet, and Stern had its auditor, Touche Ross & Co. (Touche), do so. The firm issued an unqualified audit report. Subsequently, the company went bankrupt and it was alleged that false accounting entries had been made to conceal the company's problems. Ultramares alleged that Touche had been both negligent and fraudulent in its audit of Stern. Because the privity relationship did not exist for Ultramares and Stern, the fraud charges against Touche were dismissed. However, the jury ruled that Touche had been negligent and awarded about $186,000 in damages.

The importance of the *Ultramares* decision is that third parties (Ultramares) without privity could sue if negligence was so great as to constitute gross negligence, also known as *constructive fraud.* The opinion of the New York Court of Appeals was written by Judge Benjamin Cardozo:

> If a liability for negligence exists, a thoughtless slip or blunder, the failure to detect a theft or forgery beneath the cover of deceptive entries, may expose accountants to a liability in an indeterminate amount for an indeterminate time to an indeterminate class [third parties]. The hazards of a business on these terms are so extreme as to [raise] doubt whether a flaw may not exist in the implication of a duty that exposes to these circumstances.

The *Ultramares* decision was the first of three different judicial approaches to deciding the extent of an accountant's liability to third parties. The other two are the *Restatement (Second) of the Law of Torts* approach and the foreseeable third-party approach. Both are described in the following text.

Liability to Third Parties

Near-Privity Relationship

While the *Ultramares* decision established a strict privity standard, a number of subsequent court decisions in other states had moved away from this standard over time. Following years of broadening the auditor's liability to third parties to include those who were "foreseen" and "reasonably foreseeable" (to be discussed) in a 1985 decision the court seemed to move the pendulum back in favor of limiting the liability of accountants to third parties based on the privity standard. The New York Court of Appeals expanded the privity standard in the case of *Credit Alliance v. Arthur Andersen & Co.*[13] to include a *near-privity relationship* between third parties and the accountant. In the case, Credit Alliance was the principal lender to the client and demonstrated that Andersen had known Credit Alliance was relying on the client's financial statements prior to extending credit.

The court also ruled that there had been direct communication between the lender and the auditor regarding the client.

The *Credit Alliance* case establishes the following tests that must be satisfied for holding auditors liable for negligence to third parties: (1) knowledge by the accountant that the financial statements are to be used for a particular purpose; (2) the intention of the third party to rely on those statements; and (3) some action by the accountant linking him or her to the third party that provides evidence of the accountant's understanding of intended reliance. The 1992 New York Court of Appeals decision in *Security Pacific Business Credit, Inc. v. Peat Marwick Main & Co.*[14] sharpens the last criterion in its determination that the third party must be known to the auditor, who directly conveys the audited report to the third party or acts to induce reliance on the report.

Foreseen Third Parties

The "middle ground" approach followed by the vast majority of states (and federal courts located within those states) expands the class of third parties that can successfully sue an auditor for negligence beyond near privity to a person or limited group of persons whose reliance is (*actually*) *foreseen,* even if the specific person or group is unknown to the auditor.[15]

The courts have deviated from the *Ultramares* principle through a variety of decisions. For example, a federal district court in Rhode Island decided a case in 1968, *Rusch Factors, Inc. v. Levin,*[16] that held an accountant liable for negligence to a third party not in privity of contract. In that case, Rusch Factors had requested financial statements prior to granting a loan. Levin audited the statements, which showed the company to be solvent when it was actually insolvent. After the company went into receivership, Rusch Factors sued and the court ruled that the *Ultramares* doctrine was inappropriate. In its decision, the court relied heavily on the *Restatement (Second) of the Law of Torts.*

Restatement (Second) of the Law of Torts

The *Restatement (Second) of the Law of Torts* approach, sometimes known as *Restatement 552,*[17] expands accountants' legal liability exposure for negligence beyond those with near privity to a small group of persons and classes who are or *should be foreseen* by the auditor as relying on the financial information. This is known as the *foreseen third-party* concept because even though there is no privity relationship, the accountant knew that party or those parties would rely on the financial statements for a specified transaction.

Section 552 states: "The liability . . . is limited to loss (a) suffered by the person or one of the persons for whose benefit and guidance he intends to supply the information, or knows that the recipient [client] intends to supply it; and (b) through reliance upon it in a transaction which he intends the information to influence, or knows that the recipient so intends." For example, assume that a client asks an accountant to prepare financial statements and the accountant knows those statements will be used to request a loan from one or more financial institutions. The accountant may not know the specific bank to be approached, but does know the purpose for which the statements will be used. Thus, the third parties as a class of potential users can be foreseen.

A majority of states now use the modified privity requirement imposed by Section 552 of the *Restatement (Second) of the Law of Torts.* The *Restatement* modifies the traditional rule of privity by allowing nonclients to sue accountants for negligent misrepresentation, provided they belong to a "limited group" and provided that the accountant had actual knowledge that his or her professional opinion would be supplied to that group. In some state court decisions, a less restrictive interpretation of Section 552 has been made. For example, a 1986 decision by the Texas Court of Appeals in *Blue Bell, Inc. v. Peat, Marwick,*

Mitchell & Co. held that if an accountant preparing audited statements knows or should know that such statements will be relied upon, the accountant may be held liable for negligent misrepresentation.[18]

Reasonably Foreseeable Third Parties

A third judicial approach to third-party liability expands the legal liability of accountants well beyond *Ultramares*. The *reasonably foreseeable third-party* approach results from a 1983 decision by the New Jersey Supreme Court in *Rosenblum, Inc. v. Adler*.[19] In that case the Rosenblum family agreed to sell its retail catalog showroom business to Giant Stores, a corporation operating discount department stores, in exchange for Giant common stock. The Rosenblums relied on Giant's 1971 and 1972 financial statements, which had been audited by Touche. When the statements were found to be fraudulent, and the stock was determined worthless, the investors sued Touche. The lower courts did not allow the Rosenblums' claims against Touche on the grounds the plaintiffs did not meet either the *Ultramares* privity test or the *Restatement* standard. The case was taken to the New Jersey Supreme Court and it overturned the lower courts' decision ruling that auditors can be held liable for ordinary negligence to all *reasonably foreseeable third parties* who are recipients of the financial statements for routine business purposes.

Another important case that followed this approach was *Citizens State Bank v. Timm, Schmidt & Company.*[20] In this case, the bank sued the public accounting firm after relying on financial statements for one of its debtors that had been audited by Timm. The Wisconsin court used a number of reasons for extending auditors' liability beyond privity. The following quote from the case demonstrates the court's rather liberal leanings with respect to auditor legal liability to third parties. "If relying third parties, such as creditors, are not allowed to recover, the cost of credit to the general public will increase because creditors will either have to absorb the cost of bad loans made in reliance on faulty information or hire independent accountants to verify the information received."

Since 1987 no state high court has adopted this foreseeability approach to accountants' legal liability, while a large number have approved or adopted one of the narrower standards.[21] For example, in its 1992 ruling in the *Bily* case the California Supreme Court expressly rejected the foreseeability approach in favor of the *Rusch Factors* or *Restatement* standard. The court gave a number of reasons for rejecting the *Rosenblum* foreseeability approach, including that the foreseeability rule exposes auditors to potential liability in excess of their proportionate share and the sophisticated plaintiffs have other ways to protect themselves from the risk of inaccurate financial statements (e.g., they can negotiate improved terms or hire their own auditor).[22]

However, in its 2003 ruling in *Murphy v. BDO Seidman, LLP,* the California Court of Appeals ruled that "grapevine plaintiffs," who alleged indirect reliance based on what others (e.g., stockholders and stockbrokers) told them about the financial statements, had legal claims for ordinary negligence against the auditors so long as the auditor would have reasonably foreseen that stockholders or stockbrokers would tell other people of the content of the financial statements and that the other people would rely upon the misrepresentations in purchasing the corporate stock. The court ruled that nothing in the *Bily* decision precludes indirect reliance.[23]

The *Murphy* ruling seems to stretch auditors' legal liability to third parties beyond reasonable bounds. Imagine, for example, that you are watching Jim Cramer's television show *Mad Money* on CNBC and Cramer recommends a stock that you then purchase online. Shortly thereafter, news brakes of an accounting fraud. You sue the auditors based on your belief that the auditors should have known the public would buy the stock after

EXHIBIT 6.2   **Auditor Legal Liability to Third Parties**

Legal Approach	Case	Legal Principle	Legal Liability to Third Parties
Ultramares	*Ultramares v. Touche*	Privity (only clients can sue)	Possibly gross negligence that constitutes (constructive) fraud
Near-privity relationship	*Credit Alliance*	Three-pronged approach: knowledge of accountant; intention of third party; link between accountant and third party	Ordinary negligence
Restatement (Second) of the Law of Torts	*Rusch Factors*	Foreseen third-party users	Ordinary negligence
Foreseeable third party	*H. Rosenblum*	Reasonably foreseeable third-party users	Ordinary negligence with reliance on the statements

Cramer recommended it. It makes little sense to conclude that a plaintiff may be successful in a lawsuit against the auditors based on a claim of ordinary negligence in this situation given that auditors cannot control every use of audit information.

The conflicting common-law rulings can be confusing in trying to apply legal precedent to current court cases. To assist students, we have developed a summary in Exhibit 6.2 of the primary legal issues and guiding principles addressed in important court cases in deciding the auditor's liability to third parties.

Liability for fraud is not restricted to cases where the auditor had knowledge of the deceit. Some courts have interpreted gross negligence as an instance of fraud. Gross negligence, or constructive fraud, occurs when the auditor acts so carelessly in the application of professional standards that it implies a reckless disregard for the standards of due care.

The auditor's defense against third-party lawsuits requires proof that (1) the auditor did not have a duty to the third party, (2) the third party was negligent, (3) the auditor's work was performed in accordance with professional standards, (4) the third party did not suffer a loss, (5) any loss to the third party was caused by other events, or (6) the claim is invalid because the statute of limitations has expired.

The legal liability of accountants is not limited to audited statements. In the 1967 case *1136 Tenants Corp. v. Max Rothenberg & Co.,*[24] the accounting firm was sued for negligent failure to discover embezzlement by the managing agent who had hired the firm to write up the books. The firm was held liable for failure to inquire or communicate concerning missing invoices despite a disclaiming notation on the financial statements informing users that "No independent verifications were undertaken thereon." The firm moved to dismiss the case but the court denied the motion and held that even if a CPA "acted as a robot, merely doing copy work," there was an issue as to whether there were suspicious circumstances relating to missing invoices that imposed a duty on the firm to warn the client. When the case went to trial, the court found there to be an engagement to audit and entered a judgment for more than $237,000 despite the firm's oral evidence that it was employed for $600 annually to "write up" the books.

The *1136* case affected auditing standards in two notable areas. First, the engagement letter was developed to clarify the responsibilities of accountants and auditors in performing professional services. The engagement letter formalizes the relationship between the auditor and the client. It serves as a contract detailing the responsibilities of the accountant or auditor and expectations for management. While engagement letters are not required by accounting or auditing standards, it does help clarify the obligations of professionals and any legal matters.

A second result was that the Accounting and Review Services Committee of the AICPA, a senior technical committee, was formed to formulate standards to be followed by accountants who perform two levels of service—a compilation and a review. A review provides limited assurance that the financial statements are free of material misstatements, a lower standard than the reasonable assurance requirement in the audit, while a compilation provides no assurance since the only services provided are of a bookkeeping nature.

Auditor Defenses

Common-law liability for fraud is available to third parties in any jurisdiction. The plaintiff (third party) must prove (1) a false representation by the accountant, (2) knowledge or belief by the accountant that the representation was false, (3) that the accountant intended to induce the third party to rely on false representation, (4) that the third party relied on the false representation, and (5) that the third party suffered damages.[25]

Courts have held that fraudulent intent or *scienter* may be established by proof that the accountant acted without knowledge of the false representation. However, liability for fraud is not limited to cases where the auditor was knowingly deceitful. Some courts have interpreted gross negligence or constructive fraud as an instance of fraud. *Gross negligence* is defined to be an extreme, flagrant, or reckless deviation from professional standards of due care. An important case in this area is *State Street Trust Co. v. Ernst.*[26] In this case, the auditors issued an unqualified opinion on their client's financial statements, knowing that State Street Trust Company was making a loan based on those financial statements. A month later, the auditors sent a letter to the client indicating that receivables had been overstated. The auditors, however, did not communicate this information to State Street and the client subsequently went bankrupt. The New York court ruled that the auditor's actions appeared to be grossly negligent and that "reckless disregard of consequences may take the place of deliberate intention." In such cases, while fraudulent intent or scienter may not be present, the court "constructs" fraud due to the grossness of the negligence.[27]

In *Phar-Mor v. Coopers & Lybrand,* the auditors were found guilty of fraud under both common and statutory law, even though the plaintiffs acknowledged that the auditors had no intent to deceive. Instead, the plaintiff successfully argued reckless disregard for the truth (i.e., gross negligence or constructive fraud), which gives rise to an inference of fraud. An important part of this ruling is that plaintiffs who are barred from suing for ordinary negligence because they lack a privity relationship or are not foreseen users can choose to sue the auditor for fraud because to find an auditor guilty of fraud, the plaintiffs need only prove gross negligence.[28]

In a recent case, the court ruled in *Houbigant, Inc. v. Deloitte & Touche LLP* that for an auditor to be found guilty of fraud, the plaintiffs must prove only that the auditor was aware that its misrepresentations might reasonably be relied upon by the plaintiff, not that the auditor intended to induce the detrimental reliance. The court referred to recent audit failures in its decision: "It should be sufficient that the complaint contains some rational basis for inferring that the alleged misrepresentation was knowingly made. Indeed, to require anything beyond that would be particularly undesirable at this time, when it has been widely acknowledged that our society is experiencing a proliferation of frauds perpetrated by officers of large corporations . . . unchecked by the 'impartial' auditors they hired."[29]

Statutory Liability

The most relevant sources of statutory liability for auditors are the Securities Act of 1933, the Securities Exchange Act of 1934, and the Sarbanes-Oxley Act (SOX) of 2002. These laws create potential civil liabilities for auditors for failing to adhere to the requirements of the laws in carrying out professional obligations. Criminal liability exists when an auditor defrauds a third party through knowingly being involved with falsifications in financial statements. SOX makes it a felony to destroy or create documents to impede or obstruct a federal investigation. Obstruction of justice charges were brought against Andersen in its audit of Enron, and the charge itself led to a parade of clients abandoning the firm and ultimately to its demise.

Securities Act of 1933

The Securities Act of 1933[30] regulates the disclosure of information in a registration statement for a new public offering of securities (i.e., an initial public offering, or IPO). Companies must file registration statements (S-1, S-2, and S-3 forms) and prospectuses that contain financial statements that have been audited by an independent CPA.

Section 11 of the Securities Act of 1933 imposes a liability on issuer companies and others, including auditors, for losses suffered by third parties when false or misleading information is included in a registration statement. Any purchaser of securities may sue; the purchaser generally must prove that (1) the specific security was offered through the registration statements, (2) damages were incurred, and (3) there was a material misstatement or omission in the financial statements included in the registration statement. The plaintiff need not prove reliance on the financial statements unless the purchase took place after one year of the offering.

If items (2) and (3) are proven, it is a *prima facie* case (sufficient to win against the CPA unless rebutted) and shifts the burden of proof to the accountant, who may escape liability by proving the following: (1) after reasonable investigation, the CPA concludes there is a reasonable basis to believe that the financial statements were true and there was no material misstatement (due diligence defense); (2) the plaintiff knew the financial statements were incorrect when the investment was made (knowledge of falsehood defense); or (3) the loss was due to factors other than the misstatement or omission (lack of causation defense).

Key Court Decisions

McKesson & Robbins

The *McKesson & Robbins* case[31] in 1939 was the first instance in which auditing practices were subject to significant public scrutiny. The case involved a conspiracy to defraud the company by its former president, Donald Coster. Joseph Wells, the founder and former CEO of the Association of Certified Fraud Examiners (ACFE), points out in his book *Frankensteins of Fraud* that behind the mask of Coster, the much admired CEO of McKesson & Robbins Pharmaceuticals, lurked Philip Musica, bootlegger, government snitch, and swindler. While the kindly Dr. Coster was courted for the U.S. presidency, he was living a secret life bleeding McKesson & Robbins for millions of dollars.[32]

Coster and his brothers undertook an elaborate scheme that included dummy trading companies, fictitious warehouses, and forged documents. A cynic might contend that Coster's actions served as a (negative) role model for Barry Minkow in ZZZZ Best some 40-plus years later.

A 1939 investigation by the SEC revealed that Coster and his confidants had stolen around $2.9 million of McKesson & Robbins's cash in the previous 12 years. However, due to the lack of two "then-not-required" audit procedures, physical observation of inventory and direct confirmation of accounts receivable, Price Waterhouse & Co. failed to detect $19 million nonexistent assets (out of a total assets of over $87 million) and $1.8 million gross profit on fictitious sales of $18 million that were included in McKesson's 1937 certified financial statements.

The due diligence defense available to the auditor under Section 11 requires that the auditor has made a reasonable investigation of the facts supporting or contradicting the information included in the registration statement. The test is whether a "prudent person" would have made a similar investigation under similar circumstances. There is a link to be made between the legal notion of a prudent person test and *rights theory.* Recall that the universality principle in rights theory posits that an ethical action is one in which, based on the judgment of the decision maker, others would take in similar circumstances for similar reasons.

Escott v. Bar Chris Construction Corp.

A leading case under Section 11 is *Escott v. BarChris Construction Corp.* in which the court held that the auditor's actions in reviewing events subsequent to the balance sheet date (subsequent events) were not conducted with due diligence because the senior auditor in charge of reviewing these events had not spent sufficient time and accepted unconvincing answers to key questions. The court determined that there had been sufficient warning signs that further investigation was necessary.[33]

Securities Exchange Act of 1934

The Securities Exchange Act of 1934[34] regulates the ongoing reporting by companies whose securities are listed and traded on a stock exchange such as the New York Stock Exchange and NASDAQ. The act requires ongoing filing of quarterly (10-Q) and annual (10-K) reports and the periodic filing of an 8-K form whenever a significant event takes place affecting the entity such as a change in auditors.

Section 18 of the act imposes liability on any person who makes a material false or misleading statement in documents filed with the SEC. The auditor's liability can be limited if the auditor can show that she "acted in good faith and had no knowledge that such statement was false or misleading." However, a number of cases have limited the auditor's good-faith defense when the auditor's action has been judged to be grossly negligent.[35]

The liability of auditors under the act often centers on Section 10 and Rule 10b-5. These provisions make it unlawful for a CPA to (1) employ any device, scheme, or artifice to defraud; (2) make an untrue statement of material fact or omit a material fact; and (3) engage in any act, practice, or course of business to commit fraud or deceit in connection with the purchase or sale of the security.

Once a plaintiff has established the ability to sue under Rule 10b-5, the following elements must be proved: (1) a material, factual misrepresentation or omission; (2) reliance on the financial statements; (3) damages suffered as a result of reliance on the financial statements; and (4) the intent to deceive, manipulate, or defraud *(scienter).*[36]

Ernst & Ernst v. Hochfelder

An important case that strengthens the scienter requirement is the 1976 U.S. Supreme Court reversal in *Ernst & Ernst v. Hochfelder.*[37] The U.S. Court of Appeals had ruled in favor of Hochfelder and reversed the lower court opinion. The court decision includes this statement: "One who breaches a duty of inquiry and disclosure owed another is liable in damages for aiding and abetting a third party's violation of Rule 10b-5 if the fraud would have been discovered or prevented but for the breach, and that there were genuine issues of fact as to whether [Ernst] committed such a breach, and whether inquiry and disclosure would have led to discovery or prevention of the . . . fraud."

The *Hochfelder* case involves the president of a brokerage firm who induced Hochfelder to invest in "escrow" accounts that the president represented would yield a high rate of return. The president converted those funds to personal use. The fraud came to light after the president committed suicide, leaving a note that described the brokerage as bankrupt and the escrow accounts as "spurious." Hochfelder's cause of action rested on a theory of negligent nonfeasance. The premise was that Ernst had failed to utilize "appropriate auditing procedures" in its audits of the brokerage, thereby failing to discover internal practices of the firm said to prevent an effective audit. The practice principally relied on the president's rule that only he could open mail addressed to him or to his attention at the brokerage, even if it arrived in his absence. Hochfelder argued that had Ernst conducted a proper audit, it would have discovered this "mail rule."

The U.S. Supreme Court reversed the decision ruling that a private cause of action for damages does not come under Rule 10b-5 in the absence of any allegation of scienter. The Court cited the language in Section 10 that it is unlawful for any person to use or employ any manipulative or deceptive device or contrivance in contravention of SEC rules. The Court ruled that the use of those words clearly shows that it was intended to prohibit a type of conduct quite different from negligence. The term *manipulative* connotes intentional or willful conduct designed to deceive or defraud investors, a type of conduct that did not exist in the case.

Auditor defenses under the Securities Exchange Act of 1934 include, in addition to a lack of scienter, non-negligent performance of services, a lack of duty to the third party, and the absence of any casual connection that demonstrates the third party relied on audit work and suffered damages as a result. The best defense for an auditor is to view professional responsibilities as going beyond mere adherence to the technical requirements of GAAS. The standards cannot cover every situation. Recall that when the rules are unclear or provide only vague guidance on an audit matter, the auditor should act in accordance with the ethical standards described in Chapters 1 and 2 including the Principles of the AICPA Code of Professional Conduct and ethical reasoning methods.

Court Decisions and Auditing Procedures

Equity Funding

The *Equity Funding* case changed the way that CPA firms audited clients and it brought attention to the red flags that might indicate fraud is present. Equity Funding's principal line of business was to create "funding programs" that included the sale of life insurance combined with mutual fund investment. Equity Funding derived its income from commissions on the sales. The fraud started just prior to the company's going public and it was motivated by an attempt to increase the earnings of the company. Equity Funding inflated its earnings by recording fictitious commissions from the sale of its product that the company called "reciprocals." The company also borrowed funds without recording them as liabilities; instead, the cash was recorded as payments on the loan receivable by participants in the program. By reducing the loans receivable, Equity Funding could record more fictitious commissions. The last part of the fraud involved creating fictitious insurance policies, which were then reinsured with other insurance companies. This enabled the company to obtain additional cash to pay premiums on policies, which in turn required that more fictitious policies be created on their books.[38]

Equity Funding collapsed in 1973 when a former employee disclosed the existence of the massive fraud. During the period of the fraud, Equity Funding was audited first by Wolfson Weiner, which ultimately was taken over by the CPA firm Seidman & Seidman. A lengthy audit by Touche during the bankruptcy proceedings disclosed that the company had generated more than $2 billion of fictitious insurance policies.

On November 1, 1973, a federal grand jury in California indicted 22 executives and employees of Equity Funding including Stanley Goldblum, the chair and CEO of the company. According to the indictment, Goldblum wanted to achieve a level of growth that was not attainable through legitimate business operations. He arranged for various officers and employees to make fictitious bookkeeping entries to inflate the company's income and assets. He also directed employees to create fictitious insurance policies. On November 2, 1970, an employee was instructed to write a computer program creating fictitious policies with a face value of $430 million and a total yearly premium of $5.5 million. In 1971, some phony policies were reinsured and some employees were instructed to create death claims on the policies. A cynic might say that this was yet another example of the "role models" Barry Minkow used for the ZZZZ Best fraud.

Creating phony accounting entries is relatively easy, but creating the documentation for 64,000 phony policies was a big challenge, even at Equity Funding. Management wanted to be able to satisfy the auditors, who would ask to see a sample of policies for review. The auditors would examine the policies' documentation on file, and then cross-check for premium receipts and reserve policy information. However, in all but a handful of cases, there were no policy files available. To solve this problem, management created an in-house institution—the forgery party!

At Equity Funding, policy files the auditors requested would often be "temporarily unavailable." Employees would work at night to forge the missing files to have them ready for auditor review the next day. The fact that the auditors were duped was the least of their embarrassment. One night when the auditor left his briefcase unlocked, an Equity Funding executive, in full sight of others, opened the case and took the audit plan and was able to anticipate next steps. Another time, an auditor wanted to send out policy confirmations to a sample of policyholders. Equity Funding officials, eager to help, did some clerical chores for the auditor. The result was letters addressed to branch sales managers and agents, who dutifully filled out the forms for the fictitious policyholders.[39]

Joe Wells characterized Equity Funding in *Frankensteins of Fraud* by stating that Victor Frankenstein made the dead live just as Stanley Goldblum gave life to 64,000 phony policyholders in his Equity Funding insurance scam. The lawsuit led to a verdict in California against three auditors who did not report evidence of the large-scale fraud. The court sentenced them to serve two-year prison terms, spend four years on probation, and do 2,000 hours of charity work.

Crazy Eddie

New Yorkers might remember television commercials of an electronics company called Crazy Eddie that aired during the mid- and late 1980s. The former chair and CEO, Eddie Antar, advertised that his prices were lower than the competition. An actor would come on the screen, act like a madman, and scream: "Our prices are insane." In the aftermath of the fraud at Crazy Eddie, cynics might claim that Eddie Antar was insane.

On July 16, 1990, the SEC obtained a judgment for $73,496,432 plus interest against Antar in the U.S. District Court for the District of New Jersey. Antar became a fugitive and fled to Israel in 1990. He lived under an alias until June 1992, when he was arrested. He was sent back to the United States in January 1993. The SEC initiated lawsuits in Britain, Liechtenstein, and Israel to recover misappropriated assets. With interest, the final judgment against Antar now exceeds $84 million. On February 10, 1997, the SEC announced that District Court Judge Harold A. Ackerman sentenced Antar to a federal prison term of 82 months followed by 2 years of supervised release.

According to *SEC v. Eddie Antar et al.,* Litigation Release No. 15251, that was issued on February 10, 1997, Antar pleaded guilty to the following:[40]

1. In 1985 Antar caused the value of inventory of Crazy Eddie reported to its auditors to be falsely overstated by approximately $2 million.
2. He caused the inventory counts to be artificially inflated by the falsification of count sheets or inventory tickets when Crazy Eddie took a physical inventory at the end of its fiscal year on March 2, 1986, and at the end of fiscal year 1987, thereby overstating the inventory by millions of dollars.
3. Just before the year-end 1986, he caused approximately $2 million from outside sources to be deposited into Crazy Eddie's bank accounts in such a way that the money would be booked as proceeds of retail sales.
4. His primary purpose in perpetrating these fraudulent schemes was to increase the price of Crazy Eddie stock to public investors.

Four different accounting firms audited Crazy Eddie's financial statements. Perhaps for the fourth firm if not the third, the proverbial red flag should have gone up given the unusually large number of auditor changes. In the mid-1980s, Peat Marwick became Crazy Eddie's audit firm when it merged with Main Hurdman. Following a corporate takeover of Crazy Eddie in the aftermath of the legal action against the company, the new owners replaced Peat Marwick with Touche.

One of the criticisms against Peat Marwick was that it charged a relatively modest audit fee and, allegedly, the firm lowballed the engagement to obtain Crazy Eddie as an audit client, realizing that it could make up for lost audit revenue by selling the company consulting services.[41] If this were true, Peat Marwick risked compromising its independence and objectivity because the firm may have been reluctant to go against top management when a difference of opinion on an accounting issue existed. The firm would know that the client might hold back on the consulting services pending the firm's acquiescence to the demands of top management.

Whether or not the firm cut corners in the audit and staffing because of the low fee, the court ruled against the accountants in a lawsuit brought by purchasers of the company's stock prior to the disclosure of fraudulent financial statements alleging the registration statements and prospectuses had been false and misleading in violation of Sections 11 and 13 of the Securities Act of 1933. The plaintiffs charged that the accountants had violated GAAP and GAAS by failing to uncover the fraud and fictitious activities. The court held that the plaintiffs did not have to prove fraud or negligence, only that any material misstatements in the registration statement were misleading.

On April 27, 2000, Judge Ackerman issued an order setting the amounts of disgorgement and prejudgment interest for the defendants in the case, who were ordered to pay the following amounts for their insider trading in connection with the sales of common stock in Crazy Eddie: disgorgement total—$19.38 million; interest—$54.21 million; total amount—$73.59 million. *Disgorgement* is paid by defendants, who have gained falsely obtained monies to plaintiffs to make those who have suffered financial loss at least partially whole once again. In rejecting the defendant's contention that the amount of their disgorgement should be $0, Judge Ackerman stated:

> As innovative as it was, the core of Crazy Eddie was rotten, and the investing public, once it became aware of that fact, would not have dawdled in ridding itself of the stock. The extensive fraud would certainly have driven off the investors, and the defendants' contention that the stock retained some value despite the frauds at the company simply lacks persuasiveness.[42]

Antar's nephew, Sam Antar, the former CFO of the company, was part of the mastermind of the fraud. Subsequent to his testimony for the government, Sam saw the light and joined the speakers circuit talking about how accountants can prevent frauds like Crazy Eddie from occurring in the future. On a Web site Sam posted the following comment that clearly shows his feelings of remorse over what he did to contribute to the Crazy Eddie fraud:[43]

My name is Sam Antar. I am a convicted felon, former CPA, and former Chief Financial Officer of Crazy Eddie, Inc. During the 1980s, I helped mastermind with my cousin Eddie Antar and Uncle Sam M. Antar (co-founders of the company) one of the largest securities frauds of its time. Crazy Eddie Antar was coined by U.S. Attorney Michael Chertoff as, "the Darth Vader of Capitalism." This securities fraud cost investors hundreds of millions of dollars, cost many people their life savings, cost many people their jobs and careers, cost creditors hundreds of millions of dollars, and many people's suffering that cannot be measured. I was the government's key witness in both the criminal and civil prosecutions. I also fully cooperated with all civil plaintiffs in the prosecution of their claims. I make no excuses for my criminal conduct. Nor should I receive any praise for my cooperation.

I take full and complete responsibility for my actions and apologize to all the victims of my crimes. Also, I apologize to the other persons who would never have committed a crime, if not for my efforts to recruit them into the conspiracy and convince them to lie thereafter. Furthermore, I apologize to the government lawyers, plaintiff's lawyers, government investigators, and plaintiff's investigators whose efforts in prosecuting the truth of the crimes at Crazy Eddie were hampered by my willful stonewalling prior to me relenting and later deciding to cooperate with the investigations. I apologize to anyone I deceived, directly or indirectly, including but not limited to the shareholders, employees, creditors, public accounting firms, Wall Street firms, financial analysts, the press, etc. However, my apologies, acceptance of responsibility, and the punishment imposed upon me by the court [are] not enough.

I believe that acceptance of one's personal responsibility for past actions must be accompanied by corrective action and not include exploitation for personal gain. I believe that former criminals like me must do more than just express regret for our crimes and pay whatever punishment society imposes upon us. I believe that it is our obligation and responsibility to educate society, so that society can avoid future perils caused by new generations of criminals. I also believe that any person's true test of character comes from overcoming past misdeeds and wrongdoing and trying to do something positive out of it without any personal gain or recognition.

Potential Criminal Liability

An accountant may be found criminally liable for violations of the Securities Acts of 1933 and the Securities Exchange Act of 1934, the Internal Revenue Code, and state and federal criminal codes. Under both the 1933 and 1934 acts, accountants may be subject to criminal penalties for willful violations—imprisonment of up to 10 years and/or a fine of up to $10,000 under the 1933 act and up to $100,000 under the 1934 act. SOX created new or broader federal crimes for obstruction of justice and securities fraud, with maximum prison time of 20 or 25 years, respectively. Sentences for many existing federal crimes were enhanced. Mail and wire fraud maximum penalties were quadrupled, from 5 to 20 years. The maximum sentence for some securities law violations was doubled from 10 to 20 years, and the maximum fine against a company for the same offense was increased from $2.5 to $25 million. The following is a summary of jail time sentences imposed on CEOs responsible for fraud in some of the cases discussed in this book.

CEO	Company	Jail Time
Bernie Ebbers	WorldCom	25 years
Dennis Kozlowski	Tyco	8 1/3 to 25 years
Richard Scrushy	HealthSouth	6 years, 10 months
Jeff Skilling	Enron	24 years, 4 months[44]

EXHIBIT 6.3
**Legal Cases
and Auditor
Responsibilities**

Case	Audit Procedures
Eddie Antar et al.	Procedures for taking inventory
1136 Tenants Corp.	Engagement letters; compilations and reviews
Equity Funding	Responsibilities for fraud detection
Escott v. BarChris	Due care; professional skepticism; subsequent event review
Hochfelder	"Appropriate" auditing procedures
McKesson & Robbins	Physical inventory observation; accounts receivable confirmation

Implications of Legal Decisions for Auditors' Responsibilities

Several case rulings contributed toward advancements in procedures now used by auditors in conducting an examination of the financial statements of client entities. These are summarized in Exhibit 6.3.

The Fine Line between an Auditor's Recklessness and Intent to Deceive

A 1999 decision out of the Southern District of New York explored the delicate issue of just how egregious an accounting firm's failure to comply with GAAS and GAAP must be to subject that firm to a fraud claim arising out of its audit of a clients' financial statements. The issue is a critical one because while a failure to adhere to one or more of these principles may give rise to a negligence claim (a troublesome enough predicament), a more extensive failure to comply with these industry standards can reflect such a reckless disregard for the accuracy of a client's financial representations as to satisfy the scienter element of a fraud claim against the auditor itself. Where that line is drawn can have grave consequences for accounting firms understandably eager not to end up on the receiving end of a fraud claim that, even if totally unfounded, can have a devastating impact on their stock in trade (i.e., their professional reputation). This issue was addressed in *Jacobs v. Coopers & Lybrand.*[45]

The *Jacobs* case involved a securities class action in which the plaintiff alleged that Happiness Express Inc. ("Happiness"), a publicly traded marketer of products based on children's entertainment characters, fraudulently overstated its 1995 financial performance in filings with the SEC. Coopers was sued in connection with its role as auditor of the company's financial statements. Coopers gave its unqualified approval to Happiness's financials. Plaintiffs alleged that Coopers failed to properly audit the company's accounts receivable from two of its suppliers. As a result, the company's 1995 public filings reflected almost $6.3 million in bogus sales. Plaintiffs alleged that Coopers had turned a blind eye to red flags in an extreme departure from the standards of ordinary care. Coopers's workpapers indicated that it examined certain of the suspicious documents and consciously disregarded their suspicious nature. Indeed, Coopers did not plan and perform its audit of Happiness's fiscal 1995 financial statements with an attitude of professional skepticism as required by GAAS. This audit failure, coupled with auditing procedures that were so deficient that they grossly violated GAAS, allowed Happiness to disseminate materially false and misleading "audited" financial statements and financial results to the market.

Coopers moved to dismiss the complaint for failure to state a claim. Judge Patterson observed that the plaintiff's claim under Section 10(b) of the Securities Exchange Act of 1934 would survive the motion "unless it appears beyond doubt that the plaintiffs can prove no set of facts in support of their claims that would entitle them to relief." Judge Patterson noted that a Section 10(b) argument must plead facts demonstrating that, in connection with the offering or sale of a security, the defendant (1) made a false material representation, and (2) did so with scienter (i.e., "a mental state embracing intent to deceive, manipulate, or defraud") which the plaintiff must demonstrate either by alleging facts showing that the defendant had both the motive and opportunity to commit fraud or by alleging acts that constitute strong circumstantial evidence of conscious misbehavior or recklessness.

To adequately plead a Section 10(b) violation, the court stated that "a plaintiff must plead sufficient acts amounting to recklessness such that recklessness approximates intention to deceive. The court noted that although an auditor may be found liable for a Section 10(b) violation, an auditing firm's failure to follow GAAP "without more, does not constitute a Section 10(b) violation." Coopers argued that the Section 10(b) claim should be dismissed because the complaint alleged no facts that, even if accepted as true, could support an inference of scienter and it did adhere to GAAS.

Judge Patterson flatly rejected Coopers's position. He denied the accounting firm's motion, observing that "Coopers does not offer any authority for this proposition. To the contrary," the court noted, "the Complaint details several examples of alleged departures from GAAS which amount to more than 'nitpicking attacks' as Coopers has characterized them." Judge Patterson then set forth a litany of alleged transgressions under GAAS which, when viewed collectively and accepted as true, he found sufficient to constitute a degree of recklessness so extensive as to be tantamount to a fraudulent intent to deceive. "Indeed, the Plaintiffs more than just allege that Coopers failed to adhere to GAAS in its audit of 1995 statements. They put this failure in a broader context with allegations that, taken together, paint a portrait of an audit so reckless that a jury could infer intent to defraud." In reaching this conclusion, Judge Patterson focused on, among others, the following allegations:

- Despite the fact that the company's receivables from West Coast Liquidators (West Coast) represented approximately 13 percent of its total receivable balance at fiscal year end, Coopers failed to independently confirm directly through West Coast the existence of such receivables.

- Coopers failed to sufficiently inquire into purported sales to West Coast and a second entity, Wow Wee International, Ltd. (Wow Wee). Sales to these entities purportedly amounted to 35 percent of the company's fourth quarter sales and 34 percent of the fiscal year accounts receivable. Coopers failed to inquire into the company's suspicious representation that nearly all of the purported Wow Wee sales were invoiced on the last day of the fiscal year, and all of the purported West Coast sales were invoiced within the last 36 days of the fiscal year.

- Notwithstanding its historical knowledge of Happiness's operations and the fact that Wow Wee was a supplier to the company, Coopers did not question why in fiscal year 1995 the company showed millions of dollars in sales to Wow Wee.

- Coopers did not conduct its audit in such a way as to determine why in 1994 the breakdown of the company's accounts receivable was 88 percent factored and 12 percent nonfactored, when in 1995 the breakdown was 19 percent factored and 81 percent nonfactored.

- Coopers failed to detect that Happiness had issued checks in the amount of $100,000 without supporting documentation, with these funds being used to cover the personal expenses of the company's chief financial officer.

- Coopers did not question invoices that did not identify shipping companies, customer purchase order numbers, and/or bills of lading, although it knew that the company's internal procedures required such information.

- In connection with its 1995 audit, Coopers improperly relied on information gathered during the course of its 1994 audit without independently assessing the relevant 1995 data.

The totality of the facts as alleged, the court concluded, compelled denial of the motion to dismiss. Judge Patterson observed that the complaint "alleges a situation much more grave than one in which the auditor simply failed to make further inquiries, which alone amounts only to negligence." Failing to adhere to one or two auditing standards may be only negligence, but Coopers is alleged to have disregarded many different auditing interpretations. Based on the facts as alleged, the court found that Coopers's audit was so reckless that Coopers should have known of the underlying fraud, and acted in blind disregard that there was a strong likelihood that Happiness was engaged in the underlying fraud. Judge Patterson concluded that the plaintiffs "have alleged facts sufficient to support a finding of scienter on the part of Coopers."

The Coopers audit is a poster child for inattentive auditing borne out of a desire to not look too closely to find and report fraud. It occurred during the mid-1990s, a time when the economy was booming and companies felt compelled to do whatever they could to keep up the appearance that the earnings trend was upward, matching growth in the economy. It was a period when stock prices were increasing, bonuses were higher each year, and the value of stock options made many CEOs millionaires over night.

Insider Reporting and Trading

Officers, directors, and stockholders owning 10 percent of the class of equity securities registered under Section 12 of the 1934 Securities Exchange Act must file reports with the SEC concerning their ownership and trading of the corporations' securities.[46] To discourage such insiders from using nonpublic information about their companies for their personal benefit in the stock market, Section 16(b) of the 1934 act provides for the recapture by the corporation of all profits realized by an insider on any purchase and sale or sale and purchase of the corporation's stock within any six-month period. It is irrelevant whether the insider actually uses inside information; all such short-swing profits must be returned to the corporation. Section 16(b) applies not only to stock but also to warrants, options, and securities convertible into stock.

When most people hear the term *insider trading* they think of the illegal version. However, *insider trading* can also mean the perfectly legal buying and selling of stock by a company's corporate insiders. Insider trading is legal when these corporate insiders trade stock of their own company and report these trades to the SEC. That way the insider trading is not kept a secret and anyone can find out a corporate insider's opinion of his or her company. Insider trading is illegal only when a person bases his trade of stocks in a public company on information that the public does not know. It is illegal to trade your own stock in a company based on this information, but it is also illegal to give someone that information—a tip—so he can trade the stock.

The SEC's job is to make sure that all investors are making decisions based on the same information. Insider trading can be illegal because it destroys this level playing field. According to the SEC Web site, there are almost 500 civil enforcement actions each year against individuals and companies that break securities laws. Insider trading is one of the most common laws broken. The punishment for illegal insider trading depends on the situation. The person can be fined, banned from sitting on the executive or board of directors of a public company, and even jailed.

United States v. Martha Stewart and Peter Bacanovic[47]

Samuel Waksal, the CEO of ImClone Systems, Inc., a biotechnology company, was a client of stockbroker Peter Bacanovic. Bacanovic's other clients included Martha Stewart, then the CEO of Martha Stewart Living Omnimedia (MSLO). On December 27, 2001, Waksal began selling his ImClone shares. The next day, ImClone announced that the Food and Drug

Administration had rejected the company's application for approval of its leading product, a medication called Erbitux. The government began to investigate Stewart's ImClone trades, the media began to report on the investigation, and the value of MSLO stock began to drop.

In June 2002, at a Mid-year Media Review conference attended by investment professionals and investors, Stewart said that she had previously agreed with Bacanovic to sell her ImClone stock if the price fell to $60 per share. "I have nothing to add on this matter today. And I'm here to talk about our terrific company." Her statements were followed by a 40-minute presentation on MSLO.

Subsequently, Stewart was charged with, among other things, fraud in connection with the purchase and sale of MSLO securities in violation of the SEC Act of 1934. She filed a motion for a judgment of acquittal of this charge. The court granted Stewart's motion. The court reasoned that "to find the essential element of criminal intent beyond a reasonable doubt" and conclude that Stewart lied to influence the market for the securities of her company "a rational juror would have to speculate."

Unfortunately for Stewart that was not the end of the story. She was later convicted on other charges related to her sale of ImClone stock, including obstruction of justice and lying to federal officials. Stewart was sentenced to, and has served, five months in prison and five months and three weeks of house arrest.

Private Securities Litigation Reform Act (PSLRA)

The Private Securities Litigation Reform Act (PSLRA) of 1995 changed the potential liability of accountants and other professionals in securities fraud cases. Among other things, the act imposed a new statutory obligation on accountants. An auditor must use adequate procedures in an audit to detect any illegal acts of the company being audited. If something illegal is detected, the auditor must disclose it to the company's board of directors, the audit committee, or the SEC, depending on the circumstances.[48]

Recall that Rule 301 of the AICPA Code of Professional Conduct prohibits CPAs from directly disclosing information to outside parties, including illegal acts, unless the auditors have a legal duty to do so. The PSLRA includes a requirement for fraud reporting, or whistleblowing, by the auditors. The requirements of this law apply when the client has committed an illegal act and (1) it has a material effect on the financial statements, (2) senior management and the board of directors have not taken appropriate remedial action, and (3) the failure to take remedial action is reasonably expected to warrant a departure from a standard audit report, or resignation by the auditors.

If the auditor concludes that an illegal act with a material effect on the financial statements has not been dealt with by senior management in a timely manner and with appropriate remedial actions, then the auditor should directly report its conclusions to the board of directors. If a board of directors receives such a report from its auditors, then management has one business day from the receipt of such report to inform the SEC and furnish a copy to the auditors. If the auditor fails to receive a copy of such notice within the required one-business-day period, the independent public accountant should furnish the SEC a copy of its report within the next business day following the failure to receive timely notice. Auditors are not liable in a private action for any finding, conclusion, or statement expressed in a report made pursuant to these rules.[49]

Auditors are also required to communicate illegal acts in other situations. When illegal activities cause the auditors of a public company to lose faith in the integrity of senior management, they should resign and a Form 8-K, which discloses the reasons for the auditors' resignation, should be filed with the SEC by management. The auditors must file a response to the filing indicating whether or not they agree with management's reasons, and providing the details when they disagree.

Proportionate Liability

The PSLRA changes the legal liability standard of auditors from joint-and-several liability to proportionate liability. As discussed in the opening quote of this chapter, the accounting profession had fought over time to effectuate this change because of what the profession perceived to be frivolous lawsuits that included the auditors as defendants primarily because the plaintiffs counted on out-of-court settlement by the auditors who had "deep pockets"; auditors also carry large amounts of professional liability insurance for such matters. Under the act, a party is liable only for that proportion of damages for which he is responsible. An accountant who does not participate in, and is unaware of, illegal conduct may not be liable for the entire loss caused by the illegality.

Sarbanes-Oxley (SOX) Act

We have already addressed four important provisions of the Sarbanes-Oxley (SOX) Act including Section 201 restricting certain nonaudit services for audit clients (Chapter 4); Section 302 requiring the certification of a company's financial statements by the CEO and CFO (Chapter 4); Section 404 and the related PCAOB *Auditing Standard No. 5* on conducting an audit of internal controls along with the audit of financial statements (Chapter 5); and Section 806 on whistleblowing provisions under SOX (Chapter 3). We now review some of those provisions and add a few more.

SOX (H.R. 3763) creates additional obligations and restrictions for management and auditors that change the landscape of legal liability. The relevant provisions of the act are described in the following sections.

Section 302. Corporate Responsibility for Financial Reports

This section requires the certification of periodic reports filed with the SEC by the CEO and CFO of public companies. The certification states that "based on the officer's knowledge, the report does not contain any untrue statement of a material fact or omit to state a material fact necessary in order to make the statements, in light of the circumstances under which such statements were made, not misleading." The HealthSouth fraud was the first case where the SEC brought action against company officers for a false certification.

Section 308. Fair Funds for Investors

In a securities action brought by the SEC against a public company, the court order may grant disgorgement against a member of top management, such as the CEO and CFO, for violation of the law or SEC regulations. These funds are typically returned to the parties that were harmed (i.e., investors) because the statements made or actions taken by the CEO or CFO caused the harm.

Section 401. Disclosures in Periodic Reports

Section 401 amends the Securities Exchange Act of 1934 to include the requirement that each financial statement filed with the SEC reflect all material correcting adjustments that have been identified by the audit firm in accordance with GAAP and the rules and regulations of the commission. The rule extends the disclosure requirements in securities laws to include all material off-balance sheet transactions and any other transaction with a material current or future effect on financial condition or changes thereto, operating results, liquidity, capital expenditures, capital resources, or significant components of revenues or expenses. Recall that Enron had established off-balance sheet entities to hide debt, improve liquidity, enhance financial position, and mask operating results.

Section 801. Corporate Criminal Fraud Accountability

Section 801 makes it clear that anyone who "knowingly alters, destroys, mutilates, conceals, covers up, falsifies, or makes a false entry in any record, document, or tangible object with the intent to impede, obstruct, or influence the investigation" is subject to fine, imprisonment for not more than 20 years, or both. Auditors are required to retain workpapers for a minimum of five years from the end of the fiscal period in which the audit or review was concluded.

Section 806. Protection for Employees of Publicly Traded Companies Who Provide Evidence in Fraud Cases

This so-called whistleblower provision protects employees who provide information on a fraud by prohibiting the discharge, demotion, discrimination, suspension or threatening or harassing action against an employee who provides information in a federal or regulatory investigation or to Congress or to the employee's supervisor. A person who alleges discharge or discrimination under this section can file a complaint with the secretary of labor. An employee who brings a successful action will be entitled to "reinstatement with the same seniority status that the employee would have had, but for the discrimination; the amount of back pay with interest; and compensation for any special damages sustained as a result of the discrimination, including litigation costs, expert witness fees, and reasonable attorney fees."

The Department of Labor delegated to the Occupational Safety and Health Administration (OSHA) enforcement authority over the whistleblower provisions of SOX. OSHA's regulations require that an employee must first establish a *prima facie* case of retaliation. This is generally interpreted as meaning that the employee must be engaged in a protected activity or conduct; that the employer knew "actually or constructively" that the conduct occurred; that the employee suffered an unfavorable personnel action; and that the circumstances "were sufficient to raise the inference that the protected activity was a contributing factor to the unfavorable action."

Section 807. Criminal Penalties for Defrauding Shareholders of Publicly Traded Companies

Section 807 provides that anyone who knowingly commits fraud with respect to securities registered under the Securities Exchange Act of 1934 will be subject to fine or imprisonment not more than 25 years, or both. Bernie Ebbers, the former CEO of WorldCom, was sentenced to 25 years in prison on July 13, 2005, for his role in the $11 billion fraud. Even with possible time off for good behavior, Ebbers, who was 63 years old at the time of sentencing, would remain locked up until 2027, when he would be 85.

Section 906. Corporate Responsibility for Financial Reports

Section 906 establishes penalties for the false certification of financial statements under Section 302. The maximum fine is $1 million and maximum imprisonment is 10 years, or both. If the false certification was made willfully, the penalties go up to $5 million and 20 years, or both.

Other Provisions of the Act

1. The maximum penalty under Section 801 for tampering with records or otherwise impeding investigations under the act is a 20-year prison sentence, fine, or both.
2. The SEC can prohibit persons such as CEOs and CFOs from serving as officers or directors of public companies as part of a cease-and-desist order.
3. Anyone who retaliates against an informant providing information under Section 806 is subject to a fine, imprisonment of not more than 10 years, or both.

First Whistleblower Lawsuit under SOX

Winning a lawsuit for dismissal and/or discrimination as a result of whistleblowing activity is easier said than done under SOX. On June 5, 2007, five years after becoming the first person to win protection under the whistleblower provision of the act, former Cardinal Bankshares CFO David Welch lost his case. The Department of Labor's Administrative Review Board ruled that it would not adopt an administrative law judge's recommendation to reinstate Welch and award him back pay. The reason was that the judge erred legally, according to the board. A complete set of facts in this case are presented in Case 6-8 at the end of the chapter.[50]

Welch claimed that he was fired from the bank holding company after he raised questions about the bank's accounting policies and internal controls and later refused to certify its financial results. The bank argued that Welch was suspended and later fired solely because he refused to meet with an independent auditor and an attorney representing the company if his lawyer wasn't present. In a charge upheld by the administrative law judge's ruling, Welch also contended that Cardinal's external auditor, Larrowe & Company, didn't communicate enough with him about financial matters that fell under Welch's job description. Instead, Welch charged that the auditor went straight to Cardinal's CEO, Ronald Leon Moore—and around Welch.

Welch's allegations in large part seemed to hinge on certain loan recoveries that Welch had asserted were misclassified as "income." Cardinal argued that because Welch had previously signed financial statements and Federal Reserve call reports without objecting to the entries, he could not have reasonably believed that the ledger entries were "improper." Welch also complained about the company's internal controls. He contended that "too many individuals without financial expertise were making journal entries without the CFO's review," according to the administrative law judge, who concurred with Welch's view.

The appeals board countermanded Welch's contentions on all those points, reasoning that some of his charges were not protected under SOX, as the administrative law judge had opined. "Welch's concerns that Cardinal misclassified loan recoveries and consequently misled investors do not constitute protected activity because Welch could not have reasonably believed that Cardinal misstated its financial condition," according to the review board's May 31 ruling. "Likewise, Welch's complaints about access to [auditor] Larrowe & Co. and about Cardinal's internal accounting controls are not SOX-protected activity because they do not relate to the federal securities laws." Therefore, since Welch has not demonstrated that he engaged in protected activity, an essential element of his case, the board denied his complaint.

From our perspective, the fact that Welch seemingly had initially gone along with the fraud by signing financial statements and Federal Reserve filings did not help support his claims that he did not know about faulty internal controls and misclassified entries. Moreover, as the CFO, Welch should have known more about what was going on in the company and not rely on external auditor communication. In short, Welch seemed to fail in his fiduciary obligations to the company and its shareholders.

Perspective on SOX

The stringent penalties under SOX may, over time, help reduce instances of financial statement fraud. However, the SEC has had an arsenal of laws at its disposal for many years and it does not seem to have made much of a difference. As described in Chapter 4, the history of accounting frauds is as old as the commission's tenure. The "bottom line" may be that the government will not be successful in its effort to legislate ethics. This is no surprise since being ethical comes from one's desire to do the right thing and courage to carry out an ethical action in the face of pressure and resistance from one's superiors. Still, a set of civil and criminal deterrents is an important part of a healthy securities regulatory system.

Other Laws Affecting Accountants and Auditors

In addition to the PSLRA and SOX, three other laws have influenced audit procedures, legal liability, and ethics requirements under the due care principle. These include (1) the Foreign Corrupt Practices Act, (2) the U.S. Federal Sentencing Guidelines, and (3) the Racketeer Influenced and Corrupt Organizations (RICO) Act.

Foreign Corrupt Practices Act (FCPA)

The Foreign Corrupt Practices Act (FCPA) establishes standards for the acceptability of payments made by U.S. multinational entities or their agent to foreign government officials. The act was motivated when, during the period of 1960 to 1977, the SEC cited 527 companies for bribes and other dubious payments that were made to win foreign contracts. Lockheed Corporation was one of the companies caught in the scandal. It was determined that Lockheed had made about $55 million in illegal payments to foreign governments and officials. One such payment of $1.7 million to Japanese Premier Tanaka led to his resignation in disgrace in 1974.

The FCPA makes it a crime to offer or provide payments to officials of foreign governments, political candidates, or political parties for the purpose of obtaining or retaining business. It applies to all U.S. corporations, whether they are publicly or privately held, and to foreign companies filing with the SEC. The Department of Justice is responsible for all criminal enforcement and for civil enforcement of the antibribery provisions with respect to domestic entities and foreign companies and nationals. The SEC is responsible for civil enforcement of the antibribery provisions with respect to registrants.

Under the FCPA, a corporation that violates the law can be fined up to $1 million while its officers who directly participated in violations of the act or had "reason to know" of such violations can be fined up to $10,000, imprisoned for up to five years, or both. The act also prohibits corporations from indemnifying fines imposed on directors, officers, employees, or agents. FCPA does not prohibit "grease payments" to foreign government employees whose duties are primarily ministerial or clerical, since such payments are sometimes required to persuade recipients to perform their normal duties.[51]

As a result of the criticisms of the antibribery provisions of the 1977 FCPA, Congress amended the act as part of the Omnibus Trade and Competitiveness Act of 1988 to clarify when a payment is prohibited.[52]

1. A payment is defined as illegal if it is intended to influence a foreign official to act in a way that is incompatible with the official's legal duty.
2. The "reason to know" standard is replaced by a "knowing" standard, so that criminal liability for illegal payments to third parties applies to individuals who "knowingly" engage in or tolerate illegal payments under the act.
3. The definition of *permissible facilitating,* or "grease" payments, is expanded to include payments to any foreign official that facilitates or expedites payments for the purpose of expediting or securing the performance of a routine governmental action.
4. Examples of acceptable payments under item number 4 include (a) obtaining permits, licenses, and the official documents to qualify a person to do business in a foreign country; (b) processing governmental papers, such as visas or work orders; (c) providing police protection, mail pickup, and delivery, or scheduling inspections associated with contract performance or inspections related to the transit of goods across country; (d) providing telephone service, power, and water, unloading and loading cargo, or protecting perishable product or commodities from deterioration; and (e) performing actions of a similar nature.

Two affirmative defenses for those accused of violating the act are that the payment is lawful "under the written laws" of the foreign country and the payment can be made for "reasonable and bona fide expenditures." These include lodging expenses incurred by or for a foreign official to promote products or services or execute the performance of a contract.

Individuals can be prosecuted under the 1988 amendment even if the company for which they work is not guilty. Penalties for violations were raised to $2 million for entities and $100,000 for individuals. The maximum term of imprisonment is kept at five years. A new $10,000 civil penalty was enacted.

Internal Accounting Control Requirements

The law requires all SEC registrants to maintain internal accounting controls to ensure that all transactions are authorized by management and recorded properly. As discussed in earlier chapters, Section 404 of SOX requires management to prepare a report on its internal controls and auditors must assess that report and issue their own opinion along with the audit opinion (integrated audit).

The SEC has clarified that an effective internal program to deal with violations of the act can help deter any penalty. In October 2001, the commission settled a nonbribery action against Gisela de Leon-Meredith, the controller of the Chestnut Hill Farms subsidiary of Seabord Corp. She was charged with causing inaccuracies in Seabord's books and covering up her actions. However, de Leon-Meredith only had to agree to a cease-and-desist order and the SEC took no action against the company. In providing reasons for its lenient treatment, the SEC credited Seabord's cooperation—specifically coming forward with details of its internal investigation, not involving attorney–client privilege, and promptly notifying the commission of the company's restatement plans.[53]

The SEC set forth in its proceeding against de Leon-Meredith some of the criteria it will consider in determining whether, and how much, to credit self-policing, self-reporting, remediation, and cooperation. These have implications for the "due diligence" requirement under the Federal Sentencing Guidelines that is discussed in the following text. It may also provide insight into the nature of the corporate culture that, at least in the view of the SEC, strengthens the internal control environment that is so critical to establishing a strong system of internal controls. As discussed in Chapter 5, the due diligence requirement has important implications for auditors who must evaluate the control environment under GAAS. These criteria are shown in Exhibit 6.4.[54]

The scope of the FCPA goes beyond events that already have occurred. The act also influences prospective events as well. For example, in September 2004 Lockheed Martin, the world's largest defense contractor, announced an agreement to purchase Titan, a defense technology company, for an estimated $1.8 billion. The merger fell apart after both companies jointly disclosed to the Department of Justice and SEC potential FCPA concerns uncovered during due diligence. They related to payments made by Titan to foreign consultants involved in the sale of the company's radio systems to foreign military and security services. These payments were made in Africa, Asia, and the Middle East—areas of the world with historical corruption problems.[55]

Federal Sentencing Guidelines

We previously discussed the *Caremark* ruling with respect to director and management responsibilities. In 1991, state and federal authorities began to investigate Caremark International for alleged violations of Medicare's antireferral law. The investigations led to indictments, substantial fines, and a shareholder's derivative suit alleging that the company directors had breached their fiduciary duty of care.

EXHIBIT 6.4
SEC Criteria to
Assess Due Diligence

1. What is the nature of the misconduct involved? Did it result from inadvertence, honest mistake, simple negligence, reckless or deliberate indifference to indicia of wrongful conduct, willful misconduct, or unadorned venality? Were the company's auditors misled?

2. How did the misconduct arise? Is it the result of pressure placed on employees to achieve specific results, or a tone of lawlessness set by those in control of the company? What compliance procedures were in place to prevent the misconduct now uncovered? Why did those procedures fail to stop or inhibit the wrongful conduct?

3. Where in the organization did the misconduct occur? How high up in the chain of command was knowledge of, or participation in, the misconduct? Did senior personnel participate in, or turn a blind eye toward, obvious indicia of misconduct? How systemic was the behavior? Is it symptomatic of the way the entity does business, or was it isolated?

4. How long did the misconduct last? Was it a one-quarter, or one-time, event, or did it last several years? In the case of a public company, did the misconduct occur before the company went public? Did it facilitate the company's ability to go public?

5. How much harm has the misconduct inflicted upon investors and other corporate constituencies? Did the share price of the company's stock drop significantly upon its discovery and disclosure?

6. How was the misconduct detected and who uncovered it?

7. How long after discovery of the misconduct did it take to implement an effective response?

8. What steps did the company take upon learning of the misconduct? Did the company immediately stop the misconduct? Are persons responsible for any misconduct still with the company? If so, are they still in the same positions? Did the company promptly, completely, and effectively disclose the existence of the misconduct to the public, to regulators, and to self-regulators? Did the company cooperate completely with appropriate regulatory and law enforcement bodies? Did the company identify what additional related misconduct is likely to have occurred? Did the company take steps to identify the extent of damage to investors and other corporate constituencies? Did the company appropriately recompense those adversely affected by the conduct?

9. What processes did the company follow to resolve many of these issues and ferret out necessary information? Were the Audit Committee and the Board of Directors fully informed? If so, when?

10. Did the company commit to learn the truth, fully and expeditiously? Did it do a thorough review of the nature, extent, origins, and consequences of the conduct and related behavior? Did management, the Board, or committees consisting solely of outside directors oversee the review? Did company employees or outside persons perform the review? If outside persons, had they done other work for the company? Where the review was conducted by outside counsel, had management previously engaged such counsel? Were scope limitations placed on the review? If so, what were they?

11. Did the company promptly make available to SEC staff the results of its review and provide sufficient documentation reflecting its response to the situation? Did the company identify possible violative conduct and evidence with sufficient precision to facilitate prompt enforcement actions against those who violated the law? Did the company produce a thorough and probing written report detailing the findings of its review? Did the company voluntarily disclose information not directly requested by the SEC, information that might not have been otherwise uncovered? Did the company ask its employees to cooperate with [the investigation] and make all reasonable efforts to secure such cooperation?

12. What assurances are there that the conduct is unlikely to recur? Did the company adopt and ensure enforcement of new and more effective internal controls and procedures designed to prevent a recurrence of the misconduct? Did the company provide [the investigators] with sufficient information for it to evaluate the company's measures to correct the situation and ensure that the conduct does not recur?

13. Is the company the same company in which the misconduct occurred, or has it changed through a merger or bankruptcy reorganization?

When the proposed settlement of the derivative action reached the Delaware Court of Chancery, it ruled in *Caremark International Derivative Legislation* that directors have an affirmative fiduciary obligation to ensure that adequate information and reporting systems exist in a corporation to provide timely and accurate information to the board and management about compliance with legal requirements. The *Caremark* view of this duty of care goes beyond the more passive standard that allows a board to rely on the integrity of employees to comply with legal and regulatory requirements. In this sense it contributes toward an effective corporate governance system.

Of special interest is the court's discussion of the increasing tendency to employ criminal law to ensure corporate compliance. On November 1, 1991, the U.S. Sentencing Commission's *Amendments to the Sentencing Guidelines* for U.S. courts became effective. The guidelines provide scheduled fines and a complex formula for determining how a company will be sentenced after being charged with committing federal crimes.[56]

The guidelines allow federal judges to mitigate any sentence imposed on a company according to a mathematical formula tied to conduct that the government seeks to encourage. Important factors in reducing a fine or sentence are:

- The presence of an effective compliance program.
- Voluntary disclosure of an offense or noncompliance.
- Cooperation with regulatory investigations.
- Assumption of responsibility for the misconduct.
- After an offense has been detected, the company must take all "reasonable steps" to respond "appropriately" to the offense and to prevent further similar offenses.

Considering the impact of the sentencing guidelines on corporate compliance, the *Caremark* court opined that "any rational person attempting in good faith to meet an organization's governance responsibility would be bound to take [the sentencing guidelines] into account." We would hope this would be the case in the business world today, but evidence suggests that the corporate governance systems envisioned in the sentencing guidelines either did not exist or broke down during the scandals of the late 1990s and early 2000s.

Application of the sentencing guidelines in securities fraud cases can be tricky business. Under the guidelines, a recommended sentence range is determined based mainly on how much money investors lost as a result of the conduct for which the defendant was found guilty. In the case of Bernie Ebbers, former CEO of WorldCom, the stock price declined from $64.50 on June 21, 1999, to $0.83 on June 25, 2002, before the accounting restatements were announced. Given that it was common knowledge there were financial statement credibility problems well before the announced restatement, the 25-year sentence given to Ebbers in all likelihood reflects the 99 percent decline in value.

Though the Federal Sentencing Guidelines were styled as mandatory, the Supreme Court's 2005 decision in *United States v. Booker* found that the guidelines, as originally constituted, violated the Sixth Amendment's constitutional right to a trial by jury and the remedy chosen was to delete those provisions of the law establishing the guidelines as mandatory.[57] In the aftermath of *Booker* and other Supreme Court cases, such as *Blakely v. Washington,* guidelines are now considered advisory only, on both the federal and the state levels. Judges must consider the guidelines when determining a sentence but are not required to issue sentences within the guidelines. Those sentences are still, however, subject to appellate review.[58]

Racketeer Influenced and Corrupt Organizations (RICO) Act

The RICO law was enacted by Congress in 1970 to combat the infiltration of legitimate business by organized crime. From time to time it is used against auditors although, thankfully, such claims tend to be dismissed by the courts. RICO provides civil and criminal sanctions for certain types of illegal acts. A major factor in bringing an action under RICO is that the law provides for treble damages (i.e., three times the actual loss) in civil RICO cases. Racketeering activities include a long list of federal and state crimes with mail fraud and wire fraud the most common allegations against auditors.[59]

Generally, a single instance of racketeering is not sufficient to establish a pattern of racketeering. In the case of *Reves v. Ernst & Young,* the Supreme Court established an "operations and management test" for auditors that requires that the plaintiff prove that the accounting firm participated in the operation or management of the client's business.[60]

In 1993, the U.S. District Court for the Southern District of Florida upheld investors' right to sue a company's auditors for alleged securities fraud and RICO violations in connection with private and public security offerings. The investors alleged that all the defendants had engaged in a conspiracy—known as "the Project"—to falsely represent the plaintiff's true financial condition and induce investment in the company. To further the project, defendants allegedly created false invoices, forged clients' names, altered confirmation letters, and set up a separate computer program to mask the fraud. The scheme was discovered after the company began an internal investigation in response to notice the SEC was looking into its accounting practices. Shortly after public announcement of the scheme, the company's common stock was cast into a free-fall and the company sought Chapter 11 reorganization.

Concluding Thoughts

We end this chapter the same way we began by linking the Private Securities Litigation Reform Act to a successful effort by the accounting industry to limit legal liability. Some blame the passage of the act, at least in part, for accountants and auditors feeling freer to play loose with GAAP rules since the likelihood of having to settle lawsuits out-of-court to avoid deep-pocket claims was lessened after changes in the legal liability standard from joint and several liability to proportionate liability. In this regard, Congress may have unwittingly contributed to the environment in the accounting profession between 1995 and 2003 that may have led to a reduction in audit quality, perhaps because the firms no longer had to fear being blamed for all of the damages in a fraud lawsuit.

Robert Mednick's comments at the beginning of the chapter seem to reflect the tenor of the debate in the early and mid-1990s that the deep-pockets-motivated lawsuits had to stop or auditors may restrict the dissemination of financial information that investors and creditors have a need, and an ethical right, to know. Even though the PSLRA was adopted and auditor liability rules changed, the statement is a troubling one since it implies that auditors may place their own self-interest (self-protection under the law) above the public's interest to receive accurate, reliable, and transparent financial information. Reasoning in this way reflects Stages 2 or 3 on Kohlberg's scale, not very admirable for a profession that prides itself on public service.

Only time will tell whether the audit profession has finally learned its lesson following the most recent round of congressional investigations that led to the passage of SOX. We worry that future bouts of accounting fraud similar to those in the period of the 1970s through early 2000s may lead to even more government regulation of the accounting profession than has already occurred under SOX.

Discussion Questions

1. Distinguish between common-law liability and statutory liability for auditors. What is the basis for the difference in liability?

2. In a lawsuit brought by a plaintiff against a defendant (auditor) in West Virginia, the court stated its interpretation of the relevant legal principle as follows: "In order to establish a prima facie case of negligence . . . , it must be shown that the defendant has been guilty of some act or omission in violation of a duty owed to the plaintiff. No action for negligence will lie without a duty broken." Using the AICPA Code of Professional Conduct and generally accepted auditing standards as your guide, interpret this statement in the context of auditor (CPA) ethical obligations to clients.

3. What is meant by the auditors' "near-privity" relationship? How does this differ from the "privity" relationship with a client with respect to establishing an auditor's legal liability to a client?

4. Distinguish between the legal concepts of actually foreseen third-party users and reasonably foreseeable third-party users. How does each concept establish a basis for an auditor's legal liability to third parties?

5. Describe what the law requires with respect to the legal ruling in *Credit Alliance v. Arthur Andersen & Co.* Do you think the ruling establishes a fair basis for an auditor's legal liability to third parties?

6. Compare and contrast the legal principles established in the following three cases: (1) *Murphy v. BDO Seidman;* (2) *Citizens State Bank v. Timm, Schmidt & Co.;* and (3) *Section 552 of the Restatement (Second) of the Law of Torts.*

7. A subsequent event is one that occurs after the date of the financial statements (i.e., December 31, 2010) but prior to the auditor having dated (or possibly issued) the audit report (i.e., March 15, 2011). One type of subsequent event is where additional evidence becomes available before the statements have been issued that sheds light on certain estimates previously made in the statements. A good example is additional evidence about the collectibility of a receivable that relates to its valuation in the December 31, 2010, financial statements but is not uncovered until January 31, 2011. Why is it important from an auditing perspective that an auditor be required to adjust the financial statement amounts for some material subsequent events? If an auditor fails to live up to this standard, what is the potential liability exposure for the auditor?

8. What are the legal requirements for a third party to sue an auditor under Section 10 and Rule 10b-5 of the Securities Exchange Act of 1934? How do these requirements relate to the *Hochfelder* decision?

9. Sam Antar is the former CFO of Crazy Eddie and a convicted felon. He is now teaching students and prosecutors how to spot fraud in public companies. Antar is the nephew of "Crazy Eddie" Antar, the founder of the New York City area consumer electronics chain. Sam Antar also joined the speaker's circuit to present his point of view about the fraud at his former company and provide suggestions to accountants about how to avoid such frauds in the future. Comment on the ethicality of the following:

   a. An ex-con uses his "expertise" to teach students and professionals how to spot fraud.

   b. An ex-con goes on the speaker's circuit to share his views on fraud at his company and (1) he is paid money for his speech, or (2) the money he would otherwise earn goes into a victim's restitution fund.

10. Distinguish between legal and illegal insider trading. Evaluate the ethics of the practice.

11. Section 401 of SOX requires that each financial statement filed with the SEC reflect all material correcting adjustments that have been identified by the audit firm in accordance with GAAP and the rules and regulations of the commission. How does this requirement relate to the auditors' legal liability for reporting illegal acts? What are the procedures to be followed by an auditor upon discovering that the client has committed an illegal act?

12. How does SOX Section 806 promote whistleblowing? Do you think it is ethically proper for a piece of legislation to encourage whistleblowing on the part of corporate employees? Why or why not? How do legal considerations relate to a CPA's ethical responsibilities for whistleblowing under the AICPA Code?

13. The U.S. Federal Sentencing Guidelines establish a duty of care requirement for corporations and their employees. Some have labeled this law the "good parenting" statute. Explain what you think might be meant by this statement.

14. Do you think it is ethically appropriate for a plaintiff to be able to bring a lawsuit against an auditor for RICO violations? Do you think an auditor should be held legally liable under the RICO law? Why or why not? Use ethical reasoning in answering this question.

15. The following quotation was in the court ruling in the case of the *Public Employees' Retirement Association of Colorado v. Deloitte & Touche, LLP:*

    > It is not an accountant's fault if its client actively conspires with others in order to deprive the accountant of accurate information about the client's finances. It would be wrong and counter to the purposes of the PSLRA to find an accountant liable in such an instance.

    a. Evaluate this statement from the perspective of the *scienter* requirements discussed in the text.

    b. Explain the implications of the PSLRA for audit responsibilities and auditor legal liability.

16. On December 31, 2009, the SEC sued Alameda, California–based telecommunications company UTStarcom, Inc., with violations of the Foreign Corrupt Practices Act for authorizing millions of dollars in unlawful payments by its wholly owned Chinese subsidiary to foreign government

officials in Asia. UTStarcom agreed to settle the SEC's charges and pay a $1.5 million fine to the SEC and another $1.5 million to the Department of Justice. One of the items cited as violating the FCPA was a payment of nearly $7 million between 2002 and 2007 for hundreds of overseas trips by employees of Chinese government-controlled telecommunications companies that were customers of UTStarcom, purportedly to provide customer training. In reality the trips were entirely for sightseeing.[61]

a. Why would such payments by UTStarcom violate the FCPA?

b. Review the court opinion in the *UTStarcom* case and the alleged violations of the FCPA. Explain why each of the cited violations violated the act.

Questions 17 and 18 require you to do some research about provisions in the PSLRA with respect to forward-looking information.

Forward-looking information is probably most evident in the management's discussion and analysis (MD&A) that is included with any SEC filing containing a financial statement. In MD&A, companies discuss information currently known to management that could materially impact key trends embodied in the company's financial statements. Clearly, this requirement calls upon management to make forward-looking projections. Additionally, the SEC's expanded disclosure requirements calling for increased quantitative and qualitative information about market risk call for companies to include forward-looking information about their market-risk sensitive financial instruments and derivatives.

17. Give two examples of forward-looking information and why they are considered to be important enough to include in the MD&A. What are the auditor's professional and ethical responsibilities to audit such information?

18. Explain the "safe harbor" provision in the PSLRA and how it establishes the auditor's legal liability with respect to forward-looking information.

Questions 19 and 20 are based on the following information with respect to the Oregon Steel Mills lawsuit against Coopers & Lybrand.

Oregon Steel Mills, Inc. (OSM), sold some of the stock that it owned in one of its subsidiaries in 1994. On advice from its auditors, Coopers & Lybrand, OSM reported the transaction as a $12.3 million gain on its 1994 financial statements. OSM planned a public offering of its own stock on May 2, 1996; it filed the necessary documents, which included the 1994 statements, with the SEC in February 1996. The SEC concluded that the accounting treatment of the 1994 transaction was incorrect and required OSM to restate its 1994 statements. Because of the delay, the public offering did not occur on May 2, when OSM's stock was selling for $16 per share, but on June 13 when, due to unrelated factors, the price was $13.50. OSM filed a suit in an Oregon state court against Coopers, claiming that its advice regarding the 1994 transaction was incorrect, it gave the advice negligently, and this caused a delay that resulted in the stock being sold at a lower price.

The court issued a summary judgment for Coopers, which was then reversed by a state intermediate appellate court. Coopers appealed to the Oregon Supreme Court that concluded: "Defendant breached its duty to plaintiff by failing to provide competent accounting services," but "defendant had no duty to protect plaintiff against market fluctuations in plaintiff's stock price. The decline in plaintiff's stock price in June 1996 was, as a matter of law, not reasonably foreseeable, and defendant cannot be liable for damages based on that decline." The court reversed the lower appellate court's decision and affirmed the trial court's judgment.[62]

19. In its decision, Justice Balmer writing for the Oregon State court stated: "The critical issue is whether OSM's market losses were a reasonably foreseeable result of the defendant's wrongful conduct." If we assume that Coopers genuinely believed its accounting for the $12.3 gain was correct under GAAP, is it reasonable to conclude, as did the Oregon State court, that Coopers should have foreseen the market decline in OSM's stock price? What if Coopers knew that the accounting treatment was not in conformity with GAAP?

20. The Oregon Supreme Court concluded that "defendant breached its duty to plaintiff by failing to provide competent accounting services." This supported the claim by OSM that Coopers's advice regarding the 1994 transaction was incorrect and that it gave the advice negligently. How should courts decide whether professional accounting services have been competently provided?

Endnotes

1. U.S. Court of Appeals for the Seventh Circuit, *Cenco, Inc. v. Seidman & Seidman,* 686 F.2d 449, 453 (7th Cir. 1982).
2. James L. Craig Jr., "The War on Accountants' Legal Liability," *The CPA Journal,* March 1990.
3. H.R. 1058, The Private Securities Litigation Reform Act, www.lectlaw.com/files/stf04.htm.
4. John C. Coffee Jr., *What Caused Enron? A Capsule Social and Economic History of the 1990s,* Columbia Law School Working Paper Series, www.law.columbia.edu/law-economicsstudies.
5. *Caremark International Derivative Legislation,* 1996 De. Ch LEXIS 125 (Del. 1996).
6. *Stone v. Ritter,* No. 93, 2006, http://caselaw.lp.findlaw.com/data2/Delawarestatecases/93-2006.pdf.
7. Available at www.delawarelitigation.com>ChanceryCourtUpdates.
8. *Stone v. Ritter.*
9. Available at www.delawarelitigation.com>ChanceryCourtUpdates.
10. Zoe-Vonna Palmrose, *Empirical Research in Auditor Litigation: Considerations and Data, Studies in Accounting Research No. 33* (Sarasota, FL: American Accounting Association, 1999).
11. William F. Messier Jr., Steven M. Glover, and Douglas F. Prawitt, *Auditing and Assurance Services: A Systematic Approach* (New York: McGraw-Hill Irwin, 2010).
12. *Ultramares v. Touche,* 174 N.E. 441 (N.Y. 1931).
13. *Credit Alliance v. Arthur Andersen & Co.,* 483 N.E. 2d 100 (N.Y. 1985).
14. *Security Pacific Business Credit v. Peat Marwick Main & Co.,* 165 AD2d 622, 626), July 1, 1992, www.law.cornell.edu/nyctap/I92_0135.htm.
15. Messier et al., pp. 692–693.
16. *Rusch Factors, Inc. v. Levin,* 284. F.Supp. 85, 91.
17. *Restatement (Second) Law of Torts,* Section 652-A-E (1997), www.tomwbell.com/NetLaw/Ch05/R2ndTorts.html.
18. *Blue Bell, Inc. v. Peat, Marwick, Mitchell & Co.,* 715 S.W. 2d 408 (Dallas 1986).
19. *Rosenblum, Inc. v. Adler,* 93 N.J. 324 (1983).
20. *Citizens State Bank v. Timm, Schmidt & Company* (1983), www.wisbar.org/res/capp/2007/2006ap002290.htm.
21. Dan M. Goldwasser and Thomas Arnold, *Accountants' Liability* (New York: Practising Law Institute, 2009).
22. *Bily v. Arthur Young,* 834 P. 2d 745 (Cal. 1992).
23. *Murphy v. BDO Seidman, LLP* (2003), www.precydent.com/citation/CA+App+(2nd)/B154584M.
24. *1136 Tenants Corp. v. Max Rothenberg & Co.,* 27 App. Div. 2d 830, 277 NYS 2d 996 (1967).
25. Messier et al., pp. 696–698.
26. *State Street Trust Co. v. Ernst,* Court of Appeals, N.Y. (1938), 278 N.Y. 104. 15 N.E.2d 416.
27. Messier et al., p. 697.
28. *Phar-Mor v. Coopers & Lybrand,* www.cases.justia.com/us-court-of-appeals/F3/22/1228/579478/.
29. Available at http://caselaw.findlaw.com/data/ny/cases/app/64opn08.pdf.
30. Securities Act of 1933, Title 18 of the U.S. Code.
31. *United States of America before the Securities and Exchange Commission in the Matter of McKesson and Robbins, Inc. (Accountancy in transition)* (New York: Garland Publishing, 1982).
32. Joseph T. Wells, *Frankensteins of Fraud: The 20th Century's Top Ten White-Collar Crimes* (Austin, TX: ACFE, 2000).
33. *Escott v. BarChris Construction Corp.,* U.S. District Court for the Southern District of New York, 1968, 283 F.Supp. 643.
34. Securities Exchange Act of 1934, Title 15 of the U.S. Code.
35. Messier et al., pp. 701–702.

36. Securities Exchange Act of 1934.

37. *Ernst & Ernst v. Hochfelder,* 425 U.S. 185 (1976).

38. Raymond L. Dirks and Leonard Gross, *The Great Wall Street Scandal* (New York: McGraw-Hill, 1974).

39. "A Scandal Unfolds," *The Wall Street Journal,* April 2, 1973, p. 14.

40. *Securities and Exchange Commission v. Eddie Antar, Sam E. Antar, Mitchell Antar, Isaac Kairey, David Panoff, Eddie Gindi, and Kathleen Morin,* Civil Action No. 89-3773 (JCL), Litigation Release 15251, February 10, 1997, www.sec.gov/litigation/litreleases/lr15251.txt.

41. M. I. Weiss, "Auditors: Be Watchdogs, Not Just Bean Counters," *Accounting Today,* November 15, 1993, p. 41.

42. Securities and Exchange Commission, Litigation Release No. 16544, May 9, 2000, www.sec .gov/litigation/litreleases/2000/lr16544.htm.

43. Available at www.whitecollarfraud.com/.

44. On January 6, 2009, the U.S. Court of Appeals for the Fifth Circuit affirmed Skilling's conviction but vacated the sentence. The case was remanded for resentencing in 2010.

45. *Jacobs v. Coopers & Lybrand, LLP,* No. 97 Civ. 3374 (RPP), 1999, U.S. District 234, 254 (S.D.N.Y. 1997), www.content.lawyerlinks.com/library/sec/. . ./aai_pharma_brief_073007_165.pdf.

46. 15 United States Code (U.S.C.) Section 78.

47. U.S. District Court Southern District of New York, *United States v. Martha Stewart and Peter Bacanovi,* Superseding Indictment, http://news.findlaw.com/hdocs/. . ./mstewart/usmspb10504sind .html.

48. 15 U.S.C. Section 78u-4(g).

49. 15 United States Code (U.S.C.) Section 78.

50. *Welch v. Cardinal Bankshares Corp.,* 454 F.Supp. 2d 552 (W.D. Va. 2006).

51. FCPA available at http://library.findlaw.com.

52. Richard D. Ramsey and A. F. Alkhafaji, "The 1977 Foreign Corrupt Practices Act and the 1988 Omnibus Trade Bill," *Management Decision* 29, no. 6.

53. Securities and Exchange Commission, Accounting and Auditing Enforcement Release No. 1471, *In the Matter of Gisela de Leon-Meredith,* www.sec.gov/litigation/admin/34-44970 .htm.

54. Securities and Exchange Commission, Accounting and Auditing Enforcement (AAER) No. 1470, October 23, 2001, www.sec.gov/litigation/investreport/34-44969htm, 69 Fed. Reg. 52114.

55. "Does Your Target have Clean Hands Overseas?" *Mergers & Acquisitions: The Dealmakers Journal,* April 1, 2005, www.foley.com.

56. Available at www.ussc.gov/guidelin.htm.

57. *United States v. Booker,* 543 U.S. 220 (2005), http://laws.findlaw.com/us/000/04-104.html.

58. *Blakely v. Washington,* 542 U.S. 296 (2004), http://caselaw.lp.findlaw.com/scripts/getcase. pl?court=US.

59. United States Code (U.S.C.) Section 78 dd (1982).

60. U.S. Supreme Court, *Reves v. Ernst & Young,* 494 U.S. 56 (1990).

61. U.S. District Court Northern District of California San Francisco Division, *Securities and Exchange v. UTStarcom, Inc.,* CV 09 go94, December 31, 2009.

62. *Oregon Steel Mills, Inc. v. Coopers & Lybrand, LLP,* Oregon Supreme Court (2000), 336 Or. 329, 83 P.3d 322.

Chapter 6 Cases

Case 6-1

SEC v. Halliburton Company and KBR, Inc.

On February 11, 2009, the SEC announced settlements with KBR, Inc., and Halliburton Company to resolve SEC charges that KBR subsidiary Kellogg Brown & Root LLC bribed Nigerian government officials over a 10-year period, in violation of the Foreign Corrupt Practices Act, in order to obtain construction contracts. The SEC also charged that KBR and Halliburton engaged in books and records violations and internal controls violations related to the bribery.[1]

The SEC had alleged that beginning as early as 1994, members of the joint venture determined that it was necessary to pay bribes to officials within the Nigerian government in order to obtain the construction contracts. The former CEO of the predecessor entities, Albert "Jack" Stanley, and others involved in the joint venture met with high-ranking Nigerian government officials and their representatives on at least four occasions to arrange the bribe payments. To conceal the illicit payments, the joint venture entered into sham contracts with two agents, one based in the United Kingdom and one based in Japan, to funnel money to Nigerian officials.

The SEC complaint describes a "cultural committee" to decide how to carry out the bribery scheme. The committee decided to use the United Kingdom agent to make payments to high-ranking Nigerian officials and to use the Japanese agent to make payments to lower-ranking Nigerian officials. The joint venture took payments on a construction project and, in turn, made payments to the Japanese agent and to the Swiss and Monaco bank accounts of the United Kingdom agent. The total payments to the two agents exceeded $180 million. After receiving the money, the United Kingdom agent made substantial payments to accounts controlled by Nigerian government officials, and beginning in 2002 paid $5 million in cash to a Nigerian political party.

The SEC's complaint also alleged that the internal controls of Halliburton, the parent company of the KBR predecessor entities from 1998 to 2006, failed to detect or prevent the bribery, and that Halliburton records were falsified as a result of the bribery scheme. In September 2008, Stanley pleaded guilty to bribery and related charges and entered into a settlement with the SEC. Stanley's high profile and punishment—he faces a potential seven-year sentence, the longest in the history of the federal statute outlawing the bribing of foreign officials—also signal the federal government's willingness to seek long prison terms rather than fines and court injunctions.

Without admitting or denying the SEC's allegations, KBR and Halliburton consented to be permanently enjoined from violating the antibribery, records, and internal control provisions in SEC laws. The SEC also imposed an independent consultant for Halliburton to review its policies and procedures as they relate to compliance with the FCPA.

As a result of the indemnity and the KBR subsidiary's criminal plea, Halliburton has agreed to pay $382 of $402 million in criminal fines payable by KBR with KBR consenting to pay the remaining $20 million. Halliburton also agreed to be jointly and severally liable with KBR and, as a result of the indemnity, to pay to the SEC $177 million in disgorgement.

Questions

1. According to one who has lived in Nigeria, becoming corrupt in Nigeria is almost unavoidable, as morality is relaxed, because to survive people have to make money. The *1996 Study of Corruption* by Transparency International and Goettingen University ranked Nigeria as the most corrupt nation among 54 nations listed in the study, with Pakistan as the second highest. As if this was not bad enough, in the 1998 Transparency International corruption perception index (CPI) of 85 countries, Nigeria placed 81 out of the 85 countries. And in the 2001 corruption perception index (CPI), the image of Nigeria slipped further south (ranked 90, out of 91 countries pooled), with second position as the most corrupt nation, with Bangladesh coming in first.[2]

   Given the apparent corrupt culture in Nigeria, why shouldn't U.S. businesses just consider payoffs to Nigerian officials as a cost of doing business in that country and not a payment in violation of the FCPA?

2. Use ethical reasoning to respond to the following statement by a U.S. executive:

   > Bribery is bad for business. Bribery is inefficient; it's wasteful. It often doesn't accomplish what its original purpose was. You may be competing with another company that may ultimately out-bribe you. And then at the end of the day, of course, there is a huge risk that the bribery is uncovered, that you are the subject of a protracted investigation. And the costs can be quite, quite high at the end of the day.

[1]Securities and Exchange Commission, Accounting and Auditing Enforcement Release No. 2935A , February 11, 2009, *SEC v. Halliburton Company and KBR, Inc.*, www.sec.gov/litigation/litreleases/2009/lr20897a.htm.

[2]Sources include the Transparency International corruption perception index, 1998; Lipset, Seymour Martin, and Salman Lenz, "Corruption, Culture, and Markets," in *Culture Matters*, ed. L. E. Harrison & S. P. Huntington (New York: Basic Books, 2000), p. 113; and the Transparency International corruption perception index, 2001, pp. 234–236.

Case 6-2

Hewlett-Packard[1]

Legal Settlement

On December 8, 2006, California's attorney general announced a settlement with Hewlett-Packard (HP) over its corporate spying scandal. The civil settlement involved a lawsuit the state filed against the computer giant in Santa Clara County Superior Court. Under the agreement, HP will pay $13.5 million to create a "privacy and piracy" fund to help state and local law enforcement fight privacy and intellectual property violations. The rest of the money will go to damages and to pay for the investigation.

The scandal broke in September when HP acknowledged in an SEC filing that investigators probing internal HP leaks to the media had gained access to board members' personal phone records by impersonating the board members, a practice known as "pretexting." HP's investigators also conducted physical and electronic surveillance of board members and reporters, according to HP documents.

Pretexting violates a California criminal law banning the use of "false and fraudulent pretenses" to obtain confidential information from a phone company, stated Attorney General Bill Lockyer. California civil law also considers criminal acts unlawful business practices, which was the basis of the state's civil action.

Mark V. Hurd, HP's chair and chief executive, hailed the deal. "We are pleased to settle this matter with the attorney general and are committed to ensuring that HP regains its standing as a global leader in corporate ethics and responsibility," he said.

Insider Trading

HP investors sued some of the computer maker's directors, claiming they sold $38 million in company stock shortly before publicly acknowledging an internal probe into boardroom leaks. The directors, including CEO Mark Hurd, exercised options and sold shares during a 2 1/2-week period beginning August 21, 2006. HP began its internal investigation after boardroom discussions about ex-CEO Carly Fiorina were quoted in news stories.

The flap over the probe cost Dunn and two HP executives their jobs and sparked investigations by U.S. regulators. The company said on November 16 that the SEC stepped up its examination of the company's tactics and the Federal Communications Commission had requested documents related to the leak probe.

California prosecutors had charged Dunn, HP's former CEO, with conspiracy and fraud for directing the boardroom

[1]The case is *The 1199 SEIU Greater New York Pension Fund, et al. v. Patricia C. Dunn, et al.,* CA No. 06-071186, Santa Clara County Superior Court (San Jose).

spying. They also charged Kevin Hunsaker, an in-house lawyer and former director of ethics, as well as three private investigators who participated in the probe.

Board members, worried about negative publicity over the leak probe, took steps to protect the company's stock by approving a $6 billion share buyback program less than a month before the spying became public. That brought the amount of shares HP was authorized to buy back to $11.7 billion, according to the complaint. The investors alleged that the share buybacks were prompted by defendants' illegal misconduct.

Ethics Compliance Officers

According to Forbes.com, "Chief ethics officers and compliance officers have become trendy in recent years, but some experts fear they act mainly as window dressing." Chief ethics officers began appearing in defense contractor organizational structures in 1986, when a self-governing Defense Industry Initiative was created as a recommendation of the Packard Commission championed by President Reagan.

Companies began creating more chief ethics officers in 1991 when the Federal Sentencing Guidelines went into effect. When companies employ "effective" ethics compliance programs, penalties for ethical violations can be reduced to 5 percent of fines levied. Penalties can be increased up to 400 percent where evidence demonstrated that an effective program did not exist.

Many believe having a chief ethics officer is a "requirement for good governance." But according to Efrem Grail, ethics officers are sometimes "just a mask for the company to hide behind." According to Forbes, most corporations hire an attorney to fill the chief ethics officer position—while attorneys generally receive training in professional responsibility, they are not specialists in ethics.

Corporate Governance and Ethics Issues

The original lawsuit claimed "breach of fiduciary responsibilities" by HP executives. It alleged that the executives' spylike tactics to uncover boardroom leaks harmed the company. The suit claimed that the group engaged in insider trading just before news of the spying incident became public. Specifically, the suit claims that they sold off $41.3 million worth of stock two weeks before the scandal broke. The lawsuit also alleged that the group approved stock buybacks in the months preceding the scandal in an effort "to keep the company's stock price propped up while insiders were selling."

HP also agreed to strengthen in-house monitoring to ensure that future investigations launched by HP or its contractors would comply with legal and ethical standards and protect privacy rights. HP further agreed to hire an independent director, expand the duties of its chief ethics officer and chief privacy officer, beef up staff ethics training, and create a compliance council to set policies for ethics programs.

In the lawsuit, Attorney General Bill Lockyer was quoted as saying:

> With its governance reforms, this settlement should help guide companies across the country as they seek to protect confidential business information without violating corporate ethics or privacy rights. The new fund will help ensure that when businesses cross the legal line they will be held accountable. Fortunately, Hewlett-Packard is not Enron. I commend the firm for cooperating instead of stonewalling, for taking instead of shirking responsibility, and for working with my office to expeditiously craft a creative resolution.

The settlement's corporate governance reforms aimed to strengthen in-house monitoring and oversight to ensure compliance with legal and ethical standards, and protection of privacy rights, during any investigations launched by HP or outside firms hired by HP. "This settlement creates a template for other companies seeking to protect confidential business information without violating corporate ethics or privacy rights," stated Lockyer.

Major Governance Reforms

The major governance reforms included the following:

- A new independent director will serve as the board's watchdog on compliance with ethical and legal requirements. The director will have specific responsibilities in carrying out that oversight function, and report violations to the board, other responsible HP officials, and the attorney general.

- HP's chief ethics and compliance officer (CECO) will have expanded oversight and reporting duties. The CECO will review HP's investigation practices and make recommendations to the board on how to improve the practices by July 31, 2007. The CECO, who previously reported only to the general counsel, now also will report to the board's audit committee. Additionally, the CECO will have authority to retain independent legal advisors.

- HP will expand the duties and responsibilities of its chief privacy officer to include review of the firm's investigation protocols to ensure they protect privacy and comply with ethical requirements.

- HP will establish a new Compliance Council, headed by the CECO and also comprised of the chief privacy officer, deputy general counsel for compliance, head of internal audit, and ethics and compliance liaisons. The council will develop and maintain policies and procedures governing HP's ethics and compliance program, and provide periodic reports to the CEO, audit committee, and board.

- HP will beef up the ethics and conflict-of-interest components of its training program. The training redesign will be directed and monitored by the CECO, Compliance Council, independent director, and chief privacy officer. HP also will create a separate code of conduct, for use by outside investigators that addresses privacy and business ethics issues.

Questions

1. The original lawsuit filed in the HP case claimed that the executives breached their fiduciary responsibilities. What are the fiduciary responsibilities of executives and members of the board of directors to shareholders? How were these obligations violated in the HP case?

2. Pretexting violates a California criminal law banning the use of "false and fraudulent pretenses" to obtain confidential information from a phone company. California civil law also considers criminal acts unlawful business practices, which was the basis of the state's civil action against HP. From an ethical perspective, why should such bans exist especially if pretexting enables an investigator to uncover fraud in the financial statements?

3. An important part of the settlement with HP deals with strengthening corporate governance systems at the company including having a chief ethics and compliance officer. Some companies use an attorney to fill that position because of legal implications. In the HP case, the company seemed to favor the approach of having an independent director fill that position. Evaluate the pros and cons of having an attorney, independent director, or some other person serve as chief ethics and compliance officer.

Case 6-3

XTO Energy, Inc.

On December 14, 2009, the Exxon Mobil Corporation announced its intention to take over XTO Energy, Inc., in an all-stock transaction valued at $41 billion. On December 14, XTO Energy filed an 8-K Form with the SEC pursuant to its takeover by Exxon Mobil. Under the terms of the agreement, Exxon Mobil was to issue 0.7098 common shares for each common share of XTO. According to XTO Energy, the boards of directors of both companies approved the agreement and the offer represented a 25 percent premium to XTO stockholders.[1]

Exxon is already the largest publicly traded energy company and would become the top U.S. natural gas producer after the XTO acquisition goes through. "This deal provides Exxon with some domestic momentum it didn't have," John Olson, a fund manager at Houston Energy Partners, said. "They are getting a huge acreage spread, with lots of shale gas plays."

The bid spurred expectation of a wave of consolidation in the energy industry as cash-rich companies such as Exxon move to snap up smaller players with attractive assets. "There will be more of these deals, and it will make the industry more resilient to volatility in natural gas prices," said Fadel Gheit, an analyst at Oppenheimer & Company.

The deal, which is subject to XTO shareholder approval and expected to close in the second quarter of 2010, would be Exxon's biggest since it purchased Mobil in 1999, and the eighth largest ever in the energy and power sector. The purchase values XTO's proved reserves at about $2.93 per thousand cubic feet of gas equivalent, just over half the current natural gas futures price.

Breach of Fiduciary Duties

On December 17, 2009, the Shareholders Foundation, Inc.,[2] announced that a lawsuit had been filed in Tarrant County (Texas) District Court on behalf of current investors in XTO Energy, who purchased their XTO shares before December 14, 2009, over alleged breach of fiduciary duty by the board of directors of XTO Energy.

According to the complaint, the plaintiff alleges breaches of fiduciary duty by the board of directors of XTO Energy arising out of their attempt to sell XTO Energy to Exxon Mobil. The plaintiff claims that the XTO management and directors agreed to sell the company through "an unfair process" and that XTO Energy is worth more because of likely future global warming regulations that could curtail carbon emissions.

Previous investigations by law firms examined the following: (1) whether the XTO Energy board of directors breached their fiduciary duties to XTO shareholders by agreeing to sell XTO at an unfair price thereby harming the company and its shareholders; (2) whether the directors of XTO may have breached their fiduciary duties by not acting in XTO shareholders' best interests; and (3) whether the company may not have adequately shopped itself around before entering into this transaction and, pursuant to this proposed transaction, Exxon Mobil may be underpaying for XTO thereby unlawfully harming XTO shareholders. Exxon's shares fell 4.3 percent to $69.69 after the announcement, while XTO shares jumped more than 15 percent to $47.86 on the New York Stock Exchange.

About XTO Energy

XTO Energy, Inc., located in Fort Worth, Texas, along with its subsidiaries is engaged in the acquisition, development, exploitation, and exploration of both producing oil and gas properties and unproved properties, and in the production, processing, marketing, and transportation of oil and natural gas. The company's estimated proved reserves at December 31, 2008, were 11.80 trillion cubic feet of natural gas, 76 million barrels of natural gas liquids, and 268 million barrels of oil. On an energy-equivalent basis, its proved reserves were 13.86 trillion cubic feet equivalent at December 31, 2008. On a thousand cubic feet of natural gas equivalent basis, 64 percent of proved reserves were proved developed reserves at December 31, 2008. During the year ended December 31, 2008, its average daily production was 1.91 billion cubic feet of gas, 15.6 million barrels of natural gas liquids, and 56 million barrels of oil. As of December 31, 2008, the company owned an interest in 33,285 gross (18,235.7 net) producing wells.

XTO is one of the leading developers of unconventional resources including shale oil and gas or gas trapped in sands with low permeability that require advanced drilling techniques to recover. These resources have emerged as a potentially huge new resource in North America, and their development has so far been dominated by independent U.S. exploration and production companies. But now, big oil companies like Exxon are starting to look for reserves around the world. "Natural gas is expected to be the fastest growing of the major energy sources; it's going to grow at a substantially faster rate than oil or coal," according to Rex Tillerson, Exxon's CEO.

---

[1]Securities and Exchange Commission Form 8-K Report, pursuant to Section 13 or 15(d) of the Securities Exchange Act of 1934, December 14, 2009, XTO Energy, Inc., www.faqs.org/sec-filings/091215/XTO-ENERGY-INC_8-K/#ixzz0aB07OOKm.

[2]The Shareholders Foundation, Inc., is an investor advocacy group that does research related to shareholder issues and informs investors of securities class actions, settlements, judgments, and other legal related news to the stock/financial market. The group offers help, support, and assistance for every shareholder, and investors find answers to their questions and equitable solutions to their problems.

XTO's resource base is the equivalent of 45 trillion cubic feet of gas and includes shale gas, tight gas, coal bed methane, and shale oil and is intended to complement Exxon Mobil's holdings in the United States, Canada, Germany, Poland, Hungary, and Argentina. According to Tillerson, Exxon is going to bring XTO's expertise to bear on many of Exxon's acquisitions.

XTO has been one of the fastest-growing energy producers in the United States and it expects its production to climb 23 percent by the end of 2009. Exxon, like other major oil companies, has struggled to increase its oil and gas reserves in recent years as state-owned energy companies held fast to the new energy discoveries. The purchase of XTO would increase the company's resource base about 10 percent.

XTO Energy reported in 2007 total revenue of $5.513 billion with a net income of $1.691 billion, and in 2008 total revenue of $7.695 billion with a net income of $1.912 billion.

Approval by U.S. Congress

The Energy Information Administration (EIA) has stated that Exxon Mobil Corp. will emerge as the largest producer of natural gas in the United States after its expected acquisition of XTO in 2010. The EIA based its estimate by combining production figures reported by the two companies in their 2008 Form 10-K filings with the SEC. Representative Ed Markey, chair of the House Energy and Environment Subcommittee, said he will hold hearings into Exxon Mobil Corp.'s takeover of XTO Energy Inc.

According to *The Wall Street Journal,* the hearings will explore the deal's effect on competition in the natural gas industry, the role of natural gas in U.S. energy, and environmental questions surrounding production of gas from shale-rock formations. One argument for the deal is that it secures more domestic energy in the hands of a U.S.-based player in the quest for energy independence.[3]

An important part of the merger agreement is payments to be made to officers and members of the board of directors at XTO. Given the distaste for large payout packages to corporate insiders during the period of the financial crisis in 2008–2009, it will be interesting to see whether the arrangements detailed in Exhibit 1 will influence Congress in giving its approval for the merger of XTO into Exxon Mobil.

[3]Russell Gold, "Exxon Bets Big on Gas with Deal for XTO," December 15, 2009, http://online.wsj.com/article/SB100014 2405274870486930457459571 0440167726.html.

Exhibit 1
Form 8-K Filing with the SEC on Officer/Board Member Payments

Consulting Agreements & Amendments to Share Grant Agreements

In connection with the Merger and pursuant to negotiations with Exxon Mobil, Messrs. Simpson, Hutton, Vennerberg, Baldwin, and Petrus (each an "Officer" and collectively, the "Officers") have agreed to waive their employment and change in control protections under their existing arrangements with the Company and enter into consulting agreements with the Company and Exxon Mobil which were executed on December 13, 2009, and will become effective at the time of the Merger. Pursuant to their existing employment agreements (for Messrs. Simpson, Hutton and Vennerberg) or the Third Amended and Restated Management Group Employee Severance Protection Plan (for Messrs. Baldwin and Petrus), upon the occurrence of a change in control transaction, which would include the Merger, each of the Officers was entitled to receive a lump sum cash payment, within 45 days after the change in control, generally equal to three times (2.5 times for Messrs. Baldwin and Petrus) the sum of his (1) annual base salary, (2) annual cash bonus, and (3) for Mr. Simpson only, annual grant of the Company's common stock. Each Officer, other than Mr. Simpson, was also entitled to receive a gross-up payment for any excise taxes imposed under Section 280G of the Internal Revenue Code ("280G Excise Taxes"). In connection with entering into the Consulting Agreements, each Officer generally agreed to (i) waive his right to receive a portion of the Change in Control Payments; (ii) subject all or a portion of the remainder of his Change in Control Payments, as retention payments, to the continued performance of consulting services and continued compliance with agreed restrictive covenants (relating to confidentiality, noncompetition, and nonsolicitation) and (iii) relinquish his right to any Gross-Up Payment due.

The waiver of the existing arrangements and effectiveness of the new Consulting Agreements among the Officers, the Company, and Exxon Mobil will be contingent on the closing of the Merger. Under the Consulting Agreements, the Officers will retire as employees of the Company upon completion of the Merger and continue to serve the Company thereafter as consultants on a full time basis. The initial term of the Consulting Agreements will end, unless earlier terminated, on the first anniversary of the Merger. The Consulting Agreements are each renewable for an additional one-year period upon the mutual agreement of the Officer and ExxonMobil, in consultation with the Company.

The Company will provide each Officer with an annual consulting fee equal to one-half of the Officer's current base salary. Each Officer will also be entitled to receive an annual cash bonus equal to one-half of the Officer's current base salary, generally subject to the Officer's continued service to the payment date (for reference, the Officers' current base salaries are: Simpson—$3,600,000; Hutton—$1,400,000; Vennerberg—$900,000; Baldwin—$500,000; Petrus—$475,000). Also under the Consulting Agreements, ExxonMobil has agreed to provide each Officer with a one-time grant of restricted ExxonMobil common stock or stock units having a grant date fair market value equal to 100% of the Officer's current base salary. One-half of the Restricted Equity will vest on the first anniversary of the Merger and one-half will vest on either the second anniversary of the Merger, or, if the Initial Term is extended, on the third anniversary of the Merger, in either case subject to service requirements and the Officer's continued compliance with the applicable restrictive covenants through the applicable vesting date.

In lieu of the payment Mr. Simpson otherwise would have received in connection with the Merger under his existing employment agreement, Mr. Simpson will receive a lump sum cash payment within five days after the Merger in an amount equal to $10,800,000 (which equals three times his current base salary). In addition, Mr. Simpson will be entitled to receive a retention payment, payable in equal installments at six and twelve months after the Merger, generally subject to Mr. Simpson's continued performance of consulting services through the payment date. Mr. Simpson's retention payment, which relates to his annual grant of the Company's common stock, will equal up to $24,750,000.

In lieu of payments each of the Officers, other than Mr. Simpson, would have received in connection with the Merger under either an existing employment agreement or the terms of the Third Amended and Restated Management Group Employee Severance Protection Plan, each of the Officers (other than Mr. Simpson and Mr. Petrus) will be entitled to receive a retention payment, payable in equal installments at six and twelve months after the Merger, generally subject to the Officer's continued performance of consulting services to the payment date. The payment for the Officers, which relates to the amount of the Change in Control Payments, will equal an amount up to the following: Mr. Hutton, $10,913,662; Mr. Vennerberg, $6,172,817; and Mr. Baldwin, $2,591,527. Mr. Petrus will not receive a retention payment.

Under pre-existing Amended and Restated Agreements with the Company, each of the Officers was entitled to certain additional lump sum cash payments in the event of a change in control transaction, which would include the Merger. On December 13, 2009, the Grant Agreements were amended to provide that the lump sum cash payments due thereunder in connection with the Merger will be made in the form of shares of the Company's common stock immediately prior to completion of the Merger. The number of Shares is as follows: Mr. Simpson, 833,333 Shares; Mr. Hutton, 687,500 Shares; Mr. Vennerberg, 583,333 Shares; Mr. Baldwin, 166,667 Shares; and Mr. Petrus 156,250 Shares.

Each Officer has agreed pursuant to the terms of the Consulting Agreements and the Grant Agreement amendments that, instead of receiving a Gross-Up Payment for any 280G Excise Taxes that might apply to the amounts the Officer is entitled to receive in connection with the Merger, the combined amount of the Shares and the retention payment will be subject to an added reduction, if necessary, so that the total value of this combined amount, when added to the value of other equity awards granted to the Officer which are vesting in connection with the Merger and, for Mr. Simpson, his lump sum payment, does not exceed 90% of the amount that could be provided to the Officer without the imposition of 280G Excise Taxes.

Upon termination of an Officer's services as a consultant either by the Company without "Cause" or by the Officer with "Good Reason" (each as defined in the Consulting Agreements) or upon an Officer's death or disability, the Officer will be entitled to receive (1) a lump sum cash payment equal to the unpaid portion of the Consulting Fee, and the Completion Bonus for the current term, and the unpaid portion of the retention payment and (2) in the case of all Officers other than Mr. Simpson, accelerated vesting of any unvested equity awards which were granted prior to the Merger.

Waiver of Rights under Outside Directors Severance Plan

The Outside Directors Severance Plan provides that, upon a change in control, each nonemployee director will receive a lump sum cash payment equal to three times the sum of the annual cash retainer and value of the company's common stock most recently granted to the nonemployee director. In February 2009, each nonemployee director received a grant of 4,166 fully vested shares of the company's common stock. The nonemployee directors received an annual cash retainer of $180,000 in respect of services performed in 2009.

On December 13, 2009, each nonemployee member of the company's board of directors voluntarily waived his right to receive the payments that otherwise would have become payable to him upon the completion of the merger under XTO Energy. Absent such a waiver, based on the closing price of the company's common stock on December 1, 2009 ($42.93), each nonemployee director would have become entitled to receive a lump sum cash payment of approximately $1,000,000 upon completion of the merger.

Questions

1. The lawsuit filed by the Shareholders Foundation alleges that the board of directors of XTO beached its fiduciary duties. Identify the duties allegedly violated in the XTO case.

2. Much has been said during the recent financial crisis about top executive salaries being way too large, especially in those companies receiving a government bailout. The Obama administration sought to rein them in through threats of taxation or other forms of "moral suasion." Do you believe the government has an ethical right to intervene in a company's executive compensation program? Support your answer with reference to ethical reasoning. Review Exhibit 1. Do you believe that the agreement in the Form 8-K about payments to officers and board members raises any ethical issues?

3. Under President Obama, a great deal has been said about "green technology" and the need to find more environmentally friendly sources of energy. The United States has been struggling for more than 30 years to become energy independent. The use of existing sources of energy such as natural gas and proven oil and gas reserves can help achieve that goal. To what extent should environmental considerations and other "social responsibility" issues influence decision making by management and the board of directors? How does such decision making relate to agency theory discussed in Chapter 3? In addressing this question, be sure to assess the environmental effects of the 2010 disaster along the Louisiana Coast when a British Petroleum deep water oil well exploded and leaked hundreds of millions of barrels of oil into the Gulf of Mexico.

Case 6-4

Anjoorian et al.: Third-Party Liability

In the case of *Paul V. Anjoorian v. Arnold Kilberg & Co., Arnold Kilberg, and Pascarella & Trench,* the Superior Court of the State of Rhode Island used prior SEC rulings to guide its decision on what is the auditor's liability to third parties. The court denied the defendant's motion for summary judgment.[1] The facts of the case described as follows focus on the legal reasoning used by the court with respect to previous common-law decisions regarding the auditor's liability to third parties.

Facts of the Case

The defendants Pascarella and Trench, general partners of the accounting firm Pascarella & Trench (P&T), asked the court for summary judgment in their favor with respect to plaintiff Anjoorian's claim that P&T committed malpractice in the preparation of financial statements, and that the plaintiff (Anjoorian) suffered pecuniary harm as a result.

Anjoorian formerly owned 50 percent of the issued shares of Fairway Capital Corporation (FCC), a Rhode Island corporation. The other 50 percent of the shares were held by the three children of Arnold Kilberg. Arnold Kilberg himself owned no stock in the corporation, but served as the day-to-day manager of the company. FCC was in the business of making and servicing equity loans to small businesses under the regulation of the U.S. Small Business Administration (SBA), and was capitalized by loans from the SBA and a $1.26 million investment by Anjoorian.

Beginning in 1990, P&T provided accounting services to FCC. The firm audited FCC's annual financial statements following the close of each calendar year between 1990 and 1994. In its representation letter (similar to current Section 302 requirement under SOX), P&T stated that FCC was "responsible for the fair presentation in the financial statements of financial position." P&T's responsibility was to perform an audit in accordance with GAAS and to "express an opinion on the financial statements" based on the firm's audit. The first page of each financial statement contained the auditor's opinion that "the financial statements referred to above present fairly, in all material respects, the financial position of FCC in conformity with generally accepted accounting principles." Each report is addressed to "The Board of Directors and Shareholders." The 1990–1994 statements indicate that "it is management's opinion that all accounts presented on the balance sheet are collectible." In addition, the 1991–1994 statements indicate that "all loans are fully collateralized" according to the board of directors.

On March 2, 1994, Anjoorian filed a complaint and motion for a temporary restraining order seeking the dissolution of FCC on various grounds. P&T was not a party to that suit. As a result of that action, the three Kilberg children exercised their right to purchase the plaintiff's shares of the corporation. The court appointed an appraiser to determine the value of Anjoorian's shares, which the other shareholders would have to pay. The bulk of FCC's assets was its right to receive payment for the loans it had made. The appraiser determined that the value of the corporation was $2,395,000, plus a payroll adjustment of $102,000, and minus a "loss reserve" adjustment to account for the fact that 10 of FCC's 30 outstanding loans were delinquent. The loss reserve adjustment reduced the total appraised value of the corporation by $878,234. Consequently, Anjoorian's 50 percent interest in the corporation was reduced accordingly by $439,117. He ultimately received a judgment for $809,382.85 against the other shareholders in exchange for the buyout of his shares.

In 1997, Anjoorian brought the lawsuit against Kilberg, Kilberg's Company, and P&T. He claimed that P&T was negligent in preparing the annual financial statements for FCC because it did not include an accurate loan loss reserve in the statements. Anjoorian argued that he relied on the financial statements prepared by the defendants, and that if the statements had included a loan loss reserve, he would have sought dissolution of the corporation much earlier than 1994 when his shares would have been more valuable. Anjoorian submitted an appraisal suggesting that the appropriate loan loss reserve figure would have been much less—and, therefore, his share value much higher—in the years 1990 and 1991. He alleged that he lost over $300,000 in share value between 1990 and March 2, 1994. Nine years later, the defendants moved for summary judgment on the grounds that P&T owed no duty to Anjoorian as a shareholder, and that his claims are barred by the statute of limitations.

Statute of Limitations

A claim for accounting malpractice must be commenced within three years from the time of the occurrence of the incident that gave rise to the action. The acts of malpractice alleged by Anjoorian are the failure of P&T to include an accurate loan loss reserve in each of four financial statements for the years 1990 through 1993. Anjoorian filed his complaint on February 27, 1997, which meant that acts of malpractice that occurred prior to February 27, 1994, were barred unless the discovery rule had applied. The *discovery rule* provides that for injuries or damages "which could not in the exercise of reasonable diligence be discoverable at the time of the occurrence of the incident which gave rise to the

[1]Superior Court, State of Rhode Island, *Paul V. Anjoorian v. Arnold Kilberg & Co., Arnold Kilberg, and Pascarella & Trench,* November 27, 2006.

action, the lawsuit shall be commenced within 3 years of the time that the act or acts of the malpractice should, *in the exercise of reasonable diligence,* have been discovered." Because the defendants did not present evidence that foreclosed this possibility, the court found that there existed a genuine issue as to when the pertinent facts were discovered, and therefore the court could not conclude that Anjoorian's claims should be barred for purposes of this summary judgment motion.

Duties Owed by Accountants in the Preparing of Financial Statements

The defendants argued that they are entitled to summary judgment on the plaintiff's negligence claim because P&T owed no duty to him as a shareholder of FCC. The Supreme Court has acknowledged that the duty of accounting professionals to third parties is an open question in Rhode Island, but it did identify at least three competing views: the foreseeability test, the near-privity test, and the *Restatement* test.[2]

There are two competing policy concerns underlying each of the tests. The first is compensation, because a person who relies on an accountant's work product should not have to bear the loss arising from that accountant's malpractice.[3] However, a second policy favors limiting liability for accountants to certain individuals or groups of individuals in order to make the risk of loss manageable. In the financial world, there is a significant potential for the widespread dissemination of the information from financial statements beyond the uses for which it was prepared.[4]

An auditor can balance the risks and rewards involved with the uses of financial information only if he knows the uses to which the information will be put.[5] "By receiving notice of the third parties to whom potential liability may be incurred, the auditor can decide whether to accept the engagement,

adjust the audit plan to meet the needs of third parties, and/or negotiate audit fees that are commensurate with the scope of liability." Therefore, many courts have placed limits on the scope of an auditor's potential liability so that they might successfully manage the risks inherent in their profession.[6]

The foreseeability test originally developed in *Rosenblum* provides the most expansive scope of liability. Under that approach, "when the independent auditor furnishes an opinion with no limitation . . . as to whom the company may disseminate the financial statements, he has a duty to all those whom that auditor should reasonably foresee as recipients" provided only that the user receive the statements from the company for "proper business purposes."[7] This rule gives little weight to the concern for limiting the potential liability for accountants and is not widely adopted.[8] Under this approach, however, P&T clearly would owe a duty to the shareholders of FCC for whom the audit is performed because it is eminently foreseeable that shareholders would rely on the company's financial statements to evaluate the status of their investment.

At the other end of the spectrum are the privity and near-privity tests. The privity test is the most restrictive and requires that "a contractual relationship . . . exist between an accountant or auditor and another party." If privity existed, there would be no need to analyze duties to third parties because the plaintiff would be the client. Under this approach, it seems clear that Anjoorian's claim must fail. Defendant Pascarella states in his affidavit that his main contact at FCC was Arnold Kilberg, that he never met or spoke with the plaintiff or any of the shareholders of FCC, that he did not know of their intended use of the financial statements, and that FCC paid for the accounting services. Defendant Trench testified similarly in his deposition. Therefore, Anjoorian is not in privity, and his claim that the financial statement was addressed "to the board of directors and shareholders" is appropriately treated as a third-party issue.

The near-privity test developed in *Credit Alliance v. Arthur Andersen & Co.*[9] expands the scope of accountants' liability from those in privity to include those third parties who rely on the accountants' work, when (1) "the accountants [are] aware that the financial reports were to be used for a particular purpose or purposes; (2) in the furtherance of which a known party or parties was intended to rely; and (3) there must have been some conduct on the part of the accountants linking them to that party or parties, which evidences the accountants' understanding of that party or parties' reliance."

The *Restatement (Second) of the Law of Torts* expands the scope of liability from the privity and near-privity approaches, but not to the extent of the foreseeability approach. It states that an accountant's liability will be limited to losses suffered "(a) by the person or one of a limited

---

[2]*Bowen Court Assocs. v. Ernst & Young,* 818 A.2d 721, 728 n.2 (R.I. 2003); see Carl Pacini, Mary Jill Martin, and Lynda Hamilton, "At the Interface of Law and Accounting: An Examination of a Trend toward a Reduction in the Scope of Auditor Liability to Third Parties in the Common Law Countries," *American Business Law Journal* 37 (Winter 2000), pp. 171, 175. (The authors noted that the standards lie on a continuum, and each may produce different results for the same set of facts.)

[3]U.S. Court of Appeals, *Rusch Factors Inc. v. Levin,* 284 F.Supp. 85, 90–91 (D.R.I. 1968).

[4]See *Restatement (Second) of Torts,* § 522, com. a (1977); see also *Ultramares Corp. v. Touche Niven & Co.,* 255 N.Y. 170, 179–180 (N.Y. 1931) (J. Cardozo noted that "if liability for negligence exists, a thoughtless slip or blunder, the failure to detect a theft or forgery beneath the cover of deceptive entries, may expose accountants to a liability in an indeterminate amount for an indeterminate time to an indeterminate class. The hazards of a business conducted on these terms are so extreme as to enkindle doubt whether a flaw may not exist in the implication of a duty that exposes to these consequences.")

[5]*Restatement (Second) of Torts,* § 522, com. a (1977).

[6]See Pacini et al., pp. 175–179.

[7]*Rosenblum, Inc. v. Adler,* 461 A.2d 138, 153 (N.J. 1983) superseded by N.J. Stat. Ann. 2A: 53A-25.

[8]See Pacini et al., p. 179.

[9]*Credit Alliance Corp. v. Arthur Andersen & Co.,* 483 N.E.2d 110, 118 (N.Y. 1985).

group of persons for whose benefit and guidance he intends to supply the information . . . and (b) through reliance upon it in a transaction that he intends the information to influence . . . or in a substantially similar transaction."[10]

Under the *Restatement* approach, when an accountant or auditor fails to exercise reasonable care, he is liable only to intended persons or classes of persons, and only for intended transactions or substantially similar transactions. The *Restatement* approach differs from the near-privity test in that it applies to not only specific persons and transactions contemplated by the accountant, but also specific classes of persons and transactions. Therefore, the *Restatement* approach does not utilize the third prong of the *Credit Alliance* test, which requires conduct on the part of the accountants linking them to the persons relying on the information.[11] The court found that the *Restatement* rule is the better-reasoned approach, and it strikes the appropriate balance between compensating victims of malpractice and limiting the scope of potential liability for those who certify financial statements.[12]

Following the *Restatement* approach, the U.S. District Court of Rhode Island in *Bowen v. Ernst & Young* found that an accountant can be held liable in negligence for "misrepresentations relied upon by *actually foreseen* and *limited* classes of persons." In that case, the plaintiff was a potential creditor of the corporation who requested audited financial statements from the corporation before advancing funds: "Although they were compensated for their services by the company," the defendant accountants "actually knew the plaintiff and prepared the balance sheets for him."[13]

The Court agreed with the holding in the *Rusch Factors, Inc.,* decision, but disagreed with Anjoorian that it adopts the foreseeability rule. Even under the *Restatement* test and perhaps the near-privity test, the facts in *Rusch Factors* would be sufficient to find a duty because the accountants prepared their financial statements with the intent that the creditor would use them in a specifically contemplated loan transaction. The foreseeability rule, conversely, would find a duty to all foreseeable persons (hardly a limited class), whether or not they were actually foreseen. Therefore, the holding that an accountant has a duty to "actually foreseen and limited classes of persons" is more consistent with the *Restatement*'s reference to "intended" persons and transactions, and in fact the *Rusch Factors, Inc.,* court cites the *Restatement* rule.

Analysis of the Facts of the Case

The court found that the addressing of the reports to the shareholders, while not conclusive, is a strong indication that

P&T intended the shareholders to rely upon them. Therefore, the court concluded that genuine issues of fact exist as to whether P&T intended for Anjoorian to rely on these financial statements. Perhaps the court would have reached a different conclusion for a widely held public corporation with a potentially unlimited number of shareholders whose identities change regularly. Here, however, FCC was a close corporation with only four shareholders, giving greater significance to the fact that the financial statements were addressed "to the shareholders."

The defendants also argued that, in order to find a duty to third parties, an accountant must have contemplated a specific transaction for which the financial statement would be used and that no such transaction was contemplated here.[14] The court found this argument unconvincing, stating that the case is unusual in that the alleged malpractice did not arise from a specific financial transaction. The typical case involves a person whose reliance on a defective financial statement induces the person to advance credit or invest new equity into the corporation.[15] When the investment is lost, or the loan unpaid, the person sues the accountant. In this case, however, Anjoorian had already invested his capital in the corporation when P&T was hired, and alleges that he used the financial statements as a tool to evaluate the value of that investment. The alleged malpractice did not result in his advancing new value to the corporation and then losing his investment, but instead resulted in Anjoorian failing to withdraw his capital from the corporation while its value was higher.

The court opined that it would have no difficulty finding a duty in this case, in the absence of a specific financial transaction, if it can be shown that P&T intended the shareholders to rely on the financial statements for the purpose of evaluating the financial health of the company and, therefore, their investment in the company. In this case, the "particular transaction" contemplated by the *Restatement* relates to the purpose for which the financial statements would be used—the shareholders' decision whether to withdraw capital or not. While it remains to be proved that P&T actually did foresee that its financial statements would be used by the shareholders in this manner, the absence of a particular financial transaction does not preclude the finding of a duty in this case. Because the value of the shareholders' investment was limited to the amounts reflected in the company balance sheets, any loss from malpractice was an insurable risk for which accounting professionals can plan.[16] Further, the accountants may have further curtailed their exposure by placing an appropriate disclaimer on the financial statements to warn shareholders that they rely on the financial

[10]*Restatement (Second) of Torts,* § 522.
[11]*Credit Alliance,* 483 N.E.2d at 119 n.11.
[12]See, e.g., *Nycal Corp. v. KPMG Peat Marwick LLP,* 688 N.E.2d 1368, 1372 (Mass.1998) (the *Restatement* test properly balances the indeterminate liability of the foreseeability test and the restrictiveness of the near-privity rule).
[13]*Bowen Court Assocs. v. Ernst & Young.*

[14]See *Restatement (Second) of Torts,* § 552(2)(b) & com h (concluding in illustration 10 that an accountant would not have a duty to a bank where he conducted an audit "of the customary scope for the corporation" and a bank subsequently relied upon it to advance credit to the corporation).
[15]See, e.g., *Rusch Factors, Inc.,* 284 F.Supp. at 86–87; *Credit Alliance,* 483 N.E.2d at 111.
[16]See *Rusch Factors, Inc.,* 284 F.Supp. at 91.

statements at their peril.[17] Therefore, the policy that would justify limits on accountant liability would not apply if the requisite intent were found.

The defendants argued that the plaintiff's theory of damages is speculative and against public policy. Anjoorian based his damage claims on the assertion that he relied on four annual audited financial statements to evaluate the status of his $1.26 million investment in FCC. Because the statements failed to include a loan loss reserve figure, he argued that the statements overstated the value of the corporation at the end of each year from 1990 to 1993. When Anjoorian sought dissolution in 1994, the value he obtained for his shares was significantly less than his expectation. He contended that if he had accurate financial information, he would have liquidated his investment earlier when his shares were more valuable. At issue was the existence and amount of the loan loss reserve. An appraiser of the value of the corporation in the dissolution action determined that the inclusion of a loan

[17]See, e.g., *First Nat'l Bank v. Sparkmon,* 442 S.E.2d 804, 806 (Ga. Ct. App. 1994) (finding disclaimers effective "to preclude any justifiable reliance by a third party upon the . . . reports they prefaced").

loss reserve in the financial statements was proper, and that created a genuine issue as to whether a breach of the duty of care occurred. The defendant had questioned the computation of the loan loss reserve but the court disagreed. (A detailed analysis of the amount of loan loss reserve has been omitted.)

Questions

1. The auditors (P&T) claimed to have no duty to Anjoorian as a shareholder of FCC. The Rhode Island Supreme Court acknowledged that the duty of accounting professionals to third parties is an open question in the state, but it did identify at least three competing views: the foreseeability test, the near-privity test, and the *Restatement* test. Briefly describe the legal reasoning with respect to each of the three liability standards and how they pertain to the facts of the case.

2. The court decision refers to the importance of the auditors' knowing about third-party usage of the audited financial statements. What role does such knowledge play in enabling auditors to meet their professional and ethical responsibilities?

Case 6-5

KnowledgeWare, Inc.

The Complaint

On September 28, 1999, the SEC filed a civil injunctive action in federal court in Atlanta, Georgia, charging seven former executives of a computer software company, KnowledgeWare, Inc., with carrying out a multimillion-dollar financial fraud scheme that materially inflated KnowledgeWare's reported earnings during fiscal year ended June 30, 1994, and charging two of those defendants with also committing illegal insider trading. Those named in the complaint include Francis A. Tarkenton, who was CEO and chair of the board of directors of KnowledgeWare; Donald P. Addington, president and COO; Rick W. Gossett, a CPA and CFO of KnowledgeWare; Lee R. Fontaine, also a CPA and manager of financial reporting at KnowledgeWare; William E. Hammersla III, who was KnowledgeWare's vice president for direct sales in the northeastern United States; Eladio Alvarez, a district sales manager in KnowledgeWare's Direct Sales group; and Edward Welch, a district sales manager in KnowledgeWare's Reseller Channel Sales group.[1]

The KnowledgeWare fraud might not be large or interesting enough a study if it were not for the fact that the CEO and chair of the board of directors was former professional football star Francis A. Tarkenton. Tarkenton played quarterback for the Minnesota Vikings for 13 years in the 1960s and 1970s. He is in the football Hall of Fame, although he had the dubious distinction back then of having led his team into three Super Bowl games—all ending in losses. Tarkenton was named the NFL's Most Valuable Player in 1975.

Since retirement, Tarkenton had taken his trademark freewheeling style of quarterbacking into the business world. He started as many as 30 separate companies, including a short-lived fast-food franchise called Scramblers. Today, Tarkenton runs several business Web sites and a sports-memorabilia Web site.

The commission's complaint alleged that Tarkenton, Addington, Gossett, Fontaine, Hammersla, Alvarez, and Welch engaged in a fraudulent scheme to inflate KnowledgeWare's financial results to meet sales and earnings projections. In all, KnowledgeWare reported at least $8 million in revenue from sham software sales. KnowledgeWare "parked" inventory with software resellers and other supposed customers that were given the right not to pay for the software, either orally or in "side letters" that were kept separate from the other sales documents. As a result of this scheme,

[1]Securities and Exchange Commission, Litigation Release No. 16306, *Securities and Exchange Commission v. Francis A. Tarkenton, Donald P. Addington, Rick W. Gossett, Lee R. Fontaine, William E. Hammersla III, Eladio Alvarez and Edward Welch,* Civil Action File No. 1:99-CV 2497 (N.D. September 28, 1999), www.sec.gov/litigation/litreleases/lr16306.htm.

KnowledgeWare falsely reported record sales revenue and dramatic increases in earnings in press releases and in quarterly reports filed with the commission and disseminated to the public in 1993 and 1994.

Even when KnowledgeWare later restated those quarterly results, the company continued to mislead the investing public by claiming, in its annual report for fiscal year 1994 and other public documents, that the restatement resulted from a problem with the "collectibility" of reseller receivables—without disclosing that KnowledgeWare had created the problem by "selling" software and simultaneously granting the "purchaser" the right not to pay for it.

Violations of Law

Tarkenton, Addington, and Gossett directed the fraudulent scheme and made materially false and misleading statements to purchasers of KnowledgeWare stock. Gossett also made materially false and misleading statements to KnowledgeWare's auditors. Hammersla, Alvarez, and Welch implemented the fraudulent scheme by creating the sham software sales. Fontaine further implemented the fraudulent scheme by helping prepare the financial statements and other materially false and misleading portions of the quarterly reports. With the exception of Fontaine, each defendant received unwarranted incentive compensation as a result of the scheme. In addition, Hammersla and Alvarez engaged in illegal insider trading by using material nonpublic information regarding the status of KnowledgeWare's prospective acquisition by Sterling Software, Inc., when they sold all their shares of KnowledgeWare stock in late August 1994.

Resolution of the Case

Tarkenton consented to the issuance of a final judgment permanently enjoining him from (1) committing securities fraud in violation of Section 17(a) of the Securities Act of 1933 (Securities Act) or Section 10(b) of the Securities Exchange Act of 1934 (Exchange Act) and Rule 10b-5; (2) falsifying corporate books and records or engaging in other conduct in violation of Section 13(b)(5) of the Exchange Act or Rule 13b2-1; and (3) engaging in conduct as a controlling person that would render him liable pursuant to Section 20(a) of the Exchange Act for violations of corporate reporting, record-keeping, and internal control provisions of the Exchange Act (Sections 13[a] and 13[b][2] and Rules 12b-20, 13a-1, and 13a-13). Tarkenton also agreed to pay a civil money penalty of $100,000 and disgorge $54,187, the amount of the incentive compensation he received in fiscal year 1994 on the basis of KnowledgeWare's materially overstated quarterly earnings, plus prejudgment interest thereon.

Addington, Gossett, Fontaine, and Hammersla settled charges with the SEC for securities acts violations and agreed to civil monetary settlements and the disgorgement of incentive compensation received during fiscal year 1994. Hammersla also settled similar charges and made monetary and disgorgement payments. In addition, he agreed to pay civil money penalties totaling $21,575, consisting of a $10,000 penalty in connection with his financial fraud violations and an $11,575 penalty in connection with his insider trading violations.

Postscript

In August 1994, Sterling Software—a Dallas-based software company that managed data processing center operations and was successful in network management—paid $143 million to acquire KnowledgeWare, which was absorbed into Sterling. KnowledgeWare did not enter the Sterling fold quietly, however. In January 1995 several former KnowledgeWare shareholders sued Tarkenton and other executives for securities fraud and breach of contract. The investors alleged that Tarkenton had deliberately misrepresented KnowledgeWare's earnings between November 3, 1993, and August 29, 1994. Sterling was forced to allocate $15 million for legal fees, and court costs negatively impacted Sterling's 1995 revenue. Nevertheless, Sterling did successfully integrate KnowledgeWare into its growing roster of acquisitions. Tarkenton remained on Sterling's board until 1997.[2]

Questions

1. Explain why revenue recognition rules were violated based on the facts of the case. How do such violations relate to the standards for legal liability under the securities acts?

2. Gossett and Fontaine are CPAs. Given the charges against them and settlement with the SEC, how did their actions violate provisions of the AICPA Code of Professional Conduct?

3. When the KnowledgeWare story of fraud broke in the press, many Viking fans and lifelong football fans of Tarkenton acted in disbelief stating that there had to be a mistake. After all, Tarkenton was their football hero for many years. Should we hold athletes to the same ethical standards as other people (a) in their chosen profession and (b) in their personal lives? Compare the reaction of Vikings fans to the public reaction after hearing about the sexual liaisons of Tiger Woods. Are these comparable situations?

[2]Available at www.fundinguniverse.com/company-histories/KnowledgeWare-Inc-Company-History.html.

Case 6-6

Con-way Inc.

Summary of Findings

Con-way is a Delaware corporation headquartered in San Mateo, California. Con-way is an international freight transportation and logistics services company that conducts operations in a number of foreign jurisdictions. During the relevant period, the company was named CNF, Inc. The company changed its name to Con-way in April 2006. Con-way's common stock is registered with the SEC pursuant to Section 12(b) of the Exchange Act and is listed on the New York Stock Exchange.[1]

Menlo Worldwide Forwarding, Inc. (Menlo Forwarding), was a wholly owned U.S-based subsidiary of Con-way that Con-way purchased in 1989. During the relevant period, Menlo Forwarding was headquartered in Redwood City, California, and had a 55 percent voting interest in Emery Transnational (Emery). Con-way sold Menlo Forwarding to United Parcel Service of America, Inc. (UPS), in December 2004.

California-based Con-way Inc., a global freight forwarder, was charged by the SEC with making payments that violated the Foreign Corrupt Practices Act. The company paid a $300,000 penalty and accepted a cease and desist order to settle the FCPA enforcement action. Con-way's FCPA violations were caused by a Philippines-based subsidiary, Emery Transnational. It made about $244,000 in improper payments between 2000 and 2003 to officials at the Philippines Bureau of Customs and the Philippine Economic Zone Area, and $173,000 in improper payments to officials at 14 state-owned airlines. In connection with the improper payments, Con-way failed to accurately record these payments on the company's books and records, and knowingly failed to implement or maintain a system of effective internal accounting controls.

Lack of Oversight over Emery Transnational

During the relevant period, Con-way and Menlo Forwarding engaged in little supervision or oversight over Emery. Neither Con-way nor Menlo Forwarding took steps to devise or maintain internal accounting controls concerning Emery, to ensure that it acted in accordance with Con-way's FCPA policies, or to make certain that its books and records were detailed or accurate.

During the relevant period, Con-way and Menlo Forwarding required only that Emery periodically report back to

[1]Securities and Exchange Commission, *In the Matter of Con-way Inc.,* Accounting and Auditing Enforcement Release No. 2867, August 27, 2008, www.sec.gov/litigation/admin/2008/34-58433.pdf.

Menlo its net profits, from which Emery then paid Menlo a yearly 55 percent dividend. Menlo incorporated the yearly 55 percent dividend into its financial results, which were then consolidated in Con-way's financial statements. Neither Con-way nor Menlo asked for or received any other financial information from Emery. Accordingly, neither Con-way nor Menlo maintained or reviewed any of the books and records of Emery—including the records of operating expenses, which should have reflected the illicit payments made to foreign officials.

Payments to Philippine Customs Officials

Emery made hundreds of small payments to foreign officials at the Philippines Bureau of Customs and the Philippine Economic Zone Area between 2000 and 2003 in order to obtain or retain business. These payments were made to influence the acts and decisions of these foreign officials and to secure a business advantage or economic benefit. By these payments, foreign officials were induced to (1) violate customs regulations by allowing Emery to store shipments longer than otherwise permitted, thus saving the company transportation costs related to its inbound shipments; (2) improperly settle Emery's disputes with the Philippines Bureau of Customs, or (3) reduce or not enforce otherwise legitimate fines for administrative violations.

To generate funding for these payments, Emery employees submitted a *Shipment Processing and Clearance Expense Report* to Emery's finance department. These reports requested cash advances to complete customs processing. The cash advances were then issued via checks made payable to Emery employees, who cashed the checks and paid the money to designated foreign officials. Unlike legitimate customs payments, the payments at issue were not supported by receipts from the Philippines Bureau of Customs and the Philippine Economic Zone Area. Emery did not identify the true nature of these payments in its books and records. During the period 2000 to 2003, these payments totaled at least $244,000.

Payments to Officials of Majority State-Owned Airlines

To obtain or retain business, Emery also made numerous payments to foreign officials at 14 state-owned airlines that did business in the Philippines between 2000 and 2003. These payments were made with the intent of improperly influencing the acts and decisions of these foreign officials and to secure a business advantage or economic benefit.

Emery Transnational made two types of payments. The first type was known as "weight-shipped" payments, which were made to induce airline officials to improperly reserve space for Emery on the airplanes. These payments were valued based on the volume of the shipments the airlines carried for Emery. The second type were known as "gain shares" payments, which were paid to induce airline officials to falsely underweigh shipments and to consolidate multiple shipments into a single shipment, resulting in lower shipping charges. Emery paid the foreign officials 90 percent of the reduced shipping costs.

Both types of payments to foreign airline officials were paid in cash by members of Emery's management team. Checks reflecting the amount of the weight-shipped and gain shares payments were issued to these managers, who cashed the checks and personally distributed the cash payments to the foreign airline officials. Emery Transnational did not characterize these payments in its books and records as bribes. During the period 2000 to 2003, these payments totaled at least $173,000. Neither Con-way nor Menlo requested or received any records of these payments, or any of Emery's expenses, during this period.

Discovery of Improper Payments and Internal Investigation

Con-way discovered potential FCPA issues in early 2003. Starting in January 2003, Menlo initiated steps to increase Emery's internal reporting requirements, including requiring Emery to begin reporting its income and expenses, in addition to its net profits. As a result, in reviewing Emery's records, Menlo employees noticed unusually high customs and airline-related expenditures.

Menlo conducted an internal investigation of the suspicious payments at Emery and determined that Emery employees had been making regular cash payments to customs officials and employees of majority state-owned airlines. Based on Menlo's investigation, Con-way conducted a broader review of all of Menlo foreign businesses and voluntarily disclosed the existence of possible FCPA violations to the staff. After completing its internal investigation, Con-way imposed heightened financial reporting and compliance requirements on Emery. Menlo terminated a number of the Emery employees involved in the misconduct, and Con-way provided additional FCPA training and education to its employees and strengthened its regulatory compliance program. In December 2004, Con-way sold Emery to UPS.

Legal Analysis

The FCPA, enacted in 1977, added Exchange Act Section 13(b)(2)(A) to require public companies to make and keep books, records, and accounts that, in reasonable detail, accurately and fairly reflect the transactions and dispositions of

the assets of the issuer, and added Exchange Act Section 13(b)(2)(B) to require such companies to devise and maintain a system of internal accounting controls sufficient to provide reasonable assurances that (1) transactions are executed in accordance with management's general or specific authorization; and (2) transactions are recorded as necessary to permit preparation of financial statements in conformity with generally accepted accounting principles or any other criteria applicable to such statements, and to maintain accountability for assets.

As already detailed, Con-way's books, records, and accounts did not properly reflect the illicit payments made by Emery to Philippine customs officials and to officials of majority state-owned airlines. As a result, Con-way violated SEC Exchange Act Section 13(b)(2)(A). Con-way also failed to devise or maintain sufficient internal controls to ensure that Emery Transnational complied with the FCPA and to ensure that the payments it made to foreign officials were accurately reflected on its books and records. As a result, Con-way violated Section 13(b)(2)(B) of the act.

Securities Exchange Act Section 13(b)(5) prohibits any person or company from knowingly circumventing or knowingly failing to implement a system of internal accounting controls as described in Section 13(b)(2)(B), or knowingly falsifying any book, record, or account as described in Section 13(b)(2)(A). By knowingly failing to implement a system of internal accounting controls concerning Emery Transnational, Con-way also violated Exchange Act Section 13(b)(5).

According to the SEC's complaint, none of Emery's improper payments were accurately reflected in Con-way's books and records. Also, Con-way knowingly failed to implement a system of internal accounting controls concerning Emery that would both ensure that Emery complied with the FCPA and require that the payments it made to foreign officials were accurately reflected on its books and records.

Questions

1. The FCPA distinguishes between so-called facilitating payments and more serious activities. Do you think such a distinction and the related penalties for violations under the act make sense from an ethical perspective? Why or why not?

2. Given the extensiveness of the illegal payments in this case, comment on the corporate culture at the offending companies by referring to the specific violations of the FCPA. What failings in ethical reasoning and decision making can you identify in this case?

3. Securities Exchange Act Section 13(b)(5), 15 U.S.C. § 78m(b)(5) prohibits any person or company from knowingly circumventing or knowingly failing to implement a system of internal accounting controls or knowingly falsifying any book, record, or account. Describe the violations of the internal controls provision of the act by Con-way.

Case 6-7

Countrywide Corporation Shareholder Litigation

Background

On March 31, 2009, Vice Chancellor Noble in *In re Countrywide Corporation Shareholders Litigation,* C.A. No 3464-VCN (Del. Ch.),[1] denied "for the time being" an application to certify a class and approve a stipulated settlement because the settlement would have improperly eliminated some investors' claims for common-law fraud.

After the January 11, 2008, announcement of Countrywide's proposed merger with Bank of America Corporation (BOA), Countrywide stockholders brought an action seeking to enjoin the merger, alleging breach of fiduciary duties by the individual director-defendants of Countrywide and aiding and abetting charges against BOA. Ultimately, a settlement was negotiated whereby the class claims would be dismissed in return for additional disclosures; there was no additional monetary consideration.

In the summer of 2007, Countrywide started experiencing financial difficulties due to, among other things, increased rates of loan defaults on residential mortgages, foreclosures due to subprime mortgages, and the need for capital and liquidity. Countrywide entered into an agreement in August 2007 with BOA to secure additional funding. BOA invested $2 billion in Countrywide and in return BOA received numerous benefits in addition to a 16 percent stake in Countrywide. The crisis continued to worsen. Countrywide's stock price continued to fall and bankruptcy rumors surfaced. The situation was so dire that Countrywide went back to BOA and on January 11, 2008, Countrywide announced that it had entered into a merger agreement. On June 25, 2008, Countrywide's shareholders voted to approve the merger, which closed on July 1, 2008.

Class Action Allegations and Settlement

After the merger announcement, stockholder actions were filed alleging that the Countrywide board had breached its fiduciary duties by (1) agreeing to a merger that did not provide fair and adequate consideration, (2) discouraging other bidders from making an offer, (3) issuing a false and misleading preliminary proxy statement, (4) agreeing to provisions in the merger agreement that allegedly insulated Countrywide's directors and officers from liability for breaches of fiduciary duty raised in pending derivative actions, and (5) entering into the merger agreement without adequately valuing certain pending

[1]Available at www.delawarelitigation.com/2009/08/articles/chancery-court-updates/chancery-court-approves-class-action-settlement-involving-countrywide-and-attorneys-fees-for-plaintiffs-attorneys-based-on-therapeutic-disclosures/print.html.

derivative claims. Within days of the plaintiffs' moving for a preliminary injunction, the parties reached an agreement to settle the consolidated actions by providing additional disclosures, which occurred on May 28, 2008, and releasing the defendants from a wide range of potential claims. A Stipulation of Settlement was filed on June 13, 2008, requesting court approval. The parties also stipulated to the propriety of certifying a non-opt-out class pursuant to Court of Chancery Rules 23(a) and 23(b)(1) or (b)(2). Several shareholders objected with respect to the limited benefits of the proposed settlement to the shareholders and the broad release of claims. In addition, one objector challenged the appropriateness of a certification without an opportunity for shareholders to opt out.

The Federal Objectors and "Two Novel Theories"

Objections to the settlement were raised by five former Countrywide shareholders (the Federal Objectors) who were plaintiffs in a federal court action brought in California against Countrywide. The Federal Objectors lost standing in California federal court to pursue the derivative claims after the close of the merger because under Delaware law, "a merger which eliminates a derivative plaintiff's ownership of shares of the corporation for whose benefit she has sued terminates her standing to pursue those derivative claims."

To avoid the impact of Delaware law, the Federal Objectors raised what the vice chancellor called "two novel theories of direct liability, both of which they argue have value equal to that of the derivative claims and, thereby, render the proposed settlement fundamentally unfair." Without any supporting case law, the Federal Objectors argued that the Countrywide directors had a fiduciary duty to (1) value the derivative claims pending against them at the time the merger was negotiated, and (2) preserve that value "either by extracting additional consideration from BOA or by assigning the derivative claims to a litigation trust that could pursue the claims for the benefit of Countrywide's shareholders." The vice chancellor, however, was not persuaded.

In discussing the applicable law, the vice chancellor noted that because this merger was a stock-for-stock transaction of two widely held corporations, the Countrywide board's decisions surrounding the merger were subject to the protections of the business judgment rule. Moreover, the court noted that the presumption protects a board-approved transaction unless the plaintiff can show that a majority of the directors were self-interested, lacked independence, were grossly negligent in failing to inform themselves, or that the transaction can be attributed to no rational business purpose. The court concluded that the Federal Objectors had failed to demonstrate "any facts suggesting their claims could overcome the insulating effects of the business judgment rule." Therefore, the court overruled the Federal Objectors' objections.

The SRM Objectors

SRM Global Fund Limited Partnership (SRM) challenged the propriety of class certification by arguing that its common-law fraud claims for money damages were individual and thus "predominate over the equitable relief found in the Delaware Complaint." SRM also argued that "to foreclose the individual common-law fraud claims of SRM by virtue of certification of a class action and approval of the Proposed Settlement would violate due process."

For factual support, SRM pointed to January 14, 2008, when, just days after the merger was announced, Kenneth Lewis, the chair, CEO, and president of BOA, in a speech to the Delaware State Chamber of Commerce, dismissed rumors of Countrywide's impending bankruptcy and asserted that Countrywide "had a very impressive liquidity plan [and] backup lines in place." SRM claimed that these Lewis Statements were false and that this misrepresentation induced SRM to hold, rather than sell, its shares of Countrywide which resulted in losses of $80 million. As a result, SRM alleged that its common-law fraud claims arising out of the Lewis Statements were uniquely individual, not shared by the named plaintiffs and the plaintiffs could not adequately raise them so they should not be dismissed. Vice Chancellor Noble agreed, finding that it was "improper to include SRM's individual claims based on the Lewis Statements within the reach of the class action and the scope of the proposed release precludes both class certification and approval of the proposed settlement."

Almost Approved but Denied for Now—with Options

Vice Chancellor Noble found that "except for the matters raised in the SRM Objections related to the Lewis Statements, the Court would certify the defined class of former Countrywide stockholders." Moreover, the court found that except for "the problems with the scope of the release, the settlement . . . would be approved." While the court denied the plaintiff's application for class certification and approval of the settlement for now, Vice Chancellor Noble did note that the parties had a number of options including (1) amending the class structure to allow for opt-out rights, (2) amending the release contained in the proposed settlement to carve out the common-law fraud claims with respect to the Lewis Statements, or (3) abandoning their efforts to settle this litigation altogether.

Legal Reasoning

In a follow-up to its original ruling, the Chancery Court reviewed its decision and affirmed it to be correct. What follows is the court's legal reasoning in this regard.

The prior decision of the Chancery Court in which the court refused to approve the class action settlement in this case was reviewed as a result of the shareholder's objections to the release of potential federal securities laws violations based on the statements of Ken Lewis. The duty of the court is to apply various factors to make an independent determination about whether the proposed settlement was fair and reasonable. Additional considerations include:

- Rule 23(a) and Rule 23(b) must also be satisfied before the court will conclude that this case should be certified as a class action—which must precede the court's approval of the proposed class action settlement.
- In certifying this case as a class action, the court did not require an opt-out right for class members.
- The court rejected the objections to the settlement and approved the settlement based on the following rulings and reasoning:
  - The absence of a monetary benefit "is not fatal to a settlement which, almost by definition, confers only a therapeutic benefit." The court found the merger price fair and that there were no other potential buyers—and that the shareholders would have done worse without the merger.
  - The court reviewed the elements that must be established for a successful fraud action based on the federal securities laws (which the objector argued should not be released), and found that those claims "possess no obvious value" (based on the unlikely success in pursuing them on the facts of this case). Thus, the court reasoned it was fair and reasonable to release them.
  - The federal securities laws claims based on the Lewis Statements did not predominate over the equitable claims.
  - The release provision in the settlement proposal is not overbroad. In reaching this conclusion, the court evaluated not only the claims in the complaint but also those that might be barred due to the release. In the case of *In Re Philadelphia Stock Exchange,*[2] the court ruled that a settlement can release claims not specifically asserted in a settled action only if those claims are "based on the same factual predicate or the same set of operative facts as the underlying action."
  - There is no requirement that a specific claim be included in a lawsuit in order for it to be released.
  - An objector is not required to present its common-law fraud claims (that it wants carved out of the settlement) with the same specificity as would be needed when pleading in a complaint.
  - Approval of a class action settlement by the Court of Chancery requires only a cursory scrutiny of the issues presented, but the Court's consideration must be the product of a logical and deductive process.

[2]*In Re Philadelphia Stock Exchange,* 945 A.2d at 1145-46 (Del Ch. 2008).

The court concluded that the class treatment was proper, the case was certified as a class action, and the proposed settlement was approved.

Questions

1. What is the duty of care required of the board of directors and its individual members? Include in your discussion the "business judgment" rule. Do you think the Countrywide board met this standard? Give specific examples to support your answer.

2. Legal rulings such as the one in *Countrywide* are based solely on legal principles. Still, ethical principles are always important factors in business decision making. From the perspective of the stakeholders, identify as many ethical issues that you can that relate to legal considerations in the *Countrywide* ruling.

3. The SRM objectors took the position that "its common law fraud claims for money damages were individual and thus predominate over the equitable relief found in the Delaware Complaint." SRM also argued that "to foreclose the individual common law fraud claims of SRM by virtue of certification of a class action and approval of the Proposed Settlement would violate due process." Discuss the common-law fraud claims raised by SRM. Do you agree that it should have been allowed to opt out of the settlement and separately pursue its charges against the Countrywide board?

Case 6-8

Welch v. Cardinal Bankshares Corp.[1]

The Reversal

In a remarkable turn of events, on May 31, 2007, the Arbitration Review Board (ARB) of the Department of Labor reversed the 2004 decision of an administrative law judge, and dismissed the complaint of the first individual to bring an initially successful whistleblower claim under Section 806 of the Sarbanes-Oxley (SOX) Act.

In *Welch v. Cardinal Bankshares Corp.,* the ARB dismissed the complaint of David Welch, the former CFO of Cardinal Bankshares Corp. (Cardinal), a small, publicly traded Virginia bank holding company, on the grounds that Welch did not have a reasonable belief that Cardinal violated any of the laws protected by SOX. In doing so, the ARB rejected Welch's broad definition of protected activity, including, significantly, his claim that Cardinal's alleged violation of GAAP standards constituted a violation of the laws protected by SOX. Thus, this decision provides employers with a significant victory and the courts with much-needed guidance in determining what constitutes protected activity.[2]

Background

Welch, a CPA, began working for Cardinal as a part-time accounting officer in February 1999. About a year later, Welch asked for a full-time position as Cardinal's CFO, and Ronald Leon Moore, Cardinal's CEO, agreed. As CFO, Welch's duties included "preparing federal, state, and local financial reports of various kinds; developing accounting control procedures; and reviewing and correcting errors and inconsistencies in financial entries, documents, and reports." Beginning in late 2001, and continuing through late 2002, Welch raised a number of issues regarding Cardinal's accounting practices and procedures.

In September 2001, Welch discovered that Cardinal had recovered amounts due on two loans (for a total of $195,000) for accounts Cardinal had previously written off. The entries were classified as income and reported as such on Cardinal's third-quarter 10-Q report to the SEC. Welch informed Moore that, under GAAP, loan recoveries should be entered in the "loan reserve" account, rather than as income. Welch further told Moore that Cardinal's misclassification of these recoveries caused Cardinal's SEC report to "overstate Cardinal's year-to-date income." (Welch later pointed out this error to Larrowe & Company, Cardinal's outside auditors, which corrected the entries.)

Welch also raised issues regarding Cardinal's internal financial controls. Specifically, in August 2002, Welch expressed his concern to Moore that Cardinal's financial

controls were deficient because too many people without accounting experience had unrestricted access to the general ledger. A month later, in September 2002, Welch provided Moore with a detailed memorandum, stating that Welch believed he was being excluded from the process of designing disclosure controls and procedures under SOX, including being excluded from consultations with Cardinal's outside auditors. In the memorandum, Welch again stated his opinion that Cardinal had overstated its year-to-date income. Welch reiterated these same concerns in a meeting of Cardinal managers on September 20, which he tape-recorded.

After the managers' meeting, Cardinal's counsel and outside auditor attempted to interview Welch and obtain a copy of the tape recording, as part of an investigation into his allegations. Welch refused to meet without his attorney, who Welch claimed was out of town. As a result, Cardinal suspended Welch. On October 1, 2002, Cardinal's counsel and outside auditor presented their findings to the board—that the information available did not support Welch's allegations—and recommended that he be terminated for failing to cooperate unconditionally in Cardinal's efforts to investigate his allegations. The board voted unanimously to terminate Welch, effective October 1. Welch then filed a complaint with the Occupational Safety & Health Administration (OSHA), U.S. Department of Labor, alleging that he had been unlawfully terminated, in violation of Section 806 of SOX.

Procedural history

After an initial investigation, OSHA dismissed Welch's complaint, finding that it was without merit. Welch appealed this finding and requested a hearing before an administrative law judge (ALJ), who concluded, after a hearing, that Cardinal had violated SOX and recommended that Welch be reinstated, with back pay. The ALJ's decision was the first finding that a company had unlawfully retaliated against an employee under SOX. Cardinal requested review by the ARB.

Welch, the first whistleblower to prevail under SOX, had been awarded $175,000—including more than $100,000 in attorney fees—and had been ordered reinstated to his position as CFO. Under Section 806 of the act, the whistleblower is entitled to get his job back even though it means that his successor will be put out of work. In addition, he will have to work closely with the very people who were the target of his complaint.

ARB Holding

The ARB held that, to prevail, Welch needed to prove, by a preponderance of the evidence, that (1) he engaged in protected activity, (2) Cardinal knew that he engaged in such activity, (3) he suffered an unfavorable personnel action,

---

[1]Some of the facts of this case are discussed in the chapter.
[2]*Welch v. Cardinal Bankshares Corp.,* 454 F.Supp. 2d 552 (W.D. Va. 2006).

and (4) the protected activity was a contributing factor in the unfavorable action. The ARB confined its review, however, solely to the issue of whether Welch had engaged in protected activity—that is, whether "he provided information to Cardinal that he reasonably believed constituted a violation of 18 U.S.C.A., sections 1341 (mail fraud), 1343 (wire, radio, TV fraud), 1344 (bank fraud), or 1348 (securities fraud), or any rule or regulation of the SEC, or any provision of federal law relating to fraud against shareholders" (defined hereinafter, and in the ARB's decision, as the "federal securities laws"). The ARB also restated the general principle that, to be protected, employee communications must "definitively and specifically" relate to the federal securities laws. The ARB reversed the ALJ's holding that Welch had engaged in protected activity, and held that Welch had failed to establish that his conduct constituted protected activity under SOX, for the reasons set forth in the following text.

The $195,000 Loan Recovery Entries

After noting that the "reasonable belief" standard contained both a subjective and an objective component—requiring Welch to prove both that he actually believed that the SEC report overstated income and that a person with his expertise and knowledge would have reasonably believed that as well—the ARB held that Welch's concerns that Cardinal misclassified the loan recoveries and consequently misled investors did not constitute protected activity, because Welch could not have reasonably believed that Cardinal misstated its financial condition. According to the ARB, whether or not the loan recoveries were misclassified as income (rather than a credit to the loan reserve amount) did not change the fact that Cardinal recovered $195,000 that it previously did not have. Thus, "an experienced CPA/CFO, like Welch, could not have reasonably believed that [Cardinal's 10-Q report to the SEC] presented potential investors with a misleading picture of Cardinal's financial condition."

GAAP Standards

The ARB also held that Welch's complaints about Cardinal's internal accounting standards were not SOX-protected activity because they did not relate to the federal securities laws. The ARB rejected Welch's argument that his complaints about the loan recoveries constituted protected activity because they concerned violations of GAAP standards. Welch had argued that violations of GAAP automatically constitute violations of the federal securities laws because those standards and the federal securities laws have the same purpose—protecting investors from financial misrepresentations. The ARB disagreed. In its first ruling on this key threshold issue, the ARB held that such an argument "amounts to a wholesale re-writing of SOX's section 1514A," which only protects whistleblowers who report about "specifically enumerated

employer conduct—violations of the federal fraud statutes, SEC rules or regulations, or federal laws relating to shareholder fraud." The ARB found no authority to support Welch's argument that Congress meant to extend SOX protection to employees who report violations of GAAP.

Internal Controls

The ARB held that Welch's complaints about deficient internal controls did not constitute protected activity because they did not relate to the federal securities laws. The ARB also rejected Welch's argument that Moore intended to mislead investors when he disregarded Welch's instructions to make changes to Cardinal's internal controls. Welch failed to explain how merely refusing to accept his advice, as CFO, supported an inference that Moore intended to deceive shareholders. The ARB also found no legal authority to support Welch's proposition that, by rejecting his advice on accounting matters, Cardinal violated or could reasonably be regarded as having violated the federal securities laws.

Access to External Auditors

Finally, the ARB held that Welch's complaints about access to Cardinal's outside auditors, Larrowe & Co., were not SOX-protected activity because they also did not relate to federal securities laws. According to the ARB, "Welch did not prove by a preponderance of the evidence how his unhappiness about access to Larrowe & Co. constituted a reasonable belief that Cardinal was violating or might violate the enumerated fraud statutes, any SEC rule or regulation, or any federal law relating to fraud against shareholders." The ARB again emphasized that, to be protected, an employee's SOX complaint must "definitively and specifically" relate to the federal securities laws and found nothing in the record to demonstrate how "insufficient access to Larrowe & Co." related to such laws.

Conclusion

The ARB's decision represents a significant victory for Cardinal, and for other employers, as it provides meaningful, favorable guidance on the breadth (and limitations) of protected activity under SOX: Simply because an employee's complaint concerns an employer's accounting procedures or practices, or financial controls, does not mean that it will be protected by SOX. Rather, to be protected, a complaint must "definitively and specifically" relate to one of the enumerated violations set forth in the statute. Complaints such as Welch's, alleging violations of GAAP standards, generally will not constitute protected activity. An employee must have both an objective and a subjective reasonable belief that a violation of the federal securities laws has occurred. Thus, employees with more experience and knowledge concerning accounting matters will be held to a higher standard in complaining about such matters than those with less experience and knowledge.

The bottom line is that the Welch case proves to be double trouble for employees. It demonstrates not only how hard it can be for an employee to prove having been unlawfully terminated, but also how difficult it can be to get a job back, even if someone can, at least initially, prove that his or her termination was unlawful.

Questions

1. Do you believe the reasoning used by the ARB conforms to the spirit and intent of Section 806 of the SOX? Why or why not?

2. Do you believe the ARB used proper logic when he ruled that Welch's complaints about Cardinal's application of GAAP and accounting and internal control standards were *not* SOX-protected activity because they did not relate to the federal securities laws? Give reasons to support your answer. Does the ruling make sense from an ethical perspective? Why or why not?

3. The ARB held that Welch's concerns that Cardinal misclassified the loan recoveries and consequently misled investors did not constitute protected activity, because Welch could not have reasonably believed that Cardinal misstated its financial condition. According to the ARB, whether or not the loan recoveries were misclassified as income (rather than a credit to the loan reserve amount) did not change the fact that Cardinal recovered $195,000 that it previously did not have. Thus, "an experienced CPA/CFO, like Welch, could not have reasonably believed that [Cardinal's 10-Q report to the SEC] presented potential investors with a misleading picture of Cardinal's financial condition." Do you believe the ARB used proper logic when he based his decision solely on "financial condition matters"? Explain how Welch might have attempted to refute the ARB's opinion in this regard.

Case 6-9

Reznor v. J. Artist Management (JAM), Inc.[1]

Michael Trent Reznor met John Malm Jr., a part-time promoter of local rock bands who also is a licensed CPA, in Cleveland, Ohio, in 1985. Malm became Reznor's manager and formed J. Artist Management (JAM), Inc. Reznor became the lead singer in the band Nine Inch Nails, which performed its first show in 1988. Reznor and Malm signed a management agreement, under which JAM was to receive 20 percent of Reznor's gross compensation.

In 1966, Malm hired a CPA, Richard Szekelyi, and his firm, Navigent Group, to provide tax consulting services to Reznor personally; his duties also included examining Reznor's financial records. Szekelyi discovered flawed accounting between the two parties to the detriment of Reznor by about $4 million. The primary cause was that Malm received tax benefits that should have gone to Reznor.[2] Reznor filed a separate lawsuit against codefendants Szekelyi and Navigent Group charging them with negligence, breach of fiduciary duty, and aiding and abetting fraud. The codefendants sought summary judgment to dismiss Reznor's claims stating they did not breach any standard of care in preparing or presenting reports of Reznor's financial status, nor did Szekelyi fail to counsel Reznor adequately concerning other transactions. The court granted the summary judgment dismissing the charges against Szekelyi and Navigent.[3] Reznor had also filed a lawsuit in 2004 in New York claiming that former manager John Malm mismanaged the band's finances and actually stole money from them. Apparently Malm had tricked Reznor into signing a contract that assigned the

manager 20 percent of gross earnings. The problem is that the assignment should have been of net income, not gross earnings. This means that Malm would have received 20 percent of all earnings, before taxes and before more important distributions like his band member payments.[4]

On June 1, 2005, a verdict was rendered in favor of Reznor. Malm was ordered to pay up to $2.9 million for allegedly cheating Reznor out of millions. The verdict also awarded trademarks back into Reznor's hands.

Questions

1. Describe the nature of the relationship between Szekelyi and Reznor. Did a privity relationship exist between the two? Why or why not?

2. What were Szekelyi's ethical obligations to Reznor given the nature of the services provided? Which of the ethics standards in the AICPA Code should have been of particular concern to Szekelyi in performing professional services for Reznor?

3. During the course of working as the manager for Nine Inch Nails, John Malm mismanaged the band's finances and was found guilty of those charges. Malm, who is a CPA, was not hired to perform any accounting services for Reznor or the band. Does that mean his actions are not enforceable under the AICPA Code of Professional Conduct? What about the fact that Malm is a licensed CPA. Would a state board of accountancy have any recourse with respect to Malm's transgressions?

---

[1]Some of the facts of the original case have been changed to better develop legal liability issues.
[2]Roger LeRoy Miller and Gaylord A. Jentz, *Business Law Today*, 7th ed. (Mason, OH: Thomson West, 2007), pp. 1087–1088.
[3]*Reznor v. J. Artist Mgmt*, 365 F.Supp.2d 565 (S.D.N.Y. 2005).

[4]Available at www.cmt.com/news/country-music/1503212/nine-inch-nails-trent-reznor-wins-case-against-his-former-partner.jhtml.

Case 6-10

SEC v. Zurich Financial Services

Background

On December 11, 2008, the SEC reached agreement with Zurich Financial Services (Zurich) to settle the commission's charges against Zurich Financial Services Group for aiding and abetting a fraud by Converium Holding AG involving the use of finite reinsurance transactions to inflate improperly Converium's financial performance. The commission's complaint alleges that Zurich aided and abetted Converium's violation of Section 10(b) of the Securities Exchange Act of 1934 and Rule 10b-5 thereunder. Under the settlement, Zurich consented to the entry of a final judgment directing it to pay a $25 million penalty plus $1 in disgorgement and, in a related administrative proceeding, consented to the entry of a cease-and-desist order against it.[1] The accounting issue in question deals with the complex topic of reinsurance. The facts of the accounting fraud have been simplified as much as possible to focus mainly on the legal liabilities of the company.

Zurich is a corporation organized under the laws of Switzerland with its principal place of business in Zurich, Switzerland. Historically, Zurich operated its reinsurance business under the brand name Zurich Re, which operated as a separate division within Zurich Insurance Company (ZIC), a wholly owned subsidiary of Zurich, and through its North American subsidiary, Zurich Reinsurance (North America) Inc. (Zurich Re North America). Prior to Converium's IPO, Zurich restructured its reinsurance operations and transferred substantially all of the reinsurance business operated under Zurich Re to Converium. In December 2001 and January 2002, pursuant to the Registration Statement and Prospectus, Zurich sold 40 million shares of Converium in the form of shares and American Depository Shares (ADSs), representing its entire stake in Converium, for proceeds of approximately $1.9 billion.

Accounting Issues

The SEC announced on December 11, 2008, the filing and settlement of charges against Zurich Financial Services Group for aiding and abetting a fraud by Converium Holding AG involving the use of finite reinsurance transactions to inflate improperly Converium's financial performance. The commission's complaint alleges that beginning in 1999, the management of Zurich Re developed three reinsurance

transactions for the purpose of obtaining the financial benefits of reinsurance accounting. However, in order for a company to obtain the benefits of reinsurance accounting, the reinsurance transaction must transfer risk. Here, Zurich Re management designed the transactions to make them appear to transfer risk to third-party reinsurers, when, in fact, no risk was transferred outside of Zurich-owned entities. For two of the transactions at issue, Zurich Re ceded risk to third-party reinsurers, but took it back through reinsurance agreements—known as retrocessions—with another Zurich entity. For the third transaction, Zurich Re ceded the risk to a third-party reinsurer but simultaneously entered into an undisclosed side agreement with the reinsurer pursuant to which Zurich Re agreed to hold the reinsurer harmless for any losses realized under the reinsurance contracts. Because the ultimate risk under the reinsurance contracts remained with Zurich-owned entities, these transactions should not have been accounted for as reinsurance.

The complaint also alleges that, in March 2001, Zurich announced its intent to spin off its reinsurance group in an initial public offering (IPO). Zurich then created and capitalized Converium, which assumed the rights and obligations of Zurich's assumed reinsurance business. On December 11, 2001, Zurich spun off Converium in an IPO. At the conclusion of the IPO, the members of Zurich Re management responsible for the three reinsurance transactions ceased to be affiliated with Zurich. As a result of the improper accounting treatment of reinsurance transactions, the historical financial statements in Converium's IPO documents, including the Form F-1 it filed with the Commission, were materially misleading. Among other things, Converium understated its reported loss before taxes by approximately $100 million (67 percent) in 2000 and by approximately $3 million (1 percent) in 2001. In addition, for certain periods, the transactions had the effect of artificially decreasing Converium's reported loss ratios for certain reporting segments—the ratio between losses paid by an insurer and premiums earned that is frequently cited by analysts as a key performance metric for insurance companies.

The complaint further alleges that Converium's misstatements were material to investors who purchased shares in the IPO. Through the IPO, which was the largest reinsurance IPO in history, Zurich raised significantly more than it would have raised had Zurich and Converium not improperly inflated Converium's financial performance.

Reinsurance Accounting Principles

In basic terms, reinsurance is insurance for insurers. Reinsurance is the transfer of insurance risk by the primary insurer to a second insurance carrier, called the reinsurer, in exchange

---

[1] Securities and Exchange Commission, *SEC v. Zurich Financial Services,* 08 Civ. 10760 (WHP) (S.D.N.Y.), Litigation Release No. 20825, December 11, 2008, Accounting and Auditing Enforcement Release No. 2910, December 11, 2008.

for a payment or premium. Whether a contract is accounted for as reinsurance depends on whether the contract indemnifies the ceding company—here Zurich and Converium—from loss or liability. Such indemnification is known as *risk transfer*. Risk is transferred when (1) the reinsurer assumes significant insurance risk and (2) it is reasonably possible that the reinsurer will realize a significant loss in the transaction. A risk transfer analysis for a contract emphasizes substance over form and GAAP requires "an evaluation of all contractual features that . . . limit the amount of insurance risk to which the reinsurer is subject." Accordingly, under GAAP, "if agreements with the reinsurer . . . in the aggregate, do not transfer risk, the individual contracts that make up those agreements also would not be considered to transfer risk, regardless of how they are structured."

Where there is insufficient risk transfer, a transaction may not be treated as reinsurance under GAAP, and must be accounted for using the deposit method, which lacks the potential accounting benefits of reinsurance accounting. Under reinsurance accounting, when losses on the ceded business are incurred, the ceding insurer records an offset to the increase in its gross loss reserves in an amount equal to the reinsurance it expects to recover from the reinsurer, thus increasing its net income by that amount. Deposit accounting has no comparable income statement benefit.

From 1999 through 2001, management of Zurich Re designed three reinsurance transactions that created the appearance of risk transfer in order to benefit from reinsurance accounting. These three transactions affected the financial statements included in Converium's IPO prospectus. In two of the three transactions, Zurich Re purchased reinsurance from Inter-Ocean, which, in turn, ceded these liabilities to a Zurich entity (the Inter-Ocean transactions), in one transaction directly and in the other transaction indirectly through a third reinsurer (Company A). Zurich Re's use of Inter-Ocean as an intermediary in the transaction helped obscure the transactions' circular structure and the fact that Zurich Re had merely moved the risk from one Zurich Re entity to another. In the third transaction, Zurich Re entered into a reinsurance transaction for which the risk transfer was negated by an undisclosed and purportedly unrelated side agreement that protected the reinsurer against losses suffered under the reinsurance contract. Zurich Re improperly accounted for these transactions using reinsurance accounting.

Although Zurich Re accounted for the transactions with Inter-Ocean and Company A as reinsurance, in reality, Zurich Re had recirculated the risk from one Zurich entity to another, while interposing intermediaries (Inter-Ocean and Company A) that obscured the transactions' circular structure. Because this transaction was circular, there was no risk transfer and Zurich Re and later Converium should not have accounted for the contract as reinsurance. As a result, and as reported in Converium's December 2001 Form F-1, Converium understated its pretax losses for the year ended December 31, 2000, by $1.36 million.

The Converium IPO

On March 22, 2001, in connection with its announcement of disappointing financial results for 2000, Zurich reported that it intended to exit the assumed reinsurance business. In a September 6, 2001, press release, Zurich announced that its reinsurance business would be spun off in an IPO, and that as of October 1, 2001, the business would operate under the name Converium.

The Registration Statement and Prospectus filed by Converium in connection with the IPO, which became effective on December 11, 2001, was derived from data from the Zurich subsidiaries combined to form Converium and failed to disclose the impact of the circular Inter-Ocean and the Z-1 Facility transactions on Converium's business operations, financial results, and shareholders' equity at the time of the IPO.

Accordingly, the statements in the prospectus regarding Converium's financial results for 2000 and the first half of 2001 were materially false and misleading. As a consequence of the circular Inter-Ocean transactions and the Z-1 Facility transactions, rather than reporting a loss before taxes of $48.8 million for 2000, Converium should have reported a loss of at least $148.4 million. Converium also overstated its $1.09 billion in reported shareholders' equity as of December 31, 2000, by at least $72.3 million (approximately 6.6 percent of the total reported shareholders' equity), an amount including the effect of $100 million attributable to the Inter-Ocean and Z-1 Facility transactions and partially offset by $27.7 million attributable to other reinsurance transactions not addressed within the complaint.

Finally, because Converium's loss ratio for its non-life reinsurance business was directly affected by the improperly recorded reinsurance obtained through the circular Inter-Ocean and the Z-1 Facility transactions, Converium materially understated its reported loss ratios.

SEC Charges

Based on the foregoing, the SEC charged Converium with violating Section 10(b) of the Exchange Act and Rule 10b-5 in that it knowingly or recklessly made false and misleading statements, or omitted to state material facts necessary in order to make the statements, in the light of the circumstances under which they were made, not misleading to purchasers of Converium securities in connection with the 2001 IPO.

Zurich substantially assisted Converium's violation of Section 10(b) of the Exchange Act and Rule 10b-5 by, among other things, entering into the finite reinsurance transactions previously described for the purpose of improperly inflating its financial performance and improperly using reinsurance accounting rules to account for the transactions with the knowledge that such accounting was improper.

Questions

1. Why do you think it is important for a reinsurance transaction to transfer risk in order for a company to obtain the benefits of reinsurance accounting? Discuss the accounting and legal issues behind such a requirement.

2. Assume the external auditors of Zurich Re and Converium knew about the Inter-Ocean and the Z-1 Facility transactions. What legal issues could have been raised by the purchasers of stock in Converium's IPO to successfully bring an action against the auditors?

3. Evaluate the ethics of Zurich Re's actions with respect to its reinsurance transactions and the transfer of economic risk.

Chapter 7

Earnings Management and the Quality of Financial Reporting

Ethics Reflection

On April 10, 1997, the SEC filed charges against five senior officers of Structural Dynamics Research Corporation (SDRC), an international supplier of mechanical design automation software and engineering services, and two audit partners from KPMG for their involvement in accounting fraud at SDRC. The commission's complaint alleged that from 1992 through September 1994, SDRC recorded premature and fictitious revenue based on, among other things, purchase orders obtained from sales representatives that contained conditional language, indicating that the sales had not been finalized. SDRC allegedly shipped the product "sold" to a warehouse of a freight company, where it was held until further instructions, if any, from SDRC's Far East Operations. When the scheme was disclosed in September 1994, approximately $30 million of SDRC product was stored in the warehouse. The complaint further alleged that during the audit of SDRC's 1993 financial statements, Tony Tolani, formerly SDRC's vice president in charge of Far East Operations, made false statements to KPMG about the validity of orders from the Far East, and Ronald H. Hoffman, formerly SDRC's CFO, and Richard J. LaJoie Jr., formerly SDRC's controller, directly or indirectly failed to disclose certain material information to the auditors.[1]

In connection with KPMG's audit of SDRC's financial statements for the year ended December 31, 1993, KPMG issued an unqualified audit opinion stating that the audit was conducted in accordance with GAAS and that the financial statements were fairly presented in conformity with GAAP; both statements were wrong. During the audit, the engagement team spent considerable time auditing accounts receivable, a critical area of the audit. Particular emphasis was placed on auditing receivables in SDRC's Far East Operations, which represented approximately 50 percent of consolidated accounts receivable at year-end 1993. While auditing accounts receivable, the engagement team identified sales with conditional language noted on the purchase orders that should have precluded revenue recognition under GAAP. The audit staff prepared a memo included in the workpapers that stated that certain purchase orders were contingent upon receipt of end-user purchase orders and thus were conditional purchase orders. The workpapers also contained the SDRC controller's explanation to the audit team about these conditional purchase orders—that is, language was included in certain purchase orders ensuring written documentation that it could substitute software modules or end users.

Despite the fact that the language clearly stated the orders were conditional and subject to cancellation, the auditors unduly relied on the controller's explanation and management's representations. Auditors' judgment lacked professional skepticism and they failed to corroborate management's representations regarding conditional purchase orders with sufficient additional evidence that these sales were properly recorded.

As you read through this chapter, think about our past discussions of the importance of professional skepticism,

(Continued)

ethical judgment, and due care, and how the failure to adhere to ethical and professional standards undermines an audit in accordance with GAAS. SDRC is just one example of many in which the auditors looked the other way as their clients managed earnings through a variety of devices. An important question to ask is, what motivates a company to manipulate earnings in violation of GAAP? (Recall this is the incentive/pressure side of the fraud triangle.)

> Increasingly, I have become concerned that the motivation to meet Wall Street earnings expectations may be overriding common sense business practices. Too many corporate managers, auditors, and analysts are participants in a game of nods and winks. In the zeal to satisfy consensus earnings estimates and project a smooth earnings path, wishful thinking may be winning the day over faithful representation.
>
> *Arthur Levitt*

This quote by former SEC chair Arthur Levitt is from a speech to the New York University Center for Law and Business on September 28, 1998. Levitt links the practice of "earnings management" to an excessive zeal to project smoother earnings from year to year that casts a pall over the quality of the underlying numbers. Levitt identifies the cause as a "culture of gamesmanship" in business rooted in the emphasis on achieving short-term results such as meeting or exceeding financial analysts' earnings expectations.[2]

> Earnings can be as pliable as putty when a charlatan heads the company reporting them.
>
> *Warren Buffett (1930–)*

This quote by the American investment entrepreneur Warren Buffet emphasizes the importance of having an ethical person at the head of a company because a CEO who practices fraud can twist earnings to make them look better than they really are, thereby deceiving the users of the financial statements. Recall that the public relies on the integrity and strong ethical values of accountants and auditors to ensure that the financial statements are accurate and reliable and that the statements include all the information investors and creditors need (have a right) to know to make informed decisions. Taken together, the statements by Levitt and Buffet point to the need for those directly involved in the financial reporting process to establish and support the existence of an ethical culture in an organization.

The accounting scandals at companies such as Enron, WorldCom, and Tyco involved the use of inside information by top management to sell shares owned at a relatively favorable current price as compared to future prices. Presumably, the executives knew the earnings had been manipulated and either the manipulation could no longer be sustained or the bubble was about to burst. While the executives sold their shares and typically enhanced their wealth, thousands of employees lost millions of dollars of accumulated wealth in stock ownership and 401-k plans. The trigger for the sale was inside information about the future viability of the company. Clearly, these managers acted illegally in violation of securities laws motivated by their own self-interest and without due regard for their fiduciary obligations to the shareholders.

Motivation to Manage Earnings

Levitt attributes the practice of earnings management to the pressure on Wall Street to "make the numbers." He identifies a pattern created by earnings management whereby "companies try to meet or beat Wall Street earnings projections in order to grow market capitalization and increase the value of stock options." He notes that on the one hand, auditors are under pressure to retain clients by the firm, and on the other, they are under pressure by management "not to stand in the way."

Levitt talks about another motivation to manage earnings: to smooth net income over time. The ideal pattern of earnings for a manager is a steady increase each year over a period of time. The results make it appear that the company is growing and doing better than it really is and the manager should be given credit for the positive results. The market reacts by bidding up the price of the stock and the manager is rewarded for the results by a performance bonus and stock options with a prospective value that increases over time because of income smoothing that triggers stock price increases.

Levitt concludes that "these practices lead to erosion in the quality of earnings and therefore, the quality of financial reporting." The notion that accounting information should represent what it purports to represent, or representational faithfulness,[3] is distorted by the use of devices such as accelerating the recognition of revenue, delaying the recognition of an expense, and creating "cookie jar reserves" to smooth net income. These earnings management techniques will be discussed later in the chapter.

Definition of Earnings Management

Earnings management occurs when companies artificially inflate (or deflate) their revenues or profits, or earnings per share figures. This is accomplished in two broad ways: (1) by using aggressive accounting techniques such as capitalizing costs that should have been expensed (e.g., WorldCom accounted for its line costs as capital expenditures rather than expensing them against revenue because they benefited only the current year) and (2) by establishing/altering the elements of an estimate to achieve a desired goal (e.g., Waste Management's lengthening of the useful lives on trash hauling equipment to slow down depreciation each year).

There is no generally accepted definition of earnings management in accounting. General agreement does exist that the end result of earnings management is to distort the application of GAAP, thereby bringing into question the quality of earnings. The question to be answered is whether the distortion is the result of appropriate decision making given that choices exist in the application of GAAP, or if it is motivated by a conscious effort to manipulate earnings for one's advantage, which is fraud.

There are a variety of definitions of earnings management. Schipper defines it as a "purposeful intervention in the external reporting process, with the intent of obtaining some private gain (as opposed to say, merely facilitating the neutral operation of the process)."[4] Healy and Wahlen define it as "when managers use judgment in financial reporting and in structuring transactions to alter financial reports to either mislead some stakeholders about the underlying economic performance of the company, or to influence contractual outcomes that depend on reported accounting numbers."[5]

Dechow and Skinner note the difficulty of operationalizing earnings management based on the reported accounting numbers because they center on managerial intent, which is unobservable. Dechow and Skinner offer their own view that a distinction should be made between making choices in determining earnings that may comprise aggressive, but acceptable, accounting estimates and judgments as compared to fraudulent accounting practices that are clearly intended to deceive others.[6]

Recall that ethical intent is an essential ingredient in making moral decisions. Schipper views earnings management as a purposeful act by management as might be the case when earnings are manipulated to get the stock price up in advance of cashing in stock options. Healy and Wahlen focus on management's intent to deceive the stakeholders by using accounting devices to positively influence reported earnings. The underlying motivation for such actions according to the authors is the pursuit of self-interest rather than the interests of shareholders and other stakeholders.

Thomas E. McKee wrote a book on earnings management from the executive perspective. He defines *earnings management* as "reasonable and legal management decision making and reporting intended to achieve stable and predictable financial results." McKee believes earnings management reflects a conscious choice by management to smooth earnings over time and it does not include devices designed to "cook the books." He criticizes Schipper, Healy and Wahlen, and Dechow and Skinner for taking "unnecessarily negative view[s] of earnings management." McKee contends that a more positive definition is needed that portrays managers' motives in a positive light rather than the negative view adopted by others.[7]

Ethics of Earnings Management

The authors of this book believe that the acceptability of earnings management techniques should be judged using the ethics framework established earlier in the book. Virtue ethics examines the reasons for actions taken by the decision maker as well as the action itself. McKee's definition is self-serving from a management perspective and does not reflect virtues such as honesty (full disclosure) and dependability (reliable numbers). The definition also ignores the rights of shareholders and other stakeholders to receive fair and accurate financial information. McKee's explanation that earnings management is good because it creates a more stable and predictable earnings stream by smoothing net income cannot overcome the fact that a smooth net income by choice does not reflect what investors and creditors need or want to know since it masks true performance. Further, McKee's explanation for the "goodness" of earnings management is nothing more than a rationalization for an unethical act.

One might be able to rationalize the ethics of earnings management from an act-utilitarian perspective. Under this view, a decision about how to account for and report a financial transaction could be made by weighing the benefits to management and the company of using a particular technique (to smooth net income) versus the costs of providing potentially misleading information to the shareholders. Under a rule-utilitarian perspective, however, financial statements should never be manipulated for personal gain.

How Managers and Accountants Perceive Earnings Management

The first survey of note about how managers view the ethics of earnings management was conducted in 1990 by Bruns and Merchant. They found that managers disagreed considerably on whether earnings management is ethically acceptable. They also found that in general the respondents thought manipulating earnings via operating decisions (for example, purposefully delaying making needed repairs to a subsequent year) was more ethically acceptable than manipulation by accounting methods. The authors were disturbed by these findings. They were concerned that these practices could be misleading to users of the information and, over time, reduce the credibility of accounting numbers thereby damaging the reputation of the accounting profession.[8]

Rosenzweig and Fischer followed up on the Bruns and Merchant survey in 1995 by asking accounting professionals about factors causing earnings management. Two of these factors involve accounting manipulation, and two involve operating decisions designed to influence reported earnings. The accounting factors include actions that influence earnings by changing accounting methods. Examples include recording an expense in the wrong year or changing an inventory valuation in order to influence earnings. Examples of operating decision manipulations are deferring necessary expenditures to a subsequent year or offering unusually attractive terms to customers at year-end to draw next year's sales into the current year.[9] (Recall the conditional purchase orders in the SDRC case.)

In a 2006 survey, Akers, Giacomino, and Bellovary surveyed accounting students and practitioners about their views of earnings management. With respect to accounting practitioners, the results show that accounting manipulation is much less acceptable ethically than operating decision manipulation. This finding parallels the attitude Bruns and Merchant found among managers.[10] Generally, the practitioners had few ethical qualms about operating decision manipulation with scores indicating an average rating between (fully) ethical and questionable. The practitioners, however, generally felt that operating decisions that influenced expenses were somewhat more suspect than those that influenced revenues.

The results of the survey by Akers et al. indicates that none of the 20 practices asked about were rated as "Totally Unacceptable." Additional findings include (1) only 5 of the 20 practices were rated as a "Serious Infraction," (2) 10 practices were rated as a "Minor Infraction," (3) 4 practices were rated as a "Questionable Practice," and (4) 1 action was rated as an "Ethical Practice"—painting ahead of schedule.

The five most serious infractions were (1) bury "scrap costs" in other expenses—no (operating) income effect; (2) request deferred billing from supplier; (3) raise return forecast (on purchases) from 22 to 35 percent, with actual of 22 percent; (4) accelerate delivery to customers by 42 days; and (5) defer supplies expense by delaying recording invoice. It is interesting to note that the most serious infraction did not even affect net income.[11] Instead, the action to bury scrap costs in other expenses shifts an operating expense into a nonoperating category thereby increasing operating income, an amount on the income statement oftentimes considered to be a more important gauge of earnings than "bottom line" net income. Other actions are clearly designed to manage earnings by either accelerating the recording of earnings or delaying the recording of operating expenses.

As to the 10 practices rated as minor infractions, the ethical significance of each is as follows: (1) reduce reserve for obsolescence to meet budget target; (2) increase reserve for obsolescence, and reduce income; (3) accelerate delivery to customer by 28 days; (4) defer expenses to meet annual budget; (5) raise return forecast from 22 to 35 percent; (6) request deferred billing from supplier; (7) accelerate delivery to customer by 16 days; (8) reduce reserve for obsolescence to continue work; (9) defer expenses to meet quarterly budget; and (10) prepay expenses to reduce income by $60,000.[12]

One unexpected result is that the second most unacceptable minor infraction leads to a decrease in income. Students may wonder why a manager might choose to reduce reported income by increasing a reserve account with an offset that increases expenses (i.e., debit: estimated loss due to obsolescence of inventory; credit: reserve for obsolescence). A good example is the case of Sunbeam Corporation where the newly hired CEO, Al Dunlap, directed the accountants to create a reserve account during his first few months as CEO based on the belief that increasing the expenses and showing an even larger net loss would work to his advantage in the long run because in future periods the company could restore the reserves to increase income. Later on, it would appear that Dunlap had worked his magic in turning a company around when the reserves were restored and net income increased. During the 1990s, these reserve practices were given the moniker of "cookie jar" reserves because a company "set aside" some reserves to be taken out of the jar and used when needed to prop up earnings.

Acceptability of Earnings Management from a Materiality Perspective

Defining Materiality

We have already discussed materiality from an audit perspective. Recall that the Financial Accounting Standards Board (FASB) defined *materiality* in *Statement of Financial Accounting Concepts Statement No. 2,* Qualitative Characteristics of Accounting Information, as "the magnitude of an omission or misstatement of accounting information that, in the light of surrounding circumstances, makes it probable that the judgment of a reasonable person relying on the information would have been changed or influenced by the omission or misstatement."[13]

Staff Accounting Bulletin (SAB) No. 99, issued by the SEC, clarifies that the exclusive use of a percentage materiality criteria to assess material misstatements in the financial statements has no basis in law and is not acceptable. The commission did state that the use of a percentage as a numerical threshold, such as 5 percent, may provide the basis for a preliminary assumption that, without considering all relevant circumstances, a deviation of less than the specified percentage with respect to a particular item on the registrant's financial statements is unlikely to be material. However, the SEC ruled that both qualitative and quantitative factors must be considered when assessing materiality.[14] Materiality judgments in lawsuits against accountants rely on the "reasonable person" standard that "a substantial likelihood that the . . . fact would have been viewed by the reasonable investor as having significantly altered the 'total mix' of information made available." If an item is material, it should be disclosed in the body of the financial statements or footnotes.

Materiality is judged both by relative amount and by the nature of the item. For example, even a small theft by the president of a company is material because it brings into question the trustworthiness of the president, may indicate other misappropriations have occurred, and such an action brings into question the tone at the top. The SEC in *Accounting Series Release* No. 159 provides that an item is material if it changed by 10 percent or more relative to the prior year. It seems this is a generous standard and counterintuitive to the fact that any knowing manipulation of earnings is unethical.

In *SAB 99,* the SEC lists some of the qualitative factors that may cause quantitatively small misstatements to become material including:

- Arises from an item capable of precise measurement
- Arises from an estimate and, if so, the degree of imprecision inherent in the estimate
- Masks a change in earnings or other trends
- Hides a failure to meet analysts' consensus expectations for the enterprise
- Changes a loss into income or vice versa
- Concerns a segment or other portion of the registrant's business that has been identified as playing a significant role in the registrant's operations or profitability
- Affects the registrant's compliance with regulatory requirements
- Affects the registrant's compliance with loan covenants or other contractual requirements
- Has the effect of increasing management's compensation—for example, by satisfying the requirements for the award of bonuses or other forms of incentive compensation
- Involves concealment of an unlawful transaction

Auditors should be on the alert for these red flags that signal qualitatively material items may not have been recorded and disclosed in accordance with GAAP.

Materiality Considerations in Evaluating Internal Control Deficiencies under Sarbanes-Oxley

The Sarbanes-Oxley (SOX) Act increased demands on management to prevent and detect material control weaknesses. To develop the controls SOX requires, CPAs need to be able to identify key control exceptions and apply a materiality concept to determine the financial impact of such exceptions. In this regard, Vorhies identifies four perspectives to help CPAs meet their responsibilities under the act including (1) the actual financial statement misstatement or error, (2) an internal control deficiency caused by the failure in design or operation of a control, (3) a large variance in an accounting estimate compared with the actual determined amount, and (4) financial fraud by management or other employees to enhance a company's reported financial position and operating results.[15]

Under Section 302 of SOX, companies are required to (1) review their disclosure controls and procedures quarterly, (2) identify all key control exceptions and determine which are internal control deficiencies, (3) assess each deficiency's impact on the fair presentation of their financial statements, and (4) identify and report significant control deficiencies or material weaknesses to the audit committee of the board of directors and to the company's independent auditor.

Examples of misstatements or errors include incorrectly recorded financial statement amounts and financial statement amounts that should have been recorded but were not. Any internal control failure could be a control deficiency. Such deficiencies usually are the result of a failure in control design or operation. A design failure occurs when management fails to establish a sufficient level of internal control or control activities to achieve a control objective; an operating failure is when an adequately designed control does not operate properly. Because estimation processes are evaluated based on their adequacy, an accounting estimation generally would not result in a control deficiency or an uncorrected/unrecorded misstatement if it was reasonable given the available technology and the process was "normal" for the industry, and the company's independent auditor reviewed and approved it. Estimating financial events and balances is a necessary evil given the accrual accounting system and need to report on the income and the state of assets at artificial points in time. As long as the estimation process is reasonable, CPAs cannot conclude a control deficiency exists when the actual amount is compared with the estimate regardless of the size of the variance. If the estimation process is flawed, broken, or unreasonable, a control deficiency exists. An uncorrected/unrecorded misstatement also may exist—the difference between the estimate calculated and recorded in error versus what the correct estimate should have been.

Current Auditing Standards and Presumptions

Statement on Auditing Standards (SAS) No. 107, Audit Risk and Materiality in Conducting an Audit,[16] includes the following guidance with respect to materiality in the context of an audit:

> The auditor's consideration of materiality is a matter of professional judgment and is influenced by the auditor's perception of the needs of users of financial statements as a group; the auditor does not consider the possible effect of misstatements on specific individual users, whose needs may vary widely. Materiality judgments are made in light of surrounding circumstances and necessarily involve both quantitative and qualitative considerations.

SAS 107 points out that the evaluation of whether a misstatement could influence economic decisions of users, and therefore be material, involves consideration of the characteristics of those users who are assumed to

- Have an appropriate knowledge of business and economic activities and accounting and a willingness to study the information in the financial statements with an appropriate diligence.
- Understand that financial statements are prepared and audited to levels of materiality.
- Recognize the uncertainties inherent in the measurement of amounts based on the use of estimates, judgment, and the consideration of future events.
- Make appropriate economic decisions on the basis of the information in the financial statements.

The determination of materiality, therefore, takes into account how users with such characteristics could reasonably be expected to be influenced in making economic decisions.

SAS 107 offers the following guidance with respect to using benchmarks to evaluate materiality: "Examples of benchmarks that might be appropriate, depending on the nature and circumstances of the entity, include total revenues, gross profit, and other categories of reported income, such as profit before tax from continuing operations. For asset-based entities (for example, an investment fund) an appropriate benchmark might be net assets. Other entities (for example, banks, and insurance companies) might use other benchmarks."

Financial statement disclosures of items deemed to be material should include:

- Significance of the related financial statement balance
- Quantitative significance of the disclosure
- Qualitative aspects of the disclosure
- "Reasonable reader" needs (i.e., would decisions about the entity change or be influenced if the disclosure were present?)
- Not applicable versus not material (when preparing disclosure checklists)
- Judgment

Each *Statement of Financial Accounting Standards* includes a caveat at the end stating that the "provisions of the Statement need not be applied to immaterial items." However, financial statement preparers should always consider the cumulative effect that numerous, immaterial (and omitted) items could have on the financial statement taken as a whole.

Gemstar-TV Guide International, Inc.

The danger of relying on only a quantitative analysis to make materiality judgments can be seen in the audit by KPMG of Gemstar-TV Guide International, Inc. Accounting and Auditing Enforcement Release (AAER) No. 2125 issued by the SEC concludes that $364 million of revenue was improperly reported and certain disclosure policies were inconsistent with Gemstar's accounting for revenue and/or did not comply with GAAP disclosure requirements. AAER No. 2125 found that the KPMG auditors concurred in Gemstar's accounting for overstated revenue from licensing and advertising transactions in March 2000, December 2000, December 2001, and March 31, 2002. Also, KPMG did not object to Gemstar's disclosure and issued audit reports stating that KPMG had conducted its audits in conformity with GAAS and that the financial statements fairly presented its results in conformity with GAAP. In reaching these conclusions, the KPMG auditors unreasonably relied on representations by Gemstar management and/or unreasonably determined that the revenues were immaterial to Gemstar's financial statements. The KPMG auditors' materiality determinations were unreasonable in that they only considered quantitative materiality factors (i.e., that the amount of revenue was not a large percentage of Gemstar's consolidated financial results) and failed to also consider qualitative materiality (i.e., that the revenue related to business lines that were closely watched by securities analysts and had a material effect on the valuation of Gemstar stock).

The SEC complaint reads like a "what's what" in earnings management and it provides insight into the techniques that some companies use to manage earnings. The complaint alleges that Gemstar materially overstated its revenues by nearly $250 million through the following means:[17]

- Recording revenue under expired, disputed, or nonexistent agreements, and improperly reporting this as licensing and advertising revenue
- Recording revenue from a long-term agreement on an accelerated basis in violation of GAAP and Gemstar's own policies that required recording and reporting such revenue ratably over the terms of the agreement (consistent with the matching theory)
- Inflating advertising revenue by improperly recording and reporting revenue amounts from multiple-element transactions
- Engaging in "round-trip" transactions whereby Gemstar paid money to a third party to advertise its services and capitalized that cost while the third party used the funds received from Gemstar to buy advertising that was 100 percent recorded as revenue by Gemstar in the period of transaction
- Failing to disclose that it had structured certain settlements for the purpose of creating cookie jar reserves of advertising revenue to smooth net income
- Improperly recording advertising revenue from nonmonetary and barter transactions even though Gemstar could not properly establish the advertising fair value

Restatements of Financial Statements

A *financial statement restatement* occurs when a company, either voluntarily or under prompting by its auditors or regulators, revises its public financial information that was previously reported. The number and varied restatements of financial statements by publicly owned companies increased significantly during the 2000–2006 period as many companies restated after disclosing accounting frauds. Since 2006, the number of restatements has gone down in part due to stricter internal control requirements under SOX Section 404 and new auditing standards established by the PCAOB. These requirements were addressed in Chapter 5.

Restatements Due to Errors in Accounting and Reporting

An analysis of causes of restatement due to errors in accounting and reporting was made by Turner and Weirich. They looked at financial statement restatements during 2005 and the first nine months of 2006 of nearly 25,000 company filings with the SEC. Companies with U.S.-listed securities filed 1,295 financial restatements in 2005, nearly double the previous year. This represents about one restatement for every 12 public companies (up from one for every 23 in 2004). Of these restatements, 100 were by foreign companies.[18]

Results from the Turner–Weirich study with respect to the kinds of accounting errors that trigger restatements are particularly relevant for our discussion in the next section of earnings management techniques. Exhibit 7.1 presents these results.

On March 19, 2009, Glass Lewis & Company, an independent research and proxy advisory firm, released financial restatement data for 2008. In its *Trend Report: Restatement Dust Settles,* Glass Lewis discovered that over the 2008 year restatements dropped to a five-year low, with restatements down 49 percent from a year earlier.[19]

Glass Lewis's study examined U.S.-listed companies with market values of at least $250 million, and found that the 2008 decline was the result of work recently completed

EXHIBIT 7.1
Accounting Errors
that Trigger Financial
Statement Restatements

Category	Cause of Restatements
Revenue recognition	Improper revenue recognition including questionable items and misreported revenue
Expense recognition	Improper expense recognition including period of recognition, incorrect amounts; includes improper lease accounting
Misclassification	Improper classification on income statement, balance sheet or cash flow statement; includes nonoperating revenue in operating category; cash outflow from operating activities in investment activities
Equity	Improper accounting for earnings per share; stock-based compensation plans, options, warrants, and convertibles
Other comprehensive income (OCI)	Improper accounting for OCI transactions including unrealized gains and losses on investments in debt and equity securities, derivatives; and pension-liability adjustments
Capital assets	Improper accounting for asset impairments, asset placed in service dates and depreciation
Inventory	Improper accounting for valuation of inventory including market adjustments and obsolescence
Reserves/allowances	Improper accounting for bad debt reserves on accounts receivable, reserves for inventory, provision for loan losses
Liabilities/contingencies	Improper estimation of liability claims, loss contingencies litigation matters, commitments, and certain accruals

at larger companies to overhaul the systems and processes they use to ensure financial reports are accurate. In the fifth year of SOX compliance, companies made fewer errors. Interestingly, one possible cause of the decline may have occurred because an SEC advisory committee in 2008 moved to relax materiality standards and streamline error corrections, making it easier for companies to avoid restatements. This is discussed further in the following text.

Key findings of the study are as follows: (1) 172 U.S.-listed companies with market values of at least $250 million filed 185 financial restatements to correct errors, a five-year low; (2) only 6 percent of companies filed restatements, down from 9 percent in 2007; and (3) returns for companies that corrected severe errors recovered least and continued to underperform six months and one year following restatement announcements.

SEC Advisory Committee on Improvements to Financial Reporting

The SEC Advisory Committee on Improvements to Financial Reporting issued its findings on November 2, 2007, providing additional guidance about materiality judgments that shift from the current model of making such judgments based on professional judgment and the "reasonable person" standard to emphasizing whether a restatement may be desirable to meet user (investor) needs. Specifically, the SEC stated that *SAB 99* is being applied too broadly (i.e., resulting in errors being deemed to be material when an investor may not find them to be important). The subcommittee believes that market reaction can be one factor relevant in evaluating materiality, and based on these studies it would appear that there may be many restatements occurring that investors do not consider important due to a lack of a statistically significant market reaction. While there are limitations to using market reaction as a proxy for materiality, the subcommittee believes that these studies indicate that a reduction in the number of restatements is appropriate and worth trying to achieve.[20]

We are concerned about the SEC's position with respect to reducing the number of restatements because users may not find the restatement information useful. While accounting does identify user needs for information as a critical factor in deciding what information to provide, we do not believe this approach should be extended to accounting restatements. The restatements are triggered by mistakes of some kind by management in accounting for and reporting financial data. This means the users have incorrect information with respect to these mistakes. Without knowledge of the restated information, how can the users adequately evaluate the competency of management and the level of trust it should place in their decision making? We believe the issue of reporting restatements should be based on ethical factors: the fact that dishonesty may be behind the restatement; questions about the integrity of management may persist; and an environment of pressure may lead to manipulating earnings that have to be restated at a later date.

The SEC advisory committee gathered input from equity and credit analysts and others about investors' views on materiality and how restatements are viewed in the marketplace. Important feedback includes:

- Bright lines are not useful in making materiality judgments. Both qualitative and quantitative factors should be considered in determining if an error is material or not.
- One of the major costs of restatements for investors is the amount of time between the restatement announcement and the final resolution of the restatement, including potential delisting of the company's stock.
- The disclosure provided on restatements is not adequate. Notably, the disclosure does not clearly explain how the error was detected and why the restatement occurred.
- Interim periods should be viewed as discrete periods for purposes of making materiality judgments.

The advisory committee believes that the goal of companies should be to record errors, excluding clearly insignificant errors and errors resulting from normal accounting conventions, no later than in the financial statements of the period in which the error was discovered. The subcommittee believes that the current disclosure surrounding a restatement is not adequate. Instead, all companies that have a restatement should be required to disclose the following information, in addition to the amount of the restatement and the periods impacted: (1) how the restatement was discovered; (2) why the restatement occurred, including clear disclosure of any control weakness that led to the restatement, even if the control weakness was not determined to be a material weakness; and (3) corrective actions, if any, taken by the company to prevent the error from occurring in the future. We support these disclosure guidelines of the SEC that attempt to ferret out the underlying cause of financial statement restatements.

FreightCar America: An Example of Disclosures about a Restatement

On July 28, 2009, FreightCar America, Inc., announced that it had recently identified historical accounting errors in accounts payable. We believe this case serves as an excellent example of the disclosures that should accompany a financial statement restatement as soon as it is known, even before the statements are corrected. The details are as follows:

- The company currently estimates that accounts payable was overstated in a range of $10 to $14 million as of March 31, 2009. The company is also reviewing the extent to which the historical accounting errors have resulted in the understatement of net earnings since the fourth quarter of 2007.
- On July 27, 2009, the audit committee of the board of directors of FreightCar America concluded that the company's previously issued audited consolidated financial statements as of and for the fiscal years ended December 31, 2008, and December 31, 2007, and related auditors' report, and unaudited interim consolidated financial statements as of and for the quarterly periods ended March 31, 2009, December 31, 2008, September 30, 2008,

June 30, 2008, March 31, 2008, and December 31, 2007, should no longer be relied upon because of these errors in the financial statements. The company intends to restate these financial statements. The company's board of directors agreed with the audit committee's conclusions.

- The errors were attributable to flaws in the design of an internal information technology and accounting process to properly account for receipt of certain goods.
- The company will likely not file its quarterly 10-Q report for the second quarter of 2009 on time as it completes its analysis and financial restatement.

Review of Accounting Errors

- The company's review of these accounting errors and their impact on the company's consolidated financial statements for each period is continuing. The accounting errors did not result from any changes in the company's accounting policies, and the company has no evidence that the errors resulted from any fraud or intentional misconduct.
- The company's review indicates that the errors were attributable to flaws in the design of an internal information technology and accounting process to account for receipt of certain goods that was implemented in the fourth quarter of 2007.
- Management identified the accounting errors in connection with the implementation of a new enterprisewide reporting and management software platform system to improve processes and strengthen controls throughout the company.

Review Process

The company's audit committee is overseeing this review. The company has not reached a final conclusion on the effect of these accounting errors on its assessment of internal control over financial reporting and disclosure controls and procedures. Given the complexity of the analysis, the company expects that the review will be completed during the third quarter of 2009, including the filing of amended quarterly reports on Form 10-Q for the quarters ended March 31, 2009, and September 30, 2008, and an amended annual report on Form 10-K for the year ended December 31, 2008, to restate the financial statements for the periods indicated previously.

Earnings Management Techniques

Schilit identifies seven common financial shenanigans. We use Schilit's framework to discuss earnings manipulations at two companies charged by the SEC with accounting fraud—Xerox and Lucent. Later we discuss what happened at Enron, including ethics and corporate governance failures.

We explain the basic financial shenanigan techniques,[21] with the number of examples in each category limited to the three most common techniques.

1. Recording Revenue Too Soon or of Questionable Quality

This may be the most common technique because many opportunities arise to accomplish the goal including recording revenue before the earnings process has been completed or before an unconditional exchange has occurred (e.g., SDRC). Examples of this shenanigan include:

- Recording revenue when future services remain to be provided
- Recording revenue before shipment or before the customer's unconditional acceptance
- Recording revenue even though the customer is not obligated to pay

2. Recording Bogus Revenue

Typically, bogus revenue transactions lead to fictitious revenue. Examples include:

- Recording sales that lack economic substance
- Recording as revenue supplier rebates tied to future required purchases
- Releasing revenue that was improperly held back before a merger

3. Boosting Income with One-Time Gains

The gains (and losses) from the sale of operating and investment assets that should be recorded in another income account can be classified in other ways if the intent is to boost operating income. These include:

- Boosting profits by selling undervalued assets
- Including investment income or gains as part of operating revenue
- Including investment income or gains as a reduction in operating expenses

4. Shifting Current Expenses to a Later or Earlier Period

A common approach to shift expenses to a later period is by capitalizing a cost in the current period and expensing it over a period of time rather than expensing the item completely in the current period. This was the technique used by WorldCom to inflate earnings by about $11 to $13 billion. Additional examples include:

- Changing accounting policies and shifting current expenses to an earlier period
- Failing to write down or write off impaired assets
- Reducing asset reserves

5. Failing to Record or Improperly Reducing Liabilities

The liability account is often used to manipulate earnings because when liabilities that should be recorded are not, the expenses also are understated. When liabilities are improperly reduced, the same affect on expenses occurs. The result is to overstate earnings. Some examples include:

- Failing to record expenses and related liabilities when future obligations remain
- Releasing questionable reserves (cookie jar reserves) into income
- Recording revenue when cash is received, even though future obligations remain

6. Shifting Current Revenue to a Later Period

Some companies act to delay the recording of revenue when the amount is relatively high in a given year. In a sense this action sets up a "rainy day" reserve that can be used to restore earnings in low-earnings years. One way to accomplish the goal is to create a reserve (cookie jar reserve) with the excess revenues and release it back into the income stream at a later date when it can do more good. Examples include:

- Deliberately overstating the allowance for uncollectible accounts and adjusting it downward in future years
- Deliberately overstating the reserve for loan losses and adjusting it downward in future years
- Deliberately overstating the estimated sales returns account and adjusting it downward in future years

7. Shifting Future Expenses to the Current Period as a Special Charge

A company might choose to accelerate discretionary expenses such as repairs and maintenance into the current period if the current years' revenue is relatively high in relation to expected future revenue or future expenses are expected to be relatively high. The motivation to shift future expenses to the current period might be to smooth net income over time.

The delay in recording repairs and maintenance is a technique that McKee would probably categorize as appropriate given the goal of providing smooth and predictable earnings. Recall that in the reported studies on earnings management the idea of managing earnings through operating decisions was not perceived to be as big a problem as altering revenue amounts. However, the decision to delay needed repairs raises several ethical issues with respect to the company's operating decisions because it creates a risk that assets such as machinery and equipment may break down prematurely. These are (1) the quality of product may suffer leading to extra quality control costs and rework costs; (2) production slows and fails to meet deadlines, thereby risking customer goodwill; and (3) the costs to repair the machines can be greater than they would have been had maintenance been completed on a timely basis. Imagine, for example, that you fail to change the oil in your car on a regular basis. The result may be serious and costly repairs to the engine later on.

Descriptions of Financial Shenanigans

In this section we describe the financial shenanigans that occurred at Xerox, Lucent, and Enron. We chose these companies because the techniques used to manage earnings vary from the relatively simple (recording revenue too soon) to the more exotic (using special-purpose entities to hide debt and inflate earnings).

The Case of Xerox

Motivation for Fraudulent Scheme of Top Management

On June 3, 2003, the SEC filed a civil fraud injunctive action in the U.S. District Court for the Southern District of New York charging six former senior executives of Xerox Corporation, including its former CEOs Paul Allaire and G. Richard Thoman, and its former CFO Barry D. Romeril, with securities fraud and aiding and abetting Xerox's violations of the reporting, books and records, and internal control provisions of the federal securities laws. The complaint charges the former executives with engaging in a fraudulent scheme that lasted from 1997 to 2000 and misled investors about Xerox's earnings to "polish its reputation on Wall Street and to boost the company's stock price."[22]

The quality of the financial reports came into question as Xerox failed to disclose GAAP violations that led to acceleration in the recognition of approximately $3 billion in equipment revenues and an increase in pretax earnings by approximately $1.4 billion in Xerox's 1997–2000 financial results. The executives agreed to pay over $22 million in penalties, disgorgement, and interest without admitting or denying the SEC's allegations.

The tone at the top was one that viewed business success with meeting short-term earnings targets. Romeril directed or allowed lower-ranking defendants in Xerox's financial department to make accounting adjustments to results reported from operating divisions to accelerate revenues and increase earnings. These individuals utilized accounting methods to meet earnings goals and predictions of outside securities analysts. Allaire and Thoman then announced these results to the public through meetings with analysts and in communications to shareholders, celebrating that Xerox was enjoying substantially greater earnings growth than the true operating results warranted.

A description of two selected fraudulent accounting devices follows.

Fraudulent Lease Accounting

Xerox sold copiers and other office equipment to its customers for cash, but more frequently entered into long-term lease agreements in which customers paid a single negotiated monthly fee in return for the equipment, service, supplies, and financing. Xerox referred to these arrangements as "bundled leases."

The leases met the criteria under *SFAS 13* to be accounted for as "sales-type" leases whereby the fair value of the equipment leased would be recognized as income in the period the lease is delivered, less any residual value the equipment is expected to retain once the lease expires. GAAP permits the financing revenue portion of the lease to be recognized only as it is earned over the life of the lease. *SFAS 13* also specifies that the portion of the lease payments that represents the fee for repair services and copier supplies be prorated over the term of the lease matching it against the financing income.

Until the mid-1990s, Xerox followed satisfactory procedures for revenue recognition. However, the company encountered growing copier sales competition around the world and perceived a need to continue reporting record earnings. The management told KPMG it was no longer able to reasonably assign a fair value to the equipment as it had in the past. The company abandoned the value determinations made at the lease inception, for public financial reporting purposes, but not for internal operating purposes, and substituted a formula which management could manipulate at will. Xerox did not test the value determinations to assess the reliability of the original method or if the new method did a better job of accurately reflecting the fair value of copier equipment.[23]

Xerox's "topside" lease accounting devices consistently increased the amount of lease revenues that Xerox recognized at the inception of the lease and reduced the amount it recognized over the life of the lease. One method was called *return on equity (ROE),* which pulled forward a portion of finance income and recognized it immediately as equipment revenue. The second, called *margin normalization,* pulled forward a portion of service income and recognized it immediately as equipment revenue. These income acceleration methods did not comply with GAAP because there was no matching of revenue with the period during which (1) financing was provided, (2) copier supplies were provided, and (3) repairs were made to the leased equipment.

"Cushion" Reserves

From 1997 through 2000, Xerox violated GAAP through the use of approximately $496 million of reserves to close the gap between actual results and earnings targets. Xerox had created reserves through charges to income prior to 1997. These cookie jar reserves were released into income to make the numbers look better than they really were. The result was a smoothing of net income over time. This practice violated *Statement of Financial Accounting Standards (SFAS) No. 5,* Accounting for Contingencies, which allows a company to establish reserves only for identifiable, probable, and estimable risks and precludes the use of reserves, including excess reserves, for general or unknown business risks because they do not meet the accrual requirements of *SFAS 5.*

Sanctions by the SEC on KPMG

The SEC issued a cease-and-desist order against KPMG on April 19, 2005, for its role in auditing the financial statements of Xerox from 1997 through 2000. Accounting and Auditing Enforcement Release No. 2234 details KPMG's consent to institute a variety of quality control measures including to provide oversight of engagement partner changes of audit personnel and related independence issues.[24]

On February 22, 2006, the SEC announced that all four remaining KPMG staff members in the commission's action in connection with the $1.2 billion fraudulent earnings manipulation scheme by Xerox from 1997 through 2000 had agreed to settle the charges against them. Three KPMG partners agreed to permanent injunctions, payment of $400,000 in penalties, and suspensions from practice before the commission. Four partners were charged with filing materially false and misleading financial statements with the SEC and aiding and abetting Xerox's filing of false financial reports. The SEC charged that the partners knew or should have known about improper "topside adjustments" that resulted in $3 billion of the restated revenues and $1.2 billion of the restated earnings.[25]

The concurring review partner on the audit engagement team was cited because the adjustments enabled Xerox to change the allocations of revenues it received from leasing photocopiers and other types of office equipment. The partner agreed to a censure by the SEC for failing to exercise due care, professional skepticism, and adhere to GAAS.

Xerox paid a record fine of $10 million. On April 20, 2005, KPMG settled with the SEC over the financial fraud at Xerox agreeing to pay $10 million in penalties, in addition to disgorging nearly $10 million in audit fees and another $2.7 million in interest.

The Case of Lucent Technologies

On May 20, 2004, the SEC charged Lucent Technologies, Inc., with securities fraud, and violations of the reporting, books and records, and internal control provisions of the federal securities laws. The commission also charged nine current and former Lucent officers, executives, and employees with securities fraud and aiding and abetting Lucent's violations of federal securities laws. The SEC complaint alleged that Lucent fraudulently and improperly recognized approximately $1.148 billion of revenue and $470 million in pretax income during the fiscal year 2000. As part of the settlement, Lucent agreed to pay a $25 million penalty for its lack of cooperation.

The Lucent case is typical of the frauds that occurred in the late 1990s and early 2000s. The company's accounting techniques violated GAAP and were motivated by its drive to realize revenue, meet internal sales targets, and obtain sales bonuses. The internal controls were either violated or circumvented by top management. The board of directors and audit committee were either not involved or turned away from their obligations.

According to the Accounting and Auditing Enforcement Release (AAER) No. 2016, Lucent officers improperly granted and/or failed to disclose various side agreements, credits, and other incentives (extracontractual commitments) made to induce Lucent's customers to purchase the company's products. The premature recognition of revenue occurred by "selling" $135 million in software to a customer that could choose from a software pool by September 29, 2001, and Lucent recognized $135 million in revenue in its fiscal year ending September 30, 2000. The parties reached an agreement to separately document additional elements of the software pool transaction that would give the customer additional value in the form of side agreements. Top management postdated three letters documenting the side agreements with fictitious dates in October 2000. The effect of the postdated letters was to create the appearance that the side agreements were reached after September 30, 2000, and were not connected to the software pool agreement.[26] The accounting for these transactions enabled Lucent to manage earnings in a way that smoothed net income over time.

Lucent's story as a separate entity began in April 1996 when AT&T spun off the company. By 1999, operating income had reached $5.4 billion, tripling in two years. Net income had grown more than 10-fold during that time period. These remarkable increases over a relatively short period of time should have raised a red flag for KPMG, but it did not. Exhibits 7.2 and 7.3 present the comparative amounts during the two-year period ended September 30, 1999.[27]

Schilit points out that Lucent's stock price increased from a low of about $14 per share on January 1, 1997, to a high of about $78 by September 1999. The stock price began to decline after that to a low of about $7 per share on January 1, 2002, as the fraud unfolded.

EXHIBIT 7.2
Lucent Technologies, Inc.: Comparative Sales and Income

	Sales and Income Amounts (in billions of dollars)		
Item	September 1999	September 1998	September 1997
Sales	$48.3	$31.8	$27.6
Operating income	5.4	2.6	1.6
Net income	4.8	1.0	0.4

EXHIBIT 7.3
Lucent Technologies, Inc.: Percentage Change in Sales and Income

	Percentage Changes in Sales and Income Amounts	
	September 1998 to September 1999	September 1997 to September 1998
Sales	52%	15%
Operating income	104	63
Net income	380	150

Exhibit 7.4 takes Lucent's earnings management techniques and classifies them into Schilit's financial shenanigan categories.

The Story of Enron

The uniqueness of the decisions and manipulations at Enron and its link to the passage of SOX warrants a detailed discussion. The story of Enron is one of structuring financial transactions to keep debt off the books and report higher earnings. The failure of its corporate governance systems is the poster child for needed changes under SOX.

In the Beginning . . .

Enron was created in 1985 through Omaha-based InterNorth Inc.'s takeover of Houston Natural Gas Corporation. InterNorth paid a huge premium for Houston Natural Gas creating $5 million in debt. The company's debt payments of $50 million a month quickly led to the sell-off of billions of dollars' worth of assets. Its debt load was so high that it forced the company into financing projects with borrowings that were kept off the balance sheet.

EXHIBIT 7.4 Lucent Technologies, Inc.: Financial Shenanigans

Technique	Description	Shenanigan Number
Recorded revenue too soon	Lucent restated year 2000 earnings, removing $679 million improperly included revenue.	No. 1
Boosted income with one-time gains	During fiscal 1998, Lucent recorded $558 million of pension income—over 50% of earnings for the year.	No. 3
Failed to write down impaired assets	Lucent reduced the allowance for doubtful accounts and released the previous reserves despite an increase in receivables of 32%.	No. 4
Shifted current expenses to a later period	Lucent reduced the allowance for inventory obsolescence although the inventory balance increased.	No. 4
Reduced liabilities by changing accounting assumptions	Lucent modified its accounting approach and assumptions for pensions.	No. 5
Released reserves into income	Lucent released $100 million of a previously recorded restructuring reserve, boosting operating income.	No. 5
Created new reserves from 10 acquisitions	Lucent wrote off $2.4 billion (58% of the cumulative purchase price) as an in-process research and development (R&D). This new reserve could later be released into earnings.	No. 7

Jeff Skilling suggested that Enron's problem were due to a fluid market for natural gas; the industry needed long-term supply contracts. But prices were volatile and contracts were available only for 30-day spot deals. Producers were unwilling to commit to the long-term, always believing the price could go up.

Skilling's "Gas Bank" Idea

Enron needed to find a way to bridge the gap between what the producers and big gas users wanted. Skilling discussed ways to pool the investments in gas-supply contracts and then sell long-term deals to utilities through a "Gas Bank." The Gas Bank called for Enron to write long-term contracts enabling it to start accounting for those contracts differently. Traditionally accounting would book revenue from a long-term contract when it came in. But Skilling wanted Enron to book all anticipated revenue immediately as if it was writing up a marketable security. The technique lends itself to earnings management because of the subjectivity involved in estimating future market value.

Counting all expected profits immediately meant a huge earnings kick for a company that was getting deeply in debt. But it also put Enron on a treadmill: To keep growing, it would have to book bigger and bigger deals every quarter. The result was to shift focus from developing economically sound partnerships to doing deals at all costs.

The marketplace didn't seem to like the Enron deals. The initial Gas Bank plan hadn't persuaded gas producers to sell Enron their reserves. To entice the producers, the company needed to offer them money upfront for gas that would be delivered later. The problem was where to get the cash.

Fastow's Special-Purpose Entities

In 1991, to revitalize the Gas Bank, Enron's CFO, Andy Fastow, began creating a number of partnerships. The first series was called Cactus. The Cactus ventures eventually took in money from banks and gave it to energy producers in return for a portion of their existing gas reserves. That gave the producers money upfront and Enron gas over time.

Fastow worked to structure ventures that met the conditions under GAAP to keep the partnership activities off Enron's books and on the separate books of the partnership. To do so the equity financing of the partnership venture had to include a minimum of 3 percent outside ownership. Control was not established through traditional means, which was the ownership of a majority of voting equity and combining of the partnership entity into the sponsoring organization (Enron), as is done with parent and subsidiary entities in a consolidation. Instead, the independent third parties were required to have a controlling and substantial interest in the entity. Control was established by the third-party investors exercising management rights over the entity's operations. There were a lot of "Monday morning quarterbacks" in the accounting profession that questioned the economic logic of attributing even the possibility of control to those who owned only 3 percent of the capital.

Bethany McLean and Peter Elkind are two *Fortune* magazine reporters credited with prompting the inquiries and investigations that brought down the Enron house of cards. McLean had written a story posing the simple question: "How, exactly, does Enron make its money?" Well, in the go-go years of the 1990s, all too often no one asked these kinds of questions or, perhaps, did not want to know the answer.

According to McLean and Elkind, a small group of investors were pulled together known internally as the Friends of Enron. When Enron needed the 3 percent, it turned to the friends. These business associates and friends of Fastow and others were independent only in a technical sense. Though they made money on their investment, they didn't control the entities or the assets within them. "This, of course, was precisely the point."[28]

The 3 percent investments triggered a "special purpose vehicle or special purpose entity (SPE)." The advantage of the independent partnership relationship was that the SPE borrowed money from banks and other financial institutions that were willing to loan money to it with an obligation to repay the debt. The money borrowed by the SPE was often "transferred" to Enron in a sale of an operating asset no longer needed by Enron. The sale transaction typically led to a recorded gain because the cash proceeds exceeded the book value of the asset sold. Exhibit 7.5 depicts the typical relationship.

The SPE enabled Enron to keep debt off its books while benefiting from the transfer and use of the cash borrowed by the SPE. To enhance the attractiveness of the structured transaction, Enron would add to its managed earnings by "selling" an underperforming operating asset to the SPE at a gain. The result was increased cash flow and liquidity and inflated earnings. The uniqueness of the transactions engaged in by Enron was that they initially didn't violate GAAP. Instead, Enron took advantage of the rules to engineer transactions that enabled it to achieve its goals for enhanced liquidity and profitability.

The Growth of SPEs

Eventually, Enron would grow addicted to these arrangements because they hid debt. Not only did the company turn to its "friends," but increasingly it had to borrow from banks and financial institutions it did business with. After all, these entities did not want to turn down a company like Enron that was, at its peak, the seventh largest in the United States. But, Enron let the risk-shifting feature of the partnerships lapse, thus negating their conformity with GAAP. Over time, the financial institutions that were involved in providing the 3 percent for the SPEs became cautious of the ability of the SPEs to repay the interest when due. These institutions asked Enron to relieve the risk of the SPEs failure to repay the investments. Later, partnership deals were backed by promises of Enron stock. Thus, if something went wrong Enron would be left holding the bag. Therefore, there was no true transfer of economic risk to the SPE and, according to GAAP, the SPE should have been consolidated into Enron's financial statements.

The Culture at Enron

The tension in the workplace grew with employees working later and later—first until 6 p.m. and then 11 p.m., even into the next morning. Part of the pressure resulted from Skilling's new employee-evaluation policy. Workers called it "rank and yank." Employees

EXHIBIT 7.5
Enron Corporation's SPEs

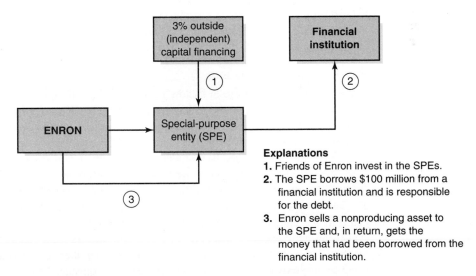

Explanations
1. Friends of Enron invest in the SPEs.
2. The SPE borrows $100 million from a financial institution and is responsible for the debt.
3. Enron sells a nonproducing asset to the SPE and, in return, gets the money that had been borrowed from the financial institution.

Journal Entries

Enron			SPE		
N/A			Cash	100m	
			Due to Bank		100m
Cash	100M		Asset	100m	
	Asset (assume)	40M	Cash		100m
	Gain on sale	60M			

were evaluated in groups, with each rated on a scale of 1 to 5. The goal was to remove the bottom 20 percent of each group every year.

Ultimately, the system was seen as a tool for managers to reward loyalists and punish dissenters. It was seen as a cutthroat system and encouraged a "yes" culture, in which employees were reluctant to question their bosses—a fear that many would later come to regret.

Let the Force Be with You

In late 1997, Enron entered a number of partnerships to improperly inflate earnings and hide debt. Enron created *Chewco,* named after the *Star Wars* character Chewbacca, to buy out its partner in another venture called *JEDI,* which was legally kept off the books. For JEDI to remain off the balance sheet, however, Chewco had to meet certain accounting requirements. But Enron skirted the already weak rules required to keep Chewco off its books. JEDI helped overstate Enron's profits by $405 million and understate debt of $2.6 billion.

Because Enron needed to close the deal by year's end, Chewco was a rush job. Enron's executive committee presented the Chewco proposal to the board of directors on November 5. But CFO Fastow left out a few key details. He failed to mention that there was virtually no outside ownership in Chewco, which he maintained was not affiliated with Enron. Nor did he reveal that one of his protégés, Michael Kopper, would manage the partnership. Indirectly if not directly, Fastow would control the partnership through Kopper. Enron had a code of ethics that prohibited an officer from becoming involved with another entity that did business with Enron. Involvement by Fastow in these related-party entities was forbidden by the code. Nevertheless, the board of directors waived that requirement so Fastow could become involved with Chewco.

The board approved the deal even though Enron's law firm, Vinson & Elkins, prepared the requisite documents so quickly that very few people actually read it before approving. Arthur Andersen, the firm that both audited Enron and did significant internal audit work for the company (pre-SOX), claimed that Enron withheld critical information. The firm billed the company only $80,000 for its review of the transaction indicating a cursory review at best. Chewco, Fastow's involvement, the board approval, and a rapid approval process all were allowed because of a lack of internal controls. The *Star Wars* transactions were the beginning of the end for Enron. Chewco was inappropriately treated as a separate entity. Other SPE transactions eventually lead to Enron's guaranteeing the debt of the SPE using its stock as collateral. When Enron finally collapsed, its off-balance-sheet financing stood at an estimated $17 billion.

Enron Just Keeps on Going

The greatest pressures were in Fastow's finance group. In 1999, he constructed two partnerships called *LJM Cayman* and *LJM2* that readily passed through the board, the lawyers, and the accountants. They were followed by four more, known as the *Raptors.* They did it once—it worked—then they did it again. It didn't take long to blur the lines between what's legal and what's not. When asked by a student what he did at Enron, one employee in the finance group answered by saying, "I remove numbers from our balance sheet and inflate earnings."

As Enron pushed into new directions—wind power, water, high-speed Internet, paper, metals, data storage, advertising—it became a different company almost every quarter. Entrepreneurship was encouraged; innovation was the mantra. The quarter-by-quarter scramble to post ever-better numbers became all-consuming. Enron traders were encouraged to use "prudence reserves," to essentially put aside some revenue until another quarter when it might be needed. Long-term energy contracts were evaluated using an adjustable curve to forecast energy prices. When a quarter looked tight, analysts were told to simply adjust the curve in Enron's favor.

Executive Compensation

Enron's goal of setting its executive pay in the 75th percentile of its peer group—including companies like Duke Energy, Dynegy, and PG&E that it compared itself with to assess overall corporate performance—was easily exceeded. In 2000 base salary, Enron exceeded the peer group average by 51 percent. In bonus payments, it outdistanced its peers by 383 percent. The stock options granted in 2000—valued at the time of grant at $86.5 million—exceeded the number granted by peers by 484 percent. Top management became accustomed to the large payouts and the desire for more became of part of the culture of greed at Enron.

While Enron was the first player into the new energy market enabling it to score huge gains, over time competitors caught on and profit margins shrank. Skilling began looking for new pastures and in 1996 he set his sights on electricity. Enron would do for power what it had done for natural gas. The push into electricity only added to the pressures boiling inside Enron. Earlier in 1996, Ken Lay, Enron's CEO, had predicted that the company's profits would double by 2000. This was a statement that would come back to haunt Lay in his civil trial in 2006 that alleged he knowingly hyped Enron's stock to keep funds flowing even though Lay knew the company was coming apart at the seams.

Lay pushed on as if nothing was wrong. Enron instituted a stock-option plan that promised to double employee salaries after eight years. Fresh off a $2.1 billion takeover of Portland General Corporation, an electric utility, Lay said his goal was nothing less than to make Enron the "world's greatest energy company."

Growth at all costs was the mantra at Enron. It encouraged executives to buy into this philosophy by giving out stock options that would provide cash over time and added the sweetener that if profits and the stock price went up enough, the schedule for those options would be sharply accelerated. It provided the incentive to find ways of increasing profits and improving stock price. It looked the other way when questions about ethics came up. Clearly, Enron and its officers pursued their self-interests to the detriment of all other interests and created a culture of greed. The environment at Enron reminds us of the famous quote by Gordon Gekko in the 1987 movie, *Wall Street:* "Greed is good. Greed captures the essence of the evolutionary spirit."

Congressional Investigation and Skilling's Departure

In 2000, Skilling was granted 867,880 options to buy shares, in addition to his salary and bonus totaling $6.45 million. In that year, he exercised and sold over 1.1 million shares from options he received from prior years, and pocketed $62.48 million. Skilling testified before Congress that he did not dump Enron shares as he told others to buy because he knew or suspected that the company was in financial trouble. Skilling's holdings of Enron shares increased because of more and more options. Even under Enron's option plan, in which options vested fully in three years, an unusually quick rate, Skilling wound up holding many Enron shares he couldn't legally sell.

Lay and Skilling used as their defense in the 2006 civil trial that Enron was a successful company brought down by a crisis of confidence in the market. The government contended that Enron appeared successful but actually hid its failures through dubious, even criminal accounting tricks. In fact, Enron by most measures wasn't particularly profitable—a fact obscured by its share price until late. But there was one area in which it succeeded like few others: executive compensation.

As the stock market began to decline in the late 1990s, Enron's stock followed the downward trend. The never-ending number of deals even as business slowed gave pause to Wall Street. By April 2001, concerns mounted whether the company was adequately disclosing financial information from its off-balance-sheet financing transactions.

The pressure continued both internally and externally from a slowing economy, competition from other entities that had caught on to Enron's gimmicks, and stock market declines. Differences of opinion exist why Skilling made the decision, but on August 14, 2001, Skilling, who just six months prior had been named the CEO of Enron, resigned. He gave as his public reason the ever popular "I need to spend more time with my family." However, Enron executive Sherron Watkins was dubious and she sent an anonymous letter to Ken Lay, the former and now current once again CEO and chair of the board of directors, warning Lay of an impending scandal.

Sherron Watkins's Role "Has Enron become a risky place to work? For those of us who didn't get rich over the last few years, can we afford to stay?" Sherron Watkins's words were in an unsigned letter sent to Ken Lay after he had encouraged employees to write about their concerns anonymously. She described in detail problems with Enron's partnerships, problems that the letter claimed would cause huge financial upheavals at the company in as little as a year. "I am incredibly nervous that we will implode in a wave of accounting scandals," Watkins wrote. "Skilling is resigning for 'personal reasons,' but I think he wasn't having fun, looked down the road and knew this stuff was unfixable and would rather abandon ship now than resign in shame in two years."[29]

Lay took a copy of the letter to James V. Derrick Jr., Enron's general counsel, who agreed it needed to be investigated. They decided to assign the task to Vinson & Elkins—which had helped prepare some of the legal documents for some of the partnerships. Enron wanted answers fast seemingly regardless of the due diligence, and the company instructed the outside lawyers not to spend time examining the accounting treatment recommended by Arthur Andersen—although that was at the heart of the letter's warnings.

Powers Committee Report

Vinson & Elkins began its investigation. Even while it investigated Fastow's role, the conflicts mounted. Kopper, who had sold his Chewco assets to Enron to deflect criticisms of Fastow's role, made a profit on the sale and then insisted that Enron cover the $2.6 million tax liability from the sale. The Powers Committee, formed by the audit committee to investigate the failure of Enron, concluded on this matter that "there is credible evidence that Fastow authorized Enron's payment to Chewco," adding that the payment—done against the explicit instructions of Enron's general counsel—was "one of the most serious issues we identified in connection with the Chewco buyout."[30]

Three days after beginning their investigation, the Vinson & Elkins lawyers investigating Watkins's warnings reported their findings to Lay and Derrick that there was no reason for concern. Everything in Fastow's operation seemed to be on the level. They promised a written report in a matter of weeks. By then, it would be too late.

The Final Days

In November 2001, Enron announced it had overstated earnings by $586 million since 1997. In December 2001, Enron made the largest bankruptcy filing ever. By January 2002, the Justice Department confirmed an investigation of Enron. The very next day, Andersen admitted to shredding documents related to its audit of Enron, an act of obstructing justice that would doom the firm following a Department of Justice lawsuit. It hardly mattered what the outcome of the lawsuit would be; Enron's clients started to abandon the firm in droves after the announcement of the lawsuit. Ultimately, the jury decided that the firm had obstructed justice, a decision that would be overturned later on due to a technicality.

The Lay–Skilling Civil Trial

Following the unanimous jury verdict on May 26, 2006, that found both Ken Lay and Jeff Skilling guilty of fraud and conspiracy, Lay was quoted as saying, "Certainly we're surprised" and Skilling commented that "I think it's more appropriate to say we're shocked. This is not the outcome we expected."[31]

Skilling was convicted of 19 counts of fraud, conspiracy, and insider trading. Lay was convicted on six counts in the joint trial and four charges of bank fraud and making false statements to banks in a separate nonjury trial before U.S. District Judge Sam Lake related to Lay's personal finances. The sentencing for Lay and Skilling, somewhat ironically, was set for September 11, 2006. If convicted on all counts, Skilling would have to serve 185 years in prison. For Lay, the fraud and conspiracy convictions carried a combined maximum punishment of 45 years. The bank fraud case added 120 years, 30 years for each of the four counts and rendered its ruling in June 2010. Unfortunately, Ken Lay passed away just weeks after the verdict.

June 2010 U.S. Supreme Court Ruling On June 24, 2010, the U.S. Supreme Court unanimously ruled in Skilling's appeal that the federal law that makes it a crime to deprive others of one's "honest services" was too broadly interpreted in the lower court decision and should have been more narrower construed to include only defined offenses of bribery and kickbacks both of which did not apply in Skilling's case. The reversal applies only to the honest services charges and not others that were part of Skilling's conviction including insider trading. The Supreme Court remanded back to the lower court for reconsideration its original decision to determine how the justice's decision affects various counts charged against Skilling. Federal prosecutors would be free to retry Skilling on some grounds, even if others are set aside.[32]

Skilling's Efforts to Overturn the Verdict On October 23, 2006, Skilling was sentenced to 24 years and 4 months in prison, and fined $45 million. The case is currently under appeal. Skilling's request to remain free during the appeal was denied by Judge Patrick Higginbotham of the Fifth U.S. Circuit Court of Appeals on December 12, 2006. In ordering Skilling's immediate imprisonment, the judge wrote, "Skilling raises no substantial question that is likely to result in the reversal of his convictions on all of the charged counts," although the order also noted "serious frailties" in the convictions. Skilling began his sentence on December 13, 2006. According to the Federal Bureau of Prisons, he is scheduled for release on February 21, 2028, when he would be 74 years old.

On April 3, 2008, Skilling's defense attorney argued with government prosecutors that Skilling's trial and the conviction itself was based on "honest services fraud" that he said did not apply to Jeffrey Skilling. This argument was based on the idea that, even though Skilling committed illegal financial maneuvers, he did so in order to save the company and did not profit from it. This in turn could lead to all of his convictions being overturned; however, the chances are very narrow. Experts believe Skilling's best chance lies in citing a parallel appeals court decision that threw out guilty verdicts on three Merrill Lynch bankers accused of helping Enron inflate profits.

On January 6, 2009, the U.S. Court of Appeals for the Fifth Circuit affirmed Skilling's conviction, but vacated the sentence and remanded for resentencing. On October 13, 2009, the Supreme Court agreed to hear Skilling's appeal in early 2010. Two questions will be before the Court. The first issue is whether the federal "honest services" fraud statute (title 18 of the United States Code, Section 1346) required the government to prove that Skilling's conduct was intended to achieve "private gain" rather than to advance the interest of his employer, and, if not, is the statute unconstitutionally vague.

The second issue—"in-house judging"—is whether, when a presumption of jury prejudice arises because of widespread community impact of defendant's alleged conduct and massive, inflammatory pretrial publicity, the government may rebut that presumption, and, if so, must the government prove beyond reasonable doubt that no juror was actually prejudiced. The Court heard arguments in March 2010 in Skilling's case and is expected to rule in June 2010.

Enron: A Review of Important Accounting Issues

The fraud at Enron was caused by a variety of factors including these:

- Improperly failing to consolidate the results of an SPE (Chewco) with Enron. Consolidation was warranted because Chewco lacked the necessary independence from Enron's management since Andy Fastow had direct or indirect control over the SPE.

- Failing to adequately disclose the related-party relationship between Enron and the SPEs, especially those that were independent of the company under GAAP.

- Overstating earnings from using mark-to-market accounting for investments in long-term gas contracts that relied on estimates of future market value to record unrealized gains.

The quality of financial reports was poor:

- Failure to adequately disclose the related-party transactions made it impossible for investors and creditors to know the full extent of these transactions and loans were made to Enron based on vastly understated debt.
- Sale of assets to SPEs in return for the transfer of borrowed funds from the SPE with the subsequent recording of a gain masked the true earnings and made it appear the company was doing better than it really was.
- Use of reserves and failure to explain the basis for creation made it impossible to judge the acceptability of these transactions.
- Failure to disclose Fastow's dual role with the SPEs and as CFO of Enron made it impossible for investors and creditors to gain the information they had an ethical right to know in order to evaluate the legitimacy of off-balance-sheet transactions and their effect on the financial statements.

Enron managed earnings through the following techniques (Schilit's shenanigans are indicated in parentheses):

- Used reserves to increase earnings when reported amounts were too low (#5)
- Used mark-to-market estimates to inflate earnings in violation of GAAP (#1)
- Selected which operating assets to "sell" to the SPEs, thereby affecting the amount of the gain on transfer and earnings effect (#3)

The lack of strong controls contributed to the fraud as evidenced by:

- Top management overrode or ignored internal controls in the approval process for Chewco, the LJMs, and the Raptors.
- Oversight by the board of directors was either negligent, as was the case with the waiving of the ethics code for Fastow, or nonexistent.
- A culture was established to make the deals at any cost, thereby diluting the due diligence process that should have raised red flags on some of the transactions.
- A culture of fear was created within Enron with its "rank or yank" policy and cutthroat competition.

FASB Rules on SPEs

While it may seem that the GAAP rules on SPEs are naïve, there are legitimate reasons for establishing the concept that an entity could isolate a business operation or some corporate assets. The idea was to control risk in a project such as investing in a new oil refinery. By following the rules to set up an SPE, an oil company could keep the large amount of debt off the books while using the funds from the SPE to construct the refinery. The off-balance-sheet effect helps control risk if the project fails. The original motivation by FASB was to establish a mechanism to encourage companies to invest in needed assets while keeping the related debt off their books.

The "creativity" of Andy Fastow was in using a not-so-well-known technique under GAAP to satisfy Enron's unique needs. Enron became the leader of structured transactions designed to meet specific goals rather than to best present financial position and the results of operations. These are nothing more than elaborate attempts to manage earnings.

FASB Interpretation 46(R)

After much debate about how to fix the original SPE ownership percentage and consolidation rules, FASB issued on December 24, 2003, a revision of its proposed Interpretation: *FASB Interpretation 46(R),* Consolidation of Variable Interest Entities.[33] Basically, *Interpretation 46(R)* requires unconsolidated variable interest entities to be consolidated by their primary beneficiaries if the entities do not effectively disperse risk among parties involved. Variable interest entities that effectively disperse risks would not be consolidated unless a single party holds an interest or combination of interests that effectively recombines risks that were previously dispersed.

The new rules apply an economic reality test to the consolidation of a variable interest entity. No longer is there a percentage ownership test. Instead, it is the dispersion of risk that determines the consolidation status. By effectively dispersing risk, the primary beneficiary controls its own risk with respect to activities of the unconsolidated variable interest entity.

Enron's Role in SOX

The Enron fraud was a direct cause, along with WorldCom, of congressional passage of SOX and efforts to reform the accounting profession. The provisions of the act that were motivated by the Enron fraud include:

- Prohibiting the provision of internal audit services for audit clients. Andersen provided the major part of internal audit services for Enron. Overall, Andersen earned from Enron in its last full year as accountants $27 million from nonaudit services and $25 million from audit services.
- Requiring that off-balance-sheet financing activities be disclosed in the notes to the financial statements. Enron's SPEs were never referred to as providing off-balance-sheet financing.
- Requiring that related-party transactions be disclosed in the notes. The activities with the SPEs qualify as related-party transactions. By some accounts Enron had over 3,000 SPEs, yet the footnote disclosure in its last year before filing for bankruptcy was limited to one page.

Enron also suffered from the same lack of controls and inadequate corporate governance that infected so many other companies during the accounting scandals. For example, the board of directors did not act independently and the audit committee members were not independent of management. The internal environment at Enron, especially the tone at the top, promoted a culture of making deals regardless of the risks.

The internal controls at Enron were either ignored or overridden by management (i.e., the board waived its ethics policy so that Andy Fastow could indirectly control Chewco while, at the same time, serving as the CFO for Enron). This created a conflict of interest that enabled Fastow to enrich himself through control of Chewco at the expense of Enron. The result was a serious breach of fiduciary responsibilities and the failure of management to meet its obligation as an agent for the shareholders.

Lessons to Be Learned from Enron

What is the moral of the Enron story? Certainly, we could say that weak internal controls equate with possible fraud. Also, we could point to the need for an ethical tone at the top to help prevent fraud. At Enron, once the company developed an appetite for establishing SPEs and keeping these transactions off the books, the company became more and more addicted to the cash provided through the SPEs. Even if it wanted to stop the transactions, Enron and its top management had set the company on a course that was difficult to change. Enron had started to slide down the ethical slippery slope and there was no turning back.

The bottom-line factor that kept the Enron fraud going well past the point of no return was greed. Skilling saw Fastow getting rich, Lay saw Skilling getting rich, all the Enron employees thought they saw Lay getting rich, and then Lay hyped Enron stock to the employees for their 401-ks as a way for them, eventually, to get rich.

Concluding Thoughts

We started discussing accounting fraud earlier in the book (before Chapter 7) because it results from a lack of professional (ethical) judgment, weak corporate governance systems, and the failure of accountants and auditors to follow the profession's principles and standards in meeting their ethical obligations. Your authors have wondered whether there is anything new under the sun in public accounting. The scandals of the 1980s repeated themselves in the 1990s and now the 2000s. Calls for stronger internal controls and an internal control report by management had gone unheeded for more than 30 years, but finally Section 404 of SOX dictated that requirement. GAAS that have called for more meaningful communication between auditors and audit committees have been ignored over the years, but now SOX requires specific communications to help prevent or detect material misstatements in the financial statements.

What will it take in the future to avoid history repeating itself once again? One thing we know is that it will take more than SOX. Ethical behavior cannot be legislated. What is needed is a strong internal control environment backed by adherence to ethical values and effective corporate governance systems. What is needed is a true commitment to ethics in one's personal as well as professional life. At the end of the day, all we have is our personal integrity and reputation for honest, hard work.

We do believe SOX is an important step in moving down the road of ensuring accurate and reliable financial reports. The act establishes important requirements to strengthen audit and audit committee independence and enhance internal controls. SOX is designed to enhance transparency and full disclosure thereby improving the quality of financial reporting. What's needed now is strict enforcement of the act, legal liabilities for violations, and the site of more and more offending CEOs and CFOs doing the "perp walk."

You have learned that earnings management was widely practiced during the accounting scandals of the late 1990s and early 2000s. The motivation during that time often was to respond to internal pressures brought about by financial analysts' earnings estimates. These pressures were driven by hungry investors who became accustomed to substantial growth and stock price returns in unusually short periods of time. An important factor that enabled the fraud to occur was stock option grants that increased in value as the current market price went up in part due to manipulated earnings.

We end this chapter with one final quote that focuses on the role of the investing public in instigating the frauds. This quote comes from Joseph E. Abbott, the vice president and controller of West Pharmaceuticals Services Inc. in Lionville, Pennsylvania: "Investors should remember that if we do see companies start hitting estimates and not beating them, that wouldn't be such a bad thing. It could mean there is less earnings management going on."

Discussion Questions

1. In Arthur Levitt's speech that was referred to in the opening quote he also said: "I fear that we are witnessing an erosion in the quality of earnings, and therefore, the quality of financial reporting. Managing may be giving way to manipulation; integrity may be losing out to illusion." Explain what you think Levitt meant by this statement.

2. Can earnings management be an ethical practice? Discuss why or why not. Give an example of when it might be ethical.

3. Comment on the statement that materiality is in the eye of the beholder. How does this statement relate to the discussion in the chapter of how to gauge materiality in assessing financial statement restatements?

4. According to the SEC Advisory Committee on Improvements to Financial Reporting, the determination of materiality with respect to financial statement disclosures should be based on an evaluation of the needs of the users of financial statements. Explain what you think the SEC

meant by this statement. Do you agree that materiality judgments should be directly influenced by the perceived needs of the users? Why or why not?

5. Under SOX Section 302, companies must review their disclosure controls and procedures quarterly. To develop the controls, SOX requires CPAs to be able to identify key control exceptions and apply a materiality concept to determine the financial impact of such exceptions. How is a materiality concept used to determine the financial impact of such exceptions?

6. On July 23, 2009, for the first time the SEC ordered an executive to return compensation awarded during years the company misstated financial results—even though the executive himself wasn't accused of wrongdoing. In a step that could have broader repercussions, the SEC told Maynard L. Jenkins, the former chief executive of CSK Auto Corporation, to give back to the company more than $4 million in bonuses and equity compensation he'd earned between 2002 and 2004. Those were years during which the Phoenix auto-parts retailer engaged in fraudulent accounting that boosted its pretax income by a total of $66 million, the SEC alleged. CSK restated its earnings for those years twice. The civil action, filed in U.S. District Court in Arizona, represents the SEC's boldest test of the "clawback" provision of SOX. That provision requires CEOs and CFOs to return incentive and equity compensation gained during a period of fraudulent financial statements.

   a. Do you think it is ethically appropriate for the SEC to be able to claw back CEO and CFO incentive and equity compensation when companies restate results because of misconduct even if they were not personally involved in any wrongdoing?

   b. The clawback provision also is being applied in the Bernie Madoff case whereby prosecutors seek to identify those investors who received returns on their investments with Madoff while others lost everything. The idea is to force those investors who received returns on their investments to turn over those amounts to the government so that they may be more equitably distributed. Do you think it is ethically appropriate for those investors who did receive returns to be forced to sacrifice them solely because other investors received no returns?

7. On January 4, 2005, Krispy Kreme Doughnuts, Inc., announced it would restate its financial statements for the 2004 fiscal year. The restatement, the company said, was due to errors in how it accounted for the repurchase of franchises. It explained that such a restatement could reduce its earnings by seven to eight cents a share and cause the company to default on its credit agreement. The company's stock price fell $1.83 that day, or about 15 percent. Explain what you believe to be the factors that cause a company's stock price to decline by a significant amount on the day of the announcement of a restatement of earnings. That is, what motivates shareholders to sell off their stock holdings after announcements such as that at Krispy Kreme?

8. Comment on the statement that what a company's income statement reveals is interesting but what it conceals is vital.

9. Explain why accrual earnings and cash flow from operating activities are different amounts. Which of the two numbers do you think is more reliable? Give an example of where the accrual amount creates questions about reliability while the cash flow amount would be a better gauge of earnings.

10. Create your own "financial shenanigan" and explain how it might work. Do not use the shenanigans described by Schilit.

    Use the following information to answer questions 11 and 12.

    Revenue recognition for multiple-element arrangements can be extraordinarily complicated. For example, a vendor may design and sell manufacturing equipment and installation services for one overall price. The arrangement consideration for the bundled sale of the equipment and the installation services calls for determining the stand-alone selling price for each of the deliverables and use it to separate out the revenue amounts. For example, assume the bundled sale of the equipment and installation services is for $250,000. The stand-alone estimates of selling prices for each element would be used to separate out revenue amounts.

11. Why do you think it is important to separate out the selling prices of each element of a bundled transaction? How might the separation affect recorded revenue in the period of sale and in future periods?

12. In an attempt to address some of the challenges surrounding separating elements, the Financial Accounting Standards Board (FASB) issued *Accounting Standards Update (ASU) 2009–13,*

Multiple-Deliverable Revenue Arrangements—a consensus of the FASB Emerging Issues Task Force—and *ASU 2009–14,* Certain Revenue Arrangements That Include Software Elements—a consensus of the FASB Emerging Issues Task Force. Review these pronouncements (www.fasb.org) and summarize the primary provisions that relate to accounting for multiple element revenue arrangements.

13. Tinseltown Construction just received a $2 billion contract to construct a modern football stadium in the City of Industry located in southern California for the new National Football League team, the Los Angeles Devils of Industry. The company estimates it will cost $1.5 billion to construct the stadium. Explain how Tinseltown can make revenue recognition decisions that enable it to manage earnings over the three-year duration of the contract.

14. Explain why off-balance-sheet-financing techniques are used by companies to keep debt off the books. In particular, how do the accounting rules for lease transactions create the potential for off-balance-sheet financing? If a company treats a lease as an off-balance-sheet debt, what steps should it take to ensure that the financial results present fairly financial position with respect to this transaction?

15. a. In the Enron case the company eventually turned to "back-door" guaranteeing of the SPE's debt to satisfy equity investors. Explain why such an action negated the transfer of economic risk requirement to keep the SPE off Enron's books.

    b. Assume the guarantee referred to was for a $16 million loan. The loan agreement required that Enron stock should not fall below $40 per share. If the share price did decline below that trigger amount, either the loan would be called by the bank or the bank could choose to increase the guaranteed number of Enron shares based on the new (assumed) $32 price. If the bank decides to increase the number of shares guaranteed, what would be (1) the original number of shares in the guarantee and (2) the new number of shares? Why would it be important for Enron to disclose information about the guarantee in its financial statements?

16. In a speech titled "A QT Report Card for High Quality Financial Reporting," at the Critical Issues in Accounting Forum program sponsored by Wake Forest University, Lynn Turner, former chief accountant of the SEC, made the following analogy to describe representational faithfulness:

    A map's representational faithfulness may be determined by how well the map describes the coastline. In the same way, a financial statement's representational faithfulness may be evaluated by how well it represents the economic resources and obligations of the company, and by how well the transactions and events that change those resources and obligations are described.

    If a company purposefully understates an estimated allowance for sales returns to inflate revenue in the current year, how does this accounting influence the representational faithfulness and quality of financial information?

17. *Statement on Auditing Standards (SAS) No. 90,* Audit Committee Communications, requires the auditor to discuss with the audit committee the quality, not just the acceptability, of the accounting principles used by an entity. Describe what should be included in a discussion about the quality of accounting principles.

18. In a Duke University survey of 400 corporate financial executives, two out of five said they would use legal ways to book revenues early if that would help them meet earnings targets. More than one in five would adjust certain estimates or sell investments to book higher income. Are you surprised by these results? Comment on the ethics of the results.

19. Who is responsible for earnings management? Is it top management that instigates the practice? Or, is it the accountants, who may go along with recording and reporting such transactions? Or, is it the auditors, who do not discover or look the other way and ignore the effects of the transactions on the financial statements? Be sure to discuss the ethical obligations of each group in answering the question.

20. What is meant by transparency in financial statements? Why is it important for financial statements to be transparent? That is, who benefits from it and how do transparent statements influence the judgments of those receiving such statements?

Endnotes

1. *Securities Exchange Commission v. Structural Dynamics Research Corporation et al.*, Litigation Release No. 15325, www.sec.gov/litigation/litreleases/1994/lr15325.htm.

2. Arthur Levitt, "The 'Numbers Game,' Remarks by Chairman Arthur Levitt, Securities and Exchange Commission, before the NYU Center for Law and Business," September 28, 1998, www.sec.gov.

3. Financial Accounting Standards Board, "Recognition and Measurement in Financial Statements of Business Enterprises," *Statement of Financial Accounting Concepts (SFAC) No. 5* (Stamford, CT: FASB, May 1986).

4. K. Schipper, "Commentary on Earnings Management," *Accounting Horizons* (December 1989), pp. 91–102.

5. P. M. Healy and J. M. Wahlen, "A Review of Earnings Management Literature and Its Implications for Standard Setting," *Accounting Horizons* 13 (1999), pp. 365–383.

6. P. M. Dechow and P. J. Skinner, "Earnings Management: Reconciling the Views of Accounting Academics, Practitioners, and Regulation," *Accounting Horizons* 14 (2001), pp. 235–250.

7. Thomas E. McKee, *Earnings Management: An Executive Perspective* (Mason, OH: Thompson Corporation, 2005).

8. William J. Bruns Jr. and Kenneth A. Merchant, "The Dangerous Morality of Managing Earnings," *Management Accounting,* August 1990.

9. K. Rosenzweig and M. Fischer, "Is Managing Earnings Ethically Acceptable?" *Management Accounting,* March 1994.

10. Michael D. Akers, Don E. Giacomino, and Jodi L. Bellovary, "Earnings Management and Its Implications: Educating the Accounting Profession," *The CPA Journal,* August 2007.

11. Akers et al.

12. Akers et al.

13. Financial Accounting Standards Board, *Statement of Financial Accounting Concepts No. 2,* Qualitative Characteristics of Accounting Information, www.fasb.org.

14. Securities and Exchange Commission, *Staff Accounting Bulletin No. 99—Materiality,* www.sec.gov/interps/account/sab99.htm.

15. James Brady Vorhies, "The New Importance of Materiality," *Journal of Accountancy,* May 2005.

16. American Institute of CPAs, *AICPA Professional Standards, Volume 1 as of June 1, 2009, Statement on Auditing Standards (SAS) No. 107,* Audit Risk and Materiality in Conducting an Audit (New York: AICPA, 2009).

17. Securities and Exchange Commission, Accounting and Auditing Enforcement Release No. 2125, *In the Matter of KPMG [v. Gemstar],* www.sec.gov/litigation/admin/34-550564.html.

18. Lynn E. Turner and Thomas R. Weirich, "A Closer Look at Financial Statement Restatements: Analyzing the Reasons behind the Trend," *The CPA Journal,* December 2006.

19. Huron Consulting Group, 2004 Annual Review of Financial Reporting Matters, www.huronconsultinggroup.com.

20. Securities and Exchange Commission, SEC Advisory Committee on Improvements to Financial Reporting, www.sec.gov.

21. Howard M. Schilit, *Financial Shenanigans: How to Detect Accounting Gimmicks and Fraud in Financial Reports,* 2nd ed. (New York: McGraw-Hill, 2002).

22. Securities and Exchange Commission, Litigation Release No. 18174, *Securities and Exchange Commission v. Paul A. Allaire, G. Richard Thoman, Barry D. Romeril, Philip D. Fishbach, Daniel S. Marchibroda, and Gregory B. Tayler,* June 5, 2003, Accounting and Auditing Enforcement Release No. 1796, www.sec.gov/litigation/litreleases/lr18174.html.

23. Securities and Exchange Commission, Litigation Release No. 17645, Accounting and Enforcement Release No. 1542, *Securities and Exchange Commission v. Xerox Corporation,* Civil Action No. 02-CV-2780 (DLC) (S.D.N.Y.) (April 11, 2002).

24. Exchange Commission, Litigation Release No. 19573, Accounting and Enforcement Release No. 2379, *SEC v. KPMG LLP et al.,* Civil Action No. 03-CV 0671 (DLC) (S.D.N.Y.) (February 22, 2006).

25. Securities and Exchange Commission, Accounting and Auditing Enforcement Release No. 2234, *In the Matter of KPMG LLP,* April 19, 2005, www.sec.gov/litigation/admin/34-51574.pdf.

26. Securities and Exchange Commission, Accounting and Enforcement Release Litigation Release No. 2016, *Securities and Exchange Commission v. Lucent Technologies, Inc., Nina Aversano, Jay Carter, A. Leslie Dorn, William Plunkett, John Bratten, Deborah Harris, Charles Elliott, Vanessa Petrini, Michelle Hayes-Bullock, and David Ackerman,* Civil Action No. 04-2315 (WHW) (D.N.J.) (filed May 17, 2004, www.sec.gov/ltigation /litreleases/lr18715.htm.)

27. Securities and Exchange Commission, Accounting and Enforcement Release No. 2380, *In the Matter of Thomas J. Yoho, CPA, Respondent,* Administrative Proceeding File No. 3-12215, February 22, 2006.

28. Bethany McLean and Peter Elkind, *The Smartest Guys in the Room: The Amazing Rise and Scandalous Fall of Enron* (New York: Penguin Books, 2003).

29. Mimi Swartz and Sherron Watkins, *Power Failure: The Inside Story of the Collapse of Enron* (New York: Doubleday, 2003), pp. 275–276.

30. Report of Investigation by the Special Investigative Committee of the Board of Directors of Enron Corp., February 1, 2002, www.news.findlaw/hdocs/docs/enron/sicreport.

31. Michael Gracyzk, "Lay Says He's 'Shocked' at Enron Verdict," www.cbsnews.com/stories/2006/05/26/ap/business/mainD8HRJ2C80.shtml.

32. Supreme Court of the U.S., *Skilling v United States,* Certiorari to the United States Court of Appeals for the Fifth Circuit. No. 08-1394. June 24, 2010. http://www.supremecourt.gov/opinions/09pdf/08-1394.pdf

33. Financial Accounting Standards Board, *FASB Interpretation 46(R),* Consolidation of Variable Interest Entities, December 24, 2003 (Norwalk, CT: FASB, 2003).

Chapter 7 Cases

Case 7-1

Nortel Networks

Canada-based Nortel Networks was one of the largest tele-communications equipment companies in the world prior to its filing for bankruptcy protection on January 14, 2009, in the United States, Canada, and Europe. The company had been subjected to several financial reporting investigations by U.S. and Canadian securities agencies in 2004. The accounting irregularities centered on premature revenue recognition and hidden cash reserves used to manipulate financial statements. The goal was to present the company in a positive light so that investors would buy (hold) Nortel stock thereby inflating the stock price. Although Nortel was an international company, the listing of its securities on American stock exchanges subjected it to all SEC regulations, along with the requirement to register its financial statements in accordance to U.S. GAAP.

The company had gambled by investing heavily on Code Division Multiple Access (CDMA) wireless cellular technology during the 1990s in an attempt to gain access to the growing European and Asian markets. However, many wireless carriers in the aforementioned markets opted for rival Global System Mobile (GSM) wireless technology instead. Coupled with a worldwide economic slowdown in the technology sector, Nortel's losses mounted to $27.3 billion by 2001, resulting in the termination of two-thirds of its workforce.

The Nortel fraud primarily involved four members of Nortel's senior management as follows: CEO Frank Dunn, CFO Douglas Beatty, controller Michael Gollogly, and assistant controller, Maryanne Pahapill. Dunn is a certified management accountant, while Beatty, Gollogly, and Pahapill are chartered accountants in Canada.

Accounting Irregularities

On March 12, 2007, the SEC alleged the following in a complaint against Nortel:[1]

- In late 2000, Beatty and Pahapill implemented changes to Nortel's revenue recognition policies that violated U.S. GAAP, specifically to pull forward revenue to meet publicly announced revenue targets. These actions improperly boosted Nortel's fourth quarter and fiscal 2000 revenue by over $1 billion, while at the same time allowing the company to meet, but not exceed, market expectations. However, because their efforts pulled in more revenue than needed to meet those targets, Dunn, Beatty, and Pahapill selectively reversed certain revenue entries during the 2000 year-end closing process.

[1]U.S. District Court for the Southern District of New York, *U.S. Securities and Exchange Commission v. Frank A. Dunn, Douglas C. Beatty, Michael J. Gollogly, and Maryanne E. Pahapill,* Civil Action No. 07-CV-2058, www.sec.gov/litigation/complaints/2007/comp20036.pdf.

- In November 2002, Dunn, Beatty, and Gollogly learned that Nortel was carrying over $300 million in excess reserves. The three did not release these excess reserves into income as required under U.S. GAAP. Instead, they concealed their existence and maintained them for later use. Further, Beatty, Dunn, and Gollogly directed the establishment of yet another $151 million in unnecessary reserves during the 2002 year-end closing process to avoid posting a profit and paying bonuses earlier than Dunn had predicted publicly. These reserve manipulations erased Nortel's *pro forma* profit for the fourth quarter of 2002 and caused it to report a loss instead.[2]

- In the first and second quarters of 2003, Dunn, Beatty, and Gollogly directed the release of at least $490 million of excess reserves specifically to boost earnings, fabricate profits, and pay bonuses. These efforts turned Nortel's first quarter 2003 loss into a reported profit under U.S. GAAP, which allowed Dunn to claim that he had brought Nortel to profitability a quarter ahead of schedule. In the second quarter of 2003, their efforts largely erased Nortel's quarterly loss and generated a *pro forma* profit. In both quarters, Nortel posted sufficient earnings to pay tens of millions of dollars in so-called return to profitability bonuses, largely to a select group of senior managers.

- During the second half of 2003, Dunn and Beatty repeatedly misled investors as to why Nortel was conducting a purportedly "comprehensive review" of its assets and liabilities, which resulted in Nortel's restatement of approximately $948 million in liabilities in November 2003. Dunn and Beatty falsely represented to the public that the restatement was caused solely by internal control mistakes. In reality, Nortel's first restatement was necessitated by the intentional improper handling of reserves, which occurred throughout Nortel for several years, and the first restatement effort was sharply limited to avoid uncovering Dunn, Beatty, and Gollogly's earnings management activities.

The complaint charged Dunn, Beatty, Gollogly, and Pahapill with violating and/or aiding and abetting violations

[2]*Pro forma* means literally as a matter of form. Companies sometimes report income to the public and financial analysts that may not be calculated in accordance with GAAP. For example, a company might report *pro forma* earnings that exclude depreciation expense, amortization expense, and nonrecurring expenses such as restructuring costs. In general, *pro forma* earnings are reported in an effort to put a more positive spin on a company's operations. Unfortunately, there are no accounting rules on just how *pro forma* should be calculated so that comparability is difficult at best, and investors may be misled as a result.

of the antifraud, reporting, books and records, internal controls, and lying to auditors provisions of the federal securities laws. Dunn and Beatty were separately charged with violations of the officer certification provisions instituted by SOX. The commission sought a permanent injunction, civil monetary penalties, officer and director bars, and disgorgement with prejudgment interest against all four defendants.

Specifics of Earnings Management Techniques

From the third quarter of 2000 through the first quarter of 2001, when Nortel reported its financial results for year-end 2000, Dunn, Beatty, and Pahapill altered Nortel's revenue recognition policies to accelerate revenues as needed to meet Nortel's quarterly and annual revenue guidance, and to hide the worsening condition of Nortel's business. Techniques used to accomplish this goal include:

1. *Reinstituting bill and hold transactions.* The company tried to find a solution for the hundreds of millions of dollars in inventory that was sitting in Nortel's warehouses and offsite storage locations. Revenues could not be recognized for this inventory because U.S. GAAP revenue recognition rules generally require goods to be delivered to the buyer before revenue can be recognized. This inventory grew, in part, because orders were slowing and, in June 2000, Nortel had banned bill and hold transactions from its sales and accounting practices. A *bill and hold transaction* is one where the customer agrees to purchase a product but the seller (here Nortel) retains physical possession until the customer can accept delivery. The company reinstituted bill and hold sales when it became clear it fell short of earnings guidance. In all, Nortel accelerated into 2000 more than $1 billion in revenues through its improper use of bill and hold transactions.

2. *Restructuring business-asset write-downs.* Beginning in February 2001, Nortel suffered serious losses when it finally lowered its earnings guidance to account for the fact that its business was suffering from the same widespread economic downturn that impacted the entire telecommunications industry. As Nortel's business plummeted throughout the remainder of 2001, the company reacted by implementing a restructuring that, among other things, reduced its workforce by two-thirds and resulted in a significant write-downs of assets.

3. *Creating reserves.* In relation to writing down the assets, Nortel established reserves that were used to manage earnings. Assisted by defendants Beatty and Gollogly, Dunn manipulated the company's reserves to manage Nortel's publicly reported earnings, create the false appearance that his leadership and business acumen was responsible for Nortel's profitability, and pay bonuses to these three defendants and other Nortel executives.

4. *Releasing reserves into income.* From at least July 2002 through June 2003, Dunn, Beatty, and Gollogly released excess reserves to meet Dunn's unrealistic and overly aggressive earnings targets. When Nortel internally (and unexpectedly) determined that it would return to profitability in the fourth quarter of 2002, the reserves were used to reduce earnings for the quarter, avoid reporting a profit earlier than Dunn had publicly predicted, and create a stockpile of reserves that could be (and were) released in the future as necessary to meet Dunn's prediction of profitability by the second quarter of 2003. When 2003 turned out to be rockier than expected, Dunn, Beatty, and Gollogly orchestrated the release of excess reserves to cause Nortel to report a profit in the first quarter of 2003, a quarter earlier than the public expected, and to pay defendants and others substantial bonuses that were awarded for achieving profitability on a *pro forma* basis. Because their actions drew the attention of Nortel's outside auditors, they made only a portion of the planned reserve releases. This allowed Nortel to report nearly break-even results (though not actual profit) and to show internally that the company had again reached profitability on a *pro forma* basis necessary to pay bonuses.

Role of Auditors and Audit Committee

In the second half of 2003, Nortel's outside auditors raised concerns about Nortel's handling of reserves and, from that point forward, defendants' scheme began to unravel. To appease the auditors, Nortel's management—led by Dunn and Beatty—conducted a purportedly comprehensive review of Nortel's assets and liabilities. This resulted in an announcement, on October 23, 2003, that Nortel would restate its financials for fiscal years 2000, 2001, and 2002.

Shortly after Nortel's announced restatement, the audit committee commenced an independent investigation and hired outside counsel to help it "gain a full understanding of the events that caused significant excess liabilities to be maintained on the balance sheet that needed to be restated," as well as to recommend any necessary remedial measures. The investigation uncovered evidence that Dunn, Beatty, and Gollogly and certain other financial managers were responsible for Nortel's improper use of reserves in the second half of 2002 and first half of 2003.

In March 2004, Nortel suspended Beatty and Gollogly and announced that it would "likely" need to further revise and restate previously filed financial results. Dunn, Beatty, and Gollogly were terminated for cause in April 2004.

On January 11, 2005, Nortel issued a second restatement that restated approximately $3.4 billion in misstated revenues and at least another $746 million in liabilities. All of the financial statement effects of defendants' two accounting fraud schemes were corrected as of this date, albeit, there remained lingering effects from defendants' internal control and other nonfraud violations.

Nortel also disclosed the findings to date of the audit committee's independent review, which concluded, among other things, that Dunn, Beatty, and Gollogly were responsible for Nortel's improper use of reserves in the second half of 2002 and first half of 2003. The second restatement, however, did not reveal that Nortel's top executives had also engaged in revenue recognition fraud in 2000.

In May 2006, in its Form 10-K for the period ending December 31, 2005, Nortel admitted for the first time that its restated revenues in part had resulted from management fraud, stating that "in an effort to meet internal and external targets, the senior corporate finance management team . . . changed the accounting policies of the company several times during 2000," and that those changes were "driven by the need to close revenue and earnings gaps."

Throughout their scheme, defendants lied to Nortel's independent auditor by making materially false and misleading statements and omissions in connection with the quarterly reviews and annual audits of the financial statements that were materially misstated. Among other things, each of the defendants submitted management representation letters to the auditors that concealed the fraud and made false statements, which included that the affected quarterly and annual financial statements were presented in conformity with U.S. GAAP and that they had no knowledge of any fraud that could have a material effect on the financial statements. Dunn, Beatty, and Gollogly also submitted a false management representation letter in connection with Nortel's first restatement, and Pahapill likewise made false management representations in connection with Nortel's second restatement.

The defendants' scheme resulted in Nortel issuing materially false and misleading quarterly and annual financial statements and related disclosures for at least the financial reporting periods ending December 31, 2000, through December 31, 2003, and in all subsequent filings made with the commission that incorporated those financial statements and related disclosures by reference.

Settlement

On October 15, 2007, Nortel, without admitting or denying the commission's charges, agreed to settle the commission's action by consenting to be permanently enjoined from violating the antifraud, reporting, books and records, and internal control provisions of the federal securities laws and by paying a $35 million civil penalty, which the commission placed in a Fair Fund for distribution to affected shareholders. Nortel also agreed to report periodically to the commission's staff on its progress in implementing remedial measures and resolving an outstanding material weakness over its revenue recognition procedures.

In settling the matter, the SEC acknowledged Nortel's substantial remedial efforts and cooperation. After Nortel announced its first restatement, the audit committee launched an independent investigation that later uncovered the improper accounting. Nortel's board took extensive remedial action that included promptly terminating employees responsible for the wrongdoing, restating its financial statements four times over four years, replacing its senior management, and instituting a comprehensive remediation program designed to ensure proper accounting and reporting practices. Nortel also shared the results of its independent investigation with the SEC. As part of the settlement, Nortel agreed to report to the commission staff every quarter until it fully implements its remediation program, and the company and its outside auditor agreed that the existing material weakness has been resolved. The commission acknowledged the assistance of the Ontario Securities Commission, which conducted its own separate, parallel investigation.

Nortel in Canada

After a four-year investigation, on June 20, 2008, Canadian authorities arrested three high-level ex-Nortel Networks executives on fraud charges for their alleged part in what has been described as the worst stock scandal in Canadian history. The Royal Canadian Mounted Police in Toronto arrested ex-CEO Frank Dunn, ex-CFO Douglas Beatty, and former corporate controller Michael Gollogly, who were each charged with seven counts of fraud. The charges include "fraud affecting public market; falsification of books and documents; and false prospectus, pertaining to allegations of criminal activity within Nortel Networks during 2002 and 2003." The three pleaded innocent and were released on bail.

On January 14, 2009, Nortel filed for protection from creditors in the United States, Canada, and the United Kingdom in order to restructure its debt and financial obligations. In June, the company announced it no longer planned to continue operations and that it would sell off all of its business units. Nortel's CDMA wireless business and LTE access technology were sold to Ericsson, and Avaya purchased its Enterprise business unit.

The final indignity for Nortel came on June 25, 2009, when Nortel's stock price dropped to 18.5¢ a share down from a high of $124.50 in 2000. Nortel's battered and bruised stock was finally delisted from the S&P/TSX composite index, ending a colossal collapse on an exchange on which the Canadian telecommunications giant's stock valuation once accounted for a third of its value.

In the end, most industry experts agreed that the former Canadian tech champion was just another casualty of capitalism. "Ultimately, we're in this not for the glory but to provide sufficient returns to shareholders," said Professor Foerster. "We have a company whose business model appears to be broken. Clearly, this is a company that destroyed value for shareholders over an extended period of time and that's reason enough to defend why we don't expect bailouts."[3]

Questions

1. Dunn is a certified management accountant. Based on the facts of the case, which provisions of the IMA's Statement of Ethical Professional Practice that was discussed in Chapter 1 have been violated?

2. What are the responsibilities of an auditor to detect fraud? How were those responsibilities compromised by the actions of Nortel's management?

3. Describe the incentives that created pressure on Nortel to manage earnings. Considering the role of Nortel's management in this regard, discuss whether it met its corporate governance obligations as discussed in previous chapters.

4. The final quote in the case characterizes Nortel's failure as "just another casualty of capitalism." Do you agree with this statement? Why or why not? How would you characterize the cause of the failure at Nortel?

Optional Question

Beatty, Gollogly, and Pahapill are chartered accountants in Canada. Research the ethical standards for chartered accountants in Canada and explain whether those standards were violated by the three with respect to their actions in the case.

[3]Theresa Tedesco and Jamie Sturgeon, with a file from Paul Vieira in Ottawa, "Nortel: Cautionary Tale of a Former Canadian Titan," *Financial Post,* June 27, 2009, www.nationalpost.com/life/travel/sun-destinations/story.html?id=1739799#ixzz0mtBaFszD.

Case 7-2

Solutions Network, Inc.

"We can't recognize revenue immediately, Paul, since we agreed to buy similar software from Data Systems Solutions (DSS)," Sarah Young stated. "That's ridiculous," Paul Henley replied. "Get your head out of the sand, Sarah, before it's too late."

Sarah Young is the controller for Solutions Network, Inc. She is meeting with Paul Henley, the CFO of the company on January 7, 2011, to discuss the accounting for a software systems transaction with Data Systems Solutions (DSS) prior to the company's audit for the year ended December 31, 2010. Both Young and Henley are CPAs.

Young has excluded the amount in contention from revenue and net income for 2010. Henley wants the amount to be included in the 2010 results. Henley told Young that the order came from the top to record the revenue on December 28, 2010, the day the transaction with DSS was finalized. Young pointed out that Solutions Network ordered essentially the same software from DSS to be shipped and delivered early in 2011. Therefore, according to Young, Solutions Network should delay revenue recognition on this "swap" transaction until that time. Henley argued against Young's position stating that title had passed from the company to DSS on December 31, 2010, when the software product was shipped with FOB shipping point terms.

Background

Solutions Network, Inc., became a publicly owned company on March 15, 2010, following a successful initial public offering (IPO). Solutions Network built up a loyal clientele in the five years prior to the IPO by establishing close working relationships with technology leaders including IBM, Apple, and Dell Computer. The company designs and engineers systems software to function seamlessly with minimal user interface. There are several companies that provide similar products and consulting services. One is DSS. However, DSS operates in a larger market providing IT services management products that coordinate the entire business infrastructure into a single system.

Solutions Networks grew very rapidly in the five years prior to its IPO. The revenue and earnings streams during those years are as follows:

Year	Revenues ($ in millions)	Net Income ($ in millions)
2005	$148.0	$11.9
2006	175.8	13.2
2007	202.2	15.0
2008	229.8	16.1
2009	267.5	17.3

Young prepared the following estimates for 2010:

Year	Revenues ($ in millions)	Net Income ($ in millions)
2010 (projected at 12/31/09)	$287.5	$17.9

The Transaction

On December 28, 2010, Solutions Network offered to sell its Internet infrastructure software to DSS for its internal use. In return, DSS agreed to ship similar software 30 days later to Solutions Network for that company's internal use. The companies had conducted several transactions together during the previous five years and while DSS initially balked at the transaction because it provided no value added to the company, it did not want to upset one of the fastest growing software companies in the industry. Moreover, Solutions Network might be able to help identify future customers for DSS's IT services management products.

The $30 million of revenue would increase net income $1.9 million over the projected amount for 2010. For Solutions Network, the revenue from the transaction was enough to enable the company to meet targeted goals and the higher level of income would provide extra bonus money at year end for Sarah Young, Paul Henley, and Ed Fralen, the CEO.

Accounting Considerations

Normally, Sarah wouldn't object to Paul's proposed accounting for the transaction with DSS. However, she knows that regardless of the passage of title to DSS on December 31, 2010, the transaction is linked to Solutions Network's agreement to take the DSS product 30 days later. While she doesn't anticipate any problems in that regard, Sarah is uncomfortable with the recording of revenue on December 31 since DSS did not complete its portion of the agreement by that date.

Sarah is also concerned about the fact that another transaction occurred during the previous year that she questioned but, in the end, Sarah went along with Paul's accounting for this transaction. On December 28, 2009, Solutions Network sold a major system for $20 million to Laramie Systems but executed a side agreement with Laramie on December 29, 2009, that gave the customer the right to return the product for any reason after January 1, 2010, and for 27 additional days. Even though Solutions Network recorded the revenue on December 29, 2009, and Sarah felt uneasy about it, she did not object because Laramie did not return the product. Sarah never brought it up again. Now, she is concerned that a pattern may be developing. She knows it's important to sort out the events and carefully consider her ethical obligations prior to meeting with Paul on January 14, 2011.

Questions

1. Describe the rules in accounting for revenue recognition in general and relate them to the two transactions mentioned in the case. Be sure to include proper citations from the pronouncements of the Financial Accounting Standards Board (FASB) and other relevant material. Do you believe the transactions have been accounted for properly?

2. a. Prepare a schedule of the percentage of net income to revenues from 2005 through the projected amounts for 2010. Use the *original amounts reported* including that for 2009 and show the percentage changes in revenue and net income each year.

   b. In addition, prepare a schedule using the same requirements as in part (a) to calculate the relevant amounts assuming: (1) the company restates the results for 2009 and (2) Solutions Network records the $30 million transaction with DSS in 2010 but does not correct the 2009 results.

c. Redo the comparative analysis required by question 2 using 2008 as the base year and show the effects on comparative revenues and net income from 2008 through 2010 assuming (1) Solutions Network was allowed to record revenue for 2009 and 2010 the way it wants and (2) the company follows GAAP rules for recording revenue in both years. Comment on the results of your percentage analyses including what may be the underlying motivation for Paul Henley and Ed Fralen to record revenue their way.

3. Given that Sarah and Paul are CPAs, describe their ethical obligations with respect to the facts of the case based on the standards in the AICPA Code of Professional Conduct.

4. Assume Sarah asks for more time to consider the matter when she meets with Paul on January 14. She points out that the auditors will not arrive until February 1, 2011; therefore, the company should be certain of the appropriateness of its accounting before that time. Paul reacts angrily and tells Sarah she can pack her bags and go if she doesn't support the company in its revenue recognition of the DSS transaction. Assume you are in Sarah's position. What ethical considerations would influence any action you might take in response to Paul's ultimatum? What would you do and why?

Case 7-3

Cubbies Cable

Ernie Binks is a big baseball fan, so it is quite natural for him, at a time like this, to recall a phrase attributed to Yogi Berra: "It was déjà vu all over again."

Binks is the partner in charge of the Cubbies Cable audit for the accounting firm of Santos & Williams LLP. Cubbies is a family-owned regional cable company headquartered in Chicago. Binks is involved in a second dispute in three years with client management. The first dispute concerned the disclosure of a contingent liability on a class action lawsuit against Cubbies for age discrimination in hiring. Cubbies did not disclose the possibility of loss even though all signs pointed to a verdict against the company. Cubbies argued there was nothing to confirm the CPA firm's position in that regard and the company would disclose only if it lost the lawsuit.

The current dispute involves the capitalization of cable construction costs that the client wants to expense. Binks reviewed a memorandum in the workpapers prepared by John Kessinger, the audit manager. The document summarizes the facts on the second dispute. This memo is presented in Exhibit 1.

Exhibit 1
Memo on Capitalization of Cable Equipment[1]

November 30, 2009

1. Cubbies Cable is a locally owned cable television company that services the neighborhoods in Chicago that surround Wrigley Field, the home of the Chicago Cubs. Cubbies Cable was incorporated as a closely held company in 2007. We have audited the company's financial statements since September 30, 2008. The audited statements are used by Chicago First National Bank in granting short-term loans to Cubbies Cable. In particular, the company has a debt covenant agreement with the bank that obligates Cubbies to maintain a specified level of liquidity as indicated by the working capital and "quick" ratios.

2. During the twelve-month period ending March 30, 2010, Cubbies constructed a new cable system in parts of Chicago that enabled it to increase its presence in that market. The revenue from the system through September 30, 2010, exceeded projections by more than 20 percent. The sharp increase over expected revenue was the cause of the conflict with the client.

3. A difference of opinion arose over the proper accounting for cable construction costs. The client wanted to expense all of the costs in the quarter ended September 30, 2010. We suspect that the client wanted to decrease net income for the year. Two different types of costs were involved:

   a. **Cable television plant:** Costs associated with constructing the *cable television plant* and providing cable service include *head-end costs, cable,* and *drop costs.* The client wanted to expense all of these costs. However, *Statement of Financial Accounting Standards No. 51, Financial Reporting by Cable Television Companies,* requires that cable television plant costs incurred during the prematurity periods be capitalized in full. We had protracted discussions with Cubbies Cable regarding this issue, and we were told there was no way the company would agree to capitalize any of the costs. Given that Cubbies was not publicly owned, our only recourse is to take the matter to the board of directors. Another concern is that nine of the eleven members of the board are family members of the CEO or past officers of Cubbies Cable. We expect this situation to work against us in convincing the client that its proposed accounting procedure is not in accordance with generally accepted accounting principles.

   b. **Interest cost:** The client initially expensed all costs during the *prematurity period.* We convinced the client to change its accounting to capitalize costs during the construction period. We used for support our reference to *SFAS 51.* This statement requires application of *SFAS No. 34,* Capitalization of Interest Cost, to interest costs incurred during the construction of an asset. The application of paragraphs 13 and 14 of *SFAS 34* to the client's situation requires that interest costs incurred during the prematurity period be capitalized in full by applying the interest capitalization rate to the average amount of accumulated expenditures for the asset during the period. The purpose of this procedure is to capitalize the amount of interest costs incurred during the prematurity period that theoretically could have been avoided if expenditures for construction of the cable television plant had not been made.

[1]See definitions in Exhibit 2 for all italicized words.

Exhibit 2
Definitions of Terms from SFAS 28, 29, and 51

SFAS No. 51, **Financial Reporting by Cable Television Companies (Paragraph 17)**

Cable television plant. This refers to the cable television system required to render services to subscribers and includes the following equipment:

Head-end. The equipment used to receive television signals, including the studio facilities required to transmit the programs to subscribers.

Cable. This consists of cable and amplifiers placed on utility poles or underground that maintain the quality of the signal to subscribers.

Drops. This consists of the hardware that provides access to the main cable in order to bring the signal from the main cable to the subscriber's television set, and devices to block channels.

Converters and descramblers. These are devices attached to the subscribers' television sets when more than 12 channels are provided, such as pay-per-view programming or two-way communication.

Prematurity period. This refers to the period of time during which the cable television system is partially under construction and partially in service. It begins with the first earned subscriber revenue and ends with the completion of the first major construction period or achievement of a specified, predetermined subscriber level at which no additional investment will be required, other than that for cable television plant.

Cubbies recently completed a major cable installation project at a condominium complex across the street from Wrigley Field in Chicago. The revenue earned from that job enabled the company to complete the third quarter of 2010 with record earnings. Revenues at September 30, 2010, exceeded revenues at September 30, 2009, by 22 percent. Net income for the nine months ended September 30, 2010, was 24 percent above the same amount in the prior year.

Binks is now preparing for a meeting with Rod Hondley, the advisory partner on the Cubbies Cable audit. Hondley has already made it known that he supports the client's position. Binks knows Santos & Williams operates by the simple philosophy that you have to let the client win one somewhere along the line or you may lose that client.

Binks contemplates his options—either to go along with the client's position (the option supported by Hondley) or to maintain his own position. It is at this point that he thinks about another "Yogi-ism"; "When you come to a fork in the road, take it."

Questions

1. Given the limited facts in this case, do you agree with the client on its position in the first dispute with respect to the treatment of the contingency? Why or why not? Use accounting reasoning and your knowledge of contingency rules to help in answering the question.

2. What do you think was the motivation for Cubbies Cable in taking the position to expense all cable costs during the nine months ended September 20, 2010? Would you question the company's integrity in this situation given that Cubbies did agree with the firm on the issue of capitalizing interest during the prematurity period? In other words, should CPAs be prepared to "horse trade" when negotiating with a client about the proper GAAP to apply in a particular situation?

3. Who are the stakeholders in this situation? Identify the major ethical issues that should be of concern to Binks in deciding whether to just go along with the firm in its support of the client, or to take some other action. What would you do at this point if you were in Binks's position? Why?

Case 7-4

Excello Telecommunications

Excello Telecommunications has been profitable for many years but recently has been faced with increased competition for its products by overseas manufacturers. For the first time in the company's history, it appears that earnings estimates will not be met. Top management is concerned about the effect on bonuses, stock options, and the share price of Excello stock. That is when Terry Reed, the CFO, learns of a transaction on December 20, 2010, that might solve the problem. On December 20, 2010, Excello sold $1.2 million of equipment to Data Equipment Systems. Typically, this type of transaction would be recorded as a sale on the date of shipment. However, the customer requested that Excello hold on to the product until January 11, 2011, because Data Equipment lacked the warehouse capacity to hold the product until then.

On December 30, Reed approaches the controller, Marty Fuller, to discuss the dilemma. Fuller explains the rules in accounting for sales where the goods are held for future delivery. Reed understands the rules, but tells Fuller he needs to come up with a creative way around the rules so that the $1.2 million can be recorded as revenue in 2010.

Fuller calls a meeting of the accounting department to discuss what can be done. He emphasizes two important points. First, the $1.2 million must be recorded in 2010. Second, whatever is decided it must be defensible from a GAAP point of view. The team comes up with the following alternatives:

1. Transfer the product to an off-site warehouse owned by Excello by December 31 and hold it until January 11 when it would be shipped to Data Equipment.

2. Transfer the product to Data Equipment by December 31 and agree that the customer could return it for a full refund after it arrives at Data Equipment's warehouse.

3. Offer Data Equipment a 10 percent discount to take the product by December 31.

Questions

1. Evaluate the GAAP conformity of each of the three alternative transactions.

2. Assume Data Equipment agrees to the third alternative but conditions its acceptance on Excello's promise to buy the same exact equipment from Data Equipment within the first two weeks of 2011. How do you think the original sale to Data Equipment and subsequent purchase from that company should be recorded by Excello under these circumstances?

3. Assume Marty Fuller is a CPA. What ethical standards should be of concern to him in deciding on a course of action given the facts in this case?

Case 7-5

Florida Transportation

Florida Transportation buys transportation equipment, sells it to leasing companies, and then leases back the transportation equipment for its own use. Florida Transportation is a privately held company headquartered in Orlando, Florida. The company recently purchased four high-speed trains from a German manufacturer for its use in the Orlando to Miami corridor. The high-speed train form of transportation has become popular for families visiting Disneyworld. The cost of a one-way ticket between the two destinations is $30 for coach class and $40 for business class. A round-trip ticket costs $55 and $75, respectively. Children under 12 ride for $15 each way and $25 round-trip. Children under 5 years old ride for free. By comparison, it would cost at least $100 to drive the 400-plus miles round-trip between the two cities.

Sale and Leaseback Agreements

Under these agreements, Florida Transportation sells the high-speed trains to Leasing Associates in an all-cash transaction and then leases it back. Part of the purpose of the sale-leaseback transaction is to provide needed financing for Florida Transportation. The terms of the sale-leaseback agreement are summarized in Exhibit 1. Exhibit 2 contains selected definitions from the relevant accounting standards to help determine how Florida Transportation should account for the lease.

Mickey Duck is a CPA and the CFO of Florida Transportation. Duck has been asked by Donald Mouse, the CEO, to determine the proper accounting for the sale-and-leaseback transaction. Duck went online and accessed from the Web site of the Financial Accounting Standards Board the provisions of *SFAS No. 28,* Accounting for Sales with Leasebacks. *SFAS 28* amends *SFAS No. 13,* Accounting for Leases, and calls for the seller-lessee to defer the profit on a sale-leaseback transaction if the seller retains substantially all of the use of the property through the leaseback. Duck downloads the two exhibits (see Exhibits 1 and 2) that he developed and he will take them to his meeting with Mouse. His position is to treat the transaction as a sale (with deferred profit) and then the leaseback of the high-speed trains as a capital lease. The deferred profit would be written off over the leaseback period. Duck believes this is the proper accounting for the transaction with Leasing Associates.

Exhibit 1
Sale-Leaseback Agreement

Cost of the high-speed train	$2,000,000
Estimated useful life	40 years
Estimated residual value	N/A
Sale price to Leasing Associates	$3,000,000

Terms of the leaseback:

Leaseback Period
- Ten-year periods, renewable four times, for a total of 40 years.
- Renewal subject to approval of the buyer-lessor.
- Seller-lessee can sell its rights to the high-speed trains at any time, but purchaser company assumes all obligations under this lease agreement, including payments to Leasing Associates.

Leaseback Rentals
- Annual payments each January 1 to Leasing Associates based on a 10% interest rate and 40-year lease is $278,889.

> **Exhibit 2**
> **Definitions of Terms from SFAS 28, 29, and 51**
>
> *SFAS NO. 28,* **Accounting for Sales with Leasebacks (Paragraph 3)**
>
> If the seller-lessee relinquishes the right to substantially all of the remaining use of the property sold (retaining only a minor portion of such use), the sale and leaseback should be accounted for as separate transactions, based on their respective terms.
>
> If the seller-lessee retains the right to substantially all of the remaining use of the property sold, the sale and leaseback should be accounted for as a continuous transaction, based on capital and operating lease criteria.
>
> **SFAS No. 28, Accounting for Sales with Leasebacks (Paragraph 3a)**
>
> ***Substantially all and minor.*** The phrase *substantially all and minor* is used in the context of the concepts underlying the classification criteria of *SFAS 13*. In that context, a test based on the 90% recovery criterion of *SFAS 13* could be used as a guideline. That is, if the present value of a reasonable amount of rental for the leaseback represents 10% or less of the fair value of the asset sold, the seller-lessee could be presumed to have transferred to the purchaser-lessor the right to substantially all of the remaining use of the property sold, and the seller-lessee could be presumed to have retained only a minor portion of such use.

Questions

1. a. From an accounting point of view, do you agree with Duck's position? Why or why not? Be sure to cite references to the *SFASs* in this case and any relevant revenue recognition rules.

   b. Assume Mouse takes the position that the sale part of the transaction should be recorded as immediate revenue and the leaseback should be treated as an operating lease. Do you believe Mouse can justify that position from an accounting perspective by reference to the relevant pronouncements?

2. Is there an earnings management element to Mouse's position? Why or why not? Is it possible to classify Mouse's position as one of the financial shenanigans identified by Schilit? If so, which one? If not, what elements are missing?

3. Assume Mouse tells Duck to quack off if he doesn't like the "Big Cheese's" position? What would you do if you were Mickey Duck? Be sure to consider your ethical obligations given the facts of the case.

Case 7-6

Sweat Hog Construction Company

Ever since the economy of southwestern Texas began to decline in 2008, Sweat Hog Construction Company has been more aggressive in seeking out new business opportunities. One such opportunity is the Computer Assistance Vocational Training School. It has contracted for a new 1-million-square-foot facility in San Marcos, Texas. Computer Assistance trains computer programmers for jobs in business and government. It is the largest computer training school in the southwestern United States.

Gabe Kotter is the passive owner of Sweat Hog Construction. The company began operating in 1997, when Kotter hired Michael Woodman to be the president of the company. Sweat Hog Construction is a family-owned business that has been very successful as a mechanical contractor of heating, ventilation, and air-conditioning systems. However, the economic downturn of 2008 put pressure on the company to diversify its operations. Although it made a profit in 2008, the company's net income for the year was 50 percent lower than in previous years. As a result of these factors, the company decided to expand into plumbing and electrical contract work.

In March 2009, Sweat Hog successfully bid for the Computer Assistance job. The company bid low in order to secure the $3 million contract that is expected to be completed by June 30, 2010. Woodman knows that the company has little margin for error on the contract. The estimated gross margin of 11.5 percent is on the low side of historical margins, which

have been between 10 to 15 percent on heating, ventilation, and air-conditioning contracts. Since it is a fixed-price contract, the company will have to absorb any cost overruns.

The Computer Assistance contract is an important one for Sweat Hog Construction. It represents about 20 percent of the average annual revenues for the past five years. Moreover, First National Bank of Texas has been pressuring the company to speed up its interest payments on a $2 million term loan payable to the bank that is renewable on March 15, 2010. The company has been late in five of its last six monthly payments. The main reason is that some of the company's customers have been paying their bills later than usual because of tight economic conditions. However, the company expects to get back on the right track very soon after the Computer Assistance job begins.

Everything started out well on the contract. For the quarter ended June 30, 2009, Sweat Hog had an estimated cumulative gross profit of $75,000 on the contract under the percentage-of-completion method. This represents a 20 percent gross margin. Costs started to increase during the September quarter and, even though cumulative gross margin decreased to 10 percent, it was still within projected amounts. Unfortunately, the $54,000 estimated gross profit for the nine months ended December 31, 2009, represents only a 3 percent gross margin for the first year of the contract. Exhibit 1 contains cost data, billings, and collections for the year.

EXHIBIT 1
SWEAT HOG CONSTRUCTION
Company Computer Assistance Contract
Year Ended December 31, 2009

	Quarter Ending		
	June 30	September 30	December 31
Costs to date	$ 300,000	$ 900,000	$1,740,000
Estimated costs to complete	2,100,000	1,800,000	1,170,000
Progress billings each quarter	250,000	600,000	950,000
Cash collections each quarter	150,000	350,000	400,000

Vinny Barbarino is a CPA and the controller of Sweat Hog Construction. Barbarino knows that cash collections on the Computer Assistance project have been slowing down—in part, because the company is behind schedule—and tension has developed between the company and Computer Assistance. He decides to contact Juan Epstein, general manager for the project. Epstein informs Barbarino that the tension between the company and Computer Assistance escalated recently when Epstein informed top management of Computer Assistance that the electrical work may not be

completed by the June 30, 2010, deadline. If the facility does not open as scheduled for the summer months, Computer Assistance may be required to return deposits from students. Consequently, it may lose out on the revenue that is projected for the July and August summer term.

Woodman calls for a meeting with Epstein and Barbarino on February 6, 2011, to discuss the Computer Assistance contract. Woodman knows that Sweat Hog's external auditors will begin their audit of the December 31, 2010, year-end financial statements in two weeks. Woodman wants to make sure the problems with the contract have been corrected. He asks Barbarino to bring him up-to-date on the recent cost increases on the contract.

Barbarino informs Woodman that the internal job cost data indicate that $420,000 was incurred for the month of January 2011. About 10 percent of the work was completed during that month. Barbarino emphasizes that this is consistent with recent trend data that indicate the estimated costs to complete the contract have been significantly understated. In fact, for the quarter ended December 31, 2010, the company lost approximately $40,000 on the contract, although there is a cumulative gross margin of about $60,000 for 2010. However, this cumulative margin represents only 2 percent of revenue, and the gross margin percentage is declining. Barbarino analyzed the cost data in preparation for the meeting. He estimates that total costs on the contract may be as high as $4.2 million. He recommends that the $1.17 million estimate to complete the contract at December 31, 2011, should be increased by at least $1 million.

Michael Woodman is stunned by this information. He cannot understand how the company got into this predicament. The company has consistently made profits on its contracts, and there has never before been any tension with clients. The timing is particularly troublesome, since First National Bank is expecting audited financial statements by March 1, 2010. Woodman asks Epstein whether he agrees with Barbarino's assessment about the anticipated higher level of future costs. Epstein hesitates, at first, but he eventually admits to the likelihood of cost overruns. He points out that the workers are not as skilled with electrical work as they are with heating, ventilation, and air-conditioning work. Consequently, some degree of learning is taking place on the job.

Woodman dismisses Epstein at this point and asks Barbarino what would happen if the company reports the estimated costs at December 31, 2009, without any adjustments. Woodman emphasizes that the company would make the necessary adjustments in the first quarter of 2010, and gross profit on the contract with Computer Assistance ultimately will be correct. This approach would enable the company to renew its loan and give it some time to rethink its business strategy.

Barbarino immediately tells Woodman that he is not comfortable with this approach, since the profit on the contract for the nine months ended December 31, 2009, would be significantly overstated. He points out that the auditors are likely to question the low cost estimates. Woodman becomes a bit irritated with Barbarino at this point. He tells Barbarino that the bank is not likely to renew the company's $2 million loan if the statements reflect what Barbarino suggests. He concludes by stating: "The auditors have never been a problem before. I do not expect any problems from them on this issue either, given that the firm has gone along with whatever we've asked of them in the past."

Question

1. Using the ethical decision-making model presented in Chapter 2, what is the appropriate course of action for Barbarino?

Case 7-7

Sunbeam Corporation

One of the earliest frauds during the late 1990s and early 2000s was at Sunbeam. The SEC alleged in its charges against Sunbeam that top management engaged in a scheme to fraudulently misrepresent Sunbeam's operating results in connection with a purported "turnaround" of the company. When Sunbeam's turnaround was exposed as a sham, the stock price plummeted, causing investors billions of dollars in losses. The defendants in the action included Sunbeam's former CEO and chair Albert J. Dunlap; former principal financial officer Russell A. Kersh; former controller Robert J. Gluck; former vice presidents Donald R. Uzzi, and Lee B. Griffith; and Arthur Andersen LLP partner Phillip Harlow.

The SEC complaint described several questionable management decisions and fraudulent actions that led to the manipulation of financial statement amounts in the company's 1996 year-end results, quarterly and year-end 1997 results, and the first quarter of 1998. The fraud was enabled by weak or nonexistent internal controls, inadequate or nonexistent board of directors and audit committee oversight, and the failure of the Andersen auditor to follow GAAS. A brief summary of the case follows.[1]

Chainsaw Al

Al Dunlap, a turnaround specialist who had gained the nickname "Chainsaw Al" for his reputation of cutting companies to the bone, was hired by Sunbeam's board in July 1996 to restructure the financially ailing company. He promised a rapid turnaround, thereby raising expectations in the marketplace. The fraudulent actions helped raise the market price to a high of $52 in 1997. Following the disclosure of the fraud in the first quarter of 1998, the price of Sunbeam shares dropped by 25 percent to $34.63. The price continued to decline as the board of directors investigated the fraud and fired Dunlap and the CFO. An extensive restatement of earnings from the fourth quarter of 1996 through the first quarter of 1998 eliminated one-half of the reported 1997 profits. On February 6, 2001, Sunbeam filed for Chapter 11 bankruptcy protection under U.S. Bankruptcy Court.

Accounting Issues

Cookie Jar Reserves

The illegal conduct began in late 1996 with the creation of cookie jar reserves that were used to inflate income in 1997. Sunbeam then engaged in fraudulent revenue transactions that inflated the company's record-setting earnings of $189 million by at least $60 million in 1997. The transactions were designed to create the impression that Sunbeam was experiencing significant revenue growth, thereby further misleading the investors and financial markets.

Channel Stuffing

Eager to extend the selling season for its gas grills and to boost sales in 1996, CEO Dunlap's "turnaround year," the company tried to convince retailers to buy grills nearly six months before they were needed in exchange for major discounts. Retailers agreed to purchase merchandise that they would not physically receive until six months after billing. In the meantime, the goods were shipped to a third-party warehouse and held there until the customers requested them. These bill and hold transactions led to recording $35 million in revenue too soon. However, the auditors (Andersen) reviewed the documents and reversed $29 million.

In 1997 the company failed to disclose that Sunbeam's 1997 revenue growth was, in part, achieved at the expense of future results. The company had offered discounts and other inducements to customers to sell merchandise immediately that otherwise would have been sold in later periods, a practice referred to as "channel stuffing." The resulting revenue shift threatened to suppress Sunbeam's future results of operations.

Sunbeam either didn't realize or totally ignored the fact that by stuffing the channels with product to make one year look better, the company had to continue to find outlets for their product in advance of when it was desired by customers. In other words, it created a balloon affect in that the same amount or more accelerated amount of revenue was needed year after year. Ultimately, Sunbeam (and its customers) just couldn't keep up and there was no way to fix the numbers.

Sunbeam's Shenanigans

Exhibit 1 presents an analysis of Sunbeam's accounting with respect to Schilit's financial shenanigans.

Red Flags

Schilit points to red flags that existed at Sunbeam but either went undetected or were ignored by Andersen including the following:[2]

1. *Excessive charges recorded shortly after Dunlap arrived.* The theory is that an incoming CEO will create cookie jar reserves by overstating expenses even though it reduces earnings for the first year based on the belief

---

[1]Securities and Exchange Commission, Litigation Release 17001, *Securities and Exchange Commission v. Albert J. Dunlap, Russell A. Kersh, Robert J. Gluck, Donald R. Uzzi, Lee B. Griffith, and Phillip E. Harlow,* 01-8437-CIV-Dimitrouleas (S.D. Fla., May 15, 2001), www.sec.gov/litigation/admin/33-7977.htm.

[2]Howard M. Schilit, *Financial Shenanigans: How to Detect Accounting Gimmicks and Fraud in Financial Reports,* 2nd ed. (New York: McGraw-Hill, 2002).

EXHIBIT 1
Sunbeam Corporation's Aggressive Accounting Techniques

Technique	Example	Shenanigan Number
Recorded bogus revenue	Bill and hold sales	No. 2
Released questionable reserves into income	Cookie jar reserves	No. 5
Inflated special charges	Litigation reserve	No. 7

that increases in future earnings through the release of the reserves or other techniques make it appear that the CEO has turned the company around, as evidenced by turning losses into profits. Some companies might take it to an extreme and pile on losses by creating reserves in a loss year believing that it doesn't matter whether you show a $1.2 million loss for the year or a $1.8 million loss ($0.6 million reserve). This is known as the "big bath theory."

2. *Reserve amounts reduced after initial overstatement.* Fluctuations in the reserve amount should have raised a red flag because they evidenced earnings management as initially record reserves were restored into net income.

3. *Receivables grew much faster than sales.* A simple ratio of the increase in receivables to the increase in revenues should have provided another warning signal. Schilit provides the following for Sunbeam's operational performance in Exhibit 2 that should have created doubts in the minds of the auditors about the accuracy of reported revenue amounts in relation to the collectibility of receivables as indicated by the significantly larger percentage increase in receivables when compared to revenues.

EXHIBIT 2
Sunbeam Corporation's Operational Performance

	Operational Performance		
	9 months 9/97 ($ in millions)	9 months 9/96 ($ in millions)	% Change
Revenue	$830.1	$715.4	16%
Gross profit	231.1	123.1	86%
Operating revenue	132.6	4.0	3215%
Receivables	309.1	194.6	59%
Inventory	290.9	330.2	12%
Cash flow from operations	(60.8)	(18.8)	N/A

4. *Accrual earnings increased much faster than cash from operating activities.* While Sunbeam made $189 million in 1997, its cash flow from operating activities was a negative 60.8 million. This is a $250 million difference that should raise a red flag even under a cursory analytical review about the quality of recorded receivables. Accrual earnings and cash flow from operating activity amounts are not expected to be equal but the differential in these amounts at Sunbeam seems to defy logic. Financial analysts tend to rely on the cash figure because of the inherent unreliability of the estimates and judgments that go into determining accrual earnings.

Questions

1. Refer to the discussion of earnings management in this chapter. Consider the underlying objectives of Dunlap and evaluate whether earnings management had occurred at Sunbeam using the approaches of (1) Healy and Wahlen, (2) Dechow and Skinner, (3) Schipper, and (4) McKee.

2. Chapter 3 addresses issues related to corporate governance and ethical management. Given the facts of the case, identify the deficiencies in ethics and corporate governance failures at Sunbeam.

3. One of the most creative methods of producing profits at Sunbeam dealt with spare parts. Sunbeam owned a lot of spare parts that were used to fix its blenders and grills when they broke. Those parts were stored in the warehouse of a company called EPI Printers, which sent the parts out as needed. To inflate profits, Sunbeam approached EPI at the end of December to sell it parts for $11 million and book an $8 million profit. EPI balked stating the parts were only worth $2 million, but Sunbeam found a way around that. EPI was persuaded to sign an "agreement to agree" to buy the parts for $11 million,

with a clause letting EPI walk away in January. In fact, the parts were never sold but the profit was posted. Along came Phillip E. Harlow, the Arthur Andersen partner in charge of the audit. He concluded the profit was not allowed under GAAP. Sunbeam agreed to cut its profit by $3 million but would go no further. Harlow decided that the remaining profit was not material. Since the audit opinion says the financial statements present fairly, *in all material respects,* the company's financial posi-tion, he could sign off on it. Do you think Harlow made a proper interpretation of materiality in the context of the EPI "transaction"? Why or why not? What might have motivated Harlow to accept only a $3 million adjustment and not the entire $11 million amount?

4. Why is it important for auditors to use analytical com-parisons such as the ratios in the Sunbeam case to evalu-ate strengths and weaknesses in financial position and operating results?

Case 7-8

Shareholders of Altris Software, Inc. v. Altris Software, Inc. and PricewaterhouseCoopers[1]

This case involves a lawsuit filed in the U.S. Court of Appeals on February 4, 2002, by appellant shareholders (those appealing a prior decision) of Altris Software LLP against Altris Software and its auditors, PricewaterhouseCoopers. In the appeal of the District Court original decision, appellants alleged that the auditors failed to properly recognize revenue on software sales because it failed to follow required auditing procedures to test the accuracy of recorded amounts. At issue in the case is whether the auditors had knowledge of the fraud (scienter) and acted recklessly with respect to its audit. The U.S. Court of Appeals revisited the issues decided in the U.S. District Court for the Southern District of California and it affirmed the initial ruling against the plaintiff-appellants. The case addresses important issues discussed in Chapter 5 (GAAS), Chapter 6 (legal liability), and in this chapter (earnings management).[2]

Issues Argued

The main legal issue in this case is whether the allegations of a seriously botched audit are sufficient to plead scienter under the heightened pleading requirements of the Private Securities Litigation Reform Act (PSLRA) and *In re Silicon Graphics, Inc.*[3] The plaintiff-shareholders of Altris alleged that the auditors failed to see the obvious—that according to GAAP, millions of dollars in revenue from software sales should not have been recognized in the financial statements. The Court of Appeals held that the complaint set out a compelling case of negligence—perhaps even gross negligence—but did not give rise to a strong inference that the auditor acted with an intent to defraud, conscious misconduct, or deliberate recklessness, as is required in a securities fraud case.

Appellants were shareholders of Altris Software, Inc., a publicly traded company that develops document management software. Appellants brought this securities fraud lawsuit against Altris's auditors, PricewaterhouseCoopers LLP, in its audit of the 1996 financial statements. In February 1997, PwC certified that Altris's 1996 financial statements complied with GAAP and that PwC had conducted its audit

in accordance with GAAS. Altris filed its Form 10-K with the SEC for 1996 and included the PwC audit opinion. The financial statements reflected net income of approximately $2.4 million for the year.

About a year later, in the course of preparing for the 1997 audit, PwC discovered that the 1996 Altris financial statements reflected revenue that should not have been recognized, and it withdrew the audit opinion. Altris then publicly announced that it had overstated its revenues, earnings and receivables for all of 1996 and the first three quarters of 1997, and trading in Altris stock was halted. Shortly thereafter, Altris formally restated its 1996 revenue, reversing $4.9 million in previously recognized revenue. This caused the financial statements to change from showing $2.4 million in net income to showing a $2.5 million loss.

Shareholder Claims

Altris's shareholders filed six related securities fraud class actions in district court against Altris and its officers and directors. After the district court consolidated the actions, the shareholders added PwC as a defendant. The district court dismissed the first consolidated complaint ruling that Appellants had failed to plead scienter properly. Appellants filed a second amended complaint. The district court dismissed the second amended complaint for the same reason but this time without leave to further amend. The district court reasoned that the amended complaint failed to sufficiently allege scienter—that PwC had actual knowledge that its audit opinion was inaccurate at the time it was issued or that the firm was deliberately reckless with respect to its accuracy. The district court ruled that further amendment of the complaint would be futile.

The court noted that to state a claim under Section 10(b), 15 U.S.C. 78j(b), and Rule 10b-5, 17 C.F.R. § 240.10b5, the appellants must allege (1) a misstatement or omission, (2) of material fact, (3) made with scienter, (4) on which the appellants relied, (5) that proximately caused their injury. The PSLRA requires appellants to "state with particularity facts giving rise to a strong inference that [Pricewaterhouse] acted with [scienter]." The appellants must "plead, in great detail, facts that constitute strong circumstantial evidence of deliberately reckless or conscious misconduct."[4]

Recklessness is defined as a highly unreasonable omission, involving not merely simple, or even inexcusable negligence, but an extreme departure from the standards of ordinary care, and which presents a danger of misleading buyers or sellers that is either known to the defendant

---

[1]*Dsam Global Value Fund; Putnam Tank Car Employee Profit Sharing Plan; Establishment Comfort; Rolando Chavez; Hank Elkins, Plaintiffs-Appellants, v. Altris Software, Inc., Defendant, and PricewaterhouseCoopers LLP, Defendant-Appellee,* 288 F.3d 385 (9th Cir. 2002), No. 00-56848.

[2]The facts of the case argued in the U.S. Court of Appeals, Ninth Circuit, reflected an appeal of the lower court ruling in *Dsam Global Value Fund v. Altris Software, Inc. LLP,* 288 F.3d 385, February 4, 2002.

[3]*In re Silicon Graphics, Inc., Sec. Litig.,* 183 F.3d 970 (9th Cir. 1999).

[4]15 U.S.C. § 78u-4(b)(2) (2002).

or is so obvious that the actor must have been aware of it.[5] To allege a "strong inference of deliberate recklessness," the appellants "must state facts that come closer to demonstrating intent, as opposed to mere motive and opportunity."

The essence of the appellants' claim was that Altris recognized revenue on software sales before critical requirements had been met, making its 1996 sales and earnings appear larger than they really were, and that PwC had failed to take the necessary steps to test those sales to provide a reasonable basis for the audit opinion it issued. For example, to demonstrate that PwC deliberately ignored the falsity of Altris's financial statement, the appellants pointed to transactions between Altris and two of its "value added resellers." A value added reseller (VAR) is an intermediary that buys product for subsequent resale. It does not pay its supplier until it has been paid by its customer. On the last day of 1996, Altris recorded revenue of $250,000 from Plexxus and $338,220 from Staffware, two of its VARs, as "start-up fees." These VAR transactions eventually required reversal and restatement. The appellants alleged that PwC audited these transactions, yet failed to see three red flags that should have alerted PwC that the recognition of revenue from these VAR transactions was highly suspicious. The first red flag was that the start-up fees were grossly exorbitant; Altris never previously had start-up fees of more than $5,000. The second was that Altris recorded both transactions on the last day of the year. The third was that the contract documents described the transaction as "special."

Accounting Issues

The appellants also identified 12 large transactions, audited by PwC, where Altris improperly recognized revenue from software sales. In this connection, the appellants alleged that in auditing the Altris financial statement, PwC deliberately ignored Altris's repeated failure to follow a GAAP—namely, Software Revenue Recognition *Statement of Position 91-1* (*SOP 91-1*). Under *SOP 91-1,* a company should not recognize revenue from software sales when there is significant uncertainty as to whether the company will ever get paid. Under this rule, software revenue should be recognized only when the following conditions exist:

1. There must be "persuasive evidence" of an agreement for the sale of the merchandise.
2. There must be an irrevocable, noncontingent obligation to pay a fixed fee, normally payable within 12 months.
3. Delivery of the software must have occurred.
4. No significant vendor obligations remain.
5. Collection must be probable.
6. Revenue should not be recognized if there is a right of return, unless it is routine and relatively minor.

[5]*Hollinger v. Titan Capital Corp.,* 914 F.2d 1564, 1569 (9th Cir. 1990).

7. If acceptance of the software has not yet occurred, lack of acceptance may preclude revenue recognition if there is significant uncertainty about the customer's acceptance of the software.

As to these 12 large transactions that passed the PwC audit, the appellants pointed to instances in which Altris recognized revenue from software sales where (1) there was no signed, fixed agreement; (2) the amount of the software license fee was not fixed, or the contract did not require payment within 12 months; (3) customers and resellers had unexpired cancellation privileges; and (4) Altris still had significant obligations to perform. The appellants alleged that in performing its audit, PwC had in its hands the very documentation that clearly showed Altris's violation of GAAP, and in particular, *SOP 91-1,* yet did not see the obvious. The appellants alleged that PwC conducted the equivalent of no audit at all.

PwC conceded that the Altris financial statement it audited did not comply with GAAP. However, the firm argued that the facts as pleaded at best show negligence, not the strong inference of scienter required to plead a case of fraud under the securities laws. The court agreed with the district judge that the appellants' allegations did not establish a strong circumstantial case of deliberate recklessness or conscious misconduct as required in previous rulings.

The court pointed out that the factual allegations in the *Altris* case were similar to the allegations the court rejected in *Software Toolworks.*[6] In that case, the plaintiffs had alleged that sales agreements were "poorly documented, informal and conditional"; the transactions were risky; management was under pressure for favorable earnings; and the accountants obtained only oral confirmations of some agreements. That court found that such allegations that an accountant failed to investigate established only a negligent audit rather than one with knowledge of the fraud (scienter).

In the *Software Toolworks* opinion, the court stated that in fraud cases it is often a matter of inference from circumstantial evidence. However, the mere publication of inaccurate accounting figures, or a failure to follow GAAP, without more does not establish scienter. Rather, scienter requires more than a misapplication of accounting principles. The plaintiff must prove that the accounting practices were so deficient that the audit amounted to no audit at all, or an egregious refusal to see the obvious, or to investigate the doubtful, or that the accounting judgments that were made were such that no reasonable accountant would have made the same decisions if confronted with the same facts. Thus, mere allegations that an accountant negligently failed to closely review files or follow GAAP cannot raise a strong inference of scienter.

The appellants argued that PwC must have consciously disregarded the improper revenue recognition because it had access to the documents that revealed Altris's improper revenue recognition at the very time it conducted the original audit. The court found, however, that the fact does not strongly

[6]*Software Toolworks,* 50 F.3d at 627.

compel an inference of intentional or deliberately reckless conduct as opposed to ordinary carelessness. The court in the case *In re Worlds of Wonder* rejected a similar claim.[7]

In that case, the plaintiffs' expert concluded that the accountant had improperly recognized revenue in violation of GAAP and the failure was "so obvious that . . . [the accounting firm] must have been aware of it." The court rejected this testimony as evidence of scienter because it was a conclusory opinion "not based on specific facts that shed light on the mental state of [the accountant's] auditors." Like the plaintiffs in *Worlds of Wonder,* the appellants had failed to allege any facts to establish that PwC knew or must have been aware of the improper revenue recognition, intentionally or knowingly falsified the financial statements, or that the audit was "such 'an extreme departure' from reasonable accounting practice that PwC 'knew or had to have known' that its conclusions would mislead investors." The court found that the appellants' allegations of negligence were insufficient to establish a strong inference of deliberate recklessness under *Silicon Graphics.*

The court ruled that the facts stated in the second amended complaint failed to give rise to a strong inference that PwC had actual knowledge that the Altris financial statement it audited was inaccurate, or that PwC was deliberately reckless. "Negligence, even gross negligence, does

[7]*Worlds of Wonder Sec. Litig.,* 35 F.3d 1407, 1426-27 (9th Cir.1994).

not rise to the level of the nefarious mental state necessary to constitute securities fraud under the PSLRA and *Silicon Graphics.*"

Questions

1. Given the facts of the case, do you think that the PwC auditors exercised the degree of professional skepticism required by GAAS? Cite specific examples of when the firm did and/or did not meet its burden in this regard.

2. In Chapter 6 there was a discussion of the case *Jacobs v. Coopers & Lybrand, LLP,* 97 Civ. 3374 (S.D.N.Y., March 1, 1999). The issues addressed by the court in that case are quite similar to those in Altris. However, the court in the *Jacobs* case sided with the plaintiffs that Coopers was guilty of fraud in failing to conduct the audit in accordance with GAAS. Review the *Jacobs* case in Chapter 6. Do you think the court in that matter had sufficient evidence to find fraud? Does the standard used by the court in that case seem similar to or different from the standard in Altris? Provide support in making your comparisons and answering the question.

Optional Question

There are several references to legal rulings in the *Altris* case. Review these opinions and explain how they relate to the findings of the court in *Altris.*

Case 7-9

CellCyte Genetics Corporation

CellCyte Genetics Corporation (CellCyte) was sued by the SEC on September 8, 2009, for making false and misleading statements in several SEC filings and other materials distributed to potential investors about the company's purportedly late-stage stem-cell research and imminent clinical trials. The SEC's action further alleges that CellCyte engaged in an illegal stock distribution by partnering with a Canadian stock promoter, who sent millions of spam e-mails, faxes, and newsletters containing false information about CellCyte. During the August–December 2007 promotional campaign, CellCyte's stock price rose from $4.00 to $7.50, briefly giving the fledgling company a market capitalization of nearly half a billion dollars. The price later crashed to under $0.10 per share. The stock now trades at less than $0.08 per share, leaving investors who were deceived by the fraudulent materials with massive losses.[1]

Background

In 2004, Gary A. Reys, cofounder of CellCyte and its CEO and chair of the board of directors through 2008, learned from a former colleague who had worked for Reys at two biotechnology companies that a scientist had made a stem-cell-related discovery that might be available for licensing. In 2001 and 2002, the scientist had observed in fewer than 10 mice that a specially formulated compound, when injected into the bloodstream before a dose of stem cells, appeared to cause the stem cells to migrate to specific organs and remain there in significant concentrations. Normally, stem cells that are injected into the bloodstream do not remain in any particular organ and are quickly flushed out of the body.

The special compound was supplied by a European biotechnology company, which also funded the scientist's research. In 2002, before the scientist could perform additional research using the compound, the biotechnology company stopped funding the research and supplying the special compound. The scientist performed no further research using the compound after 2002.

Reys also served as CellCyte's principal accounting officer until 2008. Reys and his former colleague, Ronald W. Berninger, who became CellCyte's chief scientific officer, formed CellCyte as a private company in early 2005 for the purpose of acquiring the rights to the scientist's discovery. Reys and Berninger met with the scientist for several days in January 2005 to review the details of her research findings. At the meetings and in discussions thereafter, the scientist told Reys and Berninger that she had conducted only preliminary research. The scientist also told Reys and Berninger that she had never conducted research on the compound using mice with injured organs, and therefore had no data showing that the stem cells could repair or improve function in injured organs. The scientist also disclosed that she had not yet done any toxicology studies, and that the mixture of the compound and stem cells had killed some mice during her research. Further, the scientist told Reys that CellCyte would need to obtain or develop a supply of the special compound before any further research could begin.

Summary of Facts and Charges

During 2007, CellCyte, a fledgling biotechnology company based in Bothell, Washington, and its CEO and chair Gary Reys repeatedly misled the investing public about CellCyte's key product, a purported stem-cell therapy to treat and repair damaged organs. CellCyte claimed it had received approval from the U.S. Food and Drug Administration (FDA) and was on the verge of beginning human clinical trials with a special stem-cell compound to repair the heart. Contrary to these claims, CellCyte did not even know how to produce the stem-cell compound and had not satisfied any of the FDA requirements to begin human clinical trials.

In late 2005, CellCyte paid $90,000 to license very-early-stage stem-cell technology. No research had been done using the technology since 2002. CellCyte failed in its efforts to raise money to begin conducting research, so it completed a reverse merger with a shell company controlled by a Canadian stock promoter to become a public company in March 2007. Reys agreed that the stock promoter would receive 15 million supposedly "freely tradable" CellCyte shares, about 90 percent of CellCyte's public issuance, in exchange for about $6 million in funding.

CellCyte then made false and misleading statements in several SEC filings and other materials distributed to potential investors about the Company's purportedly late-stage stem-cell research and imminent clinical trials. During fall 2007, the stock promoter conducted a promotional campaign on behalf of CellCyte that included millions of spam e-mails, blast faxes, and newsletters containing false and misleading statements, some of which originated from CellCyte's own investor materials. Reys communicated with the stock promoter about the campaign and specifically approved some of the false and misleading statements in the promotional materials. Reys then denied his involvement in the promotional campaign to others at CellCyte and in an interview with a *Seattle Times* reporter in December 2007.

[1] *Securities and Exchange Commission v. CellCyte Genetics Corp. & Ronald W. Berninger,* www.sec.gov/litigation/complaints/2009/comp21200-berninger.pdf.

CellCyte Makes False and Misleading Statements about Its Research

After CellCyte became a public company in March 2007, it made false and misleading statements about its research and development efforts and business prospects in SEC filings and in other materials that were distributed to potential investors. CellCyte made false and misleading statements in four different SEC filings, including a Form 8-K report filed April 5, 2007; a Form 10-Q quarterly report filed May 18, 2007; a Form SB-2 registration statement filed June 29, 2007; and a Form 10-Q quarterly report filed August 14, 2007. Reys signed all of these filings as CellCyte's CEO and principal accounting officer. In connection with the May and August 2007 Form 10-Q reports, Reys signed certifications stating that he had reviewed the reports and that they did not contain any untrue statements of a material fact or omit to state any material facts necessary to make the statements, in light of the circumstances under which the statements were made, not misleading.

CellCyte Makes False Statements about FDA Approval

In the SEC filings and in other investor materials that Reys approved, CellCyte stated that its stem-cell discoveries "are the first stem cell enabling drugs to enter Investigational New Drug (IND) supported by the FDA clinical trials." In reality, Reys knew that CellCyte never filed an IND application for the stem-cell technology and therefore never received FDA approval to begin clinical trials. Reys also knew that CellCyte did not obtain the necessary ingredients to attempt to formulate the special compound until May 2007, and did not begin conducting experiments using the compound in mice until October 2007. Reys knew or was reckless in not knowing that the statement was materially false and misleading.

CellCyte Misled Investors about the Advanced Stage of Its Research and Development

In the SEC filings and other materials distributed to potential investors, CellCyte portrayed its stem-cell research as having been "proven in extensive late-stage animal studies." In reality, Reys knew that the preliminary experiments in 2001 and 2002 had achieved positive results in a small number of mice and that no additional research had been conducted using the special compound since 2002. CellCyte also claimed that "the company is advancing [the heart compound] into human trials for repair of the heart with an IND submission scheduled for the second half of 2007." In reality, Reys knew that CellCyte never attempted any research nor achieved any results to prove that its stem-cell technology could repair the heart in mice, a prerequisite to beginning any clinical trial to repair the heart in humans.

CellCyte Falsely Stated That Its Drugs Had Been Shown to Improve Bone Marrow Engraftment

In the SEC filings and other materials distributed to potential investors, CellCyte claimed that during its research using the special compound, "the stem cells migrated directly to the bone marrow, therefore increasing the effective dose of stem cells available for engraftment." In reality, Reys knew that the preliminary research on the compound had not shown stem cells migrating to the bone marrow. CellCyte never conducted any research involving bone marrow, and it had no data showing that the compound caused stem cells to localize in bone marrow or improved bone marrow engraftment. Reys knew or was reckless in not knowing that the statement was materially false and misleading.

CellCyte Makes Material Omissions about Its Research and Operations

CellCyte also omitted critical information from its public statements about its research. Most significantly, CellCyte failed to disclose that it was unable to obtain the specially formulated compound from the European biotechnology company that had originally funded the stem-cell research, and that CellCyte had not determined how to properly formulate the special compound from material that CellCyte obtained from other sources. Reys knew that CellCyte needed to have a sufficient supply of the special compound before it could begin conducting the extensive additional research that was required to determine whether an IND application could be filed to begin human clinical trials.

CellCyte touted a lack of safety and toxicity concerns about the special compound, but failed to state that no safety or toxicology studies had been done or that some mice had died during the scientist's preliminary research, suggesting that some doses of the compound and stem cells were in fact toxic and even fatal. CellCyte also failed to disclose that its experiments in mice between October 2007 and March 2008 were unsuccessful. The information omitted by CellCyte, and the false and misleading statements that were made, were material to investors because they concerned the company's ultimate likelihood of success in developing stem-cell technology to repair damaged organs.

The Charges

The SEC sued CellCyte for its false and misleading statements in violation of the Securities Act of 1933, Sections 10(b) and 13(a) of the Securities Exchange Act of 1934, and Exchange Act Rules 10b-5, 12b-20, 13a-11, and 13a-13. Also named in the suit was Ronald Berninger. The SEC's action alleged that Berninger violated Section 10(b) of the Exchange Act and Rule 10b-5 thereunder, and that Berninger aided and abetted CellCyte's violations of Section 13(a) of the

Exchange Act and Rules 12b-20, 13a-11, and 13a-13. Cell-Cyte and Berninger agreed to a settlement, without admitting or denying the SEC's allegations, in which they each consented to a permanent injunction; Berninger also agreed to pay a $50,000 civil penalty and be barred from serving as an officer or director of a public company for five years.

In a separate litigated action, the SEC charged Reys with violating Section 10(b) of the Exchange Act and Rule 10b-5 and with aiding and abetting CellCyte's violations of the Exchange Act. The SEC sought injunctive relief, a monetary penalty, and an order barring Reys from serving as an officer or director of a public company.

A summary of the violations appears as follows:

- Reys, directly or indirectly, in connection with the purchase or sale of securities, by the use of means or instrumentalities of interstate commerce or of the mails, with scienter:
  a. employed devices, schemes, or artifices to defraud.
  b. made untrue statements of material facts or omitted to state material facts necessary in order to make the statements made, in the light of the circumstances under which they were made, not misleading.
  c. engaged in acts, practices, or courses of business which operated or would operate as a fraud or deceit upon other persons, including purchasers and sellers of securities.
- CellCyte violated securities laws that obligate issuers of securities registered pursuant to Section 12 of the Exchange Act to file with the commission accurate quarterly and current reports.
- Reys knowingly provided substantial assistance to Cell-Cyte's filing of materially false and misleading reports

with the commission. Reys also aided and abetted Cell-Cyte's violations of the securities laws.

The SEC asked the court to issue an order permanently restraining and enjoining Reys and those persons in active concert or participation with them, from violating, directly or indirectly aforementioned sections of the securities laws. The SEC also asked the court to issue an order directing Reys to pay a civil monetary penalty and issue an order barring Reys from serving as an officer or director of any public company.

Questions

1. From a corporate governance perspective, discuss the shortcomings in the CellCyte case that may have contributed to the disclosure fraud.

2. An important element of the charges lodged by the SEC against CellCyte and Reys is the distribution of false and misleading information to investors about the development of special compounds and potential success of its stem-cell research. Do you think CellCyte committed fraud with respect to the statements described in the case? Be sure to include in your discussion how the fraud standard was met or, if it was not fraud, how you would characterize the statements in question.

3. *Statement on Auditing Standards (SAS) No. 107,* Audit Risk and Materiality in Conducting an Audit, addresses the issue of the materiality of a misstatement. Reviewing the facts of the case, do you believe the misstatements by CellCyte meet the standard of materiality? Be sure to provide support for your answer using the facts of the case and standards of *SAS 107.*

Case 7-10

Vivendi Universal

"Some of my management decisions turned wrong, but fraud? Never, never, never." This statement was made by the former CEO of Vivendi Universal, Jean-Marie Messier, as he took the stand in November 20, 2009, for a civil class action lawsuit brought against him, Vivendi Universal, and the former CFO, Guillaume Hannezo, accusing the company of hiding Vivendi's true financial condition before a $46 billion three-way merger with Seagram Company and Canal Plus. The case was brought against Vivendi, Messier, and Hannezo after it was discovered that the firm was in a liquidity crisis and would have problems repaying its outstanding debt and operating expenses (contrary to the press releases by Messier, Hannezo, and other senior executives that the firm had "excellent" and "strong" liquidity); that it participated in earnings management to achieve earnings goals; and that it had failed to disclose debt obligations regarding two of the company's subsidiaries.[1]

The stock price of the firm dropped 89 percent from €84.70 on October 31, 2000, to €9.30 on August 16, 2002, over the period of fraudulent reporting and press releases to the media.[2]

Vivendi is a French international media giant rivaling Time Warner Inc. that spent $77 billion on acquisitions including the world's largest music company, Universal Music Group. Messier took the firm to new heights that came with a large amount of debt through mergers and acquisitions.

The Vivendi Universal case raises a few ethical issues. For example, was it wrong for Vivendi to make improper adjustments to its earnings before interest, taxes, depreciation, and amortization (EBITDA) to meet ambitious earnings targets in 2001? Was Messier correct in stating that he made some decisions that just turned out poorly and that he was not participating in an extensive fraud scandal?

In December 2000, Vivendi acquired Canal Plus and Seagram, which included Universal Studios and its related companies, and became known as Vivendi Universal. At the time, it was one of Europe's largest companies in terms of assets and revenues, with holdings in the United States that included Universal Studios Group, Universal Music Group (UMG), and USA Networks Inc. These acquisitions cost Vivendi cash, stock, and assumed debt of over $60 billion and increased the debt associated with Vivendi's Media & Communications division from approximately €3 billion ($4.32 billion) at the beginning of 2000 to over €21 billion ($30.25 billion) in 2002.

[1] *Securities and Exchange Commission v. Vivendi Universal, S.A., Jean-Marie Messier, and Guillaume Hannezo,* www.sec.gov/litigation/complaints/comp18523.htm.

[2] As of December 31, 2009, (1 Euro) €1 = $1.4406, or $1 = €0.694155.

In July of 2002, Messier and Hannezo resigned from their positions as CEO and CFO, respectively, and new management disclosed that the company was experiencing a liquidity crisis that was a very different picture than the previous management had painted about the financial condition of Vivendi Universal. This was due to senior executives using four different methods to conceal Vivendi Universal's financial problems: issuing false press releases stating that the liquidity of the company was "strong" and "excellent" after the release of the 2001 financial statements to the public, using aggressive accounting principles and adjustments to increase EBITDA and meet ambitious earnings targets, failing to disclose the existence of various commitments and contingencies, and failing to disclose part of its investment in a transaction to acquire shares of Telco, a Polish telecommunications holding company.

On March 5, 2002, Vivendi issued earnings releases for 2001, which were approved by Messier, Hannezo, and other senior executives, that their Media & Communications business had produced €5.03 billion ($7.25 billion) in EBITDA and just over €2 billion ($2.88 billion) in Operating Free Cash Flow. These earnings were materially misleading and falsely represented Vivendi's financial situation because, due to legal restrictions, Vivendi was unable unilaterally to access the earnings and cash flow of two of its most profitable subsidiaries, Cegetel and Maroc Telecom, which accounted for 30 percent of Vivendi's EBITDA and almost half of its cash flow. This attributed to Vivendi's cash flow actually being "zero or negative," making it difficult for Vivendi to meet its debt and cash obligations. Furthermore, Vivendi declared a €1 ($1.44) per share dividend because of its excellent operations for the pass year, but Vivendi borrowed against credit facilities to pay the dividend, which cost more than €1.3 billion ($1.87 billion) after French corporate taxes on dividends. Throughout the following months until Messier and Hannezo's resignations, senior executives continued to lie to the public about the strength of Vivendi as a company.

In December 2000, Vivendi and Messier predicted a 35 percent EBITDA growth for 2001 and 2002, and, in order to reach that target, Vivendi used earnings management and aggressive accounting practices to overstate its EBITDA. In June 2001, Vivendi made improper adjustments to increase EBITDA by almost €59 million ($85 million), or 5 percent of the total EBITDA of €1.12 billion ($1.61 billion) that Vivendi reported. Senior executives did this mainly by restructuring Cegetel's allowance for bad debts. Cegetel, a Vivendi subsidiary whose financial statements were consolidated with Vivendi's, took a lower provision for bad debts in the period and caused the bad debts expense to be €45 million ($64.83 million) less than it would have been under historical methodology, which in turn increased earnings by the same amount. Furthermore, after the third quarter of 2001, Vivendi adjusted earnings of UMG by at least €10.125 million ($14.77 million) or approximately 4 percent of UMG's total EBITDA of €250 million ($360.15 million) for that quarter. At that level, UMG would have been able to show EBITDA growth of approximately 6 percent versus the same period in 2000, and to outperform its rivals in the music business. They did this by prematurely recognizing revenue of €3 million ($4.32 million) and temporarily reducing the corporate overhead charges by €7 million ($10.08 million).

Vivendi failed to disclose in their financial statements commitments regarding Cegetel and Maroc Telecom that would have shown Vivendi's potential inability to meet its cash needs and obligations. They were also worried that if they disclosed this information, companies that publish independent credit opinions would have declined to maintain their credit rating of Vivendi. In August of 2001, Vivendi entered into an undisclosed current account borrowing with Cegetel, one of its subsidiaries, for €520 million ($749.11 million) and continued to grow to over €1 billion ($1.44 billion) at certain periods of time. Vivendi maintained cash pooling agreements with most of its subsidiaries, but the current account with Cegetel operated much like a loan, with a due date of the balance at December 31, 2001 (which was later pushed back to July 31, 2002), and there was a clause in the agreement that provided Cegetel with the ability to demand immediate reimbursement at any time during the loan period. If this information would have been disclosed, it would have shown that Vivendi would have trouble repaying its obligations.

Regarding Maroc Telecom, in December 2000 Vivendi purchased 35 percent of the Moroccan government–owned telecommunications operator of fixed line and mobile telephony and Internet services for €2.35 billion ($3.39 billion). In February 2001, Vivendi and the Moroccan government entered into a side agreement that required Vivendi to purchase an additional 16 percent of Maroc Telecom's shares in February 2002 for approximately €1.1 billion ($1.58 billion). Vivendi did this in order to gain control of Maroc Telecom and consolidate its financial statements with their own

because Maroc carried little debt and generated substantial EBITDA. By not disclosing this information on the financial statements, Vivendi's financial information for 2001 was materially false and misleading.

The major stakeholders in the Vivendi case include (1) the investors, creditors, and shareholders of the company and its subsidiaries—by not providing reliable financial information, Vivendi mislead these groups into lending credit, cash, and investing in a company that was not as strong as it seemed; (2) the subsidiaries of Vivendi and their customers—by struggling with debt and liquidity, Vivendi borrowed cash from the numerous subsidiaries all over the globe, jeopardizing their operations; (3) the governments of these countries—because some of Vivendi's companies were government owned (such as the Moroccan company Maroc Telecom), and these governments have to regulate the fraud and crimes that Vivendi committed; and (4) Vivendi, Messier, Hannezo, and other senior management and employees—Messier was putting his future, the employees of Vivendi, and the company itself in jeopardy by making loose and risky decisions involving the sanctity of the firm.

Questions

1. The case opens with a quote by former Vivendi CEO Jean-Marie Messier: "Some of my management decisions turned wrong, but fraud? Never, never, never." Can you explain from an ethical perspective Vivendi management's obliviousness to what was going on around them?

2. Why do financial analysts look at measures such as EBITDA and operating free cash flow to evaluate financial results? How do these measures differ from accrual earnings?

3. An important issue in the case is the extent of disclosures about the transactions undertaken by Vivendi that affected its liquidity. The company was very concerned about its potential inability to meet its cash needs and obligations. Use stakeholder analysis to identify the ethical questions raised by the facts of the case.

8

International Financial Reporting: Ethics and Corporate Governance Considerations

Ethics Reflection

The goal of trying to establish one set of accounting standards around the world began in 1973 when nine of the largest developed countries came together to form the International Accounting Standards Committee (IASC). The purpose was to facilitate international trade and investment by having one set of standards for the financial reports of multinational entities that would be better understood than if companies in each country had prepared financial statements using their own generally accepted accounting principles. The IASC established international accounting standards until April 1, 2001, when it was replaced by the International Accounting Standards Board (IASB), a body that now issues International Financial Reporting Standards, or IFRS. It is expected that by the end of 2011, 150 countries will have adopted IFRS as their own accounting standards. The United States has been lagging behind, although the SEC issued a road map that calls for the adoption of IFRS starting about 2015 with a phase-in between 2015 and around 2016.

One difference in standard setting is that in the United States a rules-based approach is followed with "bright line" rules dictating how to account for a transaction. One problem with rules-based standards is that "creative" accountants may be able to find ways around the rules. IFRS is a more principles-based approach to standard setting that

relies on broad concepts such as economic substance over legal form to guide decision making. Of course, principles cannot cover every situation so professional (ethical) judgment is still a critical component of decision making.

Corporate governance procedures differ as well. Many countries outside the United States such as those in the European Union (EU) have a two-tier board structure with the Management Board carrying out many of the responsibilities of top management, while the Supervisory Board oversees company operations in a way that is similar to the board of directors in the United States. Outside the United States, a "comply or explain" provision establishes a mechanism to report when governance provisions are not followed. In the United States, the NYSE listing requirements call for similar, although less structured, disclosures. Finally, the "present fairly" language in U.S. audit reports is replaced by "true and fair" view. The latter provides a more definitive statement about the conformity of the financial statements with IFRS and it denotes a sense of ethics in decision making.

To give a real-life dimension to the discussion in this chapter, we review corporate governance provisions in Germany, China, and India. Each country has unique aspects to its governance mechanisms and the countries also represent three of the largest or fastest growing economies.

We also use the British company, HSBC to illustrate IFRS-compliant financial statements and disclosures.

Public accounting professionals in the United States have made it clear that they expect future graduates to have a basic knowledge of IFRS. Even if IFRS were not adopted in the United States, many students who work for international CPA firms would have to be familiar with these standards because they are used by U.S. subsidiaries reporting in IFRS-compliant countries. Also, the AICPA has announced that it intends to cover international accounting issues on the CPA Exam starting in 2011.

In this chapter we focus on the basics and discuss standards that differ under U.S. GAAP and IFRS. As you read through the chapter, think about how these differences affect financial reports and the ethical challenges of operating in a global economy.

Sir David Tweedie, the chairman of the International Accounting Standards Board, speaking to the American Institute of Certified Public Accountants spring Council meeting on May 25, 2010, said the move to global accounting standards is a key element of the global financial reform agenda and long-term benefits of a single set of high-quality accounting standards far outweigh the short-term difficulties of transition. "The world is moving to a single set of high-quality global accounting standards, and this is too important an area for the U.S. not to be involved. After almost a decade of work to improve IFRS and U.S. GAAP and to seek their convergence, it's time to finish the job."

This quote from Sir David Tweedie expresses some of the frustration in the international accounting community over the slow-paced process of adopting IFRS in the U.S. The European Community first adopted IFRS in 2005. Now, more than five years later, the U.S. SEC still seems to be somewhat reluctant to give its blessing to adoption. Nevertheless, the adoption of one set of internationally-accepted accounting standards brings with it questions about ethical management and corporate governance practices in different countries that fall under the IFRS regime. We explore some of the most important differences in this chapter.

Introduction

For almost 40 years a movement has been under way to establish one set of international accounting standards for all countries around the world in order to facilitate international trade and investment. Since it is no longer unusual to have foreign companies list their stock on the New York Stock Exchange, one common set of accounting standards should go a long way toward increasing the understandability of international financial reports.

Until recently, listing rules required that non-U.S. companies must reconcile their financial statements prepared under home country standards to U.S. GAAP. This is a tedious exercise and, unless you believe that U.S. GAAP better reflects financial position and results of operations than IFRS, the cost of reconciliation probably exceeds any benefits derived.

A natural outgrowth of the movement toward IFRS has been the development of one set of auditing standards. Auditors are charged with determining whether IFRS has been properly implemented; a common set of auditing standards adds assurance of meeting that goal. The International Auditing and Assurance Standards Board (IAASB) of the International Federation of Accountants (IFAC) establishes international auditing and assurance standards including International Standards on Auditing (ISAs). These will be discussed later in the chapter.

The globalization of accounting and auditing standards has led to an examination of corporate governance standards around the world. Just as governance mechanisms in the United States help establish controls that monitor adherence to GAAP and GAAS, a similar system is needed internationally to strengthen the mechanisms needed to support conformity with IFRS and ISAs. Given that governance standards are a natural outgrowth of accounting and auditing requirements, a sound system of international corporate governance is essential to achieve quality financial reporting on a global level.

The passage of the Sarbanes-Oxley (SOX) Act in the United States and governance initiatives incorporated in the Combined Code on Corporate Governance issued by the Financial Reporting Council in the United Kingdom together deserve a great deal of credit for getting the international business community to focus on improvements in governance. Important differences still exist such as the two-tier versus unitary board of directors. In some countries the most important shareholder is represented by family ownership or by a large industrial group such as Tata Company in India. In other countries such as China, the state, through state-owned enterprises, has a prominent role to play with respect to ownership requirements and management of Chinese companies.

A common set of ethical standards would go a long way toward providing a foundation for professional judgment and support the implementation of IFRS and ISAs. We have pointed out many times in this book that GAAP conformity in the financial statements depends on a strong set of values to guide behavior, an ability to reason ethically, and adherence to ethics standards such as those in the AICPA Code of Professional Conduct. Virtues such as honesty, integrity, trustworthiness, and due care inform ethical action and ensure compliance with GAAP and GAAS. The IFAC group—International Ethics Standards Board for Accountants—has developed a Code of Ethics for Professional Accountants (Global Code) that has helped develop a common set of ethical standards for accountants and those with oversight responsibilities. The Global Code is discussed later in the chapter.

In this chapter we review key international standards with respect to independence, corporate governance provisions, and ethics standards. We use the discussion of these standards as a way to review similar requirements in the United States that were discussed in earlier chapters. In that sense, the discussion in this chapter reviews important U.S. requirements and examines standards imposed on global entities.

SEC Study of a Principles-Based System

SOX requires changes in many facets of financial reporting and oversight including (1) required certification of financial information by company CEOs and CFOs; (2) empowerment of audit committees to engage and approve the services provided by independent auditors; (3) more stringent auditor independence standards; and (4) greater oversight of auditors through the establishment of the Public Company Accounting Oversight Board (PCAOB). One lesser-known provision of SOX is for a study to be conducted of the need to adopt a principles-based approach to standard setting to replace the more rules-based system in the United States.

An SEC study notes that imperfections exist when standards are established on either a rules-based or a principles-only basis. Principles-only standards may present enforcement difficulties because they provide little guidance or structure for exercising professional judgment by preparers and auditors. Rules-based standards often provide a vehicle for circumventing the intention of the standard. As a result of its study, the SEC recommended that those involved in the standard-setting process more consistently develop standards on a principles-based or objectives-oriented basis. Such standards should have the following characteristics:[1]

- Be based on an improved and consistently applied conceptual framework.
- Clearly state the accounting objective of the standard.
- Provide sufficient detail and structure so that the standard can be operationalized and applied on a consistent basis.
- Minimize exceptions from the standard.
- Avoid use of percentage tests (bright lines) that allow financial engineers to achieve technical compliance with the standard while evading the intent of the standard. A good example is the 3 percent equity requirement for outside ownership of SPEs that enabled Enron to avoid consolidating SPE operations with those of Enron. Instead, the "dispersion of risk" requirement of FASB *Interpretation 46(R)* that was discussed in Chapter 7 provides a more conceptual basis to determine when consolidation is appropriate.

The SEC's view is that an optimal standard involves a concise statement of substantive accounting principle where the accounting objective has been included at an appropriate level of specificity as an integral part of the standard and where few, if any, exceptions or conceptual inconsistencies are included in the standard. Further, such a standard should provide an appropriate amount of implementation guidance given the nature of the class of transactions or events and should be devoid of bright-line tests. Finally, such a standard should be consistent with, and derive from, a coherent conceptual framework of financial reporting. The study concludes that objectives-oriented standard setting is desirable and that the benefit of adopting this approach in the United States should justify the costs.

In contrast to objectives-oriented standards, rules-based standards can provide a road map to avoidance of the accounting objectives inherent in the standards. Internal inconsistencies, exceptions, and bright-line tests reward those willing to engineer their way around the intent of standards. This can result in financial reporting that is not representationally faithful to the underlying economic substance of transactions and events. Representational faithfulness means the information presents what really happened or existed. In a rules-based system, financial reporting may well come to be seen as an act of compliance rather than an act of communication. Additionally, because the multiple exceptions lead to internal inconsistencies, significant judgment is needed in determining where within the myriad of possible exceptions an accounting transaction falls. In Chapter 5 we discussed how the lease accounting standards can lead to the application of the rules in a rigid manner resulting in achieving one's objective in lease accounting rather than to reflect economic reality.

At the other extreme, a principles-only approach typically provides insufficient guidance to make the standards reliably operational. As a consequence, principles-only standards require preparers and auditors to exercise significant judgment in applying overly broad standards to more specific transactions and events, and often do not provide a sufficient structure to frame the judgment that must be made. The result of principles-only standards can be a significant loss of comparability among reporting entities. Furthermore, under a principles-only standard setting regime, the increased reliance on the capabilities and judgment of preparers and auditors could increase the likelihood of retrospective disagreements on accounting treatments. In turn, this could result in increased litigation with regulators for both companies and auditors.

In contrast to these extremes, according to the SEC study, objectives-oriented standards explicitly charge management with the responsibility for capturing within the company's financial reports the economic substance of transactions and events—not abstractly, but as defined specifically and framed by the substantive objectives built into each pertinent standard. In turn, auditors would be held responsible for reporting whether management has fulfilled that responsibility. Accordingly, objectives-oriented standards place greater emphasis on the responsibility of both management and auditors to ensure that financial reporting captures the objectives of the standard better than do either rules-based standards or principles-only standards. Further, if properly constructed, the SEC believes that objectives-oriented standards may require less use of judgment than either rules-based or principles-only standards and, thus, may better facilitate consistency and compliance with the intent of the standards.

SEC Road Map for Adoption of IFRS in the United States

On November 14, 2008, the SEC released for comment a proposed road map for the adoption of IFRS that would monitor progress until 2011, when the commission plans to consider requiring U.S. public companies to file their financial statements using IFRS. On February 10, 2010, the SEC issued a statement reaffirming its support for a single set of globally accepted accounting standards, yet refrained from establishing a firm timeline for incorporating such standards into the U.S. financial reporting system. A March 3, 2010 statement by the SEC provides that, assuming certain milestones are met, the SEC will be in a position to determine in 2011 whether to transition the U.S. financial reporting system from GAAP to IFRS. If the SEC decides in 2011 that U.S. public companies should transition financial reporting to IFRS, then the statement indicates that the earliest U.S. issuers would be required to report under the new system likely would be 2015.[2] The United States is under a great deal of pressure to adopt IFRS because European countries have already done so and many other countries have or will be adopting IFRS by the end of 2011. The IASB chair Sir David Tweedie stated in August 2009 that countries having already adopted IFRS are running out of patience waiting for the SEC to decide whether to approve a road map for transitioning to IFRS and that the United States would have to commit by 2011. Moreover, in September 2009 the G-20[3] called on international accounting bodies to redouble their efforts to achieve a single set of global accounting standards within the context of their independent standards setting process and complete their convergence to IFRS by June 2011.

The SEC now permits foreign companies to use IFRS without reconciliation to U.S. GAAP. The SEC's road map assumes IFRS will replace GAAP for reporting by publicly owned U.S. companies. Notwithstanding the potential adoption of IFRS for small and medium-sized entities (SMEs) discussed later, an unresolved issue is whether GAAP in its current form will continue to be used by non-public companies. In addition, some uncertainty exists about the SEC's willingness to hold to the timeline for U.S. companies because of concerns about the quality of IFRS and the pace of the timeline. Indeed, comments about the IFRS proposal that are posted on the Web site of the American Institute of CPAs indicate that a consensus exists among those opposed to the road map that continued convergence was a better option than IFRS adoption because fuller convergence between both sets of standards would be less complex and less costly than IFRS adoption.

The final decision of the SEC to mandate IFRS starting in 2015 will be based on whether those accounting standards are of high quality and are sufficiently comprehensive. The SEC's convergence approach is based on the notion of "improve and adopt" IFRS before giving its stamp of approval. The commission has been assessing whether IFRS develops a high quality of financial reporting relative to the standards which may be replaced. A good example of the convergence process at work is the capitalization of finance costs during the period of construction of an asset. Originally, *IAS No. 23,* Capitalization of Borrowing Costs, and a revised version allowed for capitalization but identified expensing as the benchmark treatment for borrowing costs. In March 2007, the IASB issued another revised version, this time mandating capitalization to bring the standards in line with U.S. GAAP under *FASB*

No. 34, Capitalization of Interest Cost.[4] Notably, the recently issued IFRS for small and medium-sized entities that is discussed later adopts expensing as the required standard.

One concern in the United States is the loss of some sovereignty with respect to establishing accounting standards, although FASB would still work with the IASB in developing new standards. Also, while the SEC would still be legally responsible to ensure that publicly owned companies adhere to IFRS, some of its influence and that of the NYSE may be muted by the International Organization of Securities Commissions (IOSCO).[5] IOSCO adopted in 1998 a comprehensive set of Objectives and Principles of Securities Regulation (IOSCO Principles), which today are recognized as the international regulatory benchmarks for all securities markets. The organization endorsed in 2003 a comprehensive methodology (IOSCO Principles Assessment Methodology) that enables an objective assessment of the level of implementation of the IOSCO Principles in the jurisdictions of its members and the development of practical action plans to correct identified deficiencies.

In 2002, IOSCO adopted a multilateral memorandum of understanding (IOSCO MOU) designed to facilitate cross-border enforcement and exchange of information among the international community of securities regulators.[6] IOSCO's MOU is the first global multilateral information-sharing arrangement among securities regulators and sets a new international benchmark for cooperation critical to combating violations of securities laws. The MOU provides for the exchange of basic information in investigating cross-border violations, including bank, brokerage, and client identification records. Information provided through the MOU may be used to enforce compliance with securities laws and regulations, including through civil and criminal prosecutions.

Global Adoption of IFRS

About 117 countries have signed up to adopt IFRS as their accounting standards and IASB chair David Tweedie expects there to be 150 by 2011. In the EU an agreement was reached in 2005 that provided the impetus for the global adoption of one set of international accounting standards when the member states of the EU required about 7,000 listed companies to produce annual financial statements in compliance with IFRS. According to the EU Commission the number of IFRS adopters whose securities traded on a regulated market in the EU stood at 7,365, of which 5,534 were equity issuers.[7] The EU permits companies from Canada, China, India, Japan, South Korea, and the United States to use their home-country generally accepted accounting principles in financial statements of companies listed on exchanges in the EU. Notwithstanding the uncertainty about implementation in the United States, all of these countries have announced their efforts to adopt IFRS by 2011.

Two important elements of IASB's constitution are the broadening of IAS to IFRS and the movement from harmonization to the concept of convergence. Convergence implies the adoption of one set of standards internationally by reducing international differences in accounting standards. It is a natural step in the evolution of accounting standards to IFRS. The convergence project began in October 2002 as a result of the Norwalk Agreement between the FASB and the IASB that resulted in the issuance of a Memorandum of Understanding formalizing the commitment of both organizations to the convergence of U.S. GAAP and IAS.[8] Another memorandum issued on February 27, 2006, reaffirms the boards' shared objective of developing high-quality, common accounting standards for use in the world's capital markets that would enhance the consistency, comparability, and efficiency of financial statements, enabling global markets to move with less friction.[9] A recent EU commission study found that the application of IFRS has improved the comparability and quality of financial reporting and has led to greater transparency. With a limited number of exceptions, most stakeholders believe that the understandability of financial statements has generally improved.

Rules versus Principles-Based Standards

Judgments about the appropriate accounting standards to apply in a given situation are influenced by whether a rules-based or principles-based system is used. Rules-based standards prescribe for the preparer what to do in contrast to a principles-based approach that emphasizes how to decide what to do.[10] Schipper believes that "U.S. GAAP is based on a recognizable set of principles derived from the FASB's Conceptual Framework, but nonetheless contains elements that cause some commentators to conclude that U.S. accounting is 'rules-based.'" She contends that standards that are initially based on principles can become rule-based exercises when terms are defined in great detail, prescriptive explanations of the application of the standard are provided, and numerous examples given.[11]

Some professionals believe that the reason U.S. accounting standards are more rules-based than principles-based stems in large part from the emphasis put on the wording *present fairly* in the audit report and *in conformity with GAAP.* They contend that "present fairly" indicates a principles-based approach but is converted to a rules-based approach when it is defined in *Statement on Auditing Standards (SAS) No. 69* and covered in *SAS 91* and in Rule 203 of the AICPA Code. In other words, the application of officially established accounting principles as defined in these standards (GAAP) almost always results in a fair presentation of the financial statements. Exceptions may be made if circumstances warrant such as the application of another principle that more accurately reflects financial position, results of operations, and cash flows. However, these would presumably be few and far between.[12]

A relatively more principles-based standards regime requires professional judgment at both the transaction level (substance over form) and the financial statement level ("true and fair view" override). It is the latter judgment that is unique to international standards. *IAS No. 1,* Presentation of Financial Statements, provides that if the application of IFRS conflicts with the provisions of the *Framework for the Preparation and Presentation of Financial Statements* so that the financial statements do not present fairly, "then the entity should first consider the salutary effects of providing supplementary disclosures. If the disclosures are insufficient to provide a true and fair view, then the entity may conclude that it must override (ignore or contravene) the applicable accounting standard." *IAS 1* anticipates such overrides would be made only in rare circumstances.[13]

The IASB *Framework for the Preparation and Presentation of Financial Statements* (the *Framework)*[14] serves as a guide to resolving accounting issues that are not addressed directly in a standard. Moreover, in the absence of a standard or an interpretation that specifically applies to a transaction, *IAS No. 8,* Accounting Policies, Changes in Accounting Estimates and Errors, requires that an entity must use its judgment in developing and applying an accounting policy that results in information that is relevant and reliable. In making that judgment, *IAS 8* requires management to consider the definitions, recognition criteria, and measurement concepts for assets, liabilities, income, and expenses in the *Framework.*[15]

One benefit of principles-based accounting rests in its broad guidelines that can be applied to numerous situations such as the substance over form evaluation. Another advantage is that principles-based standards are simpler than rules-based standards that contain complex implementation requirements. For example, there are at least a dozen financial accounting standards, interpretations, and staff positions in the United States on lease matters. U.S. standards also contain numerous provisions that apply only to specific industries. U.S. GAAP is now spread out over 17,000 pages in the new FASB Codification, whereas IFRS is covered in 2,500 pages. David Tweedie believes that principles-based reasoning makes it easier to defend professional judgment and principles-based standards if challenged in stockholder lawsuits. One result of having less specific principles-based standards is that financial statement notes tend to be more elaborate in IFRS-based statements.

Earnings Management Concerns

One concern about a principles-based system is whether an economic substance over form concept might lead preparers of financial statements to try and justify a specific accounting outcome with reference to commercial drivers in an attempt to manage earnings. To determine if there was a difference in the magnitude of earnings management in a principles-based versus rules-based environment, Mergenthaler examined the factors that executives consider when deciding to manage earnings. He contends that the probability of being penalized for earnings management and the penalty imposed on executives who manage are factors that influence executives' estimate of the expected cost of earnings management. Mergenthaler found a positive association between rules-based characteristics and the dollar magnitude of earnings management. He argues that this is because the expected cost of managing earnings is lower in a rules-based environment.[16] An SEC study of principles-based standards seems to support Mergenthaler's contention. In the aforementioned SEC study of the adoption of a principles-based system, the commission expressed its concern that there may be "a greater difficulty in seeking remedies against 'bad' actors either through enforcement or litigation."[17]

French authors Thomas Jeanjean and Herve Stolowy examined the effect of IFRS conversion on earnings quality—specifically on management manipulation of earnings to avoid recognition of losses. Their work examined more than 1,100 firms in three countries to determine whether the earnings management appeared to increase or decrease after implementation of IFRS. The authors measured financial reporting quality as a reduction in earnings management. Earnings management was assessed as the frequency of small profits as compared to small losses, a technique used in past studies. Australia, France, and the United Kingdom were selected for examination, as these three countries were unable to adopt IFRS before the 2005 mandatory transition date, thus eliminating any early adoption benefits. Based on the authors' research, earnings management remained consistent in Australia and the United Kingdom after IFRS adoption. However, in France, earnings management appeared to increase, suggesting that overall, earnings quality was not improved by adopting IFRS.[18]

In evaluating the authors' research results, Bolt-Lee and Smith address the issue of the subjectivity of IFRS (i.e., principles-based judgments) and the use of management discretion for quality reporting. The authors suggest that the efforts of the standard-setting bodies should be focused on enhancing IFRS adoption reporting incentives and strict enforcement as opposed to "harmonizing accounting standards."[19] The principles-based judgments required by IFRS introduce an ethical dimension to decision making because these standards do not spell out all the required considerations in determining proper accounting and reporting, but rely instead on the application of basic principles such as substance over form and true and fair view.

FASB–IASB Conceptual Framework: The Role of Representational Faithfulness

On May 29, 2008, the FASB and IASB jointly issued an Exposure Draft for comment titled *Conceptual Framework for Financial Reporting*. The objective of the conceptual framework project is to develop an improved common conceptual framework that provides a sound foundation for developing future accounting standards. Such a framework is essential to fulfilling the boards' goal of developing standards that are principles-based, internally consistent, and internationally converged and that lead to financial reporting that provides the information capital providers need to make decisions in their capacity as capital providers. The new framework, which will deal with a wide range of issues, will build on the existing IASB and FASB frameworks and consider developments subsequent to the issuance of those frameworks.[20]

Financial statements should truthfully represent economic reality. In its definition of *representational faithfulness,* the FASB's *Statement of Accounting Concepts No. 2* states that representational faithfulness is "correspondence or agreement between a measure or description and the phenomenon that it purports to represent."[21] Alexander and Jermakowicz make the important observation that "truth implies an external reality, since it implies that there is a reality to which statements correspond if they are true."[22]

One difference between the Exposure Draft and the conceptual joint framework in the United States is to define the qualitative characteristics of useful information to include faithful representation. Rather than being considered an element of reliability as in the United States, the faithful representation of the economic phenomena is a foundational element of useful information in the framework. According to the joint framework, the primary qualities of decision-useful information are relevance and reliability. Faithful representation is attained when the depiction of an economic phenomenon is complete, neutral, and free from material error. Financial information that faithfully represents an economic phenomenon depicts the economic substance of the underlying transaction, event, or circumstance, which is not always the same as its legal form. A strong set of core values (virtues) is needed to make reasoned judgments about representational faithfulness and to support the professional judgments needed to ensure reliable information.

Faithful representation does not imply total freedom from error in the depiction of economic phenomenon because the economic phenomena presented in financial reports generally are measured under conditions of uncertainty. The key is to identify the appropriate inputs (i.e., fair value) and make estimates without bias and that are verifiable. Ethical principles should be followed in making such determinations including objectivity and integrity. A virtuous accountant should avoid any temptation to slant measurements one way or the other. Instead, the proper accounting should be objectively determined and pressure to do otherwise should be resisted by maintaining one's integrity.

Examples of Rules-Based versus Principles-Based Standards

Accounting for Leases

A principles-based approach to decision making is illustrated by emphasizing economic substance over legal form in lease transactions. In the United States, *Statement of Financial Accounting Standards (SFAS) No. 13* establishes rules that can undermine the substance over form concept. Recall from our discussion in Chapter 5 that if any one of four lease criteria is met, then capitalization treatment leads to recording an asset and liability on the books of the lessee using the present value of future lease payments including any guaranteed residual value. One problem with the rules-based criteria for capitalization is they rely on implementation guidance (bright-line rules) that can be manipulated. A company might engineer a lease transaction in such a way as to achieve its desired objective of keeping the liability off its books rather than faithfully representing the underlying economic substance of the transaction. For example, to keep the liability off its books the lessee simply does not have to guarantee to pay the residual value to the lessor. Consider the following: Present value of lease payments (excluding residual value), $107,000; fair value of leased asset, $120,000; present value of residual value, $2,000. If the residual value is unguaranteed (then, $107,000 is less than 90 percent of $120,000) and assuming none of the other criteria are met, then the lease is recorded as an operating lease.

International accounting standards apply a principles-based approach to lease accounting. *IAS 17* provides that if the substance of the transaction is effectively to transfer ownership to the lessee, then it is accounted for as a purchase and sale (capitalization). The standard does establish criteria that guide capitalization but the application relies on professional judgment. For example, the lease term must be for the *major part* of the economic life of the leased asset and the present value of the minimum lease payments must be at least equal to *substantially all* of the fair value of the leased asset.[23] In reality, it is difficult to see how these vaguer standards produce better results given that one company might decide that the "major part" is greater than 50 percent of the useful life of the leased asset while another may say it is 75 percent or more. The different applications of the standards may lead to a lack of comparability in financial reports. The problem is that even in a principles-based environment, rules might factor into the judgments made, thereby effectively negating the more conceptual principles approach. Still, if the accounting for leases does not conform to financial reporting requirements in the judgment of the auditor, then the true and fair view override (i.e., capitalizing a lease) should be exercised to ensure economic reality is portrayed.

Valuation and Recording of Property, Plant, and Equipment

Principles-based standards are generic and, as opposed to rules-based systems, they do not address every controversial issue but keep considerable ambiguity about such major processes as record keeping and measurement. A potential drawback of the principles-based approach is a lack of precise guidelines that could create inconsistencies in the application of standards across organizations. One example is *IAS 16* that deals with accounting for property, plant, and equipment. According to the standard, property, plant, and equipment can be accounted for under the cost method or the revaluation method. Specific rules do not exist to guide when one method should be used as opposed to the other. Moreover, the revaluations are made at fair value with little guidance to help determine this amount except that "fair value is the amount for which an asset could be exchanged between knowledgeable, willing parties in an arm's length transaction."[24] The question is whether determinations of fair value can be made objectively over time and with sufficient precision.

Comparability suffers under a revaluation method since different companies may estimate replacement value differently. Benston contends that it is not the principles-only approach that is to blame, but the inevitable and desirable lack of comparability due to different economic environments. He states that "a company's choice of accounting measurement or presentation can convey information that is valuable to investors about the managers' operational and investment approach and decisions."[25]

An important ingredient in determining the sufficiency of evidence is judging its reliability, including materiality, and relevance. As previously discussed in Chapters 5 through 7, the reasonable person standard that is used to evaluate materiality is one of the most subjective and difficult judgments to make. While a quantitative approach can be used, its application depends on the professional judgment of the decision maker. The goal should be to provide accurate and complete information. The representational faithfulness of economic information depends on it being free from material error. The FASB–IASB joint conceptual framework states that information is material if its omission or misstatement could influence the decisions that users make on the basis of an entity's financial statements. A virtuous auditor should avoid the temptation to report an event in a way that shows the company's side of the story and then attempt to justify it under the guise of it not being material.

Exhibit 8.1 presents the authors' conceptual view of the major ingredients of a principles-based approach to making accounting judgments. Notice how, in a principles-based environment, virtue-based considerations (e.g., objectivity and integrity) form the basis to evaluate representational faithfulness and to make professional judgments about the economic substance of transactions and the assessment of a true and fair view.

The Problem with Provisions and Reserves

The words *provisions* and *reserves* have different meanings in the United States and in many other countries around the world. In the United States, *reserve* always means "provision." The word *provision* means two things: (1) a liability of uncertain timing or amount

EXHIBIT 8.1
Conceptual Framework of a Principles-Based Approach to Decision Making

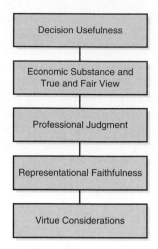

(e.g., provisions for pensions) and (2) an allowance against (or impairment of) the value of an asset (e.g., bad debt provision or provision for depreciation). It is safe to say that a provision relates to a liability that does not exist at the reporting date (e.g., contingencies), whereas an allowance reflects the decline in value of an existing asset (e.g., impairments of property, plant, and equipment).[26] Further distinctions include the following: (1) there are no legal reserves in the United States, (2) revaluation reserves relating to investments are shown as cumulative other comprehensive income if they are based on market adjustments for available-for-sale securities, (3) reserves caused by foreign currency translation are called cumulative translation adjustments and they, too, appear in comprehensive income, and (4) profit and loss account reserves are called retained earnings (e.g., appropriations of retained earnings).

The distinction between provisions and reserves is important for financial reporting because provisions are liabilities recognized by charges against profit that decrease profit and net assets (used in the United States). A reserve, on the other hand, is an element of shareholders' equity that might reflect the reduction of available profit and an increase in a corresponding equity account with no net effect on retained earnings. For many years, companies in the EU used reserves to reduce reported profits because of a statutory requirement or simply to follow conservative reporting. In IFRS and U.S. GAAP, provisions for general risks should not be established simply to smooth net income. In 1998, the IASC issued *IAS 37* stating that a provision should be recognized when, and only when, there is a liability to a third party at the balance sheet date.[27]

Another expression that is often found, particularly under the domestic rules of prudent countries (e.g., Germany) and particularly relating to banks, is *secret* or *hidden reserves*. These would arise because a company (1) failed to recognize an asset in its balance sheet, (2) deliberately measured an asset at an unreasonably low value, or (3) set up unnecessarily high provisions. Recall that in Chapter 7 we discussed the use of cookie jar reserves that were used in many of the accounting scandals in the United States to smooth earnings.

Secret reserves might be recorded in the name of prudence (conservatism) or, in some countries, in order to get tax deductions. Whatever the motivation, the result is that net assets and equity will be understated. As Nobes and Parker point out, most systems of accounting contain some degree of secret reserves. For example, the IFRS, German, and U.S. regimes do not recognize the internally generated asset research; and it is normal to value many assets at depreciated cost, which is often below fair value.[28] The former means research will be expensed rather than capitalized and amortized, thereby shifting the full expense into the first year. In the case of depreciation, accounting for that amount on a historical cost basis will lead to different charges (oftentimes lower) because the fair value (revaluation method) would provide larger depreciation amounts. Of course, a company might also lengthen the useful life (e.g., Waste Management) or overstate its salvage value to reduce depreciation charges each year and, perhaps, change the depreciation method later on, which would lead to different amounts in future years.

In the September 30, 2009 fiscal year annual report of the German company Siemens that can be found at www.siemens.com/annual/09/en/index.htm, five provisions are identified: (1) provision for contingent liabilities, (2) provisions when the estimated costs of a construction contract exceed future revenues (onerous contract), (3) provisions for asset retirement obligations, (4) provisions for warranty obligations, and (5) provisions for the eventual outcome of regulatory and legal proceedings.

The following footnote from Siemens's report describes various provisions.

Provisions—A provision is recognized in the balance sheet when the Company has a present legal or constructive obligation as a result of a past event, it is probable that an outflow of economic benefits will be required to settle the obligation and a reliable estimate can be made of the amount of the obligation. If the effect is material, provisions are recognized at present value by discounting the expected future cash flows at a pre-tax rate that reflects current market assessments of the time value of money. Provisions for onerous contracts are measured at the lower of the expected cost of fulfilling the contract and the expected cost of terminating the contract. Additions to provisions are generally recognized in the income statement. The present value of legal obligations associated with the retirement of property, plant and equipment (asset retirement obligations) that result from the acquisition, construction, development or normal use of an asset is added to the carrying amount of the related asset. The additional carrying amount is depreciated over the useful life of the related asset. If the asset retirement obligation is settled for other than the carrying amount of the liability, the Company recognizes a gain or loss on settlement.

Provisions—Significant estimates are involved in the determination of provisions related to onerous contracts, warranty costs and legal proceedings. A significant portion of the business of certain operating divisions is performed pursuant to long-term contracts, often for large projects, in Germany and abroad, awarded on a competitive bidding basis. Siemens records a provision for onerous sales contracts when current estimates of total contract costs exceed expected contract revenue. Such estimates are subject to change based on new information as projects progress toward completion. Onerous sales contracts are identified by monitoring the progress of the project and updating the estimate of total contract costs which also requires significant judgment relating to achieving certain performance standards, for example in the IT service business, the Mobility Division and the Energy Sector as well as estimates involving warranty costs.

Siemens is subject to legal and regulatory proceeding in various jurisdictions. Such proceedings may result in criminal or civil sanctions, penalties or disgorgements against the Company. If it is more likely than not that an obligation of the Company exists and will result in an outflow of resources, a provision is recorded if the amount of the obligation can be reliably estimated. Regulatory and legal proceedings as well as government investigations often involve complex legal issues and are subject to substantial uncertainties. Accordingly, management exercises considerable judgment in determining whether there is a present obligation as a result of a past event at the balance sheet date, whether it is more likely than not that such a proceeding will result in an outflow of resources and whether the amount of the obligation can be reliably estimated. The Company periodically reviews the status of these proceedings with both inside and outside counsel. These judgments are subject to change as new information becomes available. The required amount of a provision may change in the future due to new developments in the particular matter. Revisions to estimates may significantly impact future net income. Upon resolution, Siemens may incur charges in excess of the recorded provisions for such matters. It can not be excluded that the financial position or results of operations of Siemens will be materially affected by an unfavorable outcome of legal or regulatory proceedings or government investigations. See Note 30 *Legal Proceedings* for further information.

IFRS for Small and Medium-Sized Entities

On July 9, 2009, the IASB published IFRS designed for use by small and medium-sized entities (SMEs), which are estimated to represent more than 95 percent of all companies. SMEs are defined as those entities that do not have public accountability and publish general-purpose financial statements. While every entity has some public accountability including to its owners and tax authorities, public accountability in the context of IFRS for SMEs is defined to cover entities with or seeking to have securities traded in a public market or that hold assets in a fiduciary capacity as their main business activity. The definition is therefore based on the nature of the entity rather than on its size.[29]

U.S. private companies are not required, like public companies, to use a particular basis of accounting when preparing their financial statements. The factors that drive a private company's choice of which financial accounting and reporting framework to follow in preparing its financial statements depend on each company's objectives and the needs of their financial statement users. Currently, private companies in the United States can prepare their financial statements in accordance with U.S. GAAP as promulgated by the FASB, some other comprehensive basis of accounting such as cash or tax basis, or full IFRS (assuming adoption), among others. Now, with the issuance of IFRS for SMEs, U.S. private companies have an additional option.

The IFRS for SMEs is a self-contained standard of about 230 pages tailored for the needs and capabilities of smaller businesses. Many of the principles in full IFRS for recognizing and measuring assets, liabilities, income, and expenses have been simplified; topics not relevant to SMEs have been omitted; and the number of required disclosures has been significantly reduced. Examples of simplifications in *IFRS for SMEs* appear in Exhibit 8.2.

IFRS for SMEs responds to the strong international demand from both developed and emerging economies for a rigorous and common set of accounting standards for small and medium-sized businesses that are much simpler than full IFRS. These standards are separate from full IFRS and can be adopted by a jurisdiction whether or not it has adopted full IFRS. Where a transaction is not addressed by the IFRS for SMEs, management is expected to use judgment to determine its accounting policy. If such a transaction is covered in full IFRS, management may refer to the appropriate international standard if it wishes but is not required to do so.

EXHIBIT 8.2
Comparison of Accounting Rules for Full IFRS and IFRS for SMEs

Item	Full IFRS	IFRS for SMEs
Property, plant, and equipment	Cost or revaluation method	Cost method only
Goodwill and other intangibles	Reviewed for impairment and not amortized (indefinite lives)	Amortized (indefinite and definite lives); tested for impairment if indicated
Research and development costs	Research costs expensed as incurred; development costs capitalized and amortized if specific criteria met	All research and development costs expensed
Borrowing costs	Capitalized if certain criteria are met	Expensed
Pension costs	Actuarial gains or losses can be recognized immediately or amortized into profit or loss over the expected remaining working lives of participating employees	Immediate recognition and splits the expense into different components

Comparative Corporate Governance

On a basic level, the movement toward IFRS will affect corporate governance systems because in those countries transitioning to IFRS (e.g., the United States) the audit committees and board of director members will have to deal with convergence issues. IFRS will not merely be a technical accounting conversion. It will be most critical for boards to monitor the quality and robustness of the conversion process and the road map to IFRS. Ethical issues exist in corporate governance systems in different countries because business practices and cultural considerations directly affect the way in which companies are managed and controlled.

IFRS No. 1, First-Time Adoption of International Financial Reporting Standards, is applicable in an entity's first IFRS financial statements. These are the first annual financial statements in which an entity adopts IFRS. An entity selects accounting policies based on IFRS that are effective at the current reporting date, or based on the permitted early application of standards that are not yet required to be adopted. Generally those policies are applied consistently at the date of transition to restate the opening balance sheet on an IFRS basis and in each of the periods presented in the first IFRS financial statements, even if a particular standard does not require retrospective application for existing IFRS users.[30] Usually, investors and regulators look at any restatement negatively, so audit committees and board members will need to address this risk effectively. The biggest challenge will likely be to manage stakeholder expectations in terms of meeting targets and key performance indicators given the changed results under IFRS.

A major theme of this text is the need for ethical corporate governance systems to ensure that decisions are made in the public interest. We discussed various corporate governance mechanisms in Chapter 3 including the board of directors, audit committee, internal controls, the role of internal auditors, and the external audit. In this chapter we look at governance provisions that differ from those in the United States, emphasizing differences in three countries: Germany, China, and India. Germany was chosen because its system mirrors that of many European countries and includes the two-tier board of directors structure. China and India are two of the fastest-growing economies and have some unique aspects to their governance system. In China, a transition has been under way for quite a few years from a state-controlled to a more private enterprise system with state-representative shareholders. In India, large industrial groups (e.g., Tata) or family-owned entities are major shareholders.

Corporate Governance in Germany

The defining feature of German corporate governance is the two-tier board structure and extensive labor representation on the Supervisory Board. In accordance with German law, the Management Board is charged with managing the enterprise for the benefit of various stakeholder groups. The Supervisory Board, whose members are elected by shareholders at the annual meeting, consists of non-management members including employee representatives, and it appoints, supervises, and advises the members of the Management Board on policy but does not participate in the company's day-to-day management. The Supervisory Board can meet without the Management Board, if necessary, to ensure independence in decision making. In relying on a two-tier structure, Germany has formalized the distinction between managing the company and supervising the management of the company. The Supervisory Board's responsibilities are generally comparable to those of the board of directors in the United States. The Management Board generally performs the duties and responsibilities of senior management of a corporation.

The German Corporate Governance Code establishes requirements for the conduct and activities of the Management and Supervisory Boards. The Code stresses the need for transparency and clarifies shareholder rights in order to promote the trust of investors and capital market development. The Code's "comply-or-explain principle" helps foster transparency by requiring an explanation from those corporations not complying with the provisions of the Code.[31]

The following is a summary of governance in German companies as compared to that in the United States:

1. The German corporate governance system reflects concentrated ownership and insider control in addition to management including large shareholders, lenders, and labor. It builds on insider relationships, while the U.S. system relies on external participation.

2. In Germany, two-tier boards include the Management Board, which manages the enterprise for stakeholder groups, and the Supervisory Board, which oversees management policy carried out by the Management Board. In the United States, a unitary board of directors approach is used.

3. Influential stakeholders on the German Supervisory Board include shareholders owning 25 percent or more of a block of stock, other blockholders including another business enterprise, wealthy families, and large commercial banks; and there is employee representation on the board. Large institutional investors in the United States (e.g., Calpers) are the only blockholders in publicly owned companies.

4. The Management Board prepares the financial statements that are examined by the outside auditors and the Supervisory Board. In the United States, the management of the company prepares its financial statements.

5. In Germany, board and management decisions are to be made in the best interests of the company, whereas in the United States, shareholder interests are emphasized.

6. In Germany, the comply or explain principle requires an explanation of noncompliance with corporate governance provisions of the Code. In the United States, CEOs must certify compliance with corporate governance guidelines of the NYSE.

A major issue to be resolved for corporate governance in Germany is that ownership structures are complex and work against transparency in corporate control. Also, hybrid ownership groups and insider control create challenges for effective corporate governance. The traditional lack of protection for investors, in part due to the emphasis on bank financing, has been somewhat resolved with the expansion of stock financing in Germany.

Corporate Governance in China

In China, the traditional state-owned enterprise (SOE) has been undergoing a process of "corporatization" since 1984 when these enterprises were encouraged to expand production and earn profits. The traditional model of state-owned and state-managed enterprises became two-fold: state ownership of property with management rights in SOEs separated out. More than 80 percent of the SOEs are being transformed into corporate entities under the company law to facilitate stock exchange listing. According to a 2007 survey, SOEs consume close to 90 percent of 1,400 listed companies in China.[32]

Schipani and Liu point out that compared with traditional SOEs, the ownership structure of SOE-corporatized corporations includes better defined shareholder rights than its traditional counterpart along with increased efficiency and accountability.[33] The modern corporate model presents more sophisticated and difficult governance issues as China continues to transition from a planned economy to a market economy.

The Code of Corporate Governance for Listed Companies in China that was issued by the Chinese Securities Regulatory Commission, a body that carries out some of the same functions as the SEC in the United States, provides a measuring stick for corporate governance practices. The company law requires corporations to form three statutory and indispensable corporate governing bodies: (1) the shareholders, acting as a body at the general meeting; (2) the board of directors; and (3) the board of supervisors. The law also introduced two new statutory corporate positions—the chair of the board of directors and the CEO.[34]

The following is a summary of governance differences in Chinese enterprises as compared to those in the United States:

1. The state plays the role of an investor in China's corporatized SOEs; reporting practices are more often focused on meeting the needs of the major shareholder (i.e., the state) rather than the needs of investors as in the case of the United States.
2. China has a two-tier system of oversight, with overlapping responsibilities of both the supervisory board and the board of directors, and the board of directors and management compared with the unitary board in the United States.
3. Only the chair of the audit committee need be independent in China, with a majority of independent directors on the committee. In the United States, all members of the audit committee should be independent.
4. Fiduciary duties for controlling shareholders. Directors have fiduciary duties to act in the best interests of the company and its shareholders. In the United States, both management and the board of directors have fiduciary obligations with respect to the shareholders.
5. No required certification of financial statements by management or an internal control report, whereas SOX requires certification by the CEO and CFO.
6. Comply or explain gaps between existing corporate governance practices and recommendations in the corporate code, although there is no penalty for failing to do so. In the United States, CEOs must certify compliance with corporate governance guidelines of the NYSE.

The most significant issue with respect to corporate governance in China is enforcement of the many provisions that already exist in the law. Even though China has adopted many of the principles of corporate governance followed in the United States and Germany, there is no guarantee that SOEs and public companies will implement them in the best interests of investors given the critical role of the state shareholder and the government.

Corporate Governance in India

Unlike China where governance requirements exist in a corporate code, in India various committees have studied the governance and have issued a variety of recommended guidelines. For example, the Kumar Mangalam Birla Committee on Corporate Governance suggests that there should be a separate section on corporate governance compliance in the annual report highlighting non-compliance with any of the mandatory recommendations and the reasons thereof.[35] This resembles the comply or explain provision in the codes of German companies. The auditors should also attest to the compliance of the corporate governance; recommendations and certification should be submitted to the relevant stock exchange.

There are many similarities between corporate governance systems in the United States and India, probably due to the long-standing influence of the United Kingdom in India. The following addresses both similarities and differences that exist between the two sets of standards:

1. More diverse share ownership including family and some government ownership. In the United States, family ownership exists mainly in private entities and, notwithstanding the recent government bailout of some major U.S. corporations during the financial crisis of 2007–2009, government ownership is rare.
2. In India between only 33 and 50 percent of directors need to be independent, whereas a majority is required in the United States.

3. Independence of directors can be problematic in Indian systems due to the influence of family businesses and blockholder owners. For the most part this is not a problem in the United States because of SOX and the NYSE listing requirements that dictate there should be a majority of independent directors.

4. In India, the fiduciary duties of directors are to act in the best interests of the company and its shareholders, similar to the Chinese system, whereas in the United States both management and the board of directors have fiduciary obligations with respect to the shareholders.

5. Certification of annual accounts only is recommended in India, whereas in the United States it is required under SOX.

6. External auditors issue a certificate of assessment of compliance of corporate governance rules to be filed with the stock exchanges in India; similar requirements exist under NYSE listing requirements.

7. The Indian corporate governance system requires businesses to comply or explain noncompliance with mandatory recommendations. Compliance explanations are also required in the United States under NYSE listing requirements.

An important issue in India is the lack of independent members of the board of directors in practice, notwithstanding requirements to the contrary. Many companies are traditionally owned by families whose members are part of management as well as the board of directors, making it difficult to have a level of independence that serves as a check on management behavior. According to Rajagopalan and Zhang, 45 percent of all Indian companies are family controlled.[36] The key challenge for India going forward is to strictly enforce corporate governance requirements and make recommended practices mandatory.

In India, large industrial groups play a special role in corporate governance. It is not unusual to have one such group be a major shareholder of another Indian company. A good example is the Tata Group. The Tata Group is a multinational conglomerate based in Mumbai, India. In terms of market capitalization and revenues, the Tata Group is the largest private corporate group in India. It has interests in steel, automobiles, information technology, communication, power, tea, and hospitality. The Tata Group has operations in more than 85 countries across six continents and its companies export products and services to 80 nations. The Tata Group comprises 114 companies and subsidiaries in 7 business sectors, 27 of which are publicly listed. Companies that form a major part of the group include Tata Steel, Corus Steel, Tata Motors, Tata Consultancy Services, Tata Technologies, Tata Tea, Titan Industries, Tata Power, Tata Communications, Tata Teleservices, and the Taj Hotels.

Selected provisions of the Tata Group's code of conduct are presented in Appendix 1 of this chapter. The following provisions are of particular note.

1. Tata recognizes its social responsibility to India and countries that it operates in with respect to economic development and to improve the quality of life; it is sensitive to different cultures.

2. The company applies the accounting and financial reporting standards of the country in which it operates; India is committed to adopting IFRS by 2011.

3. Illegal payments are not permitted, although relatively minor gifts can be given if normal and customary practice in a particular country.

4. Stakeholder obligations are recognized and authorized directors and employees have a special role to play in disclosing information about the company.

5. Shareholder obligations are recognized and the board of directors are assigned the responsibility to keep shareholders informed about important matters.

6. Employees, full-time directors, and the CEO are obligated to adhere to ethical standards, including professionalism, honesty, and integrity, and promote transparency in all of their dealings with stakeholders.

7. Each country in which Tata operates must comply with regulatory requirements.

8. Conflicts of interest should be avoided and, if they exist, reported to the chief executive, who in turn should report such exceptional cases to the board of directors.

9. The code precludes the use of insider information obtained as a result of an employee's position in the company for personal gain.

10. The code prohibits the misappropriation of corporate assets for personal use.

11. The confidentiality of all information must be protected and not provided to outside parties without the expressed approval of management.

12. Employees should report to management and/or a third-party hotline any possible violations of the code or an event of misconduct or other action not in Tata's best interest. Employees may choose to make such reports to the chair of the audit committee or the board of directors, in which case they are protected by the company's whistleblower policy.

OECD Principles of Corporate Governance

Introduction

The 30 large industrial member countries of the Organization for Economic Cooperation and Development adopted OECD Principles of Corporate Governance in 1999 and the Principles were most recently revised in 2004. The OECD Principles have since become an international benchmark for policy makers, investors, corporations, and other stakeholders worldwide. They have advanced the corporate governance agenda and provided specific guidance for legislative and regulatory initiatives in both OECD and non-OECD countries. The Principles also provide the basis for an extensive program of cooperation between OECD and non-OECD countries and underpin the corporate governance component of World Bank/IMF Reports on the Observance of Standards and Codes (ROSC).

The Principles were most recently reviewed to take account of developments and experiences in OECD member and nonmember countries during the period of accounting fraud in the late 1990s and early 2000s. Policy makers are now more aware of the contribution good corporate governance makes to financial market stability, investment, and economic growth. Companies better understand how good corporate governance contributes to their competitiveness. Investors—especially collective investment institutions and pension funds acting in a fiduciary capacity—realize they have a role to play in ensuring good corporate governance practices, thereby supporting the value of their investments. In today's economies, interest in corporate governance goes beyond that of shareholders in the performance of individual companies. As companies play a pivotal role in our economies and we rely increasingly on private sector institutions to manage personal savings and secure retirement incomes, good corporate governance is important to broad and growing segments of the population.

Corporate Governance Recommendations

Member country compliance with OECD Principles is based on a series of recommendations for good governance. The OECD has no legal authority to enforce these provisions, although member countries agree to incorporate the recommendations into their own corporate governance regulatory policies. The following is a summary of recommendations.[37] Notice how the provisions of the corporate governance framework attempt to strengthen corporate governance mechanisms and the role of investors in the corporate governance process. This is not surprising given the OECD's emphasis on protecting the public interest against possible inappropriate behavior by top management that negatively affects shareholder interests.

1. Promote transparent and efficient markets, be consistent with the rule of law, and clearly articulate the division of responsibilities among different supervisory, regulatory, and enforcement authorities.
2. Protect and facilitate the exercise of shareholders' rights.
3. Ensure the equitable treatment of all shareholders, including minority and foreign shareholders. All shareholders should have the opportunity to obtain effective redress for violation of their rights.
4. Recognize the rights of stakeholders established by law or through mutual agreements and encourage active cooperation between corporations and stakeholders in creating wealth, jobs, and the sustainability of financially sound enterprises.
5. Ensure that timely and accurate disclosure is made on all material matters regarding the corporation, including the financial situation, performance, ownership, and governance of the company.
6. Ensure the strategic guidance of the company, the effective monitoring of management by the board, and the board's accountability to the company and the shareholders.

Global Code of Ethics

IFAC established the International Ethics Standards Board for Accountants (IESBA) to develop and issue high-quality ethical standards and other pronouncements for professional accountants for use around the world. The result was the issuance of the Code of Ethics for Professional Accountants (IFAC Code) that establishes ethical requirements for professional accountants performing services in the global business arena. A member body of IFAC or a firm from its country may not apply less stringent standards than those stated in the IFAC Code. However, if a member body or firm is prohibited from complying with certain parts of this Code by law or regulation, they should be governed by their country's requirements but comply with all other parts of the Code.

The IFAC Code contains provisions virtually identical to those embodied in the AICPA Code of Professional Conduct. The following is a brief list of similarities:[38]

1. To act in accordance with the public interest.
2. To identify threats to independence (i.e., self-interest threats, advocacy threats, self-review threats, familiarity threats, and intimidation threats) and develop safeguards to mitigate such threats.
3. To be independent in fact, meaning having a state of mind that permits the expression of a conclusion without being affected by influences that compromise professional judgment, allowing an individual to act with integrity, and exercise objectivity and professional skepticism.
4. To maintain the appearance of independence, meaning the avoidance of facts and circumstances that are so significant that a reasonable and informed third party, having knowledge of all relevant information, including safeguards applied, would reasonably conclude a firm's or a member of the assurance team's integrity, objectivity, or professional skepticism had been compromised.
5. To adhere to standards related to integrity, objectivity, professional competence and due care, confidentiality, and professional behavior.

Ethical Conflict Resolution

In the United States, conflicts between principles of behavior are resolved by placing the public interest (i.e., interests of investors and creditors) ahead of all other interests including those of the accountant, one's supervisor and employer, and the client. Conflicts with respect to the application of GAAP are addressed in Interpretation 102-4 (see Exhibit 2 in Chapter 1) of the AICPA Code and the IMA's Statement of Ethical Professional Practice (Exhibit 5 in Chapter 1). Both codes obligate the accountant to go through the chain of command all the way up to the audit committee to resolve accounting differences. The IFAC Code incorporates an ethical reasoning dimension by adopting an ethics-based approach similar to the decision-making model described in Chapter 2. It also more directly addresses the steps a professional accountant should consider if the conflict cannot be resolved.

The IFAC Code provides the following:

In evaluating compliance with the fundamental principles, a professional accountant may be required to resolve a conflict in the application of these principles. When initiating either a formal or informal conflict resolution process, a professional accountant may consider the following, either individually or together with others, as part of the resolution process:

(a) Relevant facts;
(b) Ethical issues involved;
(c) Fundamental principles related to the matter in question;
(d) Established internal procedures; and
(e) Alternative courses of action.

Having considered these issues, a professional accountant should determine the appropriate course of action that is consistent with the fundamental principles identified. The professional accountant should *also weigh the consequences of each possible course of action.* If the matter remains unresolved, the professional accountant should consult with other appropriate persons within the firm or employing organization for help in obtaining resolution. Where a matter involves a conflict with or within an organization, a professional accountant should also consider consulting with those charged with governance of the organization, such as the board of directors or the audit committee. It may be in the best interests of the professional accountant to document the substance of the issue and details of any discussions held or decisions taken, concerning that issue. If a significant conflict cannot be resolved, a professional accountant may wish to obtain professional advice from the relevant professional body or legal advisors, and thereby obtain guidance on ethical issues without breaching confidentiality. For example, a professional accountant may have encountered a fraud, the reporting of which could breach the professional accountant's responsibility to respect confidentiality. The professional accountant should consider obtaining legal advice to determine whether there is a requirement to report. If, after exhausting all relevant possibilities, the ethical conflict remains unresolved, a professional accountant should, where possible, refuse to remain associated with the matter creating the conflict. The professional accountant may determine that, in the circumstances, it is appropriate to withdraw from the engagement team or specific assignment, or to resign altogether from the engagement, the firm, or the employing organization.[39]

International Auditing Standards

IFAC established the International Auditing and Assurances Board (IAASB) to issue pronouncements that govern audit, review, and other assurance and related services engagements that are conducted in accordance with International Standards on Auditing (ISAs). ISAs do not override the local laws or regulations that govern the audit of historical financial statements or assurance engagements performed in accordance with a particular country's national standards. In the event that local laws or regulations differ from, or conflict with, IAASB's standards on a particular subject, an engagement conducted in accordance with local laws or regulations will not automatically comply with the IAASB's standards. In this case, the professional accountant should not represent compliance with the IAASB's standards unless the professional accountant has complied fully with all of those relevant to the engagement.

In conducting an audit in accordance with ISAs, the auditor should be aware of and consider International Auditing Practice Statements (IAPSs) applicable to the audit engagement. IAPSs provide interpretive guidance and practical assistance to auditors in implementing ISAs. An auditor who does not apply the guidance included in a relevant IAPS needs to be prepared to explain how the basic principles and essential procedures in the Standard addressed by the IAPS have been complied with. The auditor may also conduct the audit in accordance with both ISAs and auditing standards of a specific jurisdiction or country.

International auditing and assurance standards are quite similar to U.S. GAAS. The following is a summary of important similarities:

1. The auditor should plan and perform an audit with an attitude of *professional skepticism* recognizing that circumstances may exist that cause the financial statements to be materially misstated. An attitude of professional skepticism means the auditor makes a critical assessment, with a questioning mind, of the validity of audit evidence obtained and is alert to audit evidence that contradicts or brings into question the reliability of documents and responses to inquiries and other information obtained from management and those charged with governance. For example, representations from management are not a substitute for obtaining sufficient appropriate audit evidence to be able to draw reasonable conclusions on which to base the auditor's opinion.

2. An auditor conducting an audit in accordance with ISAs obtains *reasonable assurance* that the financial statements taken as a whole are free from material misstatement, whether due to fraud or error. Reasonable assurance is a concept relating to the accumulation of the audit evidence necessary for the auditor to conclude that there are no material misstatements in the financial statements taken as a whole. Reasonable assurance relates to the whole audit process.

3. The concept of reasonable assurance acknowledges that there is a risk the audit opinion is inappropriate. The risk that the auditor expresses an inappropriate audit opinion when the financial statements are materially misstated is known as "audit risk."

4. In planning and performing the audit to reduce audit risk to an acceptably low level, the auditor should consider the risks of material misstatements in the financial statements due to fraud. The primary responsibility for the prevention and detection of fraud rests both with those charged with governance of the entity and with management. The respective responsibilities of those charged with governance and of management may vary by entity and from country to country. In some entities, the governance structure may be more informal as those charged with governance may be the same individuals as management of the entity.

5. The ISAs call for the use of the *COSO Integrated Framework* discussed in Chapter 5 to help assess fraud risks to include obtaining an understanding of the control environment.

6. When considering materiality, the practitioner considers how the adopted presentation might influence the decisions of the intended users. Materiality is considered in the context of quantitative and qualitative factors, such as relative magnitude, the nature and extent of the effect of these factors on the evaluation or measurement of the subject matter, and the interests of the intended users. The *assessment of materiality* and the relative importance of quantitative and qualitative factors in a particular engagement are matters for the practitioner's judgment.

Audit Opinion

The auditor obtains and evaluates audit evidence to obtain reasonable assurance about whether the financial statements give a true and fair view or are presented fairly, in all material respects, in accordance with the applicable financial reporting framework (GAAP in the United States; IFRS internationally). The auditor's report should state that the audit was conducted in accordance with ISAs. The auditor's report should also explain that those standards require that the auditor comply with ethical requirements. Exhibit 8.3 illustrates the wording of an audit report based on the application of ISAs.

EXHIBIT 8.3
Independent Auditor's Report

[Appropriate Addressee]
Report on the Financial Statements

We have audited the accompanying financial statements of ABC Company, which comprise the balance sheet at December 31, 20X1, and the income statement, statement of changes in equity and cash flow statement for the year then ended, and a summary of significant accounting policies and other explanatory notes. Management is responsible for the preparation and fair presentation of these financial statements in accordance with International Financial Reporting Standards. This responsibility includes designing, implementing, and maintaining internal control relevant to the preparation and fair presentation of financial statements that are free from material misstatement, whether due to fraud or error; selecting and applying appropriate accounting policies; and making accounting estimates that are reasonable in the circumstances. Our responsibility is to express an opinion on these financial statements based on our audit. We conducted our audit in accordance with International Standards on Auditing. Those standards require that we comply with ethical requirements and plan and perform the audit to obtain reasonable assurance whether the financial statements are free from material misstatement.

An audit involves performing procedures to obtain audit evidence about the amounts and disclosures in the financial statements. The procedures selected depend on the auditor's judgment, including the assessment of the risks of material misstatement of the financial statements, whether due to fraud or error. In making those risk assessments, the auditor considers internal control relevant to the entity's preparation and fair presentation of the financial statements in order to design audit procedures that are appropriate in the circumstances, but not for the purpose of expressing an opinion on the effectiveness of the entity's internal control. An audit also includes evaluating the appropriateness of accounting policies used and the reasonableness of accounting estimates made by management, as well as evaluating the overall presentation of the financial statements. We believe that the audit evidence we have obtained is sufficient and appropriate to provide a basis for our audit opinion.

In our opinion, the financial statements give a true and fair view of (or "present fairly, in all material respects,") the financial position of ABC Company as of December 31, 20X1, and of its financial performance and its cash flows for the year then ended in accordance with International Financial Reporting Standards.

Report on Other Legal and Regulatory Requirements
[Form and content of this section of the auditor's report will vary depending on the nature of the auditor's other reporting responsibilities.]

[Auditor's signature]
[Date of the auditor's report]
[Auditor's address]

Differences between an International Audit Report and a U.S. Audit Report

Although there are more similarities in the international audit report language than differences, some differences with U.S. requirements under GAAS do exist. These include:

1. The international report (the report) refers to IFRS.
2. The report elaborates on management's responsibilities in the introductory paragraph with respect to internal controls and acknowledgment that the financial statements should be free from material misstatement, whether due to fraud or error.
3. The report states in the scope paragraph that the selection of audit procedures requires the exercise of professional judgment including the assessment of the risks of material misstatement of the financial statements, *whether due to fraud or error.*
4. The opinion paragraph allows for the overall opinion to be couched in the terms "present fairly" or a "true and fair view" in accordance with IFRS.
5. A separate paragraph is provided for those entities required by law to report on compliance with legal and regulatory requirements.

True and Fair View versus Present Fairly

The IFAC Code seems to equate the term "true and fair view" with "present fairly." This may have been done for political reasons to placate the United States. However, there are important differences between these terms because the words convey a different meaning and level of assurance to investors and creditors. The concept of a true and fair view comes from UK law and it has influenced the IASB in its standard setting. In the EU, "true and fair view" is used as part of the Fourth Directive that guides audit reporting in the community so that it applies to all members of the EU.

A true and fair view is the governing criterion by which financial statements are to be judged. It is therefore possible, although unusual, to override the requirements of a standard in order to give a true and fair view. This is known as the true and fair view override. In the United States, "present fairly" is used in conjunction with the phrase "in conformity with generally accepted accounting principles." The governing criterion in the United States is, therefore, conformity with GAAP. This distinction may be blurred as we move toward internationalization and the primacy of IFRS is achieved.[40]

2009 European Fraud Survey

In 2006, Ernst & Young's Fraud Investigation & Dispute Services practice initiated a series of surveys of a broad range of employees at European companies that measure the perception of fraud risks and how management and board members are responding to the challenges. The survey was motivated in part by the global financial crisis and the rather negative results may be tainted by those experiences. The 2009 European fraud survey reflects the views of over 2,200 respondents in 22 countries.[41] The major findings of the survey are as follows:

- There is a disappointing tolerance of unethical behavior including making cash payments to win business and misstating financial performance in an effort to mask disappointing results.
- Respondents question the integrity of their own senior management and board members with many believing them to be untrustworthy. They call for directors to be held accountable for lapses that allow corporate fraud to take place.
- As a result of this mistrust, employees expect regulators to do more to protect them from wayward management and to ensure their business leaders are compelled to intensify their efforts to protect companies from fraud.

The survey reports the opinions of respondents who *did not* believe that their company was at increased risk of fraud. The following reasons were given: (1) processes/procedures (i.e., internal controls) that are adequate (57 percent); (2) risk areas (i.e., risk assessment) are well covered (45 percent); (3) strong culture of integrity and honesty (i.e., tone at the top) (40 percent); and (4) trust in management (39 percent). These are all areas of importance to U.S. companies as well, as discussed throughout the text. Of particular note is the emphasis on ethical behavior as reflected in items 3 and 4.

Another finding reports the procedures that companies rely on to counter fraud. These include (1) internal auditing (68 percent); (2) external auditing (54 percent); (3) stronger controls/scrutiny of expenditure (51 percent); (4) code of conduct (49 percent); (5) HR/legal counsel (38 percent); (6) legal due diligence (28 percent); (7) antifraud training (24 percent); (8) person with a position of confidentiality (24 percent); (9) whistleblowing hotline (21 percent); and (10) Web-based hotline (12 percent). One surprising result is the degree of reliance on external auditing to uncover fraud. Recall Exhibit 3.1 of Chapter 3 that reported the initial detection of fraud by the Association of Certified Fraud Examiners (ACFE). Only 16.3 percent of the respondents found that the external audit helped uncover fraud as compared to the 54 percent finding in the European fraud survey. The ACFE results also indicate that 51.7 percent of the frauds were discovered by a "tip," a much larger result than the 33 percent hotline reporting in the European fraud survey. Moreover, only 12.4 percent of those surveyed by ACFE indicated that initial detection was by internal audit compared to the 68 percent in the European fraud survey.

HSBC Holdings PLC

HSBC is one of the world's largest banking and financial services organizations. Headquartered in London, HSBC's international network comprises about 8,000 offices in 88 countries and territories in Europe, the Asia-Pacific region, the Americas, the Middle East and Africa. With listings on the London, Hong Kong, Paris and Bermuda stock exchanges, shares in HSBC are held by about 220,000 shareholders in 119 countries and territories. The shares are traded on the New York Stock Exchange in the form of American Depository Receipts.[42]

The following summarizes some of the key management, corporate governance, and financial statement information in the material excerpted from the HSBC December 31, 2009, annual report. The complete information appears in Appendix 2. As you read through it, notice how HSBC refers to its compliance with NYSE listing requirements and provisions of SOX. In particular, it references the independence of its board members, internal control review, and the disclosure of any corporate governance practices that differ from those followed in the U.S.

Corporate Governance Report

1. Reference to the Group Management Board that performs many of the management decision making responsibilities of the CEO and other top company officials in the U.S. Reference to executive and non-executive members of the board.

2. Reference to the separation of the roles of the Group Chairman (that is, Chairman of the board of directors in the U.S.) and Group Chief Executive (CEO in the U.S.).

3. Independence of the board of directors achieved by not allowing any one individual or small group to dominate decision making.

4. Group audit committee meets regularly with senior financial, credit and risk, internal audit, legal and compliance management and the external auditor to consider the company's financial reporting, the scope and nature of audit reviews and the effectiveness of the systems of internal control, compliance and risk management. Reference to NYSE listing requirements with respect to independence of directors and need to meet on a regular basis without management present. Need for a majority of directors to be independent.

5. Notably, reference to the Combined Code of Corporate Governance in the UK and its provision that a director should be independent in character and judgment and whether any relationships exist that may affect, or appear to affect, the independent judgment of directors. This link to judgment and character goes beyond that addressed by directors and in corporate governance compliance statements by U.S. companies.

6. Requirement to disclose whether any significant differences exist between corporate governance practices in HSBC and those required by the NYSE.

7. Reference to the need for companies listed on the NYSE (including HSBC) to adopt a code of ethics for directors, officers, and employees, and to disclose any waivers of code provisions. (Recall that at Enron the code was waived to enable Andy Fastow to serve both as the CFO of Enron and the managing partner of a SPE).

8. Requirement that, in the U.S., the CEO should certify compliance with corporate governance standards. While HSBC as a foreign entity is not required to meet this requirement, the CEO must promptly notify the NYSE in writing after any executive officer becomes aware of any material non-compliance with the NYSE corporate governance standards applicable to HSBC.

9. Director responsibility for internal control and reviewing its effectiveness whereas in the U.S., management is responsible for the internal controls and the audit committee reviews it with the external auditors.

Statement of Directors' Responsibilities

1. Statement distinguishing for shareholders the respective responsibilities of the Directors and the Auditor in relation to the financial statements.

2. Directors are responsible for preparing the annual report in accordance with applicable laws and regulations whereas the management (CEO and CFO) have that responsibility in the U.S.

3. Link between true and fair view and achieving a fair presentation.

4. Preparation of the financial statements in accordance with IFRS and the need to: (a) select suitable accounting policies and then apply them consistently; (b) make judgments and estimates that are reasonable and prudent; and (c) state whether the financial statements have been prepared in accordance with IFRS as adopted by the EU.

Independent Auditor's Report

1. Reference to the preparation of the financial statements using IFRS.

2. Reference to the Companies Act (legislation) in preparing financial statement information.

3. Reference to the directors' responsibility for the preparation of the financial statements and for being satisfied that they give a true and fair view.

4. The opinion with respect to the true and fair view standard and compliance with IFRS; reference to compliance with the Companies Act of 2006.

5. No exceptions to the true and fair view opinion with respect to: adequate accounting records being kept; the company is a going concern; required disclosures about director's remuneration; and compliance with corporate governance provisions.

Consolidated Financial Statements

The differences between the HSBC Report and that of a U.S. company are more of form rather than substance. Two examples follow:

1. Consolidated financial statements are not broken down into specific categories especially on the Balance Sheet where there is no separation between current and noncurrent assets and liabilities.

2. The term "share capital" differs from capital stock that is used in the U.S.

Concluding Thoughts

We end our journey at the same place we started. A strong ethics foundation is essential to act in accordance with the Principles of Professional Conduct in the United States and the Global Code of Ethics. An ability to make ethical, reasoned judgments enables the accounting decision maker to meet professional standards. Remember, it is through the application of ethical reasoning and the use of an ethical decision-making process that we can best analyze the issues and decide on a proper course of action.

The accounting profession owes its existence to the audit function. The public expects accounting professionals to be principled and to stand by their convictions. The public interest demands that a trusting relationship should exist between an auditor and investors and creditors who rely on the accuracy and reliability of financial reports for decision making.

Independence in fact and appearance is the hallmark of ethical standards when conducting an audit. A healthy dose of skepticism enables the accountant to ask the hard questions during the audit to ensure that the financial statements present fairly (a true and fair view). Objectivity and integrity provide the backbone of ethical decision making for external auditors and help to prevent and detect fraud. Internal accountants and auditors have a major role to play in preventing fraud since they are the first line of defense against such practices. It is through the exercise of integrity that accountants and auditors can withstand pressures imposed by one's supervisor or the client to go along with materially misstated financial statements.

On an international level, accountants and auditors must be familiar with IFRS and ISAs. There is no doubt that compliance with these standards will be mandated in the United States in the not-too-distant future. The question of international oversight and regulation is not as troubling as once thought because home-country regulators (e.g., SEC), with the support of IOSCO, have committed to enforcing IFRS standards in their home countries.

One final thought. It is important to commit to being ethical early on and not waver in your beliefs. Have the courage to say no when you know something is wrong. Don't compromise your ethics in the name of going along to get along. To do otherwise invites ethical relativism, inconsistency in behavior, and a trip down the ethical slippery slope.

We leave you the same way we started—with a famous quotation that speaks volumes about ethical behavior. One of the country's founders, Thomas Paine, is best known for this statement: "These are the times that try men's souls." We believe the ethical challenges that exist in today's competitive, global environment have created pressures to cut corners and violate ethical principles as never before. Students must make a long-term commitment to ethical behavior because, as we believe, this is the only way to ensure one's future success and the continuation of the free-market economy. As Paine said: "Character is much easier kept than recovered."

Discussion Questions

1. As you interview for and begin a full-time position in the accounting profession, what level of knowledge of issues related to international accounting (including IFRS) do you believe is expected of you by the accounting profession? Why do you think there is such an expectation?

2. Explain the advantages and disadvantages of establishing one set of accounting standards (IFRS) to be followed by all companies around the world.

3. Some people believe that U.S. companies should be given the choice of using either U.S. GAAP or IFRS instead of mandating IFRS. Do you think this would be a good idea? Why or why not?

4. Explain the difference between a rules-based and principles-based approach to accounting standard setting. Which model do you think helps better present financial position, results of operations, and changes in cash flows? Why?

5. What is meant by the "true and fair view" override? How and when might it be applied?

6. *International Accounting Standard No. 16* provides that property, plant, and equipment can be accounted for under the cost method or the revaluation method. Evaluate each of these methods with respect to their conformity with representational faithfulness.

7. Describe the different kinds of reserves that can be recorded. Can the accounting for reserves lead to a manipulation of earnings?

8. Explain how a "two-tier" structure for the board of directors such as the one in Germany differs from the unitary approach in the United States. Do you think the two-tier system better serves the goal of having strong and effective corporate governance?

9. What is the "comply or explain" principle? How does it relate to conformity with corporate governance principles in the United States and in other countries around the world?

10. What are the differences with respect to how corporate governance is carried out and monitored in the Chinese system versus that in the United States?

11. Read the discussion of the Tata Group Code of Conduct in Appendix 1. How do the provisions in Tata's Code measure up to the ethical and corporate governance standards discussed in the text?

12. What is the purpose of having a Global Code of Ethics? Do you think a Global Code is necessary given that codes of ethics already exist for public companies in virtually all countries?

13. Do you think any meaningful differences exist between the level of responsibility assumed by auditors in the United States and those providing audit services outside the United States? Be sure to address any meaningful differences in responsibility under the U.S. "present fairly" language and the "true and fair view."

14. One of the most controversial requirements of SOX is Section 404—management's assessment of internal controls over financial reporting. The act requires the auditor to review the assessment and issue an independent opinion integrated with the audit on the financial statements. Publicly owned companies in the United States have been following these requirements for several years. As for foreign entities that list their stock on U.S. exchanges, the implementation of Section 404 was initially delayed for accelerated (larger) filers until financial statements issued for the year-ended after December 31, 2007. Do you think foreign companies should be burdened with Section 404 requirements? How might widespread application of Section 404 standards to foreign entities affect stock listings in the United States? Should the SEC be worried about the possible implications of holding foreign entities to the same standards as U.S. companies?

15. IFRS for SMEs has been referred to as "IFRS lite." One of the differences between full IFRS and IFRS for SMEs is that full IFRS allows for judgment in making choices about proper accounting, whereas IFRS for SMEs is much more rigid.

    a. Do you think there should be a separate set of international accounting standards for small and medium-sized entities? Why or why not?

    b. How does your answer relate to accounting standards in the United States? That is, should there be two sets of GAAP standards—one for large (public) and another for smaller (private) companies?

    c. Can you identify one area in the United States where GAAP calls for a different (lesser) treatment of accounting standards for nonpublic companies?

16. Full IFRS and IFRS for SMEs do not permit recognition on the income statement of extraordinary items. What are the rules in the United States for extraordinary items? Evaluate the pros and cons of recognizing them separately on the income statement as opposed to combining them into another category.

17. In February 2010, the U.S. Department of Justice and the UK Serious Fraud Office announced a settlement with Britain's BAE Systems PLC to resolve a decade-long investigation into allegations that BAE had made illegal payments to officials in various countries to secure lucrative contracts. U.S. court documents detailed allegations that BAE used secretive offshore entities and shell companies to conceal where illegal payments were going in 1999 transactions to lease fighter jets to Hungary and the Czech Republic. The U.S. filing also alleged that BAE paid tens of millions of dollars to a Saudi government official and other associates as part of an agreement between the UK and Saudi Arabia to supply military hardware to the Saudis. Under the U.S. plea deal, BAE will pay $400 million to settle one charge of conspiracy to make false statements to the government. The plea agreement demonstrates the Justice Department's ability to impose tight ethical standards for its defense contractors, even those based overseas. It could send a message to other foreign military contractors that are trying to expand in the United

States. The settlement allows BAE to continue bidding for U.S. government contracts. As for the UK investigation, BAE will pay a penalty of £30 million (30 million British pounds, or $47 million) and plead guilty to one charge stemming from payments to a former consultant in Tanzania.

a. Why is it important for the U.S. government to be able to bring charges of illegal payments to foreign government officials and intermediaries against non-U.S. companies that do business in the United States?

b. The UK Serious Fraud Office is an arm of the UK government, accountable to the UK attorney-general. Established by the Criminal Justice Act 1987, the Serious Fraud Office is responsible for the investigation and prosecution of suspected cases of serious or complex fraud where £1 million ($1.57 million) or more are involved or the fraud covers more than one national jurisdiction. According to its Web site, fraud "is a type of criminal activity, defined as: abuse of position, or false representation, or prejudicing someone's rights for personal gain." Compare this definition to the definition of fraud in the United States. Do you think there are any meaningful differences?

18. Recent examples of foreign companies paying bribes to gain international business include:

a. Alstom, the French engineering giant, that has been investigated by French and Swiss authorities. They are looking into accusations that the company paid hundreds of millions of dollars in bribes to gain contracts in Asia and South America from 1995 to 2003.

b. The investigation of two former executives of Siemens who were convicted of bribery in connection with an Italian gas-turbine contract.

Some countries have their own antibribery laws such as the Foreign Corrupt Practices Act in the United States. Other countries including the UK have no such standards. On an international level, 37 of the developed countries have signed the 1997 antibribery convention of the OECD. Still, countries such as China and Russia are not members and have been reluctant to embrace antibribery regulations. Do you think there should be only one global standard to control bribery of foreign government officials and key facilitators? Why or why not?

19. The 2009 European fraud survey cautions against the manipulation of asset impairment write-downs due to the subjective factors used and judgment needed to draw conclusions about the proper amount of write-downs. The survey noted particularly high levels of asset write-downs in the banking and investment management sectors.

a. Why do you think the banking and investment management sectors may have been especially affected by write-downs during the time period leading up to the 2009 survey?

b. Explain how write-downs might affect income in the year of the write-down and subsequent years.

Endnotes

1. SEC, Study Pursuant to Section 108(d) of the Sarbanes-Oxley Act of 2002 on the Adoption by the United States Financial Reporting System of a Principles-Based Accounting System, 2003, submitted to the Committee on Banking, Housing, and Urban Affairs of the United States Senate and Committee on Financial Services of the United States House of Representatives, www.sec.gov/news/studies/principlesbasedstand.htm#executive.

2. http://sec.gov/rules/other/2010/33-9109.pdf.

3. The Group of Twenty Finance Ministers and Central Bank Governors (known as the G-20) is a group of finance ministers and central bank governors from 20 economies: 19 countries, plus the European Union. Collectively, the G-20 economies comprise 85 percent of global gross national product, 80 percent of world trade (including EU intratrade), and two-thirds of the world population. The G-20 is a forum for cooperation and consultation on matters pertaining to the international financial system. It studies, reviews, and promotes discussion among key industrial and emerging market countries of policy issues pertaining to the promotion of international financial stability, and seeks to address issues that go beyond the responsibilities of any one organization.

4. International Accounting Standards Board (IASB), International Accounting Standard (IAS) No. 23, *Borrowing Costs,* 2007, www.iasb.org.

5. IOSCO is an international organization that brings together the worldwide association of national securities regulatory commissions, such as the SEC in the United States and the Financial Services Authority in the United Kingdom, and about 100 other similar bodies.

6. International Organization of Securities Commissions (IOSCO), Memorandum of Understanding (MOU), www.iosco.org.

7. European Union Commission, 2008, Commission Regulation (EC) No. 1289/2008, http://ec.europea.eu.

8. IASB, Memorandum of Understanding—FASB and IASB: "The Norwalk Agreement," 2002, www.iasb.org.

9. IASB, A Road map for Convergence between IFRS and U.S. GAAP—2006–2008: Memorandum of Understanding between FASB and the IASB, 2006, www.iasb.org.

10. Marty T. Stuebs Jr. and C. William Thomas, "Improved Judgment in Financial Accounting: A Principled Approach," *The CPA Journal* (January 2009), pp. 32–35.

11. Katherine Schipper, "Principles-Based Accounting Standards" (commentary), *Accounting Horizons* 17 (2003), pp. 61–72.

12. G. J. Benston, M. Bromwich, and A. Wagenhofer, "Principles- versus Rules-Based Accounting Standards: The FASB's Standards Setting Strategy," *Abacus* 42, no. 2 (2006), pp. 165–188.

13. Barry J. Epstein and Eva J. Jermakowicz, *Interpretation and Application of International Financial Reporting Standards (IFRS), IAS 1: Presentation of Financial Statements* (New York: Wiley, 2009).

14. The IASB *Framework* is similar to FASB's concepts statements with respect to the objectives of financial reporting, qualitative characteristics of useful information, and the display in financial statements. As discussed, one change from the conceptual framework in the United States is to include the "faithful representation of the economic phenomena" as part of the qualitative characteristics of useful information.

15. Epstein and Jermakowicz, *IAS 8: Accounting Policies, Changes in Accounting Estimates and Errors* (New York: Wiley, 2009).

16. R. D. Mergenthaler, *Principles-Based versus Rules-Based Accounting Standards and Extreme Cases of Earnings Management,* a dissertation prepared for the University of Washington, 2008.

17. SEC, Study pursuant to Section 108(d) of the Sarbanes-Oxley Act of 2002.

18. Thomas Jeanjean and Herve H. Stolowy, "Do Accounting Standards Matter? An Exploratory Analysis of Earnings Management before and after IFRS Adoption," *Journal of Accounting and Public Policy* 27, no. 6 (2008), pp. 480–494.

19. Cynthia Bolt-Lee and L. Murphy Smith, "Highlights of IFRS Research," *Journal of Accountancy,* November 2009.

20. Financial Accounting Standards Board, *Conceptual Framework for Financial Reporting: The Objective of Financial Reporting and Qualitative Characteristics and Constraints of Decision-Useful Financial Reporting Information* (Norwalk, CT: FASB, 2008).

21. Financial Accounting Standards Board, *Original Pronouncements as Amended and Current Text—Volume I* (Norwalk, CT: FASB, 2008).

22. D. Alexander and E. Jermakowicz, "A True and Fair View of the Principles/Rules Debate," *Abacus* 42, no. 2 (2006), pp. 132–164.

23. International Accounting Standards Board, *IAS No. 17,* Accounting for Leases, 2007, www.iasb.org.

24. International Accounting Standards Board, *IAS No. 16,* Accounting for Property, Plant and Equipment, 2007, www.iasb.org.

25. Benston et al.

26. Christopher Nobes and Robert Parker, *Comparative International Accounting,* 10th ed. (London, England: Pearson Education Limited, 2008).

27. International Accounting Standards Board, *IAS No. 37,* Contingent Liabilities and Contingent Assets, 2007, www.iasb.org.

28. Nobes and Parker, pp. 352–353.

29. International Accounting Standards Board, *IFRS for Small and Medium-Sized Businesses,* July 2009, www.iasb.org.

30. International Accounting Standards Board, *IFRS No. 1,* First-Time Adoption of International Financial Reporting Standards, 2007, www.iasb.org.

31. German Corporate Governance Code 2009, www.corporate-governance-code.de/eng/kodex/index.html.

32. Centre for Financial Market Integrity 2007, China Corporate Governance Survey, www.cfapubs.org/doi/abs/10.2469/ccb.v2007.n3.4563.

33. C. A. Schipani and J. H. Liu, "Corporate Governance in China: Then and Now," *Columbia Business Law Review* 2002 (2002), pp. 1–69.

34. China Securities Regulatory Commission (CSRC), State Economic and Trade Commission, Code of Corporate Governance for Listed Companies in China, January 7, 2001, www.csrc.gov.cn/en/jip.

35. *Report of the Kumar Mangalam Birla Committee on Corporate Governance,* 2000, www.sebi.gov.in/commreport/corpgov.html.

36. N. Rajagopalan and Y. Zhang, "Corporate Governance Reforms in China and India: Challenges and Opportunities," *Business Horizons* 21 (2008), pp. 55–64.

37. Organization for Economic Cooperation and Development, *OECD Principles of Corporate Governance,* 2004, www.oecd.org/dataoecd/32/18/31557724.pdf.

38. International Federation of Accountants, International Ethics Standards Board for Accountants, *Code of Ethics for Professional Accountants,* July 2009, http://www.ifac.org/ethics/Pronouncements.php.

39. International Federation of Accountants, International Ethics Standards Board for Accountants, *Code of Ethics for Professional Accountants.*

40. Roger Hussey and Audry Ong, *International Financial Reporting Standards: Desk Reference* (New York: Wiley, 2006).

41. European Fraud Survey 2009, Ernst & Young, http://www.ey.com/Publication/vwLUAssets/European_fraud_survey_2009_-_Is_integrity_a_casualty_of_the_downturn/$FILE/Ernst%20&%20Young%20European%20fraud%20survey%202009.pdf

42. An American Depositary Receipt (ADR) represents ownership in the shares of a non-U.S. company that trades in U.S. financial markets. The stock of many non-US companies trade on US stock exchanges through the use of ADRs. ADRs enable U.S. investors to buy shares in foreign companies without the hazards or inconveniences of cross-border & cross-currency transactions because the underlying security is held by a U.S. financial institution overseas. ADRs carry prices in US dollars, pay dividends in US dollars, and can be traded like the shares of US-based companies.

Appendix 1

Tata Group Code of Ethics

Effective October 31, 2008

National Interest

The Tata group is committed to benefit the economic development of the countries in which it operates. No Tata company shall undertake any project or activity to the detriment of the wider interests of the communities in which it operates.

A Tata company's management practices and business conduct shall benefit the country, localities and communities in which it operates, to the extent possible and affordable, and shall be in accordance with the laws of the land.

A Tata company, in the course of its business activities, shall respect the culture, customs and traditions of each country and region in which it operates. It shall conform to trade procedures, including licensing, documentation and other necessary formalities, as applicable.

Financial Reporting and Records

A Tata company shall prepare and maintain its accounts fairly and accurately and in accordance with the accounting and financial reporting standards which represent the generally accepted guidelines, principles, standards, laws and regulations of the country in which the company conducts its business affairs.

Internal accounting and audit procedures shall reflect, fairly and accurately, all of the company's business transactions and disposition of assets, and shall have internal controls to provide assurance to the company's board and shareholders that the transactions are accurate and legitimate. All required information shall be accessible to company auditors and other authorised parties and government agencies. There shall be no willful omissions of any company transactions from the books and records, no advance-income recognition and no hidden bank account and funds.

Any willful, material misrepresentation of and/or misinformation on the financial accounts and reports shall be regarded as a violation of the Code, apart from inviting appropriate civil or criminal action under the relevant laws. No employee shall make, authorise, abet or collude in an improper payment, unlawful commission or bribing.

Gifts and Donations

A Tata company and its employees shall neither receive nor offer or make, directly or indirectly, any illegal payments, remuneration, gifts, donations or comparable benefits that are intended, or perceived, to obtain uncompetitive favours for the conduct of its business. The company shall cooperate with governmental authorities in efforts to eliminate all forms of bribery, fraud and corruption.

However, a Tata company and its employees may, with full disclosure, accept and offer nominal gifts, provided such gifts are customarily given and/or are of a commemorative nature. Each company shall have a policy to clarify its rules and regulations on gifts and entertainment, to be used for the guidance of its employees.

Government Agencies

A Tata company and its employees shall not, unless mandated under applicable laws, offer or give any company funds or property as donation to any government agency or its representative, directly or through intermediaries, in order to obtain any favourable performance of official duties. A Tata company shall comply with government procurement regulations and shall be transparent in all its dealings with government agencies.

Corporate Citizenship

A Tata company shall be committed to good corporate citizenship, not only in the compliance of all relevant laws and regulations but also by actively assisting in the improvement of quality of life of the people in the communities in which it operates. The company shall encourage volunteering by its employees and collaboration with community groups.

Tata companies are also encouraged to develop systematic processes and conduct management reviews, as stated in the Tata 'corporate sustainability protocol', from time to time so as to set strategic direction for social development activity. The company shall not treat these activities as optional, but should strive to incorporate them as an integral part of its business plan.

Public Representation of the Company and the Group

The Tata group honours the information requirements of the public and its stakeholders. In all its public appearances, with respect to disclosing company and business information to public constituencies such as the media, the financial community, employees, shareholders, agents, franchisees, dealers, distributors and importers, a Tata company or the Tata group shall be represented only by specifically authorised directors and employees. It shall be the sole responsibility of these authorised representatives to disclose information about the company or the group.

Third Party Representation

Parties which have business dealings with the Tata group but are not members of the group, such as consultants, agents, sales representatives, distributors, channel partners, contractors and suppliers, shall not be authorised to represent a Tata company without the written permission of the Tata company, and/or if their business conduct and ethics are known to be inconsistent with the Code.

Third parties and their employees are expected to abide by the Code in their interaction with, and on behalf of, a Tata company. Tata companies are encouraged to sign a non-disclosure agreement with third parties to support confidentiality of information.

Shareholders

A Tata company shall be committed to enhancing shareholder value and complying with all regulations and laws that govern shareholder rights. The board of directors of a Tata company shall duly and fairly inform its shareholders about all relevant aspects of the company's business, and disclose such information in accordance with relevant regulations and agreements.

Ethical Conduct

Every employee of a Tata company, including full-time directors and the chief executive, shall exhibit culturally appropriate deportment in the countries they operate in, and deal on behalf of the company with professionalism, honesty and integrity, while conforming to high moral and ethical standards. Such conduct shall be fair and transparent and be perceived to be so by third parties.

Every employee of a Tata company shall preserve the human rights of every individual and the community, and shall strive to honour commitments.

Every employee shall be responsible for the implementation of and compliance with the Code in his/her environment. Failure to adhere to the Code could attract severe consequences, including termination of employment.

Regulatory Compliance

Employees of a Tata company, in their business conduct, shall comply with all applicable laws and regulations, in letter and spirit, in all the territories in which they operate. If the ethical and professional standards of applicable laws and regulations are below that of the Code, then the standards of the Code shall prevail.

Directors of a Tata company shall comply with applicable laws and regulations of all the relevant regulatory and other authorities. As good governance practice they shall safeguard the confidentiality of all information received by them by virtue of their position.

Conflict of Interest

An employee or director of a Tata company shall always act in the interest of the company, and ensure that any business or personal association which he/she may have does not involve a conflict of interest with the operations of the company and his/her role therein. An employee, including the executive director (other than independent director) of a Tata company, shall not accept a position of responsibility in any other non-Tata company or not-for-profit organisation without specific sanction.

The above shall not apply to (whether for remuneration or otherwise):

a. Nominations to the boards of Tata companies, joint ventures or associate companies.

b. Memberships/positions of responsibility in educational/ professional bodies, wherein such association will benefit the employee/Tata company.

c. Nominations/memberships in government committees/ bodies or organisations.

d. Exceptional circumstances, as determined by the competent authority.

Competent authority, in the case of all employees, shall be the chief executive, who in turn shall report such exceptional cases to the board of directors on a quarterly basis. In case of the chief executive and executive directors, the Group Corporate Centre shall be the competent authority.

An employee or a director of a Tata company shall not engage in any business, relationship or activity which might conflict with the interest of his/her company or the Tata group. A conflict of interest, actual or potential, may arise where, directly or indirectly . . .

a. An employee of a Tata company engages in a business, relationship or activity with anyone who is party to a transaction with his/her company.

b. An employee is in a position to derive an improper benefit, personally or to any of his/her relatives, by making or influencing decisions relating to any transaction.

c. An independent judgement of the company's or group's best interest cannot be exercised.

The main areas of such actual or potential conflicts of interest shall include the following:

a. An employee or a full-time director of a Tata company conducting business on behalf of his/her company or being in a position to influence a decision with regard to his/her company's business with a supplier or customer where his/her relative is a principal officer or representative, resulting in a benefit to him/her or his/her relative.

b. Award of benefits such as increase in salary or other remuneration, posting, promotion or recruitment of a relative of an employee of a Tata company, where such an individual is in a position to influence decisions with regard to such benefits.

c. The interest of the company or the group can be compromised or defeated.

Notwithstanding such or any other instance of conflict of interest that exist due to historical reasons, adequate and full disclosure by interested employees shall be made to the company's management. It is also incumbent upon every employee to make a full disclosure of any interest which the employee or the employee's immediate family, including parents, spouse and children, may have in a family business or a company or firm that is a competitor, supplier, customer or distributor of or has other business dealings with his/her company.

Upon a decision being taken in the matter, the employee concerned shall be required to take necessary action, as advised, to resolve/avoid the conflict.

If an employee fails to make the required disclosure and the management of its own accord becomes aware of an instance of conflict of interest that ought to have been disclosed by the employee, the management shall take a serious view of the matter and consider suitable disciplinary action against the employee.

Securities Transactions and Confidential Information

An employee of a Tata company and his/her immediate family shall not derive any benefit or counsel, or assist others to derive any benefit, from access to and possession of information about the company or group or its clients or suppliers that is not in the public domain and, thus, constitutes unpublished, price-sensitive insider information.

An employee of a Tata company shall not use or proliferate information that is not available to the investing public, and which therefore constitutes insider information, for making or giving advice on investment decisions about the securities of the respective Tata company, group, client or supplier on which such insider information has been obtained.

Such insider information might include (without limitation) the following:

- Acquisition and divestiture of businesses or business units.
- Financial information such as profits, earnings and dividends.
- Announcement of new product introductions or developments.
- Asset revaluations.
- Investment decisions/plans.
- Restructuring plans.
- Major supply and delivery agreements.
- Raising of finances.

An employee of a Tata company shall also respect and observe the confidentiality of information pertaining to other companies, their patents, intellectual property rights, trademarks and inventions; and strictly observe a practice of non-disclosure.

Protecting Company Assets

The assets of a Tata company shall not be misused; they shall be employed primarily and judiciously for the purpose of conducting the business for which they are duly authorised. These include tangible assets such as equipment and machinery, systems, facilities, materials and resources, as well as intangible assets such as information technology and systems, proprietary information, intellectual property, and relationships with customers and suppliers.

Integrity of Data Furnished

Every employee of a Tata company shall ensure, at all times, the integrity of data or information furnished by him/her to the company. He/she shall be entirely responsible in ensuring that the confidentiality of all data is retained and in no circumstance transferred to any outside person/party in the course of normal operations without express guidelines from or, the approval of the management.

Reporting Concerns

Every employee of a Tata company shall promptly report to the management, and/or third-party ethics helpline, when she/he becomes aware of any actual or possible violation of the Code or an event of misconduct, act of misdemeanour or act not in the company's interest. Such reporting shall be made available to suppliers and partners, too.

Any Tata employee can choose to make a protected disclosure under the whistleblower policy of the company, providing for reporting to the chairperson of the audit committee or the board of directors or specified authority. Such a protected disclosure shall be forwarded, when there is reasonable evidence to conclude that a violation is possible or has taken place, with a covering letter, which shall bear the identity of the whistleblower.

The company shall ensure protection to the whistleblower and any attempts to intimidate him/her would be treated as a violation of the Code.

Appendix 2[1]

HSBC Holdings PLC: *Corporate Governance Report As of December 31, 2009*

Board of Directors

The Board

The objective of the management structures within HSBC, headed by the Board of Directors of HSBC Holdings and led by the Group Chairman, is to deliver sustainable value to shareholders. Implementation of the strategy set by the Board is delegated to the Group Management Board under the leadership of the Group Chief Executive. The developing framework for corporate governance best practice and regulation in the financial services industry is actively considered by the Board. The draft recommendations and HSBC's response to the consultation on a *Review of Corporate Governance in UK Banks and other Financial Industry Entities* led by Sir David Walker ('the Walker Review') were discussed by the Board in September 2009. Following publication of the final recommendations in November 2009, the Board agreed to actions to bring HSBC's practices into line with the review's recommendations. The principal changes were the establishment of a separate Board Risk Committee with effect from 26 February 2010 and broadening of the terms of reference of the Remuneration Committee.

HSBC Holdings has a unitary Board of Directors. The authority of each Director is exercised in Board meetings where the Board acts collectively as a unit. At 1 March 2010, the Board comprises the Group Chairman, Group Chief Executive, four other executive Directors and 15 non-executive Directors. The Group Chairman, Group Chief Executive and four other executive Directors are employees who carry out executive functions in HSBC in addition to their duties as Directors. Non-executive Directors are not HSBC employees and do not participate in the daily business management of HSBC. Non-executive Directors bring an external perspective, constructively challenge and help develop proposals on strategy, scrutinise the performance of management in meeting agreed goals and objectives and monitor the reporting of performance. The nonexecutive Directors have a wealth of experience across a number of industries and business sectors, including the leadership of large, complex multinational enterprises.

The Board is responsible for managing the business of HSBC Holdings and, in doing so, may exercise all of the

---

[1]Excerpted from: Morningstar Document Research, *Form 20-F, HSBC Holdings PLC — HBC*, Filed: March 15, 2010 (period: December 31, 2009).

---

powers of HSBC Holdings, subject to any relevant laws and regulations and to the Articles of Association. In particular, the Board may exercise all the powers of the Company to borrow money and to mortgage or charge all or any part of the undertaking, property or assets (present or future) of HSBC Holdings and may also exercise any of the powers conferred on it by the Companies Act 2006 and/or by shareholders. The Board is able to delegate and confer on certain Directors holding executive office any of its powers, authorities and discretions (including the power to sub-delegate) for such time and on such terms as it thinks fit. The Board may also, by power of attorney or otherwise, appoint any person or persons to be the agent of HSBC Holdings and may delegate to any such person or persons any of its powers, authorities and discretions (including the power to sub-delegate) for such time and on such terms as it thinks fit. HSBC Holdings was registered in Hong Kong under part IX of the Companies Ordinance on 17 January 1991.

The Board delegates the management and day-to-day running of HSBC to the Group Management Board but retains to itself approval of certain matters including operating plans, risk appetite and performance targets, procedures for monitoring and control of operations, the authority or the delegation of authority to approve credit, market risk limits, acquisitions, disposals, investments, capital expenditure or realisation or creation of a new venture, specified senior appointments, and any substantial change in balance sheet management policy.

Group Chairman and Group Chief Executive

The roles of Group Chairman and Group Chief Executive are separated and held by experienced full-time Directors. S K Green became Group Chairman at the conclusion of the Annual General Meeting in 2006 and M F Geoghegan succeeded S K Green as Group Chief Executive. The appointments were made after consulting with representatives of major institutional investors and explaining the succession planning and independent external search process undertaken. S K Green and M F Geoghegan stood for re-election at the 2006 Annual General Meeting and were both re-elected ahead of taking up their new roles from the conclusion of that Meeting.

There is a clear division of responsibilities at the head of the Company between the running of the Board and the executive responsibility for running HSBC's business. The Group Chairman's responsibilities include, in addition to the leadership of the Board, the development of relationships with governments and other significant external parties, corporate reputation and culture and performance management of the Group Chief Executive. Subject to the Group Chief Executive's recommendation, the Group Chairman approves risk, capital allocation and capital investment decisions within authorities delegated by the Board. The Group Chief Executive has responsibility for developing business plans and delivering performance against these.

Board Balance and Independence of Directors

The Board includes a strong presence of both executive and non-executive Directors such that no individual or small group can dominate the Board's decision making. The size of the Board is appropriate given the complexity and geographical spread of HSBC's business and the significant time demands placed on the non-executive Directors, particularly those who serve as members of Board committees. The Board appointed S M Robertson as the senior independent non-executive Director in 2007. The principal role of the senior independent nonexecutive Director is to support the Group Chairman in his role, to lead the non-executive Directors in the oversight of the Group Chairman and to ensure there is a clear division of responsibility between the Group Chairman and Group Chief Executive. The Board considers all of the non-executive Directors to be independent in character and judgement. W K L Fung has served on the Board for more than nine years, however, and in that respect only, does not meet the usual criteria for independence set out in the UK Combined Code on corporate governance. The Board has therefore determined S A Catz, M K T Cheung, J D Coombe, J L Durán, R A Fairhead, J W J Hughes-Hallett, W S H Laidlaw, J R Lomax, Sir Mark Moody-Stuart, G Morgan, N R N Murthy, S M Robertson, J L Thornton and Sir Brian Williamson to be independent. When determining independence the Board considers that calculation of the length of service of a non-executive Director begins on the date of his or her first election by shareholders as a Director of HSBC Holdings. Given the complexity and geographical spread of HSBC's business, the experience of previous service on a subsidiary company Board can be a considerable benefit to HSBC and does not detract from a Director's independence. In reaching its determination of each non-executive Director's independence the Board has concluded that there are no relationships or circumstances which are likely to affect a Director's judgement and any relationships or circumstances which could appear to do so were considered not to be material. In accordance with the Rules Governing the Listing of Securities on the Stock Exchange of Hong Kong Limited, each non-executive Director determined by the Board to be independent has provided an annual confirmation of his or her independence to HSBC Holdings.

Differences in HSBC Holdings/New York Stock Exchange Corporate Governance Practices

Under the NYSE's corporate governance rules for listed companies and the applicable rules of the SEC, as a NYSE-listed foreign private issuer, HSBC Holdings must disclose any significant ways in which its corporate governance practices differ from those followed by US companies subject to NYSE listing standards. HSBC Holdings believes the following to be the significant differences between its corporate governance practices and NYSE corporate governance rules applicable to US companies.

- US companies listed on the NYSE are required to adopt and disclose corporate governance guidelines. The Listing Rules of the FSA require each listed company incorporated in the UK to include in its *Annual Report and Accounts* a statement of how it has applied the principles of the Combined Code and a statement as to whether or not it has complied with the code provisions of the Combined Code throughout the accounting period covered by the Annual Report and Accounts. A company that has not complied with the Code provisions, or complied with only some of the Code provisions or (in the case of provisions whose requirements are of a continuing nature) complied for only part of an accounting period covered by the report, must specify the Code provisions with which it has not complied, and (where relevant) for what part of the reporting period such non-compliance continued, and give reasons for any non-compliance. As stated above, HSBC Holdings complied throughout 2009 with the applicable code provisions of the Combined Code. The Combined Code does not require HSBC Holdings to disclose the full range of corporate governance guidelines with which it complies.

- Under NYSE standards, companies are required to have a nominating/corporate governance committee, composed entirely of independent directors. In addition to identifying individuals qualified to become Board members, this committee must develop and recommend to the Board a set of corporate governance principles. HSBC's Nomination Committee complies with the Combined Code, which requires a majority of members to be independent. All four members of the Committee during 2009 were independent non-executive Directors. On 26 February 2010, S K Green, Group Chairman, became chairman of the Nomination Committee in succession to Sir Brian Williamson, who continues to serve as a member of the Committee. The Committee's terms of reference do not require the Committee to develop and recommend corporate governance principles for HSBC Holdings. As stated above, HSBC Holdings is subject to the corporate governance principles of the Combined Code.

- Pursuant to NYSE listing standards, nonmanagement directors must meet on a regular basis without management present and independent directors must meet separately at least once per year. During 2009, HSBC Holdings' non-executive Directors met four times as a group with the Group Chairman, but without other executive Directors present, and met once as a group without the Group Chairman or other executive Directors present. HSBC Holdings' practice, in this regard, complies with the Combined Code. In accordance with the requirements of the Combined Code, HSBC Holdings discloses in its annual report how the Board, its committees and the Directors are evaluated and provides extensive information regarding Directors' compensation in the Directors' Remuneration Report.

- NYSE listing standards require US companies to adopt a code of business conduct and ethics for directors, officers and employees, and promptly disclose any waivers of the code for directors or executive officers. In December 2009, the Board endorsed three Group Values statements underpinned by the continued use of HSBC's Business Principles, in replacement of the Group Business Principles and Values. In addition to the Group Values statements and Business Principles (and previously the Group Business Principles and Values), which apply to the employees of all HSBC companies, pursuant to the requirements of the Sarbanes-Oxley Act the Board of HSBC Holdings has adopted a Code of Ethics applicable to the Group Chairman and the Group Chief Executive, as the principal executive officers, and to the Chief Financial Officer, Executive Director, Risk and Regulation and Group Chief Accounting Officer. HSBC Holdings' Code of Ethics is available on www.hsbc.com/codeofethics or from the Group Company Secretary at 8 Canada Square, London E14 5HQ. If the Board amends or waives the provisions of the Code of Ethics, details of the amendment or waiver will appear at the same website address. During 2009, HSBC Holdings made no amendments to its Code of Ethics and granted no waivers from its provisions. The references to the standards to be followed by all employees have been updated to reflect the Board's endorsement of Group Values statements underpinned by the continued use of HSBC's Business Principles. The Group Values statements and Business Principles are available on www .hsbc.com/groupvalues.

- Under NYSE listing rules applicable to US companies, independent directors must comprise a majority of the Board of directors. Currently, two thirds of HSBC Holdings' Directors are independent. Under the Combined Code the HSBC Holdings Board determines whether a Director is independent in character and judgement and whether there are relationships or circumstances which are likely to affect, or could appear to affect, the Director's judgement. Under the NYSE rules a director cannot qualify as independent unless the board affirmatively determines that the director has no material relationship with the listed company; in addition the NYSE rules prescribe a list of circumstances in which a director cannot be independent. The Combined Code requires a company's board to assess director independence by affirmatively concluding that the director is independent of management and free from any business or other relationship that could materially interfere with the exercise of independent judgement.

- Lastly, a chief executive officer of a US company listed on the NYSE must annually certify that he or she is not aware of any violation by the company of NYSE corporate governance standards. In accordance with NYSE listing rules applicable to foreign private issuers, HSBC Holdings' Group Chief Executive is not required to provide the NYSE with this annual compliance certification. However, in accordance with rules applicable to both US companies and foreign private issuers, the Group Chief Executive is required promptly to notify the NYSE in writing after any executive officer becomes aware of any material non-compliance with the NYSE corporate governance standards applicable to HSBC Holdings. HSBC Holdings is required to submit annual and interim written affirmations of compliance with applicable NYSE corporate governance standards, similar to the affirmations required of NYSE-listed US companies.

Group Management Board

The Group Management Board meets frequently and operates as a general management committee under the direct authority of the Board. The objective of the Group Management Board is to maintain a reporting and control structure whereby all of the line operations of HSBC are accountable to individual members of the Group Management Board who report to the Group Chief Executive who in turn reports to the Group Chairman. The Board has set objectives and measures for the Group Management Board. These align senior executives' objectives and measures with the strategy and operating plans throughout HSBC.

The Group Management Board exercises the powers, authorities and discretions of the Board in so far as they concern the management and day-to-day running of HSBC Holdings in accordance with such policies and directions as the Board may from time to time determine. The Group Chief Executive reports to each meeting of the Board on the activities of the Group Management Board.

Group Audit Committee

The Group Audit Committee meets regularly with HSBC's senior financial, credit and risk, internal audit, legal and compliance management and the external auditor to consider HSBC Holdings' financial reporting, the nature and scope of audit reviews and the effectiveness of the systems of internal control, compliance and risk management. All members of the Committee are independent non-executive Directors.

The Board has determined that M K T Cheung, J D Coombe, R A Fairhead, J W J Hughes-Hallett and J R Lomax are independent according to SEC criteria. In addition, M K T Cheung, J D Coombe, R A Fairhead, and J W J Hughes-Hallett may be regarded as audit committee financial experts for the purposes of section 407 of the Sarbanes-Oxley Act and have recent and relevant financial experience.

There were eight meetings of the Group Audit Committee during 2009. Following each meeting the Committee reports to the Board on its activities. At each meeting, the Committee has the opportunity to meet with the external auditor, without management present, to facilitate the discussion of any matter relating to its remit and any issue arising from the audit. Similar arrangements have been adopted for the Committee to meet with the internal auditor. The Committee also has the opportunity to meet with the Group Chief Executive at each of its meetings. The terms of reference of the Committee, which are reviewed annually, are available at www.hsbc.com/board committees.

To ensure consistency of scope and approach by subsidiary company audit committees, the Group Audit Committee has established core terms of reference to guide subsidiary audit committees when adopting terms of reference. The Committee's endorsement is required for any proposed changes to subsidiary audit committee terms of reference and for appointments to such committees. Subsidiary audit committees are required to provide bi-annual certificates to the Committee or to an intermediate subsidiary audit committee, relating to the financial statements and internal control procedures of the relevant subsidiary audit committee.

The Group Audit Committee is accountable to the Board and assists it in meeting its responsibilities for maintaining an effective system of internal control and compliance and for meeting its external financial reporting obligations. The Committee undertakes an annual review of the effectiveness of HSBC's system of internal control. The Committee reviews the Company's financial statements before they are considered by the Board and the Interim Management Statements before they are approved by management. Regular reports are received on the risks involved in HSBC's business and how they are controlled and monitored by management which enable the Committee to review the effectiveness of HSBC's risk management framework. Each year the Committee agrees to a schedule of presentations to be made to it by management during the ensuing year on the operation of the risk control framework within the Group. The presentations specifically address risk indicators and performance measures such as indicators of credit, liquidity and interest rate risk.

The reports from the Group General Manager, Group Head of Audit include information on frauds and weakness in internal controls identified through internal audit reports, special investigations or reviews of regulatory reports and external auditors' reports. The Committee monitors and reviews the effectiveness of the internal audit function and receives summaries of periodic peer reviews of HSBC's principal internal audit functions. HSBC has adopted the Principles of the International Institute of Internal Auditors, which include a periodic external quality assurance review of the internal audit function. The first such review, undertaken by Independent Audit Limited, was presented to the Committee in 2008. The Committee receives regular updates on changes in law, regulations and accounting standards and practices and the preparations being made to respond to

those requirements. During 2009, the Committee received regular updates on the review of internal financial reporting controls required by section 404 of the Sarbanes-Oxley Act and the implementation of the Basel II capital adequacy requirements.

The Committee has approved procedures for the receipt, retention and handling of complaints regarding accounting, internal accounting controls and auditing matters. The Committee receives regular reports regarding the nature, investigation and resolution of material complaints and concerns from the Head of Group Compliance. The Committee is directly responsible on behalf of the Board for the selection, oversight and remuneration of the external auditor. The Committee reviews and monitors the external auditor's independence and objectivity and the effectiveness of the audit process, taking into consideration relevant professional and regulatory requirements.

The Committee reviews the strategy and approves the terms for the engagement of the external auditor for the audit of the Annual Report and Accounts. Regular reports on the progress of the audit facilitate the Committee's assessment of the effectiveness of the audit.

The Committee receives reports from the external auditor on its own policies and procedures regarding independence and quality control and oversees the appropriate rotation of audit partners within the external auditor. The external auditor provides the Committee with an annual confirmation of its independence in accordance with industry standards.

On the recommendation of the Committee the Board has approved a policy for the employment by HSBC of former employees of the external auditor or its affiliates. The Committee monitors this policy through the receipt of an annual report of those former employees of the external auditor employed by HSBC and the number of former employees of the external auditor currently employed in senior positions in HSBC. The reports enable the Committee to consider whether there has been any impairment, or appearance of impairment, of the auditor's judgement or independence in respect of the audit.

The Group Audit Committee has established policies for the pre-approval of specific services that may be provided by the principal auditor, KPMG Audit Plc and its affiliates ('KPMG'). These policies are kept under review and amended as necessary to meet the dual objectives of ensuring that HSBC benefits in a cost effective manner from the cumulative knowledge and experience of its auditor, while also ensuring that the auditor maintains the necessary degree of independence and objectivity. These pre-approval policies apply to all services where HSBC Holdings or any of its subsidiaries pays for the service, or is a beneficiary or addressee of the service and has selected or influenced the choice of KPMG. All services entered into with KPMG during 2009 were pre-approved by the Committee or were entered into under pre-approval policies established by the Committee. A quarterly update on non-audit services provided by KPMG is presented to the Committee by management. The pre-approved services relate to regulatory reviews, agreed-upon procedures reports, other types of attestation reports, the provision of advice and other non-audit services allowed under SEC independence rules. They fall into the categories of audit services, audit-related services, tax services and other services.

An analysis of the remuneration paid in respect of audit and non-audit services provided by KPMG for each of the last three years is disclosed in Note 9 on the Financial Statements. The Committee has recommended to the Board that KPMG Audit Plc be reappointed auditor at the forthcoming Annual General Meeting.

Internal Control

The Directors are responsible for internal control in HSBC and for reviewing its effectiveness. Procedures have been designed for safeguarding assets against unauthorised use or disposition; for maintaining proper accounting records; and for the reliability and usefulness of financial information used within the business or for publication. Such procedures are designed to manage rather than eliminate the risk of failure to achieve business objectives and can only provide reasonable and not absolute assurance against material misstatement, errors, losses or fraud. The procedures also enable HSBC Holdings to discharge its obligations under the Handbook of Rules and Guidance issued by the FSA (Financial Services Authority), HSBC's lead regulator. The key procedures that the Directors have established are designed to provide effective internal control within HSBC and accord with the Internal Control: Revised Guidance for Directors on the Combined Code issued by the Financial Reporting Council. Such procedures for the ongoing identification, evaluation and management of the significant risks faced by HSBC have been in place throughout the year and up to 1 March 2010, the date of approval of the *Annual Report and Accounts 2009*. In the case of companies acquired during the year, the internal controls in place are being reviewed against HSBC's benchmark s and integrated into HSBC's processes.

HSBC's key internal control procedures include the following:

- Authority to operate the various subsidiaries and responsibilities for financial performance against plans and for capital expenditure are delegated to their respective chief executive officers within limits set by the Board of Directors of HSBC Holdings. Delegation of authority from the Board to individuals requires those individuals to maintain a clear and appropriate apportionment of significant responsibilities and to oversee the establishment and maintenance of systems of control appropriate to the business. The appointment of executives to the most senior positions within HSBC requires the approval of the Board of Directors of HSBC Holdings.

- Functional, operating, financial reporting and certain management reporting standards are established by Group Management Office management committees for application across the whole of HSBC. These are supplemented by operating standards set by functional and local management as required for the type of business and geographical location of each subsidiary.

- Systems and procedures are in place in HSBC to identify, control and report on the major risks including credit, market, liquidity and operational risk, (including accounting, tax, legal, compliance, information, physical security and fraud risk). Exposure to these risks is monitored by risk management committees, asset and liability committees and executive committees in subsidiaries and, for HSBC as a whole, by the Group Management Board. A Risk Management Meeting of the Group Management Board, chaired by the Chief Financial Officer, Executive Director, Risk and Regulation, is held monthly to address asset, liability and risk management issues. The minutes of this meeting are submitted to the Group Audit Committee and to the Board of Directors. The Global Operational Risk and Control Committee ('GORCC'), which reports to the Risk Management Meeting of the Group Management Board, meets at least quarterly to monitor HSBC's operational risk profile and review the effective implementation of the Group's operational risk management framework. The GORCC receives quarterly reports on the Group's operational risk profile, including top risks, control issues, internal and external operational loss events and key risk indicators. The GORCC communicates the lessons learned from operational events both within HSBC and in the wider industry.

- A Disclosure Committee has been established to review public disclosures made by HSBC Holdings for any material errors, misstatements or omissions. The membership of the Disclosure Committee, which is chaired by the Group Company Secretary, includes the heads of the Finance, Legal, Risk, Compliance, Group Communications, Investor Relations and Internal Audit functions and representatives from the principal regions, customer groups and global businesses. The integrity of disclosures is underpinned by structures and processes within the Finance and Risk function that support expert and rigorous analytical review of financial reporting.

- The group financial reporting process for preparing the consolidated *Annual Report and Accounts 2009* is controlled using documented accounting policies and reporting formats, supported by a chart of accounts with detailed instructions and guidance on reporting requirements, issued by Group Finance to all reporting entities within the Group in advance of each reporting period end. The submission of financial information from each reporting entity to Group Finance is subject to certification by the responsible financial officer, and analytical review procedures at reporting entity and Group levels.

- Processes are in place to identify new risks from changes in market conditions and practices or customer behaviours which could expose HSBC to heightened risk of loss or reputational damage. During 2009, attention was focused on evolving best practice in liquidity management and stress testing; aggregating more efficiently counterparty risk data and improving the counterparty crisis management framework; rolling out successfully piloted anti-fraud systems; revised guidance on the approval/review of new products and business initiatives, with greater oversight by the Risk function; the identification of market pricing anomalies; changes in consumer protection standards within personal financial services markets and, more generally, changes in regulation and public policy towards the financial services industry, including the impact of government interventions to address the under-capitalisation and funding difficulties of certain systemically important financial institutions.

- Periodic strategic plans are prepared for key customer groups, global product groups, support functions and certain geographies within the framework of the Group Strategic Road Map. Rolling operating plans, informed by detailed analysis of risk appetite, are prepared and adopted by all major HSBC operating companies and set out the key business initiatives and the likely financial effects of those initiatives.

- Governance and oversight arrangements are in place to ensure that risk analytical models are fit for purpose, used accordingly and complemented by a variety of model-specific and enterprise-wide stress tests that evaluate the impact of severe yet plausible events and other unusual circumstances not fully captured by quantitative models.

- Centralised functional control is exercised over all IT developments and operations. Common systems are employed for similar business processes wherever practicable. Credit, market and operational risks are measured and reported on in subsidiaries and aggregated for review of risk concentrations on a Group-wide basis.

- Functional management in Group Management Office is responsible for setting policies, procedures and standards in the following areas of risk: credit; market; liquidity; operational; IT; fraud; business continuity; security; information; insurance; accounting; tax; legal and regulatory compliance; fiduciary; human resources; reputational; sustainability and purchasing. Authorities to enter into credit and market risk exposures are delegated with limits to line management of Group companies. The concurrence of Group Management Office is required, however, to credit proposals with specified higher risk characteristics.

- The establishment and maintenance of appropriate systems of internal control is primarily the responsibility of business management. The internal audit function, which is centrally controlled, monitors the effectiveness of internal control structures across the whole of HSBC focusing on the areas of greatest risk to HSBC as determined using a risk-based grading approach. The head of this function reports to the Group Chairman and the Group Audit Committee.

- Executive management is responsible for ensuring that recommendations made by the internal audit function are implemented within an appropriate and agreed timetable. Confirmation to this effect must be provided to internal audit. Executive management must also confirm annually as part of the internal audit process that offices under their control have taken or are in the process of taking the appropriate actions to deal with all significant recommendations made by external auditors in management letters or by regulators following regulatory inspections. The Group Audit Committee has kept under review the effectiveness of this system of internal control and has reported regularly to the Board of Directors. The key processes used by the Committee in carrying out its reviews include: regular business and operational risk assessments; regular reports from the heads of key risk functions including Internal Audit and Compliance; the production annually of reviews of the internal control framework applied at Group Management Office and major operating subsidiary level measured against HSBC benchmarks, which cover all internal controls, both financial and non-financial; semiannual confirmations from chief executives of principal subsidiary companies as to whether there have been any material losses, contingencies or uncertainties caused by weaknesses in internal controls; internal audit reports; external audit reports; prudential reviews; and regulatory reports. The Group Audit Committee keeps under review a 'Risk Map' of the status of key risk areas which impact the Group and considers whether the mitigating actions put in place are appropriate. In addition, where unexpected losses have arisen or where incidents have occurred which indicate gaps in the control framework or in adherence to Group policies, the Group Audit Committee has reviewed special reports, prepared at the instigation of management, which analyse the cause of the issue, the lessons learned and the actions proposed by management to address the issue. The Directors, through the Group Audit Committee, have conducted an annual review of the effectiveness of HSBC's system of internal control covering all material controls, including financial, operational and compliance controls and risk management systems and the adequacy of resources, qualifications and experience of staff of the issuer's accounting and financial reporting function, and their training programmes and budget. The Group Audit Committee has received confirmation that executive management has taken or is taking the necessary action to remedy any failings or weaknesses identified through the operation of HSBC's framework of controls.

Statement of Directors' Responsibilities in Respect of the *Annual Report and Accounts 2009* and the Financial Statements

The following statement, which should be read in conjunction with the Auditor's statement of their responsibilities set out in their report, is made with a view to distinguishing for shareholders the respective responsibilities of the Directors and of the Auditor in relation to the financial statements.

The Directors are responsible for preparing the Annual Report, the consolidated financial statements of HSBC Holdings and its subsidiaries (the 'Group') and holding company financial statements for HSBC Holdings (the 'parent company') in accordance with applicable law and regulations. Company law requires the Directors to prepare Group and parent company financial statements for each financial year. The Directors are required to prepare the Group financial statements in accordance with IFRSs as adopted by the EU and have elected to prepare the parent company financial statements on the same basis. The Directors are also required to present additional information for US shareholders. Accordingly these financial statements are framed to meet both UK and US requirements to give a consistent view to all shareholders.

The Group and parent company financial statements are required by law and IFRSs as adopted by the EU to present fairly the financial position of the Group and the parent company and the performance for that period; the Companies Act 2006 provides in relation to such financial statements that references in the relevant part of that Act to financial statements giving a true and fair view are references to their achieving a fair presentation. In addition, in order to meet certain US requirements, HSBC is required to present its financial statements in accordance with IFRSs as adopted by the International Accounting Standards Board ('IASB'). Currently, there are no differences in application to HSBC between IFRSs endorsed by the EU and IFRSs issued by the IASB. In preparing each of the Group and parent company financial statements, the Directors are required to:

- select suitable accounting policies and then apply them consistently;
- make judgements and estimates that are reasonable and prudent; and
- state whether they have been prepared in accordance with IFRSs as adopted by the EU.

The Directors are required to prepare the financial statements on the going concern basis unless it is not appropriate. Since the Directors are satisfied that the Group and parent company have the resources to continue in business for the foreseeable future, the financial statements continue to be prepared on the going concern basis.

The Directors have responsibility for ensuring that sufficient accounting records are kept that disclose with reasonable accuracy at any time the financial position of the parent company and enable them to ensure that its financial statements comply with the Companies Act 2006.

The Directors have general responsibility for taking such steps as are reasonably open to them to safeguard the assets of the Group and to prevent and detect fraud and other irregularities. Under applicable law and regulations, the Directors also have responsibility for preparing a Directors' Report, Directors' Remuneration Report and the Corporate Governance statement that comply with that law and those regulations.

The Directors have responsibility for the maintenance and integrity of the Annual Report and Accounts as they appear on the company's website. Legislation in the UK governing the preparation and dissemination of financial statements may differ from legislation in other jurisdictions.

The Directors confirm to the best of their knowledge:

- in accordance with rule 4.1.12(3)(a) of the Disclosure and Transparency Rules, the consolidated financial statements, which have been prepared in accordance with IFRSs as issued by the IASB and as endorsed by the EU, have been prepared in accordance with the applicable set of accounting standards and give a true and fair view of the assets, liabilities, financial position and profit or loss of the Group and the undertakings included in the consolidation taken as a whole; and
- the management report represented by the Report of the Directors has been prepared in accordance with rule 4.1.12(3)(b) of the Disclosure and Transparency Rules, and includes a fair review of the development and performance of the business and the position of the Group and the undertakings included in the consolidation taken as a whole, together with a description of the principal risks and uncertainties that the Group faces.

Independent Auditor's Report to the Members of HSBC Holdings plc

We have audited the Group and parent company financial statements of HSBC Holdings plc for the year ended 31 December 2009. The financial reporting framework that has been applied in their preparation is applicable law and International Financial Reporting Standards ('IFRSs') as adopted by the EU and as issued by the International Accounting Standards Board ('IASB') and, as regards the parent company financial statements, as applied in accordance with the provisions of the Companies Act 2006. This report is made solely to the company's members, as a body, in accordance with Chapter 3 of Part 16 of the Companies Act 2006 and, in respect of the separate opinion in relation to IFRSs as issued by the IASB, on terms that have been agreed. Our audit work has been undertaken so that we might state to the company's members those matters we are required to state to them in an auditors' report and in respect of the separate opinion in relation to IFRSs as issued by IASB, those matters that we have agreed to state to them in our report, and for no other purpose. To the fullest extent permitted by law, we do not accept or assume responsibility to anyone other than the company and the company's members, as a body, for our audit work, for this report, or for the opinions we have formed.

Respective responsibilities of Directors and auditors

As explained more fully in the Directors' Responsibilities Statement, the Directors are responsible for the preparation of the financial statements and for being satisfied that they give a true and fair view. Our responsibility is to audit the financial statements in accordance with applicable law and International Standards on Auditing (UK and Ireland). Those standards require us to comply with the Auditing Practices Board's ('APB's) Ethical Standards for Auditors.

Scope of the audit opinion

A description of the scope of an audit of financial statements is provided on the APB's website at www.frc.org.uk/apb/scope/UKP.

Opinion

In our opinion:
- the financial statements give a true and fair view of the state of the Group's and of the parent company's affairs as at 31 December 2009 and of the Group's profit for the year then ended;
- the Group financial statements have been properly prepared in accordance with IFRSs as adopted by the EU;
- the parent company financial statements have been properly prepared in accordance with IFRSs as adopted by the

EU and as applied in accordance with the provisions of the Companies Act 2006; and
- the financial statements have been prepared in accordance with the requirements of the Companies Act 2006 and, as regards the Group financial statements, Article 4 of the IAS Regulation.

Separate opinion in relation to IFRSs as issued by the IASB

As explained in Note 1(a) to the Group financial statements, the Group in addition to complying with its legal obligation to apply IFRSs as adopted by the European Union, has also applied IFRSs as issued by the IASB.

Opinion on other matters prescribed by the Companies Act, 2006

In our opinion:
- the part of the Directors' Remuneration Report to be audited has been properly prepared in accordance with the Companies Act 2006; and
- the information given in the Directors' Report for the financial year for which the financial statements are prepared is consistent with the financial statements.

Matters on which we are required to report by exception

We have nothing to report in respect of the following:
Under the Companies Act 2006 we are required to report to you if, in our opinion:

- adequate accounting records have not been kept by the parent company, or returns adequate for our audit have not been received from branches not visited by us; or
- the parent company financial statements and the part of the Directors' Remuneration Report to be audited are not in agreement with the accounting records and returns; or
- certain disclosures of directors' remuneration specified by law are not made; or
- we have not received all the information and explanations we require for our audit.

Under the Listing Rules of the Financial Services Authority, we are required to review:
- the directors' statement, set out on page 316, in relation to going concern; and
- the part of the Corporate Governance Statement relating to the company's compliance with the nine provisions of the June 2008 Combined Code specified for our review.

Brendan Nelson, Senior Statutory Auditor
For and on behalf of KPMG Audit Plc, Statutory Auditor
Chartered Accountants
London, England
1 March 2010

Footnotes to the following financial statements have been deleted.

CONSOLIDATED INCOME STATEMENT
For the Year Ended 31 December 2009

	2009 US$m	2008 US$m	2007 US$m
Interest income	62,096	91,301	92,359
Interest expense	(21,366)	(48,738)	(54,564)
Net interest income	40,730	42,563	37,795
Fee income	21,403	24,764	26,337
Fee expense	(3,739)	(4,740)	(4,335)
Net fee income	17,664	20,024	22,002
Trading income excluding net interest income	6,236	847	4,458
Net interest income on trading activities	3,627	5,713	5,376
Net trading income	9,863	6,560	9,834
Changes in fair value of long-term debt issued and related derivatives	(6,247)	6,679	2,812
Net income (expense) from other financial instruments designated at fair value	2,716	(2,827)	1,271
Net income (expense) from financial instruments designated at fair value	(3,531)	3,852	4,083
Gains less losses from financial investments	520	197	1,956
Gains arising from dilution of interests in associates	—	—	1,092
Dividend income	126	272	324
Net earned insurance premiums	10,471	10,850	9,076
Gains on disposal of French regional banks	—	2,445	—
Other operating income	2,788	1,808	1,439
Total operating income	78,631	88,571	87,601
Net insurance claims incurred and movement in liabilities to policyholders	(12,450)	(6,889)	(8,608)
Net operating income before loan impairment charges and other credit risk provisions	66,181	81,682	78,993
Loan impairment charges and other credit risk provisions	(26,488)	(24,937)	(17,242)
Net operating income	39,693	56,745	61,751
Employee compensation and benefits	(18,468)	(20,792)	(21,334)
General and administrative expenses	(13,392)	(15,260)	(15,294)
Depreciation and impairment of property, plant and equipment	(1,725)	(1,750)	(1,714)
Goodwill impairment	—	(10,564)	—
Amortisation and impairment of intangible assets	(810)	(733)	(700)
Total operating expenses	(34,395)	(49,099)	(39,042)
Operating profit	5,298	7,646	22,709
Share of profit in associates and joint ventures	1,781	1,661	1,503
Profit before tax	7,079	9,307	24,212
Tax expense	(385)	(2,809)	(3,757)
Profit for the year	6,694	6,498	20,455
Profit attributable to shareholders of the parent company	5,834	5,728	19,133
Profit attributable to minority interests	860	770	1,322
	US$	US$	US$
Basic earnings per ordinary share	0.34	0.41	1.44
Diluted earnings per ordinary share	0.34	0.41	1.42

CONSOLIDATED STATEMENT OF COMPREHENSIVE INCOME
For the Year Ended 31 December 2009

	2009 US$m	2008 US$m	2007 US$m
Profit for the year	6,694	6,498	20,455
Other comprehensive income (expense)			
Available-for-sale investments	10,817	(21,904)	(973)
fair value gains (losses)	9,821	(23,722)	756
fair value gains transferred to income statement on disposal	(648)	(1,316)	(1,826)
amounts transferred to the income statement in respect of impairment losses	2,391	1,779	86
income taxes	(747)	(1,355)	11
Cash flow hedges	772	124	(791)
fair value gains (losses)	481	(1,720)	625
fair value (gains)/losses transferred to income statement	808	1,754	(1,886)
income taxes	(517)	90	470
Actuarial gains (losses) on defined benefit plans	(2,608)	(1,175)	1,525
before income taxes	(3,586)	(1,609)	2,167
income taxes	978	434	(642)
Share of other comprehensive income/(expense) of associates and joint ventures	149	(559)	372
Exchange differences	4,975	(12,123)	5,946
Other comprehensive income/(expense) for the year, net of tax	14,105	(35,637)	6,079
Total comprehensive income/(expense) for the year	20,799	(29,139)	26,534
Total comprehensive income/(expense) for the year attributable to:			
shareholders of the parent company	19,529	(29,143)	24,866
minority interests	1,270	4	1,668
	20,799	(29,139)	26,534

CONSOLIDATED BALANCE SHEET
At 31 December 2009

	2009 US$m	2008 US$m
Assets		
Cash and balances at central banks	60,655	52,396
Items in the course of collection from other banks	6,395	6,003
Hong Kong Government certificates of indebtedness	17,463	15,358
Trading assets	421,381	427,329
Financial assets designated at fair value	37,181	28,533
Derivatives	250,886	494,876
Loans and advances to banks	179,781	153,766
Loans and advances to customers	896,231	932,868
Financial investments	369,158	300,235
Other assets	44,534	37,822
Current tax assets	2,937	2,552
Prepayments and accrued income	12,423	15,797
Interests in associates and joint ventures	13,011	11,537
Goodwill and intangible assets	29,994	27,357
Property, plant and equipment	13,802	14,025

CONSOLIDATED BALANCE SHEET
At 31 December 2009   (*Continued*)

	2009 US$m	2008 US$m
Deferred tax assets	8,620	7,011
Total assets	2,364,452	2,527,465
Liabilities and Equity		
Liabilities		
Hong Kong currency notes in circulation	17,463	15,358
Deposits by banks	124,872	130,084
Customer accounts	1,159,034	1,115,327
Items in the course of transmission to other banks	5,734	7,232
Trading liabilities	268,130	247,652
Financial liabilities designated at fair value	80,092	74,587
Derivatives	247,646	487,060
Debt securities in issue	146,896	179,693
Other liabilities	68,640	72,384
Current tax liabilities	2,140	1,822
Liabilities under insurance contracts	53,707	43,683
Accruals and deferred income	13,190	15,448
Provisions	1,965	1,730
Deferred tax liabilities	1,837	1,855
Retirement benefit liabilities	6,967	3,888
Subordinated liabilities	30,478	29,433
Total liabilities	2,228,791	2,427,236
Equity		
Called up share capital	8,705	6,053
Share premium account	8,413	8,463
Other equity instruments	2,133	2,133
Other reserves	22,236	(3,747)
Retained earnings	86,812	80,689
Total shareholders' equity	128,299	93,591
Minority interests	7,362	6,638
Total equity	135,661	100,229
Total equity and liabilities	2,364,452	2,527,465

CONSOLIDATED STATEMENT OF CASH FLOWS
For the Year Ended 31 December 2009

	2009 US$m	2008 US$m	2007 US$m
Cash flows from operating activities			
Profit before tax	7,079	9,307	24,212
Adjustments for:			
non-cash items included in profit before tax	31,384	41,305	21,701
change in operating assets	(20,803)	18,123	(176,538)
change in operating liabilities	14,645	(63,413)	250,095
elimination of exchange differences	(19,024)	36,132	(18,602)
net gain from investing activities	(1,910)	(4,195)	(2,209)
share of profits in associates and joint ventures	(1,781)	(1,661)	(1,503)
dividends received from associates	414	655	363
contributions paid to defined benefit plans	(974)	(719)	(1,393)
tax paid	(2,132)	(5,114)	(5,088)
Net cash generated from operating activities	6,898	30,420	91,038
Cash flows from investing activities			
Purchase of financial investments	(304,629)	(277,023)	(260,980)
Proceeds from the sale and maturity of financial investments	241,341	223,138	238,647
Purchase of property, plant and equipment	(2,000)	(2,985)	(2,720)
Proceeds from the sale of property, plant and equipment	4,701	2,467	3,178
Proceeds from the sale of loan portfolios	4,852	9,941	1,665
Net purchase of intangible assets	(956)	(1,169)	(950)
Net cash inflow/(outflow) from acquisition of or increase in stake of subsidiaries	(677)	1,313	(623)
Net cash inflow from disposal of subsidiaries	45	2,979	187
Net cash outflow from acquisition of or increase in stake of associates	(62)	(355)	(351)
Net cash inflow from the consolidation of funds	—	16,500	1,600
Proceeds from disposal of associates and joint ventures	308	101	69
Net cash used in investing activities	(57,077)	(25,093)	(20,278)
Cash flows from financing activities			
Issue of ordinary share capital	18,398	467	474
rights issue	18,326	—	—
other	72	467	474
Issue of other equity instruments	—	2,133	—
Net (purchases)/sales of own shares for market-making and investment purposes	(176)	(194)	126
Purchases of own shares to meet share awards and share option awards	(51)	(808)	(636)
On exercise of share options	12	27	104
Subordinated loan capital issued	2,959	7,094	5,705
Subordinated loan capital repaid	(4,637)	(350)	(659)
Dividends paid to shareholders of the parent company	(4,264)	(7,211)	(6,003)
Dividends paid to minority interests	(702)	(714)	(718)
Dividends paid to holders of other equity instruments	(269)	(92)	—
Net cash generated from/(used in) financing activities	11,270	352	(1,637)
Net increase/(decrease) in cash and cash equivalents	**(38,909)**	**5,679**	**69,123**
Cash and cash equivalents at 1 January	278,872	297,009	215,486
Exchange differences in respect of cash and cash equivalents	10,803	(23,816)	12,400
Cash and cash equivalents at 31 December	250,766	278,872	297,009

Chapter 8 Cases

Case 8-1

SEC v. Siemens Aktiengesellschaft

On December 15, 2008, the SEC filed a lawsuit against Siemens Aktiengesellschaft (German word for a corporation) charging the Munich, Germany–based manufacturer of industrial and consumer products with violations of the antibribery, books and records, and internal controls provisions of the Foreign Corrupt Practices Act. The SEC has the authority to bring this action because Siemens stock is listed on the New York Stock Exchange. Siemens agreed to pay a total of $1.6 billion in disgorgement and fines, which is the largest amount a company has ever paid to resolve corruption-related charges. The company also agreed to pay $350 million in disgorgement to the SEC. In related actions, Siemens will pay a $450 million criminal fine to the U.S. Department of Justice and a fine of €395 million (approximately $569 million) to the Office of the Prosecutor General in Munich, Germany. Siemens previously paid a fine of €202 million (approximately $285 million) to the Munich prosecutor in October 2007. The SEC released a summary of its litigation in this matter that is summarized in the following paragraphs.[1]

Summary of Litigation

Between March 12, 2001, and September 30, 2007, Siemens violated the FCPA by engaging in a widespread and systematic practice of paying bribes to foreign government officials to obtain business. Siemens created elaborate payment schemes to conceal the nature of its corrupt payments, and the company's inadequate internal controls allowed the conduct to flourish. The misconduct involved employees at all levels, including former senior management, and revealed a corporate culture long at odds with the FCPA.

During this period, Siemens made thousands of payments to third parties in ways that obscured the purpose for, and the ultimate recipients of, the money. At least 4,283 of those payments, totaling approximately $1.4 billion, were used to bribe government officials in return for business to Siemens around the world. Among others, Siemens paid bribes on transactions to design and build metro transit lines in Venezuela; metro trains and signaling devices in China; power plants in Israel; high-voltage transmission lines in China; mobile telephone networks in Bangladesh; telecommunications projects in Nigeria; national identity cards in Argentina; medical devices in Vietnam, China, and Russia; traffic control systems in Russia; refineries in Mexico; and mobile communications networks in Vietnam. Siemens

also paid kickbacks to Iraqi ministries in connection with sales of power stations and equipment to Iraq under the United Nations Oil for Food Program. Siemens earned over $1.1 billion in profits on these transactions. An additional approximately 1,185 separate payments to third parties totaling approximately $391 million were not properly controlled and were used, at least in part, for illicit purposes, including commercial bribery and embezzlement.

From 1999 to 2003, Siemens's Management Board was ineffective in implementing controls to address constraints imposed by Germany's 1999 adoption of the OECD antibribery convention that outlawed foreign bribery. The Management Board was also ineffective in meeting the U.S. regulatory and antibribery requirements that Siemens was subject to following its March 12, 2001, listing on the NYSE. Despite knowledge of bribery at two of its largest groups—Communications and Power Generation—the company's tone at the top was inconsistent with an effective FCPA compliance program and created a corporate culture in which bribery was tolerated and even rewarded at the highest levels of the company. Employees obtained large amounts of cash from cash desks, which were sometimes transported in suitcases across international borders for bribery. Authorizations for payments were placed on Post-it notes and later removed to eradicate any permanent record. Siemens used numerous slush funds, off-books accounts maintained at unconsolidated entities, and a system of business consultants and intermediaries to facilitate the corrupt payments.

Siemens failed to implement adequate internal controls to detect and prevent violations of the FCPA. Elaborate payment mechanisms were used to conceal the fact that bribe payments were made around the globe to obtain business. False invoices and payment documentation were created to make payments to business consultants under false business consultant agreements that identified services that were never intended to be rendered. Illicit payments were falsely recorded as expenses for management fees, consulting fees, supply contracts, room preparation fees, and commissions. Siemens inflated U.N. contracts, signed side agreements with Iraqi ministries that were not disclosed to the U.N., and recorded the after-sale-service-charges (ASSF) payments as legitimate commissions despite U.N., U.S., and international sanctions against such payments.

In November 2006, Siemens's current management began to implement reforms to the company's internal controls. These reforms substantially reduced, but did not entirely eliminate, corrupt payments. All but $27.5 million of the corrupt payments occurred before November 15, 2006. The company conducted a massive internal investigation and implemented an amnesty program to its employees to gather information.

[1] *Securities and Exchange Commission v. Siemens Aktiengesellschaft,* Case 1.08-cv-02167, Litigation Release No. 20829, Accounting and Enforcement Release No. 2911, December 15, 2008, www.sec.gov/litigation/litreleases/2008/lr20829.htm.

The success of Siemens's bribery system was maintained by lax internal controls over corruption-related activities and an acceptance of such activities by members of senior management and the compliance, internal audit, legal, and finance departments. Siemens violated Section 30A of the Securities Exchange Act of 1934 by making illicit payments to foreign government officials in order to obtain or retain business. Siemens violated Section 13(b)(2)(B) of the Exchange Act by failing to have adequate internal controls to detect and prevent the payments. Siemens violated Section 13(b)(2)(A) of the Exchange Act by improperly recording the payments in its books.

Without admitting or denying the commission's allegations, Siemens consented to the entry of a court order permanently enjoining it from future violations of the Exchange Act; ordering it to pay $350 million in disgorgement of wrongful profits, which does not include profits factored into Munich's fine; and ordering it to comply with certain undertakings regarding its FCPA compliance program, including an independent monitor for a period of four years. On December 15, 2008, the court entered the final judgment. Since being approached by SEC staff, Siemens has cooperated fully with the ongoing investigation, and the SEC considered the remedial acts promptly undertaken by Siemens. Siemens's massive internal investigation and lower-level-employee amnesty program were essential in gathering facts regarding the full extent of Siemens's FCPA violations.

Charges against the Management Board

The following charges were made against Siemens's Management Board:

1. The board was ineffective in meeting the U.S. regulatory and antibribery requirements that Siemens was subject to following its listing on the NYSE on March 12, 2001.
2. The board failed to adopt meaningful compliance measures, failed to adequately staff Siemens's compliance function and, at times, failed to adopt reasonable recommendations designed to ensure compliance procedures at the company.
3. The company failed to respond to red flags including ignoring substantial cash payments in Nigeria by senior-level employees within one of its business groups, and ignoring Siemens's outside auditor KPMG's identification of €4.12 million (approximately $5.81 million) in cash that was brought to Nigeria by a group employee. The FCPA compliance report prepared on the foregoing matters in November 2003 by Siemens's then-CFO did not lead to any disciplinary actions against those employees involved in the bribery, and the report was not provided to or discussed with the Management Board or the company's audit committee.

The company's response to bribery in Nigeria and Italy demonstrated a tone at the top at Siemens that was inconsistent with an effective FCPA compliance program and created a corporate culture in which bribery was tolerated and even rewarded at the highest levels of the company.

Illicit Payment Mechanisms Used to Pay Bribes

Siemens made thousands of payments to third parties in ways that obscured the purpose for, and ultimate recipient of, the money. The principal mechanisms used to facilitate illicit payments were business consultants, payment intermediaries, slush funds, cash, and intercompany accounts.

Through its use of business consultants and payment intermediaries, Siemens funneled more than $982.7 million to third parties, including government officials. All but $27.5 million of the payments were made prior to November 15, 2006. Business consultants were typically hired pursuant to business consultant agreements, contracts that on their face obligated Siemens to pay for legitimate consulting services. In reality, many business consultant agreements were shams in that the consultants performed no services beyond funneling bribes. One business group had specific instructions on how to use a "confidential payment system" to conceal payments to business consultants. Payment intermediaries were additional entities and individuals through which Siemens funneled bribes. In many cases, Siemens would pay the intermediary an amount and simultaneously direct that the money be transferred to a third-party bank account, less a small portion as the intermediary's fee.

Siemens also funneled more than $211 million through slush funds for use as bribes. Slush funds were bank accounts held in the name of current or former senior Siemens employees, third parties, or affiliated entities. These payments were made before September 30, 2004. The most notable slush funds were maintained by a former group manager recently convicted in Germany for his role in the payment of bribes to foreign officials, which included several slush funds held in the name of U.S. shell companies.

Siemens also used cash and cash equivalents to funnel more than $160.4 million to third parties. All but $9.2 million of the payments were made prior to September 30, 2004. Siemens employees used "cash desks" maintained by the Siemens Real Estate Group to obtain large amounts of cash to pay bribes. Often, employees would obtain hundreds of thousands of dollars and, at times, even $1 million in various currencies from the cash desks in Germany. The cash was transported, sometimes in suitcases, across international borders into various countries. At times, the cash was then stored in safes maintained by Siemens employees to ensure ready access to cash to pay bribes.

Siemens used various types of internal accounts to funnel more than $16.2 million to third parties. Approximately 99 percent of the payments were made prior to September 30, 2005. An intercompany account is a type of Siemens internal account that is used to make payments on transactions between two Siemens entities (i.e., for entity to entity business). Siemens used the intercompany accounts to make third-party payments and, in a number of instances, it maintained the accounts in the names of unconsolidated entities around the globe, including Ecuador and Nicaragua, to avoid detection. Some of the intercompany accounts maintained at unconsolidated entities were known to, and possibly created by, a former member of the Management Board who had oversight responsibility for Latin America.

As early as 2004, a Siemens corporate financial audit employee raised concerns about the use of intercompany accounts. He was phased out of his job and assigned to work on "special projects" from his home until leaving the company in 2005. Siemens thereafter began closing some of the accounts and eventually closed all of them.

Another type of internal account that employees abused was Siemens internal commission accounts. These balance-sheet accounts were intended to be used to record commissions at a business group earned on transactions with other Siemens entities. These accounts were used to make third-party payments. Many of the intercompany account payments and the internal commission account payments were done manually to bypass Siemens's automated payment system. The manual payments, executed through the system, did not require the submission of documentation in support of a payment. Siemens used a host of other schemes to make more than $25.3 million in payments to third parties. In particular, Siemens used sham supplier agreements, receivables, and other write-offs to generate payments.

Siemens made 4,283 separate payments totaling between $1 to $4 billion to bribe government officials in foreign countries throughout the world. An additional approximately 1,185 separate payments to third parties totaling approximately $391 million were not properly controlled and were used, at least in part, for illicit purposes, including commercial bribery. In total, Siemens made bribery payments directly or indirectly to foreign government officials in connection with at least 290 projects or individual sales involving business in Venezuela, China, Israel, Bangladesh, Nigeria, Argentina, Vietnam, Russia, and Mexico. Siemens employed the mails and other means and instrumentalities of U.S. interstate commerce. The corrupt payments were made to government officials or their designees for the purpose of obtaining or retaining business in connection to the above projects. The use of interstate commerce in connection with bribery included involving U.S.-based Siemens subsidiaries and their employees in the bribery schemes; financing of three underlying projects by the World Bank and the U.S. Export–Import Bank; making illegal payments through U.S. banks; using U.S.-based companies as intermediaries, business consultants, and holders of slush funds; conducting meetings in the United States in furtherance of a bribery scheme; and transmitting mail, electronic mail, and facsimile messages into and out of the United States.

Siemens Failed to Maintain Its Books, Records, and Internal Controls

Siemens failed to implement adequate internal controls to comply with the company's NYSE listing, including the detection and prevention of violations of the FCPA. Siemens made thousands of payments to third parties in ways that obscured the purpose for, and the ultimate recipients of, the payments. Despite a policy that required two signatures on company documents to authorize transactions, a significant number of business consultant agreements were entered into and a significant number of payments were authorized in violation of the policy.

Siemens paid approximately $1.4 billion in bribes to foreign government officials. Doing so involved the falsification of Siemens's books and records by employees throughout the Company. Specifically, Siemens failed to keep accurate books and records by (1) establishing and funding secret, off-books accounts; (2) establishing and using a system of payment intermediaries to obscure the source and destination of funds; (3) making payments pursuant to business consultant agreements that inaccurately described the services provided; (4) generating false invoices and other false documents to justify payments; (5) disbursing millions in cash from cash desks with inaccurate documentation authorizing or supporting the withdrawals; (6) using Post-it notes for the purpose of concealing the identity of persons authorizing illicit payments; (7) recording illicit ASSF payments as legitimate commissions in Oil for Food transactions; (8) falsifying U.N. documents in connection with the Oil for Food program; and (9) recording bribes as payments for legitimate services.

In numerous instances, officials signing documents failed to conduct any review of the documents. For example, an official who authorized payments on behalf of Siemens's Russian regional subsidiary authorized payments despite his inability to read the language in which the supporting documentation of the payments was prepared. Siemens officials frequently misused internal accounts by transferring money from one Siemens entity to another without any legitimate business purpose or proper documentation of the disposition of the funds. Siemens officials modified the format of agreements to avoid internal controls on the use of business consultants by backdating agreements, misidentifying counterparties as "agents" rather than "business consultants," and obscuring the amounts paid to business consultants by splitting the payments among separate agreements.

Siemens failed to establish adequate internal controls despite its knowledge that corruption was rampant. Siemens did not issue mandatory and comprehensive companywide controls regarding the use of business consultants until June 2005, well after senior officials were aware of widespread bribery in the company's two largest divisions, COM and PG. Despite those controls, due diligence on business consultants remained largely inadequate, and payments continued to be made without adequate proof of services rendered.

Finally, Siemens failed to establish controls over cash disbursements, allowed manual payments without documentation, and failed to ensure the proper use of intercompany accounts. Siemens failed to establish an effective central compliance function. The compliance office lacked independence and was severely understaffed. Siemens's tone at the top was inadequate for a law abiding entity, and employees engaged in bribery and other misconduct on behalf of the company were not adequately disciplined. Siemens also failed to conduct appropriate antibribery and corruption training.

Questions

1. Evaluate the ethics of actions taken by Siemens with respect to Josephson's Six Pillars of Character and virtue decision making discussed in Chapter 1.

2. In the Siemens case, the SEC charged that the "corporate culture [was] at odds with the Foreign Corrupt Practices Act" and that the "tone at the top [was] inconsistent with an effective FCPA compliance program." Explain how the corporate culture including tone at the top should have worked at Siemens with respect to the actions that might have been taken to prevent and then effectively deal with bribes paid to foreign officials.

3. The internal controls at Siemens failed on several levels. Describe those failings and indicate how a strong system of corporate governance might have mitigated the effects of those deficiencies.

Optional Question

Review the 13 cases on bribing foreign government officials described in the SEC complaint referenced below.[2] Summarize the accounting issues involved in each case and explain how the payments described violated the FCPA.

[2]*Securities and Exchange Commission v. Siemens Aktiengesellschaft,* Case 1.08-cv-02167, Litigation Release No. 20829, Accounting and Enforcement Release No. 2911, December 15, 2008, www.sec.gov/litigation/complaints/2008/comp20829.pdf.

Case 8-2

Parmalat: Europe's Enron

After the news broke about the frauds at Enron and World-Com in the United States, there were those in Europe who used the occasion to beat the drum: "Our Principles-based approach to accounting standard-setting is better than your rules-based approach." Many in the United States started to take a closer look at the principles-based approach in the European Community, which relies less on bright-line rules to establish standards, as is the case in the United States, but may have loopholes making it relative easy to avoid the rules. As discussed in the chapter, a principles-based approach relies more on objective standards that guide decision making in the application of accounting standards, supported by ethical judgment to help implement the principles.

Background

Parmalat began as a family-owned entity founded by Calisto Tanzi in 1961. During 2003 Parmalat was the eighth largest company in Italy and had operations in 30 countries. It was a huge player in the world dairy market and even more influential within the Italian business circles. It had a network of 5,000 dairy farmers who supplied milk products and 39,000 people who were directly employed by the company. The company eventually sold shares to the public on the Milan stock exchange. The Tanzi family always held a majority, controlling stake in the company, which in 2003 was 50.02 percent. Tanzi family members also occupied the seats of CEO and chair of the board of directors.[1] The structure of Parmalat was primarily characterized by the Tanzi family and the large amount of control it wielded over company operations. It was not unusual for family members to override whatever internal controls existed to perpetrate the accounting fraud.

The Parmalat scandal broke in late 2003 when it became known that company funds totaling almost €4 billion (approximately $5.64 billion) that were meant to be held in an account at Bank of America did not exist. The Parmalat situation described in the following text makes it clear that Europe is not isolated from financial fraud. It also proves that the quality of financial reporting and financial transparency are issues of global concern. At the end of the day, these issues may be more important than whether a principles-based or rules-based approach is used.

The Italians Act

On March 19, 2004, Milan prosecutors brought charges against Parmalat founder Calisto Tanzi, other members of his family, and an inner circle of company executives for their part in one of Europe's biggest corporate fraud scandals. After three months of investigation, the prosecutors charged 29 individuals, the Italian branches of the Bank of America, and the accountants Deloitte & Touche and Grant Thornton. The charges included market rigging, false auditing, and regulatory obstruction following the disclosure that €15 billion (approximately $21.15 billion) were found to be missing from the bank accounts of the multinational dairy group in December 2003. The company has since declared bankruptcy and 16 suspects, including Carlos Tanzi, are in jail. Other suspects include Tanzi's son Stafano, his brother Giovanni, former Parmalat finance chief Fausto Tonna, and lawyer Liampaolo Zini. Former internal auditors and three former Bank of America employees also have been jailed for their roles in the fraud.[2] The judge also gave the go-ahead for Parmalat to proceed with lawsuits against the auditors. Bondi is also pursuing another lawsuit against Citigroup in New Jersey state courts.

Parmalat Diverted Company Cash to Tanzi Family Members

In transactions that might engender pride on the part of Dennis Kozlowski, the former CEO of Tyco, Parmalat transferred approximately €350 million (approximately $494 million) to various businesses owned and operated by Tanzi family members between 1997 and 2003. These family members did not perform any equivalent services for Parmalat that would warrant such payments. Further, Parmalat failed to disclose that the transfers were to related-party interests.

U.S. Banks Caught in the Spotlight

Italian magistrates and officials from the U.S. Securities and Exchange Commission examined the role of lenders to Parmalat, which collapsed into bankruptcy in late December 2003 following the disclosure of major holes in the financing of the company. The SEC's inquiries focused on up to approximately €1.05 billion ($1.5 billion) of notes and bonds issued in private placements with U.S. investors. The banks investigated included Bank of America, JP Morgan Chase, Merrill Lynch, and Morgan Stanley Dean Witter. Parmalat's administrator, Enrico Bondi, helped the authorities identify all the financing transactions undertaken by Parmalat from 1994 through 2003. During the investigation it was noted that Parmalat's auditor from 1990 to 1999, Grant Thornton, did not have copies of crucial audit documents relating to the company's Cayman Islands subsidiary, Bonlat, which is at

---

[1] Available at www.madhyam.org.in/admin/tender/Parmalat's%20Fall,%20Europe's%20Enron(%20ASED).pdf.

[2] Sophie Arie, "29 Named in Parmalat Case," *The Guardian,* March 19, 2004, www.guardian.co.uk/parmalat/story/0,1172990,00.html.

the center of the scandal. The emergence of a €5.16 billions (approximately $7.28 billions) hole at Bonlat triggered the Parmalat collapse. The accounting firm has since handed over important audit documents to investigators.

Accounting Fraud

One of the most notable fraudulent actions was the creation of a completely fictitious bank account in the United States that supposedly contained $5 billion. After media reports exposing the account surfaced, the financial institution at which the deposit existed (Bank of America) denied any such account. The company's management had misled auditors by creating a fictitious confirmation letter regarding the account. In addition to misleading the auditors about this bank account, the company's CFO, Fausto Tonna, produced fake documents and faxed them to the auditors in order to hide the fact that many of the company's dealings were completely fictitious.[3]

Parmalat's management also used "nominee" entities to transfer debt and sales in order to hide them from auditors and other interested parties. A *nominee entity* is a company created to hold and administer the assets or securities of the actual owner as a custodian.[4] These entities were clearly controlled by Parmalat, and although the letter of the accounting laws was often followed in consolidation, the nominee entities hid many other issues. Parmalat had approximately 200 such companies, most of which existed only on paper. The entities had little to no real assets, operations, or structure.[5] Parmalat used these entities to accomplish many different objectives, with the sole underlying goal of making the company look solvent.

Using nominee entities the Parmalat management created a method to remove uncollectible or impaired accounts receivable. The bad accounts would be transferred to one of the nominee entities, thus keeping the bad debt expense or write-off for the valueless accounts off the Parmalat income statement. The transfers to nominee entities also avoided any scrutiny of the accounts by external or statutory auditors (Italian-designated auditors under the country's laws).

Creating revenues was another scheme in which the nominee or subsidiary entities were used; if a non-Italian subsidiary had a loss related to currency exchange rates, management would fabricate currency exchange contracts to convert the loss to a profit. Similar activities were undertaken to hide losses due to interest expense. Documents showing interest rate swaps were created to mislead the auditors or other parties. Interest rate swaps and currency exchange contracts are both instruments usually used to hedge on the financial markets and sometimes to diversify the risk of certain investments. Parmalat abused these tools by creating completely fictitious contracts after the fact and claiming that they were valid and accurate. The understatement of debt was another large component of the Parmalat fraud as was hidden debt. On one occasion management recorded the sale of receivables as "non-recourse" when in fact Parmalat was still responsible to ensure that the money was collectible.

There were many debt disguising schemes in relation to the nominee entities. With one loan agreement, the money borrowed was touted as from an equity source. On another occasion, a completely fictitious debt repurchase by a nominee entity was created, resulting in the removal of a liability from the books, when the debt was still in fact outstanding. Parmalat management also incorrectly recorded many million euros' worth of bank loans as intercompany loans. This incorrect classification allowed for the loans to be eliminated in consolidation when they actually represented money owed by the company to outsiders.[6]

The fraud methods did not stop at creating fictitious accounts and documents or even with the establishment of nonexistent foreign nominee companies and hiding liabilities. Calisto Tanzi and other management were investigated by Italian authorities for manipulating the Milan stock market. On December 20, 1999, Parmalat's management issued a press release of an appraisal of the Brazilian unit. While this release appeared to be a straightforward action, what Tanzi and others failed to disclose were the facts relating to the appraisal itself. The appraisal came from an accountant at Deloitte Touche Tohmatsu (the international name of Deloitte & Touche) and was dated July 23, 2008, nearly 19 months prior to the press release.[7] This failure to disclose information in a timely and transparent manner demonstrates yet another way that Parmalat was able to exert influence and mislead investors.

Missing the Red Flags

The fraud that occurred at Parmalat is a case of management greed with a lack of independent oversight and fraudulent financial reporting that was taken to the extreme. As an international company, Parmalat management had many opportunities to take advantage of the system and hide the fictitious nature of financial statement items. As with many frauds, the web of lies began to untangle when the company began to run out of cash. In a discussion with a firm in New York regarding a leveraged buyout of part of the Parmalat Corporation, two members of the Tanzi family revealed that they did not actually have the cash represented in their financial statements.[8]

---

[3]Securities and Exchange Commission, *Securities and Exchange Commission v. Parmalat Finanziaria SpA*, First Amended Complaint, www.sec.gov/litigation/complaints/comp18803.pdf.
[4]Available at www.businessdictionary.com/definition/nominee-company.html.
[5]*Parmalat Finanziaria SpA*.

[6]Available at www.sec.gov/litigation/complaints/comp18803.pdf.
[7]William D. Dobson, "Parmalat," http://purl.umn.edu/37555.
[8]Available at www.sec.gov/litigation/complaints/comp18803.pdf, page 14.

At the beginning of 2003, Lehman Brothers, Inc., issued a report questioning the financial status of Parmalat. Ironically, Parmalat filed a report with Italian authorities claiming that Lehman Brothers was slandering the company intending to hurt the Parmalat share price.[9] Financial institutions failed to thoroughly examine the accusations and continued to loan money to Parmalat due to the supposed strength and power wielded by the company throughout the world. (Notice the similarity with Enron whereby U.S. banks and financial institutions bought into the fraud that was Enron and didn't want to upset the then seventh largest company in the United States.) As Luca Sala, former head of Bank of America's Italian corporate finance division, observed, "When you have a client like Parmalat, which is bringing in all that money and has industries all over the world, you don't exactly ask them to show you their bank statements."[10] This attitude and similar attitudes at Citibank led both banks as well as many others to write off millions of dollars of loans after the collapse. Several Bank of America employees where charged in the Parmalat fraud, most in connection to the nonexistent U.S. bank account but also in relation to lending practices. Eventually, all of the bank's employees were acquitted leading the bank to state: "The crime of market manipulation with respect to BOA was found to be completely groundless."[11]

Failure of Auditors

The frauds continued for many years due, in large part, to the failures of the auditors. Italian law requires both listed and unlisted companies to have a board of statutory auditors as well as external auditors. The external auditor during the fraud, primarily Grant Thornton, SpA, failed to comply with many commonly accepted auditing practices and thus contributed to the fraud. The largest component of Parmalat's fraud that ultimately brought the company down was the nonexistent bank account with Bank of America in the United States, which supposedly held $5 billion. The auditors went through procedures to confirm this account, but they made one fatal mistake: they sent the confirmation using Parmalat's internal mail system. The confirmation request was intercepted by Parmalat employees and subsequently forged by Tonna or an agent acting on his behalf. The forgery consisted of creating a confirmation and printing it on Bank of America letterhead and then sending it back to the auditors.

Italian law requires the reselection of auditors by the board of directors every three years and the rotation of auditors after three consecutive selections; this rule was called the Draghi law. Grant Thornton, SpA audited Parmalat from 1990 until

1998 when Deloitte Touche, SpA, was rotated onto the audit. However, Deloitte did not take over the entire audit. Tanzi closed many of the foreign nominee entities and reopened them in a different country. By moving the entities, the Draghi law considered them completely new and thus could retain Grant Thornton as auditors.[12] The change in auditors did not seem to help uncover the fraud, at least not initially, as the fraud continued for more than five years following the auditor change. To Deloitte Touche, SpA's credit it did issue a nonstandard report every year of the auditing due to large amounts of the company being audited by other auditors.[13]

The statutory board is intended to act as a fundamental monitor within the company and check that the board of directors is complying with laws in their actions and decisions. The Parmalat board of statutory auditors was composed of three members; the number is significant as had there been more than three seats on the statutory auditor board, minority shareholders would have had the ability to elect two of the members.[14] Parmalat's board never reported any irregularities or problems despite receiving complaints because of the influence of the Tanzi family. After the fraud was discovered and resolution of the issues began, it became clear that the statutory audit board did nothing to prevent or detect the fraud.

Resolution of Outstanding Matters

Following an investigation, the founder of Parmalat, Calisto Tanzi, was sentenced in Milan to 10 years in prison in December of 2008 for securities laws violations in connection with the Italian dairy company's downfall late in 2003. Tonna, the CFO, was sentenced to 30 months in jail following a trial in 2005, and other officers reached plea bargain deals.[15] Bank of America settled a civil case brought by Parmalat bondholders for $100 million.[16]

After the accounting and business problems surfaced, a court battle ensued regarding who was responsible for the audit failures. The umbrella entities of Deloitte and Grant Thornton, Deloitte Touche Tohmatsu, and Grant Thornton International, along with the U.S. branches of both firms, were included in a lawsuit by Parmalat shareholders. Questions were raised as to whether or not the umbrella entities could be held liable for the failures of a country-specific branch of their firm. The courts held that due to the level of control that the international and U.S.-based branches wielded over the other portions of the firm, they could be

---

[9]Leonard J. Brooks and Paul Dunn, *Business and Professional Ethics for Executives, Directors, and Accountants* (Cincinnati, OH: South-Western Publishing, 2009).

[10]Kavaljit Singh, www.madhyam.org.in/admin/tender/Parmalat's %20Fall,%20Europe's%20Enron(%20ASED).pdf.

[11]Sara GayForden, "Parmalat's Tanzi Sentenced to 10 Years in Milan Trial," www.bloomberg.com/apps/news?pid=20601087& sid=alrsQE4_kBPU&refer=4home.

[12]Brooks and Dunn, pp. 398–399.

[13]Available at http://papers.ssrn.com/sol3/papers.cfm? abstract_id=563223.

[14]Andrea Melis, "Corporate Governance Failures: To What Extent Is Parmalat a Particularly Italian Case?" http://papers .ssrn.com/sol3/papers.cfm?abstract_id=563223.

[15]Sara Gay Forden, "Parmalat's Tanzi Sentenced to 10 Years."

[16]Andrew Longstreth, "Bank of America Makes Peace with Parmalat for $100 million," www.law.com/jsp/article .jsp?id=1202432604858.

included in the lawsuit.[17] The extension of liability was a huge issue for accounting firms and the external auditors were ultimately held liable. Both groups of external auditors were fined large sums; Deloitte Touche Tohmatsu and its U.S. unit, Deloitte & Touche LLP, agreed to pay $8.5 million while Grant Thornton International and its U.S. and Italian units agreed to pay $6.5 million.[18]

While the company did not sell stock in the United States, it did make extensive debt offerings during the fraud period. These offerings were made, according to the SEC, "in private placements that were exempt from registration with the commission." Thus, although these debt offerings were not registered with the SEC, because they were sold in United States an action was brought against the company by the SEC. The basis for the action was violations of the Securities Act of 1933 and of the Securities Exchange Act of 1934, specifically Rule 10(b).[19]

Parmalat's corporate governance structure consisted of a board of directors, statutory auditors, and an internal control committee. Each of these groups failed to meet their fiduciary responsibilities especially to the minority shareholders. The Tanzi family took advantage of this failure for personal gain. While the board of directors was supposed to be independent and serve as an advocate for shareholders, the fact is it was almost completely controlled by the Tanzi family members, many of whom also served in top management positions.[20] During 2003, minority shareholders began to lobby Tanzi for representation on the board of directors. This was a legal right afforded to them in Italy, but the request was denied.[21]

Legal Matters

On February 2, 2006, a U.S. federal judge allowed Parmalat to proceed with much of its $10 billion lawsuit against Bank of America including claims that the bank violated U.S. racketeering laws. Enrico Bondi was appointed as the equivalent of a U.S. bankruptcy trustee to pursue claims that financial institutions including Bank of America abetted the company in disguising its true financial condition. Bondi accused the bank of helping structure mostly off-balance-sheet transactions intended to "conceal Parmalat's insolvency" and collecting fees it did not deserve. The judge also gave the go-ahead for Parmalat to proceed with lawsuits against the

two auditors. Bondi is also pursuing another lawsuit against Citigroup in New Jersey state courts.

The lawsuit against Bank of America was dismissed.[22] Parmalat appealed the dismissal of its lawsuits accusing Bank of America and the company's auditor, Grant Thornton LLP, of fraud in the Italian dairy company's 2003 collapse. CEO Enrico Bondi filed notice of Parmalat's appeal to the U.S. Court of Appeals for the Second Circuit in New York. Bondi and the Parmalat Capital Finance Ltd. unit had accused Grant Thornton of helping set up fake transactions to allow insiders to steal from the company. Parmalat Capital made similar claims in a lawsuit against Bank of America. On September 18, 2009, U.S. District Judge Lewis Kaplan said Parmalat should not recover for its own fraud, noting that the transactions also generated millions of euros for the company. "The actions of its agents in so doing were in furtherance of the company's interests even if some of the agents intended at the time they assisted in raising the money to steal some of it," Kaplan wrote.

On December 10, 2009, a notification program began, as ordered by the U.S. District Court for the Southern District of New York, to alert domestic investors, including U.S. persons and entities, who bought Parmalat Finanziaria SpA equity securities from January 5, 1999, through and including December 18, 2003, about two partial settlements of a class action. The partial settlements resolve the case against several Deloitte & Touche parties and several Grant Thornton parties and will pay money to class members. The Deloitte & Touche settling parties agreed to pay $8.5 million and the Grant Thornton settling parties agreed to pay $6.5 million to resolve this matter; attorneys' fees, expenses, and administrative costs will also be paid from these amounts.[23]

International Issues

Subsequent to the Parmalat fraud, Italy decided to adopt IFRS as the principles used for accounting reports issued in the country. The transition was mandatory starting with the reporting year of 2006. As outlined by Michela Cordazzo, there was significant hesitation to transition from Italian generally accepted accounting principles to IRFS and many companies did not switch until the EU mandated timing.[24]

Following the Parmalat fraud, the IFAC called for greater vigilance to be exercised by all those involved in the production of financial information by calling for accounting professionals to cooperate in their Member Compliance Program. This program is designed to create a defined control structure within audit firms and help reduce quality-control problems.[25]

[17]Thomas M. Beshere, "Questions for Accounting Firm Networks," http://mcguirewoods.com/news-resources/publications/Questions%20For%20International%20Accounting%20Firm%20Networks.pdf.
[18]Chad Bray, http://online.wsj.com/article/BT-CO-20091119-713515.html.
[19]Securities and Exchange Commission, Litigation Release No. 18803, www.sec.gov/litigation/complaints/comp18803.pdf.
[20]Andrea Melis, "Critical Issues on the Enforcement of the 'True and Fair View,'" Accounting Principle: Learning from Parmalat, www.virtusinterpress.org/additional_files/journ_coc/paper03.pdf.
[21]Brooks and Dunn, p. 398.
[22]Available at www.reuters.com/article/idUSN18621482009 0918, *Cached*.
[23]Available at www.ParmalatSettlement.com.
[24]Michela Cordazzo, www.hec.unil.ch/urccf/seminar/Michela%20Cordazzo%20-%20Dec07.pdf.
[25]International Federation of Accountants, "International Accounting Profession Calls for Greater Vigilance in the Wake of Parmalat Bankruptcy," www.ifac.org/MediaCenter/?q=node/view/326.

Summarizing the Case: The SEC Charges

The SEC filed an amended complaint on July 28, 2004, in its lawsuit against Parmalat Finanziaria SpA in U.S. District Court in the Southern District of New York. The amended complaint alleged that Parmalat engaged in one of the largest financial frauds in history and defrauded U.S. institutional investors when it sold them more than $1 billion in debt securities in a series of private placements between 1997 and 2002. Parmalat consented to the entry of a final judgment against it in the fraud.

The complaint includes the following amended charges:

1. Parmalat consistently overstated its level of cash and marketable securities by at least $4.9 billion at December 31, 2002.
2. As of September 30, 2003, Parmalat had understated its reported debt by almost $10 billion through a variety of tactics including:
   a. Eliminating about $6 billion debt held by one of its nominee entities
   b. Recording approximately $1.6 billion debt as equity through fictitious loan participation agreements
   c. Removing approximately $500 million of liabilities by falsely describing the sale of certain receivables as non-recourse, when in fact the company retained an obligation to ensure that the receivables were ultimately paid
   d. Improperly eliminating approximately $1.6 billion of debt through a variety of techniques including mischaracterization of bank debt as intercompany debt
3. Between 1997 and 2003, Parmalat transferred approximately $500 million to various businesses owned and operated by Tanzi family members.
4. Parmalat used nominee entities to fabricate nonexistent financial operations intended to offset losses of operating subsidiaries; to disguise intercompany loans from one subsidiary to another that was experiencing operating losses; and recording fictitious revenue through sales by its subsidiaries to controlled nominee entities at inflated or entirely fictitious amounts, and to avoid unwanted scrutiny due to the aging of the receivables related to these sales, the related receivables were either sold or transferred to nominee entities.

In the consent agreement without admitting or denying the allegations, Parmalat agreed to adopt changes to its corporate governance to promote future compliance with the federal securities laws, including:

- Adopting bylaws providing for governance by a shareholder-elected board of directors, the majority of whom will be independent and serve finite terms and specifically delineating in the bylaws the duties of the board of directors
- Adopting a Code of Conduct governing the duties and activities of the board of directors
- Adopting an Insider Dealing Code of Conduct
- Adopting a Code of Ethics

The bylaws will also require that the positions of the chair of the board of directors and managing director be held by two separate individuals and Parmalat must consent to having continuing jurisdiction of the U.S. District Court to enforce its provisions.

Eventually the company was able to restructure and still exists today maintaining the name of Parmalat. The company now employs PricewaterhouseCoopers as its independent auditors and uses IFRS as the basis for its financial information as evidenced in its 2008 financial reports.[26]

Questions

1. Review the facts in the case, especially the charges in the complaint, and evaluate the auditors' compliance with GAAS. Do you think the auditors did all they could to detect the fraud? Evaluate whether the auditors exercised due care and the level of professional skepticism to be expected in an audit the size of Parmalat.
2. Refer to the fraud triangle in Chapter 5. Categorize the various activities and decisions by Parmalat and its top management into one of the three elements of the triangle.
3. Based on the information in the case, classify the improper transactions engaged in by Parmalat into one of the seven financial shenanigans identified by Schilit in Chapter 7. Provide a brief explanation why you selected that group and how Parmalat's accounting violates U.S. GAAP.
4. The consent agreement with the SEC calls for a variety of corporate governance initiatives to be undertaken by Parmalat. Explain the purpose of these requirements and how they should strengthen the corporate governance systems at Parmalat.

[26]Parmalat SpA annual report, www.parmalat.net/attach/content/2427/Bilancio%20ENG.pdf.

Case 8-3

Satyam: India's Enron

Satyam Computer Services is an India-based global business and information technology services company that specializes in consulting, systems integration, and outsourcing solutions. The company was the fourth largest software exporter in India until January 2009, when the CEO and cofounder, Ramalinga Raju, confessed to inflating the company's profits and cash reserves over an eight-year period. The accounting fraud at Satyam involved dual accounting books, more than 7,000 forged invoices, and dozens of fake bank statements. The total amount of losses was Rs (rupees) 50 billion ($1.04 billion).[1] This represented about 94 percent of the company's cash and cash equivalents. The global scope of Satyam's fraud led to the labeling of it as "India's Enron." Ironically, the name "Satyam" is derived from the Sanskrit word *satya,* which translates to "truth."

Although headquartered in Hyderabad, India, Satyam's stock was listed on the New York Stock Exchange since 2001. When the news of the fraud broke, Satyam's stock declined almost 90 percent in value on both the U.S. and Indian stock exchanges. Several top managers either resigned or were fired and jail terms were given to Ramalinga Raju, the cofounder and CEO, and Sirinivas Vadlamani, the CFO. The auditors—PricewaterhouseCoopers—were also implicated in the fraud and investigations against it are continuing.

Fraudulent Actions by Raju

Raju stepped down in early January 2009, admitting to falsifying financial figures of the company with respect to nonexistent cash and bank balances. Stunning his well wishers and investors, Raju revealed the real motive behind the December 16 bid to acquire Maytas companies for $1.6 billion. It was to swap the fictitious cash reserves of Satyam built over years with the Maytas assets. Raju thought the payments to Maytas could be delayed once Satyam's problem was solved. What had started as a marginal gap between actual operating profit and the one reflected in the books continued to grow over the years. It had attained unmanageable proportions as the size of the company's operations grew over the years. One lie led to another. The problem further worsened as the company had to carry additional resources and assets to justify a higher level of operations, leading to increased costs.

As things went out of hand, Raju was forced to raise Rs 1.23 billion (approximately $25.58 million) more by pledging the family-owned shares to keep the operations going. His woes were compounded with amounts due to vendors, fleet operators, and construction companies. The offloading of the pledged shares by IL&FS Trust and others

[1]$1 = Rs 44 (approximately) at December 31, 2009.

brought down the promoters' stake from 8.65 percent to a fragile 3.6 percent. By the end of the day, Raju was left facing charges from several sides. The Ministry of Corporate Affairs, the state government, and the market regulator, SEBI, decided to probe the affairs of the company and Raju's role, as well as corporate governance issues.

Going by his confessional statement to the board of Satyam in January 2009, what Raju had done over the years appears to be rather simple manipulation of revenues and earnings to show a superior performance than what was actually the case. For this, he resorted to the time-tested practice of creating fictitious billings for services that were never rendered. The offset was either an inflation of receivables or the cash in bank balance. The following is a summary of the way financial statement amounts were manipulated:

- 94 percent (Rs 5.04 billion [approximately $10.5 million]) of the cash in bank account balance in the September 30, 2008, balance sheet was inflated due largely to inflated profits and fictitious assets.
- An accrued interest of Rs 376 million (approximately $7.82 million) was nonexistent.
- An understated liability of Rs 1.23 billion (approximately $25.58 million) resulting from Raju's infusion of personal funds into the company was recorded as revenue.
- Inflated revenues of Rs 588 million (approximately $12.23 million) went straight to the bottom line.

Acquisition of Maytas Properties and Maytas Infrastructure

In December 2008, Raju tried to buy two firms owned by his sons, Maytas Properties and Maytas Infrastructure (Satyam spelled backward is Maytas) for $1.6 billion. Raju tried to justify the purchase stating the company needed to diversify by incorporating the infrastructure market to augment its software market. However, many investors thought the purchases of two firms were intended to line the pockets of the Raju family. Raju owned less than 10 percent of Satyam, whereas Raju's family owned 100 percent of the equity in Maytas Properties and about 40 percent of Maytas Infrastructure. Stock prices plunged dramatically after the announcement, so Raju rescinded his offer to buy the two companies.

With the prices of Satyam stock and the health of the company declining, four members of the board of directors of Satyam resigned within one month. In his confession, Raju took full responsibility for the accounting fraud and stated that the board knew nothing about the manipulation of financial statements. He indicated a willingness to accept the legal consequences of his actions.

A important question is how independently did the "independent" directors of Satyam act in the now highly questioned and failed decision to acquire the Maytas companies? One board member, Prof. M. Rammohan Rao, dean of the Indian School of Business, claimed the board had taken an independent view and raised concerns about the unrelated diversification, valuation, and other issues. Two views emerged. The first was why not stick to our core competencies and why venture into a risky proposition? The second issue was related to the valuation of the companies. Maytas Properties was valued much higher than $1.3 billion, the amount that Satyam's management came up with for the acquisition price. When asked whether the fact that the target companies—Maytas Properties and Maytas Infrastructure—were led by Raju's two sons made any difference to the board, Rao said, "We felt the valuation proposed by the Satyam management was lower and conservative, despite the family ties. We took an independent view on this."[2]

When asked if the board had taken into consideration the possible impact of the purchase of the two companies on shareholders' interests and the market reaction, the ISB dean responded, "There were concerns on these grounds as well, especially the market reaction for such an unrelated diversification." However, according to Rao, there was no way they could gauge the market reaction at first, so they decided to take a risk. But the way the market reacted was a bit unanticipated, he added.

Questions can be raised about corporate governance with respect to the failed acquisition of the Maytas companies. A conflict of interest arose when Satyam's board agreed to invest $1.6 billion to acquire a 100 percent stake in Maytas Properties and a 51 percent stake in Maytas Infrastructure. Both of these firms were owned by Raju's sons. They also floated 21 other companies under the Maytas brand. For example, the Raju family that ran the company also invited family or close friends to serve on the board of directors. These bonds created independence issues and questions about whether directors would be confrontational with top management when warranted.

Litigation in the United States

Securities fraud class action lawsuits were filed on behalf of a class of persons and entities who purchased or acquired the American Depositary Shares (ADSs)[3] of Satyam on the NYSE and/or were investors residing in the United States who purchased or acquired Satyam common stock traded on

Indian exchanges between January 6, 2004, and January 6, 2009 (the class period).

The complaint alleged that Satyam, certain of its directors and officers, and the company's outside auditors (PwC) made false and misleading public statements regarding Satyam's financial condition and performance, which artificially inflated the stock price. On January 7, 2009, Satyam's chair, Ramalinga Raju, sent a letter to the company's board confessing to a massive accounting fraud. Raju admitted that the company's balance sheet and other public disclosures contained numerous false statements. For example, Raju wrote that as of September 30, 2008, the company overstated revenue by approximately 22 percent, and reported cash and bank balances of 53.61 billion rupees, of which 50.4 billion rupees (over $1 billion) did not exist.[4]

Reports issued since the January 7 confession indicate that Raju likely understated the scope of the fraud, and that he and members of his family have engaged in widespread theft of Satyam's funds through a complex web of intermediary entities.

The complaint also asserted claims against PricewaterhouseCoopers International Ltd. and its Indian partners and affiliates. Satyam's outside auditors from the Indian affiliate of PricewaterhouseCoopers were aware of the fraud, but still certified the company's financial statements as accurate. A document (the charge sheet) filed in a Hyderabad court by the Indian Central Bureau of Investigation (the equivalent of the U.S. Federal Bureau of Investigation), detailing charges against numerous Satyam employees and two PricewaterhouseCoopers partners, alleged that the auditors received documentation from Satyam's banks that showed that the company's disclosed assets were greatly overstated. The charge sheet further alleged that these auditors received fees from Satyam that were exorbitantly higher than the fees similarly situated Indian companies paid to their outside auditors; the Central Bureau of Investigation cited these fees as evidence of a "well knit criminal conspiracy" between Satyam and PricewaterhouseCoopers auditors.

The complaint asserted claims against other defendants as well. In particular, the complaint alleged that members of the audit committee of the Satyam board of directors—who were responsible for overseeing the integrity of the company's financial statements, the performance and compensation of the outside auditors from PricewaterhouseCoopers, and the adequacy and effectiveness of internal accounting and financial controls—were responsible for the publication of false and misleading public statements due to their extreme recklessness in discharging their duties and their resulting failure to discover and prevent the massive accounting fraud. The complaint also alleged that Maytas Infrastructure and Maytas Properties and Ramalinga Raju's two sons were responsible for the false and misleading public statements. The Raju sons' false and misleading statements concerning Satyam's

[2]Available at www.blonnet.com/2008/12/19/stories/2008121951600400.htm.
[3]American Depositary Shares (ADSs) are U.S. dollar–denominated equity shares of a foreign-based company available for purchase on an American stock exchange. ADSs are issued by depository banks in the United States under agreement with the issuing foreign company; the entire issuance is called an American Depositary Receipt (ADR) and the individual shares are referred to as ADSs.
[4]*In re Satyam Computer Services, Ltd., Securities Litigation,* U.S. District Court, Southern District of New York, 09-MD-02027, January 2009.

financial condition and performance artificially inflated the prices of the company's publicly traded securities during the class period, and caused significant damages to investors when the prices of the company's securities both in the United States and in India experienced severe declines as a direct result of disclosures regarding Satyam's true condition.

Legal Courses of Action against Satyam

Since the Satyam case amounts to criminal breach of trust, Raju and members of the management team can be punished under the Indian Penal Code (IPC) under various offenses such as criminal breach of trust, cheating, forgery, falsifying records, criminal conspiracy, and abatement. The law provides the following:

- Section 405 IPC says the offense of criminal breach of trust is punishable under Section 406 IPC, with imprisonment of either description for a term that may extend to three years, or with fine, or with both.
- Section 420 defines the offense of cheating which is made punishable with imprisonment of either description for a term that may extend to seven years, and shall also be liable to fine.
- Section 463 defines the offenses of forgery which is made punishable under section 465 IPC, with imprisonment of either description for a term that may extend to two years, or with fine, or with both.
- Section 120A defines the offenses of criminal conspiracy which is made punishable under section 120B IPC.

Other legal considerations include:

- The executive directors of the company including the signatories to the balance sheets would, ipso facto, be liable to prosecution (subject to their proving lack of knowledge of the impugned transactions), while "independent" directors could be held liable if their complicity is apparent from the records.
- Under Section 24 of the SEBI Act, executive directors can be imprisoned for up to 10 years and imposed a fine of up to Rs 250 million (approximately $5.2 million). If they do not pay the fine, they can be jailed for a further term of anywhere between 4 months and 10 years.

Since Satyam is listed in the NYSE, there will be a number of lawsuits coming up for Raju. Already, two class action lawsuits have already been filed against Satyam by two U.S. law firms. Satyam Computer Services' former chair Ramalinga Raju can face up to 10 years imprisonment along with a fine, which may extend to Rs 250 million (approximately $5.2 million). Market regulator SEBI already has ordered an inquiry into these issues to find out if Raju has violated the various regulations pertaining to dealings in securities market. SEBI will look into various statutory violations, which

include unfair trade practices and insider trading. Under the SEBI Act, imprisonment and monetary penalty could be awarded "if any person contravenes or attempts to contravene or abets the contravention of the provision of this Act or of any rules or regulations made there under." This would mean that Raju could be punished for violating the securities regulation as well as for abetting officers of Satyam to commit financial fraud. In addition to violation of the SEBI norms, Raju can also be tried for other offenses like misappropriation of funds and breach of trust under various sections of the Indian Penal Code and Companies Act.

Actions against PwC

PwC, the auditors of Satyam, initially hid behind "client confidentiality" and stated that it was "examining the contents of the statement." Realizing that this was not enough, PwC came up with a second statement claiming that "the audits were conducted in accordance with applicable auditing standards and were supported by appropriate audit evidence." This is somewhat troublesome since an audit in accordance with generally accepted auditing standards calls for examining the contents of the financial statements. Given that the firm did not identify the financial wrongdoing at Satyam, it would appear that the firm, at the very least, was guilty of professional negligence. At a minimum, the firm missed or failed to do the following:

- Fictitious invoices with customers were recorded as genuine.
- Raju recorded a fictional interest credit as income.
- The auditors didn't ask for a statement of confirmation of balance from banks (for cash balances) and debtors (for receivables), a basic procedure in an audit.

On January 26, 2009, Indian police arrested two partners of the Indian arm of PwC on charges of criminal conspiracy and cheating in connection with the fraud investigation at Satyam. Furious Indian investors had pressured the authorities to take such an action in light of the more than $1 billion fraud. Investors couldn't understand how a reported $1 billion in cash was really only $78 million, and how it wasn't detected by PwC. The company's financial statements were signed off by PwC on March 31, 2008.[5]

Class Action Lawsuits

India

On July 17, 2009, the SEBI said it will fund a domestic investors' association that has filed a class action lawsuit against Satyam, its former promoters, auditors, and directors. The lawsuit is seeking compensation from Satyam and the

[5]Ronald Fink, "Doubt Cast on Satyam Executives' Accusations against PwC," *Financial Week*, www.financialweek.com/apps/pbcs.dll/article=/20090127/REG/901279970/10.

parties involved for the losses these investors incurred in its stock price crash, after the accounting fraud came to light in January 2009. The class action, which is a collective lawsuit presented by a representative-member before a court on behalf of a large number of investors, has been filed in the Supreme Court of India by New Delhi–based Midas Touch Investor Association.

This is the first instance in India where SEBI is financially assisting investors to legally challenge wrongdoing by companies or promoters.

The enforcement of lawsuits in Indian courts is complex and is explained in Appendix 3.

United States

On January 11, 2010, India asked the authorities in the United States to not take any action against Satyam as it would amount to punishing shareholders twice. Satyam can face punitive action in the United States because the company's shares are listed and traded on U.S. exchanges. Satyam also is contending about a dozen class action lawsuits in U.S. courts. It is also possible that the company will face charges from the SEC.

As many as 12 class action lawsuits were filed against the company by January 2009, and more are expected to be filed. The lawsuits were filed by investors in the American Depositary Shares ever since Raju confessed to having fudged the accounts of the company for at least seven years. The biggest liability that Satyam faces is from class action suits that have been filed in the United States by holders of Satyam's ADRs. While there is no way to put an exact figure on the liabilities, it could in theory be so large that it would make any recovery for the firm impossible. There is the option of an out-of-court settlement with those who have filed suits; but at the moment Satyam doesn't have the money to pay the settlement and may not have much money anytime soon.

The charges alleged against the defendants in the lawsuits filed to date are:

1. The defendants issued misleading financial information about the company including information contained in its annual reports, which were signed by the defendants and contained fairness opinions issued by Satyam's auditor, PricewaterhouseCoopers.

2. A letter was sent by Ramalinga Raju to the board of directors of Satyam and SEBI admitting to falsification of accounts, overstatement of profits and debt owed to the company, and understatement of liabilities. The purchasers of Satyam's ADSs were injured through their purchase of stock at inflated prices because they relied on the false and misleading information provided by the defendants.

3. None of the statements made by the defendants that have been alleged to be false in the lawsuit had any qualifying cautionary statements identifying factors that could cause results to differ materially from that stated.

Relief Sought

The plaintiffs have alleged that by defrauding the purchasers of Satyam's ADSs, the defendants have violated provisions of the U.S. Securities Exchange Act of 1934 and, therefore, the plaintiffs should be awarded unspecified compensatory damages. Indian market regulator SEBI announced in January 2010 that beleaguered Satyam can sell 51 percent equity stake in the company through a global competitive bidding process. Larsen & Toubro, Tech Mahindra, Spice group, the Hindujas, and some private equity firms have been in a race to acquire the tainted firm.

Questions

1. In his "mea culpa" statement, Ramalinga Raju, the CEO and cofounder of Satyam, confessed to inflating the company's profits and cash reserves over an eight-year period. He explained: "What started as a marginal gap between actual operating profit and the one reflected in the books continued to grow over the years. It has attained unmanageable proportions as the size of the company's operations grew over the years. One lie led to another. The problem further worsened as the company had to carry additional resources and assets to justify higher level of operations, leading to increased costs." Evaluate Raju's statement from the perspective of ethical behavior including stakeholder effects and moral reasoning using the discussions in Chapters 1–3 for guidance.

2. Explain how PwC failed to live up to its professional and ethical obligations in its audit of Satyam. Be sure to cite specific standards, whether ethical or GAAS, to support your answer.

3. Evaluate the corporate governance systems at Satyam using the model of Indian governance discussed in the chapter and any other "best practices" you believe should be implemented. Did the management and directors at Satyam live up to their responsibilities for corporate governance? Be specific and provide support for your answer.

Optional Question

Research the current status of all legal action against Satyam, its officers, and the PwC auditors. What changes have occurred in the facts of the case?

Appendix 1[6]

Enforcement of Foreign Court Awards in India

Section 44 A of the Indian Code of Civil Procedure, 1908 (Code) allows for the direct enforcement of foreign awards in India if the award is made by a superior court in a country that is a reciprocating territory, as defined in the Code. Currently, the Indian government has not notified the United States to be a reciprocating territory and, therefore, any judgment against Satyam in any class action law suit instituted in the United States cannot be directly enforced in India. In contrast, arbitral awards rendered in the United States are enforceable in India, subject to certain exceptions, as the Indian government has notified the United States to be a country that is a party to the Convention on the Recognition and Enforcement of Foreign Arbitral Awards, 1958 (New York Convention). Instead, a fresh lawsuit must be filed in the Indian domestic courts. The foreign judgment is considered to have value as evidence. Pursuant to Part X of Division I of the Schedule to the Limitation Act, 1963, the time limit to file such a law suit in India is within three years of the delivery of the foreign judgment.

Class Action Suit in India

The Indian government is planning to codify class action as law. A clause for filing class action suit has been included in the new Company Law bill in India. Once enacted, the provision will empower shareholders to hold companies and their managements responsible for wrong-doing. Though the principles of class or representative action by shareholders against managements have been upheld by various courts in India, these are yet to be reflected in law.

Investors Grievances Forum, headed by a former member of Parliament, Kirit Somaiya, filed a PIL in the Bombay High Court seeking appointment of a committee to make regulatory process more effective and protect small investors in the aftermath of the Satyam scam. It is alleged that Satyam's board and auditors are guilty of negligence, breach of duty, trust, and fraud. It also accused the auditors of taking no steps to verify the truth and ascertain and correct state of affairs of the firm.

[6]Available at Jotwani Associates Web site, www.hg.org/article.asp?id=6284.

Civil Law

The civil law gives creditors the right to sue for recovery of money in the civil courts (or by way of arbitration, if such agreements exist) or otherwise bring petitions for winding-up of the company (before the Andhra Pradesh High Court) on the grounds of the company's inability to pay its debts and, also, for the loss of its substratum and its continuance being repugnant to commercial morality. Tortuous suits for negligence are possible at the behest of the shareholders (similar to the class action suit already filed in the United States), who could equally explore the option of collectively approaching the Company Law board, for mismanagement action, as well as file winding-up petitions themselves.

Registrar of Companies (RoC)

The Satyam ripoff also appears to be violations of the Companies Act and may lead to action by the Registrar of Companies. According to Section 210 and Section 211 of the act, the board of directors must place before the Annual General Meeting a copy of the balance sheet and profit and loss of the company and that balance sheet and the profit and loss account of a company must reflect the true and fair view of the state of affairs of the company at the end of the financial year. Section 215 requires the balance sheet to be signed by a manager or secretary, if any, and by two directors, one of whom necessarily must be a managing director. Any director who fails to take suitable steps to ensure that provisions of Sections 210 and 211 are followed may be punished with imprisonment of up to 6 months and a fine, which may extend to INR 10,000 or more.

Under Section 628, if any return, report, certificate, balance sheet, prospectus, statement, or other document required by or for the purposes of any provisions of the act is made false or such a person omits any material fact, it shall be punishable with imprisonment for a term which may extend to two years. Further, under Section 635 of the act, the Central Government may investigate the affairs of the company including through the Serious Frauds Investigation Office. In addition, under the Companies Act, Depositories Act, and the Listing Agreement, SEBI will have a cause of action for violation of mailing a false annual report to the shareholders.

Case 8-4

Royal Dutch Shell plc[1]

From 1907 until 2005, Royal Dutch Petroleum Company, a Netherlands-based company, and the "Shell" Transport and Trading Company, plc., a UK-based company, were the two public parent companies of a group of companies known collectively as the Royal Dutch/Shell Group (Group).[2] Operating activities were conducted through the subsidiaries of Royal Dutch and Shell Transport. In 2005, Royal Dutch Shell plc became the single parent company of Royal Dutch and Shell Transport, the two former public parent companies of the group (the unification). Today, Shell is one of the world's largest independent oil and gas companies in terms of market capitalization, operating cash flow, and oil and gas production.

Proved Reserves

Petroleum resources represent a significant part of the group's upstream assets and are the foundation of most of its current and future activities. The group's exploration and production business depends on its effectiveness in finding and maturing petroleum resources to sustain itself and drive profitable production growth. The group reports its proved reserves of oil and gas to the SEC as part of its 20-F filing for a foreign company selling stock on the NYSE.

Properly reporting internal and external volumes is very important to Shell. This is based on the SEC-compliant proved reserves estimation and reporting process that enables access to funds needed for the group's capital-intensive business. The SEC requirement of "reasonable certainty" represents the high standard of evidence/confidence consistent with the meaning of the word *proved*. Proved oil and gas reserves are the estimated quantities of crude oil, natural gas, and natural gas liquids that geological and engineering data demonstrate with reasonable certainty to be recoverable in future years from known reservoirs under existing economic and operating conditions

(i.e., prices and costs as of the date the estimate is made). Prices include consideration of changes in existing prices provided by contractual arrangements, but not on escalations based upon future conditions.[3]

In 2004, Shell amended its annual report on Form 20-F/A for the calendar year 2003 financial statements following an agreement with the SEC reached on August 24, 2004, with respect to the amount of proved reserves. The SEC had charged that 4.47 billion barrels of oil equivalent, or approximately 23 percent of previously reported proved reserves, did not meet the standard set by law. Shell also reduced its reserves replacement ratio (RRR)—the rate at which production was replaced by new oil discoveries. According to the SEC complaint, Shell's overstatement of proved reserves, and its delay in correcting the overstatement, resulted from (1) its desire to create and maintain the appearance of a strong RRR, a key performance indicator in the oil and gas industry; (2) the failure of its internal reserves estimation and reporting guidelines to conform to applicable regulations; and (3) the lack of effective internal controls over the reserves estimation and reporting process.[4]

Reduction of Reserves Replacement Ratio

In a series of announcements between January 9 and May 24, 2004, Shell disclosed that it had recategorized 4.47 billion barrels of oil equivalent (boe), or approximately 23 percent, of the proved reserves it reported as of year-end 2002 because they were not proved reserves as defined in Commission Rule 4-10 of Regulation S-X. This recategorization reduced the standard measure of future cash flows by approximately $6.6 billion as reported in Shell's original 2002 Form 20-F Supplemental Information under Statement of Financial Accounting Standard No. 69.[5]

---

[1]The letters *plc* refer to a "public limited company." The company operates on the basis that liability of shareholders toward the public is limited to its shareholding and that they are not personally liable for debts of the company. If the company goes into bankruptcy, the personal assets of directors/shareholders are not liable for attachment.

[2]In the United States this would be comparable to the consolidated entity that comprises two separately operating subsidiaries. As in the United States, each subsidiary would issue separate financial statements and those statements would be consolidated and combined statements would be issued in the annual report. In the Royal Dutch Shell case, all references to the financial statements are to the consolidated (group) statements.

[3]Petroleum Resource Volume Requirements for Resource Classification and Value Realization, www.shell.com/...and.../reserves_announcement_09062005.html.

[4]*Securities and Exchange Commission v. Royal Dutch Petroleum Company and the "Shell" Transport and Trading Company, P.L.C.,* Complaint H-04-3359, August 24, 2004, www.sec.gov/litigation/litreleases/lr18844.htm.

[5]*Statement of Financial Accounting Standards (SFAS) No. 69,* Disclosures about Oil and Gas Producing Activities. This standard requires that publicly traded enterprises that have significant oil- and gas-producing activities should disclose, among other things, "proved oil and gas reserves" as of the beginning and end of the year. Revisions of previous estimates must be disclosed separately with appropriate explanation of significant changes.

On July 2, 2004, Shell filed an amended 2002 Form 20-F reflecting the restatement of its proved reserves and standard measure of future cash flows for the years 1999 to 2002 as follows:

Year	Reduction in Proved Reserves	% Reduction	Reduction in Standardized Measure	% Reduction
1997	3.13 boe	16%	N/A	N/A
1998	3.78 boe	18%	N/A	N/A
1999	4.58 boe	23%	$7.0 billion	11%
2000	4.84 boe	25%	$7.2 billion	10%
2001	4.53 boe	24%	$6.5 billion	13%
2002	4.47 boe	23%	$6.6 billion	9%

As a result of the overstatement of proved reserves, Shell also announced a reduction in its RRR for 1998 through 2002, from the previously reported 100 percent to approximately 80 percent. Had Shell reported proved reserves properly, its annual and three-year RRR over this span would have been as follows:

Year	1-Year RRR		3-Year RRR	
	Original	Restated	Original	Restated
1998	182%	134%	N/A	N/A
1999	56%	−5%	N/A	N/A
2000	69%	50%	102%	60%
2001	74%	97%	66%	48%
2002	117%	121%	87%	90%
2003	N/A	63%	N/A	94%

According to the SEC complaint, these failures led Shell to record and maintain proved reserves it knew, or was reckless in not knowing, did not satisfy applicable regulations and to report for certain years a stronger RRR than it actually had achieved in supplemental information filed along with its 10-K report. The SEC had warned about the proved reserves but Shell either rejected the warnings as immaterial or unduly pessimistic, or attempted to manage the potential exposure by, for example, delaying debooking of improperly recorded proved reserves until new, offsetting proved reserves bookings materialized.

Failure to Maintain Adequate Internal Controls

The charges against Shell include the failure to implement and maintain internal controls sufficient to provide reasonable assurance that it was estimating and reporting proved reserves accurately and in compliance with applicable requirements. These failures arose from inadequate training and supervision of the operating unit personnel responsible for estimating and reporting proved reserves and deficiencies in the internal reserves audit function. Shell's decentralized system required an effective internal reserves audit function.

To perform this function, Shell historically had engaged as group reserves auditor a retired Shell petroleum engineer who worked only part-time and was provided limited resources and no staff to audit its vast worldwide operations. Although the group reserves auditor was an experienced reservoir engineer, he received little, if any, training on such critical matters as how he should conduct his work and the rules and standards on which his opinions should be based. He also lacked authority to require operating unit compliance with either commission rules or group reserves guidelines. Moreover, he reported to the management of Shell's exploration and production division, which were the same people he audited.

The group reserves auditor visited each operating unit only once every four or more years. Subsequent to his visits, he issued reports rating the operating unit's systems, compliance with group guidelines, and audit response as "good," "satisfactory," or "unsatisfactory," opining whether the operating unit's reported reserves met group guidelines. From the start of his tenure in January 1999 until September 2003, the group reserves auditor did not issue a single "unsatisfactory" rating. The group reserves auditor also issued an annual report on the reasonableness of Shell's year-end total reserves summary. Until his February 2004 report on Shell's 2003 proved reserves, the group reserves auditor focused as much on whether group proved reserves complied with group guidelines as he did on whether they complied with SEC requirements.

Further, the group reserves auditor failed to act independently in several respects. At times, he allowed proved reserves associated with a project to remain booked because he was more "bullish" on its prospects than the local management responsible for the project. At other times, solely to support booking proved reserves for otherwise uneconomic projects, he advised local management to submit development plans that were unlikely ever to be executed. This lack of independence facilitated the booking of questionable reserves well after they should have been debooked.

Finally, the nonexecutive directors of Royal Dutch and Shell Transport, including the members of the group audit committee, were not provided with the information necessary for the boards of the two companies to ensure that timely and appropriate action was taken with respect to the proved reserves estimation and reporting practices.

Group Reserves Auditor's Report

In January 2002, the group reserves auditor's report on Shell's 2001 proved reserves stated that "recent clarifications of FASB reserves guidelines by the SEC have shown that current Group reserves practice regarding the first time booking of Proved reserves in new fields is in some cases too lenient." The auditor stated that the "group guidelines should be reviewed [and] first-time bookings should be aligned closer with SEC guidance and industry practice and they should be allowed only for firm projects with technical maturity and full economic viability."

On February 11, 2002, an internal note addressed the divergence between Shell's guidelines and the commission's rules and estimated the possible impact of this divergence on Shell's reported proved reserves. The note explicitly stated that "recently the SEC issued clarifications that make it apparent that the Group guidelines for booking Proved Reserves are no longer fully aligned with the SEC rules." Potential exposures identified in the note included approximately 1 billion boe of proved reserves relating to projects. The note failed to recommend debookings, and Shell did not take action to debook any of these proved reserves at that time.

On February 25, 2002, the CEO of the Exploration and Production (EP) division circulated a note regarding EP's 2001 performance, asking his colleagues to "keep a balanced perspective on EP performance in 2001 and not have it overshadowed by the high profile issues around production growth and reserves replacement." As one of the main issues, the note stated that in 2001 the SEC issued clarifications of the rules for reserves reporting that made it clear that the probabilistic approach still advocated in the Shell guidelines was, in many cases, too aggressive. The note indicated that this would likely impact future bookings in new fields and possibly existing booked volumes. The note failed

to recommend debookings, and Shell did not take action to de-book any of these proved reserves at that time.

In a July 2002 meeting, EP again reported that the SEC was tightening its requirements regarding proved reserves. EP, however, reported that "it is considered unlikely that potential over-bookings would need to be de-booked in the short term, but the reserves that are exposed to project risk or license expiration cannot remain on the books indefinitely if little progress is made to convert them to production in a timely manner." The minutes of this meeting, however, also reflect that the executives were advised of the concerns that had arisen within EP "that some booking practices had been too aggressive in the past."

By September 2002, the CEO of EP internally spoke in blunt terms of his perception of the operational and performance problems facing EP, noting to his colleagues that "we are struggling on all key criteria" and that "RRR remains below 100% mainly due to aggressive booking in 1997–2000." He further observed that "we have tried to adhere to a bunch of criteria that can only be managed successfully for so long" and admonished that "given the external visibility of our issues . . ., the market can only be 'fooled' if: (1) credibility of the company is high; (2) medium and long-term portfolio refreshment is real; and/or (3) positive trends can be shown on key indicators."

A month later, the group chair e-mailed the EP CEO that he was "not contemplating a change in the external promise." The next day, the EP CEO responded, "I must admit that I become sick and tired about arguing about the hard facts and also can not perform miracles given where we are today. If I was interpreting the disclosure requirements literally under the Sarbanes-Oxley Act and legal requirements we would have a real problem."

None of these events prompted Shell to debook significant volumes. To the contrary, Shell continued to make large, questionable proved reserves bookings during this period. By the summer of 2003, Shell's analysis of reserves exposures had progressed, but still no debookings were recommended even though internal information indicated that "some 1040 million boe (5%) is considered to be potentially at risk." The note concluded, however, that "at this stage, no action in relation to entries in the [proved reserves exposure] Catalogue is recommended. . . . It should be noted that the total potential exposure is broadly offset by the potential to include gas fuel and flare volumes in external reserves disclosures." The note apprised the committee of steps taken to address possible noncompliance with the SEC's regulations. However, management was advised that "much, if not all, of the potential exposure is offset by Shell's practice of not disclosing reserves in relation to gas production that is consumed on site as fuel or (incidental) flaring and venting."

According to the SEC complaint, Shell had undertaken substantial remedial efforts in connection with the reserves recategorization and had cooperated with the commission in its investigation.

Specific SEC Charges

The SEC complaint alleged the following:[6]

1. As a result of Shell's knowing or reckless overstatement of its oil and gas reserves in its financial statements, the group's commission filings, specified previously, as well as other public statements, contained materially false and misleading statements and disclosures. These filings contained untrue statements of material fact concerning the company's reported proved reserves and omitted to state facts necessary to make the statements made, in light of the circumstances under which they were made, not misleading. These statements constituted a violation of Rule 10b-5 of the Securities Exchange Act.

2. Section 13(a) of the Exchange Act requires issuers to file such annual and quarterly reports as the commission may prescribe and in conformity with such rules as the commission may promulgate. Rule 13a-1 requires the filing of accurate annual reports that comply with the commission's Regulation S-X. Rule 12b- 20 requires an issuer to include material information as may be necessary to make the required statements, in light of the circumstances under which they were made, not misleading. The following periodic reports that Royal Dutch and Shell Transport filed with the commission were not prepared in accordance with rules promulgated by the commission: Form 20-F for fiscal years 1997–2002.

3. Shell violated Section 12 of the Exchange Act in that it failed to (a) make and keep books, records, and accounts, which, in reasonable detail, accurately and fairly reflect the transactions and dispositions of its assets; (b) devise and maintain a system of internal accounting controls sufficient to provide reasonable assurances that (1) transactions are executed in accordance with management's general or specific authorization; (2) transactions are recorded as necessary to permit preparation of financial statements in conformity with generally accepted accounting principles or any other criteria applicable to such statements, and to maintain accountability for assets; (3) access to assets is permitted only in accordance with management's general or specific authorization; and (4) the recorded accountability for assets is compared with the existing assets at reasonable intervals and appropriate action is taken with respect to any differences.

Royal Dutch and Shell Transport agreed to settle the charges by consenting to a cease-and-desist order finding violations of the antifraud, internal controls, record-keeping, and reporting provisions of the federal securities laws, and by paying $1 disgorgement and a $120 million penalty in a related action. Shell also committed an additional $5 million to develop and implement a comprehensive internal compliance program under the direction and oversight of the group's legal director. The companies settled without admitting or denying the commission's substantive findings.[7]

Reserve and Financial Restatements

The Form 20-F/A amendment to the 2004 annual report explains the restatements of reserve amounts and its effect on net income in the information presented in Appendix 1.

---

[6]*Securities and Exchange Commission v. Royal Dutch Petroleum Company and the "Shell" Transport and Trading Company, P.L.C.,* Complaint H-04-3359, August 24, 2004, www.sec.gov/litigation/litreleases/lr18844.htm.

[7]U.S. Securities and Exchange Commission, Litigation Release No. 18844, August 24, 2004, www.sec.gov/litigation/litreleases/lr18844.htm.

Appendix 1

Royal Dutch Shell Form 20-F information[1]

Explanatory Note 1

This Amendment No. 1 (this Report) to the Annual Report on Form 20-F for the year ended December 31, 2004, as filed with the U.S. Securities and Exchange Commission (the SEC) on March 30, 2004 (the Original Form 20-F), amends pages ii, 48, G2, G9 and G49 of the Original 20-F to add certain

[1]Excerpted from: Morningstar Document Research, *Form 20-F, Royal Dutch Shell plc,* Filed: March 15, 2005 (period: December 31, 2004).

supplemental information on those pages and amends a limited number of other pages to correct clerical or typographical errors, as disclosed, in part, on the Report on Form 6-K furnished by the registrants to the SEC on April 8, 2005. No other information included in the Original 20-F is amended hereby. For presentation purposes only, this Report restates in its entirety the Original 20-F. Except as otherwise stated in this Report, all information presented in this Report, including forward looking statements, is as at March 30, 2004 and has not been updated for events subsequent to the date of the original filing. Certain disclosures are expressly presented as of an earlier date in accordance with disclosure requirements applicable to Form 20-F.

This Report does not amend the registrants' Annual Report on Form 20-F filed with the SEC for the year ended December 31, 2003 or any prior period.

Explanatory Note 2

Reserves Restatements

First Reserves Restatement

As announced on January 9, 2004, March 18, 2004, and April 19, 2004, the Group reviewed its proved reserves inventory (with the assistance of external consultants) during the period from late 2003 to April 2004 (collectively, the First Half Review). Following the First Half Review, 4,474 million barrels of oil equivalent (boe)2 previously booked at December 31, 2002 as proved reserves were recategorised as not proved. The results of the First Half Review were reflected in the restatement of proved reserves and of the standardised measure of discounted future net cash flows as for the periods prior to December 31, 2003 contained in the 2003 Annual Report and Accounts and the 2003 Annual Report on Form 20-F, as originally filed with US Securities and Exchange Commission (SEC) on June 30, 2004 (the First Reserves Restatement).

Second Reserves Restatement

As announced on October 28, 2004, November 26, 2004 and February 3, 2005, the Group performed reviews of its proved reserves inventory (with the assistance of external consultants) during the period from July 2004 to December 2004 (collectively, the Second Half Review). As a result of the Second Half Review, 1,371 million boe previously booked at December 31, 2003 as proved reserves were recategorised as not proved. These changes are reflected in the restatement of proved reserves and the standardised measure of future cash flows contained in this Report (the Second Reserves Restatement). The Second Reserves Restatement was also reflected in Amendment No. 2 to the 2003 Annual Report on Form 20-F, as filed with the SEC on March 7, 2005. The Second Reserves Restatement will also be reflected in the 2004 Annual Report and Accounts.

The Second Half Review reflected the implementation of certain remedial actions, designed to strengthen the controls relating to the reporting of proved reserves, undertaken following the restatement of proved reserves and of the standardised measure of discounted future net cash flows contained in the 2003 Annual Report and Accounts and the 2003 Annual Report on Form 20-F, as originally filed with the SEC on June 30, 2004. See "Controls and Procedures—Remedial Actions Taken in 2004" for an additional discussion of these remedial actions.

2The Group converts natural gas to crude oil equivalent using a factor of 5,800 standard cubic feet per barrel.

Financial Restatements

First Financial Restatement

In view of the inappropriate overstatement of unaudited[3] proved reserves information resulting in the First Reserves Restatement, it was determined to restate the Financial Statements of the Group, and each of the Parent Companies, for the year ended December 31, 2002 and prior periods (the First Financial Restatement) to reflect the impact of the First Reserves Restatement on those Financial Statements (as announced on April 19, 2004). As part of the First Financial Restatement, the financial statements were also restated to correct an inappropriate departure from US GAAP relating to certain exploratory drilling costs, to correct an inappropriate departure from US GAAP (for 2002 only) for certain gas contracts to correct an error in the calculation of earnings per share of the Parent Companies and to reflect a change in accounting principle relating to inventories. The First Financial Restatement was reflected in the 2003 Annual Report and Accounts and the 2003 Annual Report on Form 20-F, as originally filed with the SEC on June 30, 2004.

Second Financial Restatement

In view of the inappropriate overstatement of unaudited proved reserves information resulting in the Second Reserves Restatement, it was determined to restate the Financial Statements of the Group and each of the Parent Companies for the year ended December 31, 2003 and prior periods (the Second Financial Restatement) to reflect the impact of the Second Reserves Restatement on those Financial Statements (as announced on February 3, 2005). This overstatement of unaudited proved reserves information had the effect of understating the depreciation, depletion and amortisation charges related to Exploration & Production in each of the years covered by the Second Financial Restatement. As capitalised costs relating to Exploration & Production were amortised across fewer proved reserves (following the Second Reserves Restatement), depreciation, depletion and amortisation associated with annual production volumes increased proportionally. The Second Financial Restatement reduced previously reported net assets as at December 31, 2003 by $351 million. The Second Financial Restatement is reflected in this Report and also in Amendment No. 2 to the 2003 Annual Report on Form 20-F, as filed with the SEC on March 7, 2005.

The following table sets forth the adjustments made to reported results to eliminate the effect of the inappropriate overstatement of unaudited proved reserves as described above under "Reserves Restatements":

3Reserves, reserves volumes and reserves related information and disclosure are referred to as "unaudited" as a means to clarify that this information is not covered by the audit opinion of the independent registered accounting firms that have audited and reported on the financial statement of the Group or the Parent Companies.

Second Financial Restatement Effects

	$ million			
Net Income	**2003**	**2002**	**2001**	**pre 2001**
Depreciation, depletion and amortisation	(289)	(118)	(94)	(112)
Share of operating profit of associated companies	(19)	(6)	(2)	(2)
Income before taxation	(308)	(124)	(96)	(114)
Total tax	126	54	44	54
Income after taxation	(182)	(70)	(52)	(60)
Minority interest	(1)	4	3	7
Net income	(183)	(66)	(49)	(53)

Additional information in the notes to the financial statements explains the causes of the restatements as follows:

- The Group's guidelines for booking proved reserves were inadequate in several respects, including (i) containing inconsistencies with the SEC's rules and published guidance relating to proved reserves and (ii) failing to clearly and sufficiently impart these requirements and guidance to users of the guidelines. In addition, users of the guidelines in certain cases misapplied or disregarded SEC rules and published guidance and in some cases only applied changes in the guidelines prospectively rather than retrospectively. There was also insufficient knowledge and training among users of the guidelines of the SEC requirements relating to proved reserves;

- Executives and employees encouraged the booking of proved reserves, while discouraging the debooking of previously booked reserves. This fostered an atmosphere that failed to emphasise the paramount importance of the compliance element of proved reserves decisions; and

- There were other material weaknesses in the Group's controls relating to the booking of proved reserves, including insufficient resources allocated to the Group Reserves Auditor and Group Reserves Co-ordinator functions, a lack of clarity in the allocation of responsibilities between the Group Reserves Auditor and the Group Reserves Co-ordinator, and a lack of direct reporting responsibility of the Group Reserves Auditor to the Group internal audit function and of the business chief financial officers to the Group Chief Financial Officer.

Questions

1. Explain how the determination of proved reserves affected Shell's financial statements for the years 2001–2003. Which stakeholders were most affected by Shell's reporting of proved reserves?

2. On February 11, 2002, an internal note addressed the divergence between Shell's guidelines and the commission's rules and estimated the possible impact of this divergence on Shell's reported proved reserves. The note explicitly stated that "recently the SEC issued clarifications that make it apparent that the Group guidelines for booking Proved Reserves are no longer fully aligned with the SEC rules." Potential exposures identified in the note included approximately 1 billion boe of proved reserves relating to projects. The note failed to recommend debookings, and Shell did not take action to debook any of these proved reserves at that time. What motivated Shell to consistently delay debooking overestimated proved reserves even though the company knew they were not in compliance with SEC regulations?

3. Given the facts of the case, describe the failures in internal controls and how they contributed toward the financial reporting problems at Shell.

Optional Question

The following note to the financial statements of Shell for the fiscal year end December 31, 2008, appeared in its 20-F filing with SEC.

IMPAIRMENT

Other than properties with no proved reserves (where the basis for carrying costs in the Consolidated Balance Sheet is explained under "Exploration costs"), the carrying amounts of major property, plant and equipment are reviewed for possible impairment annually, while all assets are reviewed whenever events or changes in circumstances indicate that the carrying amounts for those assets may not be recoverable. If assets are determined to be impaired, the carrying amounts of those assets are written down to their recoverable amount, which is the higher of fair value less costs to sell and value in use, the latter being determined as the amount of estimated risk-adjusted discounted future cash flows. For this purpose, assets are grouped into cash-generating units based on separately identifiable and largely independent cash inflows. Assets classified as held for sale are recognized at the lower of the carrying amount and fair value less cost to sell. No further provision for depreciation is charged on such assets.

Estimates of future cash flows used in the evaluation for impairment of assets related to hydrocarbon production are made using risk assessments on field and reservoir performance and include expectations about proved reserves and unproved volumes, which are then risk-weighted utilizing the results from projections of geological, production, recovery and economic factors.

Impairments, except those related to goodwill, are reversed as applicable to the extent that the events or circumstances that triggered the original impairment have changed. Impairment charges and reversals are reported within depreciation, depletion and amortization.

Compare the standards followed by Shell that conform to IFRS with those generally accepted in the United States. Explain any differences and how such differences might impact the financial statements.

Case 8-5

Bat-A-Bing Construction Company

This case involves Bat-A-Bing Construction Company, a U.S.-based construction company that plans to go public in 2011 following its expansion into China. Beginning in the second quarter of 2009, Bat-A-Bing changed its accounting practices to recognize as income "unapproved claims" (defined in the following text) in connection with certain large construction contracts. Previously, the company recorded income from claims only after the claim was resolved between Bat-A-Bing and the customer. The change resulted in enhanced bottom-line financial performance for the company. For example, by including the unapproved claims component, its audited pretax income for 2009 was 46 percent greater than it would have been without the inclusion of unapproved claims.

Joey Fuzzarelli is a CPA and Bat-A-Bing's controller. He oversees the company's financial reporting including the claims recognition practice. Joey has known about the claims recognition practice for two years. During that time, the company failed to disclose the change or provide any other details concerning the accounting practice. Joey brought his concerns to Sally Bustarello, the CFO, who also is a CPA, but Sally was not very supportive. Sally insisted on reporting the unapproved claims using the new method and told Joey the word came from the highest levels of the company. "Besides," Sally said, "we are not publicly owned; therefore our results are only reported to the board of directors." Joey knew that meant the results were reported to the CEO, Augie Donatelli, who is chair of the board; Sally, who is also on the board; and members of the Donatelli family. She also reminded Joey that the auditors have provided an unqualified opinion on the financial statements for the past three years.

Prior to mid-2009, Bat-A-Bing generally conducted business under two types of contracts: "cost-plus" or "fixed-fee." *Cost-plus contracts* provide for reimbursement to the contractor of all reasonable costs, plus an agreed-upon profit payable to the contractor. Under *fixed-fee contracts,* contractors perform for a fixed, agreed-upon fee intended by the parties to encompass all reasonable costs foreseen at the time of the contract's execution. The contractor's profit equals the margin by which the fee exceeds the contractor's costs; if those costs exceed the fee, the contractor incurs a loss on the contract. Fixed-fee contracts offer, therefore, an opportunity to make larger profits—assuming the contractor can control its costs; conversely, fixed-fee contracts expose the contractor to greater risk of losses in the event that the contractor cannot control costs or incurs unforeseen costs. Under either type of contract, the contractor may incur costs that were not envisioned when the contract was executed; however, under a cost-plus contract, the contractor is more likely to recoup from the customer those unforeseen costs.

In early 2010, Bat-A-Bing commenced several large-scale fixed-fee projects that were greater in scope and complexity than the company's previous fixed-fee contracts. The earliest of these projects involved the construction of a gas production plant in the Middle East; the company's customer was a joint venture between a national oil company and a multinational oil company. The contract called for completion of the project by mid-2011 at a cost of approximately $169 million. By the fourth quarter of 2010, the company's estimated cost overruns placed the project in an approximate $20 million loss position, as a result of which the company recorded $20 million of losses in that quarter. The $20 million loss gave rise to a corresponding $20 million reduction in Bat-A-Bing's fourth quarter 2009 operating income.

Bat-A-Bing disclosed in the financial statements provided to the board of directors that "claims for additional compensation are recognized during the period such claims are resolved." This statement of practice never varied through the second quarter of 2009. Pursuant to the practice, before the claim was resolved the company generally recorded losses caused by project cost overruns; only after the claim was resolved would the company recognize the claim as an offset against a project's cost overruns.

The change in accounting practice involved offsetting cost overruns on the contracts with estimated recoveries on claims that had not been resolved with customers. Under this new practice, the company began offsetting project cost overruns with revenue from unapproved claims in instances in which the company believed that the claims were probable of collection, and reliably estimable "unapproved claims." As a result of the change in accounting practice, cost overruns and resulting losses on several contracts were reduced or eliminated. By reducing or eliminating the losses, Bat-A-Bing increased its income.

Joey has been quite concerned about Bat-A-Bing's financial reporting since the beginning of the second quarter of 2009 when it changed its accounting for unapproved claims. He has already been told by Sally that the new method was approved by top management and he knows that the board of directors are not likely to listen to his concerns especially since the external auditors did not raise any issues with respect to the accounting for unapproved claims. However, Joey knows the company must include in its registration statement with the SEC three years of audited financial statements and selected data for five years. He does not think those statements should be included without recognition of the change in accounting.

Questions

1. In May 2005, the Financial Accounting Standards Board issued *SFAS No. 154,* Accounting Changes and Error Corrections, that replaces *APB Opinion No. 20* and *FASB No. 3.* In the summary of the standard the FASB included the following statement:

   This Statement is the result of a broader effort by the FASB to improve the comparability of cross-border financial reporting by working with the International Accounting Standards Board (IASB) toward development of a single set of high-quality accounting standards. As part of that effort, the FASB and the IASB identified opportunities to improve financial reporting by eliminating certain narrow differences between their existing accounting standards. Reporting of accounting changes was identified as an area in which financial reporting in the United States could be improved by eliminating differences between Opinion 20 and *IAS 8,* Accounting Policies, Changes in Accounting Estimates and Errors [now covered by *IFRS No. 21*].

   Explain the generally accepted accounting principles in the United States to account and report changes in accounting policies *prior to* the issuance of *SFAS 154.* Do you think the change in the U.S. standard under *SFAS 154* to conform with *IAS 8* improves financial reporting or is it just an attempt to "give in" to the convergence process in an area that seems minimally harmful?

2. Given the facts of the case and that Bat-A-Bing will have to include three years' financial statements in its 2011 Registration Statement with the SEC, use the ethical decision-making model discussed in Chapter 2 to evaluate the alternatives open to Joey Fuzzarelli with respect to the company's accounting for unapproved claims. What would you do if you were Joey? Why?

3. Given that Bat-A-Bing plans to expand into China, provide a list of corporate governance considerations for the company with respect to differences between governance provisions in the United States and China.

Major Cases

The following major cases are more detailed than most of the cases in the book and may require students to do research in responding to case questions. We recommend assigning these cases after coverage of the indicated chapter.

Chapter 5: Major Case 1, Adelphia Communications Corporation
Chapter 6: Major Case 2, Royal Ahold N.V. (Ahold)
Chapter 7: Major Case 3, MicroStrategy, Inc.
Chapters 1–7: Major Case 4, Cendant Corporation

Major Case 1 (for use with Chapter 5)

Adelphia Communications Corporation

On July 24, 2009, the U.S. Court of Appeals for the District of Columbia upheld the SEC's finding that Gregory M. Dearlove, a CPA and formerly a partner with the accounting firm Deloitte & Touche LLP (Deloitte), engaged in improper professional conduct within the meaning of Rule of Practice 102(e). Dearlove served as the engagement partner on Deloitte's audit of the financial statements of Adelphia Communications Corp. (Adelphia), a public company, for the fiscal year ended December 31, 2000. The SEC confirmed its original ruling that Adelphia's financial statements were not in accordance with the generally accepted accounting principles (GAAP), and that Dearlove violated generally accepted auditing standards (GAAS). The administrative law judge (ALJ) also found that Dearlove was a cause of Adelphia's violations of the reporting and recordkeeping provisions of the Exchange Act. The ALJ permanently denied Dearlove the privilege of appearing or practicing in any capacity before the commission.

The Opinion for the Court was filed by Circuit Judge Ginsburg. The Opinion states that the SEC concluded Dearlove engaged repeatedly in unreasonable conduct resulting in violations of applicable accounting principles and standards while serving as Deloitte's engagement partner in charge of the 2000 audit of Adelphia Communications Corp. Dearlove had argued the SEC committed an error of law, misapplied the applicable accounting principles and standards, and denied him due process. Because the SEC made no error of law, and substantial evidence supports its findings of fact, the court denied the petition.

Background Issues

Deloitte audited Adelphia's financial statements from 1980 through 2002 with Dearlove as the engagement partner. John Rigas had founded Adelphia in 1952 and Rigas and his children were the controlling shareholders in 2000. Dearlove and the Deloitte team described the 2000 audit, like many prior audits of Adelphia, as posing "much greater than normal risk" because Adelphia engaged in numerous transactions with subsidiaries and affiliated entities, many of which were owned by members of the Rigas family. By the year 2000 Adelphia was one of the largest cable television companies in the United States. It had doubled the number of cable subscribers it served by acquiring several other cable companies late in 1999. Although its assets were growing, Adelphia's debt grew substantially as well. The SEC found that prior to 2000 Adelphia, its subsidiaries, and some Rigas Entities entered as coborrowers into a series of credit agreements. By 1999, Adelphia and the Rigas Entities had obtained $1.05 billion in credit; in 2000, they tripled their available credit and drew down essentially all of the funds available under the agreements.

Deloitte issued its 2000 independent auditor's report of Adelphia—signed by Dearlove—on March 29, 2001. In January 2002, in the wake of the Enron scandal, the SEC released a statement regarding the disclosure of related-party transactions. In March, Adelphia disclosed its obligations as codebtor with the Rigas Entities. Its share price declined from $30 in January 2002 to $0.30 in June, when it was delisted by the NASDAQ. In September 2002 the Department of Justice brought criminal fraud charges against Adelphia officials, including members of the Rigas family, and Adelphia agreed to pay $715 million into a victims' restitution fund as part of a settlement with the government. In April 2005 the SEC brought and settled civil actions against Adelphia, members of the Rigas family, and Deloitte.

In September 2005, the SEC charged Dearlove with improper conduct resulting in a violation of applicable professional standards, including his approval of Adelphia's method of accounting for transactions between itself and one or more Rigas Entities (i.e., related-party transactions). The matter was referred to the ALJ, who determined Dearlove had engaged in one instance of "highly unreasonable" conduct and repeated instances of "unreasonable" conduct, and permanently denied Dearlove the right to practice before the SEC. Upon review of the ALJ's decision, the SEC held Dearlove had engaged in repeated instances of unreasonable conduct as defined under Rule 102 and denied him the right to practice before the SEC, but provided him the opportunity to apply for reinstatement after four years. Dearlove petitioned for review of that decision, which was denied by the U.S. Court of Appeals.[1]

SEC Rule 102(e) provides the SEC may "deny, temporarily or permanently, the privilege of appearing or practicing before [the SEC] in any way to any person who is found by the Commission . . . to have engaged in unethical or improper professional conduct." The rule defines three classes of "improper professional conduct" for accountants: (1) "Intentional or knowing conduct, including reckless conduct, that results in a violation of applicable professional standards," (2) "a single instance of highly unreasonable conduct that results in a violation of applicable professional standards," and (3) "repeated instances of unreasonable conduct, each resulting in a violation of applicable professional standards, that indicate a lack of competence to practice before the Commission." The court supported the SEC's determination that Dearlove repeatedly engaged in unreasonable conduct.

GAAS require an auditor to have adequate training and audit proficiency, to maintain independence from the com-

---

[1]Securities and Exchange Commission, Accounting and Auditing Enforcement Release No. 2779, January 31, 2008, *In the Matter of Gregory M. Dearlove, CPA*, www.sec.gov/litigation/opinion/2008/34-57244.pdf.

pany being audited, and to exercise due professional care. The GAAS also set forth an auditor's obligation to plan, supervise, and gather evidence in conducting an audit. In contrast, the GAAP focus not upon an auditor's judgment but upon how specific accounting tasks should be performed.

Deloitte's Audit

Deloitte served as the independent auditor for Adelphia, one of its largest audit clients, from 1980 through 2002. The audits were complex. Several of Adelphia's subsidiaries filed their own Forms 10-K to the SEC and Adelphia frequently acquired other companies. For several years, Deloitte had concluded that the Adelphia engagement posed a "much greater than normal" risk of fraud, misstatement, or error; this was the highest risk category that Deloitte recognized. Risk factors that Deloitte specifically identified in reaching this assessment for the 2000 audit included the following:[2]

- Adelphia operated in a volatile industry, expanded rapidly, and had a large number of decentralized operating entities with a complex reporting structure.
- Adelphia carried substantial debt and was near the limit of its financial resources, making it critical that the company comply with debt covenants.
- Management of Adelphia was concentrated in a small group without compensating controls.
- Adelphia management lacked technical accounting expertise but nevertheless appeared willing to accept unusually high levels of risk, tended to interpret accounting standards aggressively, and was reluctant to record adjustments proposed by auditors.
- Adelphia engaged in significant related-party transactions with affiliated entities that Deloitte would not be auditing.

To help manage the audit risk, Deloitte planned, among other things, to increase Deloitte's management involvement at all stages of the audit "to ensure that the appropriate work is planned and its performance is properly supervised." It also proposed to heighten professional skepticism "to ensure that accounting estimates, related-party transactions and transactions in the normal course of business appear reasonable and are appropriately identified and disclosed."

On March 29, 2001, Deloitte issued its independent auditor's report, signed by Dearlove, which stated that it had conducted its audit in accordance with GAAS and that such audit provided a reasonable basis for its opinion that Adelphia's 2000 financial statements fairly presented Adelphia's financial position in conformity with GAAP.

Charges against Rigas Family and Deloitte

In the wake of Adelphia's decline, the Department of Justice brought criminal fraud charges against several members of the Rigas family and other Adelphia officials. The Department of Justice declined to file criminal charges against Adelphia as part of a settlement in which Adelphia agreed to pay $715 million in stock and cash to a victims' restitution fund once the company emerged from bankruptcy.

The SEC brought several actions related to the decline of Adelphia. On April 25, 2005, Adelphia, John Rigas, and Rigas's three sons settled a civil injunctive action in which the respondents, without admitting or denying the allegations against them, were enjoined from committing or causing further violations of the antifraud, reporting, recordkeeping, and internal controls provisions of the federal securities laws.[3] The next day, the commission instituted and settled administrative proceedings against Deloitte under Rule 102(e). Without admitting or denying the commission's allegations, Deloitte consented to the entry of findings that it engaged in repeated instances of unreasonable conduct with respect to the audit of Adelphia's 2000 financial statements. Deloitte also consented to a finding that it caused Adelphia's violations of those provisions of the Exchange Act that require issuers to file annual reports, make and keep accurate books and records, and devise and maintain a system of sufficient internal controls. Deloitte agreed to pay a $25 million penalty and to implement various prophylactic policies and procedures. The commission also settled a civil action based on the same conduct in which Deloitte agreed to pay another $25 million penalty. Senior manager Caswell consented to commission findings that he committed repeated instances of unreasonable conduct and agreed to a bar from appearing or practicing as an accountant before the commission with a right to apply for reinstatement after two years.[4]

Violation of GAAS: General, Fieldwork, and Reporting Standards

In determining whether to discipline an accountant under Rule 102(e)(1)(iv), the commission has consistently measured auditors' conduct by their adherence to or deviation from GAAS. GAAS require auditors to plan the audit adequately and to properly supervise any assistants. Auditors

[2] *Securities and Exchange Commission v. Adelphia Communications Corp., et al.,* Civil Action File No. 02-CV-5776 (PKC) (S.D.N.Y. October 30, 2008), Litigation Release No. 20795, October 30, 2008, www.sec.gov/litigation/litreleases/2008/lr20795.htm.

[3] *Securities and Exchange Commission v. Adelphia Communications Corporation, John J. Rigas, Timothy J. Rigas, Michael J. Rigas, James P. Rigas, James R. Brown, and Michael C. Mulcahy,* 02 Civ. 5776 (S.D.N.Y.) (KMW), Litigation Release No. 17837, November 14, 2002, www.sec.gov/litigation/litreleases/lr17837.htm.
[4] Accounting & Auditing Enforcement Release No. 2237, *In the Matter of Deloitte & Touche LLP,* April 26, 2005, www.sec.gov/litigation/admin/34-51606.pdf.

must exercise due professional care in performing an audit and preparing a report. They must maintain an attitude of professional skepticism, which includes "a questioning mind and a critical assessment of audit evidence." They must obtain sufficient competent evidential matter to afford a reasonable basis for an opinion with respect to the financial statements under review.

Certain audit conditions require auditors to increase their professional care and skepticism, as when the audit presents a risk of material misstatement or fraud. When an audit includes review of related-party transactions, auditors must tailor their examinations to obtain satisfaction concerning the purpose, nature, and extent of those transactions on the financial statements. Unless and until an auditor obtains an understanding of the business purpose of material related-party transactions, the audit is not complete. These standards can overlap somewhat, and one GAAS failure may contribute to another.

Dearlove asked the court to compare the reasonableness of his conduct to a standard used by New York state courts in professional negligence cases, that the standard for determining negligence by an accountant should be based on whether the respondent "use[d] the same degree of skill and care that other [accountants] in the community would reasonably use in the same situation." Dearlove believed his actions should be judged in the context of the large, complex Adelphia audit and to determine whether he exercised the degree of skill and care including professional skepticism that a reasonable engagement partner would have used in similar circumstances. Dearlove contended that this analysis "necessarily includes . . . conclusions previously reached by other professionals," a reference to the Adelphia audits Deloitte conducted from 1994 through 1999. Dearlove asserted that he could place some reliance on audit precedent. Moreover, in his view, the fact that prior auditors reached the same conclusions is "compelling evidence" that Dearlove acted reasonably. The court rejected any suggestion that the conduct of prior auditors should be a substitute for the standards established by GAAS ruling that "these standards apply to audits of all sizes and all levels of complexity and describe the conduct that the accounting profession itself has established as reasonable, provid[ing] a measure of audit quality and the objectives to be achieved in an audit." The court therefore declined to create a separate standard of professional conduct for auditors that depends in each case on the behavior of a particular auditor's predecessors.

The SEC found that prior Deloitte audits offered little support for the conclusions reached in the 2000 audit. The record did not describe how the audits of prior financial statements were performed or what evidential matter supported those audit conclusions. Moreover, Dearlove's expert, while arguing that partner rotation does not require the new auditor to perform a "de novo audit of the client," nevertheless explained that an engagement partner "would perform . . . new audit procedures or GAAP research and consultation . . . to address changed conditions or professional standards."

In 2000, Dearlove was presented with markedly different circumstances from those presented to prior teams: since 1999, Adelphia had tripled its coborrowed debt, doubled its revenues and operating expenses, and acquired more cable subscribers. The changes implicated areas of the Adelphia audit that Deloitte had specifically identified as posing high risk, namely, its rapid expansion, substantial debt load, and significant related-party transactions. Therefore, the court rejected Dearlove's argument that the similarity of prior audit conclusions lends reasonableness to his own audit, and found no reason to reject GAAS as the standard by which we judge all audits.

Violation of Accounting and Reporting Standards

Having determined Dearlove's conduct was unreasonable, the SEC turned to the applicable professional accounting and reporting standards. The GAAS required that when an audit posed greater than normal risk—as Dearlove had determined the Adelphia audit did—there must be "more extensive supervision by the auditor with final responsibility for the engagement during both the planning and conduct of the engagement." The SEC found no evidence in the audit workpapers or elsewhere in the record that Dearlove gave any consideration to the propriety of at least three separate transactions: (1) offsetting receivables and payables, (2) reporting of coborrowed debt, and (3) direct placement of stock transactions. We discuss the first two transactions and include an optional research question on the third transaction in the end-of-case questions.

Offsetting Receivables and Payables

Accounting Principles Board Opinion No. 10 states that "it is a general principle of accounting that the offsetting of assets and liabilities in the balance sheet is improper except where a right of setoff exists." Rule 5-02 of the Commission's Regulation S-X requires that issuers "state separately" amounts payable and receivable. Interpretation 39, Offsetting of Amounts Related to Certain Contracts, defines a right of setoff as "a debtor's legal right, by contract or otherwise, to discharge all or a portion of the debt of another party by applying against the debt an amount that the other party owes to the debtor. It also provides that a right of setoff exists only when all of the following four conditions are met: (1) each of the two parties owes the other determinable amounts; (2) the reporting party has the right to set off the amount owed with the amount owed by the other party; (3) the reporting party intends to set off; and (4) the right of setoff is enforceable at law."[5]

The court had concluded that Adelphia's presentation of a net figure for its related-party payables and receivables

---

[5]Financial Accounting Standards Board, *Offsetting of Amounts Related to Certain Contracts—an Interpretation of APB Opinion No. 10 and FASB Statement No. 105,* www.fasb.org.

violated GAAP. Because Adelphia netted the accounts payable and receivable of its various subsidiaries against the accounts payable and receivable of various Rigas Entities on a global basis, it did not comport with Interpretation 39's basic requirement that netting is appropriate only when two parties are involved.

Interpretation 39 of the FASB provides a party may use a credit to offset a debt on its balance sheet only when (1) each of two parties owes the other a determinable amount, (2) the reporting party has the right to set off the amount owed against the amount owed by the other party, (3) the reporting party intends to set off, and (4) the right to set off is enforceable at law. The SEC held Adelphia violated the GAAP because its netting involved more than two parties: "Adelphia netted the accounts payable and receivable of its various subsidiaries against the accounts payable and receivable of various Rigas Entities on a global basis . . . [and] netting is appropriate only when two parties are involved."

The SEC analyzed the record and determined that Dearlove's conduct was unreasonable in the circumstances and that it resulted in a violation of professional standards—both the GAAS and the GAAP. Because GAAS focus upon an auditor's performance and require him to exercise due professional care, the commission rejected Dearlove's attempt to fault the SEC for marshaling the same evidence to show his conduct was unreasonable and that he failed to exercise due professional care in performing the audit.

Coborrowed Debt

Between 1996 and 2000, several Adelphia subsidiaries and some of the Rigas Entities had entered as coborrowers into a series of three credit agreements with a consortium of banks. Although the agreements differed in the amount of credit available, their terms were substantially the same: each borrower provided collateral for the loan; each could draw funds under the loan agreement; and each was jointly and severally liable for the entire amount of funds drawn down under the agreement regardless of which entity drew down the amount. By year-end 2000, the total amount of coborrowed funds drawn under the credit agreements was $3.751 billion, more than triple the $1.025 billion borrowed at year-end 1999. Of this amount, Adelphia subsidiaries had drawn approximately $2.1 billion, and Rigas Entities had drawn $1.6 billion.

Generally, an issuer must accrue on its balance sheet a debt for which it is the primary obligor. However, when an issuer deems itself to be merely contingently liable for a debt, *Statement of Financial Accounting Standards (SFAS) No. 5* provides the appropriate accounting and reporting treatment for that liability. *SFAS 5* establishes a three-tiered system for determining the appropriate accounting treatment of a contingent liability, based on the likelihood that the issuer will suffer a loss—that is, be required to pay the debt for which it is contingently liable. If a loss is *probable* (i.e., likely) and its amount can be reasonably estimated, the liability should be accrued on the issuer's financial statements as if the issuer

were the primary obligor for the debt. If the likelihood of loss is only *reasonably possible* (defined as more than remote but less than likely), or if the loss is probable but not estimable, the issuer need not accrue the loss but should disclose the nature of the contingency and give an estimate of the possible loss or range of loss, or state that such an estimate cannot be made. The issuer still must disclose the "nature and amount" of the liability even if the likelihood of loss is only *remote* (slight).[6] From 1997 through 1999, Adelphia had included in the liabilities recorded on its balance sheet the amount its own subsidiaries had borrowed, but it did not consider itself the primary obligor for the amount that the Rigas Entities had borrowed and therefore did not include that amount on its balance sheet. Instead, Adelphia accounted for the amounts borrowed by the Rigas Entities by making the following disclosure in the footnotes to its financial statements:

> Certain subsidiaries of Adelphia are co-borrowers with Managed Partnerships (i.e., Rigas Entities) under credit facilities for borrowings of up to [the total amount of all co-borrowed debt available to Adelphia and the Rigas Entities that year]. Each of the co-borrowers is liable for all borrowings under this credit agreement, although the lenders have no recourse against Adelphia other than against Adelphia's interest in such subsidiaries.

Deloitte had approved this treatment in the audits it conducted from 1997 to 1999.

Dearlove knew that Adelphia considered the Rigas Entities debt to be a contingent liability for which its chances of suffering a loss were merely remote, making accrual on the balance sheet unnecessary pursuant to *SFAS 5*. Deloitte created no workpapers documenting its examination of Adelphia's decision. However, from the record, it appears that Deloitte considered the matter and focused its review on the likelihood, as defined by *SFAS 5,* that Adelphia would have to pay Rigas Entities's share of coborrowed debt.

Dearlove also believed that, although the Rigas family was not legally obligated to contribute funds in the event of a default by the coborrowers, the family would be economically compelled to protect their Adelphia holdings by stepping in to prevent a default by the Entities. Dearlove did not, however, conduct any inquiry into whether the family would, in fact, use their personal assets to prevent a default by Adelphia. Dearlove estimated the value of the Rigas family's holdings of Adelphia stock by multiplying the number of shares the Rigases owned by the price per Class A share, resulting in a figure of approximately $2.3 billion, which he concluded was by itself ample to cover the debt and conclude his *SFAS 5* analysis. However, Dearlove did not determine if these Rigas family assets were already encumbered by other debt; he saw no financial statements or other proof of the family's financial condition other than local media reports that the Rigases "were billionaires." Dearlove testified that he "never asked them: Are you worth 2 billion, 3 billion or 10 billion?"

[6]*Statement of Financial Accounting Standards (SFAS) No 5,* Accounting for Contingencies, www.fasb.org.

Dearlove also did not consider whether disposing of some or all of the family's stock might result in a downward spiral in the stock's value or in a change in their control of Adelphia, an event of default under the coborrowing agreements.

Dearlove testified that, at the end of the 2000 audit, he spoke to senior manager Caswell for about 15 minutes regarding the requirements of *SFAS 5*. During this meeting, they concluded that "the assets of the cable systems and the Adelphia common stock that the Rigases owned exceeded the amount of debt that was on the co-borrowed entities, and the overhang . . . exceeded the co-borrowing by hundreds of millions if not billions of dollars." Dearlove testified that, although other assets could have been included in an *SFAS 5* analysis, these two assets alone were sufficient to allow the auditors to conclude that Adelphia's contingent liability was remote. Deloitte therefore approved Adelphia's decision to exclude Rigas Entities's $1.6 billion in coborrowed debt from its balance sheet and to instead disclose the debt in a footnote to the financial statements.

When it reviewed the adequacy of the note disclosure that Adelphia planned to use (which was identical to the language it had used in previous years), the audit team initially believed the disclosure should be revised. During the 2000 quarterly reviews, audit manager Hofmann and others had repeatedly encouraged Adelphia management to disclose the specific dollar amount of Rigas Entities's coborrowings, but Adelphia continually ignored Deloitte's suggestions. Although Deloitte was unaware of it at the time, Adelphia management was purposefully working to obfuscate the disclosure of Rigas Entities's coborrowed debt.

In November 2000, at a third-quarter wrap-up meeting attended by Dearlove, Caswell, and Hofmann, Adelphia management (including Adelphia's vice president of finance, James Brown) agreed to make disclosures regarding the amounts borrowed by the Rigas Entities under the coborrowing agreements. Caswell and Hofmann subsequently suggested improvements to the note disclosure in written comments on at least six drafts of the 10-K; they proposed adding language that would distinguish the amount of borrowings by Adelphia subsidiaries and Rigas Entities, such as the following: "A total of $___ related to such credit agreements is included in the Company's consolidated balance sheet at December 31, 2000. The [Rigas] Entities have outstanding borrowings of $___ as of December 31, 2000 under such facilities."

At the end of March 2001, as Deloitte was concluding its audit of the 2000 financials, Brown—despite his agreement in November 2000 to disclose the amount of Rigas Entities borrowing—informed the audit team that he did not think the additional disclosure was necessary. Instead, Brown proposed adding a phrase explaining that each of the coborrowers "may borrow up to the entire amount available under the credit facility." Brown argued that his proposed language was more accurate than Deloitte's proposal, because the lines of credit could fluctuate and, as a result, it would be better to disclose Adelphia's maximum possible exposure. Caswell agreed to take Brown's language back to the engagement team, but he told Brown that he did not agree with Brown and did not think Deloitte would accept his proposed language.

Notwithstanding Caswell's reaction, Brown soon afterward presented his proposed language to the audit team, including Dearlove, Caswell, and Hofmann, during the audit exit meeting on March 30, 2001. Brown claimed that his proposed disclosure language had been discussed with, and approved by, Adelphia's outside counsel. Although Dearlove characterized the disclosure issue as "really one of the more minor points that [the audit team was] trying to reconcile at that point," the ALJ did not credit this testimony. Dearlove testified that he was "concerned" about "making it clear to the reader how much Adelphia could be guaranteeing," and that Brown's language was "more conservative" but "wasn't necessarily what we were attempting to help clarify." Dearlove also testified that he told Brown, "I don't understand how that [proposed change] enhances the note" but that, after "an exchange back and forth relative to that," Dearlove "couldn't persuade him as to what he wanted." Nevertheless, Dearlove told Brown that he agreed with the proposal and approved the change. Caswell and Hofmann also indicated their agreement.

Adelphia's note disclosure of the coborrowed debt, as it appeared in its 2000 Form 10-K with Brown's added language, read as follows:

> Certain subsidiaries of Adelphia are co-borrowers with Managed Entities under credit facilities for borrowings of up to $3,751,250,000. Each of the co-borrowers is liable for all borrowings under the credit agreements, and may borrow up to the entire amount of the available credit under the facility. The lenders have no recourse against Adelphia other than against Adelphia's interest in such subsidiaries.

Dearlove's Audit of Adelphia's *SFAS 5* Determination

Deloitte, with Dearlove's participation and agreement, had concluded that the Adelphia audit generally presented a "much greater than normal risk" based on several factors, including its multiple related-party transactions, recent significant growth in the company, and substantial debt load. Adelphia's accounting for coborrowed debt, specifically, implicated all of these risk factors. GAAS require that when an audit presents an increased risk, the auditor must increase the professional care and skepticism he applies to his review, which may include, for example, "increased sensitivity in the selection of the nature and extent of documentation to be examined in support of material transactions." Despite the clear need for increased care and skepticism, Dearlove conducted only a cursory review of Adelphia's accounting for Rigas Entities's share of coborrowed debt. There is no evidence in the workpapers that Dearlove or the audit team conducted an analysis of Adelphia's potential for liability under the credit agreements; nor is there any evidence in the workpapers that he directed his team to conduct such an analysis. Instead, Dearlove's conclusion was based on a series of assumptions about Rigas Entities's and the Rigas family's willingness and ability to pay the coborrowing Rigas Entities debt—assumptions that were either untested or inadequately tested.

Dearlove's failures in examining the critical assumptions underlying his *SFAS 5* determination were at least unreasonable in light of the circumstances of this audit area that clearly called for increased care and scrutiny. Adelphia's coborrowed debt was a multibillion-dollar related-party transaction used, in part, to finance recent significant growth in the company, and it represented a substantial portion of the company's total debt load of approximately $12 billion. Adelphia's accounting treatment of the debt warranted more than a brief discussion about assets potentially available for liquidation: it called, at least, for testing and analysis of the actual availability, liquidity, and encumbrances of those assets.

Each of Dearlove's failures to meaningfully review Adelphia's chances of suffering a loss, moreover, resulted in a violation of professional standards. Dearlove's cursory treatment of coborrowed debt did not comport with the generally applicable requirements of GAAS to exercise due professional care and professional skepticism, adequately plan the audit, and obtain sufficient competent evidential matter to afford a reasonable basis for his opinion that Adelphia's chances of incurring a loss were remote. Nor did Dearlove's review satisfy the GAAS requirement to apply increased professional care and skepticism to audit areas presenting increased risk. To the contrary, Dearlove failed to apply even basic— let alone heightened—scrutiny to Adelphia's accounting for coborrowed debt.

Adequacy of the Note Disclosure of Adelphia's Contingent Liability

The SEC also considered whether Adelphia's footnote disclosure of Rigas Entities's coborrowings was appropriate under GAAP. As explained, *SFAS 5* states that when the likelihood of loss arising from a contingent liability is only remote, a company need not accrue the amount of debt on its balance sheet. However, *SFAS 5* requires that a company must still disclose the "nature and amount" of the liability when it is a guarantee of another's indebtedness. Adelphia disclosed the total amount of credit available to the coborrowers ("up to" $3.75 billion) without indicating whether any portion of that available credit had actually been drawn down, much less that all of it had. This disclosure was inadequate to inform the investing public that Adelphia was already primarily liable for $2.1 billion and a guarantor for the remaining $1.6 billion that had been borrowed by Rigas Entities. Therefore, it did not comply with the requirement in *SFAS 5* to disclose the amount of the contingent liability.

The SEC concluded that Dearlove acted unreasonably in his audit of Adelphia's note disclosure, resulting in several

violations of GAAS. In high-risk audit environments such as that presented by the Adelphia engagement, GAAS specifically recommend "increased recognition of the need to corroborate management explanations or representations concerning material matters—such as further analytical procedures, examination of documentation, or discussion with others within or outside the entity" when audit risk increases. The accounting for Adelphia's coborrowed debt implicated the extensive related-party transactions and high debt load that were part of the basis for Deloitte's high-risk assessment for the Adelphia audit. Management's insistence on its own accounting interpretation was precisely the behavior identified by the audit plan as presenting a much higher than normal risk of misstatement in the audit.

Moreover, Dearlove knew that the audit team believed that the previous years' footnote disclosure was inadequate and had urged additional disclosure that would have made clear the extent of Rigas Entities's actual borrowings and Adelphia's resulting potential liability. Dearlove did not think Brown's language helped achieve Deloitte's goal of clarifying the extent of Rigas Entities's debt and Adelphia's obligation as guarantor. Yet Dearlove accepted Brown's language without probing his reasons for the change, without understanding Adelphia's reasons for rejecting Deloitte's language, and without discussing the issue with the concurring or risk review partners assigned to the audit. This unquestioning acceptance of Brown's proposed disclosure language was a clear—and at least unreasonable—departure from the requirements of GAAS to apply greater than normal skepticism and additional audit procedures in order to corroborate management representations in a high-risk environment. Dearlove's conduct resulted in violations of applicable professional standards: Dearlove failed to exercise the level of professional care called for by the high-risk account and failed to employ professional skepticism in analyzing the note disclosure, and he failed to apply audit procedures necessary to afford a reasonable basis for an opinion regarding the financial statements.

Dearlove asserted that disclosure of the amount that Rigas Entities could theoretically borrow (up to $3.75 billion) was more conservative than disclosure of the $1.6 billion that it had actually borrowed. The SEC concluded that the footnote disclosure was materially misleading to investors. "Materiality depends on the significance the reasonable investor would place on the withheld or misrepresented information." If "there is a substantial likelihood that a reasonable investor would consider the information important in making an investment decision," the information is material. A reasonable investor would think it significant that the footnote disclosure spoke only in terms of potential debt when, in fact, the entire line of credit had been borrowed and $1.6 billion of it was excluded from Adelphia's balance sheet but potentially payable by Adelphia. It was especially important for this information to appear in Adelphia's financial statements because investors had no access to the financial statements of the privately held Rigas Entities. The SEC rejected

Dearlove's argument that Adelphia's note complied with *SFAS 5*'s requirement to disclose the amount of debt that Adelphia guaranteed.

Debt Reclassification

After the end of the second, third, and fourth quarters of 2000, Adelphia's accounting department transferred the reporting of approximately $296 million of debt from the books of Adelphia's subsidiaries to the books of various Rigas Entities. In exchange, Adelphia eliminated from its books receivables owed to it by the respective Rigas Entities in the amount of debt transferred. The three transfers were in the amounts of $36 million, approximately $222 million, and more than $38 million, respectively. In each instance, the transaction took place after the end of the quarter, and each transfer involved a postclosing journal entry that was retroactive to the last day of the quarter.

A checklist prepared by Deloitte in anticipation of the 2000 audit showed that Deloitte was aware of a significant number of related-party transactions that had arisen outside the normal course of business and that past audits had indicated a significant number of misstatements or correcting entries made by Adelphia, particularly at or near year-end. An audit overview memorandum recognized as a risk area that "Adelphia records numerous post-closing adjusting journal entries" and provided as an audit response, "[Deloitte] engagement team to review post-closing journal entries recorded and review with appropriate personnel. Conclude as to reasonableness of entries posted." An audit planning memorandum provided that "professional skepticism will be heightened to ensure that . . . related party transactions . . . are appropriately identified and disclosed" and that auditors should "increase professional skepticism in [areas] where significant related party transactions could occur."

Dearlove testified that Deloitte had identified the Rigas family's control of both Adelphia and Rigas Entities as posing a special risk. Dearlove also testified that he believed it was important to know whose debt was whose, as between Adelphia and Rigas Entities. He testified that he was "generally aware the debt was audited," but that he did not review the debt workpapers directly. He also testified: "I don't recall [debt] being [a] particularly sensitive area, . . . I don't recall issues raised to me of difficulties we had. I don't recall any particular conversation I had with the team" concerning the audit of the debt. The record does not show that Dearlove knew of the three journal entries involving debt reclassification at the time of the audit.

Statement of Financial Accounting Standards (SFAS) No. 125, Accounting for Transfers and Servicing of Financial Assets and Extinguishment of Liabilities, permits a debtor to derecognize a liability "if and only if it has been extinguished." *SFAS 125* provides that a liability is extinguished if either (1) the debtor pays the creditor and is relieved of its obligation for the liability, or (2) the debtor is legally released

from being the primary obligor under the liability, either judicially or by the creditor.[7]

When the Adelphia subsidiaries posted the debt in question to their books, they acknowledged their primary liability for the amounts posted. They could not properly remove the debt from their books without first satisfying the requirements of *SFAS 125* that either (1) the Adelphia subsidiaries repaid the debt to the creditor during the relevant reporting periods, or (2) a creditor had released the subsidiaries from their liability for repayment. The evidence does not show, and Dearlove does not contend, that either of these events occurred. Adelphia's attempt to extinguish the debt unilaterally merely by shifting the reporting to Rigas Entities violated GAAP and rendered its financial statements materially misleading by making Adelphia's debt appear less than it was.

Dearlove did not dispute that "certain debt which had been posted to Adelphia was later posted to a Rigas entity." However, focusing on the statement in the initial decision that "once Adelphia's subsidiaries had posted this debt to their books they became primary obligors for the amounts posted," Dearlove argued that *SFAS 125* does not define the circumstances under which an entity recognizes debt that may be derecognized only under the *SFAS 125* criteria. He claimed that the initial decision of the commission improperly "assumed without analysis" that the posting of debt in a ledger is such a circumstance. Dearlove argued that the application of *SFAS 125* is complex where entities are jointly and severally liable for an obligation and it did not apply where an entity is secondarily or contingently rather than primarily liable. He asserted that Adelphia was arguably not required to recognize debt in cases where coborrowed funds were intended to be used by other coborrowers. He stopped short, however, of saying that the funds at issue were so intended, and our review of the record yields nothing to support such a contention. The record did not establish that all of the reclassified debt was coborrowed debt, and the ALJ correctly concluded that the impropriety of Adelphia's debt reclassification was unaffected by the question whether the debt was coborrowed. In addition, Dearlove cited no authority to support his contention that *SFAS 125* is applicable only where primary obligors were required to recognize a liability, and we are aware of none.

In any event, the original recording of the debt on the subsidiaries' books was, at a minimum, circumstantial evidence of their receipt of money, whether co-borrowed or otherwise borrowed. Moreover, Adelphia gave up something of value when it transferred the reporting of the debt: it removed from its books corresponding amounts of receivables owed to it by Rigas Entities. The removal of the receivables is most reasonably viewed as a *quid pro quo* for the transfer of debt that was properly Adelphia's. Adelphia's subsequent transfer of that debt to Rigas Entities was tied to the removal from

---

[7] *Statement of Financial Accounting Standards No. 125,* Accounting for Transfers and Servicing of Financial Assets and Extinguishment of Liabilities, www.fasb.org.

Adelphia's books of receivables owed to it by Rigas Entities and supports the conclusion that the subsidiaries received the money at issue from the lender.

The crucial question for the *SFAS 125* analysis is whether the debt was extinguished in one of the enumerated ways. If the debt was not extinguished as provided in *SFAS 125,* the debtor may not derecognize it. The SEC found that the debts were recognized when booked and that, because there was no evidence that the debts were extinguished under *SFAS 125,* the accounting treatment violated GAAP.

The commission also found that Dearlove's conduct in his audit of Adelphia's accounting for debt was at least unreasonable, resulting in several GAAS violations. As explained, Dearlove knew that Adelphia had a large number of decentralized operating entities with a complex reporting structure, carried substantial debt, and engaged in significant related-party transactions with affiliated entities that Deloitte would not be auditing. He also knew that Adelphia management tended to interpret accounting standards aggressively. Moreover, the audit plan specifically required that postclosing journal entries be examined in particular detail and that the audit team conclude as to their reasonableness. Dearlove knew that these factors, together with others, led Deloitte to identify the Adelphia audit as posing a "much greater than normal" risk of fraud, misstatement, or error. Additionally, Dearlove knew that Adelphia management netted its affiliate accounts payable and receivable and sought to reduce the amount of related-party receivables it reported.

In this context, GAAS required Dearlove to consider the "much greater than normal" risk of the audit in determining the extent of procedures, assigning staff, and requiring appropriate levels of supervision. Additionally, he was required to "direct the efforts of assistants who [were] involved in accomplishing the objectives of the audit and [to] determin[e] whether those objectives were accomplished." He was required to exercise "an attitude that includes a questioning mind and a critical assessment of audit evidence," "to obtain sufficient competent evidential matter to provide . . . a reasonable basis for forming a conclusion," and, after identifying related-party transactions, to "apply the procedures he consider[ed] necessary to obtain satisfaction concerning the purpose, nature, and extent of these transactions and their effect on the financial statements."

A reasonable engagement partner, under the circumstances present here, would have developed a much more thorough understanding of Adelphia's accounting for debt than Dearlove did and would have paid more attention to ensuring that the engagement team was asking the sorts of questions that would have brought matters like the accounting for reclassified debt to light. For example, the team should have asked questions about how Adelphia recorded debt or decided where debt belonged, how related-party receivables were audited, and how Adelphia managed to reduce the receivable line item on its balance sheet by 98 percent over the prior year. A reasonable engagement partner would have specifically ensured that the requirement in the audit plan concerning postclosing journal entries was followed. Instead, Dearlove paid only cursory attention to the audit of Adelphia's debt and thus remained unaware of the existence—and thus the accounting treatment—of the debt reclassifications.

The reclassified debt involved postclosing journal entries of a magnitude significant enough to require the auditors to confront management and request an explanation, as required by Deloitte's audit planning documents. After discussing the entries with appropriate Adelphia personnel, Deloitte should have documented management's explanation and Deloitte's conclusions as to whether the accounting treatment was reasonable in the audit workpapers. The record did not show that any of these steps was taken. The failure to take them was, at the very least, unreasonable.

As the engagement partner, Dearlove was responsible for assigning tasks to and supervising assistants. He was required to review the work performed by each assistant to determine whether it was adequately performed and to evaluate whether the results were consistent with the conclusions to be presented in the auditor's report. Dearlove could not satisfy his duty to supervise by waiting passively for his subordinates to bring these matters to his attention. The audit plan itself directed the audit team to examine related-party transactions and postclosing journal entries, and Dearlove himself admitted that he believed it was important to know whose debt was whose. In light of these facts, the SEC found that Dearlove's failure to apprise himself of the circumstances of the debt reclassification was a clear violation of his GAAS obligations to exercise due professional care, supervise assistants, and gather sufficient competent evidential matter to support his audit conclusions. Dearlove's failure to be more proactive was at least unreasonable.

Accordingly, the SEC concluded that Dearlove had acted at least unreasonably in signing an unqualified audit opinion stating that Deloitte had conducted its audit in accordance with GAAS and that such audit provided a reasonable basis for its opinion that Adelphia's 2000 financial statements fairly presented Adelphia's financial position in conformity with GAAP.

Questions

1. Describe the audit risk factors in the Adelphia case that should have led Gregory Dearlove and Deloitte to extend its audit procedures as part of the examination of the company's financial statements.

2. Identify and discuss the audit shortcomings in Deloitte's audit of Adelphia's financial statements using the 10 GAAS.

3. Assume you were asked by the SEC to summarize in one page or less the accounting issues at Adelphia with respect to offsetting assets and liabilities and the coborrowing of debt. Prepare a memo that might help the SEC win its case against Dearlove and Deloitte.

4. Considering your answers to questions 1–3, analyze what ethical standards seem to have been violated by Dearlove and Deloitte with respect to the ethical virtues and reasoning methods discussed in Chapters 1 and 2 and the AICPA Code provisions discussed in Chapter 4.

Optional Question

Review the legal proceedings in the Adelphia case referred to in footnote 1 and analyze the accounting, auditing, and ethics issues related to the "direct placement of stock transactions." Relate your analysis to your answers to questions 1–4.

Major Case 2 (for use with Chapter 6)

Royal Ahold N.V. (Ahold)

(*Note:* Case 5-10 in Chapter 5 covers many of the accounting and auditing facts of the case. We review these issues and go on to analyze the accountants' legal liability in this case.)

Summary of Ruling

The U.S. Court of Appeals for the Fourth Circuit affirmed the lower court ruling in the case *Public Employees Retirement Association of Colorado; Generic Trading of Philadelphia, LLC v. Deloitte & Touche, LLP* that Deloitte defendants lacked the necessary scienter to conclude they knowingly or recklessly perpetrated a fraud on Ahold's investors.

This class action securities fraud lawsuit arose out of improper accounting by Royal Ahold N.V., a Dutch corporation, and U.S. Foodservice, Inc. (USF), a Maryland-based Ahold subsidiary. The misconduct of Ahold and USF was not disputed in this appeal. The main issue is the liability of Ahold's accountants, Deloitte & Touche LLP (Deloitte U.S.) and Deloitte & Touche Accountants (Deloitte Netherlands), for their alleged role in the fraud perpetrated by Ahold and USF. Under the Private Securities Litigation Reform Act (PSLRA), plaintiffs must plead facts alleging a "strong inference" that the defendants acted with the required scienter. As explained by the Supreme Court in *Tellabs, Inc. v. Makor Issues & Rights, Ltd.,*[1] a strong inference "must be more than merely plausible or reasonable—it must be cogent and at least as compelling as any opposing inference of non-fraudulent intent."

The Appeals Court found that Deloitte, like the plaintiffs, were victims of Ahold's fraud rather than its enablers. In its decision, the court relied on the PSLRA and the decision in *Tellabs.* Circuit Judge Wilkinson wrote the conclusion for the court.[2]

Summary of Accounting Fraud

Beginning in the 1990s, and continuing until 2003, Ahold perpetrated two frauds that led it to significantly overstate its earnings on financial reports.

- Ahold improperly "consolidated" the revenue from a number of joint ventures (JV) with supermarket operators in Europe and Latin America. That is, for accounting purposes Ahold treated these JVs as if it fully controlled them—and thus treated all revenue from the ventures as

revenue to Ahold—when in fact Ahold did not have a controlling stake. Under Dutch and U.S. GAAP,[3] Ahold should have consolidated only the revenue proportionally to Ahold's stake in the ventures.

- USF falsely reported its income from promotional allowances (PAs). Also known as vendor rebates, PAs are payments or discounts that manufacturers and vendors provide to retailers like USF to encourage the retailers to promote the manufacturers' products. To increase its stated income, USF prematurely recognized income from PAs and inflated its reported PA income beyond amounts actually received.

- On February 24, 2003, Ahold announced that its earnings for fiscal years 2001 and 2002 had been overstated by at least $500 million as a result of the fraudulent accounting for promotional allowances at USF, and that Ahold would be restating revenues because it would cease treating the joint ventures as fully consolidated. After this announcement, Ahold common stock trading on the Euronext stock exchange[4] and Ahold American Depositary Receipts[5]

---

[1] U.S. Supreme Court, *Tellabs, Inc. v. Makor Issues & Rights, Ltd.,* 127 S. Ct. 2499 (2007).

[2] U.S. Court of Appeals for the Fourth Circuit, *Public Employees Retirement Association of Colorado; Generic Trading of Philadelphia, LLC v. Deloitte & Touche, LLP,* January 5, 2009, www.pacer.ca4.uscourts.gov/opinion.pdf/071704.P.pdf.

[3] Starting in 2005, members of the European Union (EU), including the Netherlands, adopted International Financial Reporting Standards (IFRSs) as the only acceptable standards for EU companies when filing statements with securities commissions in the EU. Subsequent to the adoption, the SEC in the United States announced it would accept IFRS-based financial statement filings for foreign companies listing their stock on the NYSE and NASDAQ without reconciliation to U.S. GAAP. The United States has not as yet adopted IFRS, although the SEC is studying the issue and has set forth a "road map" for adoption of IFRS in the United States that would begin to be phased in around 2015. We discuss these issues in Chapter 8.

[4] NYSE Euronext is the result of a merger on April 4, 2007, between the NYSE and stock exchanges in Paris, Amsterdam, Brussels, and Lisbon, as well as the NYSE Liffe derivatives markets in London, Paris, Amsterdam, Brussels, and Lisbon. NYSE Euronext is a U.S. holding company that operates through its subsidiaries. NYSE Euronext is a listed company. NYSE Euronext common stock is dually listed on the NYSE and Euronext Paris under the symbol "NYX." Each of the Euronext exchanges holds an exchange license granted by the relevant national exchange regulatory authority and operates under its supervision. Each market operator is also subject to national laws and regulations in its jurisdiction in addition to the requirements imposed by the national exchange authority and, in some cases, the central bank and/or the finance ministry in the relevant European country. Regulation of Euronext and its constituent markets is conducted in a coordinated fashion by the respective national regulatory authorities pursuant to memoranda of understanding relating to the cash and derivatives markets.

[5] An American Depositary Receipt (ADR) represents ownership in the shares of a non-U.S. company and trades in U.S.

trading on the NYSE lost more than 60 percent of their value. Subsequent to the February 2003 announcement, Ahold made further restatements to its earnings totaling $24.8 billion in revenues and approximately $1.1 billion in net income.

- As a result of the frauds, the SEC filed civil enforcement actions against Ahold and several individual defendants. Separately, 21 private class action securities and the Employee Retirement Income Security Act (ERISA) of 1974 actions were filed against Ahold, Deloitte, and other defendants. On June 18, 2003, the Judicial Panel on Multidistrict Litigation transferred these actions to the U.S. District Court for the District of Maryland, *In re Royal Ahold N.V. Securities & "ERISA" Litigation.*[6] Several more related actions were also transferred to the District of Maryland. On November 4, 2003, the district court consolidated all the actions and designated plaintiffs Public Employees' Retirement Association of Colorado and Generic Trading of Philadelphia, LLC, as lead plaintiffs.

JV Fraud

With respect to the JV fraud, both Deloittes advised Ahold on the consolidation of the joint ventures. Five joint ventures were at issue in this litigation: JMR, formed in August 1992; Bompreço, formed in November 1996; DAIH, formed in January 1998; Paiz-Ahold, formed in December 1999; and ICA, formed in February 2000. Ahold had a 49 percent stake in JMR and a 50 percent share of each of the other ventures at their respective times of formation. Prior to Ahold's entering into the first joint venture, Deloitte Netherlands and Deloitte U.S. gave Ahold advice about revenue consolidation under Dutch and U.S. GAAP. A memo explained that control of a joint venture is required for consolidation of the venture's revenue and discussed what situations are sufficient to demonstrate control. The memo indicated that control could be shown by a majority voting interest, a large minority voting interest under certain circumstances, or a contractual arrangement.

Ahold began consolidating the joint ventures as they were formed. The various JV agreements did not indicate that Ahold controlled the ventures. For example, the JMR joint venture agreement specified that decisions would be made by a board of directors, "deciding unanimously," and that the board would consist of three members appointed by Ahold and four members appointed by JMH, Ahold's partner in the

financial markets. The stock of many non-U.S. companies trade on U.S. stock exchanges through the use of ADRs. ADRs enable U.S. investors to buy shares in foreign companies without the hazards or inconveniences of cross-border and cross-currency transactions. ADRs carry prices in U.S. dollars, pay dividends in U.S. dollars, and can be traded like the shares of U.S.-based companies.
[6]U.S. District Court for the District of Maryland, *In re Royal Ahold N.V. Securities & "ERISA" Litigation,* 269 F.Supp. 2d 1362 (J.P.M.L. 2003).

venture. However, Ahold represented to Deloitte Netherlands that it nonetheless possessed the control requisite for consolidation. Deloitte Netherlands initially accepted these representations for the consolidation of JMR and Bompreço. But as consolidation continued, the Deloittes became concerned that Ahold lacked the control necessary to consolidate these first two joint ventures.

On August 24, 1998, Deloitte Netherlands partner John van den Dries sent a letter to Michiel Meurs, Ahold's CFO, advising him that Ahold's representations of control would no longer suffice, that Ahold would need to produce more evidence of control in order to justify continuing consolidation of joint venture revenue under U.S. GAAP, and that without such evidence a financial restatement would be required. In response to Deloitte Netherlands's requests, Ahold drafted a "control letter" addressed to BompreçoPar S.A., its partner in the Bompreço joint venture. The letter stated that the parties agreed that if they were unable to reach a consensus on a particular issue, "Ahold's proposal to solve that issue will in the end be decisive." After reviewing the draft letter, Deloitte Netherlands advised Ahold that if countersigned by the JV partner, the letter would be sufficient evidence to consolidate the venture. The letter was signed by Ahold and BompreçoPar in May 1999. By late 2000, Ahold had obtained similar countersigned control letters for the ICA, DAIH, and Paiz-Ahold joint ventures. Based on these letters and other evidence, Deloitte Netherlands concluded that consolidation was appropriate. However, in October 2002 the Deloittes learned of a "side letter" sent to Ahold in May 2000 by one of Ahold's ICA joint venture partners, Canica. The letter stated that Canica did not agree with the interpretation of the shareholder agreement stated in the ICA control letter.

At this point, Deloitte Netherlands and Deloitte U.S. began trying to get Ahold to obtain an amendment to the shareholder agreement in order to justify ongoing consolidation. At a February 14, 2003, meeting, Deloitte Netherlands and Deloitte U.S. told Ahold that Ahold lacked the necessary control for consolidation. On February 22, 2003, Ahold revealed to Deloitte Netherlands side letters contradicting the Bompreço, DAIH, and Paiz-Ahold control letters. Two days later, Ahold announced that it had improperly consolidated its joint ventures and would be restating its revenues.

PV Fraud

Ahold acquired USF in early 2000. Prior to the acquisition, Deloitte U.S. participated in Ahold's due diligence on USF. In a February 2000 memo, Deloitte U.S. noted that USF's internal system for recording promotional allowances received was weak because it heavily relied on vendors' figures, and that the system could "easily result in losses and in frauds." Deloitte U.S. also noted in the memo that USF's use of value added service providers, special-purpose entities that bought products from vendors and then resold them to USF for a higher price, needed to be evaluated for their "tax and legal implications and associated business risks."

After Ahold's acquisition of USF was finalized, Deloitte U.S. became USF's external auditor. When performing an opening balance sheet audit of USF, Deloitte U.S. discovered that a USF division in Buffalo, New York, had been fraudulently accounting for PA income. This fraud required a restatement of $11 million of PA income. USF also downwardly adjusted its income by $90 million as a result of Deloitte U.S.'s advice that it be less aggressive in its method for recognizing PA income. USF used at interim periods a method known as the "PA recognition rate" to estimate promotional allowance income, in which PAs were estimated as a percentage of USF's total sales. The rate used by USF was 4.58 percent at the time of Ahold's acquisition of USF, but rose as high as 8.51 percent in 2002. When USF booked final numbers, Deloitte U.S. in its audits tested USF's recognition of PAs by requesting written confirmation of PA amounts from vendors and by performing cash receipt tests. Using this confirmation process, Deloitte U.S. was able to test between 65 and 73 percent of PA receivables in its audits for 2000 and 2001.

Auditing Issues

Because USF lacked an internal auditing department, in April 2000 Ahold hired Deloitte U.S. to perform internal auditing services at USF. The internal auditors did not report to the Deloitte U.S. external auditors.[7] Instead, they reported initially to Ahold USA's internal audit director and, later, to USF's internal audit director after he was hired. The audit was managed by Jennifer van Cleave under the supervision of Patricia Grubel, a Deloitte U.S. partner. One of the internal audit's objectives was to determine whether USF's tracking of PAs was adequate. In van Cleave's attempt to verify USF's PA numbers, she requested a number of documents from USF management, including vendor contracts. Management refused to produce a number of the requested documents. Several members of management also refused to meet with van Cleave when she asked to conduct exit meetings. Van Cleave was thus unable to complete all of the audit's objectives.

In a February 5, 2001, draft report, van Cleave described how management's failure to produce requested documents resulted in her inability to complete some of the goals of the audit. Grubel instructed van Cleave to soften the report's language, and the version submitted to Michael Resnick, director of USF's Internal Audit Department, simply stated that Deloitte U.S. "was unable to obtain supporting documentation for some of the promotional allowance sample items" without more specifically detailing management's failures.

In its February 2003 external audit for 2002, Deloitte U.S. discovered through the PA confirmation process that USF had been inflating its recorded PA income. An investigation ensued. Ultimately, USF's former chief marketing officer (CMO), Mark Kaiser, was convicted on all counts of a federal indictment that alleged that he had induced USF's vendors to falsely report PA income amounts and receivable balances to Deloitte U.S., and that he had concealed the existence of written contracts with USF vendors from Deloitte U.S. Two other USF executives pled guilty to federal securities fraud charges; in their plea statements, they admitted that USF lied to and deceived Deloitte U.S., and that they induced vendors to sign false audit confirmation letters that falsely overstated PA payments. In addition, 17 individuals associated with USF vendors pled guilty to various charges, and admitted that they signed false audit confirmation letters in order to conceal the PA fraud from Deloitte U.S.

Private Securities Litigation Reform Act

In passing the PSLRA in 1995, Congress imposed heightened pleading requirements for private securities fraud actions. As a general matter, heightened pleading is not the norm in federal civil procedure. Frequently stated reasons include protecting defendants' reputations from baseless accusations, eliminating unmeritorious suits that are brought only for their nuisance value, discouraging fishing expeditions brought in the slight hope of discovering a fraud, and providing defendants with detailed information in order to enable them to effectively defend against a claim. When "alleging fraud or mistake," plaintiffs "must state with particularity the circumstances constituting fraud or mistake."

Under Section 10(b) of the Securities Exchange Act, it is unlawful "to use or employ, in connection with the purchase or sale of any security . . . any manipulative or deceptive device or contrivance in contravention of such rules and regulations as the [SEC] may prescribe."[8] Pursuant to Section 10(b), the SEC has promulgated Rule 10b-5, which forbids employing "any device, scheme, or artifice to defraud, . . . mak[ing] any untrue statement of a material fact or omit [- ting] to state a material fact . . . or . . . engag[ing] in any act, practice, or course of business which operates or would operate as a fraud or deceit upon any person." Section 10(b) creates a private right of action for purchasers or sellers of securities who have been injured by the statute's violation.

The PSLRA imposed a number of requirements designed to discourage private securities actions lacking merit. Among them is the requirement that in a private securities action "in which the plaintiff may recover money damages only on proof that the defendant acted with a particular state of mind, the complaint shall, with respect to each act or omission . . . , state with particularity facts giving rise to a strong inference that the defendant acted with the required state of mind." Complaints that do not adequately plead scienter are to be dismissed.

[7]Under the professional standards then in effect, an auditing firm could provide both internal and external auditing services to the same client. The Sarbanes-Oxley Act of 2002 subsequently prohibited internal audit services for external audit clients because of independence concerns.

[8]15 U.S.C. § 78(j)(b).

Because the PSLRA did not define "a strong inference," the courts of appeals disagreed on how much factual specificity plaintiffs must plead in private securities actions. The Supreme Court resolved that issue in *Tellabs,* in which the Court prescribed the following analysis for Rule 12(b)(6) motions to dismiss Section 10(b) actions:

- First, courts must, as with any motion to dismiss for failure to plead a claim on which relief can be granted, accept all factual allegations in the complaint as true.

- Second, courts must consider the complaint in its entirety, as well as other sources courts ordinarily examine, when ruling on Rule 12(b) motions to dismiss. The inquiry, as several Courts of Appeals have recognized, is whether *all* of the facts alleged, taken collectively, give rise to a strong inference of scienter, not whether any individual allegation, scrutinized in isolation, meets that standard.

- Third, in determining whether the pleaded facts give rise to a "strong" inference of scienter, the court must take into account plausible opposing inferences. The strength of an inference cannot be decided in a vacuum. The inquiry is inherently comparative. The inference of scienter must be more than merely "reasonable" or "permissible"—it must be cogent and compelling, thus strong in light of other explanations.

Legal Reasoning

The court held that a complaint will survive only if a reasonable person would deem the inference of scienter cogent and at least as compelling as any opposing inference one could draw from the facts alleged. To be sure, by no means did the PSLRA or the Supreme Court eliminate the private right of action in Section 10(b), which remains "an essential supplement to criminal prosecutions and civil enforcement actions brought, respectively, by the Department of Justice and the [SEC]."[9]

The "strong inference" requirement is not meant to prevent litigants with meritorious claims from continuing to uncover fraud and ensure confidence in the securities markets. Rather, the requirement aims to weed out meritless claims at the pleading stage, without forcing defendants to go through a potentially costly discovery process. Thus, as directed by *Tellabs,* the court must analyze the factual allegations raised by the plaintiffs, as well as other evidence in the record, and determine what plausible inferences we can draw from them. Having drawn all plausible inferences, the Court decided that it may reverse the district court only if it finds the inference that Deloitte Netherlands and Deloitte U.S. acted with scienter "at least as compelling" as the inference that the defendants lacked the required mental state. In this endeavor, it "must consider plausible nonculpable explanations for the defendant's conduct, as well as inferences favoring the plaintiff."

[9]*Tellabs,* 127 S. Ct.

The "strong inference" requirement and the comparative analysis of inferences still leave unanswered the question of exactly what state of mind satisfies the scienter requirement of a 10b-5 action. In *Ernst & Ernst v. Hochfelder,*[10] the Supreme Court held that a plaintiff must show that the defendant possessed the "intent to deceive, manipulate, or defraud" in an action brought under Rule 10b-5. However, the Court never made clear what mental state suffices to meet this requirement. ("We need not address here the question whether, in some circumstances, reckless behavior is sufficient for civil liability under Rule 10b-5."). The U.S. Court of Appeals held in *Ottman v. Hanger Orthopedic Group, Inc.* that "a securities fraud plaintiff may allege scienter by pleading not only intentional misconduct, but also recklessness."[11] The court defined a reckless act as one "'so highly unreasonable and such an extreme departure from the standard of ordinary care as to present a danger of misleading the plaintiff to the extent that the danger was either known to the defendant or so obvious that the defendant must have been aware of it'" (quoting *Phillips v. LCI Int'l, Inc.*).[12] A showing of mere negligence, however, will not suffice to support a 10(b) claim.[13]

Thus, the court ruled, the question is whether the allegations in the complaint, viewed in their totality and in light of all the evidence in the record, allow us to draw a strong inference, at least as compelling as any opposing inference, that the Deloitte defendants either knowingly or recklessly defrauded investors by issuing false audit opinions in violation of Rule 10b-5(b) or 10b-5(a) and (c). If we find the inference that defendants acted innocently, or even negligently, more compelling than the inference that they acted with the requisite scienter, we must affirm (the lower court's ruling). Plaintiffs must show that defendants actually made a misrepresentation or omission in their audit opinions on which investors relied.

In light of the foregoing standards, the court considered first the JV fraud. The plaintiffs alleged that Deloitte U.S. and Deloitte Netherlands allowed Ahold to consolidate the joint ventures despite knowing, or being reckless with regard to the risk, that Ahold lacked the control required for consolidation. The thrust of their argument was that the control letters and Ahold's oral representations were insufficient evidence of control under Dutch and U.S. GAAP. Thus, they argued, the defendants were complicit in the fraud. According to the plaintiffs, the secret side letters, in which the JV partners contradicted Ahold's interpretations of the JV agreements in the control letters, were irrelevant because the control letters themselves did not amend the JV agreements. The plaintiffs' arguments did not provide a basis for a strong inference that either Deloitte U.S.

[10]U.S. Supreme Court, *Ernst & Ernst v. Hochfelder,* 425 U.S. 185 (1976).
[11]U.S. Court of Appeals, *Ottman v. Hanger Orthopedic Group, Inc.,* 353 F.3d 338, 344 (4th Cir. 2003).
[12]U.S. Court of Appeals, *Phillips v. LCI Int'l, Inc.,* 190 F.3d 609, 621 (4th Cir. 1999).
[13]*Ernst & Ernst v. Hochfelder.*

or Deloitte Netherlands acted knowingly or recklessly in relation to the JV fraud. The most plausible inference that one can draw from the fact that Ahold concealed the side letters from its accountants is that the accountants were uninvolved in the fraud. Ahold produced letters attesting to Ahold's control countersigned by Ahold's partners for the ICA, Bompreço, DAIH, and Paiz-Ahold joint ventures at the Deloitte defendants' request, all the while concealing the side letters from those same defendants. These facts led to a strong inference that the Deloitte defendants were attempting to ensure that Ahold had sufficient control over the joint ventures for consolidation and that Ahold was determined to prevent them from discovering otherwise. With perfect hindsight, one might posit that the defendants should have required stronger evidence of control from Ahold. Indeed, as the district court noted, it may have been negligent for the defendants to accept as the only evidence of control Ahold's repeated representations that it controlled JMR, the one joint venture for which Ahold never produced a control letter.[14] Nonetheless, the evidence as a whole leads to the strong inference that defendants were deceived by their clients into approving the consolidation. Ahold would not have needed to go out of its way to produce false evidence of control had the Deloittes been complicit in the fraud, or had they been so reckless in their duties that their audit "amounted to no audit at all," as the Southern District of New York has described the standard in *SEC v. Price Waterhouse.*[15]

To establish a strong inference of scienter, plaintiffs must do more than merely demonstrate that defendants should or could have done more. They must demonstrate that the Deloittes were either knowingly complicit in the fraud, or so reckless in their duties as to be oblivious to malfeasance that was readily apparent. The inference we find most compelling based on the evidence in the record is not that the defendants were knowingly complicit or reckless, but that they were deceived by their client's repeated lies and artifices. Perhaps their failure to demand more evidence of consolidation was improper under accounting guidelines, but that is not the standard, which "requires more than a misapplication of accounting principles."[16]

The court then examined the PA fraud. The plaintiffs argued that Deloitte U.S. was knowingly complicit in the fraud when it ignored several red flags, including USF's lack of internal controls to track PA income and USF management's obstruction of the internal audit and the facts and the circumstances of USF CFO Ernie Smith's resignation. With respect to USF's problems with tracking income with PAs, it is not the case that Deloitte U.S. simply ignored the weak internal controls, as the plaintiffs alleged. Rather, Deloitte U.S. raised this issue numerous times with Ahold and USF management.

Deloitte U.S. designed a confirmation process to verify USF's reported PA income in which it contacted third-party vendors and received letters from them confirming PA amounts. The plaintiffs described the confirmation process as one that "confirmed nothing." Yet instead of merely relying on USF representations, as the plaintiffs asserted, Deloitte U.S. obtained corroboration from vendors for the figures provided by USF. Deloitte U.S. would not have attempted to verify USF's figures with third parties if it were complicit in the scheme; nor can it be said that it was anything but proper to attempt to check the accuracy of representations made by USF management.

The plaintiffs attempted to suggest that the confirmation process was unsound because, for example, Deloitte U.S. accepted confirmation letters via fax and the letters were sent to brokers or sale executives instead of financial officers. But even if the confirmation process was somewhat flawed—which the defendants contested—the larger fact remains that the PA fraud went undetected initially only because USF and its vendors conspired to lie to Deloitte U.S. and to conceal important documents. Indeed, it was Deloitte U.S.'s confirmation process itself that ultimately revealed the fraud. In the course of the 2002 audit, Deloitte U.S. learned in early 2003 from a vendor from which it had requested PA confirmations that employees had signed inaccurate confirmation letters.

Shortly thereafter, Ahold authorized an internal investigation that revealed the extent of the fraud. No doubt it would have been better had the fraud been discovered earlier, but the strongest inference one can draw from the evidence is that the fraud initially went undetected because of USF's collusion with the vendors, not because of wrongdoing by Deloitte U.S. As to the internal audit, the internal auditors reported not to the Deloitte U.S. external auditors but to USF, as was consistent with professional standards.[17]

The plaintiffs suggested that Grubel's editing of the language in van Cleave's initial report (two Deloitte partners) indicated scienter. They argued that Grubel's edits suggested that Deloitte U.S. was trying to cover up the fact that management had obstructed the internal audit. But as the district court noted, "while [the] language in the initial draft of the internal audit report was softened, the revised language continued to state the essential point, that the internal auditors had been unable to obtain certain documents related to promotional allowances and unable to achieve specific testing objectives."

The rest of the supposed red flags pointed to by the plaintiffs also failed to create a strong inference of scienter. With respect to the plaintiffs' allegations that Smith told Deloitte U.S. about the vendor rebate fraud, the district court twice concluded that this claim had no support in the record, and we see no reason to disagree with its conclusion. The plaintiffs alleged that facts like the high CFO turnover at USF and USF's rapid growth should have alerted Deloitte U.S. that there was fraud afoot, but they failed to explain why this was the only conclusion Deloitte could make.

[14] U.S. Court of Appeals, *In re Royal Ahold,* 351 F.Supp. 2d.
[15] *SEC v. Price Waterhouse,* 797 F.Supp. 1217, 1240 (S.D.N.Y. 1992) (citing *McLean v. Alexander,* 599 F.2d 1190, 1198 [3d Cir. 1979]).
[16] *SEC v. Price Waterhouse.*

[17] Institute of Internal Auditors, Standards for the Professional Practice of Internal Auditing, *Statement on Internal Auditing Standards Nos. 1–18.*

Conclusion

"Seeing the forest as well as the trees is essential." With respect to both frauds, the plaintiffs pointed to ways that the defendants could have been more careful and perhaps discovered the frauds earlier. But the plaintiffs could not escape the fact that Ahold and USF went to considerable lengths to conceal the frauds from the accountants and that it was the defendants that ultimately uncovered the frauds. The strong inference to be drawn from this fact is that Deloitte U.S. and Deloitte Netherlands lacked the requisite scienter and instead were deceived by Ahold and USF. That inference is significantly more plausible than the competing inference that defendants somehow knew that Ahold and USF were defrauding their investors.

The court reiterated that it is not an accountant's fault if its client actively conspires with others in order to deprive the accountant of accurate information about the client's finances. It would be wrong and counter to the purposes of the PSLRA to find an accountant liable in such an instance. The court concluded that it had found no version of the facts that would create a strong inference that the Deloitte defendants had the scienter required for a cause of action under Section 10(b); the district court rightly denied the plaintiffs' motion for leave to amend their complaint.

Questions

1. Explain the legal liability of auditors under SEC regulations. Do you agree with the commission's conclusion that the Deloitte auditors did not violate their obligations to shareholders? Why or why not?

2. Auditors rely on the cooperation and honesty of their clients to ensure that all relevant facts related to the audit including gathering the requisite evidence to render an opinion on its financial statements have been received/gathered and duly evaluated. In the Ahold case, the client made it more difficult for Ahold to achieve this objective. Explain the different areas of the audit where the client impeded Deloitte's efforts to follow GAAS.

3. As pointed out in the case, in passing the PSLRA in 1995, Congress imposed heightened pleading requirements for private securities fraud actions. The PSLRA imposed a number of requirements designed to discourage private securities actions lacking merit. Given the opening quote in Chapter 6 by Robert Mednick, discuss whether you think the changes in legal liability made by the PSLRA are a good thing for

   a. Shareholders and others who might sue accountants and auditors

   b. The accounting profession

   Use ethical reasoning in making the analysis.

4. The Court relied on the *Tellabs* ruling in assessing whether there is a strong inference that Deloitte acted with a particular state of mind with respect to each act or omission alleged in a lawsuit. Complaints that do not adequately plead scienter are to be dismissed. Relying on your answer to question 1, review the discussion of the *Tellabs* ruling in the Ahold case and explain how Ahold's actions made it difficult for Deloitte to meet *Tellabs* and other legal standards cited in the case.

Major Case 3 (for use with Chapter 7)

MicroStrategy, Inc.

Background

MicroStrategy, Inc., incorporated in Wilmington, Delaware, in November 1989 has offices all over the United States and around the world. Its headquarters are in McLean, Virginia. In the early years the company provided software consulting services to assist customers in building custom software systems to access, analyze, and use information contained in large-scale transaction-level databases. MicroStrategy began concentrating its efforts on the development and sale of data mining and decision support software and related products during 1994 and 1995.[1]

A greater part of the revenues in 1996 resulted from software license sales. The company licensed its software through its direct sales force and through value-added resellers and original equipment manufacturers (OEMs). The total sales through the latter two methods comprised more than 25 percent of the company's total revenues. Since 1996, the company revenues have been derived primarily from three sources:

- Product licenses
- Fees for maintenance, technical support, and training
- Consulting and development services

The company went public through an initial public offering in June 1998. From the third quarter of 1998, the company began to take on a series of increasingly bigger and more complicated transactions including the sale of software, extensive software application development, and software consulting services.

In 1998 the company began to develop an information network supported by the organization's software platform. Initially known as Telepath, but later renamed Strategy.com., the network delivers personalized finance, news, weather, traffic, travel, and entertainment information to individuals through cell phones, e-mail, and fax machines. For a fee, an entity could become a Strategy.com affiliate that could offer service on a co-branded basis directly to its customers. The affiliate shared with MicroStrategy the subscription revenues from end-users. MicroStrategy's market position by the end of 2004 was that of leading worldwide provider of business intelligence software.

The story of MicroStrategy reflects the larger problems of the go-go years of the 1990s. The dream of many young entrepreneurs was to create a new software product or design a new Internet-based network and capitalize on the explosion in telecommunications network capacity and computer usage. Greed may have been the sustaining factor enabling the manipulation of stock value as many CEOs and CFOs cashed in before the stock price tumbled. However, pressure to achieve financial analysts' estimates of earnings seems to have been the driving force behind the decision to "cook the books."

Restatement of Financial Statements

On March 20, 2000, MicroStrategy announced that it planned to restate its financial results for the fiscal years 1998 and 1999. MicroStrategy stock, which had achieved a high of $333 per share, dropped over 60 percent of its value in one day, going from $260 per share to $86 per share on March 20. The stock price continued to decline in the following weeks. Soon after, MicroStrategy announced that it would also restate its fiscal 1997 financial results, and by April 13, 2000, the company's stock closed at $33 per share. The share price was quoted at $3.15 per share as of January 16, 2002.

The restatements that are summarized in Table 1 reduced the company's revenues over the three-year period by about $65 million of the $312 million reported, or 21 percent. About 83 percent of these restated revenues were in 1999.

The company's main reporting failures were derived from its early recognition of revenue arising from the misapplication of AICPA *Statement of Position (SOP) 97-2*.[2] The SEC states in the Accounting and Enforcement Release: "This misapplication was in connection with multiple-element deals in which significant services or future products to be provided by the company were not separable from the up-front sale of a license to the company's existing software products." The company also restated revenues from arrangements in which it had not properly executed contracts in the same fiscal period in which revenue was recorded from the deals.

The company 10-K annual report filed with the SEC for the fiscal year ended December 31, 1998, states the following in item number 7 of Management's Discussion and Analysis (MD&A):

> Our revenues are derived from two principal sources (i) product licenses and (ii) fees for maintenance, technical support, education and consulting services (collectively, "product support"). Prior to January 1, 1998, we recognized revenue in accordance with Statement of Position 91-1, "Software Revenue Recognition." Subsequent to December 31, 1997, we began recognizing revenue in accordance with Statement of Position 97-2, "Software Revenue Recognition." SOP 97-2 was amended on March 31, 1998

---

[1]Information about the case can be found at Securities and Exchange Commission, Accounting and Auditing Enforcement Release No. 1351, December 14, 2000, *In the Matter of MicroStrategy, Inc.,* December 18, 2000, www.sec.gov/litigation/admin/34-43724.htm.

[2]Available at www.aicpa.org.

Table 1
Impact of Restatement on Revenue and Net Income

Reporting Period	Revenue ($ in thousands)		Net Income ($ in thousands)	
	Original	Restated	Original	Restated
Year ended:				
December 31, 1997	$ 53,557	$ 52,551	$ 121	$ (885)
Quarter ended:				
March 31, 1998	19,895	19,160	542	(193)
June 30, 1998	23,790	21,138	942	(1,133)
September 30, 1998	27,014	25,960	1,928	2,055
December 31, 1998	35,731	29,231	2,766	(2,984)
Year ended:				
December 31, 1998	106,430	95,489	6,178	(2,255)
Quarter ended:				
March 31, 1999	35,784	29,322	1,859	(3,804)
June 30, 1999	45,638	40,465	3,211	(3)
September 30, 1999	54,555	35,309	3,794	(12,774)
December 31, 1999	69,352	46,162	3,756	(17,162)
Year ended:				
December 31, 1999	205,329	151,258	12,620	(33,743)

by SOP 98-4 "Deferral of the Effective Date of a Provision of SOP 97-2." In December 1998, the AICPA issued SOP 98-9 "Modification of SOP 97-2, Software Revenue Recognition," which amends SOP 98-4, and is effective after December 31, 1998. Management has assessed these new statements and believes that their adoption will not have a material effect on the timing of our revenue recognition or cause changes to our revenue recognition policies. Product license revenues are generally recognized upon the execution of a contract and shipment of the related software product, provided that no significant Company obligations remain outstanding and the resulting receivable is deemed collectible by management. Maintenance revenues are derived from customer support agreements generally entered into in connection with initial product license sales and subsequent renewals. Fees for our maintenance and support plans are recorded as deferred revenue when billed to the customer and recognized ratably over the term of the maintenance and support agreement, which is typically one year. Fees for our education and consulting services are recognized at the time the services are performed.

The majority of MicroStrategy's sales closed in the final days of the fiscal period, which is common in the software industry and as stated by the company in its 10-K. The following is an excerpt from the company's 10-K for the fiscal year December 31, 1998.

The sales cycle for our products may span nine months or more. Historically, we have recognized a substantial portion of our revenues in the last month of a quarter, with these revenues frequently concentrated in the last two weeks of a quarter. Even minor delays in booking orders may have a significant adverse impact on revenues for a particular quarter. To the extent that delays are incurred in connection with orders of significant size, the impact will be correspondingly greater. Moreover, we currently operate with virtually no order backlog because our software products typically are shipped shortly after orders are received. Product license revenues in any quarter are substantially dependent on orders booked and shipped in that quarter. As a result of these and other factors, our quarterly results have varied significantly in the past and are likely to fluctuate significantly in the future. Accordingly, we believe that quarter-to-quarter comparisons of our results of operations are not necessarily indicative of the results to be expected for any future period.

SEC Investigation and Proceedings

According to the SEC investigation, the problems for MicroStrategy began at the time of its public offering in June 1998 and continued through the announced restatement in March 2000. The software company materially overstated its revenues and earnings contrary to GAAP. The company's internal revenue recognition policy in effect during the relevant time period stated that the company recognized revenue in accordance with *SOP 97-2*. The company, however, had not complied with *SOP 97-2,* instead recognizing revenue earlier than allowed under GAAP.

The closing of a majority of the company's sales in the final days of the fiscal period resulted in the contracts department receiving numerous contracts signed by customers that needed (according to company policy) to be signed by MicroStrategy. To realize the desired quarterly financial results, the company held open, until after the close of the quarter, contracts that had been signed by customers but had not yet been signed by the company. After the company determined the desired financial results, the unsigned contracts were signed and given an "effective date" in the last month of the prior quarter. In some instances, the contracts were signed without affixing a date, allowing the company to assign a date at a later time. GAAP and MicroStrategy's own accounting policies required the signature of both the company and the customer prior to recognizing revenue.

Microsoft's violations of SEC regulations included reporting provisions, record-keeping requirements, and the violation of internal control provisions. The company was required to cease and desist from committing any further violations of the relevant rules as well as take steps to comply with the rules already violated.

Role of the Auditor

The auditor of MicroStrategy in 1996 was Coopers & Lybrand and Warren Martin was the engagement partner. After Coopers merged with Price Waterhouse and became known as PricewaterhouseCoopers (PwC), Martin continued as the engagement partner until April 2000. The SEC filed administrative proceedings against him on August 8, 2003, and suspended him from practicing before the commission for two years.[3]

Martin was in charge of the audit of MicroStrategy during the period of restatement and was directly responsible for the unqualified opinions issued on the company's inaccurate financial statements. The SEC charged him with a variety of violations of professional standards of practice including the lack of an attitude of professional skepticism, the failure to obtain sufficient evidence to support revenue recognition, and demonstrating a lack of due care in carrying out professional responsibilities.

Role of Officers of the Company

The following officers came under investigation by the SEC: Michael Saylor, cofounder and CEO; Mark Lynch, the CFO; and Sanjeev Bansal, cofounder and COO. The SEC filed administrative proceedings against Saylor, Lynch, and Bansal on December 14, 2000, charging that MicroStrategy "materially overstated its revenues and earnings from the

sales of software and information services contrary to GAAP." Two other officials were cited for their role in drafting the revenue recognition policies that violated GAAP— Antoinette Parsons, the corporate controller and director of finance and accounting and vice president of finance; and Stacy Hamm, an accounting manager who reported to Parsons.[4] The SEC considered that all these officers should have been aware of the revenue recognition policies of the company. Lynch, as the CFO, had the responsibility to ensure the truthfulness of MicroStrategy's financial reports and he signed the company's periodic reports to the SEC. Saylor also signed the periodic reports.

The CEO, CFO, and COO paid approximately $10 million in disgorgement used to repay investors who were affected by this fraud, another $1 million in penalties, and they agreed to a cease and desist order regarding violations of reporting, bookkeeping and internal controls. The controller and the accounting manager agreed to a cease-and-desist order that prohibited them from violating Rules 13a and 13b of the Exchange Act. In a separate action, Lynch was denied the right to practice before the commission for three years.

On June 8, 2005, the SEC reinstated Lynch's right to appear before the commission as an accountant. Lynch agreed to have his work reviewed by the independent audit committee of any company for which he works. He is still prohibited from practicing before the commission as an independent auditor.

Post-Restatement through 2004

MicroStrategy discontinued its Strategy.com business in 2001. It now has a single platform for business intelligence as its core business. Total revenues consist of revenues derived from the sale of product licenses and product support and other services, including technical support, education, and consulting services. The company's international market is rapidly developing and it has positive earnings from operations since 2002.

For the year ended December 31, 2004, the MD&A identified its revenue recognition policy as follows:

Revenue Recognition

MicroStrategy's software revenue recognition policies are in accordance with the American Institute of Certified Public Accountants' Statement of Position ("SOP") 97-2, "Software Revenue Recognition," as amended. In the case of software arrangements that require significant production, modification or customization of software, we follow the guidance in SOP 81-1, "Accounting for Performance of Construction-Type and Certain Production-Type Contracts." We also follow the guidance provided by SEC Staff Accounting Bulletin ("SAB") No. 101, "Revenue Recognition in Financial Statements," and SAB No. 104, "Revenue Recognition," which provide

---

[3]Securities and Exchange Commission, Accounting and Enforcement Release No. 1835, *In the Matter of Warren Martin, CPA,* August 8, 2003, www.sec.gov/litigation/admin/34-48311.htm.

[4]U.S. Securities and Exchange Commission, "SEC Brings Civil Charges against MicroStrategy, Three Executive Officers for Accounting Violations," www.sec.gov/news/headlines/microstr.htm.

guidance on the recognition, presentation and disclosure of revenue in the financial statements filed with the SEC.

We recognize revenue from sales of software licenses to end users or resellers upon persuasive evidence of an arrangement, as provided by agreements or contracts executed by both parties, delivery of the software and determination that collection of a fixed or determinable fee is reasonably assured. When the fees for software upgrades and enhancements, technical support, consulting and education are bundled with the license fee, they are unbundled using our objective evidence of the fair value of the elements represented by our customary pricing for each element in separate transactions. If such evidence of fair value exists for all undelivered elements and there is no such evidence of fair value established for delivered elements, revenue is first allocated to the elements where evidence of fair value has been established and the residual amount is allocated to the delivered elements. If evidence of fair value for any undelivered element of an arrangement does not exist, all revenue from the arrangement is deferred until such time that evidence of fair value exists for undelivered elements or until all elements of the arrangement are delivered, subject to certain limited exceptions set forth in SOP 97-2.

When a software license arrangement requires us to provide significant production, customization or modification of the software, or when the customer considers these services essential to the functionality of the software product, both the product license revenue and consulting services revenue are recognized using the percentage of completion method. Under percentage of completion accounting, both product license and consulting services revenue are recognized as work progresses based upon labor hours incurred. Any expected losses on contracts in progress are expensed in the period in which the losses become probable and reasonably estimable. Contracts accounted for under the percentage of completion method were immaterial for the years ended December 31, 2004, 2003 and 2002.

If an arrangement includes acceptance criteria, revenue is not recognized until we can objectively demonstrate that the software or service can meet the acceptance criteria, or the acceptance period lapses, whichever occurs earlier. If a software license arrangement obligates us to deliver specified future products or upgrades, the revenue is recognized when the specified future product or upgrades are delivered, or when the obligation to deliver specified future products expires, whichever occurs earlier. If a software license arrangement obligates us to deliver unspecified future products, then revenue is recognized on the subscription basis, ratably over the term of the contract.

License revenue derived from sales to resellers or OEM's who purchase our products for future resale is recognized upon sufficient evidence that the products have been sold to the ultimate end users provided all other revenue recognition criteria have been met.

Technical support revenue, included in product support and other services revenue, is derived from providing technical support and software updates and upgrades to customers. Technical support revenue is recognized ratably over the term of the contract, which in most cases is one year. Revenue from consulting and education services is recognized as the services are performed.

Amounts collected prior to satisfying the above revenue recognition criteria are included in deferred revenue and advance payments in the accompanying consolidated balance sheets."[5]

In its early years MicroStrategy stated its revenue recognition policy in a single paragraph stating that it followed the relevant accounting policies. Now, the company provides a detailed analysis in its MD&A as well as the notes to financial statements. The company has implemented all the requirements of the SEC. PwC continues as the auditors for MicroStrategy and the firm has given an unqualified opinion on both the company's financial statements and its internal control report under SOX.

Online Resources

The following Web sites should help you answer the following questions.

1. American Institute of CPAs (*SAS 55* and *SOP 97-2*): www.aicpa.org/members/div/auditstd/index.htm
2. Committee of Sponsoring Organizations (COSO):
   a. *Internal Control—Integrated Framework* (Executive Summary): www.coso.org/publications/executive_summary_integrated_framework.htm
   b. *Report of the National Commission on Fraudulent Financial Reporting* (Treadway Commission Report): www.coso.org/publications/NCFFR.htm
3. Financial Accounting Standards Board:
   a. CON 5: www.fasb.org/pdf/con5.pdf
   b. Emerging Issues Task Force Pronouncement EITF 08-1, Revenue Arrangements with Multiple Deliverables: www.fasb.org
   c. Emerging Issues Task Force Pronouncement 09-3, Applicability of AICPA Statement of Position 97-2 to Certain Arrangements That Include Software Elements: www.fasb.org
4. Securities and Exchange Commission—Litigation Releases and Administrative Proceedings:
   a. AAER 1350: December 14, 2000, www.sec.gov/litigation/admin/34-43724.htm
   b. AAER 1351: December 14, 2000, www.sec.gov/litigation/admin/34-43725.htm
   c. AAER 1352: December 14, 2000, www.sec.gov/litigation/litreleases/lr16829.htm
   d. AAER 1359: January 17, 2001, www.sec.gov/litigation/admin/34-43850.htm
   e. AAER 1835: August 8, 2003, www.sec.gov/litigation/admin/34-48311.htm
   f. AAER 2255: June 8, 2005, www.sec.gov/litigation/admin/34-51802.pdf

---

[5]Securities and Exchange Commission, MicroStrategy 2004 10-K Report, available at: www.sec/gov/cgi-bn/browser-edgar.

Questions

1. Revenue recognition issues in accounting can be especially challenging because of the critical importance of the timing of revenue and related effects on earnings. A variety of sources exist to identify the rules and guidelines for revenue recognition. Begin your search by accessing the FASB Web site and review *Statement of Financial Accounting Concepts (CON) No. 5,* Recognition and Measurement in Financial Statements of Business Enterprises. Then, discuss how *SOP 97-2* reflects application of *CON 5* revenue recognition criteria. Finally, go to the FASB Web site and review EITF 08-1 and 09-3. A good summary of these pronouncements can be found on the KPMG site: "Implementing the New EITF Consensus on Multiple Element Revenue Arrangements" (http://us.kpmg.com/microsite/DefiningIssues/2009/di-09-41-eitf-september-meeting.pdf). How do these standards affect the division of deliverables into separate units of accounting when they are sold in a bundled arrangement?

2. According to the SEC's Enforcement Action against MicroStrategy (AAER No. 1350), the company's misstatement of revenue was due to

    a. Premature revenue recognition

    b. Improper execution of contracts

    For each of the MicroStrategy customers identified in Table 2, complete the information required by describing the transaction date, amount, and key issues, and give an explanation of the revenue recognition problem. A completed analysis is presented for the Primark transaction

to assist in your analysis. You should refer to the SEC Enforcement Actions and Litigation Releases to assist in answering this question.

3. a. Based on your analysis of the revenue recognition issues in the identified transactions, explain how what you have uncovered relates to the criteria discussed in question 1. For example, persuasive evidence of an arrangement did not exist in the Primark transaction as required by *SOP 97-2* because the contract was not signed until January 3, 2000, therefore, the $5.0 million of revenue was prematurely recognized in the last quarter of 1999.

    b. Based on your analysis in question 2 and response to question 3, do you believe MicroStrategy engaged in earnings management in its revenue recognition practices? Why or why not?

4. AAER No. 1350 requires MicroStrategy to institute a variety of corporate governance initiatives based on the SEC's findings that the company's governance systems broke down. In particular, the SEC found that MicroStrategy had violated Section 13(b)(2)(A) of the Exchange Act that requires registrants to maintain "books and records which accurately and fairly reflect its transactions and dispositions of assets." Compare the provisions in AAER 1350 with the requirements of *SAS No. 55,* Consideration of Internal Control in a Financial Statement Audit, and the COSO *Integrated Framework.* Do you think AAER 1350 adequately addresses the need for an effective control environment in MicroStrategy?

Table 2
Revenue Recognition Problems

Company Involved	Fiscal Period Affected	Issue with Transaction	Problem/Explanation	Revenue Improperly Recognized
Primark Corporation	12/31/99	Transaction not complete/or signed by either party.	Prior to midnight negotiations broke down over an issue that was not resolved until the following week and contract not signed by either party until January 3, 2000. The parties failed to properly execute the contract at December 31, 1999.	$5,000,000
Shopko Stores, Inc.				
Choicepoint, Inc.				
KMart Corporation				
NCR Corporation				
NCR Corporation				
Sybase, Inc.				
Exchange Applications, Inc.				

Major Case 4 (for use with Chapters 1–7)

Cendant Corporation[1]

The Merger of HFS and CUC

HFS Incorporated (HFS) was principally a controller of franchise brand names in the hotel, real estate brokerage, and car rental businesses including Avis, Ramada Inn, Days Inn, and Century 21. Comp-U-Card (CUC) was principally engaged in membership-based consumer services such as auto, dining, shopping, and travel "clubs." Both securities were traded on the NYSE. Cendant Corporation was created through the December 17, 1997, merger of HFS and CUC. Cendant provided certain membership-based and Internet-related consumer services and controls franchise brand names in the hotel, residential real estate brokerage, car rental, and tax preparation businesses.

Overview of the Scheme

The Cendant fraud was the largest of its kind until the late 1990s and early 2000s. Beginning in at least 1985, certain members of CUC's senior management implemented a scheme designed to ensure that CUC always met the financial results anticipated by Wall Street analysts. The CUC senior managers utilized a variety of means to achieve their goals including:

- Manipulating recognition of the company's membership sales revenue to accelerate the recording of revenue
- Improperly utilizing two liability accounts related to membership sales that resulted from commission payments
- Consistently maintaining inadequate balances in the liability accounts and on occasion reversing the accounts directly into operating income

With respect to the last item, to hide the inadequate balances, senior management periodically kept certain membership sales transactions off-books. In what was the most significant category quantitatively, the CUC senior managers intentionally overstated merger and purchase reserves and subsequently reversed those reserves directly into operating expenses and revenues. CUC senior management improperly wrote off assets—including assets that were unimpaired—and improperly charged the write-offs against the company's merger reserves. By manipulating the timing of the write-offs and by improperly determining

[1] The information for this case comes from a variety of litigation releases on the SEC Web site including: www.sec.gov/litigation/admin/34-42935.htm (June 14, 2000); www.sec.gov/litigation/admin/34-42934.htm (June 14, 2000); www.sec.gov/litigation/admin/34-42933.htm (January 24, 2001); www.sec.gov/litigation/litreleases/lr16587.htm (April 30, 2003); and www.sec.gov/litigation/complaints/comp18102.htm (April 30, 2003).

the nature of the charges incurred, the CUC senior managers used the write-offs to inflate operating income at CUC. As the scheme progressed over the course of several years, larger and larger year-end adjustments were required to show smooth net income over time. The scheme added more than $500 million to pretax operating income during the fiscal years ended January 31, 1996; January 31, 1997; and December 31, 1997.

SEC Filings against CUC and Its Officers

SEC complaints filed on June 14, 2000, alleged violations of the federal securities laws by four former accounting officials including Cosmo Corigliano, CFO of CUC; Anne M. Pember, CUC controller; Casper Sabatino, vice president of accounting and financial reporting; and Kevin Kearney, director of financial reporting. The allegations against Corigliano included his role as one of the CUC senior officers who helped engineer the fraud, and he maintained a schedule that management used to track the progress of their fraud. Corigliano regularly directed CUC financial reporting managers to make unsupported alterations to the company's quarterly and annual financial results. The commission alleged that Corigliano profited from his own wrongdoing by selling CUC securities and a large number of Cendant securities at inflated prices while the fraud he helped engineer was under way and undisclosed.

The commission alleged that Pember, the former CUC controller, was the CUC officer most responsible for implementing directives received from Corigliano in furtherance of the fraud including implementing directives that inflated Cendant's annual income by more than $100 million, primarily through improper use of the company's reserves. According to the SEC, Pember profited from her own wrongdoing by selling CUC and Cendant stock at inflated prices while the fraud she helped implement was under way and undisclosed.

Sabatino and Kearney, without admitting or denying the commission's allegations, consented to the entry of final judgments settling the commission's action against them. The commission's complaint alleged that Sabatino was the CUC officer most responsible for directing lower-level CUC financial reporting managers to make alterations to the company's quarterly financial results.

In the first of the three separate administrative orders, the commission found that Steven Speaks, the former controller of CUC's largest division, made or instructed others to make journal entries that effectuated much of the January 1998 income inflation directed by Pember. In a second separate administrative order, the commission found that Mary Sattler Polverari, a former CUC supervisor of financial reporting, at the direction of Sabatino and Kearney, regularly and knowingly made unsupported alterations to CUC's quarterly financial results.

In a third administrative order, the commission found that Paul Hiznay, a former accounting manager at CUC's largest division, aided and abetted violations of the periodic reporting provisions of the federal securities laws by making unsupported journal entries that Pember had directed. Hiznay consented to the issuance of the commission's order to cease and desist from future violations of the provisions.

In a fourth and separate administrative order the commission found that Cendant violated the periodic reporting, corporate recordkeeping, and internal controls provisions of the federal securities laws, in connection with the CUC fraud. Among other things, the company's books, records, and accounts had been falsely altered, and materially false periodic reports had been filed with the commission, as a result of the long-running fraud at CUC. Simultaneous with the institution of the administrative proceeding, and without admitting or denying the findings contained therein, Cendant consented to the issuance of the commission order, which ordered Cendant to cease and desist from future violations of the provisions.

On February 28, 2001, the SEC filed a civil enforcement action in the U.S. District Court for the District of New Jersey against Walter A. Forbes, the former chair of the board of directors at CUC, and E. Kirk Shelton, the former vice chair, alleging that they directed a massive financial fraud while selling millions of dollars' worth of the company's common stock. For the period 1995–1997 alone, pretax operating income reported to the public by CUC was inflated by an aggregate amount of over $500 million. Specific allegations included:

- Forbes, CUC's chair and CEO, directed the fraud from its beginnings in 1985. From at least 1991 on, Shelton, CUC's president and COO, joined Forbes in directing the scheme.

- Forbes and Shelton reviewed and managed schedules listing fraudulent adjustments to be made to CUC's quarterly and annual financial statements. CUC senior management used the adjustments to artificially pump up income and earnings, defrauding investors by creating the illusion of a company that had ever-increasing earnings and making millions for themselves along the way.

- Forbes and Shelton undertook a program of mergers and acquisitions on behalf of CUC in order to generate inflated merger and purchase reserves at CUC to be used in connection with the fraud. Forbes and Shelton sought out HFS as a merger partner because they believed the reserves that would be created would be big enough to bury the fraud. To entice HFS management into the merger, Forbes and Shelton inflated CUC's earnings and earnings projections.

- Forbes and Shelton profited from their own wrongdoing by selling CUC and Cendant securities at inflated prices while the fraud they had directed was under way and undisclosed. The sales brought Forbes and Shelton millions of dollars in ill-gotten gains.

- After the Cendant merger, Forbes served as Cendant's board chair until his resignation in July 1998. At the time of the merger, Shelton became a Cendant director and vice chair. Shelton resigned from Cendant in April 1998.

Specific Accounting Techniques Used to Manage Earnings

Loosely speaking, earnings management occurs when a company determines its net income based on meeting desired goals rather than through the application of GAAP. Companies can manage earnings in a variety of ways including accelerating the recording of revenue, delaying the recording of expenses, adjusting write-offs and write-downs, and utilizing reserves to smooth net income over time. We discussed these techniques in Chapter 7.

Making Unsupported Postclosing Entries

In early 1997, at the direction of senior management, Hiznay approved a series of entries reversing the commissions payable liability account into revenue at CUC. The company paid commissions to certain institutions on sales of CUC membership products sold through those institutions. Accordingly, at the time that it recorded revenue from those sales, CUC created a liability to cover its commissions payable obligation. CUC senior management used false schedules and other devices to support their understating of the commissions payable liability and to avoid the impact that would have resulted if the liability had been properly calculated. Furthermore, in connection with the January 31, 1997, fiscal year-end, senior management utilized this liability account by directing postclosing entries moving amounts from the liability directly into revenue.[2]

In February 1997, Hiznay received a schedule from the CUC controller setting forth the amounts, effective back-dates, and accounts for a series of postclosing entries reducing the commissions payable account by $9.12 million and offsetting that reduction by increases to CUC revenue accounts. Hiznay approved the unsupported entries and had his staff enter them. They all carried effective dates spread retroactively over prior months. The entries reversed the liability account directly into revenues, a treatment that, under the circumstances, was not in accordance with GAAP.

---

[2]*Postclosing journal entries* means entries that are made after a reporting period has ended, but before the financial statements for the period have been filed, and that have effective dates spread retroactively over prior weeks or months.

Keeping Rejects and Cancellations Off-Books: Establishing Reserves

During his time at CUC, Hiznay inherited, but then supervised, a long-standing practice of keeping membership sales cancellations and rejects off CUC's books during part of each fiscal year. Certain CUC membership products were processed through various financial institutions that billed their members' credit cards for new sales and charges related to the various membership products. When CUC recorded membership sales revenue from such a sale, it would allocate a percentage of the recorded revenue to cover estimated cancellations of the specific membership product being sold, as well as allocating a percentage to cover estimated rejects and charge-backs.[3] CUC used these percentage allocations to establish a membership cancellation reserve.

Over the years, CUC senior management had developed a policy of keeping rejects and cancellations off the general ledger during the last three months of each fiscal year. Instead, during that quarter, the rejects and cancellations appeared only on cash account bank reconciliations compiled by the company's accounting personnel. The senior managers then directed the booking of those rejects and cancellations against the membership cancellation reserve in the first three months of the next fiscal year. Because rejects and cancellations were not recorded against the membership cancellation reserve during the final three months of the fiscal year, the policy allowed CUC to hide the fact that the reserve was dramatically understated at each fiscal year-end. At its January 31, 1997, fiscal year-end, the balance in the CUC membership cancellation reserve was $29 million; CUC accounting personnel were holding $100 million in rejects and $22 million in cancellations off-books. Failing to book cancellations and rejects at each fiscal year-end also had the effect of overstating the company's cash position on its year-end balance sheet.

SEC Settlements

Between Hiznay's arrival at CUC in July 1995 and the discovery of the fraudulent scheme by Cendant management in April 1998, CUC and Cendant filed false and misleading annual reports with the commission that misrepresented their financial results, overstating operating income and earnings and failing to disclose that the financial results were falsely represented.

The commission's complaint alleged that Sabatino, by his actions in furtherance of the fraud, violated, or aided and abetted violations of, the antifraud, periodic reporting, corporate record-keeping, internal controls, and lying to auditors provisions of the federal securities laws. Sabatino consented to entry of a final judgment that enjoined him from future

violations of those provisions and permanently bar him from acting as an officer or director of a public company.

Kearney consented to entry of a final judgment that enjoined him from future violations of those provisions, ordered him to pay disgorgement of $32,443 in ill-gotten gains (plus prejudgment interest of $8,234), and ordered him to pay a civil money penalty of $35,000. Kearney has also agreed to the issuance of a commission administrative order that barred him from practicing before the commission as an accountant, with the right to reapply after five years.

Corigliano, Pember, and Sabatino each pleaded guilty to charges pursuant to plea agreements between those three individuals and the SEC. Pursuant to his agreement, Corigliano pleaded guilty to a charge of wire fraud, conspiracy to commit mail fraud, and causing false statements to be made in documents filed with the commission including signing CUC's periodic reports filed with the commission and making materially false statements to CUC's auditors. Pember pleaded guilty to a charge of conspiracy to commit mail fraud and wire fraud. Sabatino, pursuant to his agreement, pleaded guilty to a charge of aiding and abetting wire fraud.

In another administrative order, the commission found that Paul Hiznay aided and abetted violations of the periodic reporting provisions of the federal securities laws, in connection with actions that he took at the direction of his superiors at CUC. Among other things, the commission alleged that Hiznay made unsupported journal entries that Pember had directed. Additional orders were entered against lower-level employees.

Actions against Cendant and Walter A. Forbes, Former Board Chair

The commission found that Cendant violated the periodic reporting, corporate recordkeeping, and internal controls provisions of the federal securities laws, in connection with the CUC fraud in that the company's books, records, and accounts had been falsely altered, and materially false periodic reports had been filed with the SEC.

On December 29, 2009, the SEC announced a final judgment against Walter A. Forbes, the former chair of Cendant, arising out of his conduct in the Cendant fraud.[4] The commission alleged that Forbes orchestrated an earnings management scheme at CUC to improperly inflate the company's quarterly and annual financial results during the period 1995 to 1997. CUC's operating income was improperly inflated by an aggregate amount exceeding $500 million.

The final judgment against Forbes, to which he consented without admitting or denying the commission's allegations, enjoined him from violating relevant sections of the securities laws and bars him from serving as an officer or director of a public company.

---

[3]Rejects resulted when the credit card to be charged was over its limit, closed, or reported as lost or stolen. Charge-backs resulted when a credit card holder disputed specific charges related to a particular membership program.

[4]*Securities and Exchange Commission v. Walter A. Forbes et al.,* District Court N.J. filed February 28, 2001.

Allegations against the Officers

Kenneth Wilchfort and Marc Rabinowitz were partners at Ernst & Young (EY), which was responsible for audit and accounting advisory services provided to CUC and Cendant. During the relevant periods, CUC and Cendant made materially false statements to the defendants and EY about the company's true financial results and its accounting policies. CUC and Cendant made these false statements to mislead the defendants and EY into believing that the company's financial statements conformed to GAAP. For example, as late as March 1998, senior Cendant management had discussed plans to fraudulently use over $100 million of the Cendant reserve to create fictitious 1998 income, which was also concealed from the defendants and EY. CUC and Cendant made materially false statements to the defendants and EY that were included in the management representation letters and signed by senior members of CUC's and Cendant's management. The statements concerned, among other things, the creation and utilization of merger-related reserves, the adequacy of the reserve established for membership cancellations, the collectibilty of rejected credit card billings, and income attributable to the month of January 1997.[5]

The written representations for the calendar year 1997 falsely stated that the company's financial statements were fairly presented in conformity with GAAP and that the company had made available all relevant financial records and related data to EY. Those written representations were materially false because the financial statements did not conform to GAAP and, as discussed further, the company's management concealed material information from the defendants and EY.

In addition to providing the defendants and EY with false written representations, CUC and Cendant also adopted procedures to hide its income-inflation scheme from the defendants and EY. Some of the procedures that CUC and Cendant employed to conceal its fraudulent scheme included (1) backdating accounting entries; (2) making accounting entries in small amounts and/or in accounts or subsidiaries the company believed would receive less attention from EY; (3) in some instances ensuring that fraudulent accounting entries did not affect schedules already provided to EY; (4) withholding financial information and schedules to ensure that EY would not detect the company's accounting fraud; (5) ensuring that the company's financial results did not show unusual trends that might draw attention to its fraud; and (6) using senior management to instruct middle and lower level personnel to make fraudulent entries. Notwithstanding CUC and Cendant's repeated deception, defendants improperly failed to detect the fraud. They were aware of numerous practices by CUC and Cendant indicating that the financial statements did not conform to GAAP and, as a consequence,

they had a duty to withhold their unqualified opinion and take appropriate additional steps.

Improper Establishment and Use of Merger Reserves

The company completed a series of significant mergers and acquisitions and accounted for the majority of them using the pooling-of-interests method of accounting.[6] In connection with this merger and acquisition activity, Company management purportedly planned to restructure its operations. GAAP permits that certain anticipated costs may be recorded as liabilities (or reserves) prior to their incurrence under certain conditions. However, here CUC and Cendant routinely overstated the restructuring charges and the resultant reserves and would then use the reserves to offset normal operating costs—an improper earnings management scheme. The company's improper reversal of merger and acquisition related restructuring reserves resulted in an overstatement of operating income by $217 million.

The EY auditors provided accounting advice as well as audit services to CUC and Cendant in connection with the establishment and use of restructuring reserves. The auditors excessively relied on management representations concerning the appropriateness of the reserves and performed little substantive testing despite evidence that the reserves were improperly established and utilized.

One example of auditor failures with reserve accounting is the Cendant reserve. Cendant recorded over $500 million in merger, integration, asset impairment, and restructuring charges for the CUC-side costs purportedly associated with the merger of HFS and CUC. The company recorded a significant portion of this amount for the purpose of manipulating its earnings for December 31, 1997, and subsequent periods and, in fact, Cendant had plans, which it did not disclose to defendants and EY, to use a material amount of the reserve to artificially inflate income in subsequent periods.

In the course of providing accounting and auditing services, the auditors failed to recognize evidence that the company's establishment and use of the Cendant reserve did not conform to GAAP. For example, CUC and Cendant provided EY with contradictory drafts of schedules when EY requested support for the establishment of the Cendant reserve. The company prepared and revised these various schedules, at least in part, as a result of questions raised and information provided by the defendants. The schedules were inconsistent with regard to the nature and amount of the individual components of the reserve (i.e., component categories were added, deleted, and changed as the process progressed). While the component categories changed over

[5]Available at www.sec.gov/litigation/complaints/comp18102.htm.

[6]*Statement of Financial Accounting Standards (SFAS) No. 141, Business Combinations*, which eliminated the pooling methods for business combinations. The purchase method must now be used for all acquisitions.

time, the total amount of the reserve never changed materially. Despite this evidence, the auditors did not obtain adequate analyses, documentation, or support for changes they observed in the various revisions of the schedules submitted to support the establishment of the reserves. Instead, they relied excessively on frequently changing management representations.

The company planned to use much of the excess Cendant reserve to improperly increase operating results in future periods. During the year ended December 31, 1997, the company wrote off $104 million of assets that it characterized as impaired as a result of the merger. Despite the size and timing of the write-off, the defendants never obtained adequate evidence that the assets were impaired as a result of the merger and, therefore, properly included in the Cendant reserve. In fact, most of the assets were not impaired as a result of the merger.

Cash Balance from the Membership Cancellation Reserve

CUC and Cendant also inflated income by manipulating their membership cancellation reserve and reported cash balance. Customers usually paid for membership products by charging them on credit cards. The company recorded an increase in revenue and cash when it charged the members' credit card. Each month, issuers of members' credit cards rejected a significant amount of such charges. The issuers would deduct the amounts of the rejects from their payments to CUC and Cendant. CUC and Cendant falsely claimed to EY auditors that when it resubmitted the rejects to the banks for payment, it ultimately collected almost all of them within three months. CUC and Cendant further falsely claimed that for the few rejects that were not collected after three months, it

then recorded them as a reduction in cash and a decrease to the cancellation reserve. The cancellation reserve accounted for members who canceled during their membership period and were entitled to a refund of at least a portion of the membership fee, as well as members who joined and were billed, but never paid for their memberships.

At the end of each fiscal year, the company failed to record three months of rejects (i.e., it did not reduce its cash and decrease its cancellation reserve for these rejects). CUC and Cendant falsely claimed to the defendants and EY that it did not record rejects for the final three months of the year because it purportedly would collect most of the rejects within three months of initial rejection. According to CUC and Cendant, the three months of withheld rejects created a temporary difference at year-end between the cash balances reflected in the company's general ledger and its bank statements. The rejects were clearly specified on reconciliations of the company's numerous bank accounts, at least some of which were provided to EY and retained in its workpapers. CUC and Cendant falsely claimed to the defendants and EY that the difference between the general ledger balance and bank statement balance did not reflect an overstatement of cash and understatement in the cancellation reserve since it collected most rejects. In fact, the majority of rejects were not collected. By not recording rejects and cancellations against the membership cancellation reserve during the final three months of each fiscal year, CUC and Cendant dramatically understated the reserve at each fiscal year-end and overstated its cash position. CUC and Cendant thus avoided the expense charges needed to bring the cancellation reserve balance up to its proper amount and the entries necessary to record CUC and Cendant's actual cash balances.

The rejects, cancellation reserve balance, and overstatement of income amounts for the period 1996–1997 are as follows:

		($ in millions)	
Date	Rejects	Cancellation Reserve Balance	Understated Reserve/ Overstated Income
1/31/96	$ 72	$37	$35
1/31/97	100	29	28
12/31/97	137	37	37

The EY defendants did not adequately test the collectibility of these rejects and the adequacy of the cancellation reserve and instead relied primarily on management representations concerning the company's successful collection history and inconsistent statements concerning the purported impossibility of substantively testing these representations.

Membership Cancellation Rates

The company also overstated its operating results by manipulating its cancellation reserve. The cancellation reserve accounted for members who canceled during their membership period. A large determinant of the liability associated with cancellations was CUC and Cendant's estimates of the cancellation rates. During the audits, CUC and Cendant intentionally provided EY with false estimates that were lower than the actual estimated cancellation rates. This resulted in a significant understatement of the cancellation reserve liability and an overstatement of income. To justify its understated cancellation reserve, CUC and Cendant provided to EY small, nonrepresentative samples of cancellations, which understated the actual cancellation rates. The defendants allowed the company to choose the samples. EY did not test whether the samples provided were representative of the actual cancellations for the entire membership population.

Audit Opinion

EY issued audit reports containing unqualified audit opinions on, and conducted quarterly reviews of, the company's financial statements that, as already stated, did not conform to GAAP. The Securities Exchange Act requires every issuer of a registered security to file reports with the commission that accurately reflect the issuer's financial performance and provide other information to the public. By reason of the foregoing, the firm aided and abetted violations of the securities laws.

Class Action Lawsuits

A class action suit by stockholders against Cendant and its auditors, with the largest pension funds in the lead, alleged that stockholders paid more for Cendant stock than they would have if they had known the truth about CUC's income. The lawsuit ended in a record $3.2 billion settlement. Details of the settlement follow.

The law firm of Barrack, Rodos and Bacine (BR&B) was one of two lead counsels for the class in *In re Cendant Corporation Litigation*. That firm was retained by the two largest state pension funds and the largest municipal pension funds in the country—the New York State Common Retirement Fund, California Public Employees' Retirement System, and New York City Pension Funds—to represent it in the lawsuits. Each of the funds had suffered losses in the range of $30 million. Through its prosecution of the case, BR&B succeeded in certifying a class of purchasers of Cendant and CUC publicly traded securities during the period from May 31, 1995, through August 28, 1998, and recovering for the class nearly four times more than had ever been recovered in the history of federal securities law class actions. By the time the dust had settled, BR&B had achieved recoveries of more than $3.3 billion for the class, as well as highly significant corporate governance changes negotiated as part of the settlement with Cendant. Notably, the $3.3 billion recovery represented nearly 40 percent of the damages suffered by class members, and provided very significant payments—in a number of cases, in excess of

$100 million—for the largest claimants, many of which were public pension funds.[7]

By December 1999, BR&B announced on behalf of the lead plaintiffs the landmark $2.85 billion settlement with Cendant that far surpassed the recoveries in any other securities law class action case in history. Until the settlements reached in the WorldCom case in 2005, this stood as the largest recovery in a securities class action case, by far, and clearly set the standard in the field. In addition to the cash payment by Cendant, which was backed by a letter of credit that the company secured to protect the class, the Cendant settlement included two other very important features. First, the settlement provided that in the event Cendant or the former HFS officers and directors were successful in obtaining a net recovery in their continuing litigation against EY, the class would receive one-half of any such net recovery. As it turned out, that litigation lasted another seven years—until the end of 2007—when Cendant and EY settled their claims against each other in exchange for a payment by EY to Cendant of nearly $300 million. Based on the provision in the Cendant settlement agreement and certain further litigation and a court order, in December 2008 the class received another $132 million. This brought the total recovered from the Cendant settlement to $2.982 billion.

Second, Cendant was required to institute significant corporate governance changes that were far-reaching and unprecedented in securities class action litigation. Indeed, these changes included many of the corporate governance structural changes that would later be included within the Sarbanes-Oxley Act of 2002. They included the following:

- The board's audit, nominating, and compensation committees would be comprised entirely of independent directors (according to stringent definitions, endorsed by the institutional investment community, of what constituted an independent director).

- The majority of the board would be independent within two years following final approval of the settlement.

- Cendant would take the steps necessary to provide that, subject to amendment of the certificate of incorporation declassifying the board of directors by vote of the required super-majority of shareholders, all directors would be elected annually.

- No employee stock option could be "re-priced" following its grant without an affirmative vote of shareholders, except when such re-pricings were necessary to take into account corporate transactions such as stock dividends, stock splits, recapitalization, a merger, or distributions.

---

[7]*In Re: Cendant Corporation Litigation*, 264 F3d 201 264 F.3d 201 (3rd Cir. 2001), http://openjurist.org/264/f3d/201/in-re-cendant-corporation-litigation.

The Settlement with Ernst & Young

Ten days after reaching agreement on the Cendant settlement, BR&B finalized negotiations of an equally impressive settlement with EY. On December 17, 1999, it was announced that EY had also agreed to settle the claims of the class for $335 million. This recovery was and remains today as the largest amount ever paid by an accounting firm in a securities class action case. The recovery from EY was significant because it held an outside auditing firm responsible in cases of corporate accounting fraud. The claims against EY were based on EY's "clean" audit and review opinions for three sets of annual financial statements, and seven quarterly financial statements, between 1995 and 1997, but that it had failed to review quarterly reporting packages by CUC subsidiaries; it did not require adequate documentation for the company's merger reserves and "top-side" adjustments; and it failed to review the company's general ledgers.

The district court approved the settlements and plan of allocation in August 2000, paving the way for Cendant and EY to fund the settlements. Approximately one year later, in August 2001 the settlements and plan of allocation were affirmed on appeal by the U.S. Third Circuit Court of Appeals. And, in March 2002 the U.S. Supreme Court determined that it would not hear any further appeals in the case.

Questions

1. Briefly summarize the accounting techniques used by Cendant to manipulate financial results. Categorize each technique into one of Schilit's financial shenanigans.

2. Describe the failings of EY with respect to conducting an audit in accordance with GAAS. Include in your discussion any violations of the AICPA Code of Professional Conduct.

3. Evaluate the actions of Cendant management with respect to its obligations to shareholders. Did it meet those obligations? Why or why not?

4. The corporate governance requirements for Cendant that were stipulated in the class action lawsuit seem to emphasize the need for independence of the board of directors and audit committee. Using the corporate governance provisions in the Sarbanes-Oxley Act and NYSE listing requirements, identify the additional governance requirements that could have been imposed on Cendant. What should they be designed to accomplish?

Optional Question

The rules in accounting for merger and other restructuring reserves were changed after the frauds at companies like Cendant and Lucent. Research the new rules and explain how they differ from the rules in effect at the time of the Cendant fraud and why the rules were changed.

Name Index

Locators with n indicate notes.

Meurs, M., 458
Meyer, M. J., 31n32, 31n38, 31n44
Miller, N., 134
Miller, R. L., 319n2
Mill, J. S., 18
Minkow, B., 188–190, 218, 275, 278
Mintz, S. M., 2, 10n, 22, 30n3, 31n29, 32n47
Monus, M., 78
Moody-Stuart, M., 412
Moore, R. L., 287, 316–317
Morgan, G., 412
Morgenthau, R., 221
Moro, J., 141n4
Morse, G., 3, 66
Moss, J., 156, 158
Mulcahy, M. C., 449n3
Muralidhar, S., 144n12
Murray, B. P., 164–165
Murthy, N. R. N., 412
Musica, P., 275
Myers, D., 66–67

N

Narvaez, D., 63nn8–9, 63n13, 64n21
Nelson, B., 418
Nelson, M., 55, 64n35
Nixon, R., 11, 149
Nobes, C., 388, 406n26, 406n28
Noble, John W., 313, 314
Normand, T., 68
Noyce, R., 93

O

Obama, B., 13, 95
O'Brien, S., 128
O'Connor, R., 137
Olsen, D., 111
Olson, J., 301
Ong, A., 407n40
Owens, W. T., 166–167, 193, 194

P

Pacini, C., 306n2, 306n6, 306n8
Pahapill, M. E., 354n1
Paine, T., 403
Palmrose, Z.-V., 269, 295n10
Pany, K., 236nn4–7, 236n9, 236n20, 236n25
Parker, R., 388, 406n26, 406n28
Parkinson, J. E., 117n15
Parsons, A., 465
Patterson, Jacob M., 281–283
Pember, A., 468–470
Pennino, C. M., 63n12
Perle, R., 149
Petrus, 302–303

Pincoffs, E. L., 12, 31n22
Plaff, R., 174
Plato, 4, 22
Plumlee, D., 55–56, 64n37
Polverari, M. S., 469
Ponemon, L. A., 51, 63n13, 63n14, 63n15, 64nn16–18
Prawitt, D. F., 178n7, 236n8, 269n, 295n11
Prior, W. J., 30n9
Pulliam, S., 30n4

Q

Quarles, R., 258

R

Rabinowitz, M., 471
Radler, D., 147–153
Raines, F., 256, 257–258
Rajagopalan, N., 394, 407n36
Raju, R., 433–436
Ramsay, R. J., 216, 236nn21–23
Ramsey, R. D., 296n52
Rao, M. R., 434
Rappaport, J. B., 183n4
Reagan, R., 149, 299
Rehnquist, W., 154
Reich, M. R., 145n18
Reimers, J. L., 55, 64n36
Reingold, J., 63n1, 178n1
Renneboog, L., 93, 117n16
Resnick, M., 459
Rest, J. R., 51–53, 54, 56, 63nn8–9, 63n13, 64n19, 64n21
Reys, G. A., 373–375
Rezaee, Z., 96, 117n27, 117n30
Reznor, M. T., 319
Richards, A., 90
Rigas, J. J., 152, 448, 449
Rigas, J. P., 449n3
Rigas, M. J., 449n3
Rigas, T., 114, 449n3
Robertson, S. M., 412
Rokeach, M., 117n36
Romeril, B. D., 336
Rosenthal, R., 174
Rosenzweig, K., 327, 351n9
Ross, B., 31n25
Rowzee, J. M., 133
Ruble, R. J., 174
Rudman, W., 257–258

S

Sabatino, C., 468–470
Safer, M., 222
Sala, L., 430

Saylor, M., 465
Scalzo, R. P., 223
Schilit, H. M., 334–336, 338–339, 351n21, 367–368
Schipani, C. A., 392, 407n33
Schipper, K., 325–326, 351n4, 384, 406n11
Schwartz, R., 31n25
Schwarzenegger, A., 160
Scrushy, R., 166–167, 193, 280
Shad, J., 157
Shanks, T., 31n32, 31n38, 31n44
Shapira, D., 78
Shaub, M. K., 63n14
Shaw, W. H., 30n10
Shelton, E. K., 469
Shibut, L., 178n12
Shleifer, A., 93, 116n14
Shrivastava, P., 144n14
Simpson, 302–303
Sinason, D. H., 216, 236nn21–23
Singh, K., 430n10
Skilling, J., 52–53, 280, 340, 342, 343–344, 345, 348
Skinner, P. J., 325–326, 351n6
Smith, A., 1, 30n1
Smith, E., 461
Smith, G., 66–68
Smith, L. M., 385, 406n19
Socrates, 4
Solomon, D., 30n4
Somaiya, K., 437
Speaks, S., 468
Spencer, L. G., 257
Stanley, A., 298
Stein, J. M., 174
Stewart, M., 283–284
Stolowy, H. H., 385, 406n18
Stone, W. C., 2
Strawser, J. R., 216, 236nn21–23
Strong, G., 194
Stuebs, M. T., Jr., 406n10
Styron, W., 21, 31n43
Sullivan, S., 3, 66–68, 100, 217
Swartz, M., 53, 64nn22–23, 219, 224, 352n29
Szekelyi, R., 319

T

Tanaka, K., 288
Tanzi, Calisto, 428–432
Tanzi, Carlos, 428
Tanzi, G., 428
Tanzi, S., 428
Tarkenton, F. A., 309–310
Tate, J., 249–250
Thoman, G. R., 336
Thomas, C. W., 406n10
Thoma, S. J., 63n10
Thompson, J., 149

Subject Index

Locators with n indicate notes